CASE WHITE

OSPREY
PUBLISHING

DEDICATION

To Józef Franczak, last of the 'cursed soldiers',
who continued to resist the Soviet occupation in
Poland from 1945 until killed in action on
21 October 1963. Franczak, a simple soldier,
continued the fight long after others had given up
and demonstrated that the enemy occupation
had not broken Poland's spirit.

CASE
WHITE

THE INVASION OF POLAND, 1939

ROBERT FORCZYK

OSPREY PUBLISHING
Bloomsbury Publishing Plc
PO Box 883, Oxford, OX1 9PL, UK
1385 Broadway, 5th Floor, New York NY 10018, USA
E-mail: info@ospreypublishing.com
www.ospreypublishing.com

OSPREY is a trademark of Osprey Publishing Ltd

First published in Great Britain in 2019

A catalogue record for this book is available from the British Library.

ISBN: HB 978-1-4728-3495-9; PB 978-1-4728-3497-3; eBook 978-1-4728-3494-2;
ePDF 978-1-4728-3493-5; XML 978-1-4728-3496-6

19 20 21 22 23   10 9 8 7 6 5 4 3 2 1

Maps by www.bounford.com
Index by Zoe Ross

Typeset by Deanta Global Publishing Services, Chennai, India
Printed and bound in Great Britain by CPI (Group) UK Ltd, Croydon CRO 4YD

Front cover: Panzer Assault Badge 1st grade. (Photograph by Stewart Larking)

Osprey Publishing supports the Woodland Trust, the UK's leading woodland
conservation charity.

To find out more about our authors and books visit **www.ospreypublishing.com**.
Here you will find extracts, author interviews, details of forthcoming events and
the option to sign up for our newsletter.

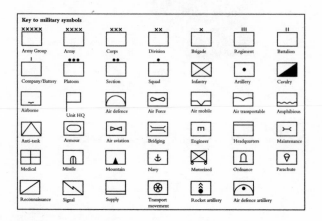

Contents

Introduction

*'We, the Poles, do not understand war as a symbol
but as a real fight.'*
Władysław Sikorski, Polish prime minister-in exile, 1939

The standard historiography of the Second World War starts with the assertion that Adolf Hitler ordered the invasion of Poland in September 1939, but hoped to fight only a localized conflict and avoid a general European war at this point in time. However, Hitler's action did spark a wider conflict because Great Britain and France honoured their security guarantees to Poland and decided to declare war upon Germany after Hitler ignored their demands to cease the invasion. The Anglo-French declaration of war was mostly symbolic, intended to put Hitler on notice that the Western democracies would no longer tolerate his aggressive land-grabbing behaviour or his broken diplomatic promises. This orthodoxy has been convenient, because it lays the blame for the start of the war solely at Hitler's feet and it exonerates the Western Allies as having done the best they could to impede the tide of Fascist aggression. In this heterodoxy, Poland is regarded as an unfortunate martyr and broken Allied promises on its behalf are easily forgotten.

Unfortunately, the standard heterodoxy has been little more than a version based on wartime propaganda and driven by post-war political necessities to avoid conflict with the Soviet Union. The truth is that after joint consultation, both Germany and the Soviet Union invaded Poland in September 1939, but the Western Allies only chose to acknowledge

Hitler's transgression. Furthermore, Allied promises of military support to Poland were never sincere and their leaders aggravated this dereliction by consistently failing to protect Poland's sovereignty or territorial integrity in later negotiations with the Soviet Union. Rather than a martyr for the Allied cause, Poland was victimized by both its foes and its friends – but then left to pay the bill at Tobruk, Monte Cassino, Mont Ormel, the Falaise Gap and Arnhem. In signing the Molotov–Ribbentrop Pact on 23 August 1939, both Hitler and Stalin thumbed their noses at the Western Allies and intended this diplomatic agreement to enable them to annex other people's land. Hitler wanted to destroy Poland so he could avoid a two-front war in the short run, then prevail in a localized European war against the Anglo-French at a later date. In contrast, Stalin sought to incite a general world war – using German militarism as his preferred instrument – in order to see the West irretrievably weakened, thereby setting the stage for subsequent Soviet expansion into an enfeebled Europe. Although Hitler and Stalin did not agree on much, one sentiment they did share was a fervent desire to destroy the Polish state and crush its people's spirit forever. The Polish state, with its appreciation for education and freedom of thought, was anathema to all the totalitarian principles they held dear. Communist post-war rationalizations that the Molotov–Ribbentrop Pact was an unfortunate necessity to buy time for the Soviet Union to prepare its military for an inevitable clash with the Third Reich do not wash, because Stalin was presented with the opportunity to sign an agreement with the Anglo-French, but rejected it out of hand. Had Molotov instead signed a pact with the Anglo-French, Hitler would have been confronted with the prospect of a two-front war, which Germany could not afford in 1939–40. A pact with the Allies could also have gained the Soviet Union a respite to prepare – but at the cost of no land concessions in eastern Europe. Consequently, my contention is that Hitler and Stalin bear equal responsibility for the outbreak of the Second World War and that their covert agreement to divide eastern Europe between themselves was the greatest criminal conspiracy of the 20th century, condemning millions to death or slavery.

Nor did it help improve the accuracy of Second World War historiography about Poland that the Western Allies were unaware of the provisions of the secret protocol signed by Molotov and Ribbentrop in August 1939 – until a copy was found in captured German archives in 1945. Although there was plenty of circumstantial evidence in 1941 to support the notion of German–Soviet collusion to destroy Poland, the

Western Allies refused to seriously consider it due to fear of upsetting their new-found ally, Josef Stalin. Even after the war, it was easier for Anglo-American historians to minimize the German–Soviet collusion in invading Poland and thereby avoid affixing any Soviet responsibility for the outbreak of war. Meanwhile, Soviet historians continued to deny the existence of the secret protocol for 50 years, until August 1989.[1] In April 1990, the Russian government also admitted responsibility for the Katyń Forest massacre and that Stalin had ordered the execution of 20,000 captured Polish prisoners; this admission further highlighted the similar methods used by both the Third Reich and the Soviet Union in exterminating enemies of their regimes. From the Polish point of view – with its citizens being rounded up by both Gestapo and NKVD during 1939–41 – there was never any doubt that Germany and the Soviet Union were equally guilty in starting a war of aggression with the purpose of destroying the Polish state.

Although the Second World War in Europe started with the invasion of Poland – which the Germans designated as *Fall Weiss* (Case White) – the actual military campaign has not been well covered in the historiography of the Second World War until recently. Most general histories of the conflict (e.g. Basil Liddell Hart, John Keegan, Max Hastings) typically provide only a few pages on the 1939 campaign in Poland, often littered with generalizations about the rapid collapse of the Polish Army. In contrast, German wartime propaganda claims about the campaign in Poland – intended to bolster the image of an invincible Wehrmacht – continue to infect even major accounts. Historical research into the 1939 Polish campaign has been seriously hindered by several factors. First, ignorance of the Polish language and Polish sources has limited use of materials from that side. Although the Polish Central Military Archives (Centralne Archiwum Wojskowe or CAW) was evacuated to the West in 1939, its reconstitution in Warsaw during the Soviet period kept it in the shadows until the 1990s. A second important factor impacting the study of *Fall Weiss* is the incomplete nature of German military records from the campaign. Many of the German division- and corps-level diaries from 1939 were damaged or destroyed by Allied bombing during the war. Even many pages in the archives are half-burned and some division-level *Kriegstagebücher* (war diaries or KTB) for 1939 are missing entirely. Due to the relative dearth of official documents and the bias towards German accounts, a number of misconceptions about the 1939 Polish campaign have lingered for many decades, despite some efforts to debunk them. The three primary misconceptions about the campaign are:

1. The Luftwaffe succeeded in destroying the Polish Air Force (Lotnictwo Wojskowe or LW) at the onset of the war and mostly on the ground.
2. Polish doctrine was foolish, outdated and too reliant on horsed cavalry, as demonstrated by examples of Polish cavalry charging German tanks.
3. The Polish armed forces were equipped with obsolete equipment and lacked the means to develop modern weapons.

Examples of the first misconception occurred when Martin Gilbert claimed in his 1989 history that 'air attacks destroyed much of the defender's air force while it was still on the ground.'[2] Even Donald Watt's magisterial *How War Came* made a similar claim.[3] A year later, John Keegan made a similar claim that 'by the end of 1 September, the Polish air force had largely ceased to exist, many of its aircraft having been caught on the ground and destroyed by the Luftwaffe.'[4] In his monumental history of the Second World War (1994), Gerhard Weinberg claimed that 'in the first days of the campaign, the Luftwaffe swept the skies clear of what few modern planes the Polish Air Force could deploy.'[5] Antony Beevor repeated these claims about the destruction of the Polish Air Force in his 2012 history, writing that 'The Luftwaffe, having eliminated the bulk of the Polish Air Force [on the first day], now concentrated on flying close support for the Wehrmacht ground forces.'[6] In fact, the Polish Air Force lost only 7 per cent of its operational aircraft on the first day of the war and remained actively in the fight for a total of 17 days – until the Soviet invasion.

The second misconception about Polish doctrine and tactics hinges on myths created by Nazi propaganda about Polish cavalry charging German tanks. Although specialist historians are aware that these claims are false, it has appeared frequently over the years. For example, the American historian Hanson Baldwin wrote in 1976 that 'the magnificent horsemen of the Pomorze Cavalry Brigade died in droves charging German tanks.'[7] The myth is based on a well-documented minor skirmish at Krojanty on 1 September 1939, which did not even involve German tanks. Even the renowned British historian Richard J. Evans stated in 2009 that 'stories of Polish cavalry squadrons quixotically charging German tank units were most probably apocryphal', which made it seem that perhaps the myth was not completely untrue.[8] In addition to the cavalry charge myth, some historians have asserted that even if the cavalry charges did not occur, the Polish military was doctrinally unprepared to deal with modern warfare, particularly tanks and aircraft.

The third misconception about the obsolete nature of Polish weaponry is alive and well, thanks to lazy scholarship in the West. Weinberg claimed that the Polish military suffered from 'the absence of modern military equipment, with no prospect of Poland either producing it herself or obtaining it by purchase.' He also stated that 'her [Poland's] industries were not yet up to the production of the planes, tanks and artillery that would be needed to hold off a German attack.'[9] Beevor wrote that 'the Polish army was severely handicapped ... by its obsolete weaponry...'.[10] In fact, the Polish Army was not only equipped with significant numbers of state-of-the-art Bofors 37mm anti-tank guns and 40mm anti-aircraft guns, but it was actually exporting them to Great Britain in the summer of 1939.[11] Richard Evans claimed that Poland 'possessed few tanks and little modern equipment ... it possessed a total of only 100 anti-aircraft guns for the whole of the country', but in fact the Polish armed forces had a total of 358 modern 40mm and 52 75mm anti-aircraft guns at the start of the war.[12] The Polish 7TP light tank was better than the bulk of the lightly armed German tanks, and better-armed tanks like the 9TP and 10TP were about to enter serial production in late 1939. Medium tanks and heavier artillery were in development and due to begin entering service in 1940. Indeed, the Polish Army had far more gun-armed tanks than the British Expeditionary Force in France possessed at the outset of the war, but no historian has referred to the BEF as equipped with obsolete weaponry. Polish industry built the PZL.37 Łoś bomber, which was superior to the British Blenheim or German Do 17 light bombers. The Polish Rkm wz. 28 light machine gun was a modified version of the same weapon, the Browning Automatic Rifle (BAR), that would be carried by American infantry throughout the Second World War. The only area where the Polish military was seriously deficient was in deploying a modern fighter that could counter the Luftwaffe's Bf 109E, but the French and Soviet militaries were in the same situation in 1939. By the standards of the day, the Polish armed forces possessed modern arms, but not in the quantities needed to stop a massive two-front invasion.

While Polish technical deficiencies are oft-mentioned, it is rarely noted that Polish intelligence succeeded in breaking into the German Enigma secure communication system – one of the great technological feats of the war – well before the war began. Poland bequeathed this technological breakthrough to England *gratis*, without receiving any financial or material support for its own war effort in return.

Meanwhile, Wehrmacht operations in Poland are usually depicted as the exemplars of a revolution in military tactics and technology, ignoring the fact the bulk of the German Army's artillery was still pulled by horses (as it would be in 1945) and the heavy dependence upon captured Czech equipment. Indeed, the German invasion appears in the history books as a slick operation, pre-destined to succeed, with *Panzer-Divisionen* (tank divisions) advancing with great speed in converging pincer movements. In reality, three days into the campaign the Oberkommando des Heeres (Army High Command or OKH) decided to tinker with the plan, diverting General der Panzertruppe Heinz Guderian's XIX Armeekorps (mot.) (XIX Army Corps (mot.)) away from Warsaw to advance instead towards Brześć (Brest). The great double pincer meeting at Warsaw – which appears on so many maps – never actually occurred in this manner. In fact, the vaunted Panzer-Division – often depicted as unstoppable in 1939–40 – suffered several tactical defeats in the short Polish campaign, including Panzer-Division Kempf at Mława on 1 September and 4. Panzer-Division in the suburbs of Warsaw on 9 September 1939. The even more disastrous battles at Ruszki and Kiernozia on 16 September 1939 are noticeably absent from existing English-language accounts. Whenever the Germans tried to assault fortified lines or urban areas with tanks, the results were predictably poor. Close examination of modern histories indicates that Beevor, Evans, Hastings, Keegan and Weinberg relied heavily upon German accounts but did not use any Polish-language sources. To date, only a few specialist histories, like Steven Zaloga and Victor Madej's *The Polish Campaign 1939* (1985) and David G. Williamson's *Poland Betrayed* (2009), have attempted to provide more balanced accounts of Case White. William Russ' *Case White* (2017) is an invaluable reference but is entirely German-centric and has some important omissions. Richard Hargreaves' *Blitzkrieg Unleashed* (2010) is based almost entirely on German contemporary accounts and includes a fair amount of wartime propaganda. Consequently, lazy or lopsided scholarship even from renowned historians has allowed wartime propaganda and biased stereotypes to shape the existing narrative of the 1939 campaign in Poland into little more than a victory parade for the Wehrmacht.

Nothing has done more to distort the nature of the German campaign in Poland than the use of the artificial term *Blitzkrieg* by historians, which has emphasized technology at the expense of doctrine, tactics,·

organization and actual battlefield leadership. The Wehrmacht had learned a bit about small unit ground and air tactics with the Legion Condor in Spain in 1936–39, but the forces committed were too small to validate operational-level methods. Thus, the Polish campaign was a grand experiment for the Heer (German Army) and the Luftwaffe, with many details of organization and methods still in flux. The question of whether tanks were best used as an independent mobile strike force or in close support of infantry formations had not been resolved at the start of the campaign. Even the mechanized divisions were in a transitional state; the Panzer-Divisionen had too many tanks but not enough infantry, while the *leichte-Divisionen* (light divisions) quickly proved to be an unsatisfactory formation. For the Luftwaffe, the state of air–ground co-operation fell far short of what was claimed by Nazi propagandists. In modern parlance, the Wehrmacht of September 1939 was a 'Beta-version' that was still working out technical, operational and organizational issues. Unlike later German campaigns, the Heer in September 1939 was not a battle-hardened force and was forced to use an assortment of Police and Border Guard regiments as part of the invasion force. The upper ranks of the OKH held justified concerns about front-line morale, which they reported back to Hitler. Indeed, most of the German troops involved in *Fall Weiss* were not aware that they were going to war until the last moment; instead, they had been told they would be participating in extended field manoeuvres. The naval infantry company assigned to seize the Westerplatte facility in Danzig deployed with practice grenades. Hitler wanted to conduct a full-scale invasion of Poland rather than a limited coup against just Danzig because he needed to see confirmation that the Wehrmacht was capable of rapidly accomplishing operational objectives, before embarking upon a major campaign against the Anglo-French in the West.

Once at war, the Poles regarded combat in a completely different light than the rest of their Western Allied partners, which has also contributed to misperceptions. Unlike the British, the Poles did not view war as a symbolic act or a sporting affair but as an existential, life-or-death event for their nation. Unlike the war-weary French, the Poles did not shrink from the idea of close combat, but often fought with great gusto and willingly accepted war as the price of national existence. Furthermore, from the outset the Poles recognized that their enemies sought their utter destruction and so they fought in a ruthless manner which sometimes appalled their allies. Western historians have struggled with the question of why Poland did not just acquiesce to Hitler's demands and surrender Danzig, because the stubborn Polish national character appears alien to the prevalent avoid-war-at-any-cost mentality that became entrenched in the West after the First World War. Unlike Neville Chamberlain, Poles recognized that acquiescence to an aggressor had not worked for the Czechs in 1938 and that Hitler's word was not to be trusted. Whether Poland surrendered Danzig willingly or not, both Germany and the Soviet Union ultimately intended to partition and smash the Polish republic. Poland's behaviour in the face of even overwhelming threats is conditioned by an innate national stubbornness which few outsiders can comprehend. Even when defeated in their homeland in 1939, Poles refused to accept defeat. It has often perplexed foreign historians why Poles would fight and suffer enormous losses – even when defeat was certain, such as in the 1944 Warsaw Uprising – but this stubbornness and unwillingness to surrender proved to be at the root of their eventual national salvation. While Hitler and Stalin conquered territory in 1939 and murdered thousands of Poles, they never came close to breaking the Polish spirit. After 50 years of brutal occupation, Poland was able to regain its freedom, while its erstwhile conquerors ended up in the dustbin of history – a testament to the value of perseverance.

My intent is to examine *Case White* in the context of sources from both the German and Polish side and to expand and update upon the interpretations put forth in Steven Zaloga's landmark work over 30 years ago. Although I intend to employ a mix of German and Polish sources, I seek to be as impartial as possible. Polish mistakes made in the campaign – or exaggerations made after the fact – will not be given a pass. Likewise, German errors will also be scrutinized. Yet the intent of this book is not just to add more military details about *Case White*, which is mere exposition of fact. As a neophyte historian, in college, I learned from Herodotus and other classical historians that the purpose of historical writing should not just be to catalogue facts, but to develop insightful analysis as to why events had particular outcomes. Nor is it adequate to just explain the 'why' of an event, it is also necessary to establish the 'so what?' – why an event was important and what relevance it possesses for future generations. Not all readers enjoy this approach and some may wonder why I just don't get on with it and get straight to the rolling of Panzers and the scream of Stukas. Yet I believe that putting *Case White* in proper context means discussing events that occurred well before September 1939, since military power is not created from thin air. Rather, modern military power is the result of years of industrial policies, doctrinal debates, economic prioritization, social preparation and national heritage.

Similarly, the meaning of historical events is often not confined to a specific moment; the Polish military defeat in September 1939 and the subsequent Soviet murder of thousands of captured Polish officers had international repercussions for decades afterward. Indeed, understanding the past is an essential element in evaluating the present. Poland's reactions to Russian aggression in eastern Ukraine in 2014–16 were heavily influenced by its memory of Stalin's land-grabbing tactics of 1939–40, which are but faintly remembered in Western Europe. It is no wonder that Poland is currently embarked upon a costly defence build-up, since its leadership do not intend to be caught militarily unprepared again or to be dependent upon empty foreign guarantees. Similarly, efforts by the EU to pressure Poland into accepting refugees from the Middle East are unpalatable to most Poles, who worry about demographic changes that could weaken their claims to historically Polish-held land. In eastern Europe, demography is destiny. Continued accusations about alleged widespread collaboration between Polish citizens and the Nazi occupation has also caused strident reactions within Poland. Unlike other countries, Poland has not forgotten that collaboration was widespread in other occupied countries and that the Waffen-SS was able to recruit 40,000 Belgians, 25,000 Dutch, 20,000 French, 6,000 Danes and 6,000 Norwegians to serve in their ranks. Furthermore, the Polish armed resistance continued for a decade after the Second World War – against the Soviets – and without any help from the West. Consequently, the idea of collaboration with any foreign occupier has long been anathema to Poles. In our time, the history of Poland's relationship with its neighbours in 1918–39 will continue to influence decision-making in eastern Europe, particularly in moments of crisis.

CHAPTER 1

Poland is Not Lost

*'The heroic characteristics of the Polish race must not blind
us to their errors, which over centuries have led
them through measureless suffering.'*
Winston S. Churchill[1]

Rise and Decline of the Polish State, 1241–1918

*'When I finish with Poland, there will not be a
papist in the land ...'*
Charles X of Sweden, 1655

'We ask you, Lord, for a world war for the freedom of nations.'
Adam Mickiewicz, 1832

If history reveals any immutable truths, it is that Poland has no real friends,
but it does have plenty of implacable foes. Poland is situated in a bad
neighbourhood, historically sandwiched between bullying Germanic
powers to the west and a rapacious Russia to the east. Throughout its
tortured history, Poland has been invaded and ransacked by some of the

greatest armies ever raised, including the Mongols (1241), the Teutonic Knights (1228–1462), the Swedes (1621, 1655, 1702) and the Turks (1672–76). Indeed, in a geo-political sense, the Polish nation was created amidst one of the most war-torn areas of the planet, with threats arising from all corners of the compass. The Mongols burned Kraków in 1241 and the Teutonic Knights slaughtered the Polish population of Gdańsk in 1308. Nevertheless, Poles succeeded in building a resilient nation-state that was able to rebuild quickly, even after disastrous defeats. It is important to spend some time making the case – in contrast to later rhetoric from British politicians like David Lloyd George and other unsympathetic spectators – that Poland had a long, established tradition of self-rule and was not just some half-baked by-product of the 1918 Treaty of Versailles.

During the mid-14th century, King Casimir III 'the Great' (1333–70) laid a solid foundation for a Polish state by making peace with the Teutonic Knights and then using the respite to revitalize Poland's military forces and its economy. He also created legal codes that paved the way for a more civil society, adopted an official policy of tolerance towards non-Catholics and established the Jagiellonian University in Kraków to promote education. Queen Jadwiga (1384–99) continued to improve Poland's stature and established dynastic ties with Lithuania through marriage. With the threat of further aggression by the Teutonic Knights judged likely, Poland's leadership sought to forge a close alliance with Lithuania. When battle was renewed, Poland and its Lithuanian allies finally broke the power of the Teutonic Knights at the battle of Tannenberg in 1410. Thereafter, Poland's power and influence in eastern Europe grew, eventually compromising a total population of more than seven million spread across a territory of roughly 1 million square kilometres. Having secured its territory, Poland turned to peaceful pursuits, which were profoundly influenced by the Renaissance (1440–1569). Poles developed a keen interest in learning, the arts and science, with the nobility investing considerable money in schools and libraries. The foremost exemplar of Poland's Renaissance was the astronomer Nicolaus Copernicus (1473–1543), whose theories revolutionized mankind's understanding of the solar system. Poland's stature was further boosted by a formal political union with Lithuania in 1569, thereby creating the Polish–Lithuanian Commonwealth. As a result of the union, most of the Ukraine also fell under Polish rule. Thereafter, the Polish–Lithuanian Commonwealth enjoyed its best years in the late 16th century. In 1573, the Sejm (the Polish National Assembly) approved an act granting religious freedom – a first in Europe.

However, the commonwealth political system had an intrinsic weakness which contributed to its decline: the Polish–Lithuanian nobility (*szlachta*) could freely elect (*wolna elekcja*) kings, particularly when no direct heirs were available. Since even non-Poles were eligible to be elected to the throne, this tradition set the stage for embroiling Poland in open-ended dynastic conflicts and power struggles which did not involve true national interests. It also allowed foreign powers to interfere in Poland's leadership selection process by trying to influence the outcome through bribing some members of the nobility. By one of the odd quirks of history, Sigismund, the crown prince of Sweden, was elected to the Polish throne in 1587, after the death of his uncle, King Stephen Bathory (himself an ethnic Hungarian). Seven years later, Sigismund III also became king of Sweden when his father died and he allied himself with the Austrian Hapsburgs by marriage. However, it proved intolerable for Lutheran Sweden to be ruled by a Catholic monarch during the Counter-Reformation, so Sigismund III was forced to abdicate the Swedish crown. Consequently, Sigismund III embroiled Poland in a series of wars with Sweden in a vain effort to regain that crown. King Gustavus Adolphus, one of the great 'soldier kings', led a professional army which succeeded in seizing much of Livonia (modern Estonia and Latvia) away from the commonwealth, before agreeing to a peace treaty in 1629. Meanwhile, Polish–Russian tensions had been brewing over control of the Ukraine and other border areas, which caused Sigismund III to invade Russia in 1609. Although Polish forces briefly occupied Moscow and the Kremlin, the war ended in defeat and Russia was now added to the list of Poland's enemies. While Sigismund III was pre-occupied with Russia, Sweden and the Hapsburgs, the Turks took the opportunity to invade and occupy part of eastern Ukraine. Despite these multiple threats, Sigismund's son, Władysław IV (1632–48) managed to fend off a Russian invasion and restore one last brief period of prosperity.

Poland's equanimity was shattered by a major Swedish invasion from their Livonian bridgehead in July 1655, a national catastrophe which became known as 'The Deluge'. At the head of a well-trained and professional army, King Charles X managed to overrun most of the commonwealth in just three months, including the capture of both Warsaw and Kraków. Swedish forces burned and looted their way across Poland, inflicting great destruction and loss of life. It is important to note that religion was an important factor in this campaign, with Charles X determined to crush Catholic Poland. Prior to the German–Soviet invasions of 1939, the Deluge was the most traumatic event in Polish history. Having suffered heavy losses in contending with a recent Cossack rebellion in Ukraine, the remnants of the Polish regular army was unsuccessful against the Swedes, but the Polish population responded with a ferocious guerrilla warfare which drained the enemy's will. Popular resistance to foreign invasion was epitomized by the Siege of Jasna Góra in December 1655, where a scratch force of Polish civilian volunteers successfully defended the monastery in Częstochowa against a numerically superior Swedish force.

Amazingly, the commonwealth was able to partially recover from the Deluge within just two decades and Polish forces under King Jan III Sobieski played a key role in stopping the Turkish advance into central Europe at the battle of Vienna (1683). However, by the early 17th century, the commonwealth was sliding into a period of decline, caused by foreign interference with the monarchy after Sobieski's death. August II of Saxony, backed by Russia, was elected king of Poland in 1697, but replaced by a Swedish-backed candidate in 1704, then was re-elected to the throne with Peter the Great's support in 1709. During the reign of Augustus II, Russian influence over Poland increased considerably and Poland's army was reduced to 18,000 troops. When August II died in 1733, a 30,000-man Russian army invaded Poland and installed his son, Augustus III, on the throne, despite French efforts to prevent this. Under nearly six decades of inept Saxon rule, by kings who spent more time in Saxony than Poland, Poland's independence began to evaporate. In 1763, Stanisław Poniatowski, with strong financial and military backing by Russia's Catherine II, was elected king of Poland. As king, Poniatowski proved to be a *de facto* Russian surrogate and he further reduced Poland's army. After Russia's ambassador bluntly stated that Poland was now in Russia's 'sphere of influence', the Polish nobility made an effort to stand up to Poniatowski and his Russian backers in 1768. With equivocal French support, the nobles formed the Confederation of the Bar, gathered a militia army around Kraków and declared war on Russia. Unfortunately, the Russians were able to dispatch one of their most able generals, Alexander Suvorov, who quickly captured Kraków. French assistance to Poland was negligible. It still took the Russians four years to suppress the Bar Confederation, after which it was clear that Poland could not be run as a client state. During this conflict, both Prussia's Frederick II and the Austrian Hapsburgs moved in to gain their share of the spoils. After signing diplomatic conventions in February 1772, which apportioned spheres of influence, the three great empires began seizing chunks of Polish territory. The only resistance to the First Partition was from final hold-outs of the Bar Confederacy, like Casimir

Pulaski at Częstochowa, which were eliminated by August. Afterwards, both the Russians and Prussians began efforts to suppress Polish identity; Frederick II moved 26,000 German colonists into Pomerania, while Catherine II exiled 5,000 Poles to Siberia.

Reduced to the monarch of a rump Polish state after the First Partition, Poniatowski allowed some efforts to regain Polish independence. In 1788, the Great Sejm voted to create a new 100,000-man army. However, the Sejm only provided enough funding to raise the army to about 37,000 troops, but some quality officers were promoted, including the military engineer Tadeusz Kościuszko. Hoping to gain assistance from Prussia after Frederick II's death, Poland agreed to sign a defensive alliance with Prussia in May 1790; Prussia asked for Gdańsk (Danzig) as a condition of the alliance, but was rebuffed.[2] In order to lay the groundwork for internal political reforms, the Great Sejm approved a new constitution in May 1791, which emulated lessons learned from the US Constitution. Among other things, the new constitution eliminated the *wolna elekcja,* in order to prevent foreign interference in Polish elections. Incensed by signs of Polish efforts to escape from its sphere of influence, Russia launched a massive invasion of Poland in May 1792. Although greatly outnumbered, the Polish armies managed to fight a successful delaying campaign back from the eastern regions, but were betrayed by their ostensible Prussian allies, who refused to honour the defensive alliance. Poniatowski cravenly threw in the towel and capitulated to the Russians before any major Polish cities were even besieged. Prussia and Russia now worked together to impose the Second Partition upon a betrayed Poland in January 1793, with Prussia seizing Gdańsk. The occupiers demanded that most of the remaining Polish army be disbanded and its leaders imprisoned.

Tadeusz Kościuszko resigned his commission after the king's capitulation and avoided arrest by fleeing to Saxony, where he gathered other Polish émigrés. When a Russian attempt to disband Polish cavalry brigades sparked resistance, Kościuszko returned to Poland in March 1794 to lead a national insurrection. Kościuszko succeeded in inflicting some tactical defeats on the Russians and their garrisons in Warsaw and Vilnius were eliminated. Spontaneous riots broke out in many areas and traitors who had colluded with the Russians were publicly hanged in Warsaw. Furthermore, Kościuszko sought to create a truly national uprising involving the peasantry by pledging civil reforms to enhance their living conditions. However, the Polish military situation became critical once Prussian and Russian armies began working together, which led to the rapid loss of Kraków. Kościuszko himself was defeated in battle and captured by the Russians in October. In November Russian troops under Suvorov stormed Warsaw and slaughtered thousands of its civilians. After eight months, the Kościuszko Uprising was crushed and both Prussia and Russia moved to ensure that there would no reoccurrences. Poniatowski was forced to abdicate and packed off to virtual house arrest in Russia, where he would die three years later. Austria was brought into the conspiracy and all three powers signed treaties making the Third Partition official in October 1795. With this stroke of a pen, an independent Polish state disappeared from the map of Europe.

During the next 123 years of foreign occupation, the only foreigner who supported the revival of a Polish state was Napoleon Bonaparte, who, after defeating Austria and Prussia, created the satellite Duchy of Warsaw in 1807. Although Napoleon was sympathetic to the Poles and desired their military co-operation in his conquests, he failed to endorse a fully independent state and the Duchy of Warsaw ceased to exist after his own defeat. Nevertheless, the Poles stubbornly refused assimilation into the Russian Empire and launched two full-blown rebellions (1830 and 1863), both of which were brutally crushed. After the January Uprising was put down in 1864, the Russians abolished the Polish language in their section of occupied Poland in an effort to suppress Polish identity. Meanwhile, in the Prussian-occupied areas of north-west Poland, the Prussian government enacted numerous laws in efforts to suppress Polish culture and the Catholic Church; these efforts were less than successful and only increased Polish resentment. The Prussians also encouraged German emigration into formerly Polish territory, to manage large farming estates in rural areas and the limited amount of industry in the cities. In contrast, the Austrians had a fairly *laissez-faire* attitude towards managing their zone in southern Poland, although they were just as willing to use force to suppress anyone advocating Polish independence.

Meanwhile, the rest of Europe simply ignored the demise of Poland. A number of Polish intellectuals relocated to Paris during the 19th century, where they were free to discuss the idea of Polish independence, but this did not lead to any immediate meaningful results. A certain cultural affinity continued to develop between France and Poland during the 19th century – which set the stage for later co-operation – but prior to the First World War French politicians were more interested in forming alliances with Russia than creating controversy by supporting the idea of a resurrected Polish state. Attitudes towards Poland were even more apathetic in London. During the two centuries prior to the final partition of Poland in 1795, only very limited diplomatic and economic contact had occurred between the Polish–Lithuanian Commonwealth and Great Britain. When Poland was being carved up by its neighbours, neither King George III nor his ministers offered even the slightest diplomatic protest about this outcome. Newspapers in London actually printed caricatures about Russian Cossacks beheading Polish civilians in Warsaw in 1794. Looking through the narrow lenses of Anglican parochialism, English politicians would consistently prove as hostile to the idea of Polish independence as they were to the idea of Catholic self-rule in Ireland.

Resurrection, 1918–26

'An independent Polish state should be erected which should include the territories inhabited by indisputably Polish populations, which should be assured a free and secure access to the sea, and whose political and economic independence and territorial integrity should be guaranteed by international covenant.'
President Woodrow Wilson's Fourteen Points, 8 January 1918

The resurrection of Poland simultaneously occurred on both a military and a political dimension, driven in large part by two charismatic revolutionaries. In the military realm, Józef Piłsudski, scion of a wealthy Polish–Lithuanian family, provided the main impetus for the re-creation of an independent Polish Army. In the political realm, Roman Dmowski, product of a Warsaw blue-collar family, worked to develop a sense of Polish nationalism at home and lay the groundwork for international recognition of a Polish state. However, neither Piłsudski nor Dmowski could have achieved much success unless fate had thrown them an unusually fortunate set of international circumstances. As long as Imperial Germany, Russia and Austria-Hungary were strong, Poles could not hope to regain their freedom. However, the assassination of Austria's Archduke Franz Ferdinand in June 1914 set in motion a sequence of events that would eventually incapacitate all three of Poland's occupiers.

Both Piłsudski and Dmowski spent their youth in the Russian-occupied region of Poland, but later relocated to the Austrian-occupied region in the decade prior to the outbreak of the First World War. From the beginning, Piłsudski followed the path of violence and hoped to lead another armed insurrection against Russian rule. He rejected any idea of co-operation with the Russians, regarding it as tantamount to collaboration. Consequently, young Piłsudski quickly ran afoul of the Russian police and spent five years in Siberian exile. After his exile, Piłsudski became involved in socialist politics and joined the Polish Socialist Party (Polska Partia Socjalistyczna or PPS), while simultaneously engaging in underground revolutionary activities. By 1904, Piłsudski was able to gather some like-minded individuals and formed a paramilitary unit within the PPS. In contrast, Dmowski believed that armed rebellion was doomed to failure and considered some degree of co-operation with the Russians as essential if Poles were ever to achieve any kind of local autonomy. Since the Russians did not look kindly on Poles forming political organizations, Dmowski was forced to found his National Democratic Party (known as *endecja*) as a covert organization. When revolution in Russia spread to Poland in 1905, Piłsudski and Dmowski found themselves on opposite sides. Dmowski formed a militia that worked with the Russians to suppress the rebellion, which helped to foster permanent enmity with Piłsudski. Furthermore, Piłsudski's preference for armed rebellion led to a split in the PPS.

Following the failed 1905 Revolution, Piłsudski relocated to Austrian-controlled Kraków with his remaining confederates while Dmowski joined the Russian Duma as a Polish delegate. The Austrians regarded Piłsudski as useful and allowed him to form several small Polish paramilitary organizations, which could be used to conduct sabotage and terrorist-style raids into the Russian-controlled region of Poland. Hauptmann Włodzimierz Zagórski, an ethnic Pole serving in the Austro-Hungarian General Staff, served as primary liaison between the Austrian military and Piłsudski's paramilitaries. Piłsudski had a tendency to resent professional military officers, since he lacked their training, and his methods seemed more like gangster tactics. In September 1908, Piłsudski led a successful raid near Vilnius which robbed a Russian mail train of about 200,000 rubles; Piłsudski used the funds to expand his covert organizations.[3] Piłsudski's long-term vision was to create a pool of armed and trained Poles who could be used to eventually fight for Polish independence. However, the Austro-Hungarian Army was not keen on subsidizing international train robberies and thereafter tried to keep Piłsudski on a short leash. Nevertheless, by the time that Gavrilo Princip assassinated the Austrian Archduke Franz Ferdinand in June 1914, Piłsudski had a solid cadre of Polish insurgents, which he wanted to march into Poland to instigate an anti-Russian rebellion. Without asking permission from the

Austrian authorities, Piłsudski launched his own invasion with 400 troops on 6 August and occupied the city of Kielce a week later. As soon as the Austrians discovered this unauthorized military action, they demanded that Piłsudski's troops be incorporated into the Austro-Hungarian Army; after three weeks of dithering, which he used to gather more recruits, Piłsudski agreed.[4] He began forming the Polish Legions, three brigade-size units that would fight on the Eastern Front in 1914–16. In order to keep close control on Piłsudski, Hauptmann Zagórski was made chief of staff of the Legions.

Poles have tended to exaggerate the actual accomplishments of the Polish Legions, but there is no doubt that Piłsudski was able to amass a cadre of veteran soldiers who would become the backbone of Poland's armed forces for the next three decades. It is also true that the Legion officers were a picked lot; they were well-educated men who were also intensely patriotic and loyal to Piłsudski. For example, Kazimierz Sosnkowski, chief of staff of the Legions' 1st Brigade, had been with Piłsudski since his PPS days and was a scholar who could speak seven languages. Władysław Sikorski, a university-trained engineer with a reserve commission in the Austrian Army, played a major role in training the Legions' nascent officer corps. Another rising star in the Legions was Edward Rydz-Śmigły. Meanwhile, Dmowski worked within the Russian political system, trying – and failing – to gain any concessions to Polish autonomy in return for support in the on-going war.

While agreeing to work with the Austrians, Piłsudski saw this as only a temporary measure and continued his own plans to build a military apparatus that could achieve Polish independence by force. Shortly after agreeing to form the Legions, he established the covert Polish Military Organization (Polska Organizacja Wojskowa or POW), which was intended to conduct subversion and propaganda behind Russian lines in Poland. When the Germans occupied Warsaw in August 1915, the POW came out into the open and formed its first battalion. At this point, Piłsudski hoped to disband the foreign-controlled Legions and expand the POW into a Polish Army under his command. However, neither Germany nor Austria-Hungary were interested in allowing an independent Polish Army and the POW battalion was integrated into the Legions. Although Russia was clearly losing the war by 1916, the Central Powers were also beginning to run out of infantry replacements and decided to seek greater Polish participation by issuing a decree that promised to create a new Kingdom of Poland after the war was won. However, Piłsudski could see that these were empty promises and that Germany would not allow true Polish independence. After the February Revolution in 1917 and the abdication of the tsar, the Germans were eager to transfer troops west to fight the Allies. Piłsudski's Polish Legions had grown to nearly a corps-size formation and Austria-Hungary agreed to transfer these troops to German command. However, Piłsudski refused to serve under German command, as did many of his troops (the so-called 'Oath Crisis'), so he was jailed and his troops scattered. Zagórski had urged the legionnaires to take the oath, which blackened his name in the eyes of many of Piłsudski's acolytes. Other Poles, including Władysław Sikorski, either joined the German-organized Polnische Wehrmacht (Polish Armed Forces) or the Austrian-organized Auxiliary Corps.[5] Before his arrest, Piłsudski appointed Edward Rydz-Śmigły as the new head of the POW, which went underground again.

Meanwhile, Dmowski had recognized that tsarist Russia was losing the war and he went to England and France in 1917 to espouse the idea of Polish autonomy. On 15 August 1917, in France, Dmowski created a new Polish National Committee aimed at rebuilding a Polish state, which included the famed pianist Ignacy Paderewski. Within a month, the French recognized the committee as the legitimate representatives of Poland and promised to help form a Polish volunteer army in France to support the Allies. The Allied governments released expatriate Poles in their own armed forces and encouraged recruitment overseas, particularly in Canada and the United States. Generał Józef Haller, one of the brigade commanders in the Polish Legions, managed to escape to France in July 1918 and he seemed the perfect leader for the Polish expatriate army being formed. Haller's so-called 'Blue Army' was slowly trained and equipped by the French, but did not see any combat on the Western Front until July 1918. When the Armistice was announced in November, Haller had two well-equipped divisions under his command, with three more divisions and a tank regiment forming. The French were also training Polish pilots, in order to form seven aviation squadrons. Haller's Blue Army was loyal to Dmowski's Polish National Committee in Paris. Dmowski and Paderewski also helped to steer opinions in the Allied camp towards favouring the restoration of a Polish state after the war was concluded. President Woodrow Wilson's Fourteen Points clearly enunciated this aspiration in January 1918, although there was little discussion about Poland's potential borders.

While the Allies were defeating Imperial Germany, Piłsudski was cooling his heels in Magdeburg fortress for 16 months, with his deputy, Kazimierz

Sosnkowski. When revolution in Germany forced Kaiser Wilhelm II to abdicate, the caretaker government released Piłsudski and allowed him to leave by train for Warsaw. Although the Germans attempted to coerce Piłsudski into making various pledges, he refused to make any concessions. The Regency Council, established by the Germans, held residual civilian authority in Warsaw. Recognizing the need for military advice, the council selected Colonel Tadeusz Rozwadowski, an Austrian-trained artilleryman, to organize an independent Polish military force. When Piłsudski arrived in Warsaw on 10 November 1918, he was met by only a few members of the POW. Nevertheless, the next day Piłsudski managed to browbeat the council into appointing him as commander-in-chief of the Polish armed forces and to dismiss Rozwadowski. He then began forming a national government – making him a *de facto* military dictator. Aside from his titles, Piłsudski was only able to cobble together a force of about three infantry regiments (9,000 troops) under his command.[6] In contrast, the Ober Ost (German Army in the East) had over 80,000 troops in Poland (mostly from General Erich von Falkenhayn's 10. Armee, 10th Army), but their military discipline was collapsing. Piłsudski met with the local German commander and negotiated an agreement, whereby the German Army would leave the area within ten days in return for no harassment by the Poles. Piłsudski's troops eagerly began disarming the evacuating German troops, acquiring large stocks of weaponry and ammunition. A similar process occurred in southern Poland, where Austrian troops were also disarmed. Thus when the Armistice ended the First World War on 11 November 1918, the new Polish republic found itself with two groups claiming to be the legitimate government of Poland: Dmowski's in Paris and Piłsudski's in Warsaw. Five days later, Piłsudski announced the re-creation of an independent Polish state, to be known as the Second Republic. Surprisingly, Italy was the first country to recognize independent Poland.

It is important to note that Piłsudski and Dmowski had radically different visions for the new Poland; the former intended to create a socialist-tinged, secular and multi-ethnic state with expanded territorial buffers to help defend against future German and Russian aggressions. In contrast, Dmowski wanted to build a homogenous state based upon a Catholic, ethnic Polish majority. He regarded the inclusion of minorities (Czechs, Germans, Ukrainians, White Russians, Jews) as a dangerous liability who might provide grounds for Poland's neighbours to seek future border adjustments. These two competing visions were never reconciled in the Second Republic.

As Austrian, German and Russian authority evaporated in eastern Europe, the political situation became extremely fluid. In particular, the German evacuation left a vacuum in the eastern borderlands, which the Poles referred to as *Kresy Wschodnie*. Ukrainian nationalists seized part of Lwów and proclaimed a republic – which immediately sparked conflict with local Polish militiamen. In Wilno, Lithuanian nationalists were agitating to claim that city for themselves, as well. Czechs and Romanian troops also were mobilizing to seize contested border areas. Meanwhile, the Western Allies – particularly Britain – sought to impose limits upon the new Polish state by proposing the so-called Curzon Line, which would deprive Poland of both Lwów and Wilno. Piłsudski simply ignored this unsolicited proposal and mobilized as many troops as possible to fight for the eastern border regions. However, the Polish Second Republic was in poor shape from the outset, having suffered significant damage to its infrastructure after four years of fighting during the First World War: cities and towns had been looted or burned, industrial production was negligible, the agricultural situation was grim and about 450,000 Poles had died in the war.[7] Before evacuating, the Germans sabotaged much of the rail network in Poland and destroyed 940 train stations.[8] Poland was even stripped of horses, which made it difficult to form cavalry units. Furthermore, there were no arms industries in Poland because the occupying Germans and Russians had not wanted the risk that they might be seized by Polish rebels. Nevertheless, Piłsudski was able to rally just enough troops to relieve the Ukrainian siege of Lwów, but his forces were still too badly outnumbered by the Ukrainian nationalists to achieve more. Yet, Piłsudski and many Polish nationalists – aside from Dmowski's faction – were committed to recovering Kresy for the Second Republic, ensuring further bloodshed.

In addition to committing forces to secure Galicia from the Ukrainians, Piłsudski also encouraged an anti-German revolt in Poznań, which began in late December 1918. Thousands of ethnic Poles in the disintegrating German Imperial Army defected to the rebels, providing them a solid core of trained soldiers, but there were still enough residual German troops in Pomerania to contest control of the region for six months. The rebels formed a separate Polish military formation known as the Greater Poland Army (Wojska Wielkopolska), which was able to amass nearly 90,000 troops by early 1919. In response, the Germans formed Freikorps and border units (*Grenzschutz Ost*) to launch vicious counter-attacks against the Polish rebels.

In Warsaw, Piłsudski faced great difficulty in organizing a re-born Polish Army (Wojsko Polskie), which was a hodgepodge force from the beginning. The veteran troops had been trained and fought under Austrian, German and Russian command, so there was no common doctrine. Weapons and equipment came from a variety of sources and there was a persistent shortage of ammunition. Thousands of patriotic volunteers also flocked to the colours, including many Lithuanians. Nevertheless, Piłsudski only had 110,000 troops under his control at the start of 1919, which was inadequate to deal with multiple border conflicts.[9] It was not until March 1919 that the Polish government was sufficiently organized to introduce conscription. However, only 100,000 rifles and 12,000 machine guns were available, so foreign military aid was essential to build a more effective military force.[10]

The year 1919 began badly for the Second Republic. Officers loyal to Dmowski attempted a coup against Piłsudski in Warsaw, but this effort quickly failed. The Czechs took advantage of Piłsudski's pre-occupation with Galicia and internal politics to seize the Silesian border town of Teschen (Cieszyn), which actually had a Polish majority. In the north-west, German forces recaptured some territory lost to the Greater Poland Army. In Galicia, the Ukrainians went on the offensive and nearly retook Lwów, with the outnumbered Poles hanging on by their finger-nails. General Tadeusz Rozwadowski, Piłsudski's bête noire, played a major role in the defence of Lwów. Hard-pressed, the Polish garrison in Lwów was forced to employ female troops in the front line. The fighting around Lwów was also noteworthy because local Jews sided with the Ukrainians and even formed armed militia units – which would not be forgotten by the Poles. Further north, the Soviet Red Army occupied Minsk and then began tentative probes towards eastern Poland. However, the Red Army was still heavily committed countering a White Russian offensive in southern Ukraine led by Anton Denikin and could not immediately commit large forces against Poland. Even with this caveat, within three months of its re-creation, Poland found itself involved in three major wars against the Germans, Russians and Ukrainians and two hostile border disputes with the Czechs and Lithuanians. The only saving grace was that the popular Ignacy Paderewski returned to Danzig via a British cruiser and agreed to become Piłsudski's prime minister and foreign minister, which helped to prevent a Polish civil war between opposing factions.[11] Piłsudski blocked Dmowski's efforts to join the government and instead insisted that he serve as Poland's primary delegate at the Versailles peace conference. Dmowski worked assiduously with the French to get Haller's Blue Army transported to Poland and to secure material assistance for Poland's war effort.[12] Indeed, Dmowski's diplomacy quickly provided great benefits for Piłsudski when the first elements of Haller's 65,000-man Blue Army reached Poland in April 1919. Furthermore, French diplomatic pressure on the Ukrainians helped limit their advance while Polish forces were still outnumbered. Haller's army was sent directly to Galicia, where it spearheaded a counter-offensive. Ultimately, Piłsudski's forces emerged victorious and the Ukrainian-Polish War ended in July 1919, with Lwów in Polish hands. Furthermore, the important oil refinery at Drohobycz, south-west of Lwów, would provide the Polish Second Republic with vital hard currency. Likewise, the Greater Poland Army managed to hold on to Pomerania and the region – including the so-called 'Polish Corridor' – until the Allies awarded the region to Poland in the Treaty of Versailles in June 1919.

In early 1919, the Anglo-French made tentative efforts to assist the Polish Second Republic, with both Britain and France sending military missions to Warsaw. The French were sympathetic to Poland and sent 1,500 military personnel to train Piłsudski's army. In addition to the 276 artillery pieces that arrived with Haller's Blue Army, the French also delivered 350 additional 75mm guns and stocks of ammunition in August 1919. However, the British military mission accomplished very little, even according to its head, Brigadier Adrian Carton de Wiart. Although Carton de Wiart was sympathetic to the Poles, British Prime Minister David Lloyd George was not. Lloyd George was himself ignorant about conditions in eastern Europe and was influenced by the opinions of two close foreign policy advisors: Sir Lewis Namier and Edward H. Carr. Namier was born a Polish Jew in south-east Poland, but emigrated to England prior to the Great War and anglicized his name. In 1919, Namier became a member of the British delegation at Versailles and he quickly adopted a hostile attitude towards Dmowski's nationalism and Poland's border claims.[13] Carr, a Cambridge historian, was also part of the British delegation at Versailles and he became quite enamoured of the Soviet Union, which also caused him to oppose Polish territorial claims. Even though British military forces were still on Soviet territory and supporting the Whites, Lloyd George sought a way to end that commitment and he was eager to develop new trade relations with the Soviets. Despite suggestions at Versailles the Poland should gain Upper Silesia and the southern part of East Prussia, Lloyd George and his protégés opposed this, as well as Piłsudski's efforts to acquire Galicia and

Wilno – which were dubbed 'imperialistic'. Paderewski's acquiescence to British demands caused great political strife in Poland, which led to his resignation. Although some English politicians, such as Winston Churchill, were still viscerally opposed to the Soviet Union, they were unwilling to offer substantive military assistance to the Poles. Even the attempted delivery of a few dozen surplus aircraft and surplus German rifles led to protests from English trade unions, which delayed shipment of the meagre arms aid that was authorized.[14] German railroad workers worked to impede arms shipments to Poland across their territory and Czechs also blocked shipments. Consequently, British military aid to Poland in 1919 was negligible. In contrast, Italy provided the Polish government with a monetary loan and delivered a vital shipment of heavy artillery pieces to Danzig in June 1919.[15]

Nevertheless, by spending 49 per cent of Poland's national budget on his military, by early 1920 Piłsudski had managed to assemble a nominal force of nearly 200,000 men under arms.[16] He even had an armoured regiment with 120 French-made FT17 tanks and an air arm with about 200 aircraft. Although there was a shortage of trained pilots, foreign volunteers made up some of the deficiency; enough American pilots arrived to form a complete squadron, known as the Kościuszko Squadron.[17] In Paris, Dmowski directed the Polish Military Procurement Mission to purchase very large quantities of ex-German weapons as scrap and send them to Poland, although much of this equipment was worn out. Emboldened by his new armament, Piłsudski was determined to resolve the question of Poland's eastern borders by force, whether or not the Anglo-French approved. Denikin's forces had been defeated and the Red Army was now shifting massive forces to its western border to crush Poland. Piłsudski unwisely chose to strike first and took personal command of the Ukrainian Front, while Władysław Sikorski took command of the Lithuanian–Byelorussian Front. By forging an alliance with the defeated Ukrainians, Piłsudski managed to capture Kiev on 7 May 1920. However, a Soviet counter-offensive in June threatened to crush Piłsudski's over-extended forces and he was forced to withdraw westwards in haste. By early July, the Red Army had seized Vilnius and was pushing towards Warsaw. At this point, the Anglo-French realized that a Bolshevik advance into central Europe was now a distinct possibility and authorized an enlarged military mission, headed by General Maxime Weygand. Allied military aid trickled in to Poland, but no more credit would be offered to Piłsudski's government to purchase additional equipment. British diplomats impotently demanded that the Red Army stop its advance at the Curzon Line, which was blithely ignored. On 24 July 1920, the Red Army crossed the line and captured the city of Białystok, 175km north-west of Warsaw.

Anticipating a rapid military victory over the Poles, the Soviets took steps to establish a puppet government in Białystok, dubbed the Provisional Polish Revolutionary Committee or Polrevkom. Since Felix Dzerzhinsky (who was also head of the Cheka, secret police) was head of the Polrevkom, there could be little doubt for Piłsudski and his associates what their fate would be if they lost. However, the population of Białystok, which was 75 per cent Jewish, did not relish remaining under Polish jurisdiction and many were enthusiastic about the prospect of communist rule.[18] Furthermore, as Polish historian Halik Kochanski noted, 'the Polish–Soviet War had an enormous effect within Poland. It reminded the Poles that the Russians, whether tsarist or Soviet, brought repression and subjugation'.[19]

When the Anglo-French failed to provide effective diplomatic or military support, the Poles were left to fend off the Soviet offensive towards Warsaw on their own. Piłsudski lacked the training or experience to plan and co-ordinate the movement of multiple armies in a mobile campaign, so General Tadeusz Rozwadowski was brought back from Paris to serve as head of the Polish General Staff. As the saying goes, 'victory has a hundred fathers, but defeat is an orphan', so it has been difficult to accurately gauge who planned the Polish counter-attack, although it is more likely that it was the product of careful staff work, rather than amateur improvisation. In any case, the Polish Army mounted a brilliant counter-offensive which inflicted a catastrophic riposte against the Red Army in the battle of Warsaw. Sikorski's 5th Army launched a carefully timed pincer attack into the enemy's flank, spearheaded by tanks, which encircled one Soviet army and threw the rest into chaos. By carefully husbanding their remaining airpower, the Poles were able to gain air superiority around Warsaw and use aircraft to bomb and strafe the enemy. The Red Army's best units were shattered and routed. Contrary to popular perception that the battle of Warsaw was won primarily by Polish cavalry, only about 5 per cent of Piłsudski's combat forces were mounted troops. Instead, the Poles fought a modern battle, winning through use of combined arms tactics that properly meshed air operations with infantry, tanks, artillery and cavalry.[20] Shortly after the victory at Warsaw, four Polish air squadrons repulsed the Soviet 1st Cavalry Army's push towards Lwów by relentless bombing and strafing attacks. As the shattered Red Army retreated in disorder, pursued by the Poles, Lloyd George demanded that Polish forces cease their pursuit at the Curzon Line. Piłsudski ignored him.[21] Instead, in the subsequent

Treaty of Riga, the Soviet Union was forced to concede much of Kresy to Poland. Victory had not come cheap to Poland, which suffered over 170,000 military casualties in its eastern border conflicts in 1918–20.

The Polish Air Force (Lotnictwo Wojskowe or LW) also played a significant role in the defeat of the Ukrainians and Russians, by maintaining air superiority over the main battlefields. Flying a mix of Austrian, French, German and British aircraft, the LW flew a total of 5,172 combat sorties during 1918–20 and demonstrated a clear superiority over their Soviet opponents.[22] Indeed, the Poles had an easier time finding skilled pilots (often from abroad) than the Bolsheviks, since most of the tsarist-era Russian pilots opted to join the White forces.

Despite the fact that Poland had regained its independence through the efforts of its own soldiers, the Anglo-French allies subsequently fabricated a false narrative that claimed that Poland owed its existence to their efforts at Versailles and their last-minute military aid.[23] While President Wilson's Fourteen Points and Dmowski's diplomacy at Versailles set the stage for international recognition of the reborn Polish state, independence itself was achieved solely through Polish military success. Both Lloyd George and Churchill convinced themselves that Poland owed its independence to their good offices, while ignoring what Polish armies actually achieved in the field in 1919–20. By March 1921, Poland had achieved a tenuous peace and two years later the League of Nations recognized the new Russo-Polish border.

While Piłsudski had been focused on the Russian threat, yet another conflict had been developing in Upper Silesia, which possessed a large Polish population. Germany intended to keep this region, with its heavy industry and coal mines, despite Polish nationalist agitation. German forces easily crushed one Polish uprising in August 1919 and a second in August 1920, resulting in thousands of casualties. The Polish POW formed paramilitary units in Upper Silesia to counter German repression and German Freikorps units swarmed into the region, leading to frequent clashes. Once the Russo-Polish War had been resolved, Poland asked the League of Nations for a plebiscite, to determine the fate of Upper Silesia. In February 1921 the League decided to send a small Allied peacekeeping force to Upper Silesia to monitor the plebiscite and keep order.* Prior to

---

*The international force consisted of four British infantry battalions, the French 46e Division d'Infanterie (nine infantry battalions) and one Italian infantry battalion. The force was deployed to Upper Silesia from June 1921 to July 1922.

the plebiscite, the German government sent in thousands of citizens from outside the region, which skewed the results in favour of Germany. In response, the Polish politician Wojciech Korfanty organized a successful third revolt, which seized much of the eastern portion of Upper Silesia and held it against German counter-attacks. French peacekeeping forces allegedly did little to stop the Polish attacks, since the French government wanted to weaken post-war Germany as much as possible. However, Britain's leadership was of a different mind and rushed two infantry brigades to the region so it could separate the two warring sides.[24] Surprisingly, Korfanty's rebels held onto the eastern part of Upper Silesia and the League eventually recognized this area as legally part of Poland. Yet while Poland gained valuable iron and coal mines in Upper Silesia, they were virtually indefensible since they were too close to the new border.

The Polish Second Republic desperately needed a period of peaceful stability to organize itself, but this proved elusive due to political in-fighting, an anaemic economy and the persistent concern about another Soviet invasion. Independence had unleashed a cacophony of political voices across the country, each of which demanded some representation in the Sejm and the Senate. Aside from national defence, there were those who thought priority should go to agricultural reforms, while labour groups wanted to focus on driving down unemployment. Poland held its first free legislative elections in November 1922, which resulted in no clear victory for any faction, so the result was a weak coalition government. Significantly, the Bloc of National Minorities (BMN), representing Germans, Jews and Ukrainians in Poland, won the second largest majority in the election. Gabriel Narutowicz, a moderate, was elected president. Piłsudski reverted to strictly military duties, becoming Chief of the General Staff. Two days after the transfer of power, President Narutowicz was assassinated by a right-wing fanatic. In turn, Stanisław Wojciechowski, an ally of Piłsudski, was elected president of Poland and Sikorski became prime minister. Roman Dmowski led an anti-Piłsudski faction in the Sejm, intent upon limiting his powers, but Piłsudski ensured that Dmowski and his right-wing nationalists were frozen out of the government. Nor did it help the new government that the Polish economy was in terrible shape due to hyperinflation and that the primary trade partner was a resentful Germany, which started a tariff war with Poland in 1925. Amazingly, Prime Minister Władysław Grabski's government managed to partly stabilize the economy within two years by the introduction of a new currency (the *złoty*) and by stimulating coal production to earn export income. Efforts were also made to develop domestic industrial production (particularly steel and chemicals) and repair national infrastructure, although the bulk of the economy remained focused on agriculture. Unemployment was also very high – up to 12.7 per cent in 1925 – which created further social unrest. In Kraków, Polish Army troops were called in to crush a strike led by Piłsudski's own PPS; between 30 and 40 strikers were killed.[25]

Due to the threat of another Soviet invasion, Poland was obliged to maintain a very large peacetime army, with over 250,000 troops. Furthermore, Sikorski created the Border Protection Corps (Korpus Ochrony Pogranicza or KOP), of six brigades, to protect the eastern borders. While this force was sufficient to deter another Soviet invasion, it also deprived the cash-strapped military of funds for modernization. Seeking allies and aid, the Poles turned to France, which agreed to sign a defensive military alliance with Poland in February 1921. The French pledged mutual military collaboration in case of an attack by a third party, by which they meant Germany, not the USSR. In addition, France provided Poland with a loan of F 400 million for rearmament and in return, Poland promised to purchase all its arms from France.[26] However, Britain's efforts to prop up Weimar Germany served to undermine Poland's security situation. At an international conference at Locarno, Switzerland in 1925, Germany, France, Britain, Italy and Belgium pledged to respect the new borders in Western Europe, but the question of eastern borders was left unresolved. Piłsudski was livid about the Locarno Treaty and stated that it meant that Poland's borders were not regarded as inviolate by the Anglo-French.

In reaction to Locarno and the worsening economy, Piłsudski became disenchanted with the democratic experiment in Poland and plotted with former legionnaire officers to overthrow the civilian government. Piłsudski regarded the civilian government as too weak and divided to deal with the myriad of serious problems facing the country. The final straw may have been a rumour that the civilian government was about to cut the army by one-quarter as part of a fiscal austerity plan, which Piłsudski believed would compromise Poland's national security. On 12 May 1926, Piłsudski led a military coup against the government of President Wojciechowski. Although he was able to enter Warsaw with about 3,000 troops, the government held its ground in the Belwedere Palace, surrounded by a loyal infantry regiment. A number of loyalist officers, including Generał Tadeusz Rozwadowski and Generał Stanisław Haller, urged the president to resist and wait for loyal troops from outside Warsaw to arrive. When the government refused to capitulate, scattered fighting broke out in the capital between loyalist and rebel troops for two days. General Rozwadowski ordered Generał Brygady Włodzimierz Zagórski's aviation group, which remained loyal to the government, to bomb the rebels – which they did. However, Piłsudski was able to rally more troops to his side, including two regiments sent by Edward Rydz-Śmigły. In the face of further bloodshed, the legitimate government decided to surrender on the morning of 15 May. A total of 821 Polish soldiers and 478 civilians were killed or wounded in Piłsudski's two-day coup – a rather bloody affair.

Piłsudski established an authoritarian regime dubbed the Sanacja (Moral Renewal) and moved quickly to crush his opponents. Most of the senior officers who supported the legal government were arrested and imprisoned, while prominent ex-legionnaires such as Sikorski and Józef Haller had their military careers terminated. Kazimierz Sosnkowski, once Piłsudski's right-hand man, had not been informed about the coup and after hearing of it, he attempted suicide. Poland had few General Staff-trained officers at this point, but many were cashiered after the coup. General Zagórski simply disappeared after a year in incarceration – possibly liquidated. On the other hand, the officers who had sided with Piłsudski – such as Edward Rydz-Śmigły – were rewarded with positions of greater responsibility in the Sanacja regime. Piłsudski's coup imposed an authoritarian regime upon Poland which deepened already wide chasms in the body politic and created irreversible fissures in the Polish officer corps, between pro-Piłsudski and anti-Piłsudski officers. Later, about 30 senior officers – mostly from the Polish General Staff – were retired early. In essence, Piłsudski's coup was a *de facto* purge, which sidelined many of Poland's most able military officers in favour of men personally loyal to him. In order to provide the appearance of a civilian government, Piłsudski engineered the election of Ignacy Mościcki, a former chemistry professor, as the new president, so he could focus on foreign affairs and the military. Far from stabilizing Poland, Piłsudski's Sanacja regime was unable to prevent the economy from sliding into a state of near-collapse by 1927, which was only rescued by a timely emergency loan from France.

Piłsudski decided to allow free parliamentary elections in 1928, but this galvanized the opposition, which included the nascent communist party. The Sanacja regime could not gain a majority at the ballot box and was forced to work with other parties – but compromise was not in Piłsudski's lexicon. When the opposition began to gel into a real anti-Sanacja coalition known as the Centrolew, Piłsudski opted for repression against them in the

1930 election cycle. Heavy media censorship was imposed and opposition candidates harassed and ultimately arrested, including Wojciech Korfanty, who had gained part of Upper Silesia for Poland. Prominent Poles, such as Ignacy Paderewski, condemned the coup and the resulting Sanacja regime. Rather than saving Poland, the Sanacja regime served to destroy any hope for real political co-operation and the country slid into a republic in name only; this was not the country that Polish patriots had struggled and sacrificed for decades to achieve.

Piłsudski's charisma and determination – along with the sacrifices of many of his soldiers – had laid the groundwork for a resurrected Polish state. Unfortunately, like many revolutionaries, Piłsudski was imbued with a pig-headed inability to compromise or work with other strong personalities, which deprived the nation of some of its best talent. His tendency to hold grudges against those who opposed him – or favour those who supported him – meant that the Second Republic was skewed towards the views of one man. Poland needed Dmowski, Korfanty, Sikorski and Paderewski as much as it needed Piłsudski, but the man at the top of the pyramid decided that only he was essential. Due to Piłsudski's authoritarian inclinations, the Polish Second Republic was undermined by a fractured political system which left it particularly vulnerable to the machinations of its neighbours. Furthermore, Piłsudski's desire to expand Poland's borders led to the creation of friction with all its neighbours and left large numbers of resentful non-Poles within its borders, thereby providing the *casus belli* for future conflicts.

CHAPTER 2

Poland Prepares for the Next Round

'Manifestly Germany has a vital interest in seeing the world firmly convinced that Germany's eastern borders, as drawn by the Treaty of Versailles, cannot endure. Since military measures are out of the question, a change in the oppressive current situation will be possible only when the necessity of revising Germany's eastern borders in the interest of universal peace becomes the common property of public opinion in the countries that matter. Now that the question of Germany's eastern borders is becoming increasingly a subject of international discussion, contributing to the creation of such public opinion is doubtless one of the most important tasks of German policy.'

Gustav Stresemann, German foreign minister, 30 June 1925[1]

Polish Military Re-organization, 1923–30

'The Army is the glue that binds the nation together.'
Rydz-Śmigły

By the time that the League of Nations recognized Poland's new borders in March 1923, the country was an impoverished wreck. The Polish armed forces (Wojsko Polskie or WP) had begun demobilizing in October 1921 and after its completion, it was left with about 292,000 troops (including 17,000 officers). The ground forces were a collection of heterogeneous units, equipped with a wide variety of uniforms and equipment, much of which was in poor condition. The primary task of the Polish Ministry of Military Affairs (Ministerstwo Spraw Wojskowych or M.S. Wojsk), formed in August 1921, was to reduce the post-war WP to a sustainable size and to impose standardization. Poland was divided into ten corps districts with mid-level staff assigned to manage the formation and training of units assigned to their regions. Peacetime conscription would be maintained, with new recruits inducted each March and serving a two-year tour of active duty, followed by a reserve obligation until age 40.

It was the task of the Armaments and Equipment Committee (Komitetu ds. Uzbrojenia i Sprzętu or KSUS) to determine weapons requirements. The Polish infantry, for example, was equipped with 24 different types of rifles and carbines, including about 260,000 French-made 8mm Lebel M1886/93, 197,000 German-made 7.92mm Mauser Gewehr 98, 120,000 Russian-made 7.62mm Mosin-Nagants and 40,000 English-made 7.7mm Lee Enfields. In June 1921, the KSUS decided that the Mauser 7.92 x 57mm cartridge would be the standard ammunition of the Polish infantry, while the remaining non-standard weapons would be assigned to reserve units or sold to other countries.[2] The Mauser Gewehr 98 was a good weapon, but what clinched the decision was the acquisition of a Mauser production facility (Königliche Gewehrfabrik) in Danzig – which meant that the Poles could begin making their own rifles. The situation with machine guns was more complex and could not be resolved as quickly; instead, the KSUS began looking at various foreign-made machine guns in an effort to determine which model could be converted to 7.92mm and built under licence in Poland. Similarly, the KSUS made efforts to standardize the artillery branch on French-made models (75mm, 105mm and 155mm), while opting to sell off the assortment of Austrian, German, Italian and Russian pieces abroad.

The Polish Ministry of Military Affairs was run by generals, not civilians. Piłsudski placed his close ally, the capable Kazimierz Sosnkowski, as the first head of the ministry. Although Sosnkowski was good at many things – military administration, politics and diplomacy – he was too distracted to put much effort into actually developing a coherent plan to remodel the WP into a more professional force. Instead, he left detailed planning to subordinate departments (infantry, cavalry, artillery, aviation), which were also consumed with day-to-day administration. The Polish General Staff (Sztab Generalny Wojska Polskiego or SG WP) was supposed to be responsible for strategic planning, including determining requirements that would shape how the post-war WP was structured, but the leadership of the General Staff was a revolving door, with seven heads in 1918–25. Piłsudski himself was head of the General Staff in 1922–23, even though he had no General Staff training. Although the Polish Second Republic was nominally a civilian-run government once the constitution of 1921 was implemented, in reality civilians had very little say over military affairs, which is what Piłsudski had intended. Instead, the civilian government was simply supposed to supply funds and then not interfere with military decision-making. The military administration situation would become even more acute after the 1926 coup, when Piłsudski assumed the role of the head of the Ministry of Military Affairs until his death in 1935.

When he created the General Staff in 1918, General Rozwadowski also created an intelligence organization, which was eventually designated as the Second Department of the Polish General Staff (dubbed the 'Dwojka' or Division II, Oddział II). Division II played an important role in the Russo-Polish War and was expanded after the war ended and worked closely with the KOP in order to monitor developments along Poland's eastern borders.[3] The General Staff was also concerned that Germany would attempt to violate the Treaty of Versailles and directed Division II to establish an intelligence collection network in Germany as well. The Polish Second Republic put considerable effort into building up its intelligence collection capabilities in the inter-war period and managed to recruit some very capable young officers, such as Jerzy Sosnowski.

Oddly, given the fact that the Polish Second Republic in 1921 had a demographic mix that included 3.8 million Ukrainians, 1 million Byelorussians and 769,000 Germans, the WP did not create any specialized units for internal security.[4] Indeed, ethnic Poles represented only 69 per cent of the population in the Second Republic and some minority members had loyalties to foreign regimes. In the eastern Kresy border regions, the Polish Communist Party (Komunistyczna Partia Polski or KPP), with support from the Comintern in Moscow, was actively recruiting members among labour union personnel. In the western regions, German nationalists such as the Deutscher Volksverband (German People's Union) were also agitating against Polish rule in Danzig and Upper Silesia. Polish intelligence personnel in Division II did have the mission to collect on subversive activities within Poland, but no security units were created – which would be a significant weakness in 1939.

In order to professionalize the Polish Army, the French military mission helped to establish officer and NCO training schools in 1922. A Higher Military School (Wyższa Szkoła Wojenna or W.S. Woj), with a two-year course, was established to train junior officers for the General Staff. Initially, training was based mostly on French methods, but the appointment of Generał Brygady Tadeusz Kutrzeba to command the school in 1928 marked a distinct change towards a uniquely Polish approach. Kutrzeba, an engineer officer and graduate of the Austrian General Staff Academy, was a brilliant military theorist who was quick to appreciate modern technology. However, Piłsudski got personally involved in the establishment of the Centre for Higher Military Studies (Centrum Wyższych Studiów Wojskowych or CWSW), a senior-level course intended to train Polish division-level commanders in operational art. He appointed Generał Broni Lucjan Żeligowski to head the centre, even though Żeligowski had gained most of his experience in the Russian Imperial Army and had no special staff training. Piłsudski also ensured that most of the officers selected for the nine-month CWSW course were ex-legionnaires.[5]

Based on French recommendations, the Polish field army was restructured from 21 'square' (each with four infantry regiments) infantry divisions in 1921 to 30 'triangular' (each with three infantry regiments) infantry divisions in 1923. However, this re-organization meant that few of the active divisions could be maintained near full strength and an infusion of reservists would be needed to bring most units up to authorized strength in wartime. Later, in 1930, the Polish Army re-organized its infantry regiments into three categories: Category III at close to full strength, Category II at about 60 per cent of establishment and Category I at 30–50 per cent of establishment. Likewise, peacetime artillery regiments were typically reduced to about 50 per cent of authorized strength. In consequence, few Polish divisions would be fully combat-effective until they could be brought up to strength with recalled reservists, which was estimated to require a minimum of two weeks after mobilization was begun.

The other main combat components of the Polish Army consisted of ten cavalry brigades, one tank regiment and ten heavy artillery regiments. In 1924, the existing cavalry brigades were formed into four cavalry divisions and five independent brigades were created. Expecting another conflict with the Soviet Union, the WP wanted a strong mobile reserve and cavalry was the only force that could fit this role. Yet aside from a single chemical defence battalion, very few support units were to be retained in the post-war regular army. Instead, most of the combat support units (engineers, signals), quartermaster, medical and maintenance units were shuffled off into the reserves. The decision was based on the assumption that these kinds of specialist units were not necessary in peacetime and could be mobilized if needed from the reserves, thereby saving funds for the combat units. Considerable effort was invested in forming the Border Protection Corps (Korpus Ochrony Pogranicza or KOP) in 1924–27, which was regarded as vital for the protection of the eastern borders. Altogether, the KOP had six brigades with 25,000 troops, most of whom were required to be ethnic Poles. Significant funds were invested in building border camps, watchtowers and other facilities to meet the needs of the KOP. Initially, the KOP was subordinate to the Ministry of Internal Affairs, but it was dependent upon the Army for equipment, personnel and training.

During the 1920s, the Ministry of Military Affairs attached great importance to the development of Poland's domestic arms industry and the Central Board of Military Manufacture (Centralny Zarząd Wytwórni Wojskowych or CZWW) was established in April 1922 for this purpose. A plethora of small arms workshops had been established during 1918–20, but these had very little capacity and it was imperative to create a coherent national arms industry that could eventually meet all of the WP's equipment needs. The CZWW funded the creation of an artillery factory at the Starachowice Works, a small arms production facility at the State Rifle Factory in Warsaw, an ammunition factory in Skarżysko and the Łucznik Arms Factory in Radom, as well as a testing facility in Warsaw. Most of the new facilities were built in the Kielce–Radom–Lublin triangle, in an effort to keep them away from vulnerable border areas. The creation of these state-run facilities was a considerable investment, with 58 million zł ($11.1 million) spent in 1926 alone. While creating the infrastructure for defence manufacturing, the CZWW also sought to secure licences to build foreign-designed weapons in Poland. The Czech Skoda works provided a licence for their 100mm howitzer to be built at Starachowice, but the French Schneider firm proved resistant and preferred to export its artillery pieces to Poland. The British 81mm mortar was also built under licence in Warsaw. However, some foreign vendors proved less than honest in dealing with the Polish government. The Polish Army was very interested in acquiring the rights to produce both the Browning Automatic Rifle (BAR) and the Browning M1917 heavy machine gun, converted to use the 7.92mm round. Under false pretences, the Belgian company Fabrique Nationale (FN), which was making both weapons itself, offered to sell the licence for the BAR to Poland. In fact, FN did not have the right to sell the licence to other countries. Negotiations dragged on for five years, until it became apparent that FN could not fulfil its obligations, which delayed the start of Polish domestic machine-gun manufacture until 1930. A licence for the BAR was eventually obtained and the Polish-made version entered service in 1930 as the Rkm wz. 28, but production of the Browning heavy machine gun was begun in 1931 without a licence.[6] In 1927, the CZWW was re-organized and an effort was made to encourage more privatization within the arms industry in order to reduce the financial burden on the government.

Given the limited funds available for defence investments, the Ministry of Military Affairs hoped that arms exports could earn hard currency in order to assist the Polish domestic arms industry. In November 1926, a joint venture known as SEPEWE (Syndykat Eksportu Przemysłu Wojennego) was established to promote Polish arms exports. After a slow start, SEPEWE was able to launch some lucrative arms deals with China and Greece in 1931.[7] Eventually, Poland become a major arms exporter, which would help fund its own military modernization programmes.

The Polish Air Force (LW) also faced the challenge of standardization in the post-war period. In 1921, the LW had 13 squadrons with a motley collection of 86 fighters and reconnaissance aircraft. After the foreign volunteer pilots went home, the LW was dreadfully short of trained pilots. The Department of Aeronautics under the Ministry of Military Affairs was responsible for organizing the LW but unfortunately lacked professional leadership in the first years of independence. In an effort to be helpful, the French military mission offered a sapper officer, Colonel François-Lèon Leveque, to head the aviation department in January 1923. Colonel Leveque had no prior aviation experience and had only been granted a pilot's licence a few months prior – he knew nothing about organizing an air force. However, along with Colonel Leveque, the French also provided a F 100 million loan to rebuild the LW, so he was acceptable for the time being. At this point, the only military aviation maintenance facility in

Poland was the Central Aviation Workshops (Centralne Warsztaty Lotnicze or CWL) in Warsaw, which had very limited fabrication capabilities.

Leveque developed a ridiculous plan to expand the LW to 50 squadrons and 572 aircraft within just three years, which was well beyond Poland's ability – even with French help – to achieve. Furthermore, Leveque envisioned most of the LW's strength would be based on reconnaissance aircraft in individual squadrons attached to army units. He invested a good portion of the French loan in purchasing the rights to produce the Potez XV and French-designed engines in Poland, while some of the money went into upgrading the CWL and purchasing machine tools. With French help, the Poles set up a new aviation production facility known as the Podlasie Aircraft Factory (Podlaska Wytwórnia Samolotów or PWS) in Biała Podlaska, east of Warsaw. By 1925, the CWL was manufacturing the Potez XV under licence. The Potez XV was an unspectacular aircraft of limited capability and the LW still had to rely upon the French for fighters and bombers. French industry regarded Poland as an ideal market for military exports and sold over 250 Bréguet XIX light bombers to the LW. Unfortunately, French aircraft exports were based more on the French desire to help their own aviation industry, not meet the LW's actual operational requirements. The purchase of rights to produce the SPAD 61C fighter proved to be a financial and technical fiasco, which quickly created a backlash against relying too heavily on the French. Piłsudski's faction was quick to smear the large-scale purchase of French aircraft and alleged corruption (the so-called Francopol scandal), despite lack of any evidence.[8]

When Generał Brygady Władysław Sikorski took over the Ministry of Military Affairs in February 1924, the re-organization of the Polish military took a more professional turn. Józef Haller, former commander of the 'Blue Army', also played a vital role as head of the General Staff. The French had provided additional funds to re-organize the Polish Army and Haller and Sikorski wanted to use this money to build the foundation for a modern, professional armed force. Together, they developed an ambitious ten-year armament plan, with particular emphasis upon integrating modern weaponry and building up a strong air force. Consequently, Leveque was sent back to France and Sikorski placed Generał Brygady Włodzimierz Zagórski in charge of the aviation department. Zagórski proved an energetic leader and quickly realized that he needed to correct the LW's low standard of training or the mass of new aircraft on order would not have enough qualified pilots to fly them. At his direction, an

Officer Aviation School was established and began to train large numbers of pilots and observers; by 1925 the school could produce up to 250 pilots a year. Although he knew that the LW was dependent upon French aircraft deliveries for the time being, Zagórski worked to bolster indigenous aircraft design and production. Rather than accept the French concept that aviation should be subordinate to the army, Zagórski envisioned brigade-size units of fighters and bombers which could provide concentrated airpower to achieve operationally decisive results. Zagórski also recognized the need to impress Poland's neighbours with the growing potential of Polish airpower and in July 1925 he personally led a flight of six aircraft in an aerial exhibition flight from Warsaw to Spain and back. By this time, there were enough trained pilots and new French-built aircraft to outfit 26 squadrons with over 200 aircraft, making the LW the strongest air force in central Europe. Unfortunately, Piłsudski was an enemy of Zagórski and managed to smear him with allegations of corruption, which resulted in his removal in March 1926.

After Piłsudski's coup, Generał Brygady Ludomił Rayski was placed in charge of the aviation department. Rayski was another ex-legionnaire with close ties to Piłsudski. Although he was a qualified fighter pilot, Rayski was overly political and lacked the kind of organizational vision required to nurture Polish airpower. Piłsudski rejected Zagórski's plans for the LW and cut its budget by 73 per cent in 1926. In October 1926, Piłsudski issued a directive that capped the size of the LW at 28 squadrons and shortly thereafter the pilot training school was shut down. While Poland's economic difficulties played a significant role in the LW's cutbacks, Piłsudski did not support the idea of a strong, independent air force. Instead, he wanted the LW configured for army co-operation missions, with light, cheap aircraft built in Poland. Consequently, Rayski focused most of his efforts in 1927–28 on assisting the development of the domestic aviation industry. In 1928, a new factory, the State Aviation Works (Państwowe Zakłady Lotnicze or PZL) was established in Warsaw to design and build modern combat aircraft. In order to gain experience in modern all-metal fabrication techniques, PZL engineers used a licence to build a small number of French-designed Wibault 70C1 fighters, then in 1929 set out to develop an all-new fighter for the LW. As part of the new fighter programme, Rayski decided to drop reliance on French-designed engines and look for alternatives.

The international recognition of Poland's new borders meant that the WP also gained the mission to defend 140km of Baltic coastline. The small naval forces employed during the Russo–Polish War were based almost entirely on the small craft of the Pinsk and Vistula river flotillas, which were of little use to defending the northern coast. As part of the disbandment of the Imperial Germany Navy, the Allies transferred six small ex-German torpedo boats and four minesweepers to Poland in September 1921. The Polish Navy (Marynarka Wojenna) was now placed under the Naval Directorate (Kierownictwo Marynarki Wojennej or KMW) within the Ministry of Military Affairs and it was decided to establish an interim base at Danzig (Gdańsk). However, since Danzig was a free city and not Polish territory, the Polish Navy was only offered the right to base its fledging naval force there for three years. Consequently, the Polish government decided to develop the small port of Gdynia in order to expand the infrastructure for economic trade and provide a long-term home for the Polish fleet. In order to protect Gdynia, the Naval Ministry also planned to develop a system of coastal defences. Wiceadmiral Kazimierz Porębski, who had extensive naval experience in the Russian Imperial Navy, was made head of the KMW in 1922 and entrusted with organizing the nascent Polish Navy. Porębski hoped to acquire at least a few modern warships, but Poland's rudimentary ship-building facilities could not yet build major warships on its own. Instead, the Polish Navy would have to rely upon French-built warships, but sufficient funds were not available until 1926. Eventually, the Poles ordered two destroyers from France for 22 million zł ($2.4 million), but the results were disappointing; it took the French six years to complete both vessels and they suffered from numerous defects. Like Zagórski, Porębski was one of the victims of Piłsudski's coup and he was relieved of command.

Sikorski's removal after the coup was a serious blow to the re-organization and modernization programmes in the WP. In order to cement his personal control over all military issues, Piłsudski assumed the role of General Inspector of the Armed Forces (Generalny Inspektor Sił Zbrojnych or GISZ), which put him over the General Staff. Piłsudski had a paternalistic attitude towards 'his' armed forces and he sought to make them as strong as possible, but he lacked the higher-level staff training or technical literacy to run both strategic planning, organizational reforms and modernization programmes on his own. Adding to his own limitations, Piłsudski tended to rely too heavily on his ex-legionnaire comrades (particularly those who supported him in the 1926 coup), which created something of an echo chamber at the top of the military pyramid. A modern military simply cannot be built upon the personality of one man – it is a team effort – but unfortunately Piłsudski rejected this approach. The result was that the WP did achieve a certain level of standardization of equipment and training in the 1920s, but it was still a force that was being reshaped primarily to fight a conflict with conditions similar to the Russo-Polish War.

Polish Strategic Planning and Policy, 1922–36

'Peace is a precious and a desirable thing. Our generation, bloodied in wars, certainly deserves peace. But peace, like almost all things of this world, has its price, a high but a measurable one. We in Poland do not know the concept of peace at any price. There is only one thing in the lives of men, nations and countries that is without price. That thing is honour.'

Józef Beck, Polish foreign minister, 5 May 1939

Although Poland had won almost all its border conflicts in 1918–20, it could not afford to rest on its laurels. Both the Polish military and political leadership recognized that neither the Germans nor the Russians were likely to accept their territorial losses and that they needed to prepare plans to counter future aggressions from either quarter. Unlike Britain or France, Polish leaders could not afford the luxury of a 'ten-year rule' mentality, consigning the possibility of war to a distant future. Nor could the Polish people adopt the tenets of pacifism or anti-militarism, which would only leave the nation vulnerable to foreign aggression. Rather, the Second Polish Republic had to plan its policies on the principle that war was a distinct possibility and could occur with relatively little notice. Given the military disarmament imposed upon Germany after the Treaty of Versailles, Piłsudski and many others reasonably regarded the Soviet Union as the most likely opponent in the near term. Furthermore, the Soviet threat was not just military in nature, but included espionage and subversive activities in the Kresy borderlands.[9] Polish foreign policy was directed to support four primary national objectives: (1) strengthening strategic co-operation with France, (2) increasing Poland's international trade, (3) developing closer relations with Hungary and Romania and (4) preventing the emergence of any anti-Polish coalitions.

The military accord that Poland signed with France on 19 February 1921 only provided for military co-operation in the event of a German attack on either signatory, but Piłsudski pressed for a commitment in the event of another Soviet attack on Poland – which was included in a secret protocol.[10] Piłsudski was also annoyed by the economic aspects of the accord, which seemed exploitive. For example, the French demanded that the Poles pay for military hardware with supplies of oil from the Drohobycz refinery and reduce their tariffs on French imports. Eager to stimulate their own post-war civilian economy, the French forced Poland to import luxuries such as jewellery and perfume, instead of essential items, like machine tools.[11] Having gained independence of the Germans and Russians, Piłsudski had no intention of allowing Poland to become little more than a French colony. Nor did it help the relationship with France that Maréchal Ferdinand Foch, France's senior soldier, openly attached little value to the Polish alliance.

Unfortunately, the dust had barely settled from the Russo-Polish War when Germany and the Soviet Union signed the Treaty of Rapallo in April 1922. The treaty laid the groundwork for normal political and economic relations between these two nations, although it had no immediate military significance – despite media-fed speculation about secret military clauses.[12] Although Germany was interested in covert military co-operation with the Soviet Union in order to avoid the restrictions of the Treaty of Versailles, it would be another three years before any substantive military co-operation began. Nevertheless, Rapallo was a poignant reminder that German–Russian co-operation against Poland could emerge with little notice. Four months after Rapallo, the French and Polish General Staffs held joint talks to discuss planning for future military co-operation. While Rapallo had caused the Poles to become nervous about the prospect of a 'two-front' war with both Germany and the Soviet Union, the French were entirely focused on the German threat. In January 1923, the French Army occupied the Ruhr due to German cessation of reparations, which further heightened war anxiety. During staff talks in May 1923, Maréchal Foch pushed the Poles to adopt an aggressive strategy. In the event of war with Germany, Foch wanted the Polish Army to advance west along the Poznań–Berlin axis, while the French advanced eastwards from the Ruhr. However, Piłsudski had no intention of boldly committing the Polish Army to a punitive campaign in central Germany and instead suggested more realistic scenarios, whereby the Poles could potentially occupy Danzig or parts of East Prussia in event of war.[13] From the start, Franco-Polish strategic planners were talking past each other and never built a solid framework, which left actual military commitments vague and unrealistic.

Furthermore, Piłsudski recognized that the Treaty of Versailles had neutered German military capabilities for the time being and he insisted that Polish military planning should stay focused on the Soviet Union and this is where the Polish General Staff invested its resources. The idea of preparing for a potential 'two-front' war was quietly dropped. General Haller, as chief of staff, recognized that Poland would need up to a month to mobilize its reserves in event of another war and developed a 'Shield Plan', in which the KOP and regular army units would screen the border areas during the mobilization period. Cavalry units were best suited for this role and were given a prominent role in the planning; their function was delay, not shock action. Once fully mobilized, it was expected that the WP would be in a better position to launch a massive counter-stroke to defeat an enemy invasion, similar to the 1920 battle of Warsaw. Although the Poles expected military assistance from the French in the event of a German attack, they did not expect much foreign help in response to an attack only by the Soviet Union. Given that many of the Polish reserves were in central and western Poland, it was essential to defend these regions from the outset of a war. Indeed, the imperatives of the 'Shield Plan' would help shape Polish strategy in 1939; early territorial losses meant fewer reserves would be mobilized.

Under Haller, the General Staff worked concurrently on the outline of two basic mobilization plans, one for the west (Plan *Zachód*) against Germany and one for the east (Plan *Wschód*) against the Soviet Union. Both plans identified likely enemy courses of actions but did not specify Polish responses. In the 1920s, Polish strategic planning did not extend beyond the initial phase of a conflict and left operational details intentionally vague. Instead, the primary planning document in 1926–35 was simply mobilization Plan 'S', which focused on mobilizing the reserves as quickly as possible in order to bring the field army up to authorized strength. Like the French, the Poles adopted a two-tiered approach to reserves, with Category A (physically fit, age 23–40) reserves used to fill out the active army units and possibly create additional reserve units. Category B recruits were in the same age category but conditionally fit (i.e., only capable of limited service), and unlike the French system there were no Category B units. Category C and D reserves were older, less fit and often had little or no prior military training; these personnel would be used for auxiliary duties or as militia. While Poland could theoretically mobilize about 1.5 million troops, it could never equip more than 600–800,000 with available equipment stocks.[14] Given the poor communications and transportation infrastructure in Poland in the 1920s, full mobilization was expected to take up to 30 days to complete.

Although the Soviet Union was the likely opponent, the General Staff could not discount the possibility that either Czechoslovakia or Lithuania – both hostile to Poland – might co-operate with the Soviets in the event of another conflict. The failure of Poland to invest serious effort into improving relations with either of these neighbouring nations was easily one of the greatest failings in its pre-war diplomacy. On the other hand, the Polish Second Republic invested considerable effort into developing military ties with its one friendly neighbour – Romania. Like the Poles, the Romanians were worried about Soviet aggression and they signed a five-year bi-lateral military alliance in March 1921 (renewed in 1926). Although Romania's military resources were even more limited than Poland's, the alliance was regarded as an insurance policy. Remarkably, the Polish–Romania relationship would prove to be critical in 1939, making it the most worthwhile Polish diplomatic investment of the inter-war period. In April 1924, a tripartite (Polish–French–Romanian) military conference was held in Warsaw to discuss strategic co-operation in event of war. The French remained focused on the Germans, the Poles and Romanians on the Russians. As a result, the General Staff developed a new war plan that allowed for the possibility of a two-front war. In that eventuality, the WP would adopt a hold-win-win strategy, with the main effort being made to first defeat the invading Soviets while holding off the Germans, then shifting to reverse any German gains in Pomerania or Upper Silesia. Polish strategy was essentially geared towards playing for time until they could mount a successful counter-offensive, as in August 1920. The General Staff regarded the defence only as a means to economize on forces in less critical sectors and to delay an enemy.[15] A great part of the General Staff's calculations were based upon Poland's theoretical use of interior lines, even though the road and rail infrastructure was inadequate in most of the border areas. The assumptions about Poland's advantage in interior lines might have been true in 1924, but 15 years later, they proved false.

After Piłsudski's 1926 coup, he assigned Generał Dywizji Jan Romer to head a new staff study on potential enemy courses of action in order to flesh out the existing war plans. Romer, a professional artilleryman but without higher staff training, made some astute observations about a potential German invasion. First, he did not believe Germany would be capable of mounting a serious offensive operation until at least five to ten years after beginning rearmament. Second, Romer did not expect the French to lend any substantive military assistance until 60 days after they began mobilizing. Consequently, he expected the Germans to plan on achieving a rapid victory over Poland by means of a double pincer offensive, with the left wing coming from Pomerania/East Prussia and the right wing from Silesia.[16] Romer's staff study was remarkably prescient and Piłsudski took it seriously. One of the main practical results of Romer's study was that Piłsudski directed the WP to begin investing serious effort into developing defences to protect the Polish Corridor and the port of Gdańsk.

However, as a result of its experiences in eastern Galicia and the Russo-Polish War, the Polish General Staff did not initially put much thought into border fortifications or the necessity of maintaining a continuous front against an opponent. Unit densities had been low in these conflicts, with armies spread across vast areas. Rather than set-piece combat like the Western Front in 1914–18, the Poles expected military operations to be fluid and mobile, but geared towards defending key cities, such as Warsaw. Since fortifications had not fared well on the Eastern Front in the First World War, the Poles were not eager to invest in fixed defences when they expected mobile warfare to be the norm.

Nor did the General Staff invest much effort in the 1920s on integrating air and naval capabilities into their war plans. In October 1926, Piłsudski issued a directive which stated that 'the aviation at the time of war shall be used principally for the purpose of reconnaissance and liaison.'[17] Consequently, the LW was regarded as merely a supporting branch for the army, which diverged greatly from Zagórski's concept of a more independent and powerful air force. Since the General Staff expected that the Soviets might attempt amphibious landings on the Baltic coast in event of war, the Polish Navy was tasked with developing the capabilities to contest such an operation. Likewise, in event of a Polish–German conflict, the navy would prevent the enemy from sending reinforcements to East Prussia. However, since the army did not intend to commit substantial forces to defend the Polish Corridor region, it was highly unlikely that the navy could operate from Gdynia for very long. Air, ground and sea missions were not co-ordinated at the top, which meant that each service would fight essentially on its own.

When thinking about the next major conflict, the Ministry of Military Affairs did anticipate that an aggressor might use chemical weapons, so considerable emphasis was placed on preparing the WP to fight on a potential chemical battlefield. In 1922, a chemical weapons research institute was established in Warsaw and four years later, a production facility was established at Skarżysko (the WWR plant), near Radom. The Poles focused on researching and developing two chemical weapons: the blister agent sulphur mustard (HD) and the choking agent phosgene (CG); by 1931 the WWR plant had stockpiled 104.5 tonnes of mustard and 106.7 tonnes of phosgene. In 1932, the Polish Army began weaponizing these agents by filling 700 75mm artillery shells with HD and 2,000 155mm shells with CG. Firing tests of chemical weapons were conducted near Zgierz. A year later, Polish chemists synthesized a new weapon, Phosgene Oxime (TSD). By the mid-1930s, Polish industry had the ability to produce several hundred tonnes of chemical weapons per month, although actual stockpiles were kept small.[18] The Ministry of Military Affairs decided that these chemical weapons would only be used in retaliation and only the supreme commander could authorize their use.

While the Polish General Staff grappled with military strategy, the Polish Foreign Ministry tried to improve regional harmony and trade. However, Piłsudski refused to accept the credentials of the first two Soviet ambassadors, which delayed signature of a trade treaty until two years after the Russo–Polish War ended. By 1926/27, Soviet–Polish trade only amounted to about $16.7 million per year, which was one-tenth of the value of Soviet–German trade. When the next Soviet ambassador to Poland was assassinated in Warsaw in June 1927 by a Russian monarchist sympathizer, Stalin nearly broke off diplomatic relations with Poland. Instead, the Soviets increased anti-Polish propaganda and there was no diplomatic progress for another seven years. Polish–Soviet relations were locked in a frozen state of mutual, implacable hatred.

Relations between Poland and Weimar Germany seemed to start off on a better foot, when Ulrich Rauscher arrived as the first German ambassador in Berlin in 1922. Rauscher pushed for improved relations for the benefit of both countries, which led to an agreement on trade. By 1925, Germany was Poland's top trade partner, accounting for about 80 per cent its coal exports and 50 per cent of its overall trade. Other significant Polish trade partners were Austria, Belgium, Czechoslovakia and the Scandinavian countries. Yet despite Rauscher's affability in Warsaw, the Weimar government refused to officially recognize Poland's borders and even before the Locarno Treaty was signed it began to take steps to de-legitimize Polish claims to the 'Polish Corridor' and Upper Silesia. Gustav Stresemann, the German foreign minister, wrote a confidential memorandum in June 1925 which stated that the objective of the German government was to use economic and diplomatic coercion to regain its lost territories in the east. Stresemann also talked openly of 'liquidating' the

Polish Corridor and returning Danzig to Germany. Under the Treaty of Versailles, Germany was supposed to purchase a certain amount of coal and agricultural products from Poland, but Stresemann took steps to initiate a 'customs war' with Poland that sharply reduced Polish imports. The still-weak Polish economy was badly hurt, which is what Stresemann intended, and he hoped it would cause the Second Republic to become destabilized and open to economic blackmail. Instead, Piłsudski seized power and ordered Polish exports to find new markets, such as exporting coal to the United Kingdom.[19] He backed further investments in the port of Gdynia to expand trade and to show his resolve to hold onto the Polish Corridor. Britain and France did nothing to restrain Stresemann's coercive tactics, which reinforced Piłsudski's belief that neither could be counted upon in a crunch. Stresemann died in 1929, but Weimar Germany continued its trade conflict with Poland until its dissolution and its relations with Poland were never fully normalized. In August 1930, a German minister, Gottfried Treviranus, gave a speech demanding the revision of the Polish–German border and the return of Pomerania – which outraged the Poles.[20]

German rhetoric about revising their eastern borders and continued Soviet hostility led Piłsudski to revisit the idea of border fortifications. Some small machine-gun bunkers had already been constructed in border areas to support the requirements of the 'Shield Plan', but Poland lacked the financial resources to lavish on large fortification projects. An elderly engineer officer, Generał Brygady Józef Burhardt, was brought out of retirement and led a staff study that examined the efficacy of creating border fortifications in vulnerable sectors of Poland's border regions. Burhardt's study was completed in 1930 and it recommended that a modest level of local fortifications could be built to assist in the defence of key frontier areas, particularly Upper Silesia.[21] However, Burhardt did not recommend building fortifications in the Polish Corridor, which was judged to be indefensible. In 1931, Piłsudski approved most of Burhardt's recommendations, although very little work began until 1933. While Piłsudski authorized the creation of the Fortified Region of Silesia (Obszar Warowny Śląsk or OWS) to protect the city of Katowice and the approaches to Kraków, he also made it a priority to fortify the Wilno (Vilnius) sector, which was far less vital. Indeed, very little work was done on Poland's border fortifications prior to 1935.[22] Eventually, 14 million zł ($2.6 million) was spent building the OWS during 1934–39, although the Polish Army was unwilling to place great faith in fortified lines that could be easily outflanked.

Given negative attitudes in Britain about the Polish annexation of eastern Galicia and Upper Silesia, relations between Poland and Great Britain virtually evaporated after 1921. Brigadier Carton de Wiart, the head of the British military mission in Warsaw, noted that 'our own mission in Upper Silesia was so pro-German that I kept away from them.'[23] Afterwards, Carton de Wiart retired to an estate in eastern Poland, while the rest of his staff went home. Piłsudski regarded the British ruling class as hostile or indifferent to Poland's national interests and he had not forgotten that British labour unions had tried to block military aid to Poland in 1918–20. Nor did Britain develop much in the way of trade relations with Poland, until domestic strikes forced the importation of Polish coal. Consequently, diplomatic relations between the two nations were icy until Piłsudski's death. Fortunately, the British government did not obstruct arms sales to Poland in the inter-war period, which had a significant effect upon Polish military modernization. The Ministry of Military Affairs was particularly interested in acquiring armoured vehicles and airplane engines from British companies. In 1927, a Poland technical delegation visited Vickers to examine its armoured vehicles, which resulted in the purchase of ten Carden-Loyd Mk VI tankettes in 1929 and 50 Vickers Mk. E light tanks in 1931. After technical evaluations in Poland, it was decided to redesign and improve both vehicles, then begin licensed production. Another Polish delegation visited Bristol Aviation in 1929 and purchased a licence to build the Jupiter VIIF radial engine, which was essential for a new Polish-designed fighter.

In December 1931, Piłsudski finally convinced the French to withdraw their military mission from Warsaw. From this point onwards, he wanted Poland to adopt a more independent geopolitical course beyond just being a pillar in France's *cordon sanitaire* against Germany, which might not always agree with the policies determined in Paris and London. In one case, Piłsudski decided to flout the League of Nations decision to prevent the Polish Navy from visiting the port of Danzig without the approval of its German-dominated senate. The destroyer *Wicher*, the Polish Navy's new flagship, was sent to Danzig in June 1932 at the same time as a Royal Navy visit and Piłsudski directed the ship's commander to use force if any attempt was made to interfere with its unauthorized visit. No violence occurred, but the *Wicher* affair reinforced English opinion that Poland was a regional bully. The incident also provided the Polish Navy with a rationale to justify more funding for new warships.

Piłsudski remained hostile to the Soviet Union, which Stalin reciprocated by directing an unrelenting campaign of anti-Polish propaganda. In 1923, the Soviet Union sent a diplomatic note to Poland saying that since eastern Galicia had been annexed 'by violent means' the Soviet Union could not remain indifferent to the fate of its fellow countrymen in the region. This type of démarche served notice that Moscow regarded the Treaty of Riga as just a scrap of paper and might use the ethnic Byelorussian and Ukrainian populations in Kresy as an excuse to invade at any time.[24] On the other hand, by the late 1920s Stalin was shifting towards a less hostile course, in hope of ending the USSR's international isolation and increasing foreign trade. In 1928, the Soviet foreign minister, Maxim Litvinov, invited Poland, Romania, Finland and the Baltic States to sign a symbolic protocol renouncing war as a means to settle disputes. Poland signed the Litvinov Protocol, which guaranteed nothing but opened the door to normalization of relations. After glacial diplomatic progress, Poland finally signed a three-year Non-Aggression Pact with the Soviet Union in 1932. Two years later, the treaty was extended to 1945 and Poland was allowed to establish an embassy in Moscow. However, the Soviet–Polish border remained tense with regular incidents; in mid-1936, Polish fighters shot down a Soviet reconnaissance aircraft that crossed into Polish airspace.[25] Piłsudski did not want to bet Poland's future on treaties with Stalin or the League of Nations, but recognized that flexibility in diplomacy might buy the time that Poland desperately needed to gather its strength.

Since his coup, Piłsudski had been promoting the careers of those who supported him in that crisis, particularly one of his ex-legionnaire comrades, Józef Beck. When August Zaleski retired as foreign minister in November 1932, Piłsudski replaced him with Beck. Piłsudski hoped to use Polish diplomacy to drive a wedge between its two natural enemies, which meant adopting a flexible attitude. Beck was tasked with normalizing relations with both German and the Soviet Union and thereby reducing the chance of conflict with either, at least for another decade. Beck's 'balancing strategy' was not well-regarded in either Paris or London, where there were concerns about Poland pursuing too independent a line.

The real game-changer occurred in January 1933, when Adolf Hitler became chancellor of Germany. Hitler's decision to quit the League of Nations made it clear that he intended to repudiate the Treaty of Versailles, which posed a direct threat to Poland's western borders. In response, Piłsudski ordered the head of the General Staff's Division II (intelligence) to make an immediate assessment of German capabilities and intentions. However, Hitler was initially more focused on domestic issues and his priority was improving Germany's economy, which meant ending Stresemann's trade war.[26] Hitler could be quite accommodating and flexible, when he had a weak hand. Piłsudski and Beck were not blind to the danger of Hitler's right-wing nationalist ideology, but they also saw him as someone who was not wedded to Germany's Prussian-dominated past. In *Mein Kampf,* Hitler had stated that previous efforts to Germanize Poles had been a mistake, which suggested possible flexibility on the eastern borders.[27] In fact, Hitler meant that incorporating Poles into the Reich would cause racial pollution – but that was not clear in 1934. However, Hitler could not ignore the fact the Poland possessed the fourth largest army in Europe and was allied with France, which would have made any premature aggressive moves on his part dangerous. Ever the gambler, Hitler opted to normalize relations with Poland and thereby reduce the threat of a Franco-Polish preventative war. In January 1934, without consulting the French, Poland signed a ten-year Non-Aggression Pact with the Third Reich. Follow-on economic agreements were also good news for the Polish economy. If this meant no war with Germany before 1944, the treaty would provide time for Poland to strengthen both its economy and military.

Piłsudski's health was fading in 1933–34 and he regularly expressed concerns about to whom he might turn the Polish Army over – apparently, he fretted much less about who would run the rest of the country. In the end, he settled upon the stalwart loyalist Edward Rydz-Śmigły as his military successor, despite doubts about his capabilities. On 12 May 1935, Piłsudski died, but his Sanacja regime would continue for four more years. By this point, Poland had apparently normalized relations with its two hostile neighbours and it appeared that the 'balancing strategy' might help keep the peace at least until the end of the decade. However, there was also a growing recognition that Germany could become a serious threat in the near future. In April 1936, Rydz-Śmigły (who was now GISZ) directed the General Staff to conduct new studies on both German and Soviet military capabilities in order to assess the relative military balance. The results of these studies were reviewed in July 1936 and they were sobering; intelligence reports indicated that both Germany and the USSR were building mechanized forces and aircraft in large numbers which would put the WP at a severe disadvantage in a conflict against either one. Generał Brygady Tadeusz Kutrzeba, one of the senior officers involved in this analysis, assessed that in event of war with Germany, Poland's armed forces could only resist for six weeks – unless France launched a major offensive in the West.[28]

Consequently, Rydz-Śmigły ordered the creation of modernization plan to provide the WP with more and better equipment as soon as possible. Unfortunately, the plan was estimated to cost about 574 million zł (about $110 million), which meant that it would take at least six years to complete. According to the plan, there would be partial motorization of some infantry divisions, at least four cavalry brigades would be mechanized, improved artillery and air defence would be fielded and enough ammunition would be stockpiled for six months of operations. In addition, the LW would receive new fighters and more bombers. However, Poland's recognition of the threat fell short of its ability to counter the danger. In order to modernize its military to adequately match German and Soviet developments, Poland would have needed at least another 250–300 million zł (about $50 million) per year in 1936–39.

In addition to the modernization plan, Rydz-Śmigły directed the General Staff to develop new operational contingency plans which could counter aggression against either Poland's eastern or western borders – but not both simultaneously. Based on the staff studies, it was assessed that in the event of a German invasion, the enemy would make their main effort in the north from Pomerania and East Prussia.

Military Modernization, 1930–39

Silni, zwarci, gotowi! [Strong, united, ready!]
Polish Army pre-war propaganda slogan

By 1930, the WP was re-organized and professionalized, a small but growing defence industrial base had been created in Poland and strategic planning had identified the most likely adversary courses of action. By mid-1936, the WP was embarking upon a lengthy modernization programme in order to transform itself into a modern force that could successfully deter its neighbours from committing armed aggression. It was now a race against time to begin equipping and training the WP to fight a modern war before either Germany or the Soviet Union decided to act against Poland. Unfortunately, the combination of German trade warfare and the Global Depression had hit Poland's economy very hard, reducing its Gross Domestic Product (GDP) by over 20 per cent in 1930–33.[29] When Rydz-Śmigły approved the modernization plan, the Polish economy was still in poor condition and the government was only saved from bankruptcy by French loans. Financial limitations greatly delayed the WP's modernization plan, forcing leaders to choose between investing in research on new weapons or manufacture/modification of existing designs. The decisions made in 1936 determined what kind of military capabilities Poland would have in the 1939 campaign.

In order to employ a rational schema for examining Poland's modernization in the 1930s, I will use the 'Battlefield Operating Systems (BOS)' methodology. The BOS was developed by the US military in the 1990s in order to help military analysts understand the seven key functions that need to occur on the modern combined arms battlefield. How armies understand and employ the BOS functions, determines how they can use and sustain combat power in a campaign.[30] The seven BOS functions are manoeuvre, fire support, air defence, mobility/counter-mobility, intelligence, command and control (C^2) and combat service support. By carefully integrating the various BOS to work together, armies can achieve combat synergy where the power produced exceeds the sum of its individual components. Indeed, this was the essential element that made the German Panzer-Divisionen so successful in 1939–41; these formations were not just powerful in tanks and motorized infantry (manoeuvre), but they also integrated fire support, intelligence and C2 better than their opponents.

Manoeuvre

Poland's ground manoeuvre forces in 1930 consisted of 30 infantry divisions, 12 cavalry brigades and one armoured battalion. Like the French Army, Polish active infantry divisions were not kept at full strength in peacetime, in order to reduce costs. Once mobilization was declared, each infantry division would receive 6,000 or more reservists to bring the formation up to authorized strength. The Polish infantry division had a nominal strength of 16,500 troops and was triangular in structure, with three infantry regiments, each with three infantry battalions. Two divisions were organized as mountain infantry. The Polish infantry were almost entirely 'leg' in composition, totally reliant on marching for tactical manoeuvring and rail transport for operational movements. Well-trained troops were supposed to be capable of marching 25–35km per day, but reservists often arrived out-of-condition and could not sustain rapid, long marching in full kit until properly re-trained – which could take weeks.[31] Although Poland began licensed production of the Italian-designed Fiat 621L 2.5-tonne truck in 1932 and had built nearly 10,000 of them by

1939, very few went to infantry units, which were forced to rely primarily upon horse-drawn carts to move their support weapons (mortars and heavy machine guns). While the Polish Army had 270 infantry battalions in its active force and another 90–100 in the reserves, by 1939 it only had four motorized infantry battalions against 69 for the Germans.

In functional terms, the Polish Army often had difficulty massing combat power because it did not use corps-size formations and it had a pronounced tendency to split its available units into operational groups (*grupa operacyjna*) and separate detachments (*oddział wydzielony*). These *ad hoc*, mission-oriented groupings lacked the cohesiveness, staff officers and support assets of a normal corps-size formation. Furthermore, the mindset of the Polish Army was offensively oriented, which meant that it regarded the battlefield in more fluid terms – which were ill-suited to defensive missions. The Poles regarded the defence as a temporary situation until they could launch a decisive counter-attack, as in 1920. The concepts of continuous fronts and defence in depth that the French Army espoused meant little to Polish officers. In practice, this offensive mindset undermined the ability of Polish formations to develop effective tactical defences in 1939.

In 1930, when the Reichsheer was prohibited from having artillery pieces larger than 75mm, the Polish Army held a clear edge in firepower. However, as Germany began to rearm and violate the Treaty of Versailles, the Polish superiority in firepower vanished. Although often derided as being equipped with obsolete weaponry, the Polish infantry did receive a considerable amount of new equipment during the 1930s (Table 1), including the Rkm. wz. 28 automatic rifle (10,700 built in 1930–39), the Ckm wz. 30 heavy machine guns (8,400 built in 1931–39), the 81mm wz. 30 Brandt mortar (905 from 1935–39), the 46mm wz. 30 and wz. 36 mortars (3,850 built 1932–38) and the wz. 35 anti-tank rifle (3,500 in 1938–39).[32] In terms of organic firepower, most Polish infantry weapons were comparable to those in contemporary American, British, French and German units, but the level of issue was generally less. Consequently, by 1939 Polish infantry only had about 70 per cent as much firepower as German units at the battalion level and only 53 per cent at the regimental level. Overall, a Polish infantry division had about 60 per cent of the firepower of a German infantry division. In some cases, the German superiority was quite pronounced, such as the belt-fed, high cyclic rate MG34 light machine gun against the magazine-fed Rkm wz. 28 rifle (although the MG34 was still in short supply in September 1939). In an effort to catch up,

Table 1: Modernization of Key Weapons in Polish
Infantry Units, 1930–39

Echelon	Direct Fire Weapons	Indirect Fire Weapons	Anti-Tank Weapons
Infantry Regiment	36 × Ckm wz. 30 machine guns 81 × Rkm. wz. 28 automatic rifles	6 × 81mm wz. 30 mortars 27 × 46mm mortars	9 × 37mm wz. 36 anti-tank guns 27 × wz. 35 anti-tank rifles
Infantry Battalion	12 × Ckm wz. 30 machine guns 27 × Rkm. wz. 28 automatic rifles	2 × 81mm wz. 30 mortars 9 × 46mm mortars	9 × wz. 35 anti-tank rifles
Infantry Company	9 × Rkm. wz. 28 automatic rifles	3 × 46mm mortars	3 × wz. 35 anti-tank rifles
Infantry Platoon	3 × Rkm. wz. 28 automatic rifles	1 × 46mm mortar	1 × wz. 35 anti-tank rifle

the Polish infantry were expected to begin receiving additional new equipment during the winter of 1939/40, including a new semi-automatic rifle (the wz. 38M), a sub-machine gun and a 20mm cannon. In particular, the ground-mounted 20mm Nkm wz. 38 cannon offered an excellent light anti-tank capability. The wz.38M semi-automatic rifle, just entering production in July 1939, would have significantly increased the firepower of Polish infantry.

The Polish Army placed great faith in its cavalry, both for its mobility in border areas and for the traditional élan of its troopers. Given the lack of roads and marshy terrain in eastern Poland, cavalry units were ideally suited for screening, delay and rearguard operations. In theory, a cavalry brigade could move up to 40km or more in a day, which was an attractive feature to an army that had few motorized units. However, maintaining cavalry units was very expensive; the annual cost of feeding and caring for just the horses in a cavalry brigade with four regiments was about 1 million zł ($192,000). Like the infantry, Polish cavalry brigades were modernized in the 1930s with new weaponry, including 37mm anti-tank guns. However, given that a cavalry brigade had 6,000–7,000 men and over 5,000 horses, it had only marginally more firepower than a 3,200-man infantry regiment. Lacking mortars and artillery at the regiment level, Polish cavalry units lacked the organic firepower needed on the modern battlefield. In order to partially redress this imbalance, by the mid-1930s

Polish cavalry brigades received an armoured group equipped with 13 TKS tankettes and eight armoured cars. Seven of 11 cavalry brigades were also provided with an infantry battalion, further increasing their organic firepower – but at the cost of reduced mobility.

As the French Army began to partially mechanize their own cavalry divisions in the mid-1930s, the Polish Army decided to begin testing the integration of armoured vehicles into an existing cavalry unit. The General Staff conducted a study in November 1936 which recommended a 3,800-man brigade equipped with a battalion of tanks, one of motorized infantry, a machine-gun battalion, a sapper battalion and an anti-tank battalion. In February 1937, the 10th Cavalry Brigade was selected for motorization. The actual composition of the 10th Cavalry Brigade was considerably less than the recommended structure; it was given a company of obsolete Vickers E light tanks and two companies of TKS tankettes, along with two motorized infantry battalions, a motorized engineer unit, a motorized anti-tank battery and a 40mm anti-aircraft battery. Aside from the lack of modern armoured vehicles, the artillery support provided to the 10th Cavalry Brigade – just eight guns – was completely inadequate. Nevertheless, the 10th Motorized Cavalry Brigade (10 BK) was a step in the right direction of modernizing Poland's cavalry arm and it was virtually the only true combined arms formation in the Polish Army of 1939. In June 1939, the Ministry of Military Affairs decided to create an additional motorized cavalry formation, designated as the Warsaw Armoured-Motorized Brigade. This second formation was similar in organization to the 10 BK, but was only partially equipped at the start of the war. It was expected that both mechanized brigades would be equipped with new vehicles as they became available, although the cost was estimated to be about 20 million zł ($3.8 million) to outfit each brigade. In sum, the Polish Army had developed the correct organizational formula to upgrade its cavalry into effective combined arms units by 1939, but it did not commit adequate resources to expand these experimental brigades into an operationally significant division-size force.

Since the arrival of the 1st Tank Regiment with Haller's Blue Army in 1919, the Polish Army had maintained a small tank corps. Once the French FT17 tank became obsolete, the Ministry of Military Affairs purchased suitable new vehicles in Britain, which were developed into the TK3 and TKS tankettes in 1931–34, followed by the 7TP light tank in 1935. The tankettes were formed into armoured reconnaissance groups for the cavalry brigades or as independent reconnaissance companies.

A small number of the TKS were equipped with the new 20mm cannon, which would demonstrate their effectiveness against German armour in the 1939 campaign. The 7TP tanks were formed into two light tank battalions, which were intended to be used as army-level reserves for counter-attacks. By the standards of 1939, the 7TP was an effective vehicle that was well-armed and mobile. Under the 1936 expansion plan, the Polish Army hoped to field up to eight tank battalions, but the domestic production of the 7TP was too low to reach this goal. Although the Polish Army would employ over 500 armoured vehicles in the 1939 campaign, at no point would it be able to mass more than two to three tank companies on one battlefield.

In sum, the Polish Army's efforts at modernization had succeeded in providing its manoeuvre forces with weapons that were qualitatively comparable to those employed by the enemy. Polish tactical doctrine was offensively oriented, with an emphasis on short, sharp counter-attacks to be delivered against over-extended opponents. However, Polish units were not equipped on the same scale as their enemies, which meant their units generally had much less tactical firepower. Furthermore, the lack of adequate tactical mobility – except in two experimental brigades – left the Polish Army ill-suited for manoeuvre warfare under the conditions of 1939.

Fire Support

The Polish Army's artillery train consisted primarily of French-made 105mm and 155mm howitzers from the Great War. These weapons were intended for positional warfare and had a maximum range of 12km. Like the French Army, the Poles still relied too heavily on the venerable 75mm gun; in 1939, the Polish had 1,374 75mm guns with a reserve of 2.25 million rounds. The best available artillery piece was the Skoda 100mm howitzer wz. 1914/19, which was built under licence at the Starachowice Works. Polish divisional artillery consisted of a light artillery regiment equipped with 24 75mm guns and 12 100mm howitzers, plus a heavy artillery squadron (battalion) with three 105mm and three 155mm howitzers. In contrast, the typical German divisional artillery consisted of four battalions, equipped with a total of 36 10.5cm guns and 12 15cm howitzers. Thus, Polish divisional artillery was significantly smaller both in terms of numbers and weight of shell compared to German divisional artillery.

During manoeuvres in the mid-1920s, the Polish Army identified an urgent requirement to develop and field new long-range-artillery to replace its obsolescent French howitzers. In 1928, the Armaments and Equipment Committee (KSUS) settled on 155mm as the best calibre for a new weapon but the only foreign-made weapon that met the requirement was the Czech-made 149.1mm Skoda K-series howitzers. This was an excellent weapon and KSUS placed an order for 60 howitzers (at a cost of nearly $137,000 per howitzer) plus a production licence, but the order was later cancelled because of insufficient funds. Indeed, the exorbitant prices charged by the Czechs for modern military equipment soured the Poles on seeking further technological assistance from Skoda. Instead, the Polish Army decided to purchase more obsolescent 155mm howitzers from Schneider.[33] It was not until mid-1936 that Poland could begin to develop its own 155mm howitzer. Tests were conducted in 1938 and in early 1939, the 155mm wz. 40 howitzer was approved for production. When the Germans invaded only two prototype howitzers were in existence, with serial production set to begin in the winter. Consequently, the Polish Army was left with fire support assets that were left-overs from the Great War.[34]

As already noted, Polish infantry units only had about 60 per cent of the firepower available to German manoeuvre units. Furthermore, when the Wehrmacht began introducing several new families of artillery pieces (10.5cm l.FH18, 10cm s.K18 and 15cm s.FH18) in the mid-1930s, they achieved a clear qualitative advantage as well. The new German howitzers had better range and better rates of fire and were more mobile than their Polish counterparts. The Polish Army also had eight heavy artillery regiments, which were usually attached to field armies; these regiments had a mix of 105mm, 120mm, 155mm and 220mm pieces. Aside from obsolescence, Polish artillery support was hindered by inadequate mobility and inadequate communications to support manoeuvre units. An effort was made to deploy several hundred artillery tractors in the mid-1930s to increase the mobility of some guns, but most artillery pieces in 1939 would still be horse-drawn. Perhaps the best fire support asset available to the Polish Army was its ten armoured trains, which were armed with a mix of 100mm and 75mm guns, as well as numerous machine guns and a platoon of tankettes. While the armoured trains were vulnerable to air attack, they did provide field armies with some mobile firepower that could be effective under the right circumstances.

The one area of fire support where the Poles made significant progress in the 1930s was in terms of anti-tank defence. In the early 1930s, the WP conducted anti-tank tests at the Thorn proving ground with a 75mm wz. 1897 field gun. Experiments determined that artillery could engage tanks up to 1,000m, but the optimal range was 400–500m. Although funding was problematic, in 1935 the KSUS was finally able to place an order for 300 Bofors 3.7mm anti-tank guns and a production licence. Two factories were set up in Poland and serial production began in 1936. Under the 1936 modernization plan, the Ministry of Military Affairs intended to provide each infantry division with up to 48 37mm anti-tank guns and 18 for each cavalry brigade. Standardized as the 37mm anti-gun wz. 36, the Bofors-designed weapon was a state-of-the-art weapon which would inflict considerable losses on German Panzers in 1939. However, due to shortages of materials and funds, only 1,200 37mm anti-tank guns were in service by September 1939, instead of the 3,038 intended. The Polish Army also continued to experiment with the 75mm field gun and discovered that by improving the sights and traversing rods, they could significantly improve its performance against a moving tank. However, it was not until late July 1939 that the Ministry of Military Affairs initiated a crash programme to modify 800 75mm guns to improve their performance in the anti-tank role; only a small number of weapons were updated prior to the outbreak of war.[35]

Nor could the Polish Army expect much close air support from the LW. Each field army was assigned one squadron of ten PZL.23b Karaś scout bombers. The Karaś was a decent aircraft for its day, being able to deliver four 100kg bombs, but there were too few available to provide more than a small number of daily sorties. Furthermore, inadequate communications between ground and air units made it difficult to co-ordinate air support against fleeting targets. The LW's Bomber Brigade (Brygada Bombowa), with its 50 PZL.23b and 36 PZL.37b Łoś bombers, was intended to provide the main aerial punch, but its mission was battlefield interdiction, not close air support.

Air Defence
Although enemy air attacks had not been a serious problem in the Russo-Polish War, the Polish Army was keenly aware of the aerial threat in a future conflict and made it a priority to strengthen its capabilities in this regard. In addition to purchasing the 37mm anti-tank gun from Bofors, the KSUS also negotiated a deal to purchase 40 of the new 40mm anti-aircraft guns in 1935. Podpułkownik Feliks Kaminski led the programme to get the new anti-aircraft weaponry into service by establishing an air defence training centre near Warsaw, which evolved into the 1st Anti-Aircraft Regiment. In 1937, licensed production of the Bofors 40mm anti-aircraft gun began at the Starachowice Works, which had the capability to build up

to 35 guns per month. Several problems appeared along the way, notably difficulty with manufacturing the sensitive fuses, but the weapon was in serial production by 1938. The Bofors 40mm anti-aircraft gun was the best low-altitude air defence weapon available throughout the Second World War and Poland had acquired the ability to mass produce it. Each Polish Bofors gun was towed by a C2P tractor, providing excellent mobility. However, the Bofors 40mm was a very expensive weapon and only 414 were built by 1939, instead of the 840 planned. The Polish Army hoped to provide each infantry division with a battery of six 40mm guns and four for each cavalry brigade, but this was not achieved before the outbreak of war. The 1st Anti-Aircraft Regiment kept 40 40mm anti-aircraft guns to defend Warsaw and others were deployed to defend airfields and other urban areas, leaving the field armies with a tissue-thin amount of air defence. In addition, the Ministry of Military Affairs also wanted a larger weapon for medium-altitude air defence and funded the development of a new 75mm anti-aircraft gun, which entered service in mid-1937 as the 75mm wz. 36. The Ministry of Military Affairs wanted to deploy 70 air defence batteries with a total of 280 75mm guns, but production lagged and did not really get going until late 1938. Even then, only 52 75mm anti-aircraft guns would be completed by September 1939.[36]

Each Polish field army was provided with one or two squadrons of fighters – either the PZL P.7a or PZL P.11c – for local air defence. While 10–20 fighters was not much, it was considered adequate to deal with enemy reconnaissance aircraft and inflict some losses on enemy ground support missions. Against an enemy like the Soviet Air Force (Voyenno-Vozdushnye Sily or VVS), this might have been somewhat effective, but against the better-armed and equipped Luftwaffe, it was a disaster. Consequently, Polish field armies were left exposed to enemy air attacks from the onset of the campaign.

Mobility/counter-mobility

Of the 30 active Polish infantry divisions, 28 were provided with an organic sapper battalion. In addition, there were seven army-level motorized sapper battalions. Like most Polish support units, the sapper units were often only kept at cadre strength in peacetime and relied heavily upon reservists to fill their ranks. Polish division-level sapper units were hindered by lack of mobility and lack of equipment; only ten of 28 division-level battalions were outfitted to the Type II standard.[37] The army-level sapper battalions were partly motorized. In defensive or retrograde operations, Polish sappers were capable of assisting with counter-mobility by destroying bridges and cratering roads, but apparently most emphasis was on mobility support (e.g. tactical bridging of water obstacles). In truth, Polish war planning neglected to incorporate counter-mobility operations into their scheme of defence, leaving it up to local commanders to choose how to employ their sappers. Oftentimes, they were simply used as extra infantrymen.

French tactical experiments in the early 1930s indicated that obstacles, covered by anti-tank guns and artillery, could stop armoured attacks.[38] Anti-tank mines were regarded as an economical means to create anti-tank barriers – but for reasons not clear they were not manufactured in quantity. Poland developed the Anti-Tank Mine wz. 1937, which was capable of disabling any German tank, but only about 1,500 were built by 1939 – barely enough to protect a single division-wide sector.

Intelligence

Polish tactical intelligence capabilities were rather limited. Each infantry division had a 216-man bicycle company and a 258-man light cavalry squadron (equipped with just one radio) for reconnaissance purposes. Each infantry regiment also had a mounted scout company. Given the lack of radios and limitations of horse-mounted scouts, Polish divisions were only capable of localized reconnaissance efforts, barely a few kilometres beyond their main lines of resistance. Each army had two squadrons of biplane reconnaissance aircraft, which had very poor survivability in contested air space. At the operational level, the LW could use bombers to conduct reconnaissance missions with some chance of success, but co-ordination between ground and air units had not been rehearsed pre-war to any great degree. Consequently, Polish field armies had poor situational awareness about enemy operational-level movements, which made them vulnerable to surprise attacks.

At the strategic level, the Second Department of the Polish General Staff ('Dwojka'), had enjoyed considerable success against the Germans in the inter-war period. Jerzy Sosnowski had succeeded in establishing a spy network in Berlin in 1926 and for the next seven years he was able to acquire a number of classified Reichswehr planning documents.[39] Among other things, the documents indicated that the Reichswehr had begun drafting offensive plans against Poland in the late 1920s and that the Nazi regime was continuing this planning effort. Sosnowski was finally arrested by the Gestapo in early 1934, but later exchanged back to Poland for three incarcerated German citizens. Unfortunately, the Second Department put little stock in Sosnowski's intelligence coup, regarding him as a potential double agent.[40] In terms of signals intelligence, the Second Department's Cipher Bureau (Biuro Szyfrów) was second to none, and it spent considerable effort attacking the encryption methods used by the German Enigma code machine. Thanks to co-operation with the French Deuxième Bureau (military intelligence), a team of three Polish mathematicians was able to break into Enigma in December 1932. During the mid-1930s, the Polish Cipher Bureau was able to learn a great deal about German military preparations because the security settings on early Enigma models were relatively low, but these were enhanced as war became more imminent. As late as 1938, the Poles claimed that they were decrypting up to 75 per cent of intercepted Enigma traffic, although this is likely an exaggeration, given the limited technical resources available. However, by early 1939 Polish codebreakers were only reading Enigma traffic on rare occasions.[41] Nevertheless, the Polish penetration of Enigma gave the Polish General Staff a unique and invaluable source of information about overall German plans and the kind of forces they could employ against Poland.

Command and Control (C^2)

In the mid-1920s, the Polish Army purchased about 100 RKA/G and 400 RKD radios from France for a total of 6.75 million zł ($1.3 million); the RKA/G was used for higher-level communications between armies, while the RKD was used for division-level communications. Both these radio systems were very heavy (up to 1,100 kg for the RKA/G) and not well-suited to mobile operations. Units below division-level usually relied on field telephones via wire for communications. During the early 1930s, Polish industry became capable of making its own military radios and the ROD wz. 33 portable radio was introduced in 1933 to work with the division-level RKD stations during mobile operations. As part of the 1936 modernization programme, military communications received considerable funding to produce a new generation of tactical radios, beginning with the N2 radio. The Polish Army hoped to deploy the N2 radio down to battalion-level units and 10,000 were ordered, but only 1,400 were delivered by the outbreak of war. Nevertheless, the N2 was an advanced design for its day and the Germans liked it so much that they adopted it for their own use and kept it in production. The N1 radio, intended for division-level communications, entered production in June 1939 but only 65 of 500 ordered were delivered by the outbreak of war. In terms of tactical communications, the Polish Army had invested heavily in a new generation of field telephones, such as the AP-36, which was a good-quality device of modern design. About 20,000 AP-36 field telephones were delivered before the German invasion. However, wire communications were better suited to a war of position and the Polish Army lacked sufficient tactical radios to sustain adequate C^2 in the mobile campaign it was forced to fight. Furthermore, both the Army and LW were still overly reliant on easily disrupted civilian telephone networks.

The Polish commander-in-chief and the General Staff received the new medium frequency W1 radio for operational-level communications just before the start of the war. The W1 could either be used as a fixed system in Warsaw or transported by six Fiat 621 trucks to alternate headquarters. Although the W2 required five hours or more to set up, it could provide radiotelephone communications up to 500km or telegraph up to 1,500km. In addition to breaking into Enigma, the Polish Cipher Bureau also built its own cipher machine known as the Lacida, but it was still experimental in 1939.

While the Polish Army did possess some modern tactical radios, its operational-level C^2 was woefully inadequate compared to the Wehrmacht's for two reasons. First, the Polish Army did not employ corps headquarters to co-ordinate divisions, as the Germans did. Instead, the Poles relied upon mission-oriented operational groups, which lacked the staff found in a German *Armeekorps*. While the operational group structure had been adequate for the Russo-Polish War in 1919, it proved a failure in the 1939 campaign. A second factor that undermined Polish C^2 was the lack of pre-war communications training and a lack of interest by senior officers in radio exercises. For example, Pułkownik Tadeusz Komorowski, who would later lead the 1944 Warsaw Uprising, acknowledged that he had never even used a radio until late in the war. Unlike the Wehrmacht division and corps leaders, who were thoroughly familiar with commanding units by radio thanks to pre-war exercises, the Polish mid-level commanders were generally not accustomed to using radios much.

Combat Service Support (CSS)

In order to function on campaign, an army needs regular resupply of fuel, ammunition and food, as well as medical care for its casualties. Due to financial constraints, almost all the Polish Army's service support personnel were reservists, available only after mobilization. Furthermore, virtually all of the combat service support elements relied upon horse-drawn transport, possessing very few motor vehicles. Each infantry division had a field hospital, plus commissary and quartermaster units, totalling about 1,500 troops and 1,440 horses. The Polish CSS units had limited mobility and would quickly fall behind in any retrograde (retreat) movements. At army-level there were a few motorized logistic units, but not enough to fill the gap in capabilities at lower levels. On active campaigning, Polish units were repeatedly plagued by fuel and ammunition shortages due to the inadequacies of their CSS services and rapid loss of fixed logistic depots, such as the massive one at Dęblin. Given that Poland produced over 10,000 Fiat 621L 2.5-tonne trucks in 1935–39, but neither the combat nor support units had any substantial amount of motorization, it is difficult to comprehend what the majority of these vehicles were doing during the 1939 campaign.

Aside from the various material defects of the Polish Army, the General Staff was also worried about simply having enough troops to create a solid defence. Even when fully mobilized, the regular army and reserves would be thinly spread across Poland. In order to add further numbers to the field army, in late 1936 the Ministry of Military Affairs authorized the creation of a National Defence (Obrona Narodowa or ON), consisting of 50,000 troops in 82 battalions. The battalions would be formed from volunteers and surplus reservists, some of whom would be trained. Once mobilized, the ON battalions would be formed into brigade-size units and attached to reinforce regular divisions. In general, the ON troops were equipped with fewer and older weapons which, combined with their limited training, made these units extremely fragile.[42]

When the German invasion did come in September 1939, it caught the Polish Army in a period of transition, before it could be fully re-equipped with modern weapons and equipment. However, it is clear that Polish industry was producing a number of state-of-the-art weapons – including the 7TP tank, the Bofors 37mm anti-tank gun and 40mm anti-aircraft gun and the N2 radio – which were the equivalent of contemporary German weapons. Nevertheless, not enough modern equipment had yet reached the field armies to enable Polish units to withstand superior German numbers and firepower.

Constraints upon Modernization

Although Poland's economy recovered and grew after 1936, the government's financial resources remained completely inadequate to support rapid military modernization. During 1935–37, Polish defence spending averaged about 730 million zł per year ($140 million) – about 10 per cent of the GDP – and this was only increased to 830 million zł ($160 million) after the Munich Crisis.[43] Even amid this tiny budget, only about 8–10 per cent could be allocated towards procurement of new equipment; the rest went to cover upkeep of existing forces and infrastructure. Consequently, the Ministry of Military Affairs was forced to look for alternative sources of funding to finance its modernization programmes, namely foreign loans, arms sales and popular subscriptions. While these alternative sources did provide enough funds to jumpstart modernization programmes, they were insufficient to advance the timetable of the 1936 modernization plan.

France was the obvious source for military loans but after Piłsudski ousted the French military mission in Warsaw in 1931, there was less enthusiasm in Paris for investing scarce financial resources in Poland. However, Hitler's reoccupation of the Rhineland in March 1936 caused France to recognize that conflict with Germany was now possible and in that eventuality, France would need allies. In August, Maréchal Maurice Gamelin, the French military commander-in-chief, visited Warsaw for discussions with Marszałek Rydz-Śmigły. Although little was agreed upon, France agreed to provide more funds for Polish military modernization. In return, the Poles agreed to share intelligence about Germany with the French.[44] In September 1936, under the terms of the Rambouillet Accord, France granted Poland a loan of ₣ 2.6 billion over five years, to be delivered in annual allotments of ₣ 500 million (about 160 million zł or $31 million) each. The infusion of French funding came at a critical moment and enabled the Ministry of Military Affairs to initiate serial production of the Bofors 37mm anti-tank gun and 40mm anti-aircraft gun.[45] In theory, the French Rambouillet loans should have helped accelerate the 1936 modernization programme, but in reality the effects were diluted by two factors. First, the French required most of the funds to be spent on French-built weapons, in order to help the French domestic arms industry. Second, the Polish government was forced to spend a good portion of the funds on industrial development and infrastructure (e.g. new rail lines and power plants to serve Polish arms factories). When the KSUS sought to purchase modern French-built aircraft and tanks, the French were less than forthcoming, citing that their own defence needs had priority. More than two years would pass before the French agreed to sell Poland any modern weapons.

Poland managed to secure some commercial loans from the United States in the late 1920s and mid-1930s, but these were too small and at very steep terms, so the benefit was negligible.[46] Indeed, Poland was running a serious trade imbalance with the United States, which made it unable to secure further financial loans. Likewise, Poland could not secure any substantial loans from Great Britain. Even though Poland had the sixth largest economy in Europe in 1939, with a GDP Product of approximately 24 billion zł ($4.63 billion), there was little British interest in investing money in Poland.[47] Unable to secure adequate foreign funding to support its rearmament plans, Poland turned to arms sales to close the gap.

After Piłsudski's 1926 coup, the Polish government created SEPEWE (Syndykat Eksportu Przemysłu Wojennego) an arms export company designed to sell Polish weapons abroad. Initially, SEPEWE focused on trading small stockpiles of surplus non-standardized weapons to other eastern European countries; the first substantial sale occurred in 1928, with 4,950 Lee-Enfield rifles sold to Estonia. By the early 1930s, Poland was selling 15–30 million zł ($2.5-5 million) per year of surplus weapons to Nationalist China, Greece and various Latin American regimes. When the Spanish Civil War broke out, SEPEWE was able to greatly increase its arms sales, up to 120 million zł ($23 million) in 1937 – equivalent to one-sixth of the national defence budget. Altogether, Poland exported over 300 million zł ($55 million) worth of arms in the 1930s, 63 per cent of which went to Spain and the Balkans. Although SEPEWE proved to be a money-maker, it was addictive and when the stockpiles of old weapons ran out, Poland began to start selling its latest weapons abroad. In 1936, PZL began selling the PZL P.24, an export version of the PZL P.11c, to Romania and Turkey. In 1938, PZL signed a deal to sell 50 PZL P.43 light bombers to Bulgaria – the last of which were delivered in August 1939. The new Bofors 37mm anti-tank guns and 40mm anti-aircraft guns were hot export items and SEPEWE readily agreed to export them to Britain, France, the Netherlands, Peru, Romania and Turkey. Most of these weapons were never delivered, but France did receive 20,000 40mm rounds and Britain received 260 37mm guns (with 150,000 rounds) and 58 40mm guns before the outbreak of war. Even Poland's most modern aircraft, the PZL P.37c bomber, was offered for export to Bulgaria, Romania and Yugoslavia.[48] While SEPEWE brought in valuable funds, it also ended up diverting valuable military hardware away from the WP at a critical moment. Although some Polish officers – particularly in the LW – opposed these arms exports, they were overruled because cash-strapped Poland needed the revenue.

Another alternative source of revenue for the Polish military was encouraging patriotic donations from the public. The Polish Navy, languishing for lack of funds, encouraged the formation of the Maritime Defence Fund (Funduszu Obrony Morskiej or FOM) in 1933. During 1934–39, the FOM was able to raise 10.5 million zł ($2 million), which went for the construction of new warships. In 1936, the National Defence Fund (Fundusz Obrony Narodowej or FON) was established to provide additional funding for both the Army and the LW. The FON was a major success, providing tens of millions in extra funding. The FON was also able to attract contributions from Polish expatriates in the United States and elsewhere. In early 1939, the Polish government began to sell specialized defence bonds, such as the Antiaircraft Defence Fund (Fundusz Obrony Przeciwlotniczej or FOP), to boost particular weapons programmes. Overall, the Polish public responded well to these fund-raising schemes, even though it was still peacetime. Altogether, arms sales and public donations eventually helped to redress the worst shortfalls in the Polish defence budget, but it is not clear that all these non-budgeted funds were channelled where they were needed most. Indeed, considerable amounts of funds were still siphoned off to support industrial development projects, rather than support the military's modernization plans.

The biggest industrial project was the Central Industrial Region (Centralny Okręg Przemysłowy or COP), which was intended to further enhance domestic armaments production as well as to alleviate high unemployment. The basic concept was that the COP would be built in the area south of Sandomierz, between the San and Vistula Rivers, because this area was furthest from the German and Soviet borders. In the event of war, the Ministry of Military Affairs believed that the COP could be protected, at least from ground attack. During 1937–39, about 1.9 billion zł ($365 million) was devoted to the COP project, although virtually none of the new factories were operational by September 1939. While the COP was a sound long-term strategic investment, in the short run it deprived the WP of valuable financial and material resources in the lead-up to war.

Poland also needed more than just funds, it needed raw materials to build weapons in its own factories. Indeed, lack of raw materials proved to be a critical roadblock for increasing domestic arms production. By 1937, mineral resources were in high demand by Britain, France and Germany for their own rearmament programmes, which caused spikes in prices. Poland had great difficulty purchasing enough raw materials for its own needs and production at key armaments factories was less than half of capacity. In April 1938, the Ministry of Military Affairs finally recognized the constraints imposed by resource shortages upon its modernization programme and directed the formation of a company known as TISSA (Towarzystwo Importu Surowców Spółka Akcyjna) to import raw materials critical for the Polish armaments industry. The government provided TISSA with 2.5 million zł ($480,000) in capital and directed it to build up a three-month war reserve of critical materials, particularly aluminium, copper and magnesium. Over the next 14 months, TISSA was able to import over 20,000 tonnes of critical raw materials.[49] However, Poland failed to import enough resources to ensure maximum production of its best weapons.

By 1938, the Ministry of Military Affairs also recognized that there was a growing technology gap between Poland and Germany, particularly in the fields of aviation and tanks. Generał Brygady Józef L. Zając, commander of the LW, recognized that the German Bf 109D and Bf 109E models, which became available in 1938, clearly outclassed not only the existing PZL. P.11c fighter, but even its replacement, the PZL.50. The LW had begun development of the PZL.50 fighter in 1937, but in testing it could not even reach 480km/h, which meant that it could not counter high-speed interceptors like the Bf 109D/E. As regional tensions mounted in late 1938, Zając pointed out the urgency of fielding new fighters and recommended purchasing foreign-built fighters to match the Bf 109.[50] There were only four available foreign-built fighters with speeds above 480km/h: the American-built Curtiss P-36, the British Hurricane and Spitfire fighters and the French MS.406 fighter. Even though the P-36 was a good design and available for export, the Poles were not interested because the aircraft was expensive and deliveries from the United States would take too long. Neither Britain nor France was interested in selling copies of their best fighter to Poland until war was imminent. Finally, on 27 July 1939, the French agreed to sell ten MS.406 fighters to Poland, to be followed by 40 more in October and 70 more during the winter of 1939/40. The French also agreed to sell Poland the D.520 fighter when it became available in 1940. However, the French had encountered serious problems with the development of the MS.406 and it did not enter serial production until early 1939, so few were available. The LW sent a small test group to Paris to examine French fighters, which ended tragically when the test pilot Kapitan Andrzej Wlodarkiewicz was killed flying an MS.406, which failed to come out of a dive. It was not until 29 August 1939 that the first batch of 20 MS.406 fighters was sent by sea to the port of Constanta in Romania; by the time the ship arrived, Poland had been invaded and the Romanians refused to allow the aircraft to be unloaded. The French MS.406 fighters were instead sold to Turkey.

Britain proved even less willing to provide modern fighters to Poland, despite the security guarantee that Chamberlain announced on 30 March 1939. While Britain had sold 20 Hurricanes to Belgium and promptly delivered them in the summer of 1939, there was no eagerness to provide the Hurricane to Poland. After much discussion, the British government finally agreed to provide a single squadron of Hurricanes and one Spitfire for the Poles to examine – there was no discussion of further British aircraft deliveries. At literally the last minute, on 30 August, the British vessel SS *Lassell* left Great Britain with 14 Hurricanes, one Spitfire and seven Fairey Battles aboard. By the time that the *Lassell* reached the Mediterranean en route to Constanta, Poland was already invaded and the ship was redirected to Istanbul. Most of the equipment aboard was later sold to Turkey.

Poland had even less success in seeking foreign-made tanks to bolster its army. In 1938, the French offered two R35 tanks for trials, which the Polish Army found inadequate in terms of firepower and mobility. Instead, the Poles preferred to purchase the more modern Somua S35 medium tank, but the French were unwilling to sell it. Instead, in April 1939 the French offered 100 R35 tanks to Poland. The Polish Army didn't want the R35s but at this point there was no alternative, so they agreed to the sale. In early June 1939, the first batch of 50 R35 and three H35 tanks was delivered by sea to Poland, at a cost of F 54.8 million (about 8.1 million zł or $1.5 million). The tanks arrived with a bare minimum support package and it would take weeks to train Polish tankers on the new vehicles. Unfortunately, the first Polish battalion of R35 tanks was not yet operational by 1 September 1939. Thus, Polish efforts to acquire Anglo-French military technology proved far too little and too late to affect the 1939 campaign.

Aside from difficulties in gaining access to foreign financial loans and technology, the Poles had made some serious mistakes on their own, which constrained the modernization of the WP. Although Piłsudski had been opposed to spending on the Polish Navy, the Naval Directorate (KMW) gradually managed to gain some support for a naval expansion programme. In August 1933, the Ministry of Military Affairs agreed to provide 6.5 million zł ($1.25 million) for new warship construction, which got the ball rolling. In 1935, the KMW ordered two destroyers to be built in Britain and in 1936, two submarines were ordered from the

Netherlands. Altogether, these four warships would cost about 45 million zł ($8.6 million) – enough to fund the establishment of four more tank battalions. In addition to purchasing more warships, in 1935 the KMW began sinking considerable funds into creating the Hel Fortified Area on the Hel Peninsula. A battery of four modern 152mm coastal defence guns was installed on the peninsula and extensive underground works built, along with a seaplane base. While the Hel Fortified Area would prove to be a tough nut to crack for the Germans, it was not linked to the defence of greater Poland. Altogether, the Ministry of Military Affairs spent about 60 million zł ($11.5 million) on the Hel Fortified Area in 1935–39.[51] Given the lack of survivability of the Polish Navy in the face of enemy air superiority, the expenditure of more than 100 million zł ($19.2 million) on these projects appears to have been a luxury that the Second Republic could not afford. Unable to purchase or produce enough modern weaponry due to constraints beyond its control, the WP was unable to complete its 1936 modernization goals prior to the outbreak of war in September 1939.

CHAPTER 3

The Threat Emerges

Hitler's Frantic Rearmament Alters the Balance of Power

'The extent of the military development of our resources
cannot be too large, nor its pace too swift ....'
Hitler, August 1936[1]

As a result of the Treaty of Versailles, in 1921 Weimar Germany's post-war Reichswehr was reduced to a 100,000-man establishment with a total force structure of just seven infantry and three cavalry divisions. Most heavy weaponry, including all tanks and armoured cars, was scrapped and the Reichswehr was left with just 288 artillery pieces (204 77mm and 84 105mm guns).[2] The Allies deliberately stripped the Reichswehr of its tactical firepower, limiting it to a total of fewer than 2,000 machine guns and 252 mortars. Furthermore, an 11,240-man Reichswehr infantry division in 1921 was 25 per cent smaller than a 1918 division. Since the treaty also prohibited Germany from possessing or developing military aircraft, Reichswehr ground troops would have no air support. The Allies also forced the disbandment of the Großer Generalstab (Great General Staff) – thereby depriving the Reichswehr of its operational-planning staff – and placed strict limits on German industry to inhibit its ability to develop new weapons. Altogether, the Treaty of Versailles stripped the Reichswehr of its offensive capabilities and reduced Germany to the status of a third-rate military power. Furthermore, Germany was convulsed with economic and political chaos in 1920–23, which shoved Reichswehr needs to the bottom of priorities. Although many Germans remained angry about the loss of territory and population to Poland, the Reichswehr lacked the strength to threaten Poland and only had a single infantry division deployed in East Prussia.

Despite all the Versailles-imposed limitations, the Germans did have some advantages for rebuilding their military power. Unlike the difficulties faced by the larger Polish Army, the German Army (Reichsheer) was a homogenous force in terms of language, training and traditions. From the beginning, General Hans von Seeckt, commander of the Reichswehr in 1920–26, structured his force to be a training laboratory and test bed. Seeckt ensured that the Reichsheer had a hand-picked officer corps which contained many General Staff-trained officers and a solid core of professional non-commissioned officers (NCOs). Since he could not have quantity, Seeckt ensured that he at least had a high-quality professional army, which could be used as the bedrock for future expansion. Seeckt set about rebuilding German ground combat power by intensively studying the lessons of the First World War, which led to the conclusion that offensive action through mobile warfare was the key to success on the battlefield. Analysis also indicated that the Western Allies had used aircraft and tanks to restore mobility to warfare on the Western Front in 1918 and Germany would need such capabilities in a future conflict. Seeckt connived to create a hidden staff within the army bureaucracy, including a small air staff to study aviation technology.[3] Initially funds were quite limited; during 1925–32, German defence spending was less than 2 per cent of Gross National Product (GNP) (around RM 700 million) – yet even this small figure was still 20 per cent more than Poland was spending on defence.

Germany's domestic armaments industrial base was also in a good position to support rearmament, despite temporary limitations imposed by Allied inspections and post-war austerity. Unlike Poland, German industry still possessed the knowledge base and skills to conduct research and development on advanced weaponry. Germany's critical infrastructure – transport, electrical power generation and mining – was also intact. After the Treaty of Rapallo normalized Soviet–German relations in 1922, Seeckt organized a covert group known as Sondergruppe R, to conduct military technical collaboration with the Soviet Union.[4] Sondergruppe R was able to lay the preparations for establishing secret testing facilities in the Soviet Union, out of sight of Allied inspectors. The Reichswehr's first covert military mission to the USSR arrived in February 1923. In 1924, the Reichswehr began providing flight instructors to help train Soviet pilots and with the help of German industrialists, the Reichswehr was able to covertly purchase 50 Fokker D.XIII fighters from Holland and ship them to Lipetsk in the USSR in mid-1925.[5] By April 1926, the Reichswehr was able to open the Kampffliegerschule Lipezk (Lipetsk flying school) and begin a fighter training course and ground attack experiments using the D.XIIIs.[6] The role of the Lipetsk facility was critical in shaping future German doctrines for the use of fighters and close air support aircraft.[7] Over the course of the next seven years, 130 German fighter pilots and 80 air observers were trained at Lipetsk.[8] In summer 1929, the Panzerschule Kama (Kama tank school) was opened with Oberst Oswald Lutz as its head and Germany began testing experimental tanks in the Soviet Union.[9] A number of German officers attended training in the Soviet Union, including Heinz Guderian, allowing them to keep abreast of modern technological developments.

In addition to covert testing in the Soviet Union, German companies used foreign subsidiary companies to conduct research and design work that could not be conducted on German soil. For example, Rheinmetall-Borsig purchased a controlling interest in the Swiss ammunition firm Solothurn AG in 1929 and Krupp made a similar effort to acquire part of the Swedish Bofors company. Krupp referred to its illicit arms production as *schwarze Produktion* (black production).[10] Junkers, one of the premier German aircraft design firms, operated a factory in Moscow during 1922–25, in co-operation with the Soviet Tupolev Design Bureau.[11] Through these foreign companies, German engineers were able to conduct important design work on new weapons. As a result, several new weapons were developed during 1928–30, including the 7.5cm l.IG18 infantry gun, the 88cm Flak 18 anti-aircraft gun, the 3.7cm PaK anti-tank gun and the MG 13 light machine gun. In addition, the Reichswehr made a considerable investment in developing tactical communications.[12]

Seeckt and his successors were particularly adamant about laying the groundwork for a new air force, although there were serious political and technical hurdles. The Allies had placed heavy restrictions on the German aviation industry, particularly in regard to developing new engines that would be suitable for military aircraft. However, the vigilance of Allied inspections waned after 1925 and engine development began to emerge from the shadows. Indeed, the Allied leadership was completely oblivious, even when indicators of secret German rearmament became public. For example, in December 1926 information about the Junkers secret aircraft plant in Moscow and German–Soviet military co-operation was leaked – but there was no reaction in London or Paris.[13] In the face of this kind of apathy, BMW introduced the 500hp BMW VI aero-engine, which was used on early military prototypes. By 1928–29, German firms were also able to obtain licences to produce two foreign radial engines – the 750hp Pratt & Whitney Hornet and the 480hp Bristol Jupiter VI. Eventually, the British sold supercharger technology to German companies, which enabled German engineers to stay abreast of the latest technological developments.[14] During the period 1926–32, the Reichswehr spent RM 170 million (about $40 million) on aviation programmes. Assisted by infusions of Anglo-American technology, Daimler-Benz and Junkers took the lead in developing new piston engines, but they would not be ready until 1932.

The Reichswehr's intensive study of the First World War and its appreciation for modern technology led it towards a new operational-level doctrine, which emphasized manoeuvre warfare conducted by the close co-operation of motorized ground forces and close air support. The inculcation of *Stosstruppen* infiltration tactics from 1918 into the doctrinal mix led to a less linear mindset about operational manoeuvre. During the late 1920s, experiments conducted with motorized infantry and tactical radios proved promising. By 1929, the Reichswehr also began to put serious effort into developing tanks and the doctrine on how to best employ them.[15] In 1930, General Kurt von Hammerstein-Equord became the new head of the Reichswehr and he made serious plans to expand the army in violation of the Versailles limits, including the creation of motorized units. In 1932, Generalmajor Oswald Lutz was put in charge of the new army motorization programme and he established a requirement to build a tracked armoured vehicle for training purposes. Contracts were signed with Krupp and by July 1932 a prototype that would evolve into the Pz I tank was ready. Lutz envisioned the Pz I only as a training tank, to be followed by more capable 15-tonne medium tanks, in due course. The evolving German doctrine was formalized in a new field manual named *Truppenführung* (Troop Leadership), which was issued by Generalleutnant Ludwig Beck's Truppenamt (Troop Office) in 1933. The new manual stressed initiative, offensive action, manoeuvre and combined arms warfare.

In particular, the *Truppenführung* emphasized the importance of using tanks in the offensive with the full support of tactical aviation, artillery, motorized infantry and engineers, plus anti-tank troops.[16] However, the resource-poor Reichswehr could only dream about motorized warfare; when Hitler came to power in 1934, the Reichswehr only had a total of 5,667 motor vehicles.[17]

Weimar Germany was a politically divided nation and not everyone supported rearmament. The Reichswehr had to be careful to conceal its covert programmes from socialist and communist politicians in Berlin, who would move to oppose funding and alert the media. Hammerstein-Equord was among those ardently opposed to the emerging Nazi Party, but it did not stop him from laying the groundwork for transforming the Reichswehr into a much more combat-capable force. In June 1932, Kurt von Schleicher, formerly of Sondergruppe R, became the new defence minister and Germany began moving towards open rearmament. Schleicher authorized the Umbau Plan, a programme to expand the army to 21 divisions, although the active army would only increase to 147,000 troops and reserves would make up the difference.[18] Thus, it is important to note that years before Adolf Hitler came to power, the Reichswehr was aggressively pursuing the development of offensive weaponry in violation of the Versailles restrictions and developing an operational doctrine clearly intended to pursue revanchist objectives. While the military and political leadership in the Weimar Republic era was careful to avoid displaying aggressive intent towards the Anglo-French, this restraint did not apply to Poland. Seeckt openly regarded Poland as an enemy and in a September 1922 memo, he wrote that its existence was 'intolerable and incompatible with the survival of Germany. It must disappear and it will disappear through its own internal weakness and through Russia – with our assistance.'[19]

Meanwhile, the Weimar Republic was slowly disintegrating and the threat of Bolshevism caused many Germans to hunger for stability and national revival. Adolf Hitler's National Socialist Party (NSDAP or Nazis) offered both – at a price. On 26 January 1932, Fritz Thyssen, one of Germany's leading industrialists, invited Hitler to speak at the Industry Club in Düsseldorf. Hitler delivered one of his best speeches, outlining his basic vision for reviving Germany by creating a strong, centralized government which filled 'its followers with an unrestrained aggressive spirit (*Kampfsinn*) and possessed the will to do whatever was necessary to protect German interests'. Although he did not include any provocative remarks about Germany's neighbours, he made it clear that he sought *Lebensraum* (living space) and that the new Germany should be 'intolerant against anyone who will not acknowledge its vital interests'.[20] Hitler's Düsseldorf speech provided a glimpse into his vision, which was clearly revanchist and expansionist.

One year later, with the financial assistance of a number of German industrialists, Hitler became chancellor of Germany. He immediately made it clear that rearmament was a priority. Four months later, Hitler's closest ally, Herman Göring, oversaw the creation of the Reichsluftfahrtministerium (Air Ministry or RLM), ostensibly to supervise commercial aviation but in reality to pave the way for an independent air force and to jump-start the German aviation industry. Göring directed the RLM, headed by Erhard Milch, to invest large sums in the aviation industry, which in the course of a single year quadrupled the work force.[21] In June 1933, Hitler's cabinet approved an allocation of RM 35 billion for rearmament over the next eight years, which meant increasing defence spending to nearly 10 per cent of GNP. Under this plan, the first phase of rearmament would see the RLM build an air force equipped with 2,000 aircraft by 1935 and the army expand to 300,000 men in 21 divisions by 1937. In the second phase, Germany would develop an offensive strike capability, to be ready by 1941.[22] After President Hindenburg's death in August 1934, Hitler gained total control over Germany and began eliminating those who opposed his vision.

Even with increased funding, it took time for German industry to begin tooling up for Hitler's rearmament programme. In 1934, Germany built just 54 Pz I tanks and 190 combat aircraft (109 fighters, 61 bombers and 20 dive-bombers), all of which were inferior to the equipment possessed by other major powers. Indeed, the Arado 65 biplane fighters were significantly slower than the current Polish PZL. P.7a fighter. The first clandestine bomber unit, dubbed the Hanseatische Fliegerschule (Hanseatic Flying School), was equipped with 24 Ju 52/3m transports, which had been converted to carry a small bombload.[23] Hitler decided to keep the new tanks and aircraft – both violations of the Versailles Treaty – out of sight until they were available in quantity. Another reason to initially keep the rearmament programme semi-covert was that German industry still needed infusions of foreign technology to close the technological gap. The RLM purchased two US-built F11C Goshawk dive-bombers in 1933 for a total of $23,000, while Junkers managed to purchase ten state-of-the-art Rolls-Royce Kestrel engines for £20,514.[24] The Rolls-Royce engines would be used to power the prototypes of both the Ju 87 dive-bomber and the Bf 109 fighter. The government of Ramsay MacDonald was fully aware of the export of aero-engines to Germany because it allowed export licences to be granted, but insisted on believing the German explanation that the engines would only be used for civilian purposes. Yet the existence of a covert Luftwaffe was already out of the bag, as reported by British media outlets such as *The Times*, in December 1932.[25]

On 9 March 1935, Hitler publicly revealed the existence of the heretofore-secret Luftwaffe. Although Göring boasted that he had 2,500 aircraft, in fact he only had 1,800 and most were trainers or reconnaissance machines. The Luftwaffe's actual combat strength totalled 674 combat aircraft, consisting of three squadrons of biplane fighters (Ar 65 and He 51) and five squadrons of bombers (Do 11 and Ju 52).[26] Six days later, Hitler announced the re-introduction of conscription and his intent to increase the army to 36 divisions with 500,000 men; in May the Reichswehr was renamed the Wehrmacht. By October 1935, Hitler dropped all pretence and announced the formation of three Panzer-Divisionen. In fact, the Heer only had 300 Pz I tanks available at this point and each division was supposed to have 500 light tanks; the first three Panzer-Divisionen were not completely equipped until late 1938.[27] Furthermore, the Panzer-Divisionen would have no gun-armed tanks until early 1938, either. Indeed, the Wehrmacht of 1935 was a cardboard force, partly equipped with second-rate equipment. However, Hitler had succeeded in violating the Versailles restrictions without any serious repercussions from the Anglo-French and in August 1936 he revealed the next phase – a Four Year Plan, in which he stated that 'the extent of the military development of our resources cannot be too large, nor its pace too swift …'.[28] From this point on, Germany embarked upon an all-out effort to achieve military supremacy in central Europe.

Although Hitler had opened the floodgates for defence spending, German rearmament efforts were slowed by a host of lingering technical problems in developing new weapons and the limited capacity of German industry to build these weapons in quantity. Even more problematic was the shortage of raw materials and skilled labour. Germany imported most of its chromite, copper, iron ore, manganese, rubber and tungsten from the Anglo-French, which had to be paid for in foreign currencies. However, Germany was very short on foreign currency reserves in the mid-1930s and was not able to import the amounts of critical raw materials required. By defaulting on Germany's foreign debt, Hitler could not borrow from foreign lenders. Consequently, even major weapons programmes had to be scaled back to reflect available resources. By February 1937, a severe shortage of steel forced German industry to ration this key resource, thereby delaying the goals of Hitler's Four Year Plan.

German armament priorities were heavily influenced by the offensive operational doctrine developed by the Reichswehr, which laid great stress upon manoeuvre and shock action. The Pz I was an adequate design for 1934, when there were few other foreign gun-armed tanks in existence. Yet while useful for infantry support and as a training vehicle, the 5-tonne Pz I was obviously too slow and under-armed to comprise the spear tip of the kind of manoeuvre warfare envisioned by Seeckt. Likewise, the He 51 biplane fighter was already inferior to a new generation of foreign monoplane fighters such as the French D.500 and Soviet I-16 *Rata*. Without a modern fighter to ensure air superiority over critical sectors, the Luftwaffe's bombers and ground attack aircraft could suffer heavy losses and the army's Panzers would not get the vital air support they needed to ensure decisive results. Thus it was the concurrent quest for better tanks and a modern air superiority fighter that shaped the outcome of Hitler's rearmament plan.

Based upon lessons learned at Panzerschule Kama in the Soviet Union, Generalmajor Oswald Lutz, inspector for motor transport troops, believed that the new *Panzertruppen* (tank troops) should be based on two distinct types of medium tanks: a tank equipped with a high-velocity 3.7cm cannon to engage enemy armoured vehicles and a tank equipped with a low-velocity 7.5cm howitzer to engage buildings and fortifications. On 11 January 1934, the Heereswaffenamt Wa Prüf 6 (Army Weapons Department, Panzer Office) issued a requirement for two new medium tanks, based upon Lutz's recommendations. These two tanks would evolve into the Pz III armed with a 3.7cm gun and the Pz IV armed with a 7.5cm howitzer. Both tanks would be powered by the 250hp Maybach HL 108 TR gasoline engine. As envisioned by Lutz and his chief of staff Heinz Guderian, the future German *Panzer-Abteilung* (tank battalion) would be based on these two tanks, with the ratio of 3 Pz III to each Pz IV.[29] By the end of 1934, Daimler-Benz and Rheinmetall-Borsig had been awarded the contract to develop the Pz III while Krupp was awarded the contract to develop the Pz IV. Although it was a top priority, the German medium tank programme underwent a long drawn-out development process in 1935–36 and the first pre-production models were not available until 1937. Krupp had some earlier experience building tank prototypes for

Panzerschule Kama and opted for a conservative design, which proved less problematic. The initial Pz IV Ausf A model proved basically sound and Krupp began building the Pz IV Ausf B model in May 1938, with a more powerful engine and better frontal armour protection. By September 1938, the basic production model, the Pz IV Ausf C, was just beginning low-rate production. A year later, a total of 211 Pz IV tanks were in service.

In contrast, the Pz III tank programme – which was supposed to be the Wehrmacht's main battle tank – was something of a fiasco. Daimler-Benz experienced great difficulty perfecting the tank's suspension, shifting from coiled springs to leaf springs to torsion bars. The first four models of the Pz III had considerably different suspensions, ranging from five to eight road wheels and were only built in token quantities. After much technical fumbling, Daimler-Benz finally had a basic production model, the Pz III Ausf E, ready for low-rate production by December 1938. On top of its sluggish development process, Daimler-Benz also experienced great difficulty ramping up Pz III production, so Henschel and M.A.N. were brought in to share the effort. Nevertheless, by September 1939 a total of only 98 Pz III tanks had been built, of which 50 were the Ausf E model. At the outset of the war, the critical Pz III programme was over a year behind schedule. Thus, the Panzer-Divisionen of 1939 would not have battalions comprised entirely of medium tanks as Lutz and Guderian had envisioned in 1933; rather, the small number of medium tanks had to be sprinkled across the entire Panzertruppe, diluting their impact. Furthermore, Germany embarked upon a major European war before either of its best medium tanks had begun serial production, which meant that the Wehrmacht would receive only 30–60 new medium tanks per month for the rest of 1939. At that rate, it would take at least another two years to completely re-equip the existing German Panzer-Divisionen with medium tanks.

Fortunately for the Wehrmacht, the Heereswaffenamt (Army Weapons Department) took out an insurance policy by issuing a requirement for an improved light tank to supplement the Pz I. In 1935, Daimler-Benz and MAN began developing the Pz II, armed with a 2cm cannon to give it a limited anti-tank capability. Daimler-Benz encountered similar suspension problems with designing the Pz II but finally succeeded in developing a production-ready model by July 1937. The main appeal of the 8.9-tonne Pz II was that it could be built in quantity: 200 in 1937, then 600 in 1938 and 250 in the first part of 1939. Without the Pz II, Germany's *Panzerwaffe* (tank force) in 1939 would have been a large force of under-armed tankettes with just a handful of medium tanks. Another fortuitous break came with the occupation of Czechoslovakia in March 1939. In addition to capturing over 200 LT vz. 35 tanks intact, the Germans acquired the production line for the new LT vz. 38 tank. Both Czech tanks would prove to be useful substitutes for the missing German medium tanks in the campaigns of 1939–41. Had the Czechs possessed the mettle to sabotage their tanks and the Skoda facility, it would have done more damage to the German war effort than all the RAF bombing of 1940–41.

While the Heer struggled to build a combat-capable Panzer force, the Luftwaffe sought to field the next generation of combat aircraft in order to intimidate Germany's potential foes. Even before the He 51 biplane fighter entered production, the Technical Department (C-Amt) of the Reich Air Ministry (RLM) issued the Rüstungsflugzeug III (Armed Aircraft III) requirement in March 1933, calling for a new single-seat monoplane fighter with a top speed of at least 250mph (400km/h) at 20,000ft (6096m). The RLM also wanted the new fighter equipped with a 2cm cannon, if feasible. In fact, the RLM requirement was rather conservative since Poland and France would both soon have fighters capable of achieving 400km/h. Given the relative inexperience of the German aviation industry and the technological challenges of building an all-metal monoplane fighter, the RLM moved cautiously and did not decide to award small development contracts to Arado, Bayerische Flugzeugwerke (BFW), Heinkel, and Focke-Wulf until early 1934. The RLM wanted a German-designed engine on the new fighter but since the Junkers Jumo 210 was not yet ready, the prototypes would have to use the British-designed 695hp Rolls-Royce Kestrel V engine.

Heinkel was the inside favourite to win the fighter competition from the start. Erhard Milch, the head of the RLM, had a personal grudge against BFW's chief designer, Willy Messerschmitt, and tried to prevent BFW from being awarded any large Luftwaffe contracts. Furthermore, Messerschmitt had no experience designing combat aircraft, unlike Arado and Heinkel. However, BFW managed to attract Arado's top engineer, Walter Rethel, just prior to the development contacts, which provided Messerschmitt with the insight to design a high-speed fighter. Another serendipitous break occurred when Messerschmitt was allowed to design a high-speed sports aircraft for the fledgling Luftwaffe, which was designated the Bf 108A and adopted as a trainer. In August–September 1934, four Bf 108As were sent to participate in an aerial competition, the Challenge International de Tourisme, in Warsaw. Three of the Bf 108As were flown by veteran military pilots, including Hauptmann Theo Osterkamp (32 victories in the First World War) and Werner Junck (one of the instructors at Lipetsk). Although the Poles won the three week-long competition, the Bf 108As performed brilliantly, particularly in terms of speed. Consequently, the lessons learned from the Bf 108 heavily influenced the fighter prototype designed by Messerschmitt and Rethel, which would become the Bf 109. Messerschmitt also adopted a riskier design approach by adding leading edge slats – designed in Britain in 1918 – on the wings, allowing for higher angles of attack. By May 1935, BFW had built the first prototype, the Bf 109 V1, equipped with the Kestrel V engine. Four months later, the Bf 109 V1 prototype was delivered to the Luftwaffe test centre at Rechlin, along with its competitors: Heinkel's He 112, Arado's Ar 80 and Focke-Wulf's Fw 159.

Both the Ar 80 and Fw 159 prototypes were found unsatisfactory in trials during October 1935, which left only the Bf 109 and the He 112 in serious contention. Both BFW and Heinkel built additional prototypes, all of which would be equipped with the new Junkers Jumo 210 engine. In February 1936, Luftwaffe test pilots began a 'fly off' competition to directly compare the newest prototypes, the Bf 109 V2 against the He 112 V2. Unexpectedly, the Bf 109 V2 demonstrated a clear superiority in terms of speed and manoeuvrability, but Milch's RLM balked. Tests continued but two months later, the He 112 V2 was destroyed when it failed to come out of a spin. Still, the RLM was reluctant to award the production contract outright to BFW and instead ordered more prototypes from each and recommended that Heinkel make adjustments to put the He 112 on a better footing against the Bf 109. However, each Bf 109 prototype proved better than the last, while redesigning the He 112 was not producing much improvement. It was not until famed aviator Ernst Udet (in charge of research and development for the Luftwaffe) and Göring himself recognized the Bf 109's superior qualities, that Milch's resistance was overcome. Nevertheless, Milch managed to delay awarding the production contract to BFW – with no official fanfare – until October 1936 and the initial contract called for BFW to build only 144 fighters.

Having won the contract, BFW encountered significant delays in ramping up production and built only 21 fighters in the first six months. A new production facility, Messerschmitt GmbH, was built in Regensburg, which began low-rate production of the Bf 109B model in early 1937. In April 1937, the RLM finally awarded a contract for over 1,300 Bf 109 fighters to be built within the next 17 months, although fewer than

300 were built in all of 1937. The RLM helped to jump-start Bf 109 production at several other plants including the Erla Machinenwerk GmbH (Leipzig) and the Gerhard Fieseler Werke in Kassel. During 1938, a total of 834 Bf 109s were built, including 500 of the new D model. During the initial production phase, Messerschmitt received another serendipitous boost when Hitler decided to intervene in the Spanish Civil War, sending an expeditionary force known as Legion Condor. In August 1936, Jagdgruppe 88, equipped with He 51 fighters, arrived in Spain to support the Nationalists. At first, the He 51s performed well against older Republican fighters but when the Soviet Union decided to intervene in the conflict and sent I-15 and I-16 fighters to Spain, the He 51s were at a disadvantage. The Luftwaffe took the bold step of sending 12 Bf 109B fighters to Spain in March 1937 and to entirely re-equip Jagdgruppe 88 as soon as more Bf 109s rolled off the production line. Given that the Bf 109 was just starting low-rate production and was not yet a mature design, sending them off to combat was a very risky decision. However, the risk paid off handsomely. The Bf 109B proved superior to the Soviet fighters and enabled Legion Condor to achieve air superiority over critical sectors. Furthermore, the experience gained in actual combat allowed BFW to mature the Bf 109 more quickly than would normally occur in peacetime. By December 1938, an improved model equipped with the Daimler-Benz DB601 engine, the Bf 109E, was entering serial production. The Bf 109E was significantly superior to virtually all Anglo-French fighters in existence, except the British Spitfire, few of which were available. By early 1939, the Luftwaffe had re-equipped all of its first-line fighter units with the Bf 109 and all would have the improved E model by the end of the year.

The ability of German industry to develop, deploy and refine the Bf 109 fighter into a mature design that could be built in quantity was a great success and it was a game changer for the balance of power in Europe. In just two years, the Luftwaffe's fighter arm transformed itself from a force equipped with a few hundred biplanes to an aerial juggernaut equipped with over 1,000 of the best air superiority fighter in Europe. Furthermore, German industry proved capable of building the new fighter in quantity, which meant reserves could be created and combat losses replaced.

In addition to fighters, the Luftwaffe also developed and deployed a new generation of level-bombers and ground attack aircraft that provided real offensive punch. The Reichswehr had secretly funded Dornier's development of several bomber prototypes in the early 1930s, but when limited numbers of the Do 11 entered service in 1932, they proved unsatisfactory. Instead, the nascent Luftwaffe pressed the humble Ju 52 transport into service as a bomber in its first few years. Once Hitler opened the spigot for funding to the Luftwaffe, Dornier began developing the twin-engine Do 17 bomber, while Heinkel developed the He 111. Both new bombers began entering service in 1936–37 and by September 1939, the Luftwaffe had 1,250 of these modern bombers. By the summer of 1939, Dornier had the improved Do 17Z in serial production and Heinkel had the He 111H in serial production; altogether, Germany was building about 150 medium bombers per month. Both were decent but not great designs, which would serve the Luftwaffe well in its opening campaigns. Junkers had also begun its own bomber programme, but the Ju 86 proved a disappointment and instead the company shifted to development of a new fast bomber, which would become the Ju 88A. The Ju 88A would in fact become one of the best medium bombers in the 1940–42 timeframe, but in 1939 it had just entered low-rate production and only a single experimental unit had been formed.

Having been conceived and guided by army officers, the Luftwaffe put considerable effort into developing tactical support aircraft. Ernst Udet, in charge of technology development for the RLM, pushed the dive-bomber concept after witnessing demonstrations of this tactic in the United States in 1931. In February 1934, the RLM issued a requirement for a dive-bomber, which resulted in the Heinkel He 50 in 1935, followed by Henschel's Hs 123 in 1936. Both of these aircraft were biplanes, but the Hs 123 was clearly superior. In 1937, the Junker Ju 87 dive-bomber entered service and the RLM decided that this would be the Luftwaffe's primary dive-bomber, although small numbers of the Hs 123 remained in service as well. During 1938–39, the Luftwaffe conducted a number of tactical training exercises with the Heer, particularly Panzer units, in order to refine their close support capabilities.[30] Under ideal visibility conditions, the Ju 87 Stuka could deliver 50 per cent of its bombs within 25m of an intended aim point (i.e. its Circular Error Probability or CEP was 25), compared to 250m for a level-bomber.[31] It was this unique precision-strike capability that made the Luftwaffe fall in love with the Stuka.

In the space of just five years, Hitler was able to revive German military power in an expansion programme that was unprecedented in its scale and frenetic pace. In 1934, the Reichswehr had fewer tanks and aircraft than Poland, but five years later the Wehrmacht had achieved a decisive superiority in tanks and aircraft. Starting from the base 100,000-man

Reichsheer with ten divisions, the Heer was expanded seven-fold to a 750,000-man force with 45 divisions by the time of the Munich Crisis in September 1938. In virtually every major category, by 1939 the Germans had achieved numerical superiority, although the quality of their weapons still lagged in some areas. It is also important to note that the Luftwaffe had completely re-equipped its front-line units with modern fighters, bombers and dive-bombers, which were in serial production, and improved models were in development. In contrast, the Heer was struggling to get modern tanks and equipment into its field units, but production was lagging and improved models would not be available for some time.

Nor did rapid expansion come without costs. Even by 1937, German industry could not build enough motor transport to motorize more than about 10–12 per cent of the Heer. Thus, most of the new German divisions still relied upon horses to pull their artillery and supplies. Indeed, the Wehrmacht was never able to break its dependence upon the horse, which meant that only the handful of motorized units could conduct rapid manoeuvre warfare. Nor could industry supply enough modern infantry weapons, tactical radios and a myriad of other pieces of equipment for the army. Germany had been forced to begin rationing steel in February 1937 and army programmes were only getting 72 per cent of the steel needed to reach the goals of Hitler's rearmament plan. While the Heer's major re-equipment programmes – artillery, anti-tank guns and small arms – were in serial production by 1938, there would only be sufficient quantities available for the active divisions. Many of the Wehrmacht's best weapons were just entering service in 1939, such as the MG 34 light machine gun, which was only adopted on 24 January 1939.[32] German reserve and Landwehr (militia) units would just have to make do with obsolescent weapons like the MG 08 machine gun and 10.5cm FH16 howitzer, or captured foreign weapons. Consequently, the limitations of the German rearmament programme led to the bifurcation of the Wehrmacht into a small number of highly capable divisions, such as the Panzer and motorized infantry, and a larger number of less capable formations better suited for secondary tasks.

In addition to material deficiencies in the field army, shortages of raw materials hindered Germany's ability to prepare for protracted warfare. While the incorporation of Austria and Czechoslovakia in 1938–39 temporarily eased the German shortages of foreign exchange and raw materials, the long-term outlook in terms of iron ore, copper, petroleum and rubber was inauspicious.[33] At the outset of the Polish campaign,

Table 2: The Evolution of the Military Threat to Poland, 1933–39

YEAR	Germany			Soviet Union		
	Army Manpower[36]	Tanks[37]	Combat Aircraft[38]	Army Manpower[39]	Tanks[40]	Combat Aircraft
1933	102,000	0	25	534,000	3,500	3,156
1934	240,000	54	215	940,000	4,000	4,800
1935	480,000	318	674	1,300,000	5,000	6,600
1936	520,000	1,217	1,300	1,300,000	6,000	7,300
1937	550,000	1,718	1,900	1,433,000	7,000	8,139
1938	570,000	2,426	2,800	1,513,000	8,000	10,000
1939	730,000	3,257	3,163	1,800,000	10,000+	12,677

Germany had stockpiled enough raw materials to continue modest levels of military production for six months.[34] Ammunition production was particularly hard hit by the shortage of steel and the Wehrmacht would go to war in September 1939 with only enough ammunition for about one month of heavy combat.[35] Essentially, Germany was already forced to begin curtailing some of its rearmament programmes before the war even started and it could not sustain adequate armament production unless some *deus ex machina* appeared; it was this economic weakness which drove Hitler to seek an accommodation with Stalin prior to embarking upon *Fall Weiss*.

The Wehrmacht Builds a Combined Arms Team

'Man schlägt jemanden mit der Faust und nicht mit gespreizten Fingern'
[Hit them with your fist, not with your fingers spread]
Heinz Guderian[41]

It is not enough to build aircraft, artillery and tanks in order to develop effective combat capability – one must know how to use them together in concert. Given the rapid changes in technology since 1918, all the major powers struggled to integrate new weapons, while operational-level doctrine would remain in flux until the test of combat could validate the choices made in structuring and training units. Although the Reichswehr had extensively studied the lessons of the First World War and conducted realistic tactical experiments, it still had little practical experience to validate its manoeuvre warfare doctrine. The Wehrmacht did gain some valuable combat experience in Spain, particularly in air-to-air combat and close air support, but it was very small scale. For example, the Legion Condor's infamous bombing of Guernica in April 1937 involved fewer than 30 aircraft. During 1936–38, a total of 26 Legion Condor pilots achieved 'ace' status and these men returned to Germany and helped to refine Luftwaffe fighter tactics with the introduction of the *Vierfingerschwarm* (Finger-Four) formation. German bomber and Ju 87 Stuka crews were also able to refine their tactics in Spain. In another operation in April 1937, Legion Condor conducted a mass attack on Republican positions near Bilbao; 60 tonnes of bombs were dropped in two minutes, which caused enemy resistance to break.[42] Altogether, the Luftwaffe component of the Legion Condor suffered about 131 killed in action or missing in Spain. In Spain, Luftwaffe leaders learned how to handle a small, mixed expeditionary force in a situation where there was essentially no German ground force to support, so they could conduct a virtually independent air campaign. The Spanish Nationalist forces that the Luftwaffe supported conducted a war of position, where the front changed very little on a daily basis. Under these circumstances, the Luftwaffe's experience in Spain yielded few operational-level lessons and had limited direct relevance to the Wehrmacht's manoeuvre warfare doctrine.

The Luftwaffe had formed its first large-scale air unit in 1935, the 1. Flieger-Division, but most of the newly forming *Staffeln* (squadrons) were assigned to single-type *Gruppen* (groups) of 30–40 aircraft, then eventually to *Geschwader* (wings) of 90–120 aircraft. Initially, these building blocks were assigned to various regional air districts (*Luftgaue*), which provided administrative and logistic support. During the mid-1930s, there was considerable difference of opinion on how best to organize an air force for war. The French opted to provide some fighter and reconnaissance squadrons to directly support individual field armies, but the bulk of their air power was reserved for use by air force zone commanders. In May 1936, Britain's Royal Air Force divided itself into Bomber Command (for strategic air attacks) and Fighter Command (for the air defence of Great Britain), which essentially divided British air power into two boxes that could not co-ordinate with each other. Like the French, the Polish LW assigned some air units directly to support the army, but concentrated their best aircraft into a Fighter Brigade and a Bomber Brigade to conduct operational-level missions. The Luftwaffe was influenced by the Reichswehr's thinking on the necessity of ground support, but the leadership recognized the need to accomplish other missions such as air superiority and battlefield interdiction. Rather than building up tribal communities of pure-fighter and pure-bomber units, the Luftwaffe sought to unite all aerial capabilities under a single commander – although the path to this goal was not a straight line.

In early 1938, the Luftwaffe proceeded to the next level by forming large-scale air groups, which was followed by the creation of four air fleets (*Luftflotten*) in February 1939. The creation of these Luftflotten – during the initial stage of planning for *Fall Weiss* – was an important indicator of German intentions that was missed by Allied intelligence. Each Luftflotten consisted of two *Flieger-Divisionen* with mixed composition of bombers, ground attack and reconnaissance aircraft, along with attached *Flak-Artillerie*, signal and maintenance units. The Luftflotte was intended to be a self-contained aerial combat force, with up to 1,000 aircraft, to provide operational-level effects in support of campaign objectives. The only serious defect was the manner in which the fighter force (*Jagdwaffe*), was not properly integrated into Luftflotten. Instead, the individual *Jagdgruppen* (fighter groups), might report either to *Luftgaukommandos* (air district tactical commands) or a *Jagdfliegerführer*, a fighter commander with semi-independent status in 1939. A large part of the reason for this disconnect was that the Jagdgruppen were averse to being directly integrated into the Luftflotten because they didn't want to be dragged into constantly escorting daylight bomber missions, which they saw as a distraction from their air superiority mission. It was not until after the 1940 French campaign that Luftflotte commanders would 'own' their own fighter units and the air fleets become truly aerial combined arms formations.

The Heer's experience in Spain was even less useful for refining its operational art because the Legion Condor's ground element, under the command of Oberstleutnant Wilhelm Ritter von Thoma (who would later command Panzer-Regiment 3 in the Polish campaign), consisted of just 267 men when it arrived in Spain on 7 October 1936. Gruppe Thoma deployed with 41 Pz I tanks and 24 3.7cm PaK anti-tank guns but its primary mission was to train and advise Spanish troops, not to be directly involved in combat.[43] Of the 646 German ground troops who served in Spain in 1936–39, only seven were killed in action. Limited numbers of German advisors did directly participate in ground combat in Spain, but the tanks were used in small groups, often without benefit of supporting arms. Thoma's troops did learn that the Pz I was inferior to Soviet-made tanks and highly vulnerable to anti-tank guns, which put greater pressure on the Heereswaffenamt to accelerate the Pz III and Pz IV programmes. Consequently, the Spanish experience was of negligible value for organizing or training the large-scale Panzer units that were forming in Germany.

The primary technological question facing armies in the early 1930s was what kind of tanks should be built, which derived from the range of missions envisioned for mechanized units. There were four basic views regarding the best use of tanks: pure tank units (primarily for shock effect/ breakthrough on the battlefield), infantry tanks to support infantry units in the attack, mechanized cavalry (using tanks in the traditional cavalry roles such as reconnaissance, screening and pursuit) and mobile combined arms (creating well-rounded combat teams for manoeuvre warfare, particularly exploitation or deep operations). The Anglo-French and the Soviets primarily embraced the infantry support and cavalry roles for their tanks, but they also experimented with the other two roles as well. In the Reichswehr, Generalmajor Oswald Lutz and his chief of staff Oberst Heinz Guderian argued vehemently for the mobile combined arms role and insisted that all tanks should be massed into division-size all-arms formations. However, this idea – considered radical in 1934 – ran into resistance from more conservative officers. General der Artillerie Ludwig Beck, chief of the Army General Staff, was opposed to the Panzer-Division concept and favoured creating independent army-level (*Heerestruppen*) regimental- or brigade-size tank units, which could be attached to reinforce individual army corps. The Heerestruppen were tank-pure units that could fulfil either the breakthrough or infantry support roles. Oberst Erich von Manstein, Beck's chief of staff, even wrote a memorandum, recommending that each infantry division should receive its own armour support – which became the genesis of the *Sturmartillerie* (assault artillery) concept. Beck, an artillery officer, ensured that the Sturmartillerie would not be under the control of Lutz's Panzertruppen. Although Hitler supported the creation of *Panzer-Divisionen*, Beck ensured that the Wehrmacht expansion plans included the creation of several independent *Panzer-Brigaden* as well as Sturmartillerie units. On top of this, the cavalry branch entered the equation and pressed for some of its units to be motorized in order to keep division-size units within the force structure (and to provide command slots for senior cavalry officers). Thus, in June 1936 the OKH authorized the creation of three *leichte-Divisionen*, each of which would get its own *Panzer-Abteilung*, to perform typical cavalry missions, such as reconnaissance, screening and pursuit.[44]

As a result of these competing agendas, there were three different types of German mechanized units in 1936–39, each configured for different purposes. While the Heerestruppen and leichte-Divisionen were not resource intensive formations – which was one of the reasons that the OKH championed them – Lutz opted for over-stuffed Panzer-Divisionen, which meant that only three could be created prior to 1938. The original Panzer-Division structure was unnecessarily complex, with a Panzer-Brigade headquarters controlling two Panzer-Regimenter, which in turn controlled two or three Panzer-Abteilungen; the result was too many mid-level leaders trying to issue orders over too many radio command nets. In the 1935 Panzer-Division, a single light tank company was authorized 30 tanks – far too many for effective tactical control by one officer – and battalions had 115 tanks. Lutz and Guderian envisioned the Panzer-Divisionen as massing enough tanks at the main point or *Schwerpunkt* to achieve decisive results, but attempting to flood the battlefield with a dense swarm of tanks was actually counter-productive since a force of this size was difficult to manoeuvre or conceal. Providing logistical support to 400 tanks and 2,000 other vehicles, operating along a single axis of advance, would also prove a serious challenge.

As it would turn out, the Panzer-Brigades of 1939–40 were not the most effective units within the Panzer-Division, but rather the far more mobile *Kradschützen Bataillon* (motorcycle infantry) and *Aufklärungs-Abteilung* (mot.) (reconnaissance battalion). Both of these units were used in the spearhead role, seeking out gaps in the enemy lines and reporting the information back to the Panzer and motorized infantry commanders.

Table 3: Comparison of Inter-war Mechanized Formations, 1935–37

Unit	Tank Bn.	Infantry Bn.	Recon Bn.	Artillery Bn.	Tanks
1935 Panzer-Division	4	3	1	2	484
1937 leichte-Division	1	3	2	2	115
French DLM (1936)	2	3	1	3	262
UK Mobile Division (1937)	6	1	0	1	350
Soviet Mechanized Corps (1935)	6	5	1	2	463

The 959-man Kradschützen Bataillon was a very mobile unit, capable of moving 100km or more in a day, and equipped with enough weaponry to seize and hold key objectives. Likewise, the 753-man Aufklärungs-Abteilung (mot.), was very mobile and its 24 armoured cars added further combat power to divisional vanguard units. The Heer did experiment with the idea of creating larger, more capable reconnaissance units for mechanized corps – akin to the US concept of an armoured reconnaissance regiment – but lacked the resources to implement this idea.

It is important to recognize that infantry also formed the vital bedrock of the German combined arms team. Infantry was not only intended to defend ground captured by the fast-moving Panzer units but to be capable of seizing secondary objectives on its own. Starting with the Reichsheer's seven original infantry divisions, the Heer expanded to 35 active divisions, which were designated as 1. Welle (1st formations). Outfitting these 35 divisions required enormous effort, since they required a total of 620,000 troops, 170,000 horses and 35,000 motor vehicles to bring them up to strength. Even after Hitler dramatically increased the size of the Wehrmacht, each 1. Welle Division still comprised 18 per cent reservists and 4 per cent Landwehr. Nevertheless, these 35 divisions were gradually brought up to strength and (nearly) fully equipped, making them the cream of the Heer's ground combat forces. However, this left very few resources for wartime expansion of the Wehrmacht. The 2. Welle divisions raised in 1939 would comprise 94 per cent reservists and Landwehr, with only a leavening of active duty soldiers. Furthermore, the 2. Welle divisions often lacked vital equipment, such as mortars and were often equipped with foreign or obsolete substitutes.[45] During the course of the Second World War, the Heer would raise a total of 31 waves of divisions, each wave less well-equipped than its predecessors. The hidden weakness within Germany's combined arms team was that its capabilities rested upon a core of elite divisions and their personnel, which were vulnerable to attrition.

In 1937, the Oberkommando des Heeres (Army High Command or OKH) decided to motorize four of its 1. Welle infantry divisions (2, 13, 20 and 29) in order to provide a force of mobile infantry which could follow the Panzers and hold key terrain. Each of these divisions was equipped with three times the amount of motor transport assigned to a standard infantry divisions; in total, it took over 10,000 motor vehicles to outfit these four motorized infantry divisions – almost one-third of the Wehrmacht's total motor pool at the time.[46] However, the question of how the Panzer-Divisionen would work with the motorized divisions was not fully worked out prior to *Fall Weiss*. Guderian opted to include two of the motorized infantry divisions with the 3. Panzer-Division in his XIX Armeekorps (mot.), but the other two were placed in the XIV Armeekorps (mot.) without armour support. The OKH did not form any more division-size mechanized units until after the 1938 Munich Crisis, when two new Panzer-Divisionen (4, 5) and four leichte-Divisionen (1–4) were stood up. In addition, the Heerestruppen were increased to two independent Panzer-Brigaden and two independent battalions; at this point, over 40 per cent of the German armour was not assigned to Panzer-Divisionen. Even before the leichte-Divisionen had been fully formed, it was apparent that these formations were too large for reconnaissance missions but lacked the combat power to conduct breakthrough operations. It was not long before even the OKH recognized that this was far from an optimal force structure and Generaloberst Walther von Brauchitsch, commander-in-chief of the Heer (Oberbefehlshaber des Heeres), issued guidance in November 1938 that the leichte-Divisionen would be converted to Panzer-Divisionen and some of the Heerestruppen units formed into new divisions by late 1939, thereby yielding a total force of nine Panzer-Divisionen.[47] A few tank-pure Heerestruppen units would be retained for infantry support. Thus, when the Wehrmacht invaded Poland in 1939, it went to war with three different types of mechanized units and aside from a few Panzer zealots like Guderian, it had not fully decided how to use them in a campaign. In particular, conservative officers like Generaloberst Gerd von Rundstedt still believed it was desirable to keep the Panzer-Divisionen closely leashed to their accompanying infantry, rather than chasing off like a pack of hounds after their prey.

By 1939, the Wehrmacht had created the rudiments of combined arms teams in the four Luftflotten and five Panzer-Divisionen, but they had yet to work together. The bedrock of the team was the 1. Welle infantry divisions, which intended to use tactics that were only slightly different from 1918 methods. Pre-war tactical experiments helped with refining basic air-ground communications procedures, but the Luftwaffe still had no practical experience in handling close air support from Panzer-Divisionen or other German ground units. Consequently, the Luftwaffe preferred to strike targets well beyond the front line in order to avoid fratricide. Likewise, German commanders had only manoeuvred mechanized forces in training exercises, not on battlefields. Conducting logistic support on a mobile battlefield – with an unco-operative enemy – was still a large unknown. Given the revolutionary combined arms nature of the new

German operational-level doctrine, theory and exercises could only go so far in revealing the strength and limitations of this new form of warfare. An actual field campaign would be required to validate the effectiveness of this team.

Stalin's Great Leap Forwards

'Hitler's generals, raised on the dogma of Clausewitz and Moltke, could not understand that war is won in the factories.'
Stalin, 1949

The Red Army that advanced upon Warsaw in August 1920 consisted primarily of infantry and cavalry, with only a handful of armoured cars and light artillery and minimal air support. During the First World War, the Russian economy had been unable to provide its soldiers with adequate weapons, ammunition or even boots. After the First World War and the subsequent Russian Civil War, the Soviet Union's economy was even more devastated and the new regime appeared to be an international pariah with little hope of attracting foreign assistance. Lenin's New Economic Policy of 1921 attempted to attract foreign capital, but largely failed to improve the Soviet economy. Although the Soviet Red Army remained a persistent potential threat to Poland, its limited capabilities in the 1920s did not encourage Lenin or Stalin to seek a rematch. Stalin had a great anathema for the Poles but also recognized that their fierce nationalism would make them a difficult nut to crack. Once he came to power in 1924, he preferred to focus on domestic policy and put off dealing with Poland until more favourable circumstances arose. Thus, the Soviet Union's economic and military weakness provided Poland with a temporary respite.

Stalin had great plans for the Soviet Union and he was determined to enhance Soviet economic – and then military power – by any means necessary. Despite the ideological divide between the communist and non-communist worlds, Stalin recognized that foreign technological assistance was a vital prerequisite for turning the Soviet Union into a great power. In 1929, Stalin initiated the First Five Year Plan, with emphasis upon heavy industry and forced agricultural collectivization. Foreign corporations and individual technicians were invited in to the Soviet Union to help develop key manufacturing industries. Most of the foreigners were American, but there were British, French, German and

Swiss technicians as well. Given the bleak economic environment of the Depression-era early 1930s, the lure of new business in the Soviet Union was appealing to many Western firms. Stalin made business offers even more appealing by providing payments in gold; over 1.5 billion rubles in gold was made available to jump-start foreign technical assistance programmes. The Soviets were particularly interested in American-style assembly line and mass production techniques and paid US engineers to design, construct and outfit similar assembly plants in the Soviet Union to produce trucks, agricultural tractors and steel. The Freyn Engineering Company of Chicago was one of the first to get in on the Soviet gravy train and agreed to build a large steel plant in Central Asia.[48] The Ford Motor Company was also a major player, agreeing in May 1929 to establish a truck assembly line in Gorky. The US government made no effort to block these ventures.

By 1930, the Soviet Union had signed 104 contracts, 81 of which were with American or German companies.[49] Two year later, there were 1,700 American and 1,600 German industrial technicians working in the Soviet Union and in the same year, the Soviets purchased 90 per cent of all machinery exported from Britain.[50] Freyn's engineers built a great industrial centre in the Ural-Kuznetsk region (later renamed the Stalin Plant, of course), which began producing iron, steel, aluminium and zinc within a few years. Freyn also provided Soviet engineers with the design for a blast furnace, which was replicated in 14 Soviet steel plants. Two other American companies, the Arthur G. McKee & Company (of Cleveland, Ohio) and General Electric were brought in to design and build a giant steel plant at Magnitogorsk, which became partly operational in 1933.[51] American engineers also modernized the Soviet coal, iron ore and petroleum industries in the early 1930s, introducing modern techniques and equipment, which greatly enhanced output. Other foreign engineers worked to expand the production of machine tools and other industrial projects which would soon be used to help rearm the Red Army. American and German engineers helped to build the Stalingrad Tractor Plant, as well as similar plants in Kharkov and Chelyabinsk, which would later be converted to produce tanks.[52] The Soviets assiduously copied every piece of foreign technological hardware they got their hands on, often making simplified versions that were easier to produce. Standardization allowed for the kind of rapid industrial expansion that Stalin desired. Once the foreign engineers completed their projects, they departed and Soviet engineers took over. Thanks to the infusion of foreign technology, Soviet heavy industry made rapid progress. Between 1929 and 1937, Soviet coal output increased 360 per cent, steel production over 400 per cent and electricity output by 700 per cent.[53]

Even before the industrialization process was in full swing, the Revolutionary Military Council (RVS), chaired by Kliment Voroshilov, began setting priorities for military modernization. Military aviation and mechanization were both high priorities, followed by artillery. The pathetic collection of Russian aircraft had been virtually impotent in the Russo-Polish War and the period of 1920–24 was one of chaos and disorganization for Soviet aviation. Virtually all of the 300-odd aircraft still in service in the early 1920s were foreign-built, since many aviation engineers had emigrated abroad. In 1925, the Red Army's air force was renamed the VVS (Voyenno-Vozdushnye Sily) and the RVS began sorting out the aviation sector by reforming design bureaus, such as Polikarpov and Tupolev. The Soviet Union's first indigenous fighter, the I-2, entered service with a copy of the 400hp American Liberty L-12 engine; the aircraft was not a success and only 211 were built. Soviet industry had particular trouble manufacturing aircraft engines and had to settle for producing limited numbers of copies of American, British, French and German engines for some time. By the late 1920s, Soviet industry was beginning to produce larger numbers of fighters and reconnaissance aircraft, although quality control was poor and the VVS was handicapped by limited numbers of qualified pilots.

However, the First Five Year Plan had a major impact upon the Soviet aviation sector, which began to produce better aircraft designs such as the I-5 fighter in 1930 (the I-5 was powered by a copy of the British-designed Jupiter engine). Two years later, the Tupolev Design Bureau unveiled its TB-3 heavy bomber, powered by German engines, which could carry 2,000kg of bombs up to 1,600km. Tupolev was also able to produce this large bomber in quantity; the VVS received over 600 TB-3 bombers in 1932–34, leading to the creation of a Long-Range Aviation branch within the VVS. Soviet aviation technology increased as well, as more foreign technology was purchased or purloined, including a licence for the new American-designed Wright Cyclone 9 engine (the same engine which would later be used on the B-17 bomber). In 1934, Polikarpov mated the Wright Cyclone engine with his latest fighter, leading to the excellent I-16, one of the best fighters of the mid-1930s.[54] By 1935, Soviet industry was manufacturing modern aircraft in quantity and the VVS was already the largest air force in the world. Yakov I. Alksnis, the dynamic leader of the VVS, pushed to organize his various aviation regiments into larger combat formations and in 1936 he formed three air armies, comprised of mixed fighter, bomber and reconnaissance units. The VVS had also developed an airborne force, beginning with one brigade in 1932 and followed by two more in 1936. Soviet paratroopers practised jumping from TB-3 bombers and later Li-2 transports (a copy of the American DC-3). By early 1937, the VVS had roughly 8,000 aircraft in service and within less than a decade it had evolved into a potent force, capable of conducting a wider variety of missions than any other air force on earth.

Voroshilov also set modernization priorities for the ground forces, beginning with tanks. The only tanks that the Red Army possessed in the mid-1920s were a small number of captured French Renault FT tanks, about 70 British-built Mk V and 12 Whippet tanks, few of which were operational. Soviet engineers at the Bolshevik Plant No. 232 in Leningrad succeeded in reverse-engineering the French Renault FT and built a copy known as the T-18 (or MS-1), which entered low-rate production in 1928. However, the T-18 performed poorly in field tests and was clearly based on obsolescent technology.[55] The Red Army wanted new weapons, not copies of old weapons. Unfortunately, Soviet engineers lacked the ability to design new tanks from scratch. In 1929, the RVS authorized a group of Soviet engineers to travel abroad and inspect foreign tank developments, then purchase any that could be built in the Soviet Union. The commission was headed by Andrei I. Khalepsky, who was head of the Red Army's Office of Mechanization and Motorization (UMM), which was responsible for drafting technical requirements for tanks. One team from the Soviet tank commission visited the United States and was impressed with the mobility of the privately designed Christie tank (M1928); two samples and a production licence were purchased for $160,000 in April 1930. Khalepsky's team arrived in England and he decided to purchase 16 copies of the Vickers 6-tonne light tank and 26 of the Carden-Loyd Mk VI tankette, for a total amount of £205,000 ($975,000). By early 1931, the American and British armoured vehicles had arrived in the Soviet Union and – after minor modifications were made – Soviet factories began producing upgraded copies of them.[56]

The Vickers 6-tonne required the least modification and was built at the Bolshevik plant in Leningrad as the T-26 light tank, with about 100 completed before the end of 1931, The Bolshevik plant modified the Carden-Loyd Mk VI tankette and began serial production of the T-27 tankette, with 393 built in 1931, The Soviets encountered greater difficulty with the Christie tanks – which arrived in the USSR without turrets – so only a handful of pre-production models were built at the KhPZ plant in Kharkov in 1931. Eventually, KhPZ was able to develop the

BT-2 cavalry tank from Christie's incomplete design and this tank entered limited production in 1932.[57] Initially, all of these armoured vehicles were only armed with machine guns, but the Soviets purchased samples of the German 3.7cm PaK anti-tank gun, which was redesigned and entered Soviet service as the 45mm Model 1932 gun. A tank version was quickly developed and by early 1933, the latest versions of the T-26 and BT-5 were equipped with the new gun. The Red Army's tank force grew rapidly, from a single mechanized brigade in 1930 to four by 1932. At that point, the RVS directed that these brigades would be formed into two mechanized corps, each with 430 tanks, plus attached motorized infantry, reconnaissance, sappers and artillery – the first large-scale, mechanized combined arms units in the world. In 1933, five more independent mechanized brigades were created and two more mechanized corps in 1934. By 1935, the Red Army had the largest armoured forces in the world, with over 2,500 tanks. Meanwhile, Khalepsky's Office of Mechanization and Motorization had already issued requirements for a new generation of medium and heavy tanks, which would far surpass these early models.

Not only was the Red Army building tanks in large numbers by the mid-1930s, but its leadership was on the cusp of developing a radical new doctrine for mobile warfare, dubbed *glubokiy boy* (Deep Battle). Vladimir K. Triandafillov and Mikhail Tukhachevsky both wrote about Deep Battle and co-ordinating tanks and air support to break through an enemy's defences.[58] Although Triandafillov died in 1931, a brilliant military theorist at the Frunze Military Academy, Georgy Isserson, expanded upon Deep Battle and developed a more sophisticated version known as *glubokaya operatsiya* (Deep Operations). Isserson envisioned using tanks and aircraft not only to breach an enemy's front, but to send mechanized forces through and exploit to depths of up to 200km.[59] Tukhachevsky accepted Isserson's theories and they were adopted as official doctrine in 1935. During the summer of 1936, the Red Army tested the doctrine with a complete mechanized corps and even threw in paratroops to see how they could support Deep Operations. The results of the tests were promising and the Red Army's Field Service Regulations for 1936 (PU-36) fully incorporated mechanized warfare and Deep Operations into campaign planning. Thus by the end of 1936, the Red Army had managed to assemble a large mechanized force and to create a revolutionary doctrine on how to use them to achieve decisive operational results – which was a grave development for Poland's security.

Just as Stalin's Five Year Plans succeeded in creating the largest mechanized and aviation forces on earth, reaching an apex in early 1937, Stalin became insanely paranoid that military modernization could undermine his authority by creating a professional military class. Clever military men like Tukhachevsky, Isserson, Khalepsky and Alksnis were useful, but worried Stalin, since he doubted their loyalty to him. Instead, he preferred less-capable but subservient subordinates such as Voroshilov and Lavrentiy Beria, head of the NKVD. Voroshilov, a technical imbecile, claimed that mechanization was a scheme to undermine the communist party's control over the Red Army. He also accused Tukhachevsky of 'wrecking', alleging that the mechanized corps were intended to spearhead an internal military coup as part of a 'right-wing-Trotskyist military conspiracy'. In May 1937, Stalin moved ruthlessly to root out the alleged 'traitors' in the Red Army, beginning with Tukhachevsky, who was arrested along with eight other senior generals. After a brief trial, Tukhachevsky and the other generals were shot. Stalin's purge quickly spread across the Red Army leadership and spilled over into the armaments industry.[60] Khalepsky and Alknis were both shot in 1938. Isserson, one of the fathers of Deep Operations doctrine, was sent to a forced labour camp for ten years. Senior engineers working in the aviation and tank design bureaus were also arrested, some shot, others imprisoned. Voroshilov and other reactionary elements in the Red Army ensured that the mechanized corps were broken up and the individual brigades dispersed in the infantry support role. He also ensured the PU-36 and Deep Operations were buried, although they were not forgotten.

The result of Stalin's purges of the military and armaments industry in 1937–38 was that the Red Army was left with plenty of modern equipment, but most of the remaining military leaders lacked the competence to use them properly. This organizational decline was not apparent to external observers until after the invasion of Poland, when the subsequent Russo-Finnish War in 1939/40 exposed the utter incompetence of the Red Army's senior leadership. Nevertheless, Stalin's Five Year Plans had laid the basis for mass production of modern military hardware, ensuring that the Red Army would be well equipped and prepared to fight a protracted war, even against Germany. Yet like the Third Reich, the Soviet Union could not have made such rapid progress without substantial technical assistance from the Western democracies.

CHAPTER 4

Countdown to War

Hitler's Territorial Ambitions

'It is the last territorial claim which I have to make in Europe ...'
Hitler referring to the Sudetenland, 26 September 1938[1]

Throughout his political career, Hitler was remarkably consistent about his strategic objectives: he wanted to make Germany economically and militarily strong so it could throw off the Versailles Treaty restrictions, then punish those whom he blamed for laying Germany low in 1918 (the French and the Jews), then create a super German nation extending well into eastern Europe (*Lebensraum*). Any states that sided with France against Germany – Belgium, Czechoslovakia and Poland – would be dealt with accordingly. On the path to greatness, Hitler intended to re-incorporate all ethnic Germans back into the Reich, including those in his native Austria and in other countries (Alsace, Czechoslovakia, Lithuania and Poland). Prior to coming to power, Hitler made it clear in a landmark speech at the Industry Club in Düsseldorf in January 1932 that he did not intend to rely upon capitalism or trade to rebuild Germany:

> In my view, it is putting the cart before the horse to believe today that Germany's position of power can be recovered using business

methods alone instead of realizing that a position of power constitutes the prerequisite for an improvement in the economic situation as well ... A prosperous economy cannot subsist if it is not backed by the protection of a prosperous, powerful State; that there would have been no Carthaginian economy without a Carthaginian fleet and no Carthaginian trade without the Carthaginian army.[2]

Although Hitler employed deception, opportunism and tactical flexibility – like most politicians – he did not waver from his essential objectives once he came to power in 1933. For example, on the first page of his book *Mein Kampf*, he stated that 'German-Austria must be restored to the great German Motherland' and this became one of the early pillars of his foreign policy. For the most part, British and French politicians did not take Hitler seriously and initially didn't bother to read *Mein Kampf*. One of the few who did, Horace Rumbold, British ambassador in Berlin, wrote a synopsis of *Mein Kampf* and sent it by dispatch to the Foreign Ministry and the Cabinet. Rumbold warned that Hitler intended to restore Germany 'by force of arms' and any talk of peace was mere deception to conceal his true intention, which was war. Although alarmed by Rumbold's dispatch, Prime Minister Ramsay MacDonald and his cabinet adopted a 'wait and see' attitude about Hitler's intentions.[3] Hitler helped to allay some apprehensions by making loud speeches about his peaceful intentions. In May 1933, he addressed the Reichstag stating that 'our boundless love for and loyalty to our own national traditions makes us respect the national claims of others and makes us desire ... to live with them in peace and friendship.'

Whether or not one believed that *Mein Kampf* or his Reichstag speeches were indicative of Hitler's true intentions, his actions soon demonstrated his contempt for international law. Using the refusal of the Anglo-French delegations at the World Disarmament Conference to allow Germany to acquire weapons denied by the Versailles Treaty, Hitler terminated Germany's membership in the League of Nations on 14 October 1933; there was no significant international response. Soon thereafter, in June 1934, Hitler further demonstrated his contempt for legal norms by ordering the mass execution of those he regarded as enemies of the regime, including senior members of the SA paramilitary organization and former Chancellor Kurt von Schleicher. In their haste to gun down Schleicher, the assassins from the Sicherheitsdienst (Security Service or SD) also gunned down his wife, further demonstrating the indiscriminate nature of Nazi violence. Another victim of the purge was Erich Klausener, a German politician and head of Catholic Action, who had openly criticized the repressive tactics of the regime. A few senior members of the Reichswehr criticized the murders, but for the most part, the generals bit their lips and opted to kneel before Hitler's broken cross.

While international opinion was still stunned by the brutal nature of the Nazi domestic purge, Hitler decided to support a violent coup by members of the Austrian Nazi Party (DNSAP), which attempted to overthrow the Austrian government on the night of 25 July 1934. Although the rebels managed to storm the chancellory and assassinate Chancellor Engelbert Dollfuss, the Austrian Army remained loyal and quickly crushed the coup, with a total over 200 persons killed. This time, international reaction was immediate and harsh. Benito Mussolini, who regarded Austria as part of his own sphere of influence, moved 75,000 Italian troops towards the Brenner Pass and threatened military action if Germany moved into Austria.[4] Yugoslavia also announced its intent to mobilize its army if Austria's territorial integrity was violated. Faced with resolute force, Hitler was forced to back down – one of the few times this occurred – and disavow support for the coup because he lacked the military or economic strength to push his agenda further. However, the Austrian Nazis – who sought refuge in Germany – continued a terrorist-style campaign against the Austrian government, which kept the pot boiling.

Indeed, Hitler was forced to face the reality that the Third Reich in mid-1934 was on the brink of economic collapse due to its shortage of foreign currency reserves and its difficulty in securing foreign loans.[5] In 1930, Germany had RM 2.8 billion in gold and foreign currency reserves, but this had fallen to only RM 165 million by 1934.[6] Only six months after becoming chancellor. Hitler had announced a *de facto* default on its long-term debts (mostly to the United States), which made it more difficult for Germany to secure credit.[7] Without the ability to purchase raw materials overseas – particularly from the British Empire – Hitler's rearmament plans would be stillborn. Despite Hitler's support for violence both at home and abroad, Britain's Prime Minister Ramsay MacDonald was more concerned that Germany might default on its short-term debts to British investors and thereby cause considerable economic damage in England. Neville Chamberlain, Chancellor of the Exchequer, argued in favour of offering inducements for Hitler to keep Germany as a reliable trade partner, rather than trying to isolate Germany and thereby drive Hitler towards more rash acts.[8] Later, this was called economic appeasement. Consequently, Britain signed two trade agreements with Germany between July and November 1934, including a loan for £750,000 (which Chamberlain concealed from the British public) and other provisions which aided Germany in purchasing raw materials from within the British Empire.[9] Additional short-term financial credits from Britain would be extended until 1939. In short, Chamberlain ended up easing Germany out of its financial straitjacket and helped to jumpstart the first phase of Hitler's rearmament plan.[10]

For the next two years, Hitler shifted to a less aggressive tone in his foreign policy, while the Wehrmacht gathered its strength and Germany finessed short-term loans from other countries, such as the Netherlands and Switzerland. Meanwhile, the Anglo-French shifted their attention to Mussolini, who had his heart set on acquiring Ethiopia for his empire. After Italy invaded Ethiopia in October 1935 – in open violation of the covenants it had signed to join the League of Nations – the League imposed limited economic sanctions on Italy in November. However, neither Britain nor France were willing to impose tougher sanctions, including an oil embargo, over what they regarded as a colonial issue. Instead, British and French diplomats laboured to develop a diplomatic solution to Mussolini's aggression by offering to award Italy large chunks of Ethiopia in return for peace (the so-called Hoare–Laval plan). Not only did this diplomatic effort fail completely, since Mussolini continued his aggression, but the League of Nations was revealed to be ineffectual and Britain and France unreliable in protecting the interests of smaller states. Italy even dared to use outlawed chemical weapons in Ethiopia, but when the League was made aware of this violation of international law, it did nothing but 'deplore' the act.[11] Once Italy achieved a partial military victory, the limited economic sanctions were removed in July 1936, having achieved nothing.[12] Hitler paid close attention to the Abyssinia Crisis and concluded that the Anglo-French were unwilling to risk more than symbolic gestures against a serious aggressor.

After the Anglo-French failure to stop Mussolini from conquering Ethiopia, Hitler decided it was time to start rolling back the Versailles and Locarno treaties in regard to Germany's borders. Hitler timed his move when the British and French were most at odds as a result of the Abyssinia Crisis. He also decided to use the ratification of the Franco-Soviet treaty of mutual assistance on 27 February 1936 as a justification, claiming that it was an attempt to create a military alliance against Germany. Within a week of the treaty's ratification, Hitler made his move. Now that he had a few hundred Pz I tanks and several squadrons of He 51 biplane fighters, Hitler was more willing to take risks than two years earlier. On 7 March 1936, he sent three German infantry battalions into the Rhineland, in direct violation of both the Versailles and Locarno treaties. The French government was overwrought about Hitler's action, but was restrained both by its own military unpreparedness and by its diplomatic inability to gather support from other nations to oppose Hitler. Général Maurice Gamelin, the French commander-in-chief, sent 50,000 troops towards the border with Germany as a covering force but claimed that the French Army could not conduct a punitive operation without full mobilization, which the politicians were loath to authorize.[13] Nor would Britain lend any military or diplomatic support to force Hitler to vacate the Rhineland. Some members of the French cabinet favoured economic sanctions against Germany, but neither Britain nor the League of Nations would support this recommendation.[14] Poland's foreign minister, Józef Beck, informed the French ambassador in Warsaw that Poland would honour its treaty obligations and attack Germany, if France went to war with Germany. The Polish offer was ignored.[15] Instead, the French political leadership decided to bring the issue to the League of Nations, which had just failed to do anything useful to stop Mussolini. As a result of Anglo-French inaction, Hitler scored a cheap foreign policy victory. Furthermore, Hitler learned that the Anglo-French political leaders were divided and often working at cross purposes, so effective responses were not likely in the future. He also reckoned that after this display of impotence, Stalin would think twice about depending upon French promises. Indeed, the lack of Allied response in the Rhineland Crisis of 1936, as well as the Abyssinia Crisis, helped shape Hitler's attitude towards the Danzig Crisis in 1939.

The German occupation had several implications for Poland. First, Hitler ordered the creation of the West Wall fortifications, to protect Germany's border against French attack. Once complete, the West Wall would allow Hitler to concentrate more forces in the east, with the knowledge that his western border was secure.[16] Second, the Ruhr industries could be fully integrated into the rearmament programme, which accelerated the pace of weapons development and production. Finally, Poland witnessed the French military's inability to respond to a direct crisis in a timely or resolute manner – a very bad harbinger for French guarantees.

After his bloodless coup in the Rhineland, Hitler re-embarked upon his 'charm offensive' to convince the West that the Third Reich was not a threat. He publicly stated that he had re-occupied the Rhineland only to re-affirm German national integrity, not as a rejection of the Locarno Treaty. Now that the Rhineland was returned to Germany, Hitler offered to help create a new peaceful order in Europe and to rejoin the League of Nations. In other words, his actions had not been meant to wreck the balance in Europe but rather, to create a new balance with Germany as a co-operative partner. In an interview with a British newspaper, Hitler stated that his foremost desire was the preservation of peace in Europe.[17] Some British politicians, like David Lloyd George, admired Hitler's audacity but the government as a whole did not take his peace plan seriously. On the other hand, the re-occupation of the Rhineland was immensely popular in Germany, which convinced Hitler that more successes of this kind could bolster support for his regime.

Following the Rhineland Crisis, Hitler's gaze turned towards Austria and Czechoslovakia. As part of his peace overtures, in July 1936 he promised to recognize Austria's full sovereignty and to refrain from interfering in its internal affairs – as long as the Austrian government accepted some Austrian Nazis into senior government posts. Kurt Schuschnigg, the new Austrian chancellor, rejected this suggestion. In August 1936, Hitler personally drafted the Four Year Plan, intended to accelerate the pace of rearmament in order to gain clear military superiority over the Anglo-French by 1940. Under the plan, the Wehrmacht would be increased to a strength of 102 divisions and Germany industry would prepare for war by expanding its production of synthetic fuel and synthetic rubber. However, only the top leadership such as Generalfeldmarschall Werner von Blomberg and Göring were aware of the full details of the Four Year Plan and that its intent was to prepare Germany for a war of aggression.[18]

Hitler's foreign policy objectives were briefly distracted by the outbreak of the Spanish Civil War in mid-1936, which afforded him an opportunity for unscheduled military intervention. The Austrian question was placed on the back-burner for nearly a year, during which time Mussolini acquiesced to German involvement in Austria in return for a free hand in the Mediterranean. On the evening of 5 November 1937, Hitler held a military conference in Berlin with his top military advisors (Blomberg, Generaloberst Werner von Fritsch, Göring, Großadmiral Erich Raeder) and his foreign minister, Konstantin von Neurath, to discuss future strategic plans. Hitler was concerned that his rearmament plans were threatened by Germany's strained finances and insufficient access to raw materials, which led him to conclude 'Germany's problems could be solved only by the use of force'. The only question in Hitler's mind was where Germany could strike to achieve the best results at the lowest cost; he decided that Austria and Czechoslovakia were the obvious targets and they should be attacked in 1938.[19] He believed that localized aggressions, with the proper political rationalizations framed by propaganda campaigns, would be tolerated by the Anglo-French and that annexation of these neighbours would provide much-needed economic and industrial resources to the Reich. Hitler expected Poland to remain neutral at this point and that very morning, he had assured the Polish ambassador in Berlin, Józef Lipski, that he recognized that 'Danzig is bound up with Poland.'[20] However, both Blomberg and Fritsch, representing the army, objected to Hitler's intentions and stated that the Wehrmacht was not yet prepared to conduct even local wars of aggression. Instead, they recommended that war should not be risked before the existing rearmament plans were completed in 1940. Neurath also objected to Hitler's plans and argued that France would not simply stand by while Germany devoured Austria and Czechoslovakia.

Hitler came away from the conference convinced that his assessments were correct and those of his advisors were unduly pessimistic, even timid. He resolved to clean house before making his move against either Austria or Czechoslovakia. Both Blomberg and Fritsch were forced to resign in January–February 1938, while Neurath was replaced by Joachim von Ribbentrop. The Defence Ministry was replaced by the Oberkommando der Wehrmacht (High Command of the Armed Forces or OKW) headed by General der Artillerie Wilhelm Keitel, while Generaloberst Walther von Brauchitsch became commander-in-chief of the Heer. Both Keitel and Brauchitsch were selected because they were compliant in acceding to Hitler's plans, not because they were particularly competent officers. Satisfied that the Wehrmacht was now headed with men who would follow orders, Hitler forced a show-down with Austria first. On 12 February 1938, Hitler met with Schuschnigg at Berchtesgaden and demanded that Austrian Nazis now be included in the government, but he was willing to accept gradual implementation. Schuschnigg agreed to take a few Austrian Nazis, such as Arthur Seyß-Inquart, into the government but he provoked Hitler by calling for a popular referendum on the issue of union with Germany. Infuriated that his will might be thwarted by a popular vote, Hitler demanded that Schuschnigg resign immediately and hand over the government to the Austrian Nazis, or Germany would invade. On the evening of 10 March, Hitler ordered the OKW to activate the 8. Armee for intervention in Austria within 48 hours. Generaloberst Fedor von Bock, commander of the 8. Armee, was forced to quickly improvise an intervention plan, dubbed *Unternehmen Otto* (Operation *Otto*).

Schuschnigg resigned on the evening of 11 March, leaving the Austrian government in virtual free-fall. Seyß-Inquart stepped into the vacuum in Vienna and was coerced by Göring into asking for German assistance in restoring order.[21] Bock had less than 36 hours to prepare his invasion before his troops began crossing the Austrian border around 0900 hours on 12 March 1938. The 8. Armee consisted of 117,000 troops (7, 10 and 27 Infanterie-Divisionen, three *Gebirgsjäger* (mountain infantry) regiments and three Waffen-SS regimental groups) and was spearheaded by the 2. Panzer-Division. Since the 60,000 Austrian Army (Bundesheer) did not resist, Bock's troops saw no action and *Otto* became a victory march to Vienna. German Panzers were covered with flowers and cheered on by numerous pro-*Anschluss* civilians. Yet Guderian noted that the 2. Panzer-Division's advance was hindered by lack of mobile supply columns, which was only partly corrected afterwards.[22] The Austrian Anschluss was another bloodless foreign policy success for Hitler but it revealed that the Wehrmacht was far from ready for war, since numerous motor vehicles and tanks had broken down in what was an unopposed advance. Nor did the Luftwaffe learn anything from *Otto*, since there were no targets to bomb nor enemy fighters to shoot down.

In additional to gaining another cheap political victory, the Anschluss also provided Hitler with a valuable short-term windfall in material terms. The assets of the Austrian national banks were seized, yielding RM 782 million in gold and foreign currency – which was used by Germany to ease its own strained balance of payments and purchase additional raw materials for the armaments industry.[23] Austria also produced small amounts of iron ore and crude oil, which provided a 'free' supplement to Germany's own resources. In 1938, the oil fields near Vienna were already annually producing about 63,000 tonnes of crude oil and German engineers were able to increase this by more then ten-fold over the next four years. In human terms, the Anschluss added nine million citizens to the Reich. Over 50,000 trained Austrian troops were absorbed into the Wehrmacht, enabling the rapid formation of five new divisions; the Austrian Schnelle Division was re-equipped and converted into the 4. leichte-Division while Austrian mountain troops enabled the creation of two high-quality Gebirgsjäger-Divisionen (2. and 3. Gebirgsjäger-Divisionen).

After the absorption of Austria, Czechoslovakia was now nearly surrounded on three sides by the Third Reich and Hitler was quick to shift gears to move against this new target. One of the lessons that he had learned from the Austrian Anschluss was the value of having a home-grown resistance movement within the country he was trying to destabilize. The Austrian Nazis had helped to bring Schuschnigg's regime down and now Hitler sought help from the Sudeten Germans, the ethnic German minority living in the western Czech border regions of Bohemia. Altogether, there were about 3.5 million Sudeten Germans, who comprised 22 per cent of the total Czech population. After the disintegration of Austria-Hungary in 1918, the Sudeten Germans claimed that they were discriminated against inside Czechoslovakia and were hostile towards the new republic. In an effort to head off trouble, the Czech government outlawed the Sudeten version of the Nazi Party in 1933, but it simply re-emerged as other right-wing nationalist groups. Konrad Henlein, a veteran of the First World War, became the leader of the 'Sudeten German Home Front' (Sudetendeutsche Heimatfront or SHF), which evolved into the Sudeten German Party (*Sudetendeutsche Partei* or SdP). Germany had been providing covert funds to Henlein for several years and now Hitler invited him to Berlin on 28 March 1938 to discuss strategy. It is important to note that Hitler's interest in the Sudeten Germans was purely strategic; he was not particularly sympathetic to their cause. Hitler instructed Henlein to create a permanent state of unrest in the Sudetenland and to agitate for greater autonomy for his people. However, Hitler did not want a peaceful solution, telling Henlein that, 'we must always demand so much that we can never be satisfied'. On 24 April 1938, Henlein publicly demanded greater autonomy for the Sudeten Germans (the so-called Karlsbad programme). Three days prior to Henlein's speech, Hitler had instructed the OKW to begin drafting plans for an attack on Czechoslovakia.[24]

Keitel and his operations chief, Oberst Alfred Jodl, wrote *Fall Grün* (*Case Green*) for the invasion of Czechoslovakia.[25] The OKW had previously developed contingency plans in case of war with Czechoslovakia, but *Fall Grün* was premised on Hitler's requirement for a rapid, violent assault from multiple directions that would achieve decisive results within four days. Hitler's intent was to smash Czechoslovakia before France or the Soviet Union could interfere. However, *Fall Grün* was highly ambitious, given that the Czechs had a large, well equipped army with 26 divisions, including about 450 tanks (many of which were superior to German tanks). Furthermore, the Czechs had heavily fortified the border region in the Sudetenland, building forts and bunkers that were similar in design to those in the French Maginot Line. In 1938, the Heer had very little heavy artillery and were not sure that their existing howitzers could penetrate the Czech defences. According to *Fall Grün*, once Hitler gave the word, five German armies (2., 8., 10., 12. and 14.), consisting of a total of 42 divisions, would attack from north, west and south in order to overrun Bohemia. The invasion force would employ three Panzer-Divisionen and all four leichte-Divisionen, but the mechanized forces were spread out rather than massed to achieve decisive effect – a lesson not yet learned by the Wehrmacht. The Luftwaffe, which outnumbered the Czech Air Force by 2:1, would support the invasion with just over 1,000 aircraft. On paper, the Wehrmacht seemed to have enough of an advantage to win, but given that the Wehrmacht would have to mount frontal attacks against border fortifications set in the mountainous terrain of Bohemia, it was likely to be a difficult and even risky operation if the Czechs decided to fight.

While Keitel and Jodl were still drafting *Fall Grün*, General der Artillerie Ludwig Beck, chief of the Army General Staff, became convinced that any premature action against Czechoslovakia would lead to a disastrous war with the Anglo-French. In a memorandum sent to Brauchitsch and the OKW senior leadership on 5 May, Beck assessed that Anglo-French intervention was likely in case of a German move against Czechoslovakia and that the Wehrmacht was not prepared to fight a long war.[26] Beck was on solid ground in his assessment of the Wehrmacht's shortcomings and other senior generals were fully aware that the rearmament plan was behind schedule – most preferred to avoid taking risks that could lead to a wider war until all the mechanized divisions were fully equipped and reserve stocks of fuel and ammunition had been built up. However, Beck had little basis for assessing the likelihood of foreign intervention or their capabilities, it was simply the innate fear of a two-front war buried deep in his General Staff-trained brain. At first, the OKW kept Beck's inflammatory memo out of Hitler's sight, but it did succeed in planting a seed of doubt within the upper ranks of the Heer. On 20 May, Keitel presented the *Fall Grün* plan to Hitler; he approved of the plan but set no date for its implementation.

As part of the effort to build a legal case for military intervention in Czechoslovakia, Josef Goebbels' Propaganda Ministry accused the Czechs of committing violent atrocities against the Sudeten Germans – a tactic dubbed *Gräuelpropaganda* (atrocity propaganda) – which quickly ratcheted up tensions between Berlin and Prague.[27] Hitler had a personal loathing for the Czechs from his early days in Vienna and despised the multi-national composition of the Czech Republic. Nazi propaganda was used to mask German preparations to dismember Czechoslovakia by focusing international attention on the 'crimes' committed against the Sudeten Germans. Ultimately, a suitable violent incident would be used to justify German military intervention to 'save' the population in the Sudetenland. However in this case, German propaganda got a bit ahead of itself. Although the OKW had not yet mobilized any forces for *Fall Grün*, the vitriolic nature of German propaganda frightened the Czech government into believing that an invasion was imminent and it declared a partial mobilization of 180,000 troops on 20 May. The so-called 'Weekend Crisis' alerted the British Foreign Ministry that German action against Czechoslovakia might be imminent, causing Lord Halifax to inform Ribbentrop that Britain might not remain neutral in case of war. Unfortunately, 'maybe' is not a very effective deterrent. Ribbentrop ignored Halifax and made no effort to reduce tensions. Instead, he made blood-curdling threats that Germany would attack Czechoslovakia and 'that there would not be a living soul left in that state'. He also made clear Germany's willingness to fight the Anglo-French over the Czech Crisis.[28] Ribbentrop's threats were clearly intended to accentuate war fears in London and Paris, thereby reducing opposition to Hitler's objectives in Czechoslovakia. Essentially, Ribbentrop's violent war rhetoric succeeded, because politicians in London and Paris came to accept the notion that if Germany could not be deterred, the Czechs should be forced to make a compromise to avoid touching off another European war. Some, such as Lord Beaverbrook, were actually pro-German in attitude. As a result of the partial Czech mobilization, Hitler ordered that the Wehrmacht should be prepared to execute *Fall Grün* no later than 1 October. In the revised planning document, Hitler stated that 'it is my unalterable decision to smash Czechoslovakia by military action in the foreseeable future.'[29]

While the Sudeten Crisis continued to fester, Beck made a naïve and forlorn effort to try and de-rail the preparations for war by encouraging organized resistance from the German officer corps. He wrote several more memoranda in June and July to Brauchitsch and senior OKW leadership, criticizing the prospects for *Fall Grün*, and even suggesting mass resignations to impede Hitler's intended aggression. However, Beck had misjudged the situation and the bulk of the German officer corps were unwilling to get involved in political matters or sacrifice their careers. Indeed, the idea of eliminating Czechoslovakia as a potential threat was accepted as necessary by much of the officer corps – the only issue that was being debated was the timing of that action. When Hitler belatedly learned in August of Beck's behind-the-scenes machinations, Beck was forced to resign (he would later be one of the key leaders in the anti-Hitler resistance). He was replaced by General der Artillerie Franz Halder who as it turned out, was also covertly involved in the evolving conspiracy to remove Hitler from power. Within days of taking his new position, Halder began planning a military coup to arrest Hitler if he tried to start a war with Czechoslovakia. Halder also sent a representative, Major Ewald von Kleist-Schmensin, to London in August 1938 to meet with Robert Vansittart (chief diplomatic advisor to the prime minister) and Winston Churchill. Kleist informed the British that Hitler was determined upon war over Czechoslovakia and that the Wehrmacht leadership was taking steps to stop him. Chamberlain was made aware of this visit but made no adjustments to his position on the issue.[30] Indeed, Chamberlain paid more heed to the views of Sir Neville Henderson, British ambassador in Berlin, who said that it was unjust that Germany had lost the Sudetenland as a result of Versailles.

In early September 1938, the Sudeten Crisis came to a head, with Britain pushing Czechoslovakia to grant concessions to the Sudeten Germans in order to avoid a conflict. However, Hitler ordered Henlein not to accept any deals, causing negotiations to collapse. The SS covertly provided arms to the Sudeten Germans, who formed an armed paramilitary group known as the Freiwilliger Schutzdienst (volunteer protective service), which began attacking Czech policemen.[31] The German military intelligence (Abwehr) also dispatched saboteurs from the Bataillon Ebbinghaus into the Sudetenland to create additional trouble. In response, the Czech government declared martial law in the Sudetenland, which gave German propagandists more opportunity to vent spleen against the republic. As the situation spiralled into a *de facto* armed insurgency in the Czech borderlands, Neville Chamberlain, now Britain's prime minister, embarked upon personal diplomacy with Hitler to resolve the crisis. Early on, it was clear that Chamberlain's foremost objective was to avoid war at all costs and he was willing to accept Hitler's demand for the Sudetenland to be handed over to Germany. Hitler deliberately used bellicose language during negotiations in order to browbeat his adversaries into submission. The Czech president, Edvard Beneš, wavered between resistance and conciliation. On 23 September, Beneš ordered general mobilization and on the next day, Prime Minister Eduard Daladier announced that France would stand by its alliance with the Czechs and ordered partial mobilization – which brought the pot to a boil. However, Chamberlain was unwilling to risk war over 'a quarrel in a far away country between people of whom we know nothing.' A study by the Royal Air Force Bomber Command – Britain's trump card – informed Chamberlain that it could do nothing to prevent Czechoslovakia from being overrun, which influenced him towards sacrificing the Sudetenland.[32] Another reason for British reticence to make a military guarantee to Czechoslovakia was the lack of a viable military commitment from the Soviet Union, which had also signed a military agreement with the Czechs. The Soviets claimed that they had 30 divisions on the Soviet–Polish border and were willing to provide military support to the Czechs, but they required permission to transit through Poland. However, Stalin knew that the Poles would refuse transit rights and no formal request was ever made.[33] After another week of hand-wringing by various diplomats, Hitler – with valuable aid from Mussolini – manoeuvred Britain and France into signing the Munich Agreement on 30 September, which gave him the Sudetenland. The Czechs did not participate in the final negotiations, but were told that they could no longer expect any help from Britain, France or the Soviet Union. Adding insult to injury, the Czech government was obliged to give Germany 14.5 tonnes of gold to cover currency conversion expenses in the newly acquired Sudetenland areas.

Although most narratives about the Munich Agreement focus on the pusillanimous behaviour of the Anglo-French leaders, Czechoslovakia was primarily the victim of its own spineless government. After learning that Germany would get the Sudetenland, the Czech leadership folded and decided not to offer the slightest resistance. General Jan Syrový, the defence minister, informed the Czech people that they could not resist because they had no allies and were outnumbered, even though he had nearly one million troops under arms. He also cravenly stated that resistance was futile because Czechoslovakia would suffer heavy casualties if it fought; in any case, Syrový would survive the next seven years of German occupation but over 300,000 of his fellow Czechs would not. Had the Czechs resisted, even without allies, the Wehrmacht would have suffered significant losses and consumed a substantial part of its limited stockpile of ammunition. The destruction of Czech military hardware, particularly tanks, would prevented the Wehrmacht from forming at least two additional Panzer-Divisionen. At the very least, Hitler's open aggression against an independent state would have likely led to economic sanctions and an acceleration of Anglo-French rearmament programmes.

Instead, the Czech collapse encouraged Hitler that he was infallible and incited him to commit further acts of aggression. Likewise, the Czech collapse stifled the resistance movement within the German officer corps for the time being, since their predictions had proved entirely false.

On 1 October, German troops under the command of Generaloberst Wilhelm Ritter von Leeb began gradually moving into the Sudetenland in stages, because Czech troops still occupied the region. There were a few small skirmishes, resulting in the death of three German and 11 Czech soldiers, until the Czech High Command ordered its troops to withdraw. As German troops marched across the border, they dismantled the Czech customs barriers, while international correspondents watched. One soldier spotted a Czech army mobilization order affixed to the side of a customs house and handed it to a nearby American correspondent as a souvenir. Guderian's XVI Armeekorps (mot.), with the 1. Panzer-Division and two motorized infantry divisions, was part of the advance guard marching into the Sudetenland. Although the advance was unopposed, Guderian found it to be a useful experience to manoeuvre all three of his divisions simultaneously.[34]

The Czech unwillingness to defend their national sovereignty also invited contempt from their other neighbours. Seeing that the Anglo-French would not lift a finger to save Czechoslovakia from dismemberment, both Poland and Hungary moved in to secure disputed border regions for themselves. On the same day that the Munich Agreement was signed, Józef Beck issued an ultimatum to Czechoslovakia demanding the return of the Silesian border region of Teschen, which the Czechs had seized by force in 1919. When no reply was received from the Czech government, Polish troops marched into Teschen on 2 October.* Hungary also annexed sections of border territory from Czechoslovakia. Hitler supported the Polish and Hungarian actions, inasmuch as it made Germany not look solely guilty for the violation of Czech sovereignty. However, Britain took a dim view of Poland seizing land from Czechoslovakia and this cooled already tepid relations considerably during the winter of 1938/39. From the Polish perspective, Czechoslovakia was an artificial state that was in the process of imploding and the Anglo-French were acquiescing to this development. In the words of Polish-American historian Anna M. Cienciala, under these circumstances, Beck decided that 'Poland should

---

*The Polish invasion force was designated Independent Operational Group Śląsk (GO Śląsk) and consisted of 35,000 troops, including the 4th Infantry Division and regiments from six other divisions.

follow the course of "individual solutions" and pull what she could from the wreckage.' Thus, Beck regarded the industrialized Teschen region and its ethnic Polish majority as better off in Polish hands, rather than Nazi ones.[35]

Amazingly, Hitler wasted no time in shifting from his annexation of the Sudetenland to his next project: the recovery of Danzig. This was a surprising move, since up to this point, Hitler had shown very little interest in Danzig and in November 1937 he had publicly stated that Polish rights in the Free City would not be infringed and that the legal status of the city would not be violated. As recently as 14 January 1938, Hitler had personally told Beck that he was not interested in making an issue out of Danzig.[36] Now, just three weeks after the Munich agreement was signed, Ribbentrop met with Józef Lipski, the Polish ambassador in Berlin, and for the first time, officially proposed that Danzig should be re-incorporated into the Reich. Ribbentrop also stated that Germany wanted to establish road and rail links across the Polish Corridor, joining East Prussia to the Fatherland. In return, he stated that the German–Polish Non-Aggression Pact would be extended 25 years. Ribbentrop also suggested that Poland might be invited to join the Anti-Comintern Pact, thereby aligning Poland with Germany against the Soviet Union. At this point, Hitler appears merely to have been feeling out Poland and to have had no immediate plans to undermine its national sovereignty. He was still primarily involved in the assimilation of the Sudetenland and weeding out Beck's confederates from the OKH. Nor were Ribbentrop's proposals to Poland made public. Indeed, Ribbentrop was not even in a hurry to receive the Polish response and it was not until 19 November that Józef Beck was able to deliver Poland's reply. Beck suggested a bi-lateral German–Polish agreement to guarantee Danzig's existence as a Free City and to protect the rights of the German minority in the Polish Corridor, but stated that any attempt by Germany to seize Danzig would lead to conflict. On the surface, the reaction in Berlin was unusually mild and Ribbentrop simply sought to continue discussions on 'Polish–German issues'.[37]

Meanwhile, Beck was working to smooth over differences with the Soviet Union, which had threatened military action if Poland attacked its ally, Czechoslovakia. Instead, the Soviets did nothing when Teschen was occupied. Beck managed to get the Soviets to re-affirm the Non-Aggression Pact with Poland on 26 November, thereby demonstrating that both countries still valued this relationship. Thus, Beck's policy of 'balancing' between Germany and the Soviet Union appeared to be working in

November 1938. However, unknown to Beck, on 29 November, Hitler ordered the OKW to begin planning a military coup to seize Danzig at an opportune moment.

Chamberlain's Guarantee, March 1939

'How lucky you are! Who would have thought six months ago
that you would have Britain on your side as an ally?'
British Minister to Count Edward Raczyński, Polish ambassador in
London, 3 September 1939

In his 1933 novel *The Shape of Things to Come*, the British science-fiction writer H. G. Wells imagined a second European Great War breaking out on January 5, 1940, with Germany fighting Poland over Danzig. Early in the novel, Wells criticized the settlement that took Danzig from Germany and established the Polish Corridor, which he refers to as 'absurd'. He also wrote how the desire to recover Danzig was 'burnt into the German imagination' and became the most significant territorial issue driving them towards war.[38] Wells would prove remarkably prescient about where and when the next major European war would begin, although that was not appreciated until later. Winston Churchill was an avid reader of H.G. Wells' books and like many Englishmen of the inter-war period, concurred that the Polish Corridor was absurd and that the loss of Danzig had been unnecessarily harsh upon Germany. Certainly the pro-appeasement British ambassador in Berlin, Sir Nevile Henderson, felt that way and regularly stated that German claims upon Danzig were just. Otherwise, British foreign policy and popular opinion essentially ignored Danzig until Hitler took an interest in it.

Danzig had actually been a Nazi-dominated city since June 1933, when Albert Forster, a Bavarian Nazi and member of the SS (Schutzstaffel), was elected as *Gauleiter* (district leader). Forster immediately began a purge of non-Nazi political groups in the city and gained control over the local constabulary force, the Schutzpolizei.[39] Arthur Greiser, an SS official, became president of the Danzig senate. The Danzig SA group was gradually expanded to regimental size and armed with machine guns. Although the League of Nations maintained nominal control over Danzig, the Nazi-controlled senate and SA units actually controlled the city. Forster began to single out the Jews of Danzig for persecution, which evoked protests from the League Commissioner in Danzig, the Irish diplomat Sean Lester. Lacking any kind of support, Lester was forced to resign in June 1936. Forster followed up by delivering a speech to local Nazi party members, in which he declared that Germany was preparing for war and that both the League and Poland would soon be eliminated. However, Forster had gone too far and he received orders to tone down his bellicose rhetoric for the moment. Germany and Poland agreed to the appointment of a new League Commissioner for Danzig, the Swiss diplomat Carl Jacob Burckhardt.[40] In addition to Burckhardt, the League also established a committee of three, with representatives from Britain, France and Portugal, to monitor events in Danzig. However, Forster returned to his aggressive tactics after the Munich Crisis and moved to enforce Nazi racial policies in Danzig, which humiliated Burckhardt and the League mandate. Amazingly, Burckhardt refused to see the Nazi threat to Danzig and in mid-1938 he continued to believe that 'it is possible that gradually the more violent and dangerous elements and personalities in the [Nazi] Party might be eliminated, and give way to more modest and sober ones.'[41]

Meanwhile, the Polish presence in Danzig was led by Commissioner-General Marian Chodacki, a protégé of Józef Beck and a Polish reserve officer with a background in Section II intelligence work. The Polish customs officials worked behind the so-called 'Green Line' in Danzig, but had to interact with Nazi officials in the city on a regular basis – a constant source of friction. Since German dockyard workers in Danzig in 1919–20 had refused to unload munitions destined for Poland, Poland had secured permission from the League of Nations in 1925 to construct a military transshipment depot on the island of Westerplatte, a former beach resort, in Danzig harbour. The purpose of this facility was to enable Poland to import or export military material via a controlled storage area, not to provide a military base within Danzig. Under the conditions set by the League, Poland was only allowed a total of 88 troops on Westerplatte.

After Ribbentrop's failure to gain any concessions from Poland over Danzig in November 1938, Hitler decided to get personally involved in the situation soon after the New Year. As usual when he wanted to impress a foreign dignitary, Hitler invited Józef Beck to his retreat at the Obersalzberg, in Bavaria on 5 January 1939. Hitler told Beck that Poland had nothing to fear from Germany, but he repeated Ribbentrop's proposals to return Danzig to the Reich and to provide unfettered access across the Polish Corridor. He stated that a new type of corporation (*Körperschaft*) might be created in Danzig, to safeguard both German and Polish interests. Hitler also alluded to potential German–Polish military co-operation against the Soviet Union. However, Beck was not receptive to Hitler's entreaties and in a follow-up meeting with Ribbentrop, Beck told him that for the first time that he was 'in a pessimistic mood' and saw no possibility of agreement.[42] Ribbentrop visited Warsaw on 25–27 January to continue discussions, but Beck made it clear that Poland would not agree to Danzig reverting to Germany or to the construction of a German highway across the Polish Corridor. Although Ribbentrop did not press the issue, it was clear that both sides had arrived at a diplomatic impasse. Recognizing that Hitler could easily change his mind about peacefully resolving the Danzig issue, Beck felt that Poland needed a stronger hand, particularly in light of its post-Munich diplomatic isolation. During January–February 1939, Beck worked to improve relations with France and Great Britain, but both proved indifferent to Polish interests in the Danzig question.

Nevertheless, further threats of German armed aggression in Europe caused the British government to reconsider its heretofore negative attitude towards Poland. After the Munich Crisis and Ribbentrop's bellicose rhetoric, rumours abounded about new German targets of aggression. In January 1939, rumours of a lightning German attack on Holland provoked a brief war scare, even though there was no on-going Dutch–German crisis.[43] British intelligence also had warning about German intentions to invade the rump Czech state. According to the Munich Agreement, all the signatories were supposed to guarantee Czechoslovakia's security, but this was put off until later. In February, Hitler directed the OKW to plan an operation against the remaining Czech state. Since the Munich Agreement, the Czech Republic, particularly its army, was in a state of disintegration as ethnic Hungarians and Slovaks deserted the colours. Hitler took up the cause of Slovak nationalists, using this as a pretext to dismantle the remainder of Czechoslovakia. On 14 March 1939, Hitler summoned Emil Hacha, the Czech president, to Berlin, where he was brusquely told that Germany was about to invade. Göring told Hacha if there was any Czech resistance, the Luftwaffe would flatten Prague. After suffering a heart attack, Hacha agreed to Hitler's conditions. As it turned out, Hitler did not wait for Hacha's surrender and German troops actually began to cross into Czech territory on the evening of 14 March. In only one place did the Czech Army resist – a 40-minute long skirmish at Frydek-Mistek which left up to six German soldiers dead – and everywhere else there was apathetic resignation. The Czech

Army was disbanded and only a few thousand troops chose to escape to Poland or Romania. On 15 March, Hitler arrived in Prague. Bohemia and Moravia became German protectorates, while Slovakia became a quasi-independent German satellite.[44]

The Poles used the German violation of the Munich agreement to sneak some additional reinforcements into the military depot at Westerplatte: 23 soldiers under Podporucznik Leon Pająk. Major Henryk Sucharski, the Polish commander on Westerplatte, quietly began to fortify his position with trenches and field works in order to prevent a German surprise coup against the island. Seven fortified positions were created on Westerplatte during the summer of 1939, without alerting the League of Nations or the Germans.

In London, Chamberlain responded to the German invasion of Czechoslovakia by making another appeasement-style speech before the House of Commons, ridiculously asserting that 'no aggression had taken place' and that the Czech government had agreed to everything that transpired. However, this attitude no longer played well in Parliament and there was considerable public anger against Germany's open violation of the Munich Agreement. It was clear that Hitler had lied at Munich and was intent upon seizing more and more land in eastern Europe. Two days after Hitler's entry into Prague, Chamberlain was forced to modify his perceptions, admitting that normal diplomacy might not suffice with Hitler. There was also a public outcry when it was revealed that the Bank of England had helped the Nazis to loot Czech gold. Once Prague was occupied, the Germans forced the directors of the Czech central bank to sign a transfer request for 23 tonnes of gold (worth £5.6 million) held at the Bank of England and send it to a German-controlled account. Montagu Norman, head of the Bank of England, was a close friend of Hjalmar Schacht, Hitler's finance minister; he approved the transfer request, even though it was likely made under duress. The gold transfer sparked brief outrage in Parliament, with Winston Churchill demanding to know how the government could ask its citizens to enlist in the military when it was 'so butter-fingered that £6 million worth of gold can be transferred to the Nazi government'.[45]

On top of this, Ribbentrop handed an ultimatum to Lithuania's foreign minister on 20 March, informing him that the Memel territory (lost under the terms of the Versailles Treaty) must be returned to Germany forthwith. Again, Göring threatened to bomb Lithuania's capital unless it complied. Three days later, Hitler and a large entourage (including

Himmler, Blomberg and Raeder) arrived in Memel aboard the pocket-battleship *Deutschland*, along with a strong Kriegsmarine squadron. Inside Memel, Hitler delivered a rousing speech to the crowd, stating:

> You were once forsaken by a Germany which had succumbed to disgrace and shame. Now you have come home to a mighty new Germany. It upholds once more its unshakeable sense of honor. It shall not entrust its destiny to foreigners; it stands ready and willing to master its own destiny, to fashion it, whether or not this suits an outside world. Eighty million Germans today stand up for this one new Germany. You shall now partake in the surge of our national life, our work, our faith, our hopes, and, should it become necessary, you shall partake in our sacrifices.[46]

The Poles reacted at once to the German occupation of Memel, with the Ministry of Military Affairs ordering a secret, partial mobilization of 'black' units on 23 March. The Ministry had two mobilization plans, Plan *Zachód* (Plan West) and Plan *Wschód* (Plan East), both of which relied upon a colour-coded scheme for units: the 'red' group to cover the eastern border, the 'blue' group to cover the western border, 'black' units to support operational units in an endangered zone, 'yellow' units to strengthen covering forces on either border, and 'brown' and 'green' groups consisted of reinforcements. The colour groups were mixed inside corps areas (each known as a *Dowództwo Okręgu Korpusu* or DOK) and the Ministry of Military Affairs could order selective mobilizations. In this case, the 'black' group from two districts in eastern Poland was mobilized and rushed to defend the western borders. Three infantry divisions, 9th, 20th and 30th Infantry Divisions (9, 20 and 30 DP) and the Nowogródek Cavalry Brigade from the IX Corps District (DOK IX) in Brześć (Brest) plus the 26th Infantry Division (26 DP) from the IV Corps District (DOK IV) in Łódź were mobilized. Some additional KOP units were also mobilized. Deploying these units took time: the 20 DP and the Nowogródek Cavalry Brigade had to move over 450km by rail from eastern Poland to reinforce the Sierpc sector north-west of Warsaw. Furthermore, Poland did not have reserve stocks of vehicles and horses to outfit mobilized units; instead, combat units requisitioned transport from the civilian sector – which took time. Nor was this partial mobilization inexpensive; the British embassy in Warsaw estimated it cost the Polish government an extra 57 million zł ($10.9 million) per month.[47]

Rydz-Śmigły also took this moment to organize his forces into five task groups that were dubbed 'armies': Modlin, Pomorze (Pomerania), Poznań, Łódź and Kraków.[48] Basic defensive responsibilities were assigned to each army for its sector, but detailed operational guidance was surprisingly lacking. Furthermore, the German occupation of the rest of Czechoslovakia invalidated much of the defensive planning made to date and Rydz-Śmigły recognized that adjustments needed to be made – there was simply too much border to properly defend. Since the Munich Agreement, a planning group of senior officers (Tadeusz Kutrzeba, Juliusz Rómmel, Władysław Bortnowski and Leon Berbecki) had been working on updating the Polish operational war plan but now the revised guidance was obsolete before it was even issued.

While the Poles mobilized in secret, the British and French debated what to do next. Between the blatant display of military might deployed to bully a neutral state and Hitler's open references to 'sacrifices', it was now evident – even to Neville Chamberlain – that quiet diplomacy and economic incentives had failed to reign in Hitler's aggressive ambitions. It slowly dawned upon the British government that a new approach was needed before the international situation deteriorated even further. However, the international situation was slipping fast. Just before Memel was annexed, Ribbentrop met with ambassador Lipski in Berlin to further discuss Danzig. Lipski affirmed the Polish position that any move to change the status of Danzig represented a *casus belli*, while Ribbentrop retorted that Germany would assert its rights in Danzig by any means necessary, including force. After the Polish rebuff, Hitler informed Keitel that at an opportune moment, he would attack Poland.[49] The next day, German newspapers begin reporting Polish 'atrocities' against German civilians in Poland, using the same formula of *Gräuelpropaganda* that had worked so well in Austria and Czechoslovakia.

It was Lord Halifax, Britain's foreign secretary, who first reached out to Beck through the British embassy in Warsaw, with a vague message that Britain would regard a threat to Polish independence with 'grave concern'.[50] In assessing Lord Halifax's message, the Poles were quick to note that there had been no history of trust or common purpose between Poland and Britain in the previous two decades. It was also odd that Halifax asked Beck to keep any discussions between Poland and Britain about a security agreement secret from the French, who were formally allied with Poland. Unknown to the Poles, Chamberlain's cabinet was stumbling towards the creation of a security agreement with Poland in an environment that was filled with rumours and devoid of sound military advice. Between 27 and 29 March, the British Cabinet met to develop diplomatic courses of action that would restrain Germany from making a sudden move again Danzig. During these discussions, Britain's military intelligence (MI6) received what it regarded as credible information from a British journalist that a German coup against Danzig was imminent. On the same day, the US embassy in Warsaw passed along similar information that a German move against Danzig was about to occur.[51] Under these circumstances, the British cabinet moved precipitously in an effort to head off what it thought was imminent German aggression against Danzig. Amazingly, the British military leadership were not consulted on their views during the cabinet discussions. Instead, Chamberlain and Halifax drove the Cabinet to announce a security guarantee to Poland premised on rumours and flimsy intelligence that a German move against Danzig – or somewhere – could occur in a matter of days.[52]

At 1500 hours on 31 March, Chamberlain spoke before the House of Commons and announced the bi-lateral security agreement with Poland. The guarantee stated that 'in the event of any action which clearly threatened Polish independence, and which the Polish government accordingly consider it vital to resist with their national forces, His Majesty's Government would feel themselves bound at once to lend the Polish Government all support in their power.'[53] Chamberlain hoped that this overt warning would suffice to deter Hitler from aggression against Poland, although he made no policy provisions in case it did not. Chamberlain still failed to understand that Hitler could not be swayed from his course by vague words, even words that carried the hint of a wider conflict. Furthermore, the lack of concrete commitment on Britain's part reinforced the idea that Chamberlain was unwilling to make any sacrifices on Poland's behalf.

When Hitler learned of Chamberlain's guarantee, he angrily retorted that, 'I'll cook them a stew that they'll choke on.'[54] However, Hitler was not so furious as to postpone his scheduled holiday cruise aboard the cruise ship *Robert Ley* in the Baltic. Instead, while he enjoyed the sea air, he ordered the OKW to prepare three contingency plans in regard to Poland: (1) a strictly defensive plan with increased border and air security; (2) *Fall Weiss* – a major invasion of Poland; and (3) a *coup de main* to seize Danzig. Hitler told Keitel that the Wehrmacht must be ready to execute any of these plans no later than 1 September.[55] At this point, Hitler was still undecided whether he should limit his aggression merely to the seizure of Danzig or whether he should seek to eliminate Poland entirely. Ultimately his decision was shaped by the reality that Poland was now firmly moving into the anti-German camp and that he believed that Britain was unwilling to back up its guarantee to Poland. Consequently, it now made no sense to start a war with Poland just to gain Danzig and the Polish Corridor. After returning from his holiday, Hitler informed the OKW on 11 April that he had selected *Fall Weiss* and that its aim was to destroy the Polish armed forces. The OKW directive explicitly stated that the intent was to limit the fighting to Poland.[56] However, Hitler adopted an increasingly anti-British tone after Chamberlain's guarantee and on 28 April he announced the abrogation of the 1935 Anglo-German Naval Agreement. On the same day, he stated that he regarded the Anglo-Polish security agreement as a violation of the 1934 German–Polish Non-Aggression Pact – which was a public demonstration that German–Polish relations were quickly deteriorating.

When Beck went to London on 4 April to discuss actual details of what Chamberlain's guarantee meant for Poland, it quickly became apparent that there was little common ground between the two sides. Beck wanted firm guarantees from Britain and France that they would help protect Polish sovereignty, backed up by increased military and financial aid. However, Chamberlain was thinking in airy diplomatic terms and his stated goal was to organize a new collective security system in eastern Europe, including not only Poland, but Romania, Yugoslavia and Greece as well. Beck had no interest in such a frivolous scheme and was impolitic enough to say so plainly. Thus, within days of Chamberlain's guarantee, the veneer had already worn thin on the nascent Anglo-Polish security collaboration. Nevertheless, on 6 April the British and French governments signed a mutual assistance pact with Poland, promising that they would send military aid to Poland in the event of a German attack. Chamberlain persisted with his collective security plan and both Britain and France offered security guarantees to Greece and Romania on 13 April.[57] Along the way, Turkey and Egypt were added into the mix. Subsequently, British diplomats announced that any British military and financial aid offered as part of this new security arrangement would be divided among Poland, Egypt, Turkey, Romania and Greece; Beck could see that British assistance was going to be marginal, at best.

On 12 May, the Polish government made a formal request to Britain for financial aid to purchase defence equipment and supplies. The Polish ambassador presented a request for a total package of £60–65 million in assistance, including £18 million for defence materials, ammunition and spare parts. Most of the rest would go to cover Polish purchases of raw materials abroad.

Although the British Foreign Office supported the notion of granting Poland at least £20 million in aid, the British Treasury Department did not.[58] This was the same Treasury Department that only two months prior had agreed to loan China £5 million to help stabilize its currency and regularly provided large cash infusions to keep Chiang Kai-Shek's corrupt regime afloat, which benefited British commercial interests in China. It was also the same Treasury Department that had continued to approve short-term credits to Germany, up until the Munich Crisis. In the month prior to Chamberlain's guarantee to Poland, Britain also tried to sell Hurricane fighters to Portugal and the Treasury Department provided a credit of £1 million to the Salazar regime in Lisbon.[59] However, the Treasury Department only looked though narrow financial lenses – there was no money to be made in Poland from trade – not Britain's larger strategic interests of preventing war. The Poles also asked the French for about £12 million in financial assistance, which the French tentatively agreed – but only if it was matched by Britain. Furthermore, Hitler could follow the inconclusive financial negotiations, which were covered in the British press, which further demonstrated the lack of real support for Poland.[60] After months of haggling, the British Treasury Office grudgingly agreed to a high-interest loan of £5.5 million – which was rejected outright by the Polish government.[61] On 19 August, the French finally agreed to provide credits amounting to just £2.6 million, but the money would have to be spent on French-built equipment. Consequently, Poland failed to secure any financial assistance from Britain or France before the German invasion began.

Keen to appear sympathetic, the French took the lead in military discussions with Poland. On 16–17 May, Général Maurice Gamelin held staff talks in Paris with a Polish military delegation headed by Generał Dywizji Tadeusz Kasprzycki, the Polish minister of war. It was in this meeting that Gamelin promised – in the event of a German attack on Poland – to start a limited offensive in the west on the third day of French mobilization. On the 16th day of French mobilization, Gamelin promised to commit 'the bulk' of French forces against Germany. Furthermore, Général Joseph Vuillemin, head of the French Armée de l'air (Air Force), promised to take 'vigorous action' to assist Poland from the beginning of a war, including sending French bombers to operate from Polish airfields. The French even signed a military agreement with the Poles, confirming their intentions to render immediate assistance. Although the Poles knew that France had quickly abandoned its ally Czechoslovakia, they wanted to believe Gamelin and Vuillemin. Unfortunately, the French commitment was just a symbolic gesture, with little substance. It was not until August that Général Louis Faury was sent to Warsaw to co-ordinate military operations with the Poles, yet Gamelin never bothered to make any specific plans for military co-operation with the Poles.[62]

Demonstrating just how unimportant Poland was to British strategic planning, the British government sent a delegation headed by a non-entity from the War Office, Colonel Edward Clayton, to hold military talks with the Polish General Staff in Warsaw on 23–30 May.[63] The Poles wanted the British to guarantee that the RAF would bomb targets in Germany in event of war, which the British were surprisingly reluctant to agree upon. Although Bomber Command had developed a plan to bomb the Ruhr, known as WA5, there was great concern that bombing industrial targets in Germany would only provoke the Luftwaffe to bomb similar targets in Britain.[64] Nevertheless, the British delegation simply lied to the Poles, assuring them that Bomber Command would attack targets in Germany if the Luftwaffe unleashed unrestricted bombing upon Poland.[65] Consequently, the Polish General Staff expected both the British and the French to provide tangible military assistance in event of war, even though the Anglo-French were really only paying lip service to this notion. In reality, Poland was on its own.

While the Anglo-French dithered, trying to decide what they could and could not offer Poland, Hitler moved to position Germany for an extended conflict – just in case. On 23 March, Ribbentrop was able to ram an economic treaty down the throats of his Romanian counterparts, which was supposed to guarantee Germany's access to the oil produced in the Ploesti refineries. Yet despite this treaty, Romania continued to supply oil to Great Britain as well, which was not stopped until July 1940.[66] On 10 May, Hitler added an additional section to the OKW directive on *Fall Weiss,* which stipulated that both the Luftwaffe and the Kriegsmarine were to make preparations for economic warfare against Britain and France, particularly merchant shipping.[67] Six days later, the OKH issued an alert to field commanders about the intent to attack Poland. While Hitler may have hoped to keep the conflict limited to Poland, *Fall Weiss* clearly included preparations for a wider war. Hitler wanted Mussolini at his side and on 22 May, Ribbentrop signed the Pact of Steel in Berlin, formalizing military-economic co-operation with Italy. Of course, the pact was primarily a propaganda coup, not a real shift in the European balance of power.[68] Mussolini was quick to privately inform Hitler that Italy would not be ready to participate in a major war prior to 1942 and recommended a protracted 'war of nerves' to wear the Anglo-French down.[69] While Hitler was aware that Italian co-operation and Romanian oil were not a war-winning formula in themselves, he hoped to demonstrate to the Anglo-French that his Third Reich was not without allies and resources of its own. In other words, as Chamberlain sought to restrain Hitler by issuing guarantees to potential victims of German aggression, Hitler sought to deter Britain or France from taking a stance against him by presenting a growing German-led alliance in central Europe. Both sides were unsuccessfully attempting to deter the other.

On 23 May, Hitler met with his key military leaders (Göring, Raeder, Brauchitsch, Keitel and Halder) in his study at the new Reich Chancellery to explain his decision to strike Poland. He stated that due to the parlous state of Germany's economy, a war of external conquest was now essential in order to gain resources. Hitler bluntly stated that:

> ... further successes cannot be attained without the shedding of blood. Poland will always be on the side of our adversaries. In spite of treaties of friendship, Poland has always had the secret intention of exploiting every opportunity to do us harm. Danzig is not the subject of the dispute at all. It is a question of expanding our living space in the East and of securing our food supplies, of the settlement of the Baltic problem. We cannot expect a repetition of the Czech affair. There will be war. Our task is to isolate Poland. The success of the isolation will be decisive. There must be no simultaneous conflict with the Western powers. If it is not certain that a German–Polish conflict will not lead to war in the West, then the fight must be primarily against England and France. Fundamentally therefore: conflict with Poland – beginning with an attack on Poland – will only be successful if the Western Powers keep out of it. If this is impossible, then it will be better to attack in the West and to settle Poland at the same time.[70]

Hitler also made clear to his generals that Germany must be prepared for a long, hard war. He said:

> ... if England intends to intervene in the Polish war, we must occupy Holland with lightning speed. We must aim at securing a new defence

line on Dutch soil up to the Zuider Zee. The war with England and France will be a life-and-death struggle. The idea that we can get off cheaply is dangerous; there is no such possibility. We must burn our boats, and it is no longer a question of justice or injustice, but of life or death for 80 million human beings. Every country's armed forces or government must aim at a short war. The government, however, must also be prepared for a war of 10–15 years' duration.[71]

Nor were Hitler's words about a long war intended as mere rhetoric. On 23 June, Göring convened a meeting of the Reich Defence Council to co-ordinate the total mobilization of German manpower and resources for the coming war. Some 35 senior military and civil leaders attended the meeting, including Reichsführer-SS Heinrich Himmler. Göring announced that Hitler had decided to draft seven million men into the armed services. Therefore, the resulting labour shortage was to be made up by forced labour, including Czechs and inmates from concentration camps. Later, the Council met to discuss speeding up efforts to complete the West Wall fortifications in order to be ready in case of a French offensive in the West.[72]

Although Hitler had set Germany on a collision course with Poland and its Anglo-French allies, he seemed to take little notice of the impending crisis in June–July 1939. During this period, he spent weeks at his Obersalzberg retreat, entertaining visitors and essentially taking an extended summer holiday.[73] Hitler also had plenty of time to visit art and theatre exhibits, and attend music festivals. He spent his nights watching films and watching the Northern Lights from his mountain retreat. Albert Speer, his architect, said that he looked nervous in this period, but Hitler boasted that 'something enormously important would happen soon.'[74]

While Hitler enjoyed his idle time at the Obersalzberg, the OKH staff laboured to perfect the *Fall Weiss* plan at the General Staff headquarters in Zossen, 30km south of Berlin. The overall concept was similar to *Fall Grün*: a massive, simultaneous pincer attack from north and south that would result in the rapid capture of Warsaw. Generaloberst Fedor von Bock was selected to lead the northern pincer with Heeresgruppe Nord attacking from East Prussia with the 3. Armee and with the 4. Armee from Pomerania. Before mobilization, Bock's command was designated as Heeresgruppenkommando 1. The 63-year-old Generaloberst Gerd von Rundstedt, who had retired after the Munich Crisis, was selected to lead the southern pincer. Once mobilization occurred, Rundstedt would be in charge of the German main effort, Heeresgruppe Süd, which would attack from Silesia, Bohemia and Slovakia with the 8., 10. and 14. Armeen. However, during the summer of 1939, Rundstedt only had a small, but high-quality planning staff (Arbeitsstab Rundstedt) consisting of Generalleutnant Erich von Manstein and Oberst Günther Blumentritt.[75] Given the tight security surrounding the preparations for *Fall Weiss,* the OKH did not wish to alert the Poles by creating large army group headquarters prior to mobilization. The Oberkommando der Luftwaffe (Air Force High Command or OKL) was also involved in planning its role in *Fall Weiss* and the Luftwaffe would support the offensive with two air fleets, Luftflotte 1 and Luftflotte 4. The rest of the Wehrmacht would remain on guard in the West, to defend the West Wall. Brauchitsch and the OKH staff were not overly concerned about Polish defensive capabilities, but their main concern was how the Anglo-French would react in the west and the Soviets in the east.

Meanwhile, Hitler's propaganda minister Josef Goebbels was busy orchestrating the campaign to make Poland look vile and guilty of crimes against ethnic Germans in the border regions. On 17 June, Goebbels went to Danzig and delivered a threatening speech before a crowd of thousands, stating that 'Danzig is a German city' and its return to the Reich was inevitable. He also warned that any power that tried to block the return of Danzig was making a mistake. Forster had already begun building up a significant military force in Danzig to supplement the Schutzpolizei. Reichsführer-SS Heinrich Himmler helped Forster to organize a local SS unit designated as the SS-Heimwehr Danzig, a supposed militia force. In order to provide a trained cadre for this unit, Himmler sent a reinforced battalion (III./SS-Regiment 4) under SS-Obersturmbannführer Hans-Friedemann Götze; these personnel arrived in civilian clothes and were ostensibly in Danzig for a sports competition. The Wehrmacht covertly supplied the SS-Heimwehr Danzig with light artillery and armoured cars from stockpiles in East Prussia. The SA formed a border protection unit, Verstärkter Grenzaufsichtsdienst (VGAD), which began building barbed wire and anti-tank obstacles around the city. Augmented with these additional troops, Forster and Greiser did their best to escalate tensions with Poland in order to set the stage for a major incident. Already, the Danzig SA were harassing Polish frontier guards and intimidating customs officials, but the incidents became increasingly violent. On 20 July, a Polish border guard, Witold Budziewicz, was shot dead by SA troops during an incident. Marian Chodacki, the Polish Commissioner-General, lodged protest after protest about the violence with both the League officials and the Danzig senate, which were ignored. He also reported the growing SA/SS presence in the city to the British, who did nothing. In response, the Polish border guards were armed, and on 25 August SA-Rottenführer Joseph Wessel was killed in another border incident.

Goebbels used the Nazi-controlled media to depict the Poles as brutal thugs and claimed that 'thousands [of ethnic Germans] had fled Polish violence for refuge in the Reich.' Of course, Goebbels made no mention that the SS had been reaching out to ethnic Germans living in Poland – just as they had in Austria and the Sudetenland – in order to organize paramilitary units useful for sabotage and black propaganda activities (i.e. attacks on ethnic Germans that could be blamed on the Poles). By the summer of 1939, covert *Volksdeutscher Selbstschutz* (self-defence units) had been formed in a number of locales and were prepared to assist the Wehrmacht once it crossed the Polish border. Selbstschutz personnel also engaged in intelligence activities (i.e. espionage), reporting details of Polish border defences to the Abwehr in Berlin. Although only a small percentage of ethnic Germans in Poland were involved in these covert pro-Nazi activities, it was enough to create the impression among Poles that no Germans could be trusted.[76]

Marszałek Rydz-Śmigły made it clear on 17 July that Poland would not give up its rights in Danzig without a fight. He stated that:

If Germany persists in her plans for Anschluss, Poland will fight, even if she fights alone and without allies. The whole nation, to the last man and woman is ready to fight for Poland's independence, for when we say we shall go to war over Danzig we shall be fighting for our independence. Danzig is necessary for Poland. Who controls Danzig controls our economic life. The taking of Danzig by the Germans would be an act which recalls to our minds the partition of Poland. In case of war every man and every woman of whatever age would be a soldier of Poland.[77]

Although committed to fight if necessary, Rydz-Śmigły was uncertain how best to deploy his limited forces. Military logic clearly pointed to making a stand behind the Vistula River as the best option, but that would mean abandoning a large portion of the Polish population without a fight. Cities like Poznań, with a population of 269,000, could not just be abandoned to the enemy, lest it encourage 'salami tactics' (slicing off undefended border regions then stopping to negotiate). Consequently,

Army Poznań, with four infantry divisions and two cavalry brigades, was left exposed in vulnerable positions along the German–Polish border. Likewise, Army Pomorze was awkwardly deployed, in order to deter a German *coup de main* against Danzig or Pomerania. Rydz-Śmigły was also concerned that the German move into Slovakia threatened to outflank the existing Polish border defences around Kraków and might enable a rapid thrust through the Dukla Pass into Galicia, which could overrun the vital Central Industrial Region (COP). In order to mitigate this potential threat, on 11 July Rydz-Śmigły authorized the formation of the Karpaty Army to cover the nearly 200km-wide sector in the Carpathian mountain region. It was not much of an army, comprised of just two mountain brigades, a separate infantry regiment and a KOP regiment; altogether barely 10,000 troops plus some additional reservists after general mobilization.[78] In reality, the Karpaty Army was little more than a screening force and its threadbare composition reveals the extent to which Polish military resources were stretched thin in 1939. On the other hand, one of the Polish Army's best units – the 1st Legions Infantry Division (1 DPL) – was left stationed in distant Vilnius right up to the outbreak of war, in order to deter any Lithuanian attempt to reclaim the city.

As part of general preparations, Polish troops began to create fieldworks in early July. Pułkownik Stanisław Sosabowski, commander of the 21st Infantry Regiment (21 PP), wrote that:

> … we managed to scrape together enough cement to build a few pillboxes for machine guns or observation posts at intervals along the dirt trenches. Earthworks were being built all over the country, not only by the troops, but also by civilian volunteers. Every hamlet, every village prepared to defend itself. Even schoolchildren turned out to help erect air-raid shelters.[79]

The Polish 20 DP built a particularly strong defensive position at Mława, 100km north of Warsaw.

General Sir Edmund Ironside was sent to Warsaw for discussions with Rydz-Śmigły during 17–21 July. The fact that Ironside held no substantive position in the British Army at the moment and that he arrived in civilian mufti did not escape the Poles. Furthermore, Ironside's innate obtuseness (his public taunt to Hitler in early 1940 to 'bring it on' is a model of military idiocy) hardly inspired confidence in the Poles and the British Cabinet did not even bother to read his trip report.[80] While the British Cabinet and its military advisors should have been focused on developing concrete plans to assist Poland, Lord Fairfax instead allowed the government to be distracted for weeks by an incident with Japan in China. Due to British financial support to the Chinese Nationalists, the Japanese Army decided to blockade the British concession at Tientsin on 14 June. Chamberlain and Fairfax redirected military planning to examine deterrent options against Japan, such as deploying a large portion of the Home Fleet to Singapore. After nearly two weeks of pointless discussion, the Cabinet finally realized that weakening the Royal Navy in European waters would only encourage Hitler to commit aggression, so the idea was dropped. Instead, Britain gave in to some Japanese demands and suffered some loss of face in return for stabilizing the situation. However, weeks of valuable time had been squandered, with nothing to show for it.[81]

Shortly after Ironside's visit, a group of senior British and French intelligence officers travelled to Warsaw to meet with members of the Polish Cipher Bureau. At this meeting on 24–25 July, the Polish General Staff revealed to their incredulous allies that they had broken into the German Enigma encoding system. Furthermore, they provided a replica of the Enigma machine to both the British and French delegations.[82] This was not an immediate 'win' for the Allies because new German countermeasures had rendered the Polish approach progressively obsolete, but it did provide the British codebreakers with a valuable jumpstart that would begin to provide dividends within a year. Meanwhile, Polish diplomats could not even secure a decent military loan from Britain.

As British diplomats listened to Hitler's increasingly strident tone about Danzig, they adopted the same attitude that they had in the lead-up to the Munich Crisis: that the threatened nation (Poland) should negotiate a settlement that essentially gave the aggressor what they wanted before an incident led to conflict. In essence, the British government recognized Danzig as a *de facto* German city and did not believe the League mandate was worth starting a war over. From the British point of view, the loss of Danzig would not seriously compromise Polish sovereignty and a negotiated settlement might defuse the entire crisis. Of course, the negotiated settlement approach did not appear viable to the Poles, who saw how Hitler had quickly violated the Munich agreement to dismember the Czech state. From the Polish perspective, the loss of Danzig would inevitably lead to the loss of the Polish Corridor, which would embolden Hitler to demand more border territories. Thus, as the Danzig Crisis unfolded in the summer of 1939, the British and Poles did not share common ground, with one side focused on conflict resolution (at no cost to itself) while the other was trying to prevent any steps that would compromise its 1921 borders. Poles regarded the Danzig Crisis as the natural result of the Locarno Treaty, which conditioned Anglo-French leaders to look at Poland's borders as less sacrosanct than their own. The British and French also kept pushing the Poles to accept Soviet military guarantees, while giving short shrift to Polish fears that Stalin could not be trusted any more than Hitler.

Had the Anglo-French leadership actually been serious about helping Poland deter German aggression, they did have the resources to make an impression on Hitler. It is important to remember that the crisis dragged on for nearly eight months, unlike the short time line witnessed in earlier international crises. First, prompt financial credits, followed by prompt delivery of at least small amounts of military equipment (such as the promised squadron of Hurricane fighters) would have demonstrated that the Anglo-French security guarantee was not mere rhetoric. Second, both the British and French could have dispatched a small but powerful joint naval squadron to Danzig along with a couple battalions of marines, as a demonstration of support for the embattled League commissioner. Why was Lord Fairfax willing to consider sending a Royal Navy squadron 15,000km to Singapore to deter the Japanese, but unwilling to send one 2,000km to Danzig to deter Hitler? Third, the Royal Air Force's Bomber Command could have publicly announced joint bombing exercises with the French Armée de l'air (Air Force) at bases near the Franco-German border, which would put heavy bombers near the Ruhr as further deterrent. Of course, there is no guarantee that any such military steps would have deterred Hitler and prevented or delayed *Fall Weiss*. However, the failure to take any material steps to aid Poland clearly left that country hanging out on a limb and encouraged Hitler to seek a violent solution.

The Pieces Fall into Place, August 1939

'Well, Ribbentrop, what do you want? The Corridor or Danzig?'
'Not that any more. We want war!'
Ribbentrop replying to Italian Foreign Minister Ciano, 11 August 1939[83]

Since the Munich agreement, Stalin had been patiently watching the Danzig situation building up, waiting for the moment where he could act to gain maximum advantage for the Soviet Union. To Stalin, the Munich agreement signalled the start of a period of lawless land-grabbing in eastern

Europe and he wanted his share of the spoils. The Anglo-French had been hoping to entice Stalin into a military agreement to contain Germany, but reports from the Soviet spy network within Britain indicated a lack of commitment to the project. Soviet intelligence was also fairly accurate about German intentions; Stalin was informed that a German attack upon Poland could occur as soon as 25 August. After much foot-dragging, the Anglo-French delegation headed by Vice-Admiral Reginald Drax finally arrived in Moscow on 11 August. Once the Soviets discovered the Anglo-French delegation did not even have the authority to negotiate a military treaty, Stalin brusquely decided to turn to the Germans for a deal.[84] Even had Vice-Admiral Drax been empowered to negotiate, Stalin could not get what he wanted from the Anglo-French: a free hand in eastern Europe. Like Hitler, Stalin had a great hunger for other people's land and he wanted to radically alter territorial boundaries in Europe, not protect them. He certainly had no wish to help protect Poland's borders. On 12 August, Stalin authorized his foreign minister Vyacheslav Molotov to begin negotiations with the Germans.

While continuing pointless talks with the Drax mission in Moscow, the Soviets began negotiations in earnest with Ribbentrop's Foreign Ministry. Despite Hitler's frequent statements about limiting the up-coming conflict to Poland, there was widespread angst within the senior military Wehrmacht leadership that an Anglo-French blockade could cripple Germany's economy at the outset of a war. However, an economic treaty with the Soviet Union – in return for German recognition of Soviet spheres of influence in the Baltic States and Finland – could neutralize the threat of an Allied blockade. Despite the large and hostile ideological divide between the Nazi and communist regimes, they could find common ground when it came to carving out spheres of influence. Once German and Soviet diplomats agreed on the broad areas of mutual interest, negotiations moved rapidly towards a settlement; on 20 August, the German–Soviet Credit Agreement was signed. Under the terms of this agreement, the Soviet Union would supply Germany with critical raw materials, while Germany extended a credit of RM 200 million ($80 million) to the USSR to purchase industrial equipment.[85] The next day, the Soviets broke off negotiations with the Drax mission and moved to expand upon the trade agreement with Germany.

Hitler was of course eager to sign a treaty with the Soviet Union and he sent a personal telegram to Stalin, asking him to receive Ribbentrop in Moscow. When Stalin agreed to accept Ribbentrop at once, Hitler was ecstatic, shouting, 'I have them! I have them!' Ribbentrop arrived in Moscow on the afternoon of 23 August and in a whirlwind of diplomatic discussions, hammered out a treaty with Molotov in less than 18 hours. The key point, only mentioned in the secret protocol, was a recognition of spheres of influence: Germany would get west and central Poland, while the Soviet Union would get eastern Poland. In addition, Germany accepted that Finland, the three Baltic States and Bessarabia fell within the Soviet sphere. Once the main points were agreed, Stalin entered to join the post-negotiation festivities and told Ribbentrop that 'in the event of military conflict between Germany and the Western democracies, the interests of the Soviet Union and German coincide completely.'[86] On 24 August, Germany announced the signing of the non-aggression pact with the Soviet Union, which would last for ten years. However, beyond the obvious improvement in German–Soviet relations, few specifics about the treaty were publicly discussed.

In reality, the German–Soviet non-aggression pact was the critical piece that now made war with Poland inevitable. As a result of the treaty, Hitler no longer had to worry about Anglo-French economic reprisals against Germany or the possibility of a two-front war. Even in the event that the Allies decided to declare war on Germany, Stalin had pointedly said to Ribbentrop that 'the Soviet Union shall never tolerate letting Germany fall into difficult straits.'[87] From Hitler's viewpoint, this was a heady affirmation that he had pulled off a game-changing coup and that the Anglo-French could no longer block his territorial ambitions. From Stalin's viewpoint, for the temporary price of providing economic and morale support to Germany's war effort, he could contribute to reducing Anglo-French influence in Europe and recover pieces of the old tsarist-era empire in eastern Europe. In retrospect, the Molotov–Ribbentrop Pact was the greatest criminal conspiracy of the 20th century, which is why it is still highly controversial. Soviet historians denied the existence of the secret protocol for decades, but then, as part of *Glasnost*, released a copy of it in 1992. However, *Glasnost* did not last and the current Putin regime has returned to denying that the Soviet Union collaborated with Nazi Germany in carving up Poland in 1939 or that the secret pact acknowledged spheres of influence. According to the 21st-century Russian version of the Molotov–Ribbentrop non-aggression pact, Poland was to blame for its fate because it first annexed the Teschen region from Czechoslovakia, then refused to allow Soviet troops onto its soil to prevent German aggression.[88]

While the diplomats were lining up the teams for the main event, the Wehrmacht was preparing for combat. On the morning of 15 August, the Luftwaffe arranged a demonstration for its senior commanders (generals Hugo Sperrle, Bruno Loerzer and Wolfram von Richthofen) of its latest dive-bombing tactics at the training range of Neuhammer, in Silesia. Two groups of Ju 87 Stukas, I./StG 76 and I./StG 2, were supposed to demonstrate high-angle attacks for the waiting dignitaries. However, a dense blanket of early morning ground fog, combined with low cloud cover over the target, precipitated an aerial disaster. The Stukas dove through the clouds, expecting clear sky with at least 900m clearance above ground, but in fact there was none. Thirteen Ju 87 Stukas plunged into the ground and exploded, killing a total of 26 aircrew. Hitler decided to keep the Neuhammer disaster secret, lest it harm morale in the Wehrmacht on the eve of *Fall Weiss*.

As part of the build-up for *Fall Weiss,* the Germans began to deploy units towards the German-Polish border regions, beginning in late June and continuing through July. The deployments were done in a gradual manner, in part to avoid detection and in part to avoid putting too much stress on peacetime *Reichsbahn* (railroad) services. The most difficult area to assemble forces was in East Prussia, since personnel and equipment could only arrive by sea. When Hitler came to power, Wehrkreis I (Military District I) only had a single infantry division and some assorted cavalry units. In 1935, two more infantry divisions were formed in East Prussia, followed by a cavalry brigade in 1937. However, even these three divisions were barely adequate to defend East Prussia and Hitler was concerned that Poland might launch a pre-emptive strike if it felt threatened. In July 1939, the 12. Infanterie-Division was transferred by sea to East Prussia, followed by Panzer-Regiment 7 and the SS-Regiment 'Deutschland' in early August. The tanks and crewmen of Panzer-Regiment 7 had been loaded at Hamburg and landed at Königsberg on 3 August. The OKH decided to form an experimental mixed Heer/Waffen-SS mobile unit and put Generalmajor Werner Kempf in charge of it, so it became Panzer-Division Kempf. On 8 August, Kempf's unique formation conducted field exercises south-west of Königsberg – the first time that the Heer and Waffen-SS ever trained together. Since the Germans could not completely conceal the fact that they had shipped over 160 tanks into East Prussia, they falsely claimed that the units were intended to participate in 25th anniversary ceremonies for the battle of Tannenberg. Between 8 and 16 August, two reserve infantry divisions began mobilizing in East

Prussia. Altogether, these units were formed into the 3. Armee, which now had the strength to assist with the seizure of the Polish Corridor and attack south towards Warsaw.

Since the Danzig Crisis began heating up in May, Hitler had been concerned that the Poles might make a pre-emptive move against Danzig to seize the city. He had serious doubts that Forster and his hodgepodge of SA, SS and police units would be militarily effective. Thus, Hitler directed the OKH to covertly send some professional officers to take charge of the paramilitary forces in Danzig and organize them into an effective combat force. Halder selected Generalmajor Georg Friedrich-Eberhardt, a reliable, veteran regular army officer, to command the military forces in Danzig. In addition, two veteran battalion commanders, Oberst Gunther Knappe and Oberst Karl-Albrecht von Groddeck, were sent to assist Eberhardt. Soon, they were followed by an assortment of junior officers and NCOs to assist with training and preparing the Danzig forces for combat. In order to conceal the creation of a quasi-Wehrmacht unit within Danzig, all the seconded personnel wore police uniforms until the outbreak of war. Eberhardt organized the six available Danzig police battalions into two regiments, which would be commanded by Knappe and Groddeck. Additional troops were provided by the SA's VGAD. Throughout the summer months, Wehrmacht personnel arrived in Danzig by sea – at night and in civilian clothes – to fill out the ranks of Brigade Eberhardt. Wehrmacht units stationed in East Prussia also covertly provided Eberhardt with medium artillery and additional automatic weapons. The creation of Brigade Eberhardt in Danzig was a gross violation of the terms of the League of Nations – but it went unnoticed by both the Polish and the Anglo-French intelligence services.

Another group of soldiers preparing for *Fall Weiss* was even more secretive. The Abwehr had formed an infiltration unit known as the Kampfverband Ebbinghaus. The unit was commanded by Hauptmann Theodore von Hippel, a veteran of the campaign in German East Africa in 1914–16 who had acquired a taste for unconventional combat. For *Fall Weiss,* Hippel recruited Polish-speaking Germans from Silesia and formed them into small teams, intended to capture key rail junctions or bridges ahead of the Wehrmacht's advance guard units. The infiltrators, known as *K-Truppen,* were armed but typically either wore Polish uniforms or civilian clothes. Some in fact were civilian volunteers. Hippel's men would be the first to cross the Polish border. During the summer of 1939, the Abwehr had also funded the creation of a battalion-size unit of Ukrainian nationalists from the Organization of Ukrainian Nationalists (OUN), under the command of Colonel Roman Sushko. Members of the Ukrainian Legion wore German uniforms, but the unit was intended to operate as a diversionary force in eastern Poland. Admiral Wilhelm Canaris, head of the Abwehr and a future leader of the anti-Hitler resistance, noted in his diary that the Ukrainian Legion could help instigate an uprising 'which would aim at the annihilation of the Jews and the Poles.'[89] However, the signing of the Molotov–Ribbentrop Pact put Ukrainian nationalist aspirations on the back burner and the Ukrainian Legion was simply attached to the 14. Armee as an auxiliary unit.

On 16–17 August, the OKH mobilized the ready reserves (2. Welle), which added three infantry divisions to the 26 already committed to *Fall Weiss*. On 26 August, additional reservists and Landwehr were mobilized (3. Welle), forming seven more infantry divisions. Altogether, 386,000 Army and 55,000 Luftwaffe reservists were mobilized for active duty in mid-August; they were told that they would be involved in annual summer manoeuvres.[90] The 2. and 3. Wellen divisions had no 5cm or 8cm mortars, no 15cm infantry guns and 11 per cent fewer machine guns than a 1. Welle division.[91] Interestingly, nine of the ten newly mobilized divisions were assigned to Bock's Heeresgruppe Nord, only one to Rundstedt's Heeresgruppe Süd. Bock was not happy with some of these new units, noting that in the 50. Infanterie-Division, 10 per cent of its troops were untrained and many of its reservists were 'very old.'[92] Bock did have nine 1. Welle divisions, but half his infantry was comprised of partly equipped reservists. In contrast, Rundstedt had the pick of the active army forces, with 17 of the 35 1. Welle divisions under his command; these units were the best equipped and trained in the Heer. Civilian resources were also mobilized to outfit the newly mobilized reserve divisions, including 200,000 vehicles and 400,000 horses – which was difficult to conceal.[93]

The OKW also had to assemble the logistics for a large invasion force without alerting the Poles – or their own troops – that war was imminent. Most of the units involved in *Fall Weiss* were provided with four basic loads of ammunition, although the 3. Armee in East Prussia was given six loads. For example, each 10.5cm howitzer would be allocated 1,200 rounds of ammunition, but only one load (300 rounds) would actually be held at the unit level; the remainder would be stored in forward ammunition depots. The OKH was extremely generous in its fuel planning, allotting units up to seven and a half VS (*Verbrauchssatz*) of fuel, instead of the normal four VS. One VS was the amount of fuel required to move each vehicle in a given division 100km, although the actual amount of fuel varied based on the type of unit. For a 1939-era Panzer-Division, one VS would equal about 100 cbm (m^3) or 74 tonnes of fuel. A division could carry a reserve of around 1 VS in its logistic columns, but the rest had to be transported from army-level fuel lagers. Rundstedt's army group was also provided an additional 1,500 tonnes of fuel, to be held as an emergency resupply on trucks, assembled near Breslau.[94] Furthermore, the Wehrmacht used multiple types of fuel which complicated logistics in the field; the Heer had two different types of petrol (Vergaser I and Vergaser II) and diesel, while the Luftwaffe needed both petrol and diesel for its ground vehicles and aviation fuel for its aircraft.[95] In terms of victuals, the OKH provided a ten-day ration for each soldier and each horse, although some of this was consumed in the final days of peace as units waited in assembly areas.

At noon on 22 August, Hitler had called a conference at the Obersalzberg for the senior commanders involved in *Fall Weiss*. He set dawn on 26 August as Y-day, for the invasion to begin. During the conference, Hitler stated that one of his reasons for seeking a military solution in Poland was to 'test the tools' prior to the showdown with the Anglo-French.[96] He needed to know that his new weapons could deliver results. Even though he referred to Chamberlain and Daladier as 'worms', it was also clear from the tasks he assigned the OKH that he expected some kind of countermove by the Anglo-French. Hitler was particularly emphatic that the invasion of Poland would be conducted with great brutality and violence. He told them, 'when starting and waging a war, it is not right that matters, but victory. Close your hearts to pity. Act brutally. Eighty million people must obtain what is their right.'[97] Many of the assembled officers warmly received Hitler's guidance and Bock wrote in his diary that the Führer's speech was 'terrific'.[98] On the other hand, other officers were worried that their commands were not yet ready for a full-scale war. Oberst Wilhelm Speidel, chief of staff of Luftflotte 1, recorded that 'I left the Fuhrer's meeting in unmistakable dismay.'[99]

Anticipating that *Fall Weiss* could lead to war with Britain, Großadmiral Raeder had already begun deploying his operational warships on 19 August. The pocket-battleship *Admiral Graf Spee* and her supply ship *Altmark* were the first to sail, followed by the pocket-battleship *Deutschland* and her supply ship *Westerwald* on the night of 23 August. Between 19 and 23 August, 34 of the Kriegsmarine's 57 U-Boats went to sea, including 16 to the Atlantic.[100] Those vessels deployed to the Atlantic, including both pocket-battleships, were told to await the signal to commence operations in the event of war with Britain. The Kriegsmarine deployment was unprecedented and had not occurred during the Munich Crisis of 1938, but it fell in line with his amendment to *Fall Weiss* to prepare for economic warfare against Britain. Furthermore, the deployment weakens the oft-repeated assertion that Hitler did not expect hostilities with the Anglo-French; at the very least, he wanted to be prepared to initiate anti-commerce attacks upon the instant of a British declaration of war. The rest of the Kriegsmarine conducted intensive training operations in the Baltic in preparation for war. Before dawn on 27 August, the Kriegsmarine suffered its own tragedy when the destroyer *Max Schultz* rammed and sank the torpedo boat *Tiger* during a refuelling exercise; two sailors were killed and six badly injured.[101]

One of the most important actions taken by the Kriegsmarine in the lead-up to war was the dispatch of the pre-dreadnought *Schleswig-Holstein* to Danzig on 21 August. Kapitän zur See Gustav Kleikamp, commander of the *Schleswig-Holstein,* was read into *Fall Weiss* by Großadmiral Raeder prior to sailing and informed of the key role that his vessel would play on the opening day of *Fall Weiss* – it would reduce the Polish garrison on Westerplatte. Although the *Schleswig-Holstein* was an elderly vessel, used primarily for cadet training, Raeder believed that the ship's four 28cm guns would prove useful for shore bombardment. Raeder may have thought that the appearance of an older warship in Danzig – unlike the Kriegsmarine's deployment of its newest warships to occupy Memel – might seem less threatening. En route to Danzig, Kleikamp conducted a night rendezvous with a German minesweeper in the Baltic on 24 August in order to pick up Oberleutnant Wilhelm Henningsen's 225-man naval assault detachment (*Marinestosstruppkompanie* or MSK).[102] Henningsen was not told that his unit would participate in an assault and was not fully equipped for combat; his mortar crews had not brought ammunition and his men had only been issued practice grenades. On the morning of 25 August, the *Schleswig-Holstein* sailed into Danzig and anchored near Westerplatte, with Henningsen's assault troops hidden below decks and out of sight. The idea of conducting a normal port visit into a city that was at the centre of a major international crisis appeared odd, but the Germans claimed that the visit was to pay homage to the sailors of the cruiser *Magdeburg*, lost in August 1914, who were buried in Danzig. On the day before the battleship arrived, the Nazi-controlled senate in Danzig declared *de facto* independence with Forster as head of the city. He immediately ordered his SA thugs to arrest senior Polish customs officials in hope of sparking an incident.[103] Once in Danzig, Kleikamp allowed normal courtesy visits – including the Polish commissioner in Danzig, Marian Chodacki – probably to add to the deception that this was a normal port call.

In Germany, the population was apprehensive about the possibility of war but most felt that Hitler would somehow pull off another bloodless Munich-style coup. News of the Molotov–Ribbentrop Pact was well received by the German populace, who saw this as a way out of the crisis – not as the spark that would ignite war. William L. Shirer, an American correspondent in Berlin, noticed that by late August the German media was putting out the most absurd claims – such as 'three German passenger planes had been fired upon by the Poles' and that 'in the corridor many German farms were in flames' – and these claims were being accepted at face value by the average German.[104] Many German civilians, bombarded by Goebbels' media, actually thought it was necessary for the Führer to respond in kind to the Poles, who were generally held in low regard.[105] On 24 August, the reality of the situation was brought home to the German people when rationing of food, coal, textiles and soap was announced.

In Poland, it was obvious that diplomacy had reached an end when the Germans recalled their ambassador from Warsaw on 10 August. The Ministry of Military Affairs decided to order an additional, quiet mobilization of the 13th and 27th Infantry Divisions (13 and 27 DP) from the DOK II (Lublin) on 13 August. These units were sent west by rail on 16–18 August, arriving near Bydgoszcz. Recognizing that the Germans were likely to attempt a coup against Danzig, the Polish Ministry of Military Affairs had decided to form an Intervention Corps (Korpus Interwencyjny) to pre-empt any such effort. Generał Brygady Stanisław Skwarczyński was put in charge of the corps and assigned the 13 and 27 DP, as well as the 1st Light Tank Battalion (1 BCL) and a few other support units. By 25 August, the units of the corps were deployed within 40km south of Danzig and Skwarczyński was ordered to be prepared to mount a hasty attack to seize the city if Forster's SA troops conducted further provocations. Of course, the Poles did not inform the Anglo-French that they were planning a pre-emptive strike against Danzig. According to Halder's diary, the OKH was alerted by Hungarian sources that the Poles were about to march into Danzig.[106]

Although the Ministry of Military Affairs was mobilizing combat units, it did a poor job ensuring that these units would be supplied with ammunition, food and fuel. Prior to the outbreak of war, Polish armies delegated most of their logistic support requirements to their local Corps

District Command (DOK). For example, Generał Brygady Aleksandr Narbut-Łuczyński was dual-hatted as the commander of DOK V and the commander of Army Kraków's logistic support command. The military districts normally supplied local units with peacetime requirements for training but did not stockpile large amounts of ammunition and other supplies unless directed by the High Command. Narbut-Łuczyński only began working on meeting Army Kraków's wartime requirements two weeks prior to hostilities and lacked the personnel (mostly reservists), vehicles (often requisitioned civilian vehicles) and infrastructure to accomplish much prior to general mobilization.[107] Nor was adequate logistic planning conducted prior to the war. Consequently, most Polish combat units would go to war with only a few days' worth of ammunition, fuel and food.[108] The bulk of supplies were still in a few large depots, which were vulnerable to bombing.

Somehow, Polish intelligence failed to fully appreciate the scale of the German military build-up on the border. Unlike the Wehrmacht, which benefited from covert aerial reconnaissance and espionage provided by ethnic Germans in Poland, the Polish intelligence services (Oddział II) had little solid information about what was going on across the border.[109] The intelligence officers in Oddział II knew that there was much activity across the border, but was it the assembly of an invasion force or merely intended to intimidate the Poles? On the evening of 22 August, Generał Brygady Wacław Stachiewicz, chief of the Polish General Staff, had a six-hour meeting with Rydz-Śmigły in which he pleaded for more troops to be mobilized. At this point, only nine of the 30 Polish active infantry divisions were fully mobilized. Rydz-Śmigły agreed to further mobilizations in stages, in an effort not to antagonize either the Anglo-French or the Germans. On 24 August, Rydz-Śmigły ordered a silent emergency mobilization. Instead of a public announcement, reservists were notified by colour-coded cards which ordered them to report. Under this mobilization order, four more cavalry brigades and 20 active infantry divisions were mobilized. The mobilization process went better for some units than others, particularly the cavalry units, which were always maintained at a higher state of readiness. For example, Pułkownik Stanisław Królicki's 7th Wielkopolska ('Greater Poland') Mounted Rifles Regiment, was stationed in the village of Biedrusko, 15km north of Poznań when it received its mobilization order at 0500 hours on 24 August. Like most cavalry units, the regiment was part of the 'yellow' contingent, intended to strengthen the covering forces on the border. It took 36 hours for the regiment to achieve full combat readiness, with about 80 per cent of its personnel. As the rest of the reservists arrived on the second day, the regiment reached 100 per cent of its authorized strength within 48 hours. In other less fortunate units, reserve personnel arrived at their mobilization stations and found there were insufficient weapons, uniforms or other material to fully equip the unit. Many reservists were surprised to see the new wz. 35 UR anti-tank rifle – a heretofore secret weapon which was only revealed to the troops at mobilization. Transport shortages also posed serious problems for Polish mobilization. The LW completed its mobilization during this period, with nearly 16,000 aviation personnel at their duty stations.

Unlike Germany, which could afford to exempt many older reservists, Poland was forced to mobilize virtually all its able-bodied males. Teachers, intellectuals, lawyers, doctors, members of the Warsaw symphony orchestra and bankers were among those mobilized. One of the thousands of Poles mobilized was Władysław Sebyła, a 37-year-old poet who worked for Radio Warsaw. Sebyła was commissioned in 1928 and after completing his military service, returned to civilian life. He kept up with his reserve training during the 1930s and was mobilized as a platoon leader in the 13 PP (8 DP) in 1939. Sebyła would be captured the Soviets and executed by the NKVD at Katyń Forest in 1940.

In Polish cities, schools were closed and citizens began to tape up their windows in case of air raids. The Polish government began issuing gas masks and requisitioned many civilian motor vehicles and horses to support the army's mobilization. Despite the threat of war, the mood was fairly upbeat in Warsaw, with many expecting the crisis to be averted at the last minute. Temporarily at least, this attitude proved correct because Hitler got cold feet as Y-Day approached. A last-minute attempt was made by Hitler, through the pro-appeasement British ambassador in Berlin, Sir Nevile Henderson, to split the British and Poles by offering negotiations, but the signing of the Anglo-Polish military alliance negated this attempt. The French ambassador also indicated that his country was willing to fight with Poland. Consequently, Hitler realized that Poland would have allies, whereas it was not clear if he would. Shortly thereafter, Hitler received a response from Mussolini, indicating that Italy would not be able to participate in a war against the Anglo-French unless it received massive material assistance from Germany.[110] Although Italian participation was essentially irrelevant to *Fall Weiss*, Hitler seized upon this disappointment as an excuse to postpone the operation at 1930 hours. In reality, Hitler was shocked by the realization that he was going to have to fight the Anglo-French as soon as Poland was crushed. Most German units were already in their attack positions on the border and it took some quick communications by the OKW staff to ensure that all aborted their attacks. General der Artillerie Walter von Reichenau, commander of the 10.Armee, had gone forwards to the border and was out of communication for several hours that evening; his army only received the abort order near midnight. However, in any complex military operation, there is always someone who does not get the word.

Hippel's infiltrators from Kampfverband Ebbinghaus had already begun crossing the Polish border and they were not in radio contact. One 30-man detachment of K-Truppen under Leutnant Hans-Albrecht Herzner was assigned to capture the Jablunkova Pass tunnel and the train station in the nearby town of Mosty. Before dawn on 26 August, the infiltrators were detected near the tunnel by troops from the Polish 21st Mountain Division (21 DPG) and fired upon. With no German troops crossing the border and the Poles alerted, the Abwehr troops retreated back across the border. At least two Polish soldiers were killed and probably some of the K-Truppen as well. The Polish division commander, General Józef Kustroń, demanded an explanation for the incident. After some delay, Generalmajor Eugen Ott, commander of the 7. Infanterie-Division, apologized to the Polish general for the regrettable 'incident caused by an insane individual'.[111] This bizarre incident only further demonstrated to the Poles that a German attack was imminent. In East Prussia, a mounted patrol from the Reiter-Regiment 2 crossed the Polish border near Ostroleka and was fired upon; a German non-commissioned officer in the patrol was killed – the first German soldier killed in the Second World War.[112] Another group of German Landespolizei stormed the Polish consulate in Marienwerder in East Prussia and arrested the consul and his staff – a clear act of war – but the Germans succeeded in concealing this fact by severing telephone links.[113]

Interestingly, had the Germans actually attacked on the morning of 26 August, they would have enjoyed a much larger numerical superiority – of the order of 3:1. Furthermore, the Polish Air Force (LW) had not yet dispersed from its peace-time airfields, so it would have been much easier for the Luftwaffe to find and destroy. However, Polish mobilization eventually reduced the German numerical advantage to 2:1 overall by 1 September. On the other hand, Heeresgruppe Süd used the delay to modify its order of battle; under the original plan, the 1. and 4. Panzer-Divisionen were split between the XIV Armeekorps and the XVI Armeekorps. Essentially, the original plan envisioned each Panzer-Division working with two 'leg' infantry divisions, which diluted German mechanized strike power. Under the updated attack plan, both Panzer-Divisionen

DISPOSITION OF POLISH AND GERMAN FORCES,
1 SEPTEMBER 1939

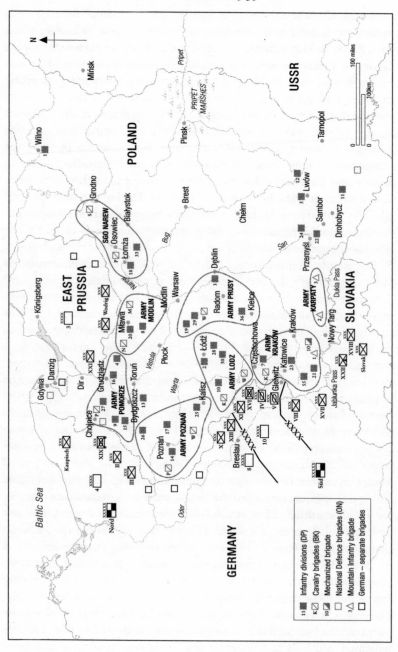

were concentrated in the XVI Armeekorps, providing the 10. Armee with a much more concentrated spearhead formation.[114] The next four days, 27–30 August, consisted of various diplomatic manoeuvres between Germany, Britain and France which amounted to nothing. However, Hitler seemed distracted from *Fall Weiss* by these antics and even briefly discussed limiting any action to just a coup against Danzig. It was clear that the Anglo-French would honour their guarantees to Poland, although he still insisted they would only conduct a sham war. The Poles were invited to conduct further negotiations in Berlin, which they refused, remembering how Hitler had used last-minute negotiations against Austria and Czechoslovakia. Finally, he informed the OKW that Y-Day would occur at 0430 hours on 1 September. During the final days, the Abwehr (military intelligence) began moving more personnel across the border; Major Hermann Baun was sent into Poland to co-ordinate their intelligence-gathering activities.[115]

Meanwhile, after the border provocations and incidents in Danzig, the Poles recognized that an invasion was imminent and tried to accelerate their mobilization efforts. On 27 August, the LW began to disperse all its operational aircraft from their peace-time bases to alternate airfields to avoid being caught by surprise by an enemy air offensive. The process took several days and cost the LW a total of three fighters and four bombers lost in operational accidents. However, by the end of August, the Luftwaffe had lost track of where most LW units were located.[116] The Polish Navy also took steps to preserve its best forces from enemy action with a contingency plan known as Operation *Peking*. Counter-Admiral Józef Unrug, the fleet commander, ordered the bulk of the Destroyer Division to prepare to depart Polish waters for Great Britain. At 1255 hours on 29 August, the destroyers *Grom*, *Blyskawica* and *Burza* sailed from Gdynia for Britain. Two medium-sized freighters, the *Kościuszko* and the *Pulaski*, accompanied the destroyers. The Kriegsmarine detected the Polish warships sailing, but did not interfere. By 31 August, the three destroyers had passed Denmark and reached the Skagerrak, well on their way to Scotland.[117] However, Unrug did not disperse the rest of his fleet. His five submarines were put on alert to conduct Operation *Worek* to defend the Hel Peninsula and Gdynia area against enemy naval forces, but these vessels remained in port until the German attack began. Likewise, Unrug could have begun naval mine laying prior to the onset of hostilities, but he did not. Indeed, many of the Polish warships that remained in the Baltic apparently did not load their wartime munitions until after hostilities had commenced.

When the Polish Army tried to shift to general mobilization, the government encountered vocal resistance from the British and French, who warned that a nation-wide mobilization could spark a war. In order to ensure that the Anglo-French did not abandon their security guarantees, Poland delayed general mobilization for four critical days after the Jablunkova Pass Incident. It was not until 31 August that Poland began general mobilization, openly calling up all its reservists. Furthermore, the Ministry of Military Affairs decided at the last moment to disband Generał Brygady Skwarczyński's Intervention Corps and transfer its units elsewhere; there would be no effort to pre-empt the Germans at Danzig.

At 0630 hours on 31 August, Hitler ordered the OKW to begin deploying all forward units into their attack positions. Six hours later, Führer Directive 1 stated that Hitler had decided on 'a solution by force' and that *Fall Weiss* would begin at 0445 hours the next morning.[118] Halder noted that Hitler accepted the notion that 'armed intervention by the Western Powers was now unavoidable', although this had been obvious for some time.[119] This time, the wheels were turning and there would be no further postponements. As part of an effort to create useful incidents to justify the up-coming German aggression, both the SS and the Abwehr attempted to stage border incidents to make the Poles look guilty. The most notable incident occurred around 2130 hours at the German Gleiwitz radio station in Silesia, where SS-Sturmbannführer Alfred Naujocks staged a mock attack on the facility and left several dead concentration camp inmates, dressed in Polish uniforms. Another six murdered concentration camp inmates, dressed in Polish uniforms, were left at the nearby Hochlinden customs station. These incidents were intended purely for internal German consumption, in order to justify the war to the German population. German K-Truppen and fifth columnists were also active along the Polish–German border during the night of 31 August/1 September. In one incident, a group of Germans attacked the Polish customs outpost at Jeziorki, 76km west of Bydgoszcz, around 0130 hours on 1 September. There was a brief firefight and in it, Kapral Piotr Konieczka from the Border Guards (Straż Graniczna or SG), was shot in the neck and then finished off by having his face smashed in with rifle butts; the mysterious attackers disappeared into the night.[120]

CHAPTER 5

Opening Moves

The Luftwaffe Strikes, 1–6 September

'I had to drop bombs onto a train station in Posen (Poznań) on the second day of the war in Poland. Eight of the 16 bombs fell in the city, right in the middle of houses. I didn't like it. On the third day I didn't care, and on the fourth day I took pleasure in it. We enjoyed heading out before breakfast, chasing individual soldiers through the fields with machine guns and then leaving them there with a few bullets in their backs.'[1]

Leutnant Pohl, bombardier on an He 111, II./KG 26

During the planning for *Fall Weiss*, the Oberkommando der Luftwaffe (OKL) operational staff under Generalmajor Hans Jeschonnek hoped to deliver an aerial knock-out blow against Poland on the first day of hostilities. Jeschonnek recognized that this would be the first time in military history that an independent air force would play more than just a supporting role to any army and he intended that the Luftwaffe would achieve decisive results from the outset. The overall air campaign, designated Operation *Ostmarkflug*, would be conducted by General der Flieger Albert Kesselring's Luftflotte 1 from its bases in Pomerania/East Prussia and by General der Flieger Alexander Löhr's Luftflotte 4 from its bases in Silesia. The massed attack on Warsaw was designated as Operation *Wasserkante*. However, in Operation *Ostmarkflug* the Luftwaffe was trying to accomplish too much, too quickly, with insufficient resources. Although Jeschonnek rightly regarded the destruction of the LW as the top priority, he also tasked the two Luftflotten to simultaneously conduct four other missions:

- destroy the Polish armaments industry
- conduct battlefield interdiction strikes against communication/ transportation hubs
- provide close air support to the army
- attack Polish naval targets and bases

The Luftwaffe had never conducted a co-ordinated, operational-level air campaign on this scale before – nobody had – but the leadership made assumptions that its units could multi-task, conducting both their primary and secondary tasks. This inability to prioritize would remain a consistent operational-level planning deficiency for the Luftwaffe throughout later campaigns, particularly the Battle of Britain in August– September 1940. Instead, the Luftwaffe planners would spread their forces across too many missions and too many targets to achieve the kind of results it desired. Furthermore, Jeschonnek's staff had not anticipated the normal frictions of war, such as marginal weather conditions, aircraft mis-identification and communication issues and the range limitations of their Bf 109s. At the start of *Ostmarkflug*, only a single Bf 109 *Gruppe* (group), Hauptmann Martin Mettig's I./Jagdgruppe (Fighter Group) 21 (I./JG 21) based in East Prussia, was within range of the Polish capital. Given that Göring wanted to conduct mass attacks against Warsaw on the first day, the failure to deploy adequate numbers of the Luftwaffe's best fighter within range suggests a failure to fully think through the requirements for establishing air superiority. The Luftwaffe's inability to appreciate the range limitations of the Bf 109 would also be replicated again over Britain.

The OKL staff also had to struggle with trying to determine how much fuel, ammunition and spare parts it would require to support a campaign involving over 1,800 aircraft. Prior to the start of *Ostmarkflug*, the Luftwaffe quartermasters were able to assemble 400,000 tonnes of aviation fuel, plus about 20,000 tonnes of bombs for the operation. In both categories, this was a large portion of the total available reserves. Air operations in Spain had been tiny in comparison and this would be the first time that the Luftwaffe would have to support an operation on this scale.

Due to Hitler's concern that the Anglo-French might attempt to intervene to interfere with *Fall Weiss,* Göring was obliged to leave substantial forces in the West to protect the Ruhr. Altogether, Luftflotten 2 and 3 possessed over 1,100 operational aircraft, including 444 fighters and 450 bombers. Over half the available Bf 109E fighters were deployed to the West and some of the Luftwaffe's best pilots, including Hauptmann Werner Mölders. Furthermore, many of the units deployed in eastern Germany were only 'loaned' to *Ostmarkflug* for a few days and the OKL began transferring air units to the western theatre well before the end of the campaign. Thus, the threat of Allied action in the west hung like a dark cloud over *Ostmarkflug* for the first ten days of the campaign.

The Polish Air Force (LW) succeeded in dispersing most of its operational aircraft prior to *Ostmarkflug* thanks to the warning provided by the border incidents on 25/26 August. For the most part, only trainers and non-operational aircraft remained at peacetime airbases by the morning of 1 September. However, the LW was not logistically prepared to fight a protracted campaign from its dispersal fields. Generał Brygady Józef L. Zając, commander of the LW, also made the cardinal mistake of dispersing his limited fighter assets in a vain effort to provide at least token air support to the army. Two-thirds of the available Polish fighters were deployed in support of the army. Consequently, the LW's only aerial combat unit with real effectiveness was the Pursuit Brigade, with 53 fighters, assigned to defend the air space over the capital. In contrast, the Polish High Command was uncertain how to use its Bomber Brigade, equipped with the modern P.37b Łos bombers, and this formation would be an under-utilized asset. While the army support squadrons were located close to the border areas and under command of the local army commanders, the fighter and bomber brigades were kept on a tight leash close to Warsaw. The Pursuit Brigade, under Pułkownik Stefan Pawlikowski, moved to the Poniatow and Zielonka airfields north-east of Warsaw with a total of 15 P.11a, 28 P.11c and ten P.7a fighters. The Bomber Brigade, under Pułkownik Władysław Heller, moved to the Podlodów and Ułęż airfields south-east of Warsaw with its 36 bombers.

As a force whose principal mission was defence, the LW established a warning network throughout Poland with over 800 observation posts. Pułkownik Pawlikowski had developed a grid system for Warsaw, which would enable observation posts to alert him by telephone to locations where enemy aircraft were spotted. Warsaw itself had a modest level of air defence, based upon 72 75mm guns (only a few of which were the new 75mm wz. 36), 24 40mm Bofors guns and seven batteries of anti-aircraft machine guns. However, the LW still had very little situational awareness beyond the capital area and had great difficulty bringing its limited strength to bear against intruding enemy aircraft. Perhaps the only real asset that the LW possessed was its pilots; they were available in quantity (about 1.4 pilots per aircraft), well trained and highly motivated to engage the enemy.

As dawn approached on the morning of 1 September (Y-Day), with *Fall Weiss* set to begin at 0445 hours, it quickly became apparent that the weather would be unfavourable for air operations. A low cloud system hung over northern and central Poland, combined with thick ground fog. The visibility was particularly poor over Luftflotte 1's airbases, which meant that only four of its 11 bomber Gruppen were able to take off prior to 0600 hours. One of Luftflotte 1's earliest raids was conducted by 20 He 111 bombers from I./Kampfgeschwader (Bomber Group) 1 (I./KG 1), which attacked the Polish naval air base at Puck around 0600 hours. The Naval Air Division (Morski Dywizjon Lotniczy) under Komandor Porucznik Edward Szystowski consisted of 13 seaplanes, only one of which was of modern design. The German bombers demolished the naval barracks, killing Szystowski and three of his men, but failed to scratch any of the nearby seaplanes. After the raid, the seaplanes evacuated across Danzig Bay to Jurata, where they were able to operate for a week without any losses. Around the same time, the Do 17s of II./KG 3 and III./KG 3 were used to strike transportation targets around Grudziadz, to disrupt the defence of the Polish 16th Infantry Division (16 DP) in this area. It was quickly apparent that the weather was affecting air operations, so at 0550 hours Göring personally cancelled *Wasserkante*.

Despite the cancellation of *Wasserkante*, Luftflotte 1 mounted a series of attacks on Warsaw with whatever forces it could launch and co-ordinate. The first major strike against the Polish capital was conducted by 34 He 111s from II./Lehrgeschwader (Demonstration Group) 1 (II./LG 1), flying from East Prussia. The bombers were escorted by 24 Bf 110Cs from Major Walter Grabmann's I(Z)./LG 1. The Bf 110C had just entered service in February 1939 and the Luftwaffe had high hopes for its new heavy fighter. Grabmann was also a very experienced pilot, having scored six victories in Spain with the Legion Condor. However, the German formation was spotted soon after it crossed the border and P.11c fighters from the 152 Eskadra (squadron) intercepted the bombers well north of Warsaw.

Pułkownik Pawlikowski was also able to get the Pursuit Brigade into the air and join the fight around 0725 hours, which became the first major aerial battle of the Second World War. The Polish fighters had difficulty catching the German bombers but managed to destroy six He 111s. However, the faster and cannon-armed Bf 110Cs inflicted considerable damage on the Polish fighters, each of which only had two machine guns. It was a long action by aerial standards, lasting approximately 50 minutes. The Poles lost at least four P.11c fighters shot down, plus many more damaged. The only consolation was that the German bombers dropped their bombs prematurely and then retreated back to their base in East Prussia. The very first bomb landed near Fort Mokotów, which had been the home of Radio Warsaw for a time. Grabmann himself was wounded but it was clear that the P.11c was no match for the Bf 110C.

Luftflotte 1 decided to send a Do 17 reconnaissance aircraft over Warsaw before the next strike, but it was shot down by a Polish fighter. It was not until 1600 hours that Luftflotte 1 was able to mount another major attack against Warsaw and it was not well co-ordinated. At this point, the Luftwaffe was still uncertain whether it was better to lead with dive-bombers or level-bombers, so it varied its tactics to try and assess what worked best. On this occasion, the second raid began at 1615 hours when 30 Ju 87 Stukas from I./Sturzkampfgeschwader (Dive-bomber Group) 1 (I./StG 1) attacked Warsaw; Polish fighters managed to knock down one Stuka. Given the persistent poor visibility over Luftflotte 1's airfields, the OKL ordered KG 27 to launch a strike against Warsaw from its bases in northern Germany, a distance of about 700km. En route to Warsaw, the three Gruppen of KG 27 joined up with an escort force provided by the Bf 110Cs of Hauptmann Schlief's I(Z)./LG 1.[2] The 22 Bf 109Ds of Hauptmann Martin Mettig's I./JG 21) based in East Prussia were also ordered to escort KG 77, but when they approached the bombers fired upon the Bf 109s – and continued to fire for some time. Although the Polish observer system failed to detect this raiding force which was flying at about 4,000m (cloud cover was as low as 600m), the Pursuit Brigade was patrolling over the Warsaw sector with 22 fighters when the enemy arrived around 1648 hours. The Polish fighters rolled in and knocked down two He 111s, but were then bounced by Schlief's Bf 110s, who shot down four P.7a fighters from the 123 Eskadra and damaged another P.7a. Mettig's Bf 109Ds also joined the fight and claimed to have shot down four more Polish fighters, although Mettig was wounded in the action. With the Polish fighters engaged, KG 27 was able to split up and strike several targets in Warsaw. The I./KG 27 dropped 52 tonnes of bombs on the Warsaw–Okęcie military airfield, which destroyed a number of aircraft under repair in the depot, while II./KG 27 bombed the civilian Warsaw–Gocław airport. The bombers of III./KG 27 attacked an ammunition plant.

It was already getting dark by the time that the German strike group started its return flight and a number of the fighter pilots were disoriented after their dogfights. Mettig's Bf 109s were also running low on fuel; five were forced to land behind Polish lines and their pilots were captured. Another Bf 109 pilot landed in Lithuania and was interned. A number of Bf 110s were also mis-oriented but their longer range enabled them to eventually reach friendly territory. Although the limited combat endurance of the Bf 109 was revealed over Warsaw on the first day of combat, the Luftwaffe leadership did not recognize the significance of this lesson. On the Polish side, Pawlikowski's Pursuit Brigade had shot down ten enemy aircraft, but lost 12 fighters and seven pilots. Furthermore, over 20 Polish fighters were damaged, leaving Pawlikowski with only 21 operational aircraft for the next day. It was clear that the LW could not sustain this kind of attritional combat for very long. It is also worth noting that the Poles did not win a single fighter-vs-fighter combat during the day, although they did damage some German fighters.

Luftflotte 1 also attacked other Polish cities. An LW air base and the main train station in Toruń were bombed without losses; Polish fighters and 40mm anti-aircraft batteries proved ineffective. Around noon, 31 He 111s from II./KG 26 bombed Poznań and this raid was followed up by an even larger raid around 1800 hours. Most of the bombs fell around the main train station, killing about 200 people (including 45 soldiers) and injuring many more.[3] Despite the fact that Poznań was defended by an anti-aircraft unit with 18 40mm Bofors guns and a squadron of P.11c fighters, the Poles only managed to down a single German bomber. These Luftwaffe raids had limited impact upon disrupting Polish mobilization efforts, but they were a shock to civilian morale.

During the late afternoon of 1 September, Luftflotte 1 continued its attacks against Polish naval targets around Gdynia and the Hel Peninsula. The Bf 109s from 5. and 6./Trägerjagdgruppe 186, which had intended to be part of the naval air group for the incomplete aircraft carrier *Graf Zeppelin*, were supposed to provide air cover for the battleship *Schleswig-Holstein* at Westerplatte but were prevented by fog. Instead, around 1400 hours they escorted Stukas from IV.(St)/LG 1 to attack the naval batteries at the Hel

Peninsula, but lost two Bf 109s to intense anti-aircraft fire. The Poles had upgraded the air defence batteries on the Hel Peninsula in July and they now had six 75mm and eight 40mm anti-aircraft guns, making it some of the best defended airspace in Poland. Another group of Stukas peeled off to attack Polish naval shipping near Gdynia and sank the gunnery training ship *Mazur* and the tender *Nurek,* both alongside piers, About 40 Polish sailors died in the attack. After this attack, the Poles were desperate to move their few major surface warships left in Polish waters – the destroyer *Wicher*, minelayer *Gryf* and two gunboats – towards the anti-aircraft defences on the Hel Peninsula. However, *Gryf* was tasked with laying several hundred mines across Danzig Bay first – a task better conducted under cover of darkness. When the Stukas of IV.(St)/LG 1 returned at 1800 hours, they caught the Polish warships out in the bay and furiously bombed the *Gryf*; the minelayer was only moderately damaged but suffered five dead (including its commander) and 17 wounded. The Polish ships abandoned the mining mission and retreated to the Hel Peninsula.

Löhr's Luftflotte 4 in Silesia was less affected by poor weather conditions on the first day of *Ostmarkflug*. The main missions conducted by Luftflotte 4 were battlefield interdiction strikes in the Kraków–Katowice areas and close support to the army, with the main effort provided to the 10. Armee. The heaviest blow fell upon Kraków, which was attacked by two Gruppen of Do 17 bombers from KG 77 at 0520 hours. The first group, I./KG 77, attacked Kraków–Rakowice airfield at medium altitude, but III./KG 77 executed a low-level attack on the airfield at just 50m off the ground, dropping SC50 and SC10 bombs. The German bombers showered the airfield with 45 tonnes of bombs, but many of the bombers from III./KG 77 were damaged by the blasts from their own bombs. There was negligible resistance and eight Polish aircraft were destroyed on the ground. During the afternoon, Kraków–Rakowice airfield was attacked again by He 111s from KG 4. This time, some of the Kraków Army fighters were able to intercept and they downed two He 111s. Several other airfields in the area were also attacked.

Generalmajor Wolfram Freiherr von Richthofen was eager to support the army with his ground attack aircraft and he committed most of them to that mission. At first light, the Hs 123s of Major Werner Spielvogel's II.(Schlacht)/LG 2 were sent to support the 10. Armee's opening attack by bombing the village of Pryzstain. This area was held by troops from the Polish 7th Infantry Division (7 DP). Soon afterwards, beginning at 0540 hours, 29 Ju 87 Stukas from Hauptmann Walter Sigel's I./StG 77 bombed the town of Wieluń, dropping 29 SC500 and 112 SC50 bombs. At least 32 Polish civilians were killed when the hospital was hit. Although the Germans would claim that Wieluń was heavily defended, there were no Polish units in the town or nearby. During the course of the day, Richthofen launched three more Stuka strikes against the town, totalling roughly 150 sorties which dropped 46 tonnes of bombs and destroyed three-quarters of Wieluń's buildings. At least 127 Polish civilians were killed in the bombing of Wieluń, perhaps more. The multiple attacks on Wieluń did nothing to support the German ground offensive, since the main action was occurring well to the south. While it is possible that Richthofen misdirected his Stukas based on false intelligence about Polish dispositions, during the day German reconnaissance aircraft confirmed that there were no Polish troops inside the town. Instead, it appears that Richthofen was attempting to use 'terror bombing' to shake Polish morale in this sector and the bombing of Wieluń was later classified as a war crime because it deliberately targeted civilians. At any rate, Richthofen wasted over 150 close air support sorties against an objective that did not fulfil *Ostmarkflug*'s objectives.

While the bombing of Wieluń was occurring, Richthofen did begin receiving requests for support from Reichenau's 10. Armee. At this point, the XVI Armeekorps (mot.) was fighting its way through the Polish border defences and this action subsequently evolved into the battle of Mokra. Richthofen decided to take a closer look at the ground battle for himself and flew forwards in his Fieseler Storch around 1100 hours, but ended up over-flying Polish positions and coming under heavy ground fire. The Polish Wołyńska Cavalry Brigade was operating as a covering force in this region and was spotted moving north towards Wieluń, causing Richthofen to redirect his Stukas against this target of opportunity. Between 1250 and 1420 hours, two Stuka Gruppen (I./StG 2 and I./StG 77) attacked the Polish cavalry unit and German sources claimed that the brigade was destroyed. While the Wołyńska Cavalry Brigade did suffer about 20 per cent casualties from all causes during the day, it was far from destroyed.[4]

The first day of *Ostmarkflug* was far from the decisive success that Göring or Jeschonnek had been hoping to achieve. Altogether, the Luftwaffe flew 2,700 sorties during the day and bombed about 30 targets, at a cost of 37 aircraft lost (including 14 lost to Polish anti-aircraft fire). In contrast, the LW only flew 280 sorties and lost 29 aircraft. While it is clear that dispersal saved the LW from immediate destruction, it does not seem that the Luftwaffe made a serious effort to destroy the LW on the first day of the invasion. Too many sorties were wasted on secondary or even tertiary targets like Gdynia and Wieluń, as well as civilian airfields. Nor was the effort put into close air support and battlefield interdiction very impressive, in large part due to inadequate reconnaissance and targeting. The Luftwaffe leadership found that the time-lag between ground commanders asking for air support and the air unit receiving the request was significantly greater than had occurred in pre-war training exercises. Essentially, the Luftwaffe kicked off the campaign by attacking mostly known targets, which were often based on outdated information. Consequently, the 2,700 Luftwaffe sorties made on the first day of the campaign did not accomplish a great deal. This difficulty in establishing target priorities and gaining reliable intelligence would plague the Luftwaffe in subsequent campaigns as well. On the other hand, the Luftwaffe demonstrated that it was flexible enough to act quickly against targets of opportunity or shift forces around.

As for the LW, its failure to mass its fighters to defend the obvious target − Warsaw − deprived it of its one chance to inflict a significant defeat upon the Luftwaffe. If the raids on Warsaw had been opposed by 100 Polish fighters instead of 20–30, the German bombers would likely have suffered a real drubbing. Furthermore, had the Poles received even a single squadron of Hurricanes in spring 1939, the Bf 110Cs would have faced a more serious challenge in the initial aerial battles over Warsaw.

On the second day of the German invasion, the weather was markedly improved. Amazingly, Luftwaffe reconnaissance had still failed to detect the location of the LW's operational units. Oberstleutnant Joseph 'Beppo' Schmid, head of the Luftwaffe's intelligence branch, erroneously concluded that the LW was all but destroyed − which was quickly adopted as truth by Josef Goebbels' Propaganda Ministry. Based upon this ridiculously optimistic assessment, the Luftwaffe decided to shift its priorities to close air support and battlefield interdiction. Having smashed defenceless Wieluń into burning rubble, Richthofen committed all three of his Stuka Gruppen to support Reichenau's 10. Armee, with the main effort provided to its spearhead formation, the XVI Armeekorps (mot.), which was advancing towards the Warta River. The Stukas bombed the rail stations at Radomsko and Piotrków, thereby preventing Polish reinforcements from reinforcing a thin defensive line attempting to form on the Warta. Major Werner Spielvogel's Hs 123 biplanes from the II.(Schlacht)/LG 2 were assigned to support the XI Armeekorps, which also advanced rapidly to the Warta. A French officer, Général Paul-François Armengaud, happened to witness the German battlefield interdiction attacks and he wrote a detailed report about their effectiveness:

> The German system consists essentially of making a breach in the front with armour and aircraft, then to throw mechanized and motorized columns into the breach, to beat down its shoulders to right and left in order to keep on enlarging it … It would be madness not to draw an exact lesson from this pattern and not to pay heed to this warning.[5]

In most cases, there was little Polish resistance to these Luftwaffe attacks, except at Łódź. When German bombers attacked the city around 1710 hours, fighters from the 161 and 162 Eskadra scrambled to intercept. Twelve escorting Bf 110s from I./ Zerstörer-Geschwader 1 (I./ZG 1) engaged the Polish fighters and destroyed two, but a P.11c shot down the Bf 110C flown by Hauptmann von Freiherr Müllenheim, the *Staffelkapitän* of the III./ZG 1.[6] In a follow-up raid, a P.7a fighter from the 162 Eskadra shot down a Bf 110C from I./ZG 76 near Łódź.[7] Even though the P.7a fighter was badly obsolescent, in the hands of a good pilot it could still occasionally score against the enemy. The Luftwaffe also continued to attack naval facilities on the northern coast and industrial facilities behind the lines. The He 111s of KG 4 conducted two large-scale raids against the aviation training centre at Dęblin and wreaked great havoc, dropping a total of 180 tonnes of bombs. Both the PWS and PZL aircraft plants were bombed, although few aircraft were actually being produced at the moment.

The only sector where the LW mounted serious resistance on the second day of the war was in the north-west, where the fighters belonging to Army Pomorze and Army Poznań attempted to repel German air raids on their lines of communications. The 141 and 142 Eskadra were able to intercept a series of raids near Bydgoszcz and shoot down five Do 17 bombers and a Bf 110 fighter. Podporucznik Stanisław Skalski of 142 Eskadra shot down two of the Dorniers and by the end of the campaign he would gain two more victories. The fighters from the 131 and 132 Eskadra claimed four enemy bombers. During the action, Marian Pisarrek from 141 Eskadra – a future ace – accidently shot down a Polish P.23 reconnaissance plane that blundered into the dogfight. As is common at the start of a war, misidentifications on both sides led to fratricide.

When intercepting unescorted bombers, the Polish fighters did well. However, Polish ground commanders tried to use their scarce aviation assets in a manner that was often unsound. Generał Bortnowski, commander of Army Pomorze, ordered Kapitan Florian Laskowski's fighter wing (141 and 142 Eskadra) to attack one of Guderian's motorized infantry column north of Bydgoszcz. Laskowski protested against the misuse of his fighters but then led the 141 Eskadra in a low-level strafing attack. The Poles discovered that the German mobile Flak, particularly 2cm guns, was particularly lethal. Of the nine Polish fighters, three were shot down and another was badly damaged; Laskowski was killed in action. The strafing attack proved only a minor nuisance to Guderian's advance.

Meanwhile, the Polish bomber brigade was held in reserve south-east of Warsaw. There was discussion about using these aircraft to bomb Königsberg in East Prussia, but this came to naught. The only commitment that was approved was to send the two squadrons from the IV/6 Group to attack General der Kavallerie Erich Hoepner's motorized columns of XVI Armeekorps (mot.) west of Częstochowa. A total of 18 P.23b Karaś conducted the attack, coming in at 600–700m, with each aircraft dropping six 100kg bombs. According to some sources, the German column suffered heavy losses and was disrupted. Yet three Polish bombers were shot down (one by a Bf 109 and two by Flak) and five more were badly shot up.[8] Another group of six Karaś attacked the column again, later in the day. On his own initiative, Wacław Buczyłko, a P.23b pilot from the Bomber Brigade's 21 Eskadra, flew across the German border south of Breslau before dawn on 2 September and dropped eight 50kg bombs on a factory near Ohlau. Buczyłko's single-sortie raid was just a stunt with no military value, although it was the first Allied air raid on German soil of the Second World War.

Overall, the Luftwaffe flew over 2,000 sorties on 2 September and lost 14 aircraft. In contrast, the Poles flew about 200 sorties and lost at least 20 aircraft. The Luftwaffe's battlefield interdiction strikes and close air support provided valuable support to the army in the sectors chosen (secondary sectors often received little or no air support). By this point, it was clear that the LW was operating as a 'guerrilla air force', striking where and when it could muster a useful combat force. However, the Luftwaffe had demonstrated that it could mount raids wherever it pleased and the best the LW could do was to pick off individual bombers. On the other hand, due to the range limitations of the Bf 109, the three Bf 110 Gruppen were carrying virtually the entire burden of escorting bombers over central Poland. The Polish fighter pilots had fared poorly on the first day of the war against the Bf 110, but they were learning and by the second day of the war they managed to destroy two of them.

On 3 September, the Luftwaffe found its stride and mounted powerful strikes against Warsaw and other aviation-related targets, while increasing its support for the army's advance. Recognizing the need for more bombers in the East, Luftflotte 3 transferred 77 He 111s from KG 54 and KG 55 to Luftflotte 4. Around 0845 hours, Luftflotte 1 resumed attacks on Warsaw. Escorted by Bf 110s from I.(Z)/LG 1, the He 111s of KG-27 bombed multiple targets around Warsaw. Having repaired a number of its damaged aircraft, the Pursuit Brigade attempted to intercept the raids but was unable to get through to the German bombers. Instead, the Poles shot down two Bf 110s but lost four of their own fighters. Altogether, Polish fighters conducted 120 sorties during the day, knocking down 15 enemy aircraft (including three fighters and six bombers) at a loss of 13 of their own.

The LW was more aggressive with its bombers, committing a total of 90 sorties, mostly in the critical Częstochowa–Radomsko sector against German motorized spearheads; nine P.23 Karaś were lost – a crippling 10 per cent loss rate. Two Gruppen of Bf 109 fighters (I./ZG 2, I./JG 76) were committed to this sector as well, on 'free hunt' missions which bagged five of the Karaś. However, the German pilots found the Karaś difficult to target due to their low speed and ability to hop just above the trees. On the other hand, the Karaś employed by army-level aviation units were split between reconnaissance and bombing missions, which greatly reduced their ability to inflict worthwhile damage on the enemy.

In the north, Luftflotte 1 unleashed Kustenfliegergruppe 506 (Coastal Group 506) to eliminate the remaining Polish naval units sheltering south of the Hel Peninsula. This formation consisted of several dozen seaplanes, supported by the Bf 109s and Ju 87s from the carrier *Graf Zeppelin's* intended air group. The German aircraft launched a series of attacks, beginning at 0900 hours and continuing until 1800 hours, which gradually smashed the destroyer *Wicher*, minelayer *Gryf* and minesweeper *Mewa* into sinking wrecks. Polish naval casualties were low on these doomed vessels but anti-aircraft fire only succeeded in knocking down a single German aircraft.

The OKL also decided to conduct a field test in Poland of its latest technical innovation – precision night bombing – on the night of 3/4 September. A specialist pathfinder unit known as Luftnachrichten-Abteilung 100 had been created with two *Staffeln* (squadrons), one equipped with 12 Ju 52/3m transport-bombers and the other with six

He 111 bombers. The aircraft carried radio gear dubbed X-Verfahren or X-Gerät, which enabled precision navigation at night. On this occasion, a small number of bombers was sent to attack the Palmiry ammunition depot north-west of Warsaw.[9] The raid failed to destroy the target, but the Germans did not know that. Nevertheless, early experiments with X-Gerät proved quite promising, with aircraft able to deliver bombs within several hundred metres of a target at night. In subsequent nights, Luftnachrichten-Abteilung 100 would conduct several more missions over Poland. No other air force in 1939 had anything like this technical capability.

By 4 September, it was clear to the Poles that the situation at the front was becoming desperate and the LW made an all-out effort to oppose the Luftwaffe wherever it could. When Luftflotte 1 mounted more punishing raids on Warsaw, the Pursuit Brigade launched 74 sorties but could not prevent the raiders from smashing Okęcie airfield and its facilities to bits. There were a large number of partly completed aircraft at Okęcie, including at least 20 PZL.23b Karaś and 20 PZL.37b Łoś bombers; most were wrecked. The damage inflicted on Okęcie also severely reduced the operational capability and logistical sustainability of the LW, which had few fuel trucks or maintenance units; most of the fixed fuel pumps were destroyed. Without special bomb lifts, the PZL.37b Łoś bombers could only carry one-third of their normal bomb-load. Altogether, Polish fighters flew 165 sorties and destroyed 11 enemy aircraft, but lost eight of their own in air-to-air combat. Luftwaffe reconnaissance finally found one of the LW's dispersal fields, Widzew east of Łódź, which was then strafed by the Bf 109Ds of I./ZG 2; five Polish fighters from the 161 Eskadra were destroyed on the ground.[10]

For the first time, the Bomber Brigade committed its PZL.37b Łoś bombers to combat, sending a total of 50 sorties throughout the day in a vain attempt to blunt the advance of the German XVI Armeekorps (mot.) in the Radomsko–Piotrków sector. Nine of the Łoś bombers were lost – the equivalent of an entire squadron. For example, three Łoś bombers from the 212 Eskadra were intercepted by eight Bf 109D fighters from I./ZG 2 near Weilun and all three bombers were shot down; seven of 12 crewmen were killed. Luftwaffe reconnaissance also discovered that the 211 and 212 Eskadra were based at the Dzierżanów airport west of Łódź and He 111 bombers attacked the airfield during the afternoon, destroying two more PZL.37b and stocks of fuel and bombs. The two Polish bomber squadrons were forced to evacuate post haste. Altogether, the LW conducted about 300 sorties on 4 September and lost 30 aircraft. In contrast, the Luftwaffe was still mounting about 2,000 daily sorties and suffering only about 1 per cent losses.

After five days of continuous combat, the LW was beginning to show signs of reduced operational effectiveness after heavy losses and insufficient logistical support. A total of only 180 sorties were flown on 5 September, including 91 fighter and 22 bomber sorties, resulting in the loss of 15 aircraft. Due to the retreat of Polish ground forces, a number of air units were beginning to displace eastwards, which also affected their readiness levels. By this point, the Luftwaffe had a clear dominance in the skies over Poland and could afford to rotate units, which allowed some rest and time to repair damaged aircraft – a luxury the LW did not have. On this day, the Luftwaffe lost seven aircraft over Poland and ten more damaged. The Luftwaffe continued to concentrate large numbers of sorties against rail centres – which proved easier to identify and attack than enemy tactical units in the field.

On 6 September, the LW tried to make a maximum effort with its fighters, flying a total of 164 sorties, which claimed 13 victories at a cost of nine losses. Altogether, the LW flew 240 sorties on 6 September and lost 23 aircraft. By evening, Generał Zając made a decision that should have been made much sooner, which was to pull back all remaining operational fighters to Lublin and use them to rebuild the Pursuit Brigade. Of course, this measure stripped the armies of their little remaining air support, but it allowed Zając to amass about 88 fighters. He also ordered all bombers to assemble at airfields near Lublin in order to strengthen the Bomber Brigade. During the course of six days combat, the LW had flown 1,610 sorties and lost 155 aircraft, or 40 per cent of their starting strength. Personnel losses were significantly lighter – only 17 fighter pilots were killed and 19 wounded, out of a total of over 220.[11] However, the Luftwaffe had only wounded the LW, not defeated it.

Despite this shortfall, the Luftwaffe had done quite well with its battlefield interdiction and close air support, enabling Heeresgruppe Süd's forces to smash their way past any serious resistance. In the first six days of the campaign, the Luftwaffe lost 126 aircraft and 315 personnel casualties, or roughly 7 per cent of their starting force. Clearly the Luftwaffe won the aerial battle of attrition. Nevertheless, the Luftwaffe had learned that operating over Warsaw was expensive, costing them 42 aircraft in the first six days. Polish anti-aircraft batteries accounted for 11 of these losses.

Polish 7TP light tanks in Teschen, October 1938. Once the Germans began carving up Czechoslovakia at Munich – with the consent of Britain and France – Poland decided to make its move to recover the Teschen region, which the Czechs had seized by force in 1919. After an ultimatum was delivered to the Czechs, the Polish Army sent a 35,000-man operational group to occupy this disputed region. (Author's collection)

A Polish anti-tank battery firing on the range before the war. The Bofors 37mm anti-tank gun was an excellent weapon that in 1939 could defeat any German tank. The Germans noted that Polish anti-tank gunners would often fight to the death, refusing to abandon their positions even as tanks closed in on them. (Author's Collection)

He 111 bombers in production prior to the outbreak of war. The pace of German rearmament caught everyone in Europe by surprise. In just four years, the Luftwaffe was able to deploy over 1,200 modern bombers. Hitler achieved this feat of rearmament by ignoring economic factors and pushing industry to prioritize a few key weapon systems such as bombers and tanks. (Bundesarchiv, Bild 101I-774-0011-34, Foto: Hanns Hubmann)

German sailors unloading equipment in Memel, 23 March 1939. Hitler's sudden occupation of Memel with a strong German naval squadron was a wake-up call for the Polish leadership, which suddenly realized that the threat of German aggression over a disputed territory like Danzig was a real possibility. On the same day, Poland began a covert partial mobilization to strengthen the forces on its western borders. (Author's collection)

A German Pz IV medium tank and MG 34 machine-gun team participate in a pre-war live-fire training exercise. Although German pre-war training was good, the Wehrmacht still had a lot to learn in Poland, particularly about tactical logistics, recovering damaged vehicles and casualty evacuation. Note the sterility of this training environment. By contrast, in Poland, German Panzer units would fight in wooded and urban areas. (Nik Cornish at www.Stavka.org.uk)

A pre-war Polish propaganda poster, for the Anti-Aircraft Defence Loan fund, which proclaims: '*Strong, united, ready!*' Although the Polish government put on a brave front in regard to the state of military preparedness, Rydz-Śmigły knew that only prompt French offensive action would enable Poland to survive a German invasion. The fact that Poland relied upon popular subscriptions to buy anti-aircraft weapons was indicative of the cash-strapped state of Poland's military defences. (Author's collection)

Marszałek Edward Rydz-Śmigły (1886–1941), Polish commander-in-chief and effectively leader of Poland since Pilsudski's death in 1935. Rydz-Śmigły was a brave and loyal military subordinate, but he lacked the ability to develop a coherent defensive strategy for Poland, which left the WP without an effective war plan. His leadership during the September campaign was simply awful, ordering retreats without thought of consequences, and he allowed the strategic reserve to be squandered without result. Rydz-Śmigły's decision to abandon Warsaw and then to flee to Romania was irresponsible and deprived Poland of strong leadership at a critical moment. He returned to Poland in October 1941 in an effort to work with the resistance, but soon died of a heart attack. (Author's collection)

Generał Dywizji Tadeusz Kutrzeba (1886–1947), commander of Army Poznań. Kutrzeba, an engineer officer and graduate of the Austrian General Staff Academy, was a brilliant military theorist who was quick to appreciate modern technology. He was involved in a General Staff study in 1936 which estimated that Poland could only hold off a German invasion for six weeks. In the September campaign, Kutrzeba led the Polish counter-offensive on the Bzura River and signed the capitulation of Warsaw. He survived five years of German captivity but died of cancer in 1947. (Author's collection)

Generał Dywizji Juliusz Rómmel (1881–1967), commander of Army Łódź. Rómmel was an artillery officer of German heritage. He was also a Lutheran in an officer corps that was almost exclusively Catholic. Rómmel's decision-making during the initial fighting on the Warta was poor and his army was soon reeling backward in disorder. He was given the two precious battalions of 7TP tanks to launch a counter-attack, but made only limited use of them. Withdrawing to the capital, Rómmel was named commander of Army Warsaw, but played only a minor role in the city's defence.
(Author's collection)

Generaloberst Gerd von Rundstedt (1875–1953), commander of Heeresgruppe Süd. Rundstedt was the archetypal *Junker* officer and Hitler valued him as a living link to the old Imperial Army and because he was apolitical. Rundstedt retired in 1938 but returned to service in May 1939. As commander of Heeresgruppe Süd, Rundstedt was capable but undistinguished and he allowed his subordinates considerable latitude. Although Rundstedt would remain in senior command billets until March 1945, his military talents were unimaginative and he tended toward a detached managerial style. Rundstedt's inattention to details contributed to 8. Armee being surprised on the Bzura River.
(Bundesarchiv, Bild 183-L08127)

General der Artillerie Georg von Küchler, commander of the 3. Armee in East Prussia at the start of *Fall Weiss*. Küchler was a career artillery officer and pro-Nazi, but he was upset by the misbehaviour of Waffen-SS units under his command in Poland. His efforts to court-martial SS personnel for war crimes were thwarted by Heinrich Himmler. After the war, Küchler was himself convicted of war crimes committed in the Soviet Union and served seven years in prison. (Bundesarchiv, Bild 183-R63872, Foto: Hans van der Piepen)

General der Infanterie Johannes Blaskowitz (1883–1948), commander of 8. Armee. Blaskowitz was initially assigned merely to protect 10. Armee's left flank but ended up being struck by the one major Polish counter-offensive during the campaign. After the battle of the Bzura, he was put in charge of the siege of Warsaw and accepted the Polish capitulation. Blaskowitz then served as military occupation commander in Poland for several months, until relieved of command for openly criticizing SS war crimes in Poland. Although he continued to serve in high-level posts until 1945, he was assigned by Hitler to secondary sectors. He committed suicide while awaiting trial at Nuremberg. (Bundesarchiv, Bild 146-2004-004-05)

General der Artillerie Walter von Reichenau (1884–1942), commander of 10. Armee, and his chief of staff, Generalmajor Friederich Paulus (right). Reichenau was part of the new breed of German officers who supported Hitler's policies of aggression. He was also one of the few senior Heer officers who joined the Nazi party and Hitler ensured that he was given choice assignments. In *Fall Weiss*, 10. Armee was the German main effort and it was Reichenau's army that would split wide open the Polish defensive screen along the Warta. (Bundesarchiv, Bild 101I-013-0054-15, Foto: Wagner)

The opening bombardment of Westerplatte seen from the deck of the *Schleswig-Holstein*. This photo demonstrates the point-blank nature of the attack. The fact that an officer in the foreground is calmly watching the bombardment demonstrates that there was no Polish return fire. However, the smoke of the bombardment quickly obscured the target area and actually made it harder for the Germans to pin-point the garrison's positions. (Author's collection)

The German pre-dreadnought *Schleswig-Holstein* bombards the Polish military transit depot on Westerplatte on the morning of 1 September 1939. Over the course of the seven-day siege, the *Schleswig-Holstein* fired 157 28cm and 309 15cm rounds at the garrison – at point-blank range – but does not appear to have killed a single Polish soldier. This was arguably the most significant yet least effective naval bombardment of the Second World War. (Süddeutsche Zeitung Photo, 00138978)

German troops prepare to assault the outer wall of the Westerplatte installation on 1 September. The assault was a fiasco, with the naval infantry company suffering heavy losses. (Author's collection)

The garrison of Westerplatte surrendered on 7 September 1939 after an epic siege. The company-size garrison managed to hold out for seven days despite repeated bombardment and ground assaults. For Poles, the defence of Westerplatte spawned the legend of a heroic defence against the odds and devotion to the nation; the fact that most of the garrison survived served to enhance the legend. In reality, the garrison was close to surrendering on the second day but the Germans failed to press their advantage. (Author's collection)

Troops from the SS-Heimwehr-Danzig, accompanied by an Austrian-built Steyr ADGZ armoured car, move toward the Polish post office in Danzig on the morning of 1 September, 1939. At least two of the SS troops are armed with MP 28 sub-machine guns. The SS attack on the Danzig post office was extremely amateurish and fell short of the propaganda coup expected by Gauleiter Albert Forster. (Bundesarchiv, Bild 146-1995-008-32)

German troops attempting to break into the Polish post office in Danzig on 1 September 1939. Note the SA Stormtrooper on the left. Despite overwhelming force, the Polish defenders under Konrad Guderski managed to hold the building for 14 hours, creating something of a legend. The defence only collapsed after the Germans set the building on fire. (Author's collection)

An He 111 bomber in flight. Although a single squadron of the new Ju 88 bombers had been formed in September 1939, the He-111 was still the most modern bomber in the Luftwaffe's arsenal. However, the He 111 carried a modest bomb-load (either 32 SC50 or 8 SC250 high-explosive bombs) and without a gyro-stabilized bombsight it was fortunate to drop its bombs within 400m of a target. After Poland, the Luftwaffe would begin experimenting with low-level tactics to improve accuracy but its ability to effectively bomb targets from medium altitudes remained impaired. (Nik Cornish at www.Stavka.org.uk)

The Bf 109B was the initial production version of the new fighter, which saw limited service with Legion Condor in Spain. Note the twin-bladed propeller on these early Bf 109s. By September 1939, most Luftwaffe fighter units had re-equipped with the more advanced Bf 109E model. Although the Bf 109E was an excellent dogfighter, it was handicapped by its limited operational range. An attempt to use Bf 109s over Warsaw from bases in East Prussia resulted in the loss of several aircraft running out of fuel. The Luftwaffe failed to make adjustments to the Bf 109, such as adding drop tanks, and this shortcoming would prove disastrous during the Battle of Britain in August 1940. (Bundesarchiv, Bild 101I-379-0015-18, Foto: Rubelt)

The Polish LW had 128 operational PZL P.11c fighters at the start of the war. The P.11c was an outstanding fighter in 1936 but it was obsolete once the Bf 109 appeared. Poland recognized that its fighter arm was in need of better aircraft and mounted a crash programme to try and develop a new fighter, but lack of time and funds made this a futile effort. Instead, Poland turned to the West for a new fighter. Although France promised the MS. 406 and Britain promised the Hurricane, none arrived before the German invasion. Nevertheless, Polish fighter pilots were able to achieve over 100 kills with their obsolete aircraft. (Author's Collection)

The Ju 87B Stuka was an excellent close-support aircraft for its day but in Poland it was primarily used for battlefield interdiction missions. Rather than have the luftwaffe drop bombs near troops in contact, army commanders preferred that the Stukas interdict enemy movements, attacking train stations, bridges and moving columns. Given that enemy fighter and anti-aircraft defences in Poland were limited, German propaganda created an aura around the Ju 87 which became a vital component in shaping the mystique around the Wehrmacht's early-war battlefield successes. (Nik Cornish at www.Stavka.org.uk)

A train bombed by Stukas and burnt out. Luftwaffe attacks upon Polish railyards and rail lines prevented the Polish General Staff from transferring any large units by rail during *Fall Weiss*. Although the actual destruction of infrastructure was limited, it was enough to paralyze the Polish rail system. (Nik Cornish at www.Stavka.org.uk)

A German soldier killed near Chojnice on 1 September. A German attempt to seize the city with a *coup de main* failed and the 2. Infanterie-Division (mot.) spent the better part of the day pushing the Polish defenders out of Chojnice. (Author's collection)

A platoon of German Pz I light tanks advancing to contact. Note commanders are buttoned up and two left-most tanks have turrets oriented left. Typically the Pz I tanks could only advance over terrain slowly, at 15–20 kilometres per hour. Although this was the most numerous German armoured fighting vehicle used in Poland, the Pz I had only been intended to be used in training, not in combat. (Süddeutsche Zeitung Photo, 00404956)

An Sd. Kfz. 232 (6-rad) armoured car, with its distinctive frame radio antenna. The reconnaissance battalion in each Panzer-Division had 33 armoured cars, of which three were Sd. Kfz. 232 (6-rad) vehicles. This armoured car, developed in the early 1930s, was already obsolescent by 1939 and suffered from poor off-road mobility. German combined-arms tactical doctrine was based on using communications to co-ordinate different units and capabilities. (Nik Cornish at www.Stavka.org.uk)

A German infantry platoon on the march in Poland. Note that the three machine gunners are equipped with the MG 13 light machine gun, which was not belt-fed like the more modern MG 34. Many of the Wehrmacht units in Poland were still equipped with older weapons or captured Czech weapons. Note also the wagon at the rear of the formation, which would carry additional supplies for the troops. (Süddeutsche Zeitung Photo, 00011670)

A column of German Pz IV medium tanks entering Grudziadz (Graudenz) in early September 1939 and being greeted by jubilant crowds with Nazi salutes. A significant percentage of the ethnic Germans in Poland were pro-Nazi and enthusiastically welcomed the invading troops. However, these jubilant crowds did not yet realize that Hitler expected them to join the Wehrmacht and participate in his next campaigns of aggression in the East. (Bundesarchiv, Bild 183-E10600)

Germany acquired over 200 Czech-made LT vz. 35 light tanks in March 1939. During *Fall Weiss*, the 1. leichte-Division was the only unit equipped with these vehicles. By the standards of 1939, these Czech-made tanks were good armoured fighting vehicles and enabled the Wehrmacht to field more Panzer formations than they could have with only their own domestic production.
(Nik Cornish at www.Stavka.org.uk)

The Polish Army had over 1,200 French-made 75mm wz. 1897 field guns in September 1939 and it was the standard weapon of light artillery regiments. A small number of the weapons had been modernized in the 1930s, such as these guns outfitted with large pneumatic tyres, allowing them to be towed by trucks. Although the 75mm gun typically fired high-explosive rounds, it did have an armour-piercing round, as well. While the 75mm gun was outclassed by German division-level artillery, its high rate of fire and dual-use capability were still useful in the defence.
(Author's collection)

A German infantry unit on the edge of a Polish village. Overall, the German infantry often failed to demonstrate the level of initiative that would be customary later in the war, often preferring to let artillery and airpower soften up targets before moving forward. In many cases, Polish units were able to break contact and retreat before the German infantry moved into towns. (Nik Cornish at www. Stavka.org.uk)

The Battle for the Northern Coast, 1 September – 2 October

'We will fight shoulder to shoulder until complete victory.'
President Ignacy Mościcki, 1 September, 1939

Although Poland's leadership was willing to go to war to hold the Polish Corridor, it was not willing to commit large forces to defend this extremely vulnerable region. Instead, naval troops, border guards and ON (National Defence) troops were ordered to defend the corridor and the northern coast, including the port of Gdynia and the Hel Peninsula. Badly outnumbered from the start and with no hope of reinforcement or retreat, the Polish troops on the northern coast were assigned a classic 'die-in-place' mission, for the sake of honour. Nevertheless, the Polish troops who fought on the northern coast demonstrated a tenacity that frequently astounded the Germans.

Prior to mobilization, the Polish Navy had two active naval rifle battalions, primarily to defend the port of Gdynia. When the Danzig Crisis began to unfold in May, both battalions were directed to begin constructing field works around Gdynia. Furthermore, Major Jan Wiśniewski's 4th Battalion KOP was assigned to defend the Hel Peninsula, which included the construction of a fortified position at the narrow neck near Jastarnia. The coastal artillerymen in the Hel Fortified Region (Rejon Umocniony Hel) were under the command of Kontradmirał Włodzimierz Steyer. The forces assigned to defend Gdynia were designated as the Land Coastal Command (Lądowa Obrona Wybrzeża or LOW) and Pułkownik Stanisław Dąbek, an experienced infantryman, was assigned to command this formation. In addition to organizing the defence of Gdynia, Dąbek was also responsible for Major Henryk Sucharski's small detachment at the military depot on Westerplatte, in Danzig. Dąbek reported to the fleet commander, Kontradmirał Józef Unrug, who relocated to the Hel Peninsula once war appeared imminent.

On 24 August, the Land Coastal Command mobilized five ON battalions assigned to the Naval Brigade of National Defence (Morska Brygada Obrony Narodowej); most of these battalions were used to expand the two regular naval infantry battalions into the 1st and 2nd Naval Rifle Regiments (1 and 2 MPS). Several incomplete battalions were also mobilized, but kept as reserves. Altogether, the Land Coastal Command was able to increase its assigned strength from fewer than 5,000 to more than 14,000 troops in a week, primarily because the ON volunteers came from the immediate area and thus mobilization could progress rapidly. However, the units in the Land Coastal Command were significantly less well-equipped than most Polish Army units, particularly in terms of artillery support. Dąbek had already decided to deploy the bulk of his troops in two areas. He created a covering force, based on Podpułkownik Kazimierz Pruszkowski's 1st Naval Rifle Regiment (1 MPS) at Wejherowo, 21km north-west of Gdynia. Pruszkowski's mission was to delay any German advance upon Gdynia from the west for as long as possible. The second group, based upon Podpułkownik Ignacy Szpunar's 2 MPS, was deployed south of Gdynia to delay any German approach from Danzig. The nearest friendly forces belonged to Army Pomorze, 50km to the south, but due to the disbandment of the Intervention Corps on 30 August there was no intent to send any reinforcements into the corridor. The Polish High Command was not under any illusions about the ability of the Land Coastal Command to fend off a full-scale German attack for more than a few days, but believed that it was strong enough deny the enemy an easy victory.

From the OKH perspective, the Germans were eager to seize full control over Danzig and establish a land link to East Prussia, but were less concerned with the seizure of the rest of the northern Polish coast. Since the primary mission of General der Artillerie Günther von Kluge's 4. Armee was to destroy Army Pomorze, only secondary forces from Generalleutnant Leonhard Kaupisch's Grenzschutz-Abschnitt-Kommando 1 (Border Sector Command 1) would move against Gdynia. The Kriegsmarine, the Brigade Eberhardt and Forster's local troops would deal with Westerplatte and the minor Polish presence in Danzig. While the Kriegsmarine would provide naval gunfire support and the Luftwaffe some air support, the German ground forces in the northern coastal sector had substantially less artillery and organic firepower than most of the other invading formations. According to information provided by Forster's paramilitary units in Danzig, the local Polish defences were negligible.

In fact, the Poles had been fortifying both the depot on Westerplatte and the main post office in Danzig for weeks, in anticipation that Forster would attempt some kind of *coup de main*. Reinforced in late August, Major Sucharski had a total of 209 troops on Westerplatte, mostly drawn from the elite 2nd Legions Infantry Division (2 DPL); only 27 men were reservists. This garrison was small, but the terrain heavily favoured the defence, since the Westerplatte depot was located on the end of a peninsula whose narrowest point was only 250m wide. Although the Germans could overlook Westerplatte from many points, the depot was surrounded by a wall and was heavily wooded. Over the course of the summer, Sucharski's troops dug trenches and laid barbed wire, creating both an outer defensive line across the narrow neck of the peninsula, as well as establishing an inner defensive stronghold centred on the concrete barracks block. In terms of defensive armament, Sucharski's company-size detachment was armed with as much firepower as a Polish infantry battalion, including one elderly 76mm field gun, two 37mm anti-tank guns, four 81mm mortars and 41 machine guns. Due to the dense tree cover on Westerplatte and the clever construction of bunkers beneath buildings, the Germans could not observe most of Sucharski's defences, even though they had outposts right outside the perimeter wall. The Germans did conduct aerial reconnaissance flights over Westerplatte, but were still uncertain about the strength of its defences. Around noon on 31 August, Podpułkownik Wincenty Sobocinski (a General Staff officer assigned to Danzig) arrived and privately told Major Sucharski that the Intervention Corps had been disbanded and that there would be no reinforcements in event of war. In that case, Sucharski was ordered to hold Westerplatte for 12 hours.

In Danzig, the Poles did the best they could to strengthen key positions, such as the post office. During the summer, the Polish Army had sent a trained engineer, Podporucznik Konrad Guderski, to fortify the post office. Guderski organized the postal workers, most of whom were military reservists, into a defensive force. Altogether, Guderski had 56 people (including two women) in the post office, with a total armament of three light machine guns, 40 assorted small arms and 60 grenades.[12]

During the night of 31 August/1 September, Kapitän zur See Kleikamp prepared his battleship *Schleswig-Holstein* for action, while Oberleutnant Henningsen's naval assault detachment (MSK) was landed on the eastern side of the Westerplatte Peninsula around 0200 hours. At 0448 hours, the *Schleswig-Holstein* opened fire on the Westerplatte garrison, from a range of less than 500m. However, the ship's two twin 28cm/40 gun turrets could only fire four rounds each per minute and the time of flight was so short that most rounds did not have time to arm. Instead, the 240kg HE projectiles smashed into the ground, in great clouds of dirt. Some of the battleship's 15cm secondary guns and a 2cm Flak gun also participated in the bombardment, which created three breaches in the eastern perimeter wall. Altogether, Kleikamp fired eight rounds of 28cm and 59 rounds of 15cm at Westerplatte. Yet amazingly, the seven-minute naval bombardment inflicted no casualties on the Polish garrison. It did succeed in setting a nearby German-owned oil storage facility on fire. At 0456 hours, the naval bombardment lifted and the German ground assault on the eastern end of the Peninsula began. Oberleutnant Henningsen's naval infantry moved through the breaches in the outer wall, deployed on line and advanced about 200m before encountering any resistance. Although there was some ground mist, the Polish fieldwork dubbed 'Prom' spotted Henningsen's men and opened a heavy fire with three machine guns. The MSK assault was repulsed with significant casualties. Two Polish soldiers were killed in the brief action, including a 39-year-old sergeant named Wojciech Najsarek – probably the first Polish military death in the Second World War.* At the same time as Henningsen's assault, the Kustenschutz der Danziger Polizei (a maritime unit of the Danzig police) attempted to seize the munitions basin on the western side of Westerplatte by crossing in small boats. However, three Polish positions on this side repulsed the police assault. The Germans had also established a number of machine-gun positions across the channel and opened heavy suppressive fire on Westerplatte. However, around 0515 hours the Poles got their 76.2mm field gun into position and silenced several machine-gun positions, including one in the Danzig lighthouse. The Poles also used their 37mm anti-tank guns to shoot at the *Schleswig-Holstein*, which shifted its position. At the same time, Polish 81mm mortars fired over 100 rounds, pounding the perimeter area where the MSK was still lurking.

Having been repulsed, Oberleutnant Henningsen reported to Kleikamp via radio that '*Verluste zu gross, gehen zurück*' ('Heavy losses, we're leaving'). He was ordered to regroup and prepare for another assault once reinforcements from the SS *Heimwehr Danzig* arrived. At 0740 hours, Kleikamp began a longer, heavier bombardment, expending 90 28cm, 47 15cm and 366 8.8cm rounds. Many of the heavy-calibre rounds ricocheted off into the sea beyond, but an 8.8cm round succeeded in knocking out the pesky Polish 76.2mm field gun. Smoke and mist obscured much of Westerplatte, making it difficult for Kleikamp to evaluate the results of his fire. At 0855 hours, Henningsen mounted a second attack, which succeeded in getting close to the 'Prom' position. Under pressure, the 20 soldiers in 'Prom' displaced rearward to the next line of defence, consisting of two fortified guard houses. When Henningsen advanced past 'Prom's' trenches, the MSK was caught in a machine-gun crossfire which inflicted heavy casualties. By noon, it was clear that the MSK lacked the strength to

---

*The Polish border guard Kapral Piotr Konieczka was killed three hours earlier, at Jeziorki. However, Najsarek was the first member of the Polish armed forces to die.

breach this position and Henningsen began pulling his men back; during the retreat he was mortally wounded.[13] Sucharski's troops had inflicted about 136 casualties upon the German assault troops – including one-third of the MSK (which suffered 15 dead, 56 wounded and three missing) – at a cost of only two Polish soldiers killed in action.[14] The Polish defences on Westerplatte were still intact and Eberhardt – who was not keen on wasting more troops on this objective – decided to ask for more firepower. He called for Luftwaffe support, but none was available due to cloud cover over Danzig.

While Henningsen's MSK was attacking Westerplatte, 6km to the south, another detachment from Gruppe Eberhardt moved to seize the post office in Danzig. The Schutzpolizei had been planning an attack on the post office since July and Polizeioberst Willi Bethke (the senior Danzig police officer) was designated to lead a 150-man assault group to seize the facility. The post office was located on the east side of a four-storey, L-shaped brick building; the west side was occupied by the Danzig Labour Office. The front entrance to the building was protected by a stout iron fence. Konrad had bricked off the passageways to the west side of the building, but Bethke planned to blast open these brick walls with grenades and gain access into the post office. Upon hearing the *Schleswig-Holstein's* opening barrage, Bethke ordered the assault to begin. A 19-man team led by SS-Untersturmführer Alfred Heinrich breached the brick wall with grenades but as they moved into the post office they were met by intense small arms fire, Heinrich was killed and his bloodied team retreated. Simultaneously, another group of Schutzpolizei tried to breach the eastern side of the building, but were also repulsed by intense fire. However, Konrad was mortally wounded in the initial attack and Alfrons Flisykowski, a reserve NCO, assumed command. Nonplussed by the failure of his assault, Bethke requested assistance from the SS *Heimwehr Danzig.*

Around 1000 hours, Albert Forster arrived, along with a photo team. He was astounded to find most of Bethke's troops resting in a courtyard. Reinforcements were beginning to arrive from the SS *Heimwehr Danzig,* including two ex-Austrian ADGZ armoured cars and two 7.5cm l.IG18 infantry guns. Forster impetuously decided to conduct a 'leaders recon' in the armoured car named 'Sudetenland', driving past the front of the post office while one his men threw grenades at the building; all of this was captured by Forster's photo team. Afterward, Forster ordered another assault on the front entrance, which was easily repulsed by heavy defensive fire. Since there obviously was no easy triumph to film here, Forster left and SS-Brigadeführer Johannes Schäfer assumed command over the motley force which now included Schutzpolizei, SS and SA troops. Rather than mounting another costly assault, Schäfer opted for siege tactics: a pioneer unit from the Eberhardt Brigade began tunnelling under the foundation of the building while the two 7.5cm guns and a single 10.5cm howitzer were positioned to support an attack on the front entrance. The 7.5cm guns blasted open the iron fence, but only damaged the building's façade. Around 1500 hours, Schäfer gave the Poles inside the post office a chance to surrender, but Flisykowski refused. At 1700 hours, the German sappers detonated a 600kg charge which blasted a hole in the front entrance. The 10.5cm howitzer fired into this gap, further collapsing the front of the building. This time, the German assault troops surged into the building, causing the Poles to retreat into the fortified basement. Schäfer opted to burn the Poles out, calling upon the local fire brigade to pour benzene into the basement, which was then set alight. Five defenders were killed outright and two more when they tried to emerge under a white flag. With the building on fire and their ammunition virtually expended, the remaining 44 defenders decided to surrender around 1900 hours. Six Poles managed to escape during the confusion, but the rest were soon tried by Gruppe Eberhardt and sentenced to death as 'illegal combatants', even though most were wearing Polish uniforms. On 5 October, 37 of the captured Polish postal workers were executed by the Schutzpolizei. The German attack on the Danzig post office was poorly executed and enabled an improvised Polish defence force to mount a 14-hour heroic stand.

While the fighting was going on at Westerplatte and the post office, Forster also moved to seize full control over the rest of the city. First on the list, he arrived with an armed detachment at the residence of Carl J. Burckhardt, the League Commissioner for Danzig, and told him that he had two hours to leave. Hustled out of his home by Gestapo officers, Burckhardt and his staff were allowed to drive through East Prussia to Lithuania.[15] Marian Chodacki, the Polish commissioner (and intelligence officer) in Danzig was arrested along with his staff. However, due to protests by Burckhardt, Forster surprisingly released Chodacki and allowed him to proceed to Lithuania. Less fortunate were the 3,000 Polish civilians in Danzig, who were roughly rounded up by the Schutzpolizei and taken to a detention camp at the Victoria School, which had been prepared ahead of time.

Meanwhile, Dąbek's Land Coastal Command was only lightly engaged by the enemy on the first day of the war, but witnessed Luftwaffe attacks against Polish naval targets around Gdynia and the Hel Peninsula. Oberst Karl-Albrecht von Groddeck's Danziger-Landespolizei-Regiment 2 crossed the border at Zoppot to seize the Polish customs office but was immediately fired upon by troops from Szpunar's 2 MPS. Groddeck had been tasked with seizing Gdynia if possible, but the defences of 2 MPS were too strong in this sector. Instead, Groddeck requested an air strike, which demolished the Polish naval barracks at nearby Kolibki, killing three naval infantrymen. However, once darkness fell, Szpunar sent combat patrols across the border to harass the Danzig policemen – inflicting several casualties – which was not at all to their liking. Thirty kilometres to the south-west, Kapitan Marian Mordawski's 4th Kartuzy ON Battalion was assigned to hold the town of Kartuzy, in an effort to keep open the lines of communication to Army Pomorze as long as possible. It is highly unusual in war for a single battalion to be deployed like this on its own, but typical of the sacrificial assignments required by the Land Coastal Command. Podporucznik Wojciech Stodulski, a platoon leader in the 3rd Company, was assigned to defend a position 8km west of Kartuzy, in anticipation of a German advance from the west. Most of his men were local farmers. In order to provide some mobile firepower, the battalion was supported by an improvised armoured train named 'the Kashubian Dragon', equipped with two 75mm guns. However, Stodulski and his men saw no action on the first day of the enemy invasion.[16] Instead, Generalleutnant Kaupisch sent the 207. Infanterie-Division across the border into the corridor, 30km south-west of the Kartuzy battalion. Otherwise, Kaupisch screened the northern section of the Polish–German border with his two border regiments, but he was not initially concerned with Polish forces around Gdynia.

Those elements of the Polish Navy that remained in Gdynia were surprisingly slow to react to the German invasion. Kontradmirał Unrug had planned to use his remaining vessels for two wartime contingency missions. First, in Operation *Rurka*, the minelayer *Gryf* was supposed to lay defensive minefields in the waters off the Hel Peninsula. Given the level of German provocations, the Poles would have been well advised to lay this minefield in late August, but instead they put it off. Nor was the *Gryf* even ready to begin the minelaying operation until 12 hours after *Fall Weiss* had begun. By the time that *Gryf* and her consorts did get under way, she was attacked by Stukas and damaged, causing Operation *Rurka* to be aborted. The second contingency mission was Operation *Worek*, which tasked the five available submarines to deploy around the Hel Peninsula in order to prevent any German landings on the northern coast and attack German merchant traffic. However, there was no German landing to contest and enemy merchant traffic had been cleared out of this area of the Baltic, leaving the Polish submarines little to do.

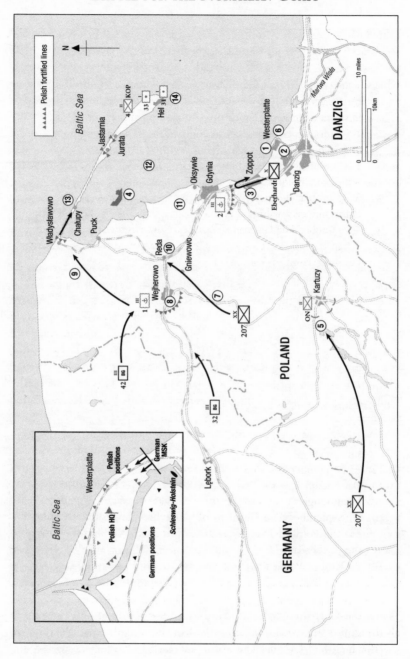

MAP KEY

1) 1 September. The German battleship *Schleswig-Holstein* fires upon the Polish military transshipment depot on Westerplatte, beginning hostilities. However, a German ground assault is repulsed.

2) 1 September. Gruppe Eberhardt attacks the Polish-held post office in Danzig, which manages to hold out for 14 hours.

3) 1 September. Gruppe Eberhardt tries to advance upon Gdynia but is blocked by Polish defences.

4) 3 September. The destroyer *Wicher* and minelayer *Gryf* – the last major Polish surface warships in Polish waters – are sunk by the Luftwaffe.

5) 4 September. The German 207. Infanterie-Division occupies Kartuzy.

6) 7 September. After another major German ground assault, the Polish garrison on Westerplatte finally surrenders.

7) 7 September. The German forces begin a co-ordinated offensive toward Gdynia, beginning with a maneouvre to isolate the Polish regiment at Wejherowo.

8) 9 September. The Polish regiment abandons Wejherowo before it is isolated and the Germans occupy the town.

9) 9 September. The German Grenzwacht-Regiment 42 isolates the Polish garrison on the Hel Peninsula.

10) 12 September. The 207. Infanterie-Division breaks the Polish position at Reda, forcing the Polish Land Coastal Command to order a retreat into the Kępa Oksywska for a final stand.

11) 19 September. The last Polish defenders in the Kępa Oksywska surrender.

12) 25 September. The German battleship *Schliesen* moves into Danzig Bay and engages the Polish batteries on the Hel Peninsula at point-blank range.

13) 30 September. The Germans overrun the strongpoint at Chalupy, but the Polish defenders create a moat across the narrow waist of the peninsula.

14) 2 October. Polish forces on the Hel Peninsula surrender.

When the German attack commenced on the morning of 1 September, all the Polish submarines were berthed in the naval base at Oksywie, on the north side of Gdynia. The Polish submarines began to sortie around 0600 hours and all reached their initial operational stations without difficulty. However, the waters around the Hel Peninsula were extremely shallow – typically 50m or less – which made it easy for German aircraft and surface vessels to detect the Polish submarines. The Kriegsmarine's Marinegruppe Ost (Marine Group East) deployed an overwhelming force off the Hel Peninsula, including ten destroyers, 21 minesweepers and six *Schnellboote*.[17] In addition, Kustenfliegergruppe 506 could conduct maritime reconnaissance and strike missions with about 40 aircraft. The Polish submarines had to remain submerged all through daylight hours and could barely move without their periscopes attracting attention. Between 2 and 5 September, each of the Polish submarines was detected, depth-charged and damaged, although none were sunk. Efforts to attack enemy shipping came to naught, with a total of only three torpedoes fired. *Orzel*, one of the most modern submarines, was ordered to attack the *Schleswig-Holstein* if it left Danzig, but never got the chance. The *Wilk* and *Zbik* both managed to lay a few mines, one of which sank the German minesweeper M-85 just before the end of the campaign. By 6 September, it was obvious that Operation *Worek* was impractical and the individual submarine commanders moved off into deeper waters in the Baltic to reduce the risk of detection. After 11 days at sea, mostly submerged, the submarines were running low on fuel and all were damaged. Kontradmirał Unrug radioed them and told them they had the option of either trying to make for Britain or seeking internment in Sweden. The *Wilk* succeeded in reaching Britain on 20 September, but *Rys*, *Zbik* and *Sep* were interned in Sweden, while *Orzel* was interned in Lithuania (but later dramatically escaped to Britain on 14 October 1939). This was a dismal end for most of the Polish submarine squadrons and it was clear that lack of prior detailed war planning had prevented them from playing any useful role in the campaign.

The second day of the war at Westerplatte began with light German harassing fire, which continued all morning. Gruppe Eberhardt was now formally attached to Bock's Heeresgruppe Nord. Hitler was disappointed by the initial failure at Westerplatte and ordered Bock not to attack again until 'the outlook for success is certain'.[18] Bock called for an assault pioneer unit commanded by Oberstleutnant Karl Henke and a battery of 21cm mortars to proceed to Westerplatte. Requests for Luftwaffe air support still met with no success, since bombing Westerplatte was not a priority for Luftflotte 1; it must also have been difficult for Kesselring to understand why Eberhardt needed air support when he had a battleship at his disposal. Major Sucharski also called for air support. In Warsaw, Generał Zając briefly considered using the Bomber Brigade to attack the

Schleswig-Holstein, but decided to conserve his precious bombers for more vital targets. By this point, the Polish High Command had clearly written off Westerplatte's tiny garrison and was not going to commit resources to a perceived lost cause. However, striking a stationary target like the *Schleswig-Holstein* might also have given a vital boost to Polish national morale in the early stages of the war. Instead, the Luftwaffe finally agreed to Eberhardt's request in the late afternoon of 2 September and over 50 Stukas from StG 2 'Immelmann' began a 30-minute attack at 1805 hours. Altogether, about 26 tonnes of bombs were dropped on Westerplatte – a very concentrated attack on a small target. On this occasion the Stukas also demonstrated pin-point accuracy, demolishing one guard house and damaging the barracks; ten Polish soldiers were killed and six wounded. Sucharski was in the barracks when it was hit by two 50kg bombs, which badly rattled him. There was great confusion in the immediate aftermath of the Stuka attack but most post-war sources agree that a shaken Sucharski wanted to surrender the garrison at this point, but was talked out of it by his second-in-command, Kapitan Franciszek Dąbrowski. It is also clear that Dąbrowski led the defence for the next five days, not Sucharski.[19] The Germans should have followed up the Stuka attack with another ground assault while the garrison was still shell-shocked, but they did not. Given a respite, the Polish garrison recovered their equilibrium and re-established their defence.

Oberstleutnant Henke's assault pioneer detachment, equipped with flamethrowers and demolition charges, arrived on the morning of 3 September. Henke assessed the Polish defence as too difficult to overcome without further reinforcements. Having first underestimated the Polish defences on Westerplatte, the Germans now seriously overestimated the Polish defences and believed that they were partly underground. Consequently, the Germans conducted only minor patrolling and harassing fire against Westerplatte on 3–5 September. On the fifth day of the siege a German 10.5cm howitzer battery bombarded Westerplatte, but many shells were improperly fused and did not explode – likely the work of reservist artillerymen not yet fully schooled in their trade. On 6 September, the Germans twice failed to set the woods on Westerplatte afire but had greater success when they brought up a battery of elderly 21cm Mörser 16 howitzers from the First World War; these weapons, designed to defeat fortifications, inflicted considerable damage on the Polish positions.

The Germans finally decided to mount another major assault against Westerplatte on 7 September, beginning at 0422 hours with another bombardment by the *Schleswig-Holstein*. By this point, most of the tree cover on Westerplatte was down and the Germans could better observe Polish positions. Rather than the big 28cm guns, it was lighter 8.8cm guns that were able to accurately engage the now-visible Polish positions. At 0500 hours, Henke's assault pioneers attacked, along with troops from the SS *Heimwehr Danzig* and the remaining MSK troops. Henke proceeded cautiously, but succeeded in knocking out one of the key Polish positions with flamethrowers by 0830 hours. Recognizing that their defence was now crumbling in the face of a co-ordinated assault, Sucharski and Dąbrowski jointly agreed to surrender around 1000 hours. An hour later, the Germans accepted that surrender. The Polish garrison on Westerplatte had held out for seven days at a cost of about 15 dead and 53 wounded, while inflicting about 200 casualties on the enemy.[20] Although the defence of Westerplatte was meaningless in the grand scheme of *Fall Weiss,* it did demonstrate how unexpected obstinate resistance could upset German plans.

On the night of 7/8 September, Albert Forster imprudently decided to hold a torch-lit victory parade in Danzig to celebrate the fall of Westerplatte. Reichsführer-SS Heinrich Himmler was in attendance. Unfortunately, the Polish Naval Air Division ruined the parade with an impromptu night bombing mission using an R.XIIIG floatplane, which took off from the water near the Hel Peninsula. The Polish aircraft had actually been sent to bomb the *Schleswig-Holstein* but was drawn to the light and noise of the parade and managed to approach at a height of just 400m. The two Polish naval aviators dropped six 12.5kg bombs on the parade, then strafed it with its machine gun before departing. German casualties were probably light due to the small size of the bombs, but the Nazi leadership was chagrined by this bold enemy action and imposed tight security on the incident.

While the Polish garrison on Westerplatte was slowly being crushed, the defenders of Gdynia and the Hel Peninsula were harassed by intermittent German air raids and naval bombardment, but enemy activity on the ground in their sector remained minimal on 2–3 September. Using materials from the shipyard in Gdynia, the Poles were able to prepare two more improvised armoured trains, equipped with machine guns and surplus naval guns. The Land Coastal Command used its armoured trains to patrol the areas west and south of Gdynia, looking for the approach of enemy forces. However, Kaupisch's forces were advancing very slowly towards Gdynia; indeed, this was the one place where the invaders were moving more slowly than the Poles had expected. Generalmajor Carl von Tiedemann, a 61-year-old Landwehr officer, commanded the 207. Infanterie-Division, which was the main element in Kaupisch's command. This division had only been formed from older Landwehr personnel at Stargard on 26 August, then had to move 180km to the German–Polish border. When the war started, the division was still sorting itself out. After significant prodding, Tiedemann's division moved across the border and finally bumped into the 4th Kartuzy ON Battalion at Kartuzy on the afternoon of 4 September. Podporucznik Wojciech Stodulski reported that although his defensive position was strong, the enemy threatened to cut off his isolated platoon and he was ordered to pull back. He said that:

> I kept my platoon for a while in the village of Cegielnia, in a small beech forest by the road, until the other platoon arrived. After a few minutes, the company's commander, Lieutenant Perkowski and his platoon joined mine. The enemy was following right behind him and soon opened fire. I ran to the company commander and said, 'Captain, let's make a counter-attack', but he responded that 'there is no time to fight, the path of retreat is closing in front of us. Send two machine guns to the hill, which are to stop the enemy, the rest will retreat.' As my platoon retreated, I said goodbye to my wife and three children, standing in front of Skrzypkowski's hut. Great pain pierced my heart! I clenched my teeth so that I would not break into tears, squeezed my revolver and marched there with the platoon, where he ordered me.[21]

Stodulski and his platoon succeeded in escaping from the pursuing Germans, and the battalion managed to force-march to link up with Pruszkowski's 1 MPS at Wejherowo by the morning of 5 September. Many troops had been lost in the retreat and the abandonment of family members to the Germans could hardly have been good for morale. Two of the improvised trains were also lost in the retreat. However, Kaupisch did not immediately follow up the capture of Kartuzy because he was waiting for his two border guard regiments to cross the border and for Brigade Eberhardt to begin advancing up the coast from Danzig to Gdynia. It was not until 7 September that Kaupisch ordered a concerted advance upon Gdynia, with Tiedemann's 207. Infanterie-Division advancing from the south-west and Groddeck's Danziger-Landespolizei-Regiment 2 from the south. Elements of the Grenzwacht-Regimenter 32 and 42 (Border Security Regiments 32 and 42), equivalent to a few battalions, crossed the Polish border north-west of Wejherowo. Given the limited number of troops available to defend an extended perimeter around Gdynia, Pruszkowski had deployed his 1 MPS with an emphasis upon blocking the most likely enemy avenue of approach – from the west. Prior to the war, his naval infantrymen had strung 16km of barbed wire, dug anti-tank ditches and built two dozen bunkers, turning Wejherowo into a fortified hedgehog. However, Pruszkowski assigned the 4th Kartuzy ON battalion to defend the area south-east of Wejherowo. On the morning of 7 September, Podporucznik Stodulski's platoon was again defending an advance outpost when elements of the 207. Infanterie-Division's reconnaissance battalion arrived. Stodulski managed to eliminate the first enemy motorcyclists with his machine guns and repulse the initial attack. However, the next morning, Tiedemann's division launched a major assault, brushing aside Stodulski's unit and advancing rapidly upon Wejherowo from the south. Polish pre-battle reconnaissance had failed to anticipate the enemy's course of action and now the Germans were able to easily push back the Polish left flank and threaten to cut off the 1 MPS's line of retreat to Gdynia. By late in the day, the German Infanterie-Regiment 322 was at Gniewowo, only 3km south of the Wejherowo–Gdynia road. Pruszkowski was reluctant to give up his fortified position without a fight, but on the night of 8 September he ordered the 1 MPS to retreat to Reda. The Polish units were forced to disengage and run a gauntlet of enemy artillery fire, which inflicted heavy casualties. Many troops became mis-oriented in the woods at night. By the time that Pruszkowski re-assembled the 1 MPS at Reda, he only had half his troops left. On the morning of 9 September, the 207. Infanterie-Division marched unopposed into Wejherowo. At the same time, the Grenzwacht-Regiment 42 marched into Puck on the Bay of Danzig and sealed off the Hel Peninsula.[22]

After occupying Wejherowo, Tiedemann's 207. Infanterie-Division pushed east towards Reda and deployed into the forests south of that town. The Poles managed to ambush the lead German battalion and inflict heavy casualties. Pruszkowski made a desperate stand at Reda and tried to block German infiltration along forest trails, but the lack of prepared positions left his troops exposed to enemy artillery fire. In addition to his own divisional artillery, Tiedemann had one attached heavy artillery regiment, giving him a total of 60 howitzers, whereas Pruszkowski had very modest artillery support. With a numerical advantage of better than 3:1, Tiedemann's infantry tried to outflank the Polish strongpoints, although the 1 MPS put up a very determined fight for two days around Reda. By

12 September, Pruszkowski had lost more than half his regiment and the Germans were just beginning to employ their full strength. Pułkownik Stanisław Dąbek decided to mount a counter-attack to try and prevent the Germans from enveloping the weakened 1 MPS, but this effort failed. The improvised armoured train 'Dragon' was supposed to support the counter-attack but was knocked out by Stukas. Consequently, on the evening of 12 September, Dąbek ordered all units in the Land Coastal Command to pull back into the Kępa Oksywska region for a final stand. After the fall of Westerplatte, Brigade Eberhardt was able to commit the bulk of its troops to this sector, pressing north from Zoppot towards Gdynia.

Once Dąbek's forces were pressed into the Kępa Oksywska, which was mostly flat terrain, with little cover, Kaupisch relied upon his artillery and Luftwaffe air strikes to reduce the defenders. The battleship *Schleswig-Holstein* was also brought up to shell the defenders from the seaward side; this was no longer a battle, but a slaughter. Despite running short of ammunition, the Poles managed to resist for another week. On 14 September, the Germans entered Gdynia and Dąbek's remaining forces were being split up into small pockets. Podporucznik Stodulski fought with the remnants of his battalion until he was badly wounded by artillery fire. By the afternoon of 19 September, when the defence crumbled, Pruszkowski's 1 MPS only had 197 of its original 1,841 men still standing. Unwilling to surrender to the Germans, Dąbek shot himself in the head. The commanders of both the 1 and 2 MPS were captured and survived the war. Altogether, the Land Coastal Command had suffered roughly 4,500 casualties in the defence of Gdynia, including about 2,250 dead or missing. Three-quarters of the Polish casualties were ON troops. German losses in the fight for Gdynia were quite heavy, despite their advantage in firepower. Tiedemann's 207. Infanterie-Division suffered nearly 1,000 casualties and the two border guard regiments a total of over 300; altogether the capture of Gdynia cost the Germans more than 400 killed in action.

The battle of Kępa Oksywska has gone down as a tragic but immortal moment of the 1939 campaign – at least according to Polish military mythology. Yet despite the fact that the Land Coastal Command had a week to perfect its defensive perimeter before the enemy arrived in force, the Polish defence was quickly outflanked by second-rate German units. Pułkownik Stanisław Dąbek bears the responsibility for the poor deployment of his forces, particularly leaving the 1 MPS exposed at Wejherowo. Although Dąbek has been lionized in Polish military history, his suicide was rather bizarre and an aberration since few Polish officers opted for suicide rather than surrender. Indeed, given that most Polish military officers were Catholic and suicide is a mortal sin for Catholics, saluting this behaviour – which effectively meant abandoning his troops – seems at odd with Polish military traditions. Many Polish officers displayed great fortitude and resiliency in German captivity, rather than seeking an easy way out. Indeed, it was the German officer corps, when faced with defeat in 1944–45, that would often opt for suicide rather than surrender.

After the fall of Gdynia, the only Polish position left on the Baltic Coast was the garrison of the Hel Peninsula. The peninsula had been isolated since 8 September when the Grenzwacht-Regiment 42 occupied the headland. However, Major Jan Wiśniewski's 4th Battalion KOP only had to defend a 300m-wide front near Chalupy. The Luftwaffe regularly attacked the coastal batteries on the Hel Peninsula, but the anti-aircraft batteries were reinforced with guns salvaged from sunken warships and a battery of 40mm guns found in a warehouse in Gdynia (these guns were in the process of being shipped to Britain); during the month of September the Polish anti-aircraft gunners shot down at least a dozen German aircraft. Amazingly, the seaplanes of the Naval Air Division were able to operate from Jurata until they were finally destroyed by a German air raid on 8 September. The Polish minesweeper squadron also remained active for a time, supporting the defence of Hel with three boats, until they too were bombed and sunk on 14 September. After the fall of Westerplatte, the Kriegsmarine deployed the battleships *Schlesien* and *Schleswig-Holstein* to shell the Hel Peninsula, beginning on 17 September. Coastal Battery 31, with its four modern Bofors 152mm gun, struck back whenever the German battleships came close enough – which was not often. Instead, the German battleships shelled the peninsula from long range with just their 28cm guns, inflicting only moderate damage. By 25 September, German minesweepers had cleared Danzig Bay of mines and the battleship *Schlesien* moved into the bay to engage Coastal Battery 31 at a range of just 1,500m. Accuracy on both sides was poor. During an 83-minute long bombardment, *Schlesien* fired 29 28cm and 86 15cm rounds, but only achieved a few near-misses on the Polish battery.[23] It was not until 27 September that Battery 31 scored a hit on the *Schleswig-Holstein,* killing six sailors and forcing the battleship to pull off. Altogether, the *Schlesien* fired 337 28cm and 512 15cm rounds at the Polish defences on Hel, but inflicted surprisingly little material damage.

Kaupisch gradually tightened his grip on the Hel Peninsula but was reluctant to make a ground assault. Instead, he used artillery and the Luftwaffe to soften up the defenders. After the fall of Gdynia, morale in the garrison began to disintegrate, as it became clear that there would be no relief. By 29 September, some of the Polish troops were refusing to fight on and had to be placed under arrest. On 30 September, the Germans overran the strongpoint at Chalupy and in response, Polish engineers detonated 83 torpedo warheads, which effectively created a moat across the narrow neck of the peninsula. However, Kontradmiral Unrug recognized that both morale and supplies were dwindling and finally requested surrender on 1 October. Some personnel attempted to flee, but the only ones who reached safety were 16 sailors on the small cutter *Batory*, which managed to reach Sweden. At 1100 hours on 2 October, the Germans occupied the Hel Peninsula and 3,600 Polish troops went into captivity. During the month-long defence, the garrison suffered about 250 casualties. In captivity, the Germans attempted to get Kontradmiral Unrug, an ethnic German, to switch sides and join the Kriegsmarine – but he refused. Indeed, although a native German speaker, Unrug refused to speak anything but Polish to his captors during interrogation.

The Germans had not bargained for a prolonged fight on the northern coast and their efforts were marred by low-quality troops and mediocre tactical leadership. In contrast to the war of manoeuvre employed elsewhere in Poland, the campaign along the Baltic coast was a war of position, in which the heavily fortified Poles could not be quickly eliminated. The Kriegsmarine's employment of two elderly battleships was unimaginative and accomplished very little against the Polish defenders. Instead, it was the combination of air strikes and artillery which gradually eroded the Polish defences. On the other hand, the Polish conduct of the campaign on the Baltic coast was not only futile but undermined by lack of effective pre-war planning. In particular, the Germans never should have been able to operate two battleships so close in to shore and under continuous Polish observation without paying a price. Despite the fact that the entire purpose of the Polish Navy was to protect the northern coast, it had remarkably few resources to contest the area. Aside from the modern 152mm battery on Cape Hel, the Navy had only a small number of ex-Russian mines and very few of these were ever deployed. The five available submarines were unsuited and poorly trained to attack the Kriegsmarine units operating near the coast. Given what Norwegian coastal defences would accomplish against the Kriegsmarine seven months later – sinking the heavy cruiser *Blucher* with ancient torpedoes – the performance of the Polish coastal defences must be judged sub-par, despite heroic efforts. If Poland was going to invest scarce resources into building a navy and coast defences to protect its bases, it should have built forces that had some ability to inflict significant damage on the enemy. Instead, the best parts of the Polish Navy fled to Britain or Sweden, leaving forlorn garrisons to defend bases that no longer served any purpose.

The Defeat of Army Pomorze, 1–3 September

'The purpose of war is not to achieve a geographical line, but to physically exterminate enemies.'

Hitler's speech at the Obersalzburg, 22 August 1939[24]

Generał Dywizji Władysław Bortnowski's Army Pomorze had the difficult task of trying to defend Pomerania, including the southern portion of the Polish Corridor. Since the Germans were expected to simultaneously attack this region from both the west and the east, Bortnowski had to divide his limited forces to fight a 'two-front' war. Consequently, he deployed his 9th and 15th Infantry Divisions (9 and 15 DP) to face the German 4. Armee in West Prussia and the Operational Group East (4 and 16 DP) to face the German 3. Armee in East Prussia. Furthermore, since the Polish High Command insisted on keeping some forces within range of Danzig for potential use by the Intervention Corps, Bortnowski had to deploy Operational Group Czersk (27 DP and Pomorska Cavalry Brigade) facing northwards. As part of mobilization, Army Pomorze would gain 15 ON battalions, which would be apportioned to reinforce the front-line divisions. However, Army Pomorze would have no appreciable reserves. The 47-year-old Bortnowski was one of the better operational commanders in the Polish Army, having plenty of combat experience from the Polish Legions and the Russo-Polish War. More recently, he had commanded the Polish operational group which re-occupied Teschen in 1938. He was also well educated in both the civilian and military spheres, including time at the French École supérieure de guerre. Bortnowski recognized that his army was poorly positioned for a defence, but the Supreme Command had mandated that Pomerania and the Corridor would be defended. Nor could Army Pomorze even create a continuous front with the Polish armies on either flank, due to the distances involved.

The primary mission of Bock's Heeresgruppe Nord was to crush Army Pomorze and quickly clear the corridor, thereby establishing a ground link with East Prussia. The main effort would be made by General der Artillerie Günther Kluge's 4. Armee, attacking from West Prussia. General der Panzertruppe Heinz Guderian's XIX Armeekorps (mot.) would spearhead the advance, supported by two infantry corps. Guderian's formation was the culmination of everything that the Reichswehr and Wehrmacht had learned about mechanized warfare in the previous 20 years. Altogether, Guderian's XIX Armeekorps (mot.) consisted of nearly 52,000 troops, 156 medium artillery pieces. 8,760 motor vehicles and 530 armoured fighting vehicles; it was a complete, combined arms force, capable of achieving independent operational-level missions. In comparison, the other five infantry divisions in 4. Armee were still tied to horse-drawn artillery and logistic columns. General der Artillerie Georg von Küchler's 3. Armee, in East Prussia, would attack Army Pomorze with its XXI Armeekorps, but the bulk of its forces would attack Army Modlin, north of Warsaw.

Bock's Heeresgruppe Nord began crossing the German–Polish border at 0445 hours on 1 September, in conjunction with the opening salvoes at Danzig. However, heavy ground fog obscured the terrain until 1000 hours. In the 3. Panzer-Division sector, Guderian decided to lead with the Panzer-Lehr-Abteilung – rather than the reconnaissance or motorcycle units as doctrine recommended – since this unit was equipped with the latest models of Pz III and Pz IV medium tanks.* Guderian was eager to see his Panzertruppe in action and he appropriated one of the brand-new SdKfz. 251 halftracks (SPW) to use as his command vehicle, but this quickly went awry. Shortly after crossing the border, Guderian's driver drove at full speed into a ditch and damaged the half-track, requiring Guderian to look for another vehicle.[25] In the meantime, the 3. Panzer-Division pushed ahead into the mist, unopposed. Bortnowski had decided

---

*The Panzer-Lehr-Abteilung was a demonstration unit, equipped with a total of 74 tanks, including 37 Pz IIIs and 14 Pz IVs. During *Fall Weiss* it was attached to Panzer-Regiment 6. In comparison, the rest of the 3. Panzer-Division only possessed a total of six Pz III and 18 Pz IV medium tanks.

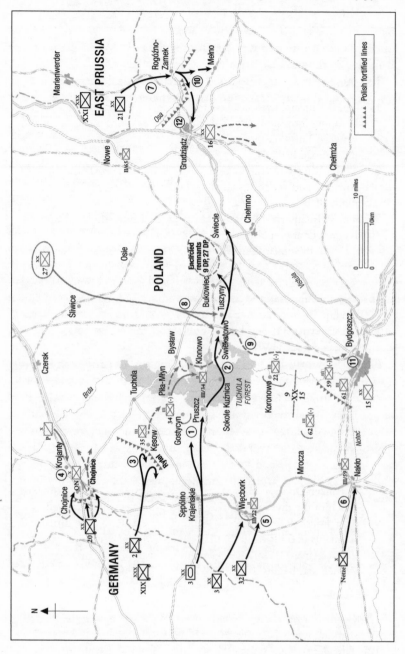

MAP KEY

1 September

1) The 3. Panzer-Division advances eastward against no resistance, until bumping into the Polish 34th Infantry Regiment at Gostycyn and Pruszcz. The Poles manage to burn Guderian's initial objective – the railroad bridge over the Brda River.

2) The 3. Panzer-Division conducts an assault river crossing at Sokole-Kuznica and reconnaissance units race to reach Swiekatowo by nightfall.

3) The 2. Infanterie-Division (mot.) attacks against the 35th Infantry Regiment are repulsed.

4) The 20. Infanterie-Division (mot.) attempts to encircle the Polish ON brigade in Chojnice, but the Polish brigade withdraws before it is isolated. During the withdrawal, the Pomorska Cavalry Brigade mounts a mounted cavalry charge at Krojanty to spoil the German pursuit.

5) The German II Armeekorps advances and destroys the Polish covering force at Wiecbork.

6) The German Brigade Netze advances but the Polish garrison of Naklo abandons the town without a fight.

7) The German XXI Armeekorps advances from East Prussia against Grudziadz, held by the Polish 16 DP, and begins assaulting the Osa line.

2 September

8) The Polish 27 DP launches an attack against the flank of the 3. Panzer-Division but fails. Some remnants escape southward, but much of the division is isolated near Bukowiec and destroyed.

9) The Polish 9 DP fights a running retreat across the Brda and remnants of 35 PP and 22 PP escape south to Bydgoszcz.

10) The German 21. Infanterie-Division crosses the Osa at Rogóźno-Zamek and begins to outflank the 16 DP's defences.

3 September

11) German fifth columnists shoot at Polish troops in Bydgoszcz, sparking reprisals against ethnic Germans in the city.

12) The German XXI Armeekorps enters Grudziadz, while the 16 DP retreats in disorder.

to keep his divisions at least 10km back from the border, where they would not immediately be exposed to surprise attack. Another reason was that this area was heavily populated by ethnic Germans and Bortnowski was concerned that they might provide information about his dispositions to the enemy. However, the Polish failure to deploy even minimal covering forces along the border was a serious tactical mistake because it deprived Polish forward units of early warning about enemy movements; even a few reservists with field telephones would have sufficed. Due to the mist, Guderian's Panzers advanced very slowly – the movement to contact took nearly five hours to move 31km. Only a few Polish border guards were spotted along the way. After passing the town of Sępólno Krajeńskie, the 3. Panzer-Division fanned out, with Panzer-Regiment 6 on the left and Panzer-Regiment 5 on the right. By 0915 hours, Panzer-Regiment 5 had reached the village of Pruscz and was approaching its initial objective – the railroad bridge over the Brda River.[26]

The Polish 9th Infantry Division (9 DP) was deployed in Guderian's path, but it was spread across a 48km-wide front (triple the maximum frontage a division could defend). During the summer, the 9 DP had built some obstacles and fortified positions along the most likely enemy avenues of approach, but it did not have a continuous front. Indeed, there was a 20km-wide gap between the 34th Infantry Regiment (34 PP) in the centre and the 22nd Infantry Regiment (22 PP) in the south. The 9 DP commander, Pułkownik Józef Werobej, placed his division bicycle company and a detached infantry company in this gap to conduct a screening mission. Oddly, Werobej had not placed any screening forces to watch the border and his first intimation that war had begun was provided by local villagers fleeing the German advance. Major Stanisław Wojtaszewski's I/34 PP was located around the village of Gostycyn, directly in Guderian's path. Panzer-Regiment 6 advanced in a long column down the road towards Wielka Klonia, which was held by a Polish combat outpost from the I/34 PP. The German tanks advanced without forward reconnaissance elements and were engaged by the Polish outpost, which had two 37mm anti-tank guns. Two German Pz II light tanks were destroyed and seven Panzertruppen were killed. Shocked by the sudden loss, the German tanks pulled back and brought up a 10.5cm howitzer battery, which bombarded the Polish position. Both anti-tank guns were destroyed and four Polish soldiers killed, causing the Polish platoon leader to withdraw the survivors towards the battalion's main position.[27]

Earlier in the morning, Werobej had decided to shift the III/34 PP to cover the Pruscz sector, but Panzer-Regiment 5 got there first. Nevertheless, a few Polish troops managed to reach the railway embankment just east of the town, which provided a real obstacle. In order to proceed towards the Brda River, just 3km to the east, German vehicles had to move single file through two U-shaped underpasses. The first vehicle through was a Pz IV medium tank, which was destroyed by point-blank fire from a Polish 37mm anti-tank gun. One German tank company tried to suppress the Polish positions but fired all its ammunition off in ten minutes. Eventually, after two hours' desultory combat, the Germans pushed through the obstacles and overran the small numbers of defenders; 22 Polish soldiers were killed in this action. Shortly thereafter, Panzer-Regiment 5 reached the railroad bridge at the Brda River, which they found had been partly burned by the Poles. Only a small number of Polish defenders were on the opposite bank, 200m away. Oddly, the 3. Panzer-Division suddenly decided to pause for a rest in front of the Brda, which infuriated Guderian when he reached Pruscz.[28] He ordered Oberstleutnant Günther von Manteuffel's Kradschützen-Bataillon 3 to move forwards and conduct an assault crossing of the Brda at Sokole-Kuźnica with rubber boats, which was accomplished by 1800 hours. Manteuffel's infantry swiftly eliminated the handful of defenders and pioneers arrived to repair the damaged bridge. As soon as the bridge was passable, Guderian despatched the Aufklärungs-Abteilung 3 and ordered it to advance through the Tuchola Forest to Swiekatowo. Werobej was unaware that the Germans had crossed the Brda for three hours and even then had no reserves available to deal with this enemy penetration.

Guderian's style of leadership from the front has often been praised by military historians, but he showed his limitations as a corps commander on the first day of the war. While he was influencing events at Pruscz – and thereby stepping on the toes of the division and brigade commanders – he paid very little heed to what was going on with the rest of his corps. Just 4km to the north, Panzer-Regiment 6 tried to advance into Gostycyn but was stopped by fierce resistance from Major Wojtaszewski's battalion. Several German tanks were damaged and fighting went on until mid-afternoon. Indeed, Major Wojtaszewski's battalion held off the 3. Panzer-Division for the rest of the day until midnight, when he was ordered to retreat to secure the crossing of the Brda at Piła-Młyn. Guderian also ignored the logistics of mobile warfare; by nightfall several of the advance battalions were out of fuel and ammunition, but the supply columns were well to the rear.

Even worse was Guderian's neglect of the two motorized infantry divisions under his command, which were supposed to be supporting the 3. Panzer-Division. The 2. Infanterie-Division (mot.) was supposed to advance to seize the town of Tuchola, which was defended by Podpułkownik Jan Maliszewski's 35th Infantry Regiment (35 PP). During the summer months, the 35 PP had constructed the fortified 'Rytel' position, complete with trenches, barbed wire and six concrete machine-gun bunkers. Approximately 82 per cent of the troops in Maliszewski's 3,300-man regiment were reservists, but the regiment was provided with substantial artillery support (20 guns, including three 155mm, three 105mm and 12 100mm howitzers). In contrast, Generalleutnant Paul Bader's 2. Infanterie-Division (mot.) was an active division with over 16,000 troops and 48 howitzers in support.[29] After crossing the border and pushing back some Polish screening units, Bader advanced towards the 'Rytel' position with all three of his regiments on line and mounted a frontal attack around 1130 hours. Right off, the German attack went badly because troops had to attack across flat, marshy terrain, while the Polish positions were concealed atop heavily wooded high ground. Polish machine guns and artillery inflicted heavy casualties upon the attacking German infantry, who were repulsed. Bader continued to attack in 1918-style, completely forgetting the superior mobility of his division. After six hours, the 2. Infanterie-Division (mot.) had failed to break through the 'Rytel' position and Maliszewski had won a tactical victory. However, he was later ordered to abandon this position in response to the penetration of the 3. Panzer-Division to the south.[30]

The attack of the 20. Infanterie-Division (mot.) was slightly more successful at Chojnice. Bortnowski had deployed an independent group to defend the transportation hub at Chojnice, consisting of three infantry battalions, three light artillery batteries and some sappers. Initially, the Germans attempted to seize the train station with a *coup de main*, using an armoured train and two platoons of concealed infantry. However, the Poles reacted quickly, disabling the train with a 75mm gun and capturing some of the raiders. Despite the fact that the defence comprised mostly ON troops and was forced to cover both the western and southern approaches to the city, the Chojnice detachment managed to hold off the 20. Infanterie-Division (mot.) until 1400 hours. The German motorized infantry gradually enveloped Chojnice on both flanks, threatening to surround the defenders. At that point, the garrison was ordered to abandon the town and withdraw to the north-east. The 18th Regiment of Pomeranian Uhlans, detached from the Pomorska Cavalry Brigade, was ordered to support the withdrawal of the Chojnice detachment. Pułkownik Kazimierz Mastalerz, the regimental commander, was ordered to counter-attack the pursuing 20. Infanterie-Division (mot.) with at least two cavalry squadrons. Around 1900 hours, Mastalerz led a mounted charge against the II./Infanterie Regiment 76 (mot.) near Krojanty, which was caught in the open and not expecting an enemy counter-attack. Initially, the Polish charge scattered the dismounted battalion but German armoured cars quickly appeared on the scene and opened fire on the Polish cavalrymen; Mastalerz was killed and the two squadrons retreated having lost one-third of their riders. Later, Nazi propaganda distorted and exaggerated the action at Krojanty, claiming that Polish cavalry had suicidally charged German tanks. In any case, the Polish cavalry counter-attack enabled the Chojnice detachment to withdraw unmolested.[31]

Meanwhile, the rest of Kluge's 4. Armee, the II and III Armeekorps, advanced slowly across the Polish border, on Guderian's right flank. The II Armeekorps (3. and 32. Infanterie-Divisionen) crossed the border and attacked the small Polish covering force at Wiecbork, the III/22 PP and an ON battalion. Both Polish battalions were destroyed in this lop-sided engagement. It was foolish to deploy such a small force so close to the border without any nearby support – the rest of the 22 PP was 30km to the east. Further south, the German III Armeekorps advanced towards Bydgoszcz, which was defended by the 15 DP. Brigade Netze, comprised primarily of German border guards with limited support weapons, advanced eastwards along the main road to Bydgoszcz. The 15 DP had only deployed insignificant forces to defend the town of Nakło, 24km west of Bydgoszcz, consisting of one regular infantry battalion and one ON battalion. However, the small number of troops had dug trenches and strung barbed wire on the main approaches to the town.[32] Nevertheless, upon learning of the German invasion, the 15 DP ordered the small garrison to evacuate the city and fall back upon Bydgoszcz – a premature and foolish decision. The bulk of the 15 DP was concentrated near Bydgoszcz and was unengaged at this point. By late afternoon, Brigade Netze reached the undefended town of Nakło. Had the 15 DP chosen to make a stand at Nakło, it is likely they could have inflicted significant casualties on a second-rate formation such as Brigade Netze. Indeed, a Polish cavalry brigade could have wreaked havoc on a lone German leg infantry unit such as this – but there was no Polish cavalry in this sector. The Wehrmacht was taking a chance using border guard units as assault troops in Poland, but in most cases, the Polish Army failed to take advantage of this risky German practice. Later in the war, the Wehrmacht would continue its habit of using second-rate allied troops in secondary sectors and they would suffer the consequences.

Army Pomorze also had to contend with an attack from East Prussia, made by 3. Armee. In this sector, the Germans actually began hostilities prior to the official start of the invasion by attempting to mount a 'Trojan horse' operation to seize the two bridges over the Vistula at Tczew. Gruppe Medem used a civilian goods train with personnel dressed in Polish railway worker uniforms but carrying a concealed company from Pionier-Bataillon 41 (Pioneer Battalion 41), followed by Armoured Train No. 7 with another pioneer company, to attempt to seize the bridges prior to 0445 hours. During the subterfuge, the German troops involved murdered a number of Polish railway and customs guards who attempted to warn the bridge security platoon – the first German war crimes committed during the Second World War. This *coup de main* was carefully timed with the first Luftwaffe attack of the war – a mission by three Ju 87s from I./ StG 1 – intended to destroy the demolition wiring for the bridges.[33] However, the Poles were alerted and prevented the train from reaching the bridge, which was defended by a platoon from the 2nd Rifle Battalion. After a brief firefight, the Poles demolished the first bridge at 0601 hours, followed by the other at 0640 hours (using 10 tonnes of explosives), thereby frustrating the intent of 3. Armee to quickly seize an intact crossing over the Vistula. However, SS-Obersturmbannführer Hans-Friedemann Götze led a battalion from the SS-Heimwehr Danzig to attack Tczew from the north-west while Gruppe Medem prepared to conduct an assault crossing from the east. By 1315 hours, Oberst Gebhard Medem's pioneers had crossed the Vistula in rubber boats and Götze's SS troops were fighting their way into Tczew, but the Polish troops managed to hold onto the town for nearly 24 hours before withdrawing.[34]

Having failed to secure the bridges at Tczew, Generalleutnant Nikolaus von Falkenhorst, the XXI Armeekorps commander, was forced to operate only on the east side of the Vistula. His mission was to capture the city of Grudziadz on the Vistula, where he was expected to establish a link with the troops of 4. Armee. The Polish 16 DP was assigned to defend a 22km-wide sector to protect Grudziadz and its left flank was anchored behind a minor tributary, the Osa

River. One battalion (II/65 PP) was placed on the west side of the Vistula. Falkenhorst advanced from assembly areas near Marienwerder and crossed the border with the 21. Infanterie-Division hugging the east side of the Vistula and the 228. Infanterie-Division on its left. The XXI Armeekorps had been reinforced with heavy artillery and had armour support in the form of the I./Panzer-Regiment 10, an independent Heerestruppen battalion. Since the Poles elected not to defend right behind the border, the XXI Armeekorps enjoyed an easy movement to contact until it encountered the 16 DP's defences around 1000 hours. Probing on their right with the divisional reconnaissance battalion, the 21. Infanterie-Division actually made its main effort in the afternoon on the left, against Rogóźno-Zamek. Initially, the Polish defences on the Osa line held, but at the cost of nearly 400 casualties. Further east, the 228. Infanterie-Division, supported by the I./Panzer-Regiment 10, also advanced to the Osa. On one occasion, the I./Panzer-Regiment 10 was engaged by a Polish artillery battery and may have had nine tanks disabled. Stymied, Falkenhorst used his artillery to pound the Polish positions while preparing for another infantry assault. This time, around 1800 hours, the German Infanterie-Regiment 24 managed to cross the Osa and seize a bridgehead, which the 64th Infantry Regiment (64 PP) was unable to eliminate.[35] Meanwhile, the 4th Infantry Division (4 DP), which was only lightly engaged by the XXI Armeekorps, transferred its 14th Infantry Regiment (14 PP) westwards to mount a counter-attack against the 21. Infanterie-Division.

By the end of the first day of the war, Army Pomorze was shaken, but still holding firm in most sectors. The loss of Chojnice was not unexpected. Bortnowski was aware that enemy reconnaissance units had crossed the Brda and something had to be done about this quickly or his army's line of retreat to the Vistula could be severed. He directed his only unengaged formations, Generał Brygady Juliusz Drapella's 27 DP and the Pomorska Cavalry Brigade, to move south, co-operate with the 9 DP and crush the enemy forces near the Brda. He put Drapella in charge of the counter-attack. The northern two regiments of the 9 DP were ordered to withdraw behind the Brda during the night of 1/2 September. In general, the Polish defence of strongpoints had been tenacious, but inter-unit co-ordination was extremely poor; each Polish regiment was essentially fighting its own independent war. On the German side, the lack of pre-battle reconnaissance proved costly on several occasions – German pre-war training had been too aggressive. Nor had the Germans learned yet to use their superior tactical mobility to full advantage by bypassing enemy centres of resistance. It is also noticeable that 4. Armee received no significant air support on the first day of the war and had to rely upon its organic artillery resources to suppress enemy defences.

During the night of 1/2 September, Manteuffel's Kradschützen-Bataillon 3 occupied Swiekatowo, followed by Aufklärungs-Abteilung 3. Guderian ordered both units to continue pushing towards the Vistula. However, Bortnowski learned about the enemy presence in Swiekatowo and re-directed the 27 DP to that location. During the night, Drapella's marching division received a series of changing orders, which made it difficult to co-ordinate his actions with the 9 DP. Indeed, Werobej's 9 DP lost communications when it began retreating to the Bdra during the night. Instead of a co-ordinated counter-attack, Drapella conducted a chaotic action, with his regiments arriving piecemeal during the morning. Initially, the 50th Infantry Regiment (50 PP) caught the Germans by surprise at Swiekatowo and almost recaptured the town. Later, the 23rd and 24th Infantry Regiments (23 and 24 PP) attacked the German position in nearby Tuszyny. In theory, the mass of the 27 DP should simply have overrun the German reconnaissance elements, but Drapella did not fight a combined arms battle, particularly since his horse-drawn artillery was slow to get into action. Just when it seemed that 27 DP might gain the upper hand, Guderian pushed the II./Panzer-Regiment 6 forwards to support his vanguard. Polish infantry was caught in the open, bereft of anti-tank support, and suffered heavy losses. Elements of the Pomorska Cavalry Brigade arrived behind the 27 DP, just in time to get mauled by the armoured cars of Aufklärungs-Abteilung 3. Once the counter-attack collapsed, Polish troops simply moved around the German-held towns, attempting to escape south to Bydgoszcz. Drapella and many of his troops escaped, but both the 27 DP and Pomorska Cavalry Brigade were badly decimated in running the gauntlet of German firepower. The only factor that saved Drapella's force from complete annihilation was that Panzer-Regiment 6 had shot off all its ammunition and was out of fuel; German battlefield logistics often failed at critical moments.

Meanwhile, Werobej's battered 9 DP fought a rearguard action at Piła-Młyn, where the bridge over the Brda was blown up at 1000 hours. Werobej attempted a counter-attack into Guderian's flank with the 35 PP at Klonowo, but this effort failed with substantial losses.[36] The

3. Panzer-Division easily pivoted and crushed these puny, unsupported efforts, while Guderian brought up the 23. Infanterie-Division to help consolidate the bridgehead over the Bdra. In the north, he pivoted the 2. and 20. Infanterie-Divisionen (mot.) to the south-east to pursue the retreating Chojnice detachment. Further south, the left wing of the 9 DP was broken by the attack of the German 32. Infanterie-Division, which overwhelmed the isolated 22 PP and forced it to withdraw towards Bydgoszcz. An ON battalion, Major Antoni Krzesiński's ON Battalion Koronowo, tried to make a valiant stand with its obsolescent French Lebel rifles against the German 3. Infanterie-Division but was quickly crushed. By evening, most of Army Pomorze was retreating south in disorder through the Tuchola Forest, hoping to reach Bydgoszcz. Guderian made little effort to create an effective cordon – which would have meant dispersing his forces – and instead remained focused on pushing on to the Vistula. The only value of Army Pomorze's unco-ordinated counter-attacks on 2 September was to delay Guderian's advance to the Vistula for 24 hours.

The situation for Army Pomorze's eastern wing at Grudziadz also deteriorated rapidly on 2 September. After Polish counter-attacks failed to dislodge the German bridgehead across the Osa River at Rogóźno-Zamek, the 21. Infanterie-Division erected a pontoon bridge and began pushing more troops across, which were used to make a major push towards the west beginning at 0900 hours. Supported by intense artillery fire, the German infantry rolled up the Polish defence along the Osa, moving from east to west. Another German spearhead, supported by tanks from the I./Panzer-Regiment 10, reached the train station in Mełno, which threatened to sever the 16 DP's lines of communications. Some Polish troops panicked, including the commander of the 16 DP, Pułkownik Stanisław Świtalski, who was relieved of command. Reinforcements from the 4 DP failed to stabilize the situation because they could not co-ordinate a counter-attack into the flank of the German penetration with local 16 DP elements. Instead, the 14 PP mounted its own counter-attack, which did succeed in inflicting some damage upon the enemy and took over 100 prisoners. Nevertheless, by the evening of 2 September, the 16 DP was in retreat towards Grudziadz.

The third day of the war was one of confusion for both sides, with most of Army Pomorze retreating towards Bydgoszcz or the Vistula, while the Germans were attempting to destroy or encircle the various fragments. Guderian ordered the Aufklärungs-Abteilung 3 and

Kradschützen elements to continue on to seize Świecie on the Vistula, but directed the bulk of his corps to crush the remnants of the 9 and 27 DP, which were retreating towards the crossing over the Vistula at Chełmno. The Polish columns stretched for over a dozen kilometres in length and were handicapped by Polish civilians attempting to flee the enemy. Unlike the previous two days, the sky was now clear over the battlefield and Guderian received his first real Luftwaffe support. Around 1200 hours, the Luftwaffe bombed the tail end of the column, smashing most of the 9 DP 's artillery units. Werobej was alerted that elements of the 3. Panzer-Division blocked his path of retreat and he tried to deploy his units for defence near the village of Bukowiec but Polish command and control was disrupted by the bombing. Shortly afterwards, the 3. Panzer-Division began attacking the Polish forces, with tanks supported by artillery. The Poles had a platoon of TKS tankettes but these were knocked out by Panzer-Regiment 6.[37] However, Polish 37mm anti-tank guns and wz. 35 anti-tank rifles succeeded in disabling a number of German tanks. In a matter of three hours, the 3. Panzer-Division carved up the trapped Polish units and captured 836 prisoners. Guderian brought the 2. and 20. Infanterie-Divisionen (mot.) up to help finish off the encircled Polish troops. Two battalions of the Polish 35 PP and the 16th Uhlans Regiment succeeded in slipping through the German cordon and crossing the Vistula, but the bulk of the 9 DP was smashed.[38] Over the course of the next 24 hours, the XIX Armeekorps would capture at least 4,000 Polish troops in mop-up operations west of the Vistula.[39]

On the east bank of the Vistula, the XXI Armeekorps attacked the eastern outskirts of Grudziadz after a punishing artillery bombardment and elements of the 21. Infanterie-Division, supported by tanks, pushed towards the city centre. At that point, the 16 DP blew up the bridge over the Vistula and abandoned the city, retreating southwards. The 4 DP retreated southwards in better order, but its 14 PP was severely mauled by a Luftwaffe bombing attack. Operational Group East was the only significant part of Army Pomorze that survived the first three days of war, but the 16 DP had been badly mauled in the battle for Grudziadz and the 14 PP had suffered 371 casualties. The German 21. Infanterie-Division also incurred significant casualties in the three-day battle, totalling about 579 dead/missing/wounded and another 140 captured.[40] By late morning on 3 September, the XXI Armeekorps had established contact with Guderian's vanguard across the Vistula.

The rest of the decimated Army Pomorze reached Bydgoszcz on the morning of 3 September, which was still held by the 15 DP. Altogether, one-third of the 2nd Infantry Division (2 DP), two battalions from the 22 PP and about one-quarter of the Pomorska Cavalry Brigade reached Bydgoszcz, but they had no chance to rest. The German 3. and 50. Infanterie-Divisionen were advancing rapidly upon the city from the north-west and Bortnowski had decided to abandon the city and create a new line south of the Bdra. The level of confusion evident in the bedraggled Polish units marching through Bydgoszcz did not escape the notice of Abwehr agents who had arrived in the city prior to hostilities. These Abwehr agents, in conjunction with Volksdeutscher Selbstschutz paramilitaries, planned to stage a divisionary action in Bydgoszcz in order to disrupt Polish efforts to defend the city. Around 1000 hours, local ethnic Germans, covertly armed by the SS, began firing on troops from the 22 PP as they passed through central Bydgoszcz. Armed with small arms and a few machine guns, the fifth columnists managed to inflict significant casualties, killing at least 20 Polish soldiers. The commander of the 15 DP promptly sent his 62nd Infantry Regiment (62 PP) to restore order in the city, but random sniping continued for much of the day. By evening, Polish troops had killed about 100 ethnic Germans – some probably innocent bystanders – and rounded up another 600 Germans. It appeared that the situation was contained. However, the next morning, 4 September, more fifth columnists began sniping at Polish troops. This time, the gloves came off and Polish troops and civilians attacked any ethnic Germans they could find in the areas where firing occurred, killing perhaps another 150 or so. Altogether, upwards of 250 ethnic Germans died in Bydgoszcz, which Josef Goebbels' propaganda machine quickly dubbed the 'Bromberg Massacre'.[41] On the night of 4/5 September the Polish troops evacuated the city and on the morning of 5 September, the German 50. Infanterie-Division marched into Bydgoszcz. Punitive measures against the local Polish population for the 'Bromberg Massacre' would soon follow.

By the time that the Anglo-French belatedly declared war on Germany on the morning of 3 September, Army Pomorze had already been decisively defeated. While Bortnowski had lost more than half his troops and equipment, Kluge's 4. Armee had suffered modest losses in return for the rapid seizure of the Polish Corridor and Pomerania. According to Guderian, the XIX Armeekorps (mot.) suffered only 150 dead and 700 wounded in the fighting in Pomerania.[42] In material terms, Guderian's spearhead – Panzer-Regiment 6 – lost about 30 of its 158 tanks in this period, mostly Pz I and Pz II light tanks. Driven by the political necessity of not allowing Hitler an easy seizure of territory in the Polish Corridor, the Polish High Command had sacrificed an entire army for very little practical benefit. Bortnowski's forces were poorly deployed for any sustained defence of Pomerania, since each division had vulnerable open flanks and the only reserves – the Operational Group Czersk – were deployed where they were least effective. Given the onset of war, Rydz-Śmigły should have ordered Army Pomorze to withdraw immediately to a more defensible line, although Guderian's motorized forces would no doubt have harried this withdrawal. On the German side, the XXI Armeekorps performed exceptionally well, but most of 4. Armee put in only an average performance. Even Guderian's XIX Armeekorps (mot.), which was a novel formation for 1939, was not used to full advantage. Luftwaffe support was vital in decimating the retreating Army Pomorze, but did not play a role in its initial defeat due to adverse weather.

Army Modlin and the Battle of Mława, 1–5 September

The Polish Army Modlin, under the commander of Generał Brygady Emil Krukowicz-Przedrzymirski, was tasked with preventing the German 3. Armee from making a rapid, direct advance against Warsaw from East Prussia. Given that the Modlin Army only had two infantry divisions (8 DP and 20 DP) and two cavalry brigades (Mazowiecka and Nowogródzka) assigned, Krukowicz-Przedrzymirski's mission was essentially to serve as a covering force, while reserve forces mobilized around Warsaw. After suitably delaying the enemy, Army Modlin was supposed to fall back to the Modlin fortress, located at the intersection of the Narew and Vistula Rivers. In order to enhance their defensive posture, the 20 DP had begun creating a fortified line north of Mława on 14 July, just 12km south of the East Prussian border. Pułkownik Wilhelm Lawicz-Liszka's 20 DP was able to build a fairly robust defensive line in six weeks – despite the shortage of materials – which included a line of trenches reinforced with 45 machine-gun bunkers, fronted by a triple row of barbed wire and anti-tank ditches. The main avenue of approach from the north was blocked by an obstacle belt made of railroad rails embedded in cement and placed in the ground at an angle. The main defensive position north of Mława was about 15km wide and held by the 78th and 80th Infantry Regiments (78 and 80 PP), while the 79th Infantry Regiment (79 PP) held a supporting position at Rzęgnowo, 6km to the east. Although the 20 DP had to defend a much wider sector than doctrine recommended, it was aided by the fact that the surrounding terrain was swampy and unsuitable for tanks.[43]

Despite the strength of the 20 DP's defensive position, its flanks were exposed. Krukowicz-Przedrzymirski assigned the Mazowiecka Cavalry Brigade to screen the eastern flank and the Nowogródzka Cavalry Brigade to screen the western flank. The 8 DP was held in reserve positions 25km south of Mława, prepared either to launch counter-attacks or cover the withdrawal of the 20 DP as needed. Krukowicz-Przedrzymirski left most of his recently mobilized ON battalions back to defend the Modlin fortress and crossings over the Vistula.

On the German side, General der Artillerie Georg von Küchler, commander of 3. Armee, rather optimistically hoped to quickly break through the Polish border defences and reach the Vistula by the end of the first day – a distance of over 100km. Amazingly, the Luftwaffe's pre-war reconnaissance flights had failed to detect the Mława defences – a significant oversight. Based upon information provided by border-crossers (either Abwehr agents or *Volksdeutsche,* ethnic Germans) on 21 August, the Germans were aware of anti-tank defences around Mława, but lacked specifics.[44] Unconcerned with rumoured anti-tank defences, Küchler intended to shove aside any Polish defenders with the infantry from Generalleutnant Walter Petzel's I Armeekorps, then exploit towards the Vistula with Panzer-Division Kempf. Korps Wodrig would support the advance and protect Petzel's left flank. Petzel's vanguard – the 11. Infanterie-Division – began crossing the border around 0500 hours and immediately encountered small detachments from the 7th Company/80 PP.[45] German reconnaissance units found obstacles created by felled trees and a few land mines. Unlike Army Pomorze which lacked screening units on the border, Army Modlin was immediately alerted that Germany had started an invasion and the 20 DP had sufficient warning time to rouse all its troops (many of whom were quartered in local villages) and get them to their assigned defensive positions.

By the time that the 11. Infanterie-Division reached the Polish main line of resistance 4km north of Mława, the 20 DP was fully alert and its defensive fire quickly halted the advance of the German infantry.

Two regiments from the 11. Infanterie Division probed the defences held by 78th Infantry Regiment (78 PP) north-west of Mława, but were stymied. Panzer-Division Kempf tried to push straight down the Nidzica–Mława road with two *Kampfgruppen* (battle groups) from SS-Regiment 'Deutschland' against the north-east sector held by the 80 PP; however the Waffen-SS troops failed to seize the village of Uniszki Zawadzkie, held by Polish covering forces. The Polish 75mm guns from the 20th Light Artillery Regiment engaged the German battle groups at a range of just 700m. According to some Polish sources, the lead enemy battalion was virtually destroyed.[46] In fact, total SS losses for the entire day were just 24 killed and 30 wounded.[47] Nevertheless, it is clear that this first Waffen-SS attack of the war was not pressed with great vigour, since only a single platoon leader was killed and most of the casualties were in a single company. The commander of SS-Regiment 'Deutschland' demanded armour support.

Normally, it is imprudent to commit tanks – bereft of engineer support – against an unbroken fortified line, but that is precisely what Generalmajor Werner Kempf decided to do. Around 1500 hours, both battalions of Panzer-Regiment 7 attacked towards Uniszki Zawadzkie, followed by the dismounted Waffen-SS infantry. Apparently, the Waffen-SS infantry failed to report the nature of the anti-tank obstacles blocking the road south from Uniszki Zawadzkie and Panzer-Regiment 7 was brought to a confused halt when it encountered a 6m-wide anti-tank ditch and rails sticking out of the ground. The German tanks then committed a tactical blunder by moving laterally across the Polish front, seeking a way to bypass the obstacles. Unless you are Frederick the Great at Leuthen, moving laterally across the front of an alert enemy is not recommended. As a result, the 80 PP's 37mm anti-tank gunners enjoyed a range shoot, firing into the flanks of German tanks at a range of about 400m. Seven German tanks (mostly Pz Is and Pz IIs) were completely destroyed and about 32 damaged. After two futile hours trying to bypass the Polish defences, the assault was terminated. A distraught Kempf reported to Küchler that, 'The attack was a disaster. Terrible losses of Panzers, number unknown. An attack here is hopeless.'[48] In fact, Kempf had little talent for the new mechanized warfare and the Poles had only scored a tactical success due to his own lack of reconnaissance.

After this setback, Küchler decided to outflank the Polish defences at Mława. However, Korps Wodrig's 1. Infanterie-Division had failed to budge the 79 PP's position at Rzęgnowska, despite the loan of some tanks from Panzer-Division Kempf; three German tanks were knocked out by the 79 PP's anti-tank gunners. The only success – and a minor one at that – was that the 12. Infanterie and 1. Kavallerie-Brigade managed to force the Mazowiecka Cavalry Brigade to pull out of the town of Chorzele, which opened a crossing over the Orzyc River. Late in the day, Polish cavalry from the Mazowiecka Cavalry Brigade skirmished with advance elements from the 1. Kavallerie-Brigade near the village of Krznowłoga Mała, 8km north-east of Rzęgnowo; this was a rare incident in the campaign of both sides using mounted cavalry. Küchler ordered Korps Wodrig to mount a major attack against the Polish right flank on 2 September, while the I Armeekorps kept up pressure on the rest of the 20 DP. On the Polish side, Krukowicz-Przedrzymirski ordered the 8 DP to begin moving forwards to support the 20 DP. Meanwhile, Pułkownik Władysław Anders' Nowogródzka Cavalry Brigade continued to hold firm on the Polish left flank, with his brigade maintaining Dzialdowo against the unaggressive German 217. Infanterie-Division.

On the morning of 2 September, Stukas from I./ StG 1 bombed the Polish trenches near Mława, inflicting some casualties, which was followed by a lengthy artillery bombardment. During the afternoon, the 11. Infanterie-Division launched two probing attacks against the 80 PP positions near Uniszki Zawadzkie, both of which were repulsed. Towards evening, the 61. Infanterie-Division conducted a probing attack against the 78 PP positions, but this was also repulsed. Korps Wodrig had better success with its late afternoon probing attacks by the 1. Infanterie-Division against the 79 PP at Rzęgnowo, which succeeded in infiltrating some elements behind the right flank of this position. Around 1800 hours, Pułkownik Józef Englicht, commander of the 79 PP, decided to refuse his right flank, pulling his regiment back towards Mława. The 12. Infanterie-Division also forced the Mazowiecka Cavalry Brigade to withdraw another 5km, which convinced Küchler that the Polish right flank was weaker.[49] He ordered Panzer-Division Kempf to move eastwards during the night of 2/3 September in order to prepare for a major attack the next day against the Polish right flank. Had the 8 DP moved forwards quickly on 2 September as ordered, the Polish situation might have been retrievable, but for reasons not entirely clear, the 8 DP was still too far away to reinforce the Polish right flank. In all likelihood, the dilatory movement of the 8 DP was due to lingering transport and C^2 problems (the 8 DP had a high proportion of reservists).

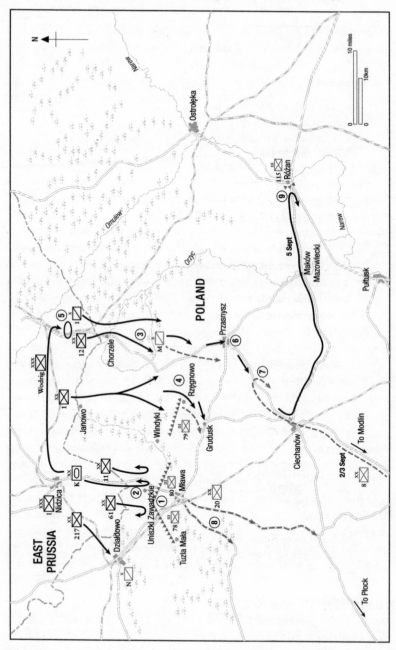

Map key

1 September

1) At the start of the war, the Polish 20 DP occupies defensive positions created north of Młava and stretching east to Rzęgnowo. Army Modlin has deployed two cavalry brigades to protect the flanks of the 20 DP.

2) The I Armeekorps attacks the Młava position but is repulsed with significant losses.

3) Korps Wodrig encounters less resistance and forces the Mazowiecka Cavalry Brigade to pull back.

2 September

4) Korps Wodrig begins to envelop the Polish right flank, forcing the 79 PP and Mazowiecka Cavalry Brigade to pull back further.

5) Night 2/3 September 1939. Panzer-Division Kempf redeploys into the Korps Wodrig sector.

3 September

6) Korps Wodrig attacks and captures Przasnysz, forcing the Mazowiecka Cavalry Brigade to retreat.

7) Army Modlin commits the fresh 8 DP to launch a counter-attack against Korps Wodrig's advance units, but this effort fails and the 8 DP retreats in disorder.

4 September

8) Once Panzer-Division Kempf occupies Ciechanow, Army Modlin orders the 20 DP to abandon the Młava position.

5 September

9) Bock redirects Korps Wodrig east to seize Rozan, but the Polish reservists put up a spirited defence.

It took Panzer-Division Kempf the entire night to move 45km eastwards, into assembly areas behind Korps Wodrig, and Kempf's formation was not ready to attack until the afternoon of 3 September. SS-Sturmbannführer Wim Brandt, commander of the SS-Aufklärungs-Abteilung attached to Panzer-Division Kempf, noted that his mechanized column was delayed moving through Chorzele because the 1. Kavallerie-Brigade was watering all its horses in the middle of the town – an image that is jarring for the normal popular mindset about the Polish campaign. After getting past the cavalry traffic-jam, Panzer-Division Kempf split into three Kampfgruppen and advanced southwards, pushing back the Mazowiecka Cavalry Brigade.[50] Around 1600 hours, Kampfgruppe Steiner occupied the town of Przasnysz, while Kampfgruppe Schmidt occupied Grudusk. The Mazowiecka Cavalry Brigade mounted a few ineffectual counter-attacks, supported by its company of TK3 tankettes, but was easily brushed aside. Once it became clear that German motorized units were outflanking the position at Mława, the 79 PP retreated further, which only allowed the German 1. Infanterie-Division to advance south-east from Grudusk. Krukowicz-Przedrzymirski ordered the 8 DP – still moving forwards – to launch an immediate counter-attack with whatever forces were available. Instead of a carefully planned and supported counter-attack, the 8 DP mounted a piece-meal effort that quickly fell apart. Pułkownik Stanisław Sosabowski led his 21 PP forwards towards Przasnysz without artillery support and with no friendly units on either flank. He was ordered to support the Mazowiecka Cavalry Brigade, which was in fact retreating away from him. Around 1400 hours, Sosabowski bumped into infantry from the 12. Infanterie-Division north-east of Ciechanów and managed to establish a defensive line, although he was under heavy pressure. When he asked for support, none came. Around 2200 hours, Sosabowski noted that C^2 collapsed within the 8 DP, losing all radio and wire contact with division headquarters.[51] In fact, the 8 DP virtually disintegrated in its movement to contact. A friendly-fire incident between the 13th and 32 Infantry Regiments led to the latter regiment retreating without orders. In the dark, for an untried unit filled with newly mobilized reservists, it did not take much to spark a panic that could not be suppressed. During the night, Sosabowski decided to pull back his still intact regiment, before he was isolated.

It did not become fully apparent to Krukowicz-Przedrzymirski until the morning of 4 September that the 8 DP had failed to stop the German outflanking manoeuvre and that the 20 DP would soon be encircled. Around 0900 hours, the 20 DP was ordered to abandon the Mława position and march southwards towards the Vistula, in conjunction with the Nowogródzka Cavalry Brigade. Pułkownik Lawicz-Liszka's 20 DP opted to leave rearguards in place to delay enemy pursuit, but the Germans were expecting the withdrawal and SS-Sturmbannführer Brandt's reconnaissance troops occupied the town of Ciechanów, while sending advance units to block the Mława–Modlin road. The Luftwaffe was called in and Stukas pounded the retreating 8th and 20 DP, inflicting great loss of material and inciting further panic. As Sosabowski withdrew southwards with his 21 PP, he 'was horrified to notice a battery of abandoned guns, with boxes of untouched ammunition lying around them. It was obvious that panic had sparked and spread through all ranks.'[52] Although Sosabowski's 21 PP and Anders' Nowogródzka Cavalry Brigade managed an orderly retreat from the battle of Mława, the rest of Krukowicz-Przedrzymirski's Army Modlin was essentially trashed after four days of combat. Most of the remnants were forced to retreat south-west towards Plock, leaving the Modlin fortress poorly defended. At this point, a rapid advance by Panzer-Division Kempf to the south-east would probably have dispersed the retreating 8 and 20 DPs and potentially have enabled the seizure of intact bridges over the Vistula at Modlin. However, Bock – who had shown little interest in 3. Armee's problems – intervened to save the remnants of Army Modlin from complete destruction. By telephone, he ordered Küchler to cease the advance of Korps Wodrig to the south-east – which he described as 'an error' – and instead ordered him to pivot the formation eastwards and seize Różan on the Narew.[53]

Bock was not interested in the Modlin fortress or even Warsaw; rather, he was focused on swinging 3. Armee wide behind the Polish defences in order to reach Lomza, then cross the Bug River. He eventually wanted to move Guderian's XIX Armeekorps (mot.) through East Prussia to support this advance to the Bug, but Bock had not yet issued this order. Instead, Panzer-Division Kempf turned eastwards and advanced to Różan on 5 September. Prior to the war, the Polish High Command had deployed the Operational Group Wyszków under Generał Brygady Wincenty Kowalski and the Independent Operational Group Narew under Generał Brygady Czesław Młot-Fijałkowski to protect the eastern border regions. Neither of these groups had any significant contact with the enemy on the first three days of the war. Różan was defended by 3,300 troops under the command of Podpułkownik Czesław Rzedzicki, consisting of two battalions of his 115th Infantry Regiment (115 PP) and a battalion of 75mm guns, part of the 41 DP (reserve) assigned to the Operational Group Wyszków. The reservists occupied three Russian forts of First World War vintage.[54] Around 1000 hours on 5 September, elements of the 12. Infanterie-Division and 1. Kavallerie-Brigade approached Różan from the west and tried to mount a hasty assault – which was repulsed. Although a German bombardment severed the telephone lines, thereby preventing Polish forward observation posts from directing artillery fire, the Polish gunners simply laid barrages in front of their forward positions (a.k.a. 'final protective fire' or FPF), which disrupted the German infantry before they could reach the Polish trenches. Around noon, once Panzer-Division Kempf arrived, the Germans mounted a major attack from three directions, supported by artillery and six He 111 bombers. However, Polish 37mm anti-tank guns and artillery succeeded in knocking out 9–12 tanks from Panzer-Regiment 7 and the German infantry failed to capture any of the forts, despite several Stuka attacks. Kempf tried to outflank the defence by sending a company from SS-Sturmbannführer Brandt's reconnaissance battalion across the Narew in rubber boats, but the Waffen-SS troops were forced to retreat back across the river after bumping into the Polish II/114 PP. By 1800 hours, the Germans ended their unsuccessful attack. At a cost of 70 casualties, a badly outnumbered group of Polish reservists had held off a Panzer-Division for six hours. Despite having a 10:1 numerical advantage and all the elements of their combined arms team in play at Różan – artillery, air support, tanks and infantry – the Germans had not achieved tactical success due to a stubborn Polish defence. Indeed, the Polish defence at Różan exemplifies Napoleon oft-quoted dictum that 'in war, the moral is to the material as three is to one'. However, Generał Kowalski recognized that Podpułkownik Rzedzicki's small command would probably be overwhelmed by an even larger German assault on the next morning, so he authorized both battalions of the 115 PP to withdraw across the Narew during the night of 5/6 September. Unfortunately, Rzedzicki's troops lacked adequate explosives to completely demolish the bridge over the Narew.[55]

When Sosabowski reached Modlin on the afternoon of 5 September, he found that his 21 PP and one battalion of the 32nd Infantry Regiment (32 PP) were the only regular units available to defend the Vistula crossings. He also found that Krukowicz-Przedrzymirski and his staff had already departed the Modlin fortress and there was a serious command vacuum in the area. Several officers claimed to be in command of forces at Modlin, but there was no overall commander at this critical moment. However, Bock's order to turn 3. Armee eastwards gave the Poles five vital days to organize a defence at Modlin; the first German units from 3. Armee did not reach the outskirts of Modlin until 10 September.

Most Polish histories tend to depict the battle of Mława as something of a Polish tactical victory and claim that 3. Armee suffered something like 5,800 casualties in three days of fighting.[56] These figures are absurd. German records show that all of 3. Armee suffered a total of only 1,698 casualties in the first four days of the war (including 596 dead or missing).[57] The 12. Infanterie-Division, which was heavily engaged at the battle of Mława, suffered a total of 39 dead in the first three days of combat. The I Armeekorps' daily casualty lists (which were probably not entirely accurate) add up to 392 casualties for 1–3 September, including 129 dead or missing. Based upon available evidence, German casualties in the battle of Mława were probably about 1,000. Polish casualties have been estimated at 2,700, including 1,200 dead; these figures are also unlikely, unless they include casualties that occurred during the retreat. Polish first-hand accounts of Mława tend to describe relatively light casualties during the actual defence. If individual attacking German divisions were only suffering a dozen or so deaths per day, it seems unlikely that two Polish divisions and two brigades were suffering 100 deaths per day. Most of Army Modlin's casualties occurred during the withdrawal from the Mława position, as a result of air and artillery bombardment. Material losses were extremely heavy in the retreat, but human losses much less.

Army Modlin was decisively defeated in the battle of Mława and this formation – after mounting a briefly successful defence – came unglued in a precipitate retreat. The inability of Krukowicz-Przedrzymirski to get 8 DP into action to properly support the 20 DP is inexplicable, as is the manner in which most of this unit disintegrated before even coming into contact with the enemy. The battle of Mława demonstrates that the Polish Army of 1939 had some good units and some good tactical commanders (such as Anders and Sosabowski) but it was deficient at the operational level. Although 3. Armee eventually won the battle of Mława through the kind of manoeuvre warfare methods which the Wehrmacht preferred, its tactical performance was marred by inadequate pre-battle reconnaissance and a tendency to use tanks against enemy strongpoints. Bock's last-second intervention deprived 3. Armee from achieving a much larger victory and served to reduce pressure against an opponent that was stumbling backwards.

Battle of the Warta River, 1–4 September

*'Soldiers! The eternal Teutonic-Prussian enemy has attacked our
country. The Wielkopolska Cavalry Brigade has the honour of
being the first in battle to defend our country's borders.
Defend your native land and your families!'*

Generał Brygady Abraham Roman

The bulk of the Wehrmacht's combat power – including 75 per cent of its
armour – was aligned with the three armies in Generaloberst Gerd von
Rundstedt's Heeresgruppe Süd. Rundstedt had a total of about 530,000
combat troops plus another 13,000 Slovak troops, which provided him
with a 2.3:1 numerical advantage against the Polish forces defending the
southern border region. According to the OKH intentions laid out in
Fall Weiss, Heeresgruppe Süd was expected to conduct several powerful,
simultaneous attacks into southern Poland to overwhelm the border
defences and open the way to Warsaw. The main effort would be made
in the centre by General der Artillerie Reichenau's 10. Armee, against
Army Łódź and the right flank of Army Kraków.[58] Generaloberst Wilhelm
List's 14. Armee, on the right, would advance upon Kraków and, in
conjunction with the Slovak Army, clear Galicia. General der Infanterie
Johannes Blaskowitz's 8. Armee, on the left flank, was primarily configured
as a flank guard for 10. Armee, with minimal armour support. German
intelligence on the disposition of Polish forces along the southern border
was fairly accurate and Rundstedt was aware that the main line of Polish
resistance would be some distance from the border. The Slovak Army, the
first of the Axis satellite forces to see combat in the Second World War,
consisted of three infantry divisions but it did not begin mobilizing until
1 September and was only lightly employed during *Fall Weiss*. Heeresgruppe
Süd enjoyed not only numerical superiority and weight of material, but
also unity of command and clear mission focus.

In contrast, the four Polish armies defending southern Poland had no
single commander to co-ordinate their actions and their missions were not
well defined. The main defence rested upon Army Łódź and Army Kraków
in the centre, which had a total of nine infantry divisions and four cavalry
brigades – roughly 200,000 troops. Rydz-Śmigły tasked these two armies
with defending the southern regions of Łódź, Kielce and Kraków, while
buying time for Army Prusy to mobilize. Once ready, Army Prusy would
be used to spearhead a counter-offensive intended to hurl the enemy back

on their heels, just as the French had done at the battle of the Marne in 1914 and the Poles at the battle of Warsaw in 1920. However, Polish operational planning was based upon the assumption that Army Łódź and Army Kraków could hold their sectors for at least a week or more. Rydz-Śmigły tasked Army Poznań to defend Wielkopolska (Greater Poland), but it was deployed in an exposed position and only had minimal contact with its neighbours, Army Pomorze and Army Łódź. The other Polish 'army' – Army Karpaty – was really just an *ad hoc* grouping of assorted units, totalling barely 20,000 troops. In Warsaw, on small-scale maps, it probably appeared to Rydz-Śmigły that he had ably deployed these four armies to defend Poland's southern borders. However, the four Polish armies had minimal contact with each other, lacked continuous fronts and were not fully organized for combat – which invited infiltration and exploitation by a mobile enemy.

Generał Dywizji Juliusz Rómmel's Army Łódź was not deployed for defence of the south-east border at the outset of the war. Consequently, during the March mobilization, Rómmel had deployed a covering force along the Warta River, designated as Operational Group Piotrków. This group, under Generał Brygady Wiktor Thommée, had the 30 DP deployed along a bend in the Warta River near Dzialoszyn and the Wołyńska Cavalry Brigade south of the Warta, near the town of Klobuck. Rómmel ordered Thommée to delay the enemy for at least three days along the Warta, while the rest of the army deployed and put itself into fighting trim. Furthermore, Thommée was ordered to maintain contact with the 7 DP from Army Kraków, which was deployed near Częstochowa. Just before the outbreak of war, Rómmel sent some additional forces to reinforce Operational Group Piotrków, including a company of TKS tankettes and Armoured Trains No. 52 and No. 53. On the opposite side of the border, Reichenau (10. Armee) intended to push towards the Warta with the infantry of the XI Armeekorps on the left and the motorized units of the XVI Armeekorps (mot.) on the right.

Around 0430 hours on 1 September, the first patrols from Infanterie-Regiment 73 (19. Infanterie-Division) crossed the border. On their left, the 18. Infanterie-Division also crossed the border. Both divisions, part of General der Artillerie Emil Leeb's XI Armeekorps, marched unopposed at first, heading towards the Warta – their objective for the first day. In one village, residents greeted the *Landsers* of Infanterie-Regiment 73 with water and shouted 'Heil Hitler'. However, around 0830 hours at the crossroads of Parzymiechy, Infanterie-Regiment 73 ran into its first real resistance. The 30 DP had deployed its 83rd Infantry Regiment (83 PP) south of the Warta to delay the German advance and this regiment's 3rd Battalion halted the lead battalion of Infanterie-Regiment 73 with heavy machine-gun and artillery fire. At first, the German infantry were at a disadvantage, since their horse-drawn artillery was still far to the rear and the Poles had two batteries of artillery in support. Two of Infanterie-Regiment 73's company commanders were killed by Polish artillery fire and the regiment floundered under enemy fire. At one point, the Poles mounted a counter-attack supported by a platoon of TKS tankettes, until driven off by a lone 3.7cm PaK anti-tank gun. Finally, after a few hours, the Germans managed to sort themselves out and Infanterie-Regiment 73 deployed all three battalions in an effort to outflank the Polish roadblock. It was not until 2100 hours that the village of Parzymiechy was in German hands, with the 83 PP withdrawing towards the Warta, having accomplished its delay mission at the cost of around 400 casualties. The troops of Infanterie-Regiment 73 were described as 'very nervous' in their own regimental war journal and sentries shot two German soldiers by mistake during the night.[59] Furthermore, the troops of Infanterie-Regiment 73 became convinced that local Polish civilians had sniped at them from windows and decided to burn the villages of Parzymiechy and Zimnowo. German soldiers indiscriminately tossed grenades into houses to set them on fire, but often killed the occupants cowering inside. Altogether, over 100 civilians – about one-quarter of whom were children – were murdered by the soldiers of the 19. Infanterie-Division.[60]

On the XI Armeekorps' left flank, the 1. leichte-Division advanced on its own towards the heavily bombed town of Wielun, but did not reach it on the first day. In order to protect the left flank of Reichenau's 10. Armee from any counter-moves by Army Poznań, Blaskowitz's 8. Armee sent its XIII Armeekorps across the border towards the boundary of Army Łódź and Army Poznań. The Infanterie-Regiment Leibstandarte SS Adolf Hitler (mot.) or LSSAH was part of this corps and this Waffen-SS unit received its baptism of fire at the village of Boleslawiec, 30km south-east of Ostrzeszow.[61] The village was defended by two troops from the 1st Cavalry Regiment KOP, reinforced with anti-tank guns and heavy machine guns. Podporucznik Lucjan Woźniak commanded a platoon deployed on the western side of the village, which around 0630 hours engaged the lead German reconnaissance element – three armoured cars and some motorcycles. A Polish 37mm anti-tank gun knocked out all three armoured cars, while the machine gunners eliminated five motorcycles.[62] Instead of deploying, the LSSAH simply bombarded the village with its 75mm infantry guns. After several hours, the KOP cavalry decided to withdraw and the Waffen-SS entered the village around 1000 hours. Apparently angered by their losses, the Waffen-SS troops murdered a number of civilians in the village, beginning the LSSAH's ledger of war crimes. Nor was the XIII Armeekorps satisfied with the tactical performance of the LSSAH, which was slow and not particularly aggressive.

Although the Luftwaffe began bombing the 30 DP's positions behind the Warta in the morning of 2 September, Leeb's XI Armeekorps was not ready to begin a river crossing operation until it had brought up all its artillery. Around 1400 hours, the 19. Infanterie-Division tried to cross the Warta at multiple points across a 9km-wide sector, but the defensive fire of the 84th Infantry Regiment (84 PP) repulsed all attempts. Likewise, efforts by the 18. Infanterie-Division to cross in the western sector held by the 82nd Infantry Regiment (82 PP) also failed. By massing artillery fire at one point, against the left flank of 82 PP near Bobrowniki, the Germans were able to suppress the defence and get across the Warta. Once across, the 19. Infanterie-Division established a firm bridgehead then began to roll up the Polish positions. By dusk, the Germans pushed into Dzialoszyn, which was held by the II/84 PP. Despite stiff Polish resistance, the 30 DP's defence began to unravel and by 2000 hours Thommée ordered the division to withdraw.

Meanwhile, General der Kavallerie Erich Hoepner's XVI Armeekorps (mot.) was simultaneously pushing towards the Warta with the 1. and 4. Panzer-Divisionen; this was the first time that two Panzer-Divisionen were employed side by side and under the same commander. The Polish 7 DP had destroyed bridges in both Krzepice and Opatow that delayed the German Panzer units right after they crossed the border, but the vanguard motorcycle and reconnaissance units pushed on nevertheless. A tactical lesson not appreciated by the defenders at the outset of the war is that obstacles are only really effective if covered by direct fire – otherwise the attackers will simply bypass or otherwise cross the obstacle. Pułkownik Julian Filipowicz's Wołyńska Cavalry Brigade (reinforced with an infantry battalion from the 30 DP) had created a strong blocking position around Mokra, which the vanguard from Generalmajor Georg-Hans Reinhardt's 4. Panzer-Division encountered at 0630 hours. The Wołyńska Cavalry Brigade was deployed with two regiments and one infantry battalion deployed in trenches, facing westwards, and two other cavalry regiments in reserve. Although the terrain was flat, most of the Polish positions were concealed in forest. Like most meeting engagements, the Germans attempted to feel out the enemy position and once they identified its flanks, they tried to envelop the vulnerable northern flank. Around 0800

Battle of the Warta River, 1–4 September 1939

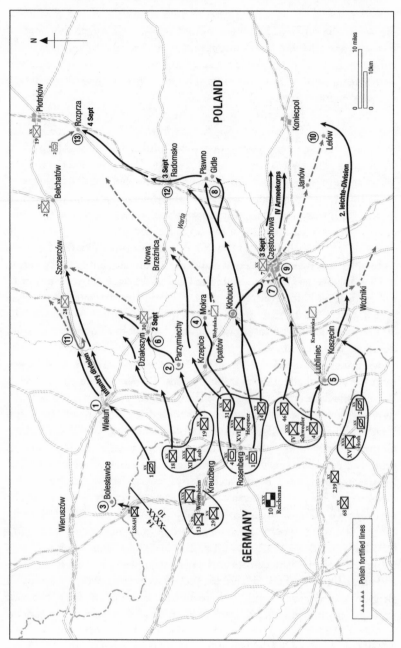

MAP KEY

1 September

1) Luftflotte 4 bombs Wielun, killing at least 127 Polish civilians.
2) Meeting engagement between 19. Infanterie-Division and 30 DP at Parzymiechy.
3) LSSAH advances to the village of Boleslawiec, where it receives its baptism of fire.
4) The 4. Panzer-Division fights a vicious meeting engagement with the Wolynska Cavalry Brigade at Mokra, suffering significant losses.
5) The 4. Infanterie-Division destroys the Polish battalion in Lubliniec.

3 September

6) The 19. Infanterie-Division crosses the Warta and captures Dzialoszyn.
7) The IV Armeekorps' initial attempt to capture Częstochowa is repulsed. However, the 7 DP withdraws toward Janow to avoid encirclement.
8) 1. Panzer-Division captures two intact bridges over the Warta.

3 September

9) The 46. Infanterie-Division occupies Częstochowa.
10) The 2. leichte-Division cuts off the escape of the 7 DP and forces it to surrender.
11) The 28 DP moves forward to try and stop the 1. leichte-Division from crossing the Warta but fails.
12) The 4. Panzer-Division occupies Radomsko.

4 September

13) Polish armoured counter-attack against the 1. Panzer-Division near Rozprza.

hours, a Kampfgruppe consisting of the I./Panzer-Regiment 36 and Schützen-Regiment 12 advanced against the 19th Uhlan Regiment, but four of its tanks were knocked out by defensive fire and the commander of I./Panzer-Regiment 36, Oberstleutnant Hans Stenglein, was badly wounded. Hauptmann Meinrad von Lauchert, a company commander, took charge of the Panzers and ordered them to withdraw, temporarily leaving the dismounted German infantry pinned down in the open. Oberstleutnant

Heinrich Eberbach, commander of Panzer-Regiment 35, noted that the initial setback – minor as it was – caused 'a panic in the rear.'[63]

Beginning around 1000 hours, the 4. Panzer-Division made a more determined effort, by launching three co-ordinated attacks which gradually forced all three Polish front-line battalions to give ground. Filipowicz committed his two reserve regiments, which slowed but did not stop the German advance. However, in choosing to use brute force rather than manoeuvre, the 4. Panzer-Division paid a heavy price to chew its way through the Polish defences. Kapral Leonard Żłób knocked out 14 German tanks with his 37mm anti-tank gun, although his battery was also eliminated in the action. Oberstleutnant Eberbach noted that his crews could not spot the defenders in the wood lines and that Polish anti-tank rifles were used effectively against his tanks. At close range, the wz. 35 anti-tank rifle could easily punch through the thin armour of the Pz I and Pz II tanks, although it took multiple hits to kill or injure the crew.[64] Pushing through the Polish trench line, the I./Panzer-Regiment 36 charged towards the rail line to attack the supporting Polish artillery battalion. Two batteries of 75mm guns were quickly destroyed by the Panzers, but the other battery engaged the oncoming German tanks with direct fire. While the 75mm gun was not particularly good in the anti-tank role, it did have a very high rate of fire. Kapral Jan Suski, a 75mm gunner, succeeded in knocking out eight German tanks, including several Pz IIs with direct hits. The Armoured Train No. 53, heavily armed with two 100mm guns, two 75mm guns and 19 machine guns also intervened in the action and was responsible for knocking out more German tanks.[65] Although the 4. Panzer-Division captured Mokra and forced the Wołyńska Cavalry Brigade to withdraw by 1700 hours, the Germans were too badly bruised to pursue. The 4. Panzer-Division had lost 62 tanks, including 24 totally destroyed, and suffered about 500 casualties. The Wołyńska Cavalry Brigade lost a good deal of its artillery and also suffered about 500 casualties. The battle of Mokra was a German tactical victory, but the 4. Panzer-Division had not been well handled. Despite the use of combined arms tactics, including some close air support, Reinhardt had decided to muscle his way through an enemy fortified position with his thin-skinned tanks. Clearly, German commanders had not yet fully appreciated the damage that modern anti-tank guns could inflict on tanks. Another lesson from Mokra – often true on any battlefield – is that much of the execution in war is caused by a relatively few steady soldiers who know their trade.

Army Kraków, under Generał Brygady Antoni Szylling, also deployed a covering force along the Warta River, consisting of the 7 DP and Krakowska

Cavalry Brigade. The primary mission of this force was to maintain the connection with Army Łódź and to defend the approaches to Częstochowa – a city of 136,000 with great religious and historical significance for Poles. Indeed, Częstochowa was probably the most heavily fortified place in Poland, with 19 large concrete bunkers and extensive field works. The approaches to the city were blocked with minefields, anti-tank ditches and barbed wire. A precious 40mm AA battery had also been provided for air defence. On 1 September, the 1. Panzer-Division and the 14. Infanterie-Division approached Częstochowa from the west, eliminated an ON battalion in Klobuck and forced elements of the 27th Infantry Regiment (27 PP) to retreat towards the city. However, the 1. Panzer-Division bypassed the city's main defensive belt and continued to the north-east – into the gap between 7 DP and Army Łódź. The main force intended to capture Częstochowa was the IV Armeekorps, with the 4. and 46. Infanterie-Divisionen along with some help from the 14. Infanterie-Division. After crossing the border, these divisions had to eliminate the Polish garrison in Lublieniec then move through a heavily forested area before reaching the outskirts of Częstochowa late on the first day.[66] The I/74 PP from 7 DP, the garrison in Lublieniec, put up stubborn resistance against a Kampfgruppe built around the Infanterie-Regiment 103, but was virtually destroyed by 0930 hours. The 4. Infanterie-Division suffered only 30 casualties.[67] Thus the right wing of Army Krakow had already failed one of its primary missions on the first day of the war – maintaining contact with Army Łódź.

On the right flank of the IV Armeekorps, General der Infanterie Hermann Hoth's XV Armeekorps (mot.) crossed the border south of Lublieniec and advanced rapidly with the 2. leichte-Division towards the town of Koszecin. The 3. leichte-Division followed in a support role. Army Kraków only had a very small covering force in this region, consisting of the 3rd Uhlans from the Krakowska Cavalry Brigade and an ON battalion. The Poles slowed the German advance with mines and by felling trees, but nevertheless Koszecin was occupied by 1245 hours. Thereafter, Hoth pivoted his corps eastwards and advanced to Lubsza, forcing the Polish cavalry screen to retreat. Altogether, Hoth advanced 20km on the first day of the war, against very light resistance.[68] German tactical mobility was impaired by the quality of Polish roads; the primary roads were asphalt but secondary roads were often composed of sand or dirt. Oberstleutnant Eberbach complained that 'our regiment [Panzer-Regiment 35] struggled to advance on bad roads' even though his unit had moved less than 80km since the start of the campaign.[69] Eberbach's attitude and the frequent mentioning of 'bad roads' in German reporting indicates that the

Wehrmacht had not trained for operating under austere field conditions. The XV Armeekorps noted that the situation was worse for the motor vehicles in the support echelons – many of which were not built for off-road mobility – a preview of problems that would be experienced on the even more primitive Russian road network in 1941.

On 2 September, the IV Armeekorps conducted reconnaissance of the 7 DP's defences around Częstochowa, while bringing up its horse-drawn artillery. The Luftwaffe's 1.(H)/41 tried to conduct aerial reconnaissance over Częstochowa, but the alert Polish 40mm anti-aircraft battery shot down at least one Hs 126 reconnaissance aircraft, perhaps more. Around noon, the Germans began probing the defences of the 27 PP in the north-west corner of the city, but were easily repulsed and several armoured cars were knocked out. However, at 1700 hours the Germans mounted a co-ordinated assault against both the north and south sides of the city, with artillery support. Nevertheless, the assaults failed to gain ground and the defence held. Later, the Poles claimed to have knocked out over 60 tanks and armoured cars in the battle of Częstochowa but the 1. Panzer-Division was not involved in the fight for the city and the IV Armeekorps only had a total of six armoured cars. While the 7 DP was fighting to defend Częstochowa, the 1. Panzer-Division advanced almost unopposed and its reconnaissance units seized two intact bridges over the Warta, at Gidle and Pławno. At the same time, Hoth's XV Armeekorps (mot.) continued to push back the Krakowska Cavalry Brigade, which abandoned Wozniki and retreated to Zawiercie. Consequently, the 2. leichte-Division was able to push past Częstochowa and German mechanized units were well-positioned to encircle the city. Upon learning that German Panzers were across the Warta and XV Armeekorps was threatening to cut off the 7 DP's lines of communication, Generał Szylling became alarmed that the 7 DP was about to be encircled within Częstochowa and he ordered the division to abandon the city and withdraw to Janów, 20km south-east of the city.[70] While this decision temporarily saved the 7 DP, it also meant giving up a heavily fortified position without much of a fight; the fact that it was Częstochowa only served to undermine Polish morale.

Army Poznań, under Generał Dywizji Tadeusz Kutrzeba, had more success defending forwards of the Warta River during the first two days of the war because it was not under heavy pressure from Blaskowitz's 8. Armee. Indeed, both Army Poznań and 8. Armee were essentially flank guards. The X Armeekorps crossed the border near Syców with a single division, Generalleutnant Friedrich Olbricht's 24. Infanterie-Division, which advanced 16km in two parallel-marching Kampfgruppen and – after a few hours of skirmishing – forced two battalions of the 10th Polish Infantry Division to evacuate the town of Ostrzeszow by 1600 hours. Olbricht's division did not pursue and stopped for the night.[71] However, the left flank of Army Poznań was not seriously threatened by this loss since Olbricht's division was the extreme left-most unit of 8. Armee and had only modest support. Indeed, the German–Polish border north of Breslau was screened by just Landwehr and border units. Kutrzeba had deployed Generał Brygady Abraham Roman's Wielkopolska Cavalry Brigade and the 55th Infantry Regiment (55 PP) to defend the border towns of Leszno, Rydzyna and Rawicz. On the first day of the war, German border troops mounted diversionary attacks against Leszno, aided by armed German fifth columnists within the town. After a Polish soldier was killed by machine-gun fire from a house in Leszno, the troopers of the Wielkopolska Cavalry Brigade killed 16 armed saboteurs and arrested 400 ethnic Germans; five who were caught carrying weapons were sentenced to death. Another German force captured the border village of Rawicz but was expelled by a Polish counter-attack.[72] Since Army Poznań was not under heavy pressure and not content to sit passively on the defence, Kutrzeba decided to mount a raid onto German territory. At 1600 hours on 2 September, a battalion-size force which included TKS tankettes and armoured cars crossed the border and occupied the German town of Geyersdorf for a few hours – a penetration of 1,700m into the Reich. A total of 28 German soldiers were captured by the Wielkopolska Cavalry Brigade before withdrawing. Despite having mounted a successful defence of the border area, the enemy success elsewhere on the Warta caused the Polish High Command to order Army Poznań to begin withdrawing eastwards on the night of 2/3 September.[73] By 4 September, the last Polish troops were leaving Poznań.

By the morning of 3 September, Reichenau's 10. Armee was across the Warta in two places and it was clear that the Polish intent to fight a protracted delaying action along the river had failed. Having cleared away the Polish covering forces and bounced the Warta fairly easily, Reichenau decided to commit some of his reserves for the next phase of the offensive. In order to reinforce his thin left flank, he brought up the XIV Armeekorps (mot.) headquarters with the 13. Infanterie-Division (mot.) and subordinated the 1. leichte-Division to this formation as well. General der Infanterie Gustav von Wietersheim's XIV Armeekorps would advance from the Wielun area towards the gap between Army Poznań and Army Łódź. In the centre, Hoepner's XVI Armeekorps (mot.) brought up the 31. Infanterie-Division to assist in expanding its bridgehead over the Warta. Once both 1. and 4. Panzer-Divisionen were fully across the Warta, Hoepner would advance to Radomsko and then towards Piotrków. That morning, the 46. Infanterie-Division from IV Armeekorps was just about to enter an undefended Częstochowa; once the city was occupied the corps would push eastwards to pursue the retreating 7 DP. On the right, Hoth's XV Armeekorps committed the 3. leichte-Division and both light divisions now advanced on line to the north-east. Blaskowitz's 8. Armee would continue to protect Reichenau's left flank with its four infantry divisions.

On the Polish side, the battle of the Warta River was turning into a disaster. Not one defended position had held for more than 48 hours and many units were retreating. Worse, there was a 30km gap between Army Łódź and Army Kraków, thanks to the abandonment of Częstochowa. The Wołyńska Cavalry Brigade managed to get behind the Warta River, but it could not maintain any sort of line with the retreating 30 DP. Generał Juliusz Rómmel, commander of Army Łódź, was desperately trying to form his main line of resistance (MLR) between Sieradz and Piotrków to defend the approaches to Łódź, but he had to decide very quickly where to deploy his three second-echelon divisions. Rómmel decided to send the 28th Infantry Division (28 DP) to the Wielun sector to delay the XIV Armeekorps, while the 10th Infantry Division (10 DP) anchored the defensive line at Sieradz. The 2nd Legions Infantry Division (2 DPL) was sent to Belchatow to help defend the eastern end of the MLR. Rómmel also sent his only substantial armour unit, Major Edmund Karpow's 2nd Light Tank Battalion (2 BCL), to help defend Piotrków. However, unless the retreating 30 DP could fill in the gap between the 10 DP and the 2 DPL, Rómmel would not even have a continuous front. Thus, it was essential that Army Łódź be reinforced.

Generał Dywizji Stefan Dąb-Biernacki's Army Prusy was supposed to be the strategic reserve that would be used to launch a concentrated counter-attack as the enemy approached Warsaw. However, Army Prusy was far from concentrated or ready for action on 3 September – it had been expected to have at least a week to form up. Nevertheless, Rydz-Śmigły was concerned about the early reverses suffered in the border battles and he directed Dąb-Biernacki to provide some forces to Army Łódź. The Wileńska Cavalry Brigade was sent to Piotrków to help organize a defence of that town, but otherwise Dąb-Biernacki committed none of his other units for the moment. Of all the Polish mistakes made in the 1939 campaign, Rydz-Śmigły's decision to entrust his operational *masse de manoeuvre* to Dąb-Biernacki was the most disastrous. Although Dąb-Biernacki had demonstrated great bravery and ability as an infantry regiment commander in the Russo-Polish War, he lacked the ability or aptitude to command larger formations and had no interest in tanks or other modern weapons. Furthermore, he was the type of commander who favoured positional warfare, rather than fast-moving battles of manoeuvre. Rydz-Śmigły did have a better candidate to direct the strategic reserve – Kazimierz Sosnkowski – but Rydz-Śmigły would not accept him due to past political differences. Eventually, Rydz-Śmigły would ask for Sosnkowski's help, but not until the situation was beyond hope.

As it was, the 7 DP was unable to escape the German pursuit after abandoning Częstochowa. The German 4. Infanterie-Division came up fast from behind while the 2. leichte- Division managed to sweep around to the south and get ahead of it. The Germans caught up with the Polish rearguard, the 74 PP, and crushed it near Lelów around 1400 hours on 3 September. Generał Brygady Janusz Gasiorowski, the 7 DP commander, tried to break through the 2. leichte-Division using his remaining forces, but the attempt failed with heavy losses. Caught in the open and surrounded, only a few troops from the 7 DP managed to escape through the German cordon. On 4 September, Gasiorowski surrendered his trapped division to the XV Armeekorps.[74] Meanwhile, the 3. leichte-Division kept the Krakowska Cavalry Brigade on the run. The northern portion of Army Kraków had disintegrated in just three days of combat.

Rómmel's Army Łódź struggled to delay Reichenau's 10. Armee on 3 September, but its forward units were fighting a series of isolated battles. After retreating from the Warta, the 30 DP made a stand at Szczerców and had a full day to prepare before the pursuing XI Armeekorps arrived. However, the fresh 28 DP moved forwards to block the advance of the 1. leichte-Division from Weilun, but one of its regiments was mauled in a meeting engagement west of the Warta. The 28 DP retreated across the Warta and tried to form a strongpoint at Konopnica, but the pursuing 1. leichte-Division managed to bounce the river before the Polish defence was fully established. In some disorder, the 28 DP retreated towards Widawa. The only other unit that Rómmel had in contact, the Wołyńska Cavalry Brigade, slowly fell back past Radomsko, trying to delay the 4. Panzer-Division. On 2 September, the Luftwaffe had bombed Radomsko, a town of 23,000, in order to hinder any Polish attempt to defend the location and at 0730 hours on 3 September, the 4. Panzer-Division occupied the town. The corridor to Piotrków and the assembly areas of Army Prusy was wide open for the XVI Armeekorps (mot.).

Fortunately for the Poles, the XVI Armeekorps (mot.) was experiencing fuel shortages by the third day of the campaign, which hindered a rapid advance. All of the German pre-war exercises with mechanized forces had occurred in relatively small training areas, like Hohenfels and Grafenwöhr in Bavaria. The Heer had not practised large-scale resupply of fuel and ammunition under austere field conditions and over longer distances – they experienced this for the first time in Poland. Both Panzer-Divisionen were using the same main supply route, so bottlenecks at damaged bridges affected each division. At this point, the Heer had not thought to ask the Luftwaffe to conduct aerial resupply of fuel for its armoured spearheads – that would come later. Nor had the Heer practised vehicle recovery or field repairs to any great extent, which meant that many vehicles damaged at the battle of Mokra took time to round up and fix, if the spare parts could be brought forwards. After springing 80km across the border in the first two days of the war, by the third day the XVI Armeekorps' two Panzer-Divisionen had difficulty moving 30km against minimal resistance. Wehrmacht commanders had much to learn about sustaining the operational tempo of mechanized warfare.

The German slow-down gave Generał Brygady Thommée a chance to order the remnants of Operational Group Piotrków to mount a spoiling attack in order to buy time for Army Łódź to establish a proper defence around Piotrków. Thommée was given a reserve infantry regiment, the 146th (146 PP), to block the main road to Piotrków and Major Edmund Karpow's 2 BCL to supplement the Wołyńska Cavalry Brigade. On the morning of 4 September, Hoepner's XVI Armeekorps (mot.) resumed its advance and reached Rozprza, just 12km south of Piotrków. At 1335 hours, Thommée ordered Major Karpow to counter-attack the German advance with his battalion and some units from the Wołyńska Cavalry Brigade; this was the combat baptism for the Polish 7TP tank. Two Polish tank companies (with a total of 32 7TPs) attacked II./Schutzen-Regiment 1 while it was attempting to cross a minor creek near Rozprza, which caused II./Panzer-Regiment 1 to intervene with about 50–60 tanks. Firing from wooded, hilly positions, the Polish light tanks and supporting artillery succeeded in knocking out about nine German tanks, for a loss of two of their own. The 7TP, armed with a 37mm gun, was clearly superior to the lightly armed Pz I and Pz II tanks. While this three-hour armoured skirmish succeeded in delaying Hoepner's Panzers for a bit, the Polish tankers had to retire for lack of support.[75] By the evening of 4 September, Thommée had established a thin screen south of Piotrków, but it could not hold against a determined attack. He had also been provided the 1 BCL, which theoretically gave him about 90 light tanks. However, the Polish Army had not adopted the mind-set of massing its tanks and even in the first combat, the 2 BCL had fought as individual companies.

While Rómmel's Army Łódź was being battered by 10. Armee and short of forces to establish a main line of resistance, Kutrzeba's Army Poznań spent 3–4 September in retreat, withdrawing eastwards towards Warsaw. Since the Germans only had minor forces in this sector, Kutrzeba's retreat was only hindered by Luftwaffe attacks, although Blaskowitz's 8. Armee was on a converging route of march from the south-east. Of all the front-line Polish armies, Army Poznań was the only one that was still relatively intact by the morning of 5 September. However, the four divisions under Kutrzeba were in the wrong place, at the wrong time. Likewise, Blaskowitz's 8. Armee was the only one of the five German armies involved in *Fall Weiss* that did not have an attached Panzer-Division, which meant that he had no mobility advantage over Kutrzeba's retreating army. By the evening of 4 September, it was clear the Polish covering forces along the Warta River had been defeated and that 10. Armee was about to seize Piotrków, which would open the doorway to Warsaw, just 130km distant.

Upper Silesia and the Carpathian Front, 1–5 September

The Polish Army had long expected a German attempt to recover the portions of Upper Silesia lost in 1921 and consequently this sector of the Polish–German border had received higher priority for defensive improvements. Construction of the Fortified Region of Silesia (Obszar Warowny Śląsk or OWS) had begun in 1933 and new bunkers were being added right up to the outbreak of war. The OWS consisted of a 22km-long chain of about 140 bunkers centred upon the city of Katowice, which was one of Poland's main coal- and steel-producing areas. Some concrete bunkers within the OWS were built with walls greater than 1m thick and could withstand artillery bombardment by weapons up to 220mm in calibre. In order to man the bunkers, the OWS was garrisoned by three infantry battalions and an artillery battalion from the 23rd Infantry Division (23 DP). Some sections of the line were fronted by anti-tank obstacles, including steel rails placed in the ground. Silesia also boasted fortifications around other border towns, such as Rybnik and more were planned after Germany annexed Czechoslovakia. On the eve of war, Generał Brygady Antoni Szylling, commander of Army Kraków, formed the Śląsk (Silesia) Operational Group with the 23 DP and the reserve 55th Infantry Division (55 DP) to defend the Katowice–Rybnik sector. The 55 DP began mobilizing in late August and was comprised almost entirely of ON troops; its task was to defend the fortified section of Mikołów southwest of Katowice. Generał Szylling also formed the Bielsko Operational Group, consisting of the 6th Infantry Division (6 DP), 21 DPG and 1st Mountain Brigade, to defend the Brzeźce–Cieszyn (Teschen)–Żywiec sector. Szylling's only mobile reserve was Pułkownik Stanisław Maczek's 10 BK, stationed near Kraków.[76]

Generaloberst Wilhelm List's 14. Armee was assigned to attack from Silesia and Slovakia in order to destroy Army Kraków. Given the nature of the hilly, rough terrain along much of the Polish–German border in this region and the limited number of useful roads, List's forces were more dispersed than 8.Armee or 10.Armee. List intended to make his main effort with General der Infanterie Eugen Beyer's XVIII Armeekorps (including the 2. Panzer-Division and 4. leichte-Division), which would advance north from Slovakia to the town of Myslenice, 25km south of Kraków, thereby enveloping the left flank of Army Kraków. At the same time, the VIII Armeekorps would attack the OWS with three infantry divisions, while its attached 5. Panzer-Division tried to envelop the southern end of the Polish fortified line. The XVII Armeekorps, comprised of three infantry divisions, would seize Teschen (Cieszyn) and dislodge the Bielsko Operational Group, then push towards Kraków. Meanwhile, the two Gebirgsjäger Divisionen in the XXII Armeekorps would attack the Polish Army Karpaty through the Carpathian passes.

Before dawn on 1 September, the advance units of the German VIII Armeekorps, commanded by General der Infanterie Ernst Busch, began crossing the border into Upper Silesia. Busch did not intend to assault the OWS with a frontal attack. Instead, Busch directed the 8. Infanterie-Division to conduct a demonstration against the 23 DP's main positions near Katowice, while the 28. Infanterie-Division marched forwards to strike the southern end of the OWS near Mikolow, held by the still-mobilizing 55 DP. The German infantry marched rapidly to seize Hill 341, a century-old heap of mining waste known as the Hałda Skalny, near the village of Wyry. The hill itself was held by the II/203 PP from 55 DP and afforded excellent observation and fields of fire, although there was almost no vegetation on the hilltop. German efforts to seize the hill failed, but by late morning the 28. Infanterie-Division managed to bypass the hill and get into the village of Gostyn while reconnaissance troops pushed even further, to Kobiór. The Polish 55 DP was under heavy pressure, but the 23 DP was not, so the commander of the Śląsk Operational Group, Generał Brygady Jan Jagmin-Sadowski, decided to transfer five battalions from the 23 DP to reinforce the faltering 55 DP. Although the Poles would not be able to mount a major counter-attack until the next day, the 55 DP managed to hold its positions.[77] The fighting in the OWS was one of the few places in the 1939 campaign where the Polish operational group concept worked properly, in large part because the local mission was well understood, the two divisions involved were in close proximity and they were allowed to fight a positional battle.

Further south, Generał Brygady Bernard Mond's 6 DP held a critical position at Pszczyna, which served as a linchpin between the Śląsk and Bielsko operational groups. Between the border and Pszczyna, Mond had established a defence in depth, with strongpoints in the towns of Rybnik and Zory. Polish sappers had also created numerous obstacles along the roads near the border. Generalleutnant Heinrich von Vietinghoff-Scheel's 5. Panzer-Division crossed the Polish border in two parallel Kampfgruppen, aiming for the first Polish strongpoint at Rybnik. Despite some modest defences, including a few mines, the lone Polish battalion from 6 DP (I/75 PP) was overrun by 1000 hours. The northern Kampfgruppe (Panzer-Regiment 15 and Schützen-Regiment 14) then pushed on, overrunning the strongpoint in Zory by 1630 hours (most of the garrison escaped to Kobiór). The southernmost Kampfgruppe (Panzer-Regiment 31 and Schützen-Regiment 13) had bypassed Zory and approached the 6 DP's main line of resistance, but the 5. Panzer-Division did not launch a serious attack until late afternoon. Mond had constructed a powerful anti-tank killing zone at the village of Brzeźce, which knocked out about 13 German tanks for the loss of a single anti-tank gun. Oberst Johann Haarde, commander of Panzer-Brigade 8, was badly wounded by Polish artillery fire and the commander of Panzer-Regiment 31, Oberst Walter Schuckelt, went temporarily missing in the chaos that ensued after the action. German armoured probes further south were also repulsed, causing Vietinghoff to temporarily call off the attack as evening fell. According to Polish sources, the 5. Panzer-Division lost about 30 tanks (out of 335) and 12 armoured cars on the first day. However, the 5. Panzer-Division had advanced over 40km against obstinate resistance and the Germans now had a good idea of where the 6 DP's main line of resistance was located.

On 2 September, the German 28. Infanterie-Division continued to exert pressure against the 55 DP at Kobiór, while the 8. Infanterie-Division tried to pin the 23 DP in the OWS positions around Katowice. The German VIII Armeekorps used all available artillery to pound Mikolow, which provoked the defending Polish artillery to launch a fierce counter-bombardment. Nevertheless, the Poles managed to begin a counter-attack with several infantry battalions, supported by Armoured Train No. 51,

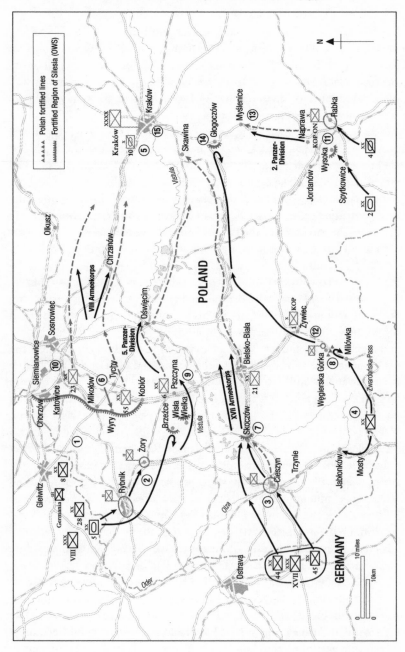

MAP KEY

1 September

1) The German VIII Armeekorps attacks the Fortified Region of Silesia (OWS) to pin the Polish 23 DP and 55 DP.
2) The 5. Panzer-Division overruns Polish garrisons in Rybnik and Zory, but its advance guard is repulsed by the 6 DP at Brzeźce.
3) The 45. Infanterie-Division occupies Cieszyn after the Polish garrison withdraws.
4) The 7. Infanterie-Division crosses the border in two separate groups.
5) Army Krakow sends Maczek's 10 BK to the Wysoka sector, just as 2. Panzer-Division approaches from the south.

2 September

6) Polish counter-attack at Mikolow achieves some success against the 28. Infanterie-Division.
7) Polish delaying action at Skoczów.
8) The 7. Infanterie-Division's initial attack on Węgierska Gorka is repulsed.
9) The 5. Panzer-Division turns the 6 DP's left flank, which precipitates a general Polish retreat.
10) Katowice is abandoned by the 23 DP and occupied the next day.
11) The German XXII Armeekorps attacks the Polish positions at Wysoka-Rabka but fails to break through. The Poles break contact and fall back to Myslenice.

3 September

12) The 7. Infanterie-Division finally overcomes the Polish garrison at Węgierska Gorka.

4 September

13) The 2. Panzer-Division reaches the corps objective at Myslenice.

5 September

14) The 21 DPG repulses initial attacks by the 7. Infanterie-Division at Glogoczów.
15) Polish forces abandon Kraków, which is occupied by the Germans the next morning.

around 1000 hours. By early afternoon, the 55 and 23 DP managed to recapture some ground – at considerable cost – from the 28. Infanterie-Division, but the success was short-lived. The Polish defence at Pszczyna was based on the notion of massing maximum firepower on the most likely avenue of approach, which was the main road that passed through Brzeźce. However, Viettinghoff demonstrated the mobility of armour by swinging south at 1000 hours, along the less optimal route, to overwhelm a single Polish company from the 20th Infantry Regiment (20 PP) east of Wisla-Wielka. The German attack was aided by dense morning fog, which helped conceal their approach. Oberst Johannes Streich led Panzer-Regiment 15 into the narrow gap in the Polish lines and turned the right flank of the 6 DP. Before Mond knew what had occurred, he received reports – which were correct – that German tanks had reached Cwiklice, behind his main line of resistance. Streich's Panzers proceeded to overrun most of the Polish divisional artillery located north-east of Pszczyna, destroying 18 75mm guns. Mond ordered the 6 DP to retreat eastwards at once to Oswiecim (the future site of the German Auschwitz death camp), but this retreat quickly turned into a rout. One battalion, the II/16 PP, bumped into German Panzers and was destroyed in the open. Four battalions from the 16 and 20 PP were trapped in Pszczyna. Bits and pieces of the battered 6 DP managed to escape eastwards through the woods, but the bulk of the division was already destroyed or encircled. Mond sent a message to Generał Sadowski, commander of the Ślask Operational Group, 'Do not count on me to protect the southern flank; my division has ceased to exist, overrun by tanks. I'm collecting the rest and going to Oswiecim.'[78] Combined with the already-mentioned retreat of the Krakowska Cavalry Brigade, both flanks of the Ślask Operational Group were now exposed.

By 1500 hours on 2 September, Generał Szylling knew that the Germans had outflanked the OWS and that the Ślask Operational Group was in danger of being encircled. He ordered the abandonment of the OWS positions and the entire Ślask Operational Group to retreat eastwards. In just two days, the Poles had lost the fight for Upper Silesia. Generał Sadowski objected to abandoning Katowice but had no choice, since all of Army Kraków would soon be in retreat. Since part of the 6 DP was still trapped in Pszczyna, the 5. Panzer-Division did not immediately pursue the other retreating fragments of the division, but instead focused on mopping up to secure its own lines of communication. The remnants of the 6 DP used the cover of night, moving through wooded areas, to escape. The 23rd and 55 DPs also disengaged during the night and retreated eastwards. Although the Polish Army abandoned the city of Katowice during the night of 2/3 September, a few rearguards from the fortress troops and several groups of armed Polish civilian volunteers managed to delay the German entry into the city, helping the Śląsk Operational Group to withdraw. Armed pro-Nazi ethnic German civilians also tried to seize control of the city, but were unsuccessful. The German 239. Infanterie-Division cautiously approached Katowice and did not begin entering the city until dusk on 3 September; the German columns were frequently fired upon from rooftops and suffered losses. It was not until noon on 4 September that the Germans had control over most of Katowice, although sporadic firing continued throughout the day. The SS-Regiment 'Germania', which had not played any significant role in the initial border fighting, entered Katowice later in the day.

While the German VIII Armeekorps had been engaged with the Śląsk Operational Group, the XVII Armeekorps moved to occupy the south-west corner of Upper Silesia and to defeat the Bielsko Operational Group. Despite much effort put into recovering Cieszyn (Teschen) in 1938 during the Munich Crisis, the Polish Army did not make a major effort to defend the border city at the outset of the war. The Polish 21 DPG was responsible for this sector, but much of the division's strength was kept back around Bielsko. Cieszyn was only held by a reinforced mountain infantry battalion (I/4th Regiment of Podhale Rifles). On 1 September, the 45. Infanterie-Division began advancing towards the city's western outskirts, while the 44. Infanterie-Division advanced north of the city. Although the Polish battalion group had a decent amount of artillery support and automatic weapons, the defending companies were too spread out to offer protracted resistance. By noontime, German troops had reached the Olza River and tried to cross, but were repulsed by machine-gun fire. Nevertheless, it was clear that the Germans had an overwhelming advantage in this sector, so the commander of the 21 DPG ordered the evacuation of the city. The Polish defenders blew up the bridges over the Olza and began retreating to Bielska, 30km to the east. Around 1600 hours, the 45. Infanterie-Division entered Cieszyn. In order to slow the advance of the XVII Armeekorps, on the morning of 2 September Polish rearguards blew up the bridges over the Vistula River at Skoczów. Two battalions of the 202nd Infantry Regiment (202 PP) then conducted a protracted delaying action along the river against the 45. Infanterie-Division, until withdrawing towards Bielsko at dusk.

The VIII Armeekorps also directed Generalmajor Eugen Ott's 7. Infanterie-Division, deployed to the Slovak town of Čadca, to clear out the Sola River valley and thereby put pressure on the left flank of the Bielsko Operational Group. After the German invasion of the rump

Czech state in March 1939, the General Inspector of the Armed Forces in Warsaw had directed Army Kraków to create a new line of fortifications to block the southern approaches to Kraków. In July, Polish engineers began construction of 20 large concrete bunkers near the village of Węgierska Gorka ('Hungarian Hill') in order to block the Sola River valley. By the end of August, five bunkers were nearly completed and due to heightened border tensions, Army Kraków ordered them garrisoned. The KOP's 1st Brigade of Mountain Rifles, commanded by Pułkownik Jan Gaładyk, was responsible for the Żywiec sector and it directed Kapitan Tadeusz Semik to form a 70-man detachment from various sources, including KOP and ON troops (designated as the 151st Fortress Company) to occupy the bunkers in Węgierska Gorka. Kapitan Semik and his men moved into four of the bunkers (he did not have enough personnel to garrison the fifth bunker) three days before the war began. Three of the bunkers were equipped with a 37mm anti-tank gun and two to four wz. 30 heavy machine guns, while the bunker 'Waligora' was equipped with two 75mm guns. The bunkers were still missing armoured cupolas for the machine guns and there were no communications between positions or with higher headquarters, but it was nevertheless a strong blocking position since the narrow valley terrain favoured the defence. In addition to Kapitan Semik's detachment, elements of the KOP Berezwecz Battalion and a company of ON troops from the Żywiec ON Battalion arrived to support the defence by digging trenches in between the bunkers.

Ott's 7. Infanterie-Division crossed the Slovak–Polish border in several places on the morning of 1 September, but the main body (Infanterie-Regimenter 19 and 62) came through the Zwardońska Pass, 15km south-west of Węgierska Gorka. Another group, led by Infanterie-Regiment 61, came through the Jablunka Pass, further west. Small detachments of KOP and ON troops put up fierce resistance and seriously delayed the German advance. It took Ott's forces all day to reach the town of Milówka, just 10km from the border. The next morning, these small detachments of KOP and ON continued to fight a successful delaying action and the 7. Infanterie-Division did not reach Węgierska Gorka until about 1300 hours on 2 September. The 7. Infanterie-Division had Infanterie-Regiment 62 on the west side of the Sola and Infanterie-Regiment 61 on the east side. Thanks to Luftwaffe reconnaissance, Ott was aware of the Polish bunkers before crossing the border, but he had no details on their garrison or armament. He decided to use his artillery to bombard the Polish bunker line, which had virtually no effect. Around 1600 hours, the Germans began a ground assault but this was quickly stopped by Polish defensive fire. Recognizing that the Polish bunker line was too strong to overcome with a frontal assault, Ott ordered his two regimental commanders to begin simultaneous infiltration attacks to get around the enemy flanks and assault the Polish bunkers from behind, supported by sappers from Pionier-Bataillon 7.[79] Once Pułkownik Gaładyk, the KOP brigade commander, learned that the Germans were approaching Bielsko and that Army Kraków was in retreat, he ordered the KOP Berezwecz Battalion and the ON troops to withdraw at nightfall. Most of the Polish troops slipped away from the position once it grew dark, but due to the lack of communications, Kapitan Semik and his bunker crews did not receive the retreat order. They remained in place.

During the night of 2/3 September, the Germans began assaults on the bunkers, which now lacked supporting infantry. On the east side, bunker Wąwóz repulsed several attacks by Infanterie-Regiment 61. However, German infantry and pioneers were able to surround Kapitan Semik and his 19-man garrison in bunker Wędrowiec and get onto the roof in order to try and throw hand grenades into the openings for the missing machine-gun cupolas. This was the weak spot in the uncompleted bunkers – the armoured cupolas had not yet been installed on the roof and the shaft was open to the sky. Although Semik was wounded, none of the bunkers were captured during the night. Before dawn, the 15 soldiers in the artillery bunker Waligóra – having exhausted all their ammunition – successfully escaped through the German cordon. The garrison in bunker Włóczęga had also exhausted their ammunition but they could not escape and surrendered at 0830 hours on 3 September. The Germans now concentrated on the last two bunkers, which continued to resist. Infanterie-Regiment 61 brought up 3.7cm PaK guns to try to shoot the doors off Kapitan Semik's bunker, but this had only limited effectiveness. Eventually, Semik surrendered at 1700 hours, once all his ammunition was gone. Amazingly, Podporucznik Czesław Chludzinski* and his 18-man garrison held bunker Wąwóz and successfully escaped around 2200 hours. Polish sources have often exaggerated German casualties in the battle of Węgierska Gorka, suggesting that the 7. Infanterie-Division suffered 500–600 casualties in the two-day battle. In fact, the 7. Infanterie-Division reported only 13 dead, four missing and 40 wounded on 2–3 September, totalling just 57 casualties. Nevertheless, four incomplete bunkers and a scratch team had inflicted a serious delay on the 7. Infanterie-Division,

---

*Executed by the Soviet NKVD at Katyń Forest in 1940.

preventing it from interfering with the withdrawal of Army Kraków from Upper Silesia. There is little doubt that if the Poles had completed all 20 bunkers in Węgierska Gorka and properly garrisoned them that the German advance in this sector would have been stopped cold.

Forty kilometres to the east, the German XVIII Armeekorps was pouring across the Slovak-Polish border near Jablonka, led by Generalmajor Alfred Ritter von Hubicki's 4. leichte-Division and a regiment from the 3. Gebirgs-Division. Generalmajor Rudolf Veiel's 2. Panzer-Division crossed the border on the corps' left flank, pushing hard for the initial objective, the town of Myslenice. The Polish defences were extremely weak in this sector, amounting to the 1st Infantry Regiment KOP, one infantry battalion (II/12 PP) from the 6 DP and two ON battalions, barely 3,000 troops, all under the command of Podpułkownik Wojciech Wójcik*, which were focused on holding the town of Rabka, 50km south of Kraków. Wójcik's forces had negligible support weapons – just a battery of 65mm mountain howitzers and six 37mm anti-tank guns. The troops in the ON Zakoplane Battalion had no uniforms or helmets – they went into battle in street clothes wearing white and red armbands – and they were armed with old German Mauser rifles. Not surprisingly, these rag-tag troops were not able to seriously delay the invaders near the border and the German motorized units made rapid progress. The vanguard of the 2. Panzer-Division approached the town of Spytkowice, less than 10km from Rabka, by late on the first day, while the 4. leichte-Division occupied Nowy Targ. The Germans also ordered the Slovak 1st Infantry to cross the border and this 6,000-man unit occupied the resort town of Zakoplane without a fight, since the Polish ON troops had retreated north to Rabka.[80] The XVIII Armeekorps appeared to be on the cusp of a major victory, which would lead to the rapid encirclement of Army Kraków.

However, Generał Szylling recognized the serious danger in this sector and without hesitation he committed his only reserve – Pułkownik Stanisław Maczek's 10 BK – at 0800 hours on 1 September to reinforce the threadbare forces around Rabka. Szylling told Maczek that he would have to hold off an entire German corps for as long as possible with his 4,100 troops. It is important to note that the 10 BK was still an experimental force, equipped with only a company of obsolete Vickers tanks instead of the battalion of new 7TP tanks it was supposed to receive in the near future. Many of the brigade's motor vehicles were also worn out.[81] Nevertheless,

---

*Executed by the Soviet NKVD at Katyń Forest in 1940.

the 10 BK moved out at once. Four hours later, Maczek reached Wójcik's headquarters near Rabka and was briefed on the enemy situation. Shortly thereafter, the first elements of the 10 BK began to arrive and Maczek deployed them on the high ground at Wysoka. In this case, the cavalry had arrived in the nick of time, since the lead Kampfgruppe (Panzer-Regiment 3) from the 2. Panzer-Division, was just approaching Wysoka from the south.[82] Polish engineers blew up a bridge over the Skawa which delayed the German advance and anti-tank guns hidden in the wood line of the high ground around Wysoka managed to hit a few German tanks. Since nightfall was approaching, the Germans decided to defer the attack on Wysoka until the next morning, which gave Maczek time to bring up the rest of his brigade and tie in with Wójcik's KOP and ON troops deployed around Rabka. Maczek used Pułkownik Kazimierz Dworak's 24th Uhlan Regiment and a battery of 37mm anti-tank guns to anchor his defence at Wysoka, but kept his own tanks in reserve. Maczek also requested that the LW's Bomber Brigade be used to attack the columns of the 2. Panzer-Division, strung out south of his position. Not content to fight a passive defence, Maczek tried to mount a night spoiling attack using the infantry battalion from the 6 DP and two squadrons of the 24th Uhlans, but this effort miscarried due to inadequate co-ordination.[83]

On 2 September, List (14. Armee) directed a reshuffling of command arrangements in the Carpathian sector: Kleist's XXII Armeekorps (mot.) would take over the three divisions advancing towards Rabka, while Beyer's XVIII Armeekorps would take control of the 1. and 2. Gebirgs-Divisionen. Normally, this kind of command rearrangement at the outset of a war is a recipe for C^2 and logistic confusion, but it apparently had negligible impact upon the German operational tempo. Yet the shift of command responsibilities one day into the war suggests that German pre-war planning – at least in 14. Armee – was not as thorough as is often claimed.

Nevertheless, Veiel's 2. Panzer-Division prepared to attack Maczek's brigade at Wysoka. Around 0530 hours, the I./Panzer-Regiment 3 advanced northwards towards Wysoka, with three tank companies in a broad wedge formation. Two battalions of German artillery pounded the high ground, but most of the shells landed on the forward slope. Initially, Maczek could only reply with eight artillery pieces against the 24 German howitzers. Nevertheless, the Polish anti-tank guns were not suppressed and they opened fire at the approaching German armour at a range of about 600m and knocked out several enemy tanks. The Polish defence was also assisted by Armoured Train No. 51, with its four 75mm guns. Under heavy fire, the German Panzers fell back to regroup. Recognizing that he was facing a strong defensive front and not a rearguard, Generalmajor Veiel was forced to commit the rest of his division and mount another assault on Wysoka around 0900 hours. Now the Germans massed fires to suppress the Polish defence. Rolf Hertenstein, a gunner on a Pz IV medium tank in the V./Panzer-Regiment. 4, was involved in this attack and claimed to have knocked out a Polish 37mm anti-tank gun with his 75mm howitzer. As the German tanks closed in, the machine-gunners in the 24th Uhlans switched to armour-piercing ammunition, which was effective against the thin armour on the Pz I and Pz II tanks. One machine gunner, Kapral Wincenty Dziechciarz, may have disabled as many as two to four German tanks before he and his crew were killed by red phosphorus rounds (the German 75mm Nbgr. Kw. K. smoke shell).[84] Another defender, Podporucznik Franciszek Dziuba, also directed a 37mm anti-tank gun which knocked out several tanks, until he too was killed.[85] The German tanks gradually pushed back the left wing of the 24th Uhlans, but Pułkownik Dworak mounted local counter-attacks that prevented a complete collapse. Around 1100 hours, Veiel mounted another offensive pulse, but shifting eastwards, hoping to exploit a perceived gap in the Polish lines between the 24th Uhlans and its sister regiment, the 10th Mounted Rifles. Veiel committed his Schützen-Brigade 2 to support this attack, which succeeded in driving a wedge into the Polish line.[86] Maczek finally committed his small armour reserve – the 121st Light Tank Company with 16 Vickers tanks – which successfully counter-attacked the German infantry penetration and prevented a breakthrough. However, the German Panzers and motorized infantry continued to press the obstinate Polish defence and managed to occupy Wysoka by 1600 hours. By late afternoon, the 24th Uhlans were falling back through Jordanow.

During the day, Hubicki's 4. leichte-Division had arrived south of Rabka and attacked Wójcik's two KOP battalions. Although the Germans did not break through in this sector, it was clear that the Germans could now employ two mobile divisions against the thin Polish defence. Consequently, Maczek converted the defence of Wysoka into a mobile delay, ordering the 10 BK and Wójcik's KOP battalion to begin falling back during the night of 2/3 September towards Myslenice. Although Polish historians acknowledge the battle of Jordanow/Wysoka as a German victory, the skilful and obstinate resistance of Maczek's 10 BK is rightly regarded with some pride. Yet claims about the battle being a German 'Pyrrhic victory' due to heavy losses are unfounded; perhaps 30 German tanks were disabled, mostly Pz I and Pz IIs, but the Germans held the battlefield and could recover their wrecks. Specific German personnel losses are unknown but were probably no more than 100 dead and wounded. Maczek's own casualties were relatively light – this was a delaying action, not a fight to the death. The main tactical point is that Maczek's 10 BK fought a successful delaying action against a superior force and was able to break contact and retreat – a feat that few Polish units could accomplish in September 1939. It also appears that German pre-war manoeuvre doctrine had focused too much on defeating static enemy defenders and not fully considered the challenges of defeating an enemy force which possessed equal mobility.

Oddly, the Germans did not mount an effective pursuit of the Polish forces – possibly due to the switch-over between controlling corps headquarters – and allowed both the 10 BK and Wójcik's units to fall back 3–4km and re-establish a new line near Naprawa by the morning of 3 September. Although both 2. Panzer-Division and the 4. leichte-Division attacked the new Polish line, they could not crush or envelop the defenders. Indeed, the Germans seemed content to push the smaller Polish forces back towards Myslenice, rather than make a serious effort to get around their open flanks and destroy them. On the night of 3/4 September, Maczek and Wójcik retreated another 10km and established blocking positions at key road junctions. On 4 September, the lead Kampfgruppe of Hubicki's 4. leichte-Division received a nasty surprise when Maczek launched a counter-attack with his armour; three German tanks and two armoured cars were knocked out for the loss of two Vickers light tanks and a TK3 tankette.[87] Yet while Maczek could slow the advance of Kleist's XXII Armeekorps (mot.), he could not stop it. By the afternoon of 4 September, Maczek's 10th Cavalry Brigade had retreated to Myslenice and the 2. Panzer-Division was hard on his heels. Around 2000 hours, German tanks broke through the thin line south of the town and caused a brief panic, before being repulsed by a prompt counter-attack. In addition to Maczek's tired brigade, only two battalions from the 12th Infantry Regiment and a KOP battalion were on hand to defend Myslenice.

While Maczek was trying to prevent Kleist's XXII Armeekorps (mot.) from enveloping Army Kraków's left flank, the bulk of Army Kraków was falling back towards that city, pursued by List's 14. Armee. The 23rd and 55 DPs managed to break contact from the German VIII Armeekorps after abandoning Katowice and fight a delaying action, while falling back towards Kraków. The Poles were successful in destroying all the bridges over the Vistula in this sector, which hindered the German pursuit. Further south, the remnants of the 6 DP tried to evade the 5. Panzer-Division but suffered further losses near Oswiecim on 3 September. The 21 DPG briefly delayed the German XVII Armeekorps along the River

Sola before withdrawing. During the night of 3/4 September, Generał Szylling received command guidance from Rydz-Śmigły to continue the retreat of Army Kraków to the north-east in an effort to try to reduce the gap between his forces and those of Army Łódź and Army Prusy. Civilian officials in Kraków were informed on the evening of 4 September that their city would soon be abandoned to the enemy. In order to prevent his retreating army from being encircled by the converging German pincers, Szylling ordered the 21 DPG to defend the south-west approaches to Krakow by creating blocking positions around Skawina, while Maczek held Myslenice. By 4 September, most of the remaining elements of Army Kraków were just west of the city. After clearing out the bunkers at Węgierska Gorka, the 7. Infanterie-Division pivoted eastwards and forced-marched towards Myslenice.

By the morning of 5 September, 14. Armee was pounding on the Polish blocking positions around Kraków. The 21 DPG made a valiant stand against the 45. Infanterie-Division at Glogoczów south of the city, repulsing three attacks. However, the 5. Panzer-Division was now approaching Kraków from the west and the hard-marching 7. Infanterie-Division managed to approach Myslenice from its unprotected western flank. Furthermore, Kleist had begun to turn his armour eastwards, sending Hubicki's 4. leichte-Division to occupy Zakliczyn. Realizing that several of his best units were about to be surrounded, Szylling ordered Maczek to abandon Myslenice and for the 21 DPG to retreat. As the Polish Army retreated, civil disorder and widespread looting occurred in Kraków, before German troops from the XVII Armeekorps entered the undefended city on the morning of 6 September.

While Army Kraków was being defeated, Army Karpaty found a side-show campaign in the Carpathians against the German 1. and 2. Gebirgs-Divisionen and the Slovaks. The Polish units along the Carpathians were too thinly spread to hold the passes and by the second day of the war the 2nd Mountain Rifle Brigade (1 KOP and three ON battalions) was in retreat towards Nowy Sącz, 73km south-east of Kraków. The two non-motorized German divisions could not pursue very rapidly and the road network was poor, which greatly reduced the operational tempo in this sector. Eventually, by 5 September the German mountain troops were closing in on Nowy Sącz but before they could mount an assault, the 2nd Mountain Rifle Brigade abandoned the town.

CHAPTER 6

Total War

'Polish civilians and soldiers are dragged out everywhere. When we finish our operation, the entire village is on fire. Nobody is left alive, also all the dogs were shot.'

German soldier from Infanterie-Regiment 41[1]

The Anglo-French Declaration of War, 3 September

'We have a clear conscience, we have done all that any country could do to establish peace.'

Neville Chamberlain, 3 September 1939

Despite signing a formal military alliance with Poland on 25 August, which stated that 'in the event of any action which clearly threatened Polish independence ... His Majesty's Government would feel themselves bound at once to lend the Polish Government all support in their power ...'. Chamberlain's cabinet took no immediate action upon learning of the German invasion. Indeed, Neville Chamberlain and his foreign minister Lord Halifax were in virtual shock that Hitler had actually made the decision for war and thereby shattered their vision of creating a new peaceful order in Europe. Halifax spent most of the morning of 1 September trying to figure out what was going on in Poland. At 1030 hours, Count Edward Raczyński, the Polish ambassador in London, informed Halifax that Warsaw had been bombed and German troops were crossing the border at multiple locations, which he said clearly met the conditions established under the terms of the military alliance. However, in a clear attempt at disinformation, at 1115 hours the German ambassador told Halifax that Warsaw had not been bombed and the only shooting along the border was being done by Polish troops.[2] At 1130 hours, Chamberlain met with his full cabinet. Chamberlain began with the statement that 'our consciences were clear, and there should be no possible question now where our duty lay.' However, Halifax stated that the situation in Poland was 'confused' and that reports of Warsaw being bombed were 'premature'. Although the Cabinet agreed to send a warning message to Hitler stating that unless Germany ceased military actions against Poland, Britain would honour its obligations to Poland, it was not an ultimatum because no deadline was included. It took nearly six hours to draft the warning into a telegram, which was not sent to Henderson in Berlin until 1745 hours. Henderson presented the warning telegram to Ribbentrop in Berlin at 2130 hours, but further diluted its meaning by emphasizing that the message was not an ultimatum.[3] Furthermore, Halifax raised the possibility within cabinet discussions of an armistice conference, which the Italian Foreign Ministry disingenuously suggested might be possible, even though Mussolini had no intention of interfering with *Fall Weiss*.[4] Some members of the Cabinet seized upon this nebulous Italian suggestion as a way to avoid making a decision for war, at least for the time being. Chamberlain's cabinet was in no hurry to honour its treaty obligations to Poland.

Even in follow-up committee meetings, Chamberlain's cabinet approached war in a highly bureaucratic manner, holding endless meetings that dealt with every subject from food rationing, to radio censorship to control of railroads and the coal industry, while avoiding the topic of Poland as much as possible.[5] Instead, the best that Chamberlain's cabinet could manage to accomplish on the first day of the war in Poland was to order full mobilization and to instruct the Royal Air Force's (RAF) Advanced Air Striking Force (AASF) to proceed to France 'forthwith'. In conjunction with mobilization, the House of Commons approved a war credit of £500 million, although the government still regarded this as a precautionary measure. Much to his personal chagrin, Chamberlain also invited his staunchest critic, Winston Churchill, to join the Cabinet as minister without portfolio; if there was to be a war, Churchill's wartime experience would be useful.

In Paris, the initial French response to the German invasion was similar – a call for general mobilization but official silence to both Germany and Poland. Georges Bonnet, the French foreign minister and perpetual advocate of appeasing Hitler, promoted the Italian mediation offer in lieu of an ultimatum. The French Council of Ministers was also keen to embrace the Italian suggestion of a peace conference, in order to gain more time for deliberation. Like Britain, France sent a warning message to Hitler, but no ultimatum. The Polish ambassador in Paris, Juliusz Łukasziewicz, quickly lost his patience with Bonnet's do-nothing mentality and demanded that France honour its treaty obligations at once.[6] In fact, the French had not even ratified the new military alliance with Poland, even though both sides had signed it in May.

On the second day of the war in Poland, both the British and French leaders continued to avoid discussing any kind of ultimatum to Hitler, even though barrage balloons were already being deployed over London and Paris. Hitler ignored the warning messages from the previous day. Daladier addressed the National Assembly and stated that 'France and England cannot stand by and watch a friendly nation destroyed ...' but avoided mentioning the necessity of a declaration of war unless Germany backed down. In order to support general mobilization, Daladier asked for F 75 billion in supplementary military credits – which was granted. In London, Halifax went round in circles most of the day about the Italian suggestion of a peace conference, which Rome claimed it might be able to arrange by 5 September. Chamberlain also preferred the idea of a peace conference and like the French, was unwilling to put any time limit on Hitler's military actions. Halifax inanely informed the Italian foreign minister that 'the British would not favour any conference while German troops remained in Poland' but left the door open to negotiations. By this point, the Poles were livid that their two erstwhile allies had still not honoured their treaty obligations and refused to consider any kind of peace conference. Germany's Foreign Ministry continued to spew out disinformation, claiming that a *de facto* cease-fire had already occurred in Poland – which some media uncritically accepted. Just prior to the British afternoon cabinet meeting, Chamberlain received a situation update from Count Raczyński, which stated that 'battle today over the whole of the front has increased in intensity' and that the Luftwaffe was bombing Polish cities. The Polish note also officially requested 'the immediate fulfilment of British obligations to Poland.'[7] Although most of the Cabinet was in favour of sending an ultimatum to Hitler at once, Chamberlain said that step should be deferred until the French were fully consulted. In Paris, Bonnet continued to prevaricate and urged delaying another 48 hours.

Up to this point, the public and the media in Britain and France had little notion of how their governments were responding to the German invasion of Poland, which led to confusion about whether or not war was imminent. It was not until Chamberlain addressed the House of Commons at 1800 hours on 2 September that it became clear that Britain had not even sent a real ultimatum to Hitler, demanding that he cease his invasion or face war. In a matter of minutes, Chamberlain's support in both the House and even his own cabinet evaporated, since his prepared statement made no mention of honouring the military commitment to Poland. Indeed, Chamberlain was shocked by the rancour in the house and was informed from multiple quarters that unless he sent an ultimatum to Hitler, his government would fall.[8] Chamberlain tried to argue that Britain should not declare war without France, which still balked at the prospect, but this did not hold sway with his cabinet. The Cabinet approved the ultimatum at a late evening meeting, but held off sending it until the next morning.[9]

The British ultimatum to Hitler was finally delivered to the Foreign Ministry in Berlin at 0900 hours on 3 September. Henderson, the British ambassador, presented the ultimatum and stated that Germany had until 1100 hours to reply. Hitler received the British ultimatum and ignored it. Two hours later, Chamberlain addressed the United Kingdom over radio and announced the declaration of war. Once the British had delivered their ultimatum and declared war, the French were left with little choice. The Germans received the French ultimatum one hour after the British declaration of war and ignored it as well, leading to a French declaration of war at 1700 hours. In Berlin, Goebbels' propaganda machine explained to the German people that it was not the Führer's fault that they now found themselves involved in another European War, but that of the Anglo-French. German news reels stated that 'for 20 years England had turned down all peaceful proposals for arbitration'. Unfortunately, by the time that Britain and France finally declared war, Polish forces had already been badly defeated on the border and were in retreat.

Even after making the decision to go to war because of the German invasion of Poland, Britain and France virtually ignored what was going on in Poland. Chamberlain held his first war cabinet meeting at 1700 hours on 3 September. Churchill was in attendance as First Lord of the Admiralty. There was no discussion of Poland in this first meeting. Instead, the main military question facing the Cabinet was how they should employ Britain's main strike force – RAF Bomber Command. The AASF had already deployed to French airfields on 2 September, comprising 12 light bomber squadrons with 120 Fairey Battles and 24 Blenheim Is. The bulk of Bomber Command – 24 squadrons with 280 operational bombers – remained at their bases in England. In late 1938, the Air Ministry (headed by Air Chief Marshal Sir Cyril Newall) had estimated that Bomber Command could deliver about 450 tonnes of bombs in a single maximum effort strike.[10] Britain's rearmament programme had invested millions in building up Bomber Command to deter war by the threat of bombing enemy cities and factories, but as war approached in 1938–39, Bomber Command's leadership became less certain of what they could actually accomplish. Just two weeks before the start of the war, Air Chief Marshal Sir Edgar Ludlow-Hewitt, in charge of Bomber Command, told Newall that if ordered to mount an all-out bomber campaign against Germany, he expected to lose all of his bombers in seven weeks.[11] Instead, Bomber Command preferred to bide its time, until it had a larger number of aircraft and better-trained aircrews. In addition to Bomber Command's reluctance to start a premature aerial offensive, most of Chamberlain's cabinet was concerned that bombing targets on German soil would provoke German retaliation against cities in Britain. Lord Halifax was particularly opposed to bombing Germany and stated before the Cabinet that 'Britain should not be the first to take the gloves off'.[12]

Furthermore, intervention from an unexpected quarter gave Chamberlain all the excuse he needed to avoid unleashing Bomber Command. On the morning of 1 September, upon learning of the invasion of Poland, President Franklin Roosevelt sent a message to the embassies of Britain, France, Germany and Poland, appealing to their respective governments 'to refrain from bombing civilians and unfortified cities'. Roosevelt's message asked for an immediate reply from each country. Lord Lothian, the British ambassador in Washington, was quick to deliver Chamberlain's response:

His Majesty's Government welcome the weighty and moving appeal of the President of the United States against the bombardment from the air of civilian populations or of unfortified cities. Deeply impressed by the humanitarian considerations to which the President's message refers, it was already the settled policy of His Majesty's Government should they become involved in hostilities to refrain from such action and to confine bombardment to strictly military objectives upon the understanding that those same rules will be scrupulously observed by all their opponents. They had already concerted in detail with certain other Governments the rules that in such an event they would impose upon themselves and make publicly known.[13]

In consequence, Chamberlain's cabinet – with the concurrence of Newall's air ministry – imposed extremely restrictive rules of engagement upon Bomber Command, which made it virtually impossible to drop any bombs on German soil. The French were more circumspect, agreeing to the bombing restriction in principle but leaving room for flexibility by replying that 'It goes without saying that the French government reserves the right to have recourse to any action which it might consider appropriate, if the adversary should not observe the restrictions to which the French government itself has subjected the operations of its air forces.' Ribbentrop also replied, claiming that the Luftwaffe would not bomb civilian targets, even as it was doing so in Poland with great enthusiasm. Roosevelt's hypocritical restrictions – which he would himself ignore when US territory was bombed in 1941 – only served to undermine the Allied war effort. Furthermore, under international law, neutral states have no right to try and impose military restrictions on combatant states. Even as the Germans were openly defying Roosevelt's entreaties, the cabinet meeting on 4 September decided that Bomber Command was only authorized to conduct air attacks on the German fleet at sea and propaganda leaflet missions over Germany. Incredibly, some of the cabinet members stated that they 'believed that these leaflets would have an important effect on German public opinion.'[14]

At 1445 hours on 4 September, Bomber Command launched its first offensive strike of the Second World War – 29 bombers were sent to bomb German warships spotted near Wilhelmshaven. According to the rules of engagement, warships could only be attacked if they were not docked, in order to avoid civilian casualties. Despite rainy weather and poor visibility, 15 Blenheim IV bombers conducted a daring low-level, daylight attack on the pocket battleship *Admiral Scheer* and the cruiser *Emden*. Three 500lb (225kg) bombs struck the *Scheer* but bounced off without exploding. All the bombs aimed at *Emden* missed. The German Flak was intense, shooting down five of the Blenheims; one swerved out of control and crashed into *Emden's* starboard side, killing 29 Kriegsmarine sailors and injuring 30. However, the damage to *Emden* was superficial and she was repaired in one week.[15] A secondary raid by Wellington bombers against Brunsbüttel failed to find any German warships. Due to a whopping 177km navigational error, one RAF bomber accidently dropped four 500lb bombs on the Danish town of Esbjerg, killing a 26-year-old woman, Edel Hansen.[16] Bomber Command's raid had negligible effect on the German war effort, but cost seven bombers and 24 aircrew killed. After this burst of bravado, Bomber Command spent most of the rest of September mounting pointless leaflet raids over Western Germany. One more attempt was made to bomb the German fleet on 29 September, resulting in the loss of five bombers and 20 aircrew for no hits.[17] Thus, aside from two small ineffective bombing raids, Britain's premier strike force sat on its hands while Poland was being crushed.

In addition to Bomber Command, Britain's other main strategic weapon was naval blockade, which it invoked shortly after the declaration of war. During the first week of the war, the Royal Navy managed to capture five German merchantmen but failed to nab the 51,000-ton passenger liner *Bremen,* returning from New York. Hitler started his own counter-blockade less than two hours after the British declaration of war, authorizing U-Boats at sea to begin attacking British – but not yet French – merchant shipping. In order to avoid the tincture of 'unrestricted submarine warfare' – which had brought the United States into the First World War – Hitler mandated that U-Boats follow the guidelines of the 1930 London Submarine Protocol, which restricted how submarines could operate. Nevertheless, at 1630 hours on 3 September, the U-30 torpedoed the British passenger liner SS *Athenia* north-west of Ireland; the liner sank and 118 persons were lost, including 28 US citizens. Since the captain of the U-30 did not report the sinking of the *Athenia* until 27 September, Germany claimed that it was not involved in the incident. On the British side, the government claimed that the sinking of the *Athenia* indicated that Germany had begun unrestricted submarine warfare.[18] Churchill directed the Royal Navy to begin anti-submarine patrols around the British Isles and destroy the U-Boats, which proved quite difficult.

Meanwhile, the French also took tentative steps to demonstrate their state of belligerency. After the French declaration of war, Maréchal Gamelin proposed air raids on German air bases and train stations near the Franco-German border. Air Chief Marshal Newall was appalled by Gamelin's suggestion and informed the Cabinet that 'it would be desirable to take steps to restrain the French from taking precipitate action in this matter'. Indeed, the Cabinet used President Roosevelt's message to torpedo any French plans for conducting air attacks against Germany, stating that 'we should not commence bombing that might mean attacking in ways involving civilian population; such bombing would be contrary to undertakings we have given (as the French have given) in reply to American President.'[19] Since the French were depending heavily upon British military co-operation against Germany, Daladier's cabinet decided to defer any efforts to strike targets near the border. On 4 September, Gamelin requested that the RAF's AASF be used to support the French Army in a ground offensive against the Saar. Newall rejected Gamelin's request and responded that 'it was important to conserve the resources of the Air Striking Force, so that it would be ready to meet any great emergency, such as heavy air attack on this country.' However, Churchill was in the Cabinet now and he seized upon Gamelin's request to urge that, 'every means possible should be employed to relieve the pressure [on Poland]. This could be done by operations against the Siegfried Line, which was at present thinly held. The burden of such operations would fall on the French Army and our Air Force.'[20] The Cabinet agreed to schedule a meeting of the Anglo-French War Council to discuss joint strategy, but this did not occur until 12 September. At the same cabinet meeting, General Sir Edmund Ironside, Chief of the Imperial General Staff (CIGS), deflated any sense of urgency by opining that 'the crushing of Poland by Germany in a few weeks was most improbable', which made it seem as if there was plenty of time for staff talks.

Even after the declaration of war, Chamberlain's ability to direct Britain's war effort was fatally undermined by his misjudging of the situation. In a letter written a week after the declaration of war, Chamberlain stated that 'I believe he [Hitler] did seriously contemplate an agreement with us … but at the last moment some brainstorm took possession of him and once he had set his machine in motion, he couldn't stop it.'[21] Chamberlain could not comprehend that war had not come as an accident but due to Hitler's deliberate desire for war. It is amazing that the fate of Great Britain at this critical juncture was in the hands of a leader as delusional and out of touch as Chamberlain, who could not understand his country's enemies or work effectively with its allies. Filled with self doubt about his ability to lead Britain in war, Chamberlain also confided to his sister that he would like 'to hand over my responsibilities to someone else'.[22]

Unlike Chamberlain, Gamelin made some attempt to help the Poles, albeit a half-hearted one. Once French mobilization began, Général André Prételat's Groupe d'Armées No. 2 was ordered to begin a limited offensive against the Saar as soon as possible. The French forces involved in the Saar Offensive were still lacking much of their vital equipment and enjoyed only modest air support, but the Germans opposing them also comprised newly raised units, including Landwehr and reservists, who were outnumbered by roughly 1.6:1. Furthermore, the French had an absolute superiority in armour, since the Wehrmacht had no Panzer units deployed in the west. On the German side, there was some apprehension that Heeresgruppe C was not well prepared to fend off a full-scale Allied offensive at the outset of the war. While Luftflotten 2 and 3 had enough Bf 109 fighters (over 400) to ensure air superiority over the Armée de l'Air, there was only a single Stuka group deployed on the western front. Since most of the limited stockpile of German artillery ammunition was deployed in the East to support *Fall Weiss*, Heeresgruppe C was not prepared to fight a protracted battle.

On 7 September, Groupe d'Armées No. 2 began probing operations along the German border and two days later, the 4e Armée (4th Army) attacked with five infantry divisions and four tank battalions. The outnumbered German 1. Armee fell back to the West Wall, allowing the French to advance 8km into Germany. However, advancing French troops were stymied when they encountered large numbers of German anti-personnel mines, which inflicted significant casualties. Although some French units got within sight of the West Wall, no attacks were actually mounted against any of its positions. Several small aerial skirmishes also occurred, resulting in the loss of ten French fighters against only six German aircraft. From the beginning, the Saar Offensive was intended to be a limited objectives operation and Gamelin was reluctant to take any risks. Heeresgruppe C was never seriously stressed by the French operation. By the time that Gamelin terminated the offensive on 12 September, the French Army had suffered about 2,000 casualties but inflicted fewer than 500 casualties on the Germans. In Zossen, the OKH barely noticed Gamelin's offensive and made no effort to divert forces from the Polish front to deal with the French operations in the Saar. Consequently, the French Saar Offensive was little more than a symbolic gesture of solidarity with the Poles.

Both Britain and France had known since early 1939 that they did not intend to provide real military support to Poland in event of

German attack, but they kept their deficiencies to themselves. Instead, their diplomats fed into the Polish wishful thinking that military guarantees would actually translate into enough of an Anglo-French military response to prevent Germany from overrunning Poland. As late as 17 September, the head of the French military mission in Poland, Louis Faury, kept telling Rydz-Śmigły that a major French offensive on the western front was imminent. In fact, both the British and French military leadership had written off Poland before the war had even started and did not intend to launch any major offensive operations until at least 1941. The Anglo-French declaration of war had more to do with making a clean public break from the embarrassing mistakes made at Munich than any intent to protect Polish sovereignty. The Anglo-French delay in honouring their treaty obligations to Poland or to 'lend all support in their power' after declaring war was a shameful moment in modern diplomatic history. In reality, Poland had no allies in September 1939.

Yet, the fact that the Anglo-French chose not to honour their treaty obligations to Poland beyond a *pro forma* declaration of war does not mean that they could not have done more. While the Allies were unprepared for robust offensive action, they did enjoy a brief period where the bulk of German combat power was facing eastwards, rather than towards them. With real leadership, Bomber Command and the French Armée de l'Air could have been used to make at least a few strong daylight raids, with fighter escort, against industrial targets in the nearby Ruhr. Aircraft losses would have been heavy, but the Germans would probably also have suffered significant civilian casualties – hurting morale far more than leaflets. Likewise, with proper air support from the AASF, Gamelin's armies might have been able to make a better showing in the Saar. The French had a nice assortment of heavy rail artillery, which could have been used to pound the West Wall bunkers into shattered concrete, enabling the capture of at least a few positions – a fine propaganda coup for the Allies. None of these actions would have saved Poland, but they would have put Hitler on notice that the West would not simply sit by and watch him conquer nations. Furthermore, the Anglo-French allies desperately needed to begin a 'weeding out' process to remove incompetent and defeatist military and political leaders in order to energize their national war efforts. In reality, this process did not start until the disastrous Norwegian campaign, but it could have begun earlier if the Allies had chosen to begin active military operation from the outset. By opting for the perceived safety of a 'Phoney War' and deferring real military operations until some ill-defined 'later', the Anglo-French leadership handed the strategic initiative to Hitler.

Retreat from Western Poland, 4–8 September

In contrast to the Anglo-French aversion to bloodshed or destruction of private property, the Wehrmacht revelled in both activities after crossing into Poland. Captured Polish soldiers were often not afforded the protections of the Geneva Convention and Polish civilians were indiscriminately murdered on numerous occasions. In the air, Luftwaffe pilots frequently strafed refugee columns or bombed defenceless towns, despite what Ribbentrop told President Roosevelt. War crimes were an integral part of Hitler's stated intent for *Fall Weiss*, since he regarded the Poles as race enemies who needed to be subjugated then eventually exterminated. Furthermore, most of the war crimes committed in Poland during *Fall Weiss* were not committed by SS troops – who comprised less than 2 per cent of the invasion force – but rather by regular Heer and Luftwaffe personnel. Given the heavy doses of pre-war anti-Slavic propaganda pumped out by Josef Goebbels' Ministry of Propaganda, many of the young German troops regarded the Poles as inferior and undeserving of any kind of sympathy. Even educated German officers, such as Hauptmann Claus Graf von Stauffenberg, a staff officer in the 1. leichte-Division, held the Poles in low regard and saw captured Poles as no more than slaves for the Reich. Stauffenberg would eventually join the anti-Nazi resistance and famously fail to assassinate Hitler in 1944, but in 1939 he viewed the Poles through the same racial lenses as the Nazis.[23] Notably, a few German officers did have enough moral character to object to this murderous brutality, but they were few in number in September 1939 and were ignored or even ridiculed.

As the Polish armies began to retreat on 2–3 September, a number of cities fell virtually undefended to the advancing Wehrmacht. Most of the extant histories of the Polish campaign fail to mention that each of the invading German armies was accompanied by an *Einsatzgruppe* (task force), each comprising about 400–800 personnel – a mix of SS, SD (Sicherheitsdienst or Security Service), Gestapo and police. Unlike the Einsatzgruppen employed in the USSR in 1941–42, the groups used in Poland consisted almost entirely of German nationals, although some were *Volksdeutsche*. Prior to the invasion of Poland, the SD and Gestapo compiled lists (*Sonderfahndungsbuch Polen*) of Polish citizens who were deemed dangerous to the Reich; these lists were based upon information provided by ethnic Germans living within Poland and amounted to over 61,000 people by 1 September.[24] As Polish cities were occupied, the Einsatzgruppen rushed in to arrest Poles on the list, as well as others picked more or less at random. In addition to the *Sonderfahndungsbuch Polen*, which was only distributed to the Einsatzgruppen, on 9 August 1939 the OKW issued a directive that ordered Wehrmacht units to arrest all suspicious civilians in Poland. In practice, all males of military age (i.e. 17–45 years) were deemed 'suspicious'.[25]

On the morning of 3 September, the German 46. Infanterie-Division marched into Częstochowa without a shot being fired. Many Poles had fled the city with the retreating 7 DP, but the remainder made no resistance. Shortly after occupying city hall, German troops began rounding up thousands of hostages, many pulled out of their homes, ostensibly to ensure that the population remained docile. While gathering Polish hostages, some of the German troops looted homes and then set them on fire. The hostages were brought to the city centre and forced to wait at an collection point, in the main square in front of the Cathedral Basilica of the Holy Family, surrounded by armed troops. Surprisingly, the first night of German occupation in Częstochowa passed relatively quietly, despite sporadic shooting – most likely caused by nervous German sentries. However, by the afternoon of 4 September, members of SS-Obersturmbannführer Emanuel Schäfer's Einsatzgruppe II arrived in Częstochowa and the occupation took a nasty turn. German soldiers were obsessed with the idea of Polish armed civilians, even though few had turned to insurgency yet. After a shooting incident – probably accidental friendly fire – German troops claimed that Poles had fired on the divisional field hospital. Either with or without orders, German troops then began shooting many of the hostages held in front of the cathedral, resulting in about 227 deaths, including 25 women and eight children. Fewer than 10 per cent of the victims were Jewish. Other civilians were executed elsewhere in the city, but numbers are less certain. It is clear that German troops, mostly from the 46. Infanterie-Division, murdered approximately 300 Polish civilians during the first day of the Częstochowa massacre.[26] Many more would be executed in subsequent days.

In the field, captured Polish soldiers were often executed by German troops. Thousands of Polish stragglers from Army Pomorze were wandering in the Tuchola Forest, hoping to reach either the Vistula River or Bydgoszcz, but they found their retreat blocked by the German III Armeekorps. On 3 September, German troops from Oberst Heinrich Wosch's Infanterie-Regiment 8 (3. Infanterie-Division), caught up with one Polish group near the village of Topolno, just short of the Vistula River. Several hundred Polish troops were captured, but approximately 80 unarmed Poles were shot soon after capture. The Polish 50 PP managed to retain some cohesion but could not cross the Vistula. On 4 September, the regiment was finally cornered near Jeżewo and was annihilated after a tough fight. Afterwards, about 3,500 captured Polish troops and civilian detainees were corralled near Serock, where they were guarded by rear-echelon troops from a road repair unit, the leichtes-Straßenbau-Bataillon 604. Many of these troops were teenagers from the Reichsarbeitsdienst (Reich Labour Service or RAD), who had only minimal military training. This labour battalion had also suffered six dead earlier in the day, in an encounter with armed Polish stragglers. Around midnight on 4 September, the German guards claimed that the prisoners were attempting to escape and machine-gunned at least 60 of them. Indeed, the firing was so wild that German officers intervened to prevent friendly casualties. Typically, German records on these incidents are sparse but when they were made, they refer to 'nervous troops' firing at prisoners who did not obey quickly enough.[27] While there is no evidence that these early incidents were ordered by German officers, the fact that German troops fired machine guns into clusters of prisoners suggests that the shooting was a team effort. Across Poland, German troops casually shot prisoners and civilians, without regard for the rules of war. Each day, it would get worse, as the normal strictures of peacetime morality evaporated.

In contrast, Poland followed the Geneva Convention in regard to captured German airmen and soldiers. About 500 survivors from Podpułkownik Jan Maliszewski's 35 PP (9 DP) managed to evade the German dragnet on the west side of the Vistula by marching west then south, keeping to the backwaters of the Tuchola Forest. On the morning of 4 September, Maliszewski's troops bumped into Sanitätskompanie 32 (Medical Company 32) from 32. Infanterie-Division, which had set up on a farm near Nowy Jasiniec. The Polish troops captured nearly 200 Germans from this medical unit, including five officers.[28] Maliszewski was not keen on being encumbered by this number of prisoners, but he firmly rejected any suggestion of shooting them. Instead, the formation continued marching southwards towards Bydgoszcz, with the Germans under guard.

However, the regiment bumped into another German unit in the woods, the I./schwere-Artillerie-Abteilung 604, and a firefight ensued. Twelve German artillerymen were killed but some of the captured medical personnel were also killed in the action. Maliszewski decided to divest himself of his prisoners, ordering them to lie down on the ground and not move for 30 minutes, while the Polish troops marched away. However, as soon as the Poles were out of sight, the German medical personnel ran and alerted another nearby German unit, Panzer-Abwehr-Abteilung 3. The Germans pursued Maliszewski's group in the woods near Stronno, pounded it with automatic weapons fire and called in an artillery barrage. For three hours, the Polish unit was pinned down and suffered at least 20 dead, but the Germans disengaged at dusk and Maliszewski led his men south. At dawn on 5 September, Maliszewski's group reached the outskirts of Bydgoszcz, only to find that the Polish Army had evacuated the city and the German 50. Infanterie-Division was approaching from the west. Skirting the city, Maliszewski led his group to a nearby railroad bridge across the Vistula, which they reached by 1100 hours. The bridge was still held by troops from the 23 PP (27 DP), who were about to blow it up. By the time that Maliszewski's 35 PP rejoined Army Pomorze, it was reduced to just 300 ragged survivors with 11 machine guns.[29]

After abandoning Bydgoszcz, Generał Bortnowski tried to regroup Army Pomorze behind the Vistula, but this proved impossible. Generał Drapella's 27 DP managed to blow up the Vistula bridges but it had lost two of its three infantry regiments and a good deal of its artillery. Bortnowski ordered the 27 DP to march south to Toruń and incorporate reserve units that were mobilizing there. Consequently, the sector of Vistula between Bydgoszcz and Chelmno was left virtually undefended. General Adolf Strauß's II Armeekorps reached the Vistula late on 3 September with the 3. and 32. Infanterie-Divisionen and attempted a river crossing the next morning. Although unopposed, both German divisions had difficulty getting across the Vistula and were unable to ferry any vehicles or artillery across until dusk. Apparently, Kluge failed to ensure that a bridging column was quickly brought up, so Strauß's corps lost a vital day getting across an undefended river. During the bridging effort, Hitler made a surprise visit to Bock to witness the 3. Infanterie-Division crossing; Hitler told Bock that he was pleased with progress and was impressed with the performance of the troops.[30] Later in the day, Hitler visited Guderian's XIX Armeekorps and was most interested in finding out how his Panzers had performed in combat.[31] Meanwhile, the two Polish divisions on the east side of the Vistula – the 4 and 16 DP – retreated south to Toruń as well. The 4 DP managed to put up a decent rearguard, which thwarted the half-hearted pursuit of Falkenhorst's XXI Armeekorps. Since the 21. Infanterie-Division was being shifted eastwards by rail to assist the push to the Narew, Falkenhorst only had the 228. Infanterie-Division to move south from Grudziadz. One Polish regiment from 4 DP was badly bombed by the Luftwaffe, suffering over 300 casualties, but these two divisions managed to make a clean break from the enemy and escape to fight another day. However, had Strauß's corps quickly gotten across the Vistula, both Polish divisions might have been blocked from reuniting with Army Pomorze near Toruń.

The 15 DP retreated along the south side of the Vistula, pursued by the 50. Infanterie-Division and slowly falling back towards Toruń. On the evening of 5 September, Kutrzeba's Army Poznań transferred the intact 26 DP to Bortnowski's command in order to help protect the left flank of Army Pomorze. The 26 DP was ordered to retreat to Inowroclaw, 33km south-west of Toruń. At this point, only the German II and III Armeekorps were actively pursuing Army Pomorze and their advance was hindered by numerous blown bridges and other obstacles. Guderian's XIX Armeekorps (mot.) was still involved in mopping up Polish stragglers west of the Vistula and was preparing to transfer to the 3. Armee area in East Prussia, so no German mechanized forces were involved in the pursuit – which was probably a mistake since Bortnowski's troops were able to stay just ahead of the German 'leg' infantry divisions chasing them. A single German motorized division could have captured Toruń and scattered Army Pomorze before it had a chance to regroup – but this did not happen. In Toruń, the 27 DP replenished itself by adding a regiment of reservists, an ON battalion and some stray artillery batteries. By 6 September, the rebuilt 27 DP occupied defensive positions around Toruń. On 6 September, Bortnowski ordered Generał Drapella to form an operational group with 27 DP and the remnants of the Pomorska Cavalry Brigade to form a rearguard for Army Pomorze, which was ordered to retreat towards Warsaw.

Bortnowski was unaware that the OKH and Heeresgruppe Nord disagreed about the next phase of *Fall Weiss*. Halder wanted to transfer the bulk of Kluge's 4. Armee to East Prussia to launch a deep pincer operation across the Narew towards Brześć. Bock argued that this would let up the pressure on the retreating Army Pomorze and leave the bulk of his forces out of action for several days. The destruction of the railroad bridge over the Vistula at Tczew would complicate this effort as well. After some deliberation, by the end of 5 September Halder allowed Bock to keep the

II and III Armeekorps pushing east along both sides of the Vistula, but the rest of 4. Armee was going to be transferred to East Prussia by road and rail movement. The OKH also committed the 10. Panzer-Division, which had been held in reserve, to move to East Prussia. These large-scale unit transfers, in part over damaged transport infrastructure, provided ample operational friction. Furthermore, Kluge was injured when his Fieseler Storch flew into a tree, so Strauß temporarily took over command of 4. Armee. Brauchitsch also got involved in the debate over courses of action and argued that Heeresgruppe Nord was trying to swing too far to the east, rather than just pushing straight onto Warsaw. Instead of just sticking to a decent plan that was working, the senior Wehrmacht leadership felt impelled to tinker with the operation in the hope of producing an ideal outcome, which Hitler tolerated when things were going well. As a result of 4. Armee's slow pursuit, Bortnowski was able to re-assemble his army around Toruń by 6 September, with 4 and 16 DP north of the Vistula and 15, 26 and 27 DP south of the river. Indeed, when the 50. Infanterie-Division encountered the 15 DP's position south-east of Toruń, they were surprised by the fierce resistance. The 50. Infanterie-Division and Brigade Netze were in fact outnumbered by the Polish forces in front of them. Nevertheless, Bortnowski pulled the 4 and 16 DP south of the Vistula, blew up the bridges and abandoned Toruń, which was occupied by the Germans on 7 September. By 8 September, Army Pomorze was concentrated near Włocławek on the Vistula.

Meanwhile, Kutrzeba's Army Poznań was trying to conform to the retreat of Bortnowski's Army Pomorze. The intent was that both armies would unite somewhere near Łódź. Kutrzeba's forces were still fairly intact, having only been lightly engaged in the first few days of the war and he wanted to use them to launch some kind of counter-stroke against the Germans. Indeed, it was galling for him to abandon the city of Poznań (population 269,000) without a fight on 4 September, when German forces were nowhere near. Since 9 per cent of the population were ethnic Germans – many of whom were Nazi sympathizers – Kutrzeba allowed the formation of a local home guard to maintain order in the city. Nevertheless, Kutrzeba's troops were sniped at by German insurgents as they retreated, while other German civilians began openly hanging Nazi flags in the city. However, no German forces reached Poznań until 10 September because Rundstedt was unwilling to divert any additional forces to this sector. Eventually, OKH ordered Rundstedt to commit the 252. Infanterie-Division from his reserves to occupy Poznań, but this was a low priority. Instead, the third-rate troops from Generalleutnant

Max von Schenckendorf's Grenzschutz-Abschnitt-Kommando 13 slowly marched towards the city. When a detachment from the Grenzschutz-Regiment 148 reached the Old Market square, they were greeted by the German inhabitants of Poznań with Nazi salutes. German civilians also help drape the city hall with a large swastika flag. A few days later, Schenckendorf arrived to become military governor, along with SS troops from Einsatzgruppe VI. Schenckendorf, an ardent Nazi, would rule Poznań with brutality and contempt for the local population. Within a month, the Germans would establish their first concentration camp in Poland, inside the abandoned Fort VII, where thousands of Poles would be tortured and executed over the next five years.

Kutrzeba suggested that Army Poznań should be used for a counter-offensive into the flank of 8. Armee instead of just retreating, but Rydz-Śmigły rejected this idea. On 6 September, Kutrzeba was ordered to transfer his remaining aviation assets to centralized control; the LW was trying to reconstitute its Fighter and Bomber Brigades by absorbing the survivors of army aviation. Kutrzeba refused this order and consequently he was now the only Polish army commander who still had his own air support. He directed the fighters of Group III/3 to provide air cover over his retreating divisions by shooting down enemy reconnaissance aircraft.[32] The decision to abandon Poznań without a fight was foolish since even a small force could have held off Schenckendorf's security troops and forced Rundstedt to divert at least one or two regular divisions to capture the city. Indeed, these division would almost certainly have come from 8. Armee, which would have weakened the Germans in the subsequent battle of the Bzura. Instead, Kutrzeba's Army Poznań was saved for the time being and after detaching the 26 DP to join Army Pomorze his three divisions (14, 17 and 25 DP) and two cavalry brigades marched 200km in four days, to reach the area around Kutno by 8 September. Although Blaskowitz's 8. Armee was pressing from the south, Army Poznań was now within 30km of Army Pomorze and for the first time in the campaign, the Poles would actually have two armies in a position to work together against less-numerous German forces.

Stand on the Narew, 6–10 September

As war approached, Rydz-Śmigły and the Polish General Staff had become increasingly concerned about a threat to Warsaw from the north, if the Germans attacked from East Prussia. While Army Modlin was intended to block the direct path to Warsaw, Operational Group Wyszków was responsible for holding the line of the Narew. Beginning in spring 1939, the Polish Army began creating a series of fortified positions along the Narew at Ostroleka, Nowogród, Łomża and Wizna. Some of the concrete bunkers boasted armoured cupolas and 1.5m-thick walls. The marshy terrain along the Narew favoured the defence. Pułkownik Stefan Kossecki's 18th Infantry Division (18 DP) was responsible for defending the critical northern section of the Narew. Kossecki* was a very capable commander and most of his troops were locally recruited, which meant they could be quickly mobilized and were tasked to defend their own communities.

On the German side, Halder and Bock became increasingly fixated on conducting a wide enveloping attack across the Narew after the end of the fighting in Pomerania. In particular, there was concern that some Polish formations would escape across the Vistula and try to form a resistance centre in eastern Poland – which is what the French had been suggesting as a 'hold-out' strategy for years. Despite the failed attempt to capture a crossing over the Narew at Różan on 5 September, Bock wanted to spring forwards to the Bug River as quickly as possible in order to envelop Warsaw from the east with Guderian's XIX Armeekorps (mot.), although repositioning units would take at least several days. In the meantime, Küchler's 3. Armee was split into two diverging groups: the I Armeekorps advancing towards Pułtusk and Korps Wodrig pushing eastwards across the Narew towards Łomża. Generalleutnant Walter Petzel's I Armeekorps advanced very slowly towards Pułtusk with the 11. and 61. Infanterie-Divisionen and was not even thinking about the Modlin fortress yet, giving the Poles five vital days to organize a strong defence.[33] At first, there were barely three to four battalions available to defend Modlin, but by the night of 7/8 September the disorganized pieces of the 8 and 20 DPs were re-assembled, which provided enough troops to form a viable defensive perimeter. Meanwhile, Podpułkownik Rzedzicki's 115 PP had abandoned Różan and Generał Kowalski's Operational Group Wyszków and Generał Młot-Fijałkowski's Independent Operational Group Narew were preparing to defend a line along the Narew against any further German eastwards advance. Although Kowalski's command mostly consisted of reserve infantry and cavalry, his command had just been augmented by the arrival of the 1st Legions Infantry Division (1 DPL) – one of the best divisions in the Polish Army – from Wilno.

---

*Executed by the Soviet NKVD at Katyń Forest in 1940.

However, in Warsaw, Rydz-Śmigły had poor situational awareness about battlefield realities due to poor communications and limited information provided by aerial reconnaissance. Rydz-Śmigły was perplexed by the German failure to pursue Army Modlin after the battle of Mława and did not yet understand that 3. Armee's spearhead had shifted eastwards. Reports from Różan suggested that Operational Group Wyszków was dealing with only a German brigade-size force. Under these uncertain circumstances, Rydz-Śmigły was worried that the Germans would strike towards the Modlin fortress and thereby expose Warsaw to attack from the north. Consequently, he ordered the Modlin garrison to establish a 360° defence in case it was encircled. Rydz-Śmigły also issued an order to Operational Group Wyszków to mount a counter-attack towards Pułtusk, assuming it would strike the flank of 3. Armee and take some pressure off Army Modlin. Operational Group Wyszków was supposed to counter-attack with the 1 DPL and the 33rd Infantry Division (33 DP), which was only a partially mobilized reserve division. The 18th and 41 DPs would continue to defend the line of the Narew River, along with two cavalry brigades. Although Rydz-Śmigły issued this order at 1815 hours on 5 September, Generał Kowalski did not receive it until 0600 hours on 6 September due to the parlous state of Polish communications.[34] Instead of mounting a deliberate defence behind a river where there was some chance of success, Kowalski now had to send his best unit across the river to mount an *ad hoc* counter-attack into the teeth of enemy resistance and thin out his defences on the Narew.

Rydz-Śmigły's order threw Operational Group Wyszków into complete disorder on 6 September. Generał Kowalski ordered the 1 DPL to march to Pułtusk, which was threatened by an attack from the advancing German I Armeekorps. Until the battle of Mława, Pułtusk had been garrisoned by the 13 PP (41 DP) but this regiment had been sent on a futile effort to reinforce the 8 DP's doomed counter-attack and was scattered.[35] The only Polish troops remaining in Pułtusk were one battalion of KOP and one ON battalion, plus a few artillery batteries. The 1 DPL arrived at Pułtusk just as the German 61. Infanterie-Division began probing the city's defences. However Rydz-Śmigły suddenly decided that he didn't want to risk the 1 DPL at Pułtusk and he ordered it to abandon the city and withdraw south of the Bug River. Generał Kowalski made an equally ill-judged decision to pull the 41 DP back from the Narew while committing the 33 DP to occupy defensive positions east of Różan; both reserve units were too inexperienced to conduct a night-time relief-in-place operation and became hopelessly entangled during the night of

6/7 September. The Podlaska Cavalry Brigade was kept back in reserve near Ostrow Mazowiecka, essentially not doing anything useful. The only solid unit with a clear mission in Operational Group Wyszków was Kossecki's 18 DP, which was holding its assigned fortified positions along the Narew from Ostroleka to Wizna.

The fog of war was also affecting the Germans. Generalleutnant Albert Wodrig was unaware that the Poles had evacuated Różan during the night of 5/6 September and spent the better part of 6 September preparing to assault an empty town. Finally, at 1600 hours the 12. Infanterie-Division advanced and occupied the deserted forts and town. Further south, the 1. Kavallerie-Brigade forded a shallow portion of the Narew and created a bridgehead, which caused the thinly held line of the 41 DP to pull back. However, it was not until nightfall that Korps Wodrig had built pontoon bridges across the Narew and could move heavy equipment across. While waiting to advance across the Narew, SS troops from Panzer-Division Kempf amused themselves by abusing then murdering 50 Jewish civilians in the village of Krasnosielec; Küchler, commander of 3. Armee, was incensed by this lawless behaviour by SS troops under his command and ordered a court-martial for two enlisted soldiers.[36] The Krasnosielec incident was reported to the OKH.[37] Once the pontoon bridge over the Narew was completed during the night of 6/7 September, Korps Wodrig began crossing the river and the vanguard advanced 10km eastwards, bumping into the disorganized 33rd and 41 DPs. On the morning of 7 September, Panzer-Division Kempf attacked the two Polish reserve divisions and scattered them; the survivors retreated south towards Wyszkow on the Bug River. Pushing ahead against negligible resistance, Panzer-Division Kempf advanced rapidly towards Ostrow Mazowiecka, held by the Podlaska Cavalry Brigade.

While Operational Group Wyszków was slowly unravelling, Bock's plan to conduct a wide envelopment was unfolding north of the Narew. Falkenhorst's XXI Armeekorps, now consisting of the 10. Panzer-Division and the 21. Infanterie-Division, had been transferred to East Prussia and was in position to begin attacking on the morning of 7 September towards Łomża on the Narew. Generalleutnant Ferdinand Schaal's 10. Panzer-Division had been formed in April 1939 and was still incomplete; the division only had one artillery battalion instead of two, no pioneers, no anti-tank battalion and limited support units. While the 10. Panzer-Division possessed 150 tanks, only ten of them were medium Pz III or Pz IV models – the rest were light Pz I and Pz IIs.[38] Since

Falkenhorst's XXI Armeekorps was already in place by the evening of 6/7 September, it would begin the grand envelopment the next day by attacking along the Narew at three points, with the main effort at Łomża. Meanwhile, Guderian's XIX Armeekorps (mot.) was having difficulty making the move to East Prussia and would not be available to join the offensive until 9 September.

On the morning of 7 September, Falkenhorst committed part of the 21. Infanterie-Division to probe the Polish defences at Łomża, which were held by Major Stanisław Wyderko's I/33 PP (18 DP) and a battalion of 12 100mm howitzers. Three forts, reinforced by 12 concrete machine-gun bunkers, were located on the eastern side of the Narew, while two forts and nine bunkers were located on the western side.[39] The Polish position was strengthened by trenches and barbed wire obstacles. On the morning of 7 September, the reconnaissance units from the 21. Infanterie-Division approached the outer defences on the east side of the Narew, but Polish anti-tank gunfire destroyed two armoured cars. Heavy machine-gun fire forced the reconnaissance troops to withdraw. It took the Germans some time to bring up their artillery and prepare for a deliberate attack. On the morning of 8 September, the Infanterie-Regiment 24 attacked Fort No. 3 (held by one Polish company), but was repulsed four times. The Poles even succeeded in capturing 57 German troops.[40] Chagrined by their failure, the Germans brought up more artillery and called for Luftwaffe support. On 9 September, the Germans heavily bombarded the outer forts and the town of Łomża itself, but failed to inflict sufficient damage. The Polish artillery on the west side of the Narew was not even silenced, enabling it to break up German infantry assaults. On 10 September, the Germans committed more troops, including Landwehr-Infanterie-Regiment 162 from the Brigade Lötzen, but nevertheless every assault was repulsed. After four days of fighting the Germans had failed to capture a single position in Łomża and Wyderko's troops had inflicted over 160 dead on the enemy for the loss of only nine of their own men.[41] Unfortunately, the 18 DP was not only hard pressed all along the Narew, but Panzer-Division Kempf was running wild south of the river. On 8 September, Panzer-Division Kempf had evicted the Podlaska Cavalry Brigade from Ostrow Mazowiecka and had turned north towards Łomża. On the evening of 10 September, Kossecki made the decision to pull Wyderko's garrison out of Łomża before it was encircled. During the night, Wyderko's blew the bridge over the Narew and retreated to the south-east.

The Polish garrison at Nowogród (III/33 PP and part of 42 PP), led by Major Józef Sikora, made an equally gallant stand against the bulk of the 21.Infanterie-Division during 7–10 September. German efforts to conduct assault crossings over the Narew were repeatedly repulsed by heavy defensive fire and prompt counter-attacks, which threw the enemy back before they could establish a bridgehead. The Polish concrete bunkers, with armoured cupolas, proved particularly troublesome until the Germans began firing 3.7cm anti-tank guns and 8.8cm Flak guns at them from across the river. After heavy artillery bombardments and liberal use of smoke, the Germans finally succeeded in getting across the river in strength on the third day of the battle. Five Polish artillery batteries pounded the crossing site. The Germans managed to capture three bunkers using pioneers to blast off the armoured doors; the defenders inside were finished off with grenades.[42] Major Sikora quickly counter-attacked, which led to two days of intense urban fighting in the burning wreckage of Nowogród throughout 9–10 September. The German 21. Infanterie-Division suffered 314 casualties in this battle, including 106 dead or missing.[43] Despite suffering about 50 per cent losses, Sikora's garrison was still holding most of its positions when he too received the order to withdraw late on 10 September. The Polish garrison in Ostrołeka, which consisted of 71 PP (18 DP) and part of the 33 DP, was not troubled much by the Germans in this period and the garrison abandoned the town on 10 September.

Although the LW had been trying to conserve Pułkownik Władysław Heller's Bomber Brigade, it was heavily committed to supporting Polish forces on the Narew, since it was recognized that defeat here would lead to the encirclement of Warsaw. On 7 September, Heller's bombers flew 41 sorties and lost nine aircraft (five P.37b Łoś and four P.23b Karaś), which was clearly unsustainable. Nevertheless, Heller's brigade flew 26 more sorties on 8 September, before withdrawing to south-east Poland with the remaining 52 bombers.[44]

Guderian did not receive his specific orders until the evening of 8 September. Bock directed him to advance east of Falkenhorst's XXI Armeekorps and cross the Narew at Wizna, where the 10. Panzer-Division had already begun crossing the river. In fact, although the 10. Panzer-Division managed to occupy the town of Wizna and get infantry across the river, the main Polish line of resistance – consisting of seven heavy bunkers – had not yet been assaulted. Kapitan Władysław Raginis commanded a garrison of just 330 troops, armed with 6 76mm guns, two 37mm anti-tank guns and 24 machine guns, which should hardly have been a major obstacle for a Panzer-Division. However, Generalleutnant Schaal had been injured on the first day of the attack and without engineers the division could not build pontoon bridges across the Narew, so no tanks could cross. The motorized infantrymen from the 10. Panzer-Division simply advanced to within range of the Polish bunkers and stopped. Without tank or artillery support, and without effective leadership, the division ground to a halt – hardly the image that Nazi propagandists wanted to promote about Panzer-Divisionen in Poland. When Guderian arrived in the bridgehead at 0800 hours on 9 September, he was incensed by the inactivity and lack of fighting.[45] He was able to energize the 10. Panzer-Division's infantry to begin assaulting the Polish bunkers, which lacked the interval troops to prevent the Germans from outflanking and overwhelming one position at a time. By late afternoon, the Germans had captured several positions, but the Polish defence was not yet broken. Guderian redirected his energy to getting his own pioneers forwards to begin building pontoon bridges over the Narew. However, this effort went awry and when the sun came up on 10 September, Guderian still only had a few operational ferries to shuttle tanks across the river. Nevertheless, with the infantry and tanks available, Guderian mounted an attack that eliminated the last Polish bunkers and broke the defence. At Wizna, two German Panzer-Divisionen and the 20. Infanterie-Division (mot.) were held up mostly by the lack of bridges, rather than the Polish defence.

Kowalski's Operational Group Wyszków had made a valiant but essentially futile stand on the Narew for several days. The XXI Armeekorps tried to bounce the river line straight off the line of march at several points and failed. The stubborn Polish defence at each location was testament to the steadiness and training of the better Polish active regiments. It was clear from the actions at Nowogród, Łomża and Wizna that German units had difficulty conducting assault river-crossing operations and reducing well-built strongpoints. A single reinforced Polish infantry regiment, the 33rd Infantry Regiment, had held off two German divisions for four days and not lost any of its positions – a rather amazing feat. Afterwards, the Germans would learn from their deficiencies on the Narew and Guderian's spearhead, including the 10. Panzer-Division, would turn in a much improved performance crossing the Meuse at Sedan in May 1940. The fighting on the Narew also revealed that overly complicated command and control arrangements had marred the German operational performance. While Falkenhorst's XXI Armeekorps was trying to get across the Narew, Küchler failed to direct Korps Wodrig to support this effort. When Guderian showed up, his XIX Armeekorps (mot.) was reporting directly to Bock, not Küchler. At one point, on 9–10 September, all three of Heeresgruppe Nord's Panzer-Divisionen were milling around the Narew without much co-ordination. If Rydz-Śmigły had not interfered with Operational Group Wyszków's deployments, the Germans would probably have faced greater delay and casualties in getting across the Narew. The oft-touted German tactical superiority was not evident on the Narew and even numerical superiority had not guaranteed success.

The Threat from the South, 5–8 September

After the rapid loss of Częstochowa, Rydz-Śmigły ordered the creation of a Warsaw Defence Command (Dowództwo Obrony Warszawy) and put Generał Walerian Czuma in charge of it. Unfortunately, Czuma had very few troops. By 5 September, the civilian government was beginning to leave the capital, including President Ignacy Mościcki, who left for Lubartów. Stefan Starzyński, mayor of Warsaw, assisted Czuma by organizing civilian volunteers to fight fires from Luftwaffe air raids and begin creating street barricades. However, Rydz-Śmigły seemed to have written off Warsaw and was already thinking about withdrawing to eastern Poland.

While pressure from Heeresgruppe Nord upon the Polish field armies decreased during 5–7 September, Rundstedt's Heeresgruppe Süd was battering Generał Rómmel's Army Łódź to pieces. Reichenau's 10. Armee was the main threat, with Hoepner's XVI Armeekorps (mot.) already at the outskirts of Piotrków by the morning of 5 September. The four divisions in Rómmel's Army Łódź were loosely deployed west of Piotrków, between Bełchatów and Sieradz, while Generał Dąb-Biernacki's Army Prusy had taken over responsibility for holding Piotrków with the 19th Infantry Division (19 DP). Due to the huge rupture between Army Łódź and Army Kraków, Dąb-Biernacki was also forced to commit the 13th and 29th Infantry Division (13 and 29 DP) and the Wileńska Cavalry Brigade to create a front extending east of Piotrków towards Radom; the Polish General Staff had intended to use the divisions of Army Prusy to mount a counter-offensive but now most of its units had been committed to a static defensive role. Piotrków itself had been heavily bombed by the Luftwaffe since the second day of the war and a good portion of the civilian population had been evacuated in anticipation of a major battle.

At dawn on 5 September, Hoepner began his push against Piotrków with 1. Panzer-Division in the lead. Two battalions of the 86 PP (19 DP), supported by artillery, were blocking the road 4km south of Piotrków. The initial German attack at 1000 hours was repulsed. While the 1. Panzer-Division was regrouping for another assault, the Poles mounted a counter-attack from the flank, using two tank companies from Major Karpow's 2 BCL and a motorized infantry battalion from the Wileńska Cavalry Brigade. The Polish 7TP tanks succeeded in knocking out 11 German tanks and several other vehicles, as well as inflicting losses upon the I./Schützen-Regiment 12. Yet the Polish counter-attack eventually was repulsed by German anti-tank and artillery fire. Major Karpow was left with only 24 of his original 7TP tanks and his dwindling supplies of ammunition and fuel severely restricted his operational capability.[46] It should be noted that the other Polish tank battalion, Major Kubin's 1 BCL, was nearby but kept in reserve. Dąb-Biernacki committed his armour in piecemeal fashion but had both tank battalions been committed simultaneously and with proper support, Hoepner's thin-skinned Panzers might have suffered debilitating losses. Having dealt with the Polish counter-attack, the 1. Panzer-Division resumed its attack at 1400 hours, supported by artillery and Luftwaffe strikes. This time, the Polish defensive line was pierced and German Panzers began to pour through. The two battalions of the 86 PP were decimated, having lost more than 80 per cent of their personnel and equipment. Hoepner committed the 4. Panzer-Division into the breach and it swung around to the north-west in an effort to envelop Piotrków, while the 1. Panzer-Division attacked into the suburbs. Hoepner also committed the 31. Infanterie-Division to attack the 2 DPL around Belchatow; after heavy fighting which lasted until dusk, the 2 DPL was pushed back 5–6km.[47] The retreat of the 2 DPL broke the tenuous link between Army Prusy and Army Łódź.

Hoepner was on the verge of capturing Piotrków on the evening of 5 September, but as night fell, the German tanks found themselves in an urban setting with limited infantry support. At least one Pz IV medium tank was knocked out and abandoned inside the city. The 19 DP still had seven infantry battalions around Piotrków and local counter-attacks threatened to cut off some German advance units. Dąb-Biernacki had also hustled the 29 DP to move towards Piotrków and Podpułkownik Stanisław Sienkiewicz' 76th Infantry Regiment (76 PP) blocked the main road south of the city. Exercising caution, Hoepner decided to pull back the 1. Panzer-Division and start afresh the next morning rather than risk a chaotic night action in a city. Dąb-Biernacki hoped to mount a night counter-attack with both the 19 DP and the 29 DP, but this effort did not come to fruition. Instead, at 2100 hours, both Rómmel and Dąb-Biernacki received an order from Rydz-Śmigły to withdraw both their armies to the Vistula. At this point, Rydz-Śmigły became more focused on saving the army, rather than trying to defend territory.

Polish communications were sporadic and some units did not receive the retreat order on the night of 5/6 September. At dawn, Podpułkownik Sienkiewicz mounted a bold counter-attack with two battalions from his 76 PP that caught the Germans by surprise. Generalleutnant Rudolf Schmidt's 1. Panzer-Division's command post, located near Milejów, was forced to retreat to avoid being overrun. Sienkiewicz personally led the I/76 PP at Longinówka, where the Poles claimed to have surprised a Panzer unit, destroying 40 tanks and inflicting 200 casualties. While it is unclear how much damage Sienkiewicz actually inflicted, there is no doubt that he had stirred up a hornet's nest and 1. Panzer-Division struck back with tanks and artillery. The Polish infantry fought desperately, at times hand to hand, but the odds were too great. Within two hours, both battalions of the 76 PP were demolished; Sienkiewicz and 683 of his men were dead. Many soldiers of the 76 PP were captured. Apparently angered by this surprise attack, soldiers from the 1. Panzer-Division shot 19 captured officers from the 76 PP, as well as a number of enlisted soldiers. Dozens of civilians from Milejów were also executed. The rest of 29 DP, reduced to a single infantry regiment and two artillery battalions, retreated towards the Vistula.

Hoepner kept part of his corps to crush the scattered battalions of the 19 DP deployed around Piotrków, but sent the vanguards of the 1. and 4. Panzer-Divisionen north-east towards Tomaszów Mazowiecki.[48] In the fighting on 6 September, the commander of the 19 DP was captured but a regimental commander, Podpułkownik Jan Kruk-Śmigli, managed to lead 7,000 survivors (five infantry battalions and 15 field guns) east across the Pilica River to temporary safety. Nevertheless, the 19 DP had lost half its strength in two days of fighting. Mop-up operations in the city continued for some time and Piotrków was not declared captured until 2000 hours. After the news of the loss of Piotrków reached Warsaw, panic set in. The rest of the civilian government left the capital on the night of 6/7 September. Rydz-Śmigły also decided to leave the capital along with the General

Staff and establish a new headquarters in Brześć, while leaving his chief of staff, Generał Brygady Wacław Stachiewicz, in Warsaw. It was a disastrous decision. Polish operational-level command and control was disrupted at a critical moment because no alternate command post had been prepared at Brześć. Although he hoped to establish a defensive line along the Vistula and San Rivers, Rydz-Śmigły could barely communicate with anyone for the next few days. Rather than provide the kind of stubborn-in-adversity leadership that kindles Polish resistance, Rydz-Śmigły instead undermined morale by fleeing and ordering remaining officials and able-bodied males to flee as well. It was a disgrace. Before leaving Warsaw, the Second Department's Cipher Bureau burned all documents related to the breaking of the Enigma code.

While Warsaw panicked, Hoepner wasted no time in attacking Tomaszów Mazowiecki. The Polish 13th Infantry Division (13 DP) had just completed moving by rail from Bydgoszcz (it had been intended to join the Intervention Corps but at the start of the war was ordered to join Army Prusy). The 13 DP established a textbook 'two-up, one back' defence at Tomaszów Mazowiecki, with its 43rd and 45th Infantry Regiments (43 and 45 PP) deployed on line and the 44th Infantry Regiment (44 PP) in reserve. Unfortunately, the 13 DP had little time to construct fieldworks or obstacles and it was struck on both flanks by Hoepner's two Panzer-Divisionen. Furthermore, the terrain in this area was flat and did not favour the defence. Amazingly, the Polish division did not buckle at once and managed to hold off the initial attacks and even knock out some German tanks. However, Hoepner brought up more of his forces and mounted a stronger attack in the afternoon which succeeded in piercing the thin Polish line. The 13 DP tried to conduct a withdrawal as night fell, but the 45 PP was virtually destroyed. The 1. Panzer-Division occupied Tomaszów Mazowiecki by dusk, while the battered 13 DP escaped to the north-east. Hoepner's Panzers were now within 100km of Warsaw and there were no intact Polish formations left to bar the way to the capital. Reichenau's 10. Armee had achieved a complete breakthrough.

Once Rydz-Śmigły left Warsaw, Generał Czuma tried to organize a defence, assisted by Mayor Starzyński. Although Rydz-Śmigły had ordered all army units to retreat east of the Vistula, Czuma ignored this order and managed to grab two battalions of Podpułkownik Józef Kalandyk's 40 PP (5 DP) and a few assorted support units as they passed through the city on 7 September. Czuma hurriedly sent Kalandyk's two battalions (II and

III/40 PP) to establish a defence in the south-west suburbs of Warsaw, while civilian volunteers set up barricades.

After the battle of Tomaszów Mazowiecki, Generalmajor Reinhardt's 4. Panzer-Division continued to press northwards and by the morning of 8 September, the division vanguard was within 45km of Warsaw. Richthofen massed five Gruppen of Stukas – about 140 Ju 77 dive-bombers – and sent them to bomb Warsaw during the morning, hoping to soften up the defenders.* Soon thereafter, Reinhardt unleashed Oberstleutnant Heinrich Eberbach's Panzer-Regiment 35 to push on to the Polish capital, although the rest of the 4. Panzer-Division was strung out for miles and needed time to refuel. The point was led by Hauptmann Meinrad von Lauchert's I/Panzer-Regiment 35 (Lauchert would become one of the best German tactical armoured leaders in the Second World War, culminating with his leading the German spearhead in the Battle of the Bulge in 1944). Although the Poles blew up two bridges to slow the German advance, resistance was light and many Polish troops encountered simply surrendered. By 1720 hours, Lauchert reached the south-west suburb of Ochota and encountered barricades. Halder's diary indicates that the OKH had monitored radio broadcasts which stated that the Polish government had left the capital, so Eberbach believed that Warsaw had been declared an 'open city' and did not expect resistance.[49] Yet when Lauchert's tanks began cautiously pushing into the city along Grójecka Street, they came under intense fire from 75mm field guns, machine guns and a few anti-tank guns from two companies of the 40 PP. After one Pz IV was knocked out by a direct hit and two other tanks damaged, Eberbach ordered Lauchert to withdraw.[50] Warsaw would not fall to a *coup de main*. On the evening of 8 September, Generał Czuma issued a defiant order over the radio that Warsaw 'would be defended until the last breath.' He ordered Polish soldiers to fight to the last man and civilians to devote all their energy to assist the army. Czuma ended with the warning that, 'leaving Warsaw at such moment will be considered cowardice' – a clear public admonishment of Rydz-Śmigły.

While Hoepner's XVI Armeekorps (mot.) was carving its way through Army Prusy's northern group, Hoth's XV Armeekorps (mot.)

*It is interesting that a number of German accounts claim that they believed Warsaw had been declared an 'open city' because of the announcement that the Polish government had evacuated the city on the previous day. Yet if the Germans believed that Warsaw was an open city, why launch a massed-Stuka raid against Warsaw?

The Polish PZL.37b Łoś bomber entered Polish service in 1938 and formed the backbone of the Bomber Brigade at the start of the war. The Łoś bomber was equipped with licence-built engines of British design but was superior to the British Bristol Blenheim light bomber. Unfortunately, Poland did not have a well thought-out plan on how to employ its bomber brigade and simply used them to attack German Panzer columns, which was wasteful. (Author's collection)

A PZL.23b Karaś reconnaissance bomber from 41 Eskadra (Army Modlin) shot down in the early days of the campaign. The Karaś was designed to be a multi-purpose aircraft but it was only moderately effective at either of its tasks. Most of the Karaś were initially controlled by the field armies, which squandered them in piecemeal attacks or high-risk reconnaissance missions. The Karaś proved highly vulnerable to enemy Flak and fighters. (Author's collection)

Soldiers from the 7. Infanterie-Division pose outside a captured Polish bunker after the battle of Węgierska Gorka. Although Polish sources have tended to exaggerate the number of casualties inflicted on the Germans in this action, there is no doubt that just four bunkers halted a German division for two days. The Polish General Staff had ordered the construction of border fortifications during the summer of 1939 and these positions were only partly completed. (Author's collection)

The Polish Army had two battalions of 7TP light tanks, which were a match for any German tanks. However, the Poles tended to use their tanks in company-size detachments, and counter-attacks only achieved local results. It was not until the battle of Tomaszów Lubelski on 18 September that the Poles were able to mass an appreciable number of armoured fighting vehicles, but by this point the campaign was lost. However, the 7TP does indicate that Poland could design and build tanks that were the equal of those built by Germany or the Soviet Union. (Author's collection)

A TKS tankette from the 10th Motorized Cavalry Brigade (10 BK) is loaded onto a truck for transport to the front. Maczek's 10 BK demonstrated superb operational mobility throughout the campaign and not only avoided destruction but managed to escape as a unit to Romania. The Wehrmacht had not prepared to fight an enemy with equivalent motorized mobility and this one brigade managed to delay an entire German motorized corps for several days. (Author's collection)

German infantry on the edge of a village. The German soldiers in Poland had an inordinate fear of being fired upon by Polish civilians, even though very few civillians had access to weapons. In fact, Polish soldiers had a higher probability of being fired upon by ethnic German civilians in Poland than German soldiers had of being fired upon by ethnic Polish civilians. This *'franc-tireur'* mentality was a hold-over from the 1870 Franco-Prussian War and was used to justify the burning of villages and execution of civilians. (Nik Cornish at www.Stavka.org.uk)

German infantry cross a water obstacle in a pneumatic raft. During *Fall Weiss*, German troops had to conduct several assault river crossings, particularly on the Narew River. Note the soldier with the Panzerbüchse 39 anti-tank rifle. (Nik Cornish at www.Stavka.org.uk)

German Pionier troops complete a pontoon bridge. The Wehrmacht was forced to build multiple pontoon bridges during the course of *Fall Weiss*, over the Vistula, Narew, Bug and San rivers. In theory, a bridging column could set up a 15-tonne pontoon bridge across a typical river in 4–8 hours, but could take much longer under actual battlefield conditions. The speed of bridging operations was one of the main inhibitors of motorized unit advances. Nevertheless, the Wehrmacht learned a great deal about tactical bridging in Poland that it would improve upon in the French campaign. (Nik Cornish at www.Stavka.org.uk)

An overturned German Pz II light tank. The Germans had their share of non-combat accidents, often due to tired vehicle crews failing to appreciate the nature of minor obstacles. The point made here, however, is that the Wehrmacht still had to recover these vehicles, and recovery assets in 1939–40 were scarce. As the war progressed, the Wehrmacht became more adept at battlefield recovery. (Nik Cornish at www.Stavka.org.uk)

A German Sd. Kfz. 232 (with radio antenna) and Sd. Kfz. 231 armoured cars from the 5. Panzer-Division's reconnaissance battalion entering Przemyśl around 16/17 September 1939. A column of motorcyclists is waiting in the square. A German Panzer-Division would typically form an advance guard unit with armoured cars and motorcycle infantry to push ahead of the main body. These tactics were successful but costly in Poland, since the Wehrmacht lost 30 per cent of its armoured cars and over 5,000 motorcycles during the short campaign. (Author's collection)

One of the weaknesses of the German Heer was its dependence upon rather primitive logistic capabilities. Here, support troops are filling 20-litre fuel cannisters from 200-litre drums, using hand pumps. The well-known , 'Jerry can' was standardized in 1937. It took seven 20-litre cannisters just to refuel one Pz I tank and two of the 200-litre drums to fill a single Pz IV tank. With a piston hand pump, it would take about 20 minutes to transfer the fuel from one fuel drum to ten cannisters. Using these methods, refueling an entire Panzer-Regiment could take the better part of a morning. (Nik Cornish at www.Stavka.org.uk)

A German Pz IV medium tank destroyed during the battle of the Bzura. On 16 September, the 4. Panzer-Division lost 23 tanks near the village of Ruszki when its vanguard was engaged by a Polish 100mm howitzer battery. On the same day, the 1. Panzer-Division lost 42 tanks near Kiernozia, including ten Pz IV tanks. A counter-attack by two Panzer-Divisionen had been stopped cold by effective anti-tank defences, although few histories of the campaign even mention these actions. (Author's collection)

Hitler meets with Generalleutnant Kurt von Briesen, commander of the 30. Infanterie-Division, on September 13, 1939. Briesen had been wounded in the battle of the Bzura. Hitler was very taken by Briesen and said he wanted him to be the first division commander awarded the *Ritterkreuz*. Briesen ended up having a short but eventful career. In June 1940 he would take the salute of the Wehrmacht victory parade in Paris. During Operation *Barbarossa* he was promoted to corps commander but was killed in action in November 1941. (Nik Cornish at www.Stavka.org.uk)

German prisoners captured in Warsaw after one of the early German assaults was repulsed. Unlike the Wehrmacht, the Polish WP scrupulously observed the Geneva Convention in regard to prisoners of war. At one point or another, the Poles managed to capture over 5,000 German prisoners during the campaign – the largest haul of German prisoners until 1942. (Author's collection)

A German motorcycle courier pauses by the side of road, with a ditch filled with dead Polish soldiers. Since the Polish corpses are still wearing helmets, field packs and entrenching tools, it is likely that they were killed by artillery fire or air attack. This photo also illustrates the casual disregard for enemy dead – as if they are merely roadside litter – commonplace in war zones. (Bundesarchiv, Bild 101I-012-0018-06A, Foto: Kliem)

German infantry advance cautiously behind a Pz II tank into the outskirts of Warsaw on 8/9 September. The German attempt to capture a major city with a Panzer-Division was a gamble that proved a costly failure. German pre-war doctrine had not addressed urban combat and the Panzer-Division was designed for rapid manoeuvre, not infantry support. However, the rapid Polish retreat emboldened Reinhardt's 4. Panzer-Division to attempt a *coup de main*. After this failure, German Panzer-Divisionen would avoid enemy cities – at least until Stalingrad in 1942. (Bundesarchiv, Bild 101I-012-0022-25, Foto: Otto Lanziger)

View from the nose of a German He 111 bomber over a Polish city. Note that the aircraft is extremely low – probably below 1,000 feet – which means that the threat of Polish anti-aircraft fire is negligible. Once the Polish Pursuit Brigade was withdrawn to the south-east, German bombers became more aggressive over Poland. (Bundesarchiv, Bild 183-S52911, Foto: Stempka)

German infantry and Pioniers advancing in a wrecked urban landscape. The Wehrmacht had not really planned for combat in major cities and was reluctant to take further casualties in Warsaw after the initial setbacks. Flamethrower teams, equipped with the Flammenwerfer 35 were used at Modlin and Gdynia. The Poles also had flamethrowers and used them on at least one occasion. (Nik Cornish at www.Stavka.org.uk)

Soviet BT-7 tanks entering Lwów on 22 September. The Germans had failed to capture the city but the garrison decided to surrender when the Red Army reached the city in force. Soviet armoured units suffered more losses from mechanical problems than from Polish resistance during their invasion. (Author's collection)

Hitler observes Warsaw under bombardment, from a church roof about 5km east of Praga. Unlike later campaigns, Hitler was very interested in observing the Wehrmacht in action and spent a good portion of the opening weeks of *Fall Weiss* in Poland. However, Hitler did not involve himself directly in operations but instead preferred to observe and discuss plans with his commanders. (Süddeutsche Zeitung Photo, 00000129)

General Tadeusz Kutrzeba arrives to sign the capitulation of Warsaw. Although the Polish military forces in Warsaw had the resources and the will to continue resistance, the heavy loss of life and the shortage of water to fight fires were key factors that caused the military leadership to accept the inevitable. It is worth noting that Poland was the only Allied power to mount a sustained defense of its capital in the Second World War (excluding the Soviet Union, which was not an Allied power). (Bundesarchiv, Bild 146-1976-032-19, Foto: Koch)

Polish prisoners of war under German escort. Although Polish senior officer POWs were sent to camps in Germany or Austria, the Wehrmacht had not prepared extensive prisoner-holding facilities prior to the beginning of *Fall Weiss* and most captured enlisted personnel remained in austere field camps in Poland during the winter of 1939/40 (with a significant number escaping). In mid-1940 the Germans began converting the Polish enlisted prisoners into forced labour in Germany. (Süddeutsche Zeitung Photo, 01044091)

Hitler and his generals review German motorized infantry in the military parade in Warsaw on 5 October 1939. Poles were forbidden from attending or viewing the parade. Hitler once said that armies 'only exist for triumphant exertion in war' and it was this kind of military triumph that he sought when he made the decision for war. (Bundesarchiv, Bild 183-S52565)

German paramilitaries – apparently policemen – pose in front of hanged prisoners in Poland. Once *Fall Weiss* began, the Volksdeutscher Selbstschutz units turned into active insurgents and then were the first to act against Poles deemed hostile to the Third Reich. Once the SS-Einsatzgruppen arrived, the Selbstschutz units served as auxiliaries and played a major role in the special actions conducted in Poland during the winter of 1939/40. (Süddeutsche Zeitung Photo, 01044027)

Hitler is saluted by the Nazi faithful after delivering his speech in Berlin on 6 October 6 1939, which made a vague peace offer to the Anglo-French. Both Britain and France rejected this offer. The Third Reich was now committed to a much larger conflict than originally intended by *Fall Weiss*. (Süddeutsche Zeitung Photo, 00404898)

The skulls of murdered Polish officers exhumed in Katyń Forest. In April 1940, the NKVD executed 4,421 captured Polish officers at this site on the orders of Stalin. Once evidence of the crime emerged in 1943, both the United States and Britain denied Soviet complicity and prevented the Polish government-in-exile from severing relations with Moscow. For the next five decades, fellow travellers in the West would deny Soviet responsibility, which contributed to the Polish feeling of betrayal by its erstwhile allies. (Author's collection)

In late October, the Soviets handed over the city of Wilno to Lithuania and set up a symbolic sawing of the border barrier. Of course this was a farce, since Lithuania had been assigned to the Soviet sphere of influence by the Molotov–Ribbentrop Pact and Stalin intended to absorb all of the Baltic states in the next six months. Just as the Anglo-French ignored the Soviet invasion of Poland, the Western allies turned a blind eye to Soviet aggression against the other states of Eastern Europe. (Author's collection)

On 17 September 1993, President Lech Wałęsa bid farewell to the last Russian soldiers to leave Polish soil. Wałęsa told them that 'Hitler lost, but Yalta gave us Stalin. Poland was struck in the back.' He stated that the Russian withdrawal meant that a 'measure of historical justice is completed.' Unlike Western Europeans, who celebrated liberation in 1944–45, Poles had to wait another five decades and accomplish it by their own resistance. Poland was one of the primary beneficiaries of the collapse of the Soviet Union. (Author's collection)

routed the three divisions (3 DPL and 12 and 36 DP) in the southern group, which had been designated as Operational Group Kielce. Dąb-Biernacki assigned Generał Brygady Stanisław Skwarczyński to lead Operational Group Kielce, which turned out to be a major mistake. The Polish forces in this sector did not have anything like a continuous front, which made them extremely vulnerable to encirclement by fast-moving forces. Furthermore, these units were still mobilizing when the Germans appeared; the 3 DPL had only three of its nine infantry battalions on hand. After destroying the retreating 7 DP on 4 September, Hoth pushed towards Kielce and the Polish armaments factories in the Central Industrial Region (COP). Generalleutnant Georg Stumme's 2. leichte-Division captured Kielce by noon on 5 September, but Operational Group Kielce had deployed two just-mobilized regiments (93 and 154 PP) to block the road just north of the city. Both regiments mounted a stubborn defence which delayed Stumme's further advance for a day, but the units were decimated in the process. Hoth brought up the 3. leichte-Division to get around the annoying Polish roadblocks and it marched rapidly through the Polish industrial region. Rundstedt also transferred part of the 29. Infanterie-Division (mot.) to reinforce Hoth's advance, while Reichenau transferred the XIV Armeekorps (mot.) with the 1. leichte-Division and 13. Infanterie-Division (mot) to add more muscle on 10. Armee's right flank. Reichenau now had five motorized divisions committed against the Operational Group Kielce.

The loss of Kielce so quickly in the campaign caused Rydz-Śmigły to create a new command, designated as Army Lublin, to organize a defence along the Vistula River south of Warsaw. Generał Dywizji Tadeusz Piskor was appointed commander of the formation, but he had very few troops assigned and they were widely dispersed. The High Command placed the 39th Infantry Division (39 DP) – a reserve unit mobilizing around Dęblin – under his command, along with a couple of infantry and cavalry regiments formed from training personnel and reservists. Pułkownik Tadeusz Komorowski (who would lead the Home Army (Armia Krajowa or AK) in the 1944 Warsaw Rebellion) headed a composite cavalry brigade. The only effective unit that Piskor was provided was Pułkownik Stefan Rowecki's Warsaw Armoured-Motorized Brigade; this well-balanced 5,000-man brigade had two motorized infantry regiments, 17 Vickers light tanks, 26 TKS tankettes, eight 75mm guns, 12 37mm anti-tanks and 600 motor vehicles. The High Command anticipated assigning Operational Group Kielce to Piskor's command once it crossed the Vistula.

On 7 September, Stumme's 2.leichte-Division surged forwards and once it was clear that Polish forces in the area were trying to retreat eastwards to the Vistula, Hoth switched the mission priority from seizing terrain to blocking the enemy's escape. Soon, both the 12th Infantry Division (12 DP) and the partially mobilized 36 DP were threatened with isolation by the German advance. The 36 DP was the first to be eliminated, losing more than half its strength trying to escape from Stumme's motorized troops. On the morning of 8 September, Generalmajor Adolf Kuntzen's 3. leichte-Division sent a Kampfgruppe under Oberst Wilhelm-Dietrich von Ditfurth to block the Polish escape route by occupying a position near the town of Iłza. Kampfgruppe Ditfurth consisted of Kavallerie-Schützen-Regiment 9, 2./Panzer-Abteilung 67 (about 20 Pz II and Pz 38t), I./Artillery-Regiment 80 (12 10.5cm howitzers) and I./Flak-Regiment 22 (2cm and 8.8cm Flak guns). Approaching Iłza from the west, Ditfurth's column came under Polish artillery fire and deployed, occupying defensive positions. German efforts to push all the way to Ilza were stopped cold by Polish defensive firepower. The commander of the 3./Panzer-Abteilung 67, Oberleutnant Otto Meisner, tried to lead an attack in his Pz 38t tank, but he was hit and killed by Polish anti-tank rifle fire. Several other German tanks were knocked out, causing the Panzers to pull back.

Around 2000 hours on 8 September, the Polish 3 DPL launched an effort to break through the German blocking position, attacking with two infantry battalions, supported by four TKS tankettes. Polish engineers also used flamethrowers in the attack. The Polish infantry fought with the courage of desperation – attacking at close quarters with the bayonet – and managed to overrun a German company, which precipitated a retreat. Ditfurth tried to organize a counter-attack, pistol in hand, but was killed by Polish machine-gun fire. Nevertheless, a battery of six 2cm Flak guns managed to repulse the 3 DPL's attack with intense direct fire. After falling back to regroup, the 3 DPL launched a bigger attack at 0410 hours on 9 September, which overran a German 8.8cm Flak battery and killed Major Bernhard Weisser, the commander of the I./Flak-Regiment 22.[51] Once again, the German 2cm Flak guns and a platoon of German tanks prevented a Polish breakthrough. Kampfgruppe Ditfurth was mauled, having suffered well over 200 casualties during the night. At dawn, the 3. leichte-Division requested air support and Richthofen provided over 150 Stuka sorties and two Gruppen of level-bombers, which relentlessly bombed Polish troop concentrations around Iłza.

The battle of Iłza on the night of 8/9 September was a chaotic action for both sides, with the Germans winning by dint of superior firepower. Most of the tactical decisions were made by Polish regimental commanders and Generał Skwarczyński exercised little influence upon the battle until the end. When 3 DPL's attacks failed to clear an escape path for the 12th or 33 DP, Skwarczyński ordered both divisions to break up into small groups and try to escape to the Vistula. All the artillery and heavy weapons of the 12 DP were abandoned, so the division virtually evaporated. The 33 DP was also reduced to small groups of fleeing survivors. Indeed, the retreat of Operational Group Kielce to the Vistula turned into a complete disaster with all three divisions disintegrating and by the end of 9 September, Army Prusy had ceased to exist. Only small numbers of troops were able to join up with Army Lublin on the east side of the Vistula. The Germans were pitiless in their pursuit, cutting off most of the escape routes to the Vistula with fast-moving motorized columns. One Polish group, survivors from the 74 PP (7 DP) led by Major Józef Pelc, was intercepted by the German III./Infanterie-Regiment 15 (mot.) near Ciepielów on the morning of 8 September. After a brief fight, about 450 Poles surrendered when their ammunition was exhausted. Unlike earlier incidents, the German commander, Oberst Walter Wessel, apparently ordered the execution of roughly 250–300 of the prisoners by the side of the road.[52] However, the exact circumstances and death toll at Ciepielów remain both murky and controversial.

Some measure of revenge was achieved when the survivors of the 19 DP, led by Podpułkownik Jan Kruk-Śmigli, ambushed a column near Opoczno on the afternoon of 10 September. Generalmajor der Polizei Georg Friedrich Wilhelm Roettig's staff car was hit by heavy machine-gun fire and he was badly wounded. He was subsequently finished off with a shot to the head. Roettig had the distinction of being the first general killed in the Second World War. Kruk-Śmigli's group continued towards the Vistula but it was eventually intercepted and only a few survivors of the 19 DP were able to make it to the east side of the river.

The advance of the XV Armeekorps (mot.) and XVI Armeekorps (mot.) was so rapid that the 'leg' infantry divisions of the IV Armeekorps were left far in the rear, unable to maintain contact with the enemy. On Reichenau's left, Blaskowitz's 8. Armee applied steady pressure on Rómmel's Army Łódź, pushing it back. The Polish 10 DP tried to make a stand behind the Warta River at Sieradz, but the German XIII Armeekorps bulled its way across the river, then fended off Polish counter-attacks. Blaskowitz also tried to outflank the 10 DP with his X Armeekorps, but Rómmel used the Kresowa Cavalry Brigade to guard his open right flank. Nevertheless, by 6 September both the 10 DP and Kresowa Cavalry Brigade were falling back towards Łódź with 8. Armee in pursuit. Rómmel abandoned his headquarters in Łódź after it was bombed. On 7 September, the 28 DP made a valiant stand at Pabianice, south of Łódź, inflicting significant losses on the German 17. Infanterie-Division. The XIII Armeekorps was forced to commit the Waffen-SS LSSAH regiment to assist the 17. Infanterie-Division at Pabianice.[53] However, as other Polish units on its flanks retreated the 28 DP was enveloped and forced to withdraw; two of its three infantry regiments were decimated during the chaotic retreat. Pułkownik Filipowicz's Wołyńska Cavalry Brigade and the 30 DP were less successful in holding off the German XI Armeekorps and fell back first towards Łódź, then towards Warsaw. By the end of 7 September, it was clear that Army Łódź was breaking up.

Blaskowitz did not intend to storm the city of Łódź (pre-war population 665,000) but rather to envelop it with the X Armeekorps while XIII Armeekorps continued to push back the disintegrating divisions of Army Łódź. The 24. Infanterie-Division reached Poddebice, north-west of Łódź and marched east along the south side of the Bzura River, slowly closing the pincers around the city.[54] Civilian morale in Łódź was fragile since about 300 civilians had already been killed in Luftwaffe raids and it was clear that the Polish Army was about to evacuate the city. On 8 September, a civilian delegation – with the concurrence of the Polish military governor – approached the 17. Infanterie-Division to negotiate the surrender of the city. Negotiations dragged on much of the day, enabling Polish units to escape. The city was finally surrendered by evening, but the 17. Infanterie-Division did not actually enter Łódź until 0500 hours on 9 September. Ethnic Germans in Łódź greeted the invaders as liberators, handing out flowers and drinks. In the next few days, these *Volksdeutsche* would assist the occupation in rounding up 1,500 citizens in Łódź who were deemed a threat to the occupation. Most of these people, including teachers and officials, would be executed.

After the collapse of Army Łódź, Rómmel and his staff headed to Warsaw, where Rydz-Śmigły's deputy Generał Stachiewicz appointed him head of the newly created Army Warsaw. Initially, Rómmel's command only included a handful of regular troops in Warsaw and the forces around the Modlin fortress, but the creation of this army served as a magnet to attract retreating Polish units towards the capital. Within a week, Rómmel would have over 100,000 troops under his command – the largest force under one Polish commander during the 1939 campaign.

The Battle of the Bzura, 9–19 September

Generał Kutrzeba had been eager to attack the Germans from the outset of the war, but his Army Poznań had done little but retreat during the first week of the campaign. Indeed, Rydz-Śmigły had ordered him to continue retreating all the way to the Vistula. As the Germans had had little contact with Kutrzeba's forces since 3 September, the OKH simply lost track of them. The Germans assumed that Army Poznań had been transferred to Warsaw by rail but their own air strikes against Polish rail yards had made this problematic, so Army Poznań simply moved east on its own resources. Despite gaining air superiority, Luftwaffe aerial reconnaissance failed to detect the approach of Army Poznań to the Bzura River. Given the rapid defeat of Army Pomorze and the loss of Łódź, along with evidence that all the Polish armies were in full retreat, the OKH convinced itself that Polish resistance west of the Vistula was broken. Having secured Łódź, Blaskowitz intended to push north with his 8. Armee and cut off the escape route of Army Pomorze, which were believed to be just tattered remnants. Yet the glaring German failure to secure the boundary between Heeresgruppe Nord and Heeresgruppe Süd with anything more than a handful of security units left Blaskowitz's 8. Armee vulnerable to a sudden riposte.

One of the hidden benefits of Rydz-Śmigły's leaving Warsaw was that he lost control over his field armies. Kutrzeba realized that he had the only intact Polish field army left and that he was now free to act independently. It was clear that once the German X Armeekorps occupied Lowicz on the Bzura, the line of communications for both Army Pomorze and Army Poznań would soon be severed. Once that happened, eight Polish infantry divisions and two cavalry brigades would be isolated. Yet while the Germans had the better operational position, General der Artillerie Wilhelm Ulex's X Armeekorps was tactically vulnerable because its units were so spread out after the capture of Łódź.[55] Ulex was an odd choice for active field command since he had already been dismissed from the service for opposition to Hitler, but was re-activated five days before the start of the war. Generalleutnant Kurt von Briesen's 30. Infanterie-Division was strung out along the south side of the Bzura, from Uniejów to Sobota, a distance of over 60km. Generalleutnant Friedrich Olbricht's

24. Infanterie-Division was more concentrated as it approached Lowicz, but it was poorly positioned to support its neighbour. Even worse, substantial remnants from Army Łódź were in the woods around Skierniewice, forcing Olbricht to divert one regiment to deal with them, while keeping the rest of his division focused on securing the last crossing sites over the Bzura. Nor did it help that Ulex's X Armeekorps had no units guarding its left flank, which was wide open. Supposedly Rundstedt's chief of staff, Generalleutnant Erich von Manstein, warned Blaskowitz, who warned Ulex to keep an eye on that vulnerable left flank, but this claim is specious. In his post-war account, Manstein only commented that he 'had a vague feeling that something was brewing on the northern flank of the army group.'[56] Ostensibly these officers were leaders, not spectators, and could have given orders to reduce this risk. Normally, when an army has an open flank, at the very least it should focus reconnaissance assets to watch in this direction to prevent surprises. Instead, through over-confidence and incompetence, the German commanders involved ignored the possibility that the Poles might do anything more than just retreat.

Kutrzeba co-ordinated with Bortnowski as best he could in order to maximize Polish combat power. He intended to use all of his own units in the initial attack, while Bortnowski held off the German III Armeekorps with just two divisions (15 and 27 DP). Kutrzeba appointed Generał Brygady Edmund Knoll-Kownacki, an artillerymen, to command the operational group that would lead the assault.[57] Unlike the rest of the Polish armies, Kutrzeba had held onto his army aviation squadrons – against orders – and his air group consisted of Major Mieczysław Mümler's composite fighter division with 16 P.11c fighters and about a dozen reconnaissance aircraft. By 8 September, the air group was deployed on grass strips north-west of Kutno and its reconnaissance aircraft were used to scout out German positions along the Bzura. If Kutrzeba could achieve a breakthrough, Bortnowski would commit his best divisions (4th, 16th and 26 DPs) to reinforce the success and open a pathway for both armies to escape to Warsaw. It was also hoped that this Polish counter-offensive would divert the Germans away from Warsaw and give more time for Czuma to organize the capital's defences. Although Polish strategy hinged on mounting a powerful counter-offensive at a judicious moment, the battle of the Bzura was a hastily planned affair and Kutrzeba was under pressure to attack before the Germans cut off their escape route. The units in Army Poznań were tired after marching over 250km, but morale was high.

Around 1400 hours on 9 September, Knoll–Kownacki began a series of attacks against the 30. Infanterie-Division all along the Bzura. Not all units were in place at this point, so some attacks occurred later in the day. Kapitan Franciszek Jastrzębski's 132 Eskadra provided limited fighter cover over the battlefield, but lost two P.11C fighters in an encounter with four Bf 109Es from I.(J)/LG 2.[58] Kutrzeba struck in the centre with his infantry (14, 17 and 25 DP) and on the flanks with his two cavalry brigades (Podolska and Wielkopolska Cavalry Brigades). For once, the Poles had a superiority in numbers and they also enjoyed an advantage in artillery. On the Polish right flank, the Podolska Cavalry Brigade, reinforced with about 2,000 survivors of the Pomorska Cavalry Brigade, advanced in the late afternoon. Briesen had left a single battalion (I./Infanterie-Regiment 46) at Uniejów, to guard his left flank. The 6th Uhlan Regiment, supported by artillery, attacked Uniejów and captured the town by at 2000 hours after a tough fight; about 25 Poles were killed, in return they captured 27 Germans, three 3.7cm PaK anti-tank guns and 11 trucks. The first attack by the Polish 25 DP against Łęczyca failed because a single Polish battalion was committed against a single German battalion (II./Infanterie-Regiment 26). Later in the day, the rest of 25 DP joined the attack and this time Łęczyca was captured.[59] Briesen directed two battalions of Infanterie-Regiment 46 to block any further advance by the 25 DP. Around 1800 hours, the Polish 17th Infantry Division (17 DP) crossed the Bzura north of Piatek and routed the single German battalion in this sector (III./Infanterie-Regiment 6) while the 14 DP advanced 5km south of the river against minimal resistance. Podpułkownik Władysław Wiecierzyński, commander of the 55 PP (14 DP), led his regiment across the Bzura. He said, 'as far as the eye could see to the left and to the right, infantry was flowing down towards the Bzura valley. They are going eagerly and briskly.'[60] On Kutrzeba's left flank, the Wielkopolska Cavalry Brigade got a late start but managed to cross the Bzura near Sobota by nightfall, using their TKS tankettes and motorcycle troops to lead the advance. Kutrzeba made a tactical mistake in employing the Wielkopolska Cavalry Brigade at Sobota, instead of using it in conjunction with the Podolska Cavalry Brigade on his right flank; cavalry was better suited to operating in open areas than assaulting defended towns. Nevertheless, by the end of the first day, Knoll–Kownacki's forces had gained multiple crossings over the Bzura and had disrupted the 30. Infanterie-Division. Yet from the German point of view, these attacks appeared to be Polish units attempting to break out to the east, which did not seem unusual.

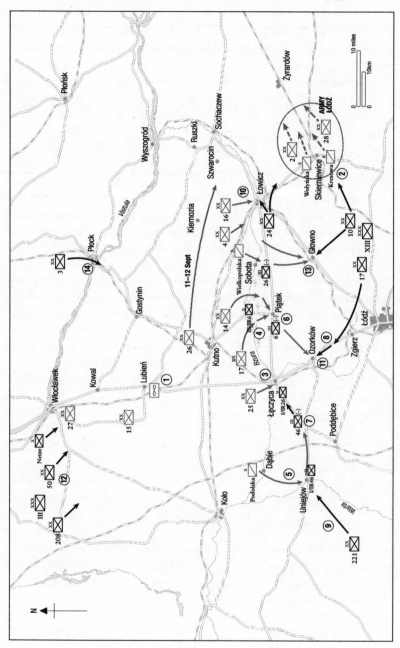

MAP KEY

8 September

1) Army Poznań's air group and main strike force (14, 17 and 25 DP) move into position.
2) German XIII Armeekorps is focused on pursuit of Army Łódź near Skierniewice.

9 September

3) The Polish 25 DP captures Łęczyca.
4) The Polish 17 DP routs a single German battalion on the Bzura while the 14 DP advances unopposed across the river.
5) Evening. The Podolska Cavalry Brigade captures Uniejów.

10 September

6) Heavy fighting around Piatek, which falls to the 14 DP.
7) The Podolska Cavalry Brigade pushes against the German left flank and raids their supply lines.
8) The German 17. Infanterie-Division marches to support the 30. Infanterie-Division and encounters the 25 DP near Ozorkow.
9) Evening. 221. Infanterie-Division committed from Heeresgruppe Süd reserves.

11 September

10) The 4 DP and 16 DP attack and push the German 24. Infanterie-Division back from Lowicz.
11) The 17 and 25 DP push the German 17. Infanterie-Division out of Ozorków.
12) The German III Armeekorps exerts greater pressure on the Polish rearguards near Wloclawek.

12 September

13) The Polish 4 DP and Wielkopolska Cavalry Brigade are stopped at Glowno. The Polish offensive has run out of steam.
   The 3. Infanterie-Division crosses the Vistula at Plock.

On 10 September, Knoll-Kownacki increased the pressure on the 30. Infanterie-Division. Heavy fighting occurred south-east of Łęczyca, where the 25 DP pushed back the Infanterie-Regiment 46. Even heavier fighting took place near Piatek, where the Infanterie-Regiment 6 tried to hold off the 14 and 17 DP.[61] Pułkownik Tadeusz Bodnar's 7th Heavy Artillery Regiment supported the attacks with 105mm and 155mm howitzer fire. Generalleutnant von Briesen set up his forward command post near Piatek, but around 1800 hours his headquarters was hit by an artillery barrage and the general was badly wounded. By evening, the 14 DP had taken Piatek and the 30. Infanterie-Division was in retreat. The Germans left a field hospital behind, with many of their wounded. On the right, the Podolska Cavalry Brigade began to harass the 30. Infanterie-Division's support units; at Stary Gostków, the cavalrymen captured a supply column with 40 prisoners and 27 trucks full of food and ammunition. Overall, the Poles claimed to have taken about 1,500 German prisoners by the end of the second day of the battle. Kapitan Jastrzębski managed to shoot down a Bf 109 but his 132 Eskdra lost two more P.11C fighters. Blaskowitz was now fully aware that a major Polish counter-offensive was under way and he ordered his XIII Armeekorps to re-orient towards the north-west and move to support Ulex's hard-pressed X Armeekorps. During the afternoon, the 17 DP had a meeting engagement with the lead elements of the 17. Infanterie-Division near Ozorków. Rundstedt released the 221. Infanterie-Division from Heeresgruppe Süd reserves and transferred it to 8. Armee so Blaskowitz could strengthen his open left flank; by the evening of 10 September the lead elements of this unit had already reached Uniejów.[62] Over the next several days, the Podolska Cavalry Brigade would conduct a tenacious delaying action to keep this German division at bay. Rundstedt also ordered Reichenau to send his XI Armeekorps to prevent any Polish forces from crossing the Bzura and reaching Warsaw. By the evening of 10 September, Kutrzeba's moment was fading.

On 11 September, Bortnowski committed his 4 and 16 DP to attack the 24. Infanterie-Division bridgehead at Lowicz. At 1500 hours, the 64 PP (16 DP) succeeded in crossing the Bzura and fought their way into Lowicz, which was defended by the German III./Infanterie-Regiment 102. Oberst Stephan Rittau, the German regimental commander, conducted a tenacious defence. Rather unusually, fighting continued in the town for much of the night, until the Poles finally managed to evict the German battalion. The 4 DP crossed the Bzura near Bielawy and joined up with the Wielkopolska Cavalry Brigade, but their further advance was stopped when they ran into the lead regiment of the 10. Infanterie-Division.[63] Knoll-Kownacki continued to attack the depleted 30. Infanterie-Division, routing part of the Infanterie-Regiment 46 at Biała Góra, 13km south-west of Łęczyca, while the 14 DP advanced south of Piatek towards Stryków. However, Blaskowitz was beginning to strike back. The 17. Infanterie-Division managed to push the 17 DP out of Ozorków, which was the high water mark of the Polish counter-offensive. Blaskowitz's urgent requests for air support resulted in the Hs 123s of II.(Schlacht)/LG 2 being provided to make low-level attacks on the 4 DP near Bielawy.[64] During the night of 11/12 September, German counter-battery fire struck the 7th Heavy Artillery Regiment near Mąkolice, killing Pułkownik Bodnar and inflicting heavy losses on this key unit.[65] The German III Armeekorps was also pushing back Army Pomorze's rearguards and the Polish armies were slowly being pushed into a corner.

German efforts to surround Army Pomorze and Army Poznań were rather clumsy and unimaginative. The battle of the Bzura was the first opportunity for the Wehrmacht to conduct a *Kesselschlacht* (cauldron battle) or pocket battle in the Second World War. Despite all the effort expended studying the concept of Kesselschlacht since the days of Moltke and Clausewitz, the Wehrmacht still had a lot to learn about the subject. In classic German military theory, Kesselschlacht was a premeditated act, brought about by superior operational-level planning. However, Rundstedt had not planned to fight a Kesselschlacht on the Bzura and was initially just reacting to events. Blaskowitz simply pushed reinforcements forwards to prevent X Armeekorps from buckling – just as the French Army would do in May 1940 – and initially devoted little thought towards Kutrzeba's open right flank. A single leichte-Division, judiciously deployed, could have driven around the open Polish flank and quickly rolled up Kutrzeba's army, but Rundstedt had committed all his motorized units to 10. Armee and 14. Armee. At a critical moment, the Wehrmacht was caught without any mobile reserves immediately available. It was not until 15 September that Rundstedt belatedly issued orders to transfer several motorized divisions to assist 8. Armee and these units would not arrive until the final stages of the battle.

The Polish counter-offensive finally began to sputter out on 12 September, as the 4 DP and Wielkopolska Cavalry Brigade fought a futile day-long battle to break through the 10. Infanterie-Division at Glowno. Luftwaffe air support was increased, with the He 111 level-bombers of KG 1, KG 4 and KG 26 being used to smash Polish troop concentrations. Kapitan Jastrzębski's fighters were still able to provide limited fighter cover and managed to shoot down two He 111s. On 13 September, 8. Armee began pushing the Polish units back to the Bzura and ran into light resistance. Most of Knoll-Kownacki's operational group and Bortnowski's forces pulled back across the Bzura, blew up the bridges and laid minefields. Instead, Polish units focused on trying to push past the 24. Infanterie-Division near Lowicz and Sochaczew. Polish tactics at this point – a mix of retreating, defending and attacking – were confusing for the Germans. At night, the Germans often found Polish units intermixed with their own. Concerned that some Polish units might escape if they could reach the Kampinos Forest east of the Bzura, Reichenau was ordered to redirect both the 4. Panzer-Division and the LSSAH westwards to secure Blonie; this town was occupied by the evening of 13 September. Reichenau also sent the 31. Infanterie-Division to assist in blocking this escape route.

Most accounts tend to depict the German response to the Polish counter-offensive on the Bzura as a rapid and decisive blow. Robert M. Citino claims that the Wehrmacht 'could stop on a dime, turn around, and [quickly] launch large-scale operations', but this is not what occurred on the Bzura. He also states that 'within a day, German reinforcements were on their way to the Bzura, including the mass of 10. Armee's armoured units.'[66] In fact, the 4. Panzer-Division was not redirected until the fourth day of the Polish counter-offensive and other motorized units were not committed until the sixth day of the battle. Fixated on Warsaw and the destruction of Polish units around Radom, Heeresgruppe Süd was slow to commit forces from outside 8. Armee to deal with the Polish counter-offensive. Instead, the German effort to crush Army Pomorze and Army Poznań was a tedious effort that went forwards in fits and starts. Until Blaskowitz received large-scale reinforcements, the attacks with his own units were purely local. He prevailed upon the OKH to pressure Heeresgruppe Nord to do more, which resulted in the 3. Infanterie-Division conducting a crossing of the Vistula at Płock on 12 September.[67] However, due to problems with bridging, the 3. Infanterie-Division did not begin attacking into the flank of Army Pomorze until 14 September. One of the main problems with German efforts to create a Kesselschlacht on the Bzura was that there was no overall commander; the battle occurred in the space between Heeresgruppe Süd and Heeresgruppe Nord and involved units from three different armies. Nor were there any hard-charging officers like Guderian or Hoth directly involved in the battle.

As Blaskowitz's 8. Armee began to recover ground along the Bzura and push towards Kutno, most of the Polish forces retreated towards the crossings at Lowicz and Sochaczew in the hope of escaping eastwards across the Bzura. Kapitan Jastrzębski relocated with his last six fighters to a remote airstrip north of Lowicz. Once Hoepner's XVI Armeekorps (mot.) with the 1. and 4. Panzer-Divisionen reached the Bzura on 15 September, Reichenau's staff planned a bold operation to finish off the nearly encircled Polish forces at one blow. Generalleutnant Rudolf Schmidt's 1. Panzer-Division would attack westwards from the bridgehead at Lowicz, while Reinhardt's 4. Panzer-Division crossed the Bzura north of Sochaczew; both divisions would converge around Kiernozia, 20km west of the Bzura.

The German attack began at 0500 hours on 16 September, but did not proceed smoothly due to traffic jams at the pontoon bridges. It was also raining, which meant no Luftwaffe support. Oberstleutnant Eberbach's Panzer-Regiment 35 finally began advancing westwards around 0700 hours and succeeded in overrunning some elements of the Wielkopolska Cavalry Brigade. However, soon afterward Panzer-Regiment 35 came under intense artillery, anti-tank and machine-gun fire from elements of 17 DP that were defending around the village of Ruszki. The German infantrymen were pinned down, but Eberbach's Panzers pressed on, hoping to come to grips with the enemy. However, one Polish artillery battery from the 17 DP, the VI/17 Light Artillery Regiment equipped with four 100mm howitzers, engaged Eberbach's Panzers and destroyed 22 of them (including most of his 6. Kompanie). The heavy 100mm projectiles tore the thin-skinned Panzers to pieces, knocking off turrets.[68] Even the Pz IV medium tanks proved vulnerable. Eberbach's Panzers eventually ran out of ammunition and had to retreat by 1700 hours. Since the Poles controlled the battlefield – a rarity – they had their sappers blow up all the German wrecks.[69] Panzer-Regiment 35 lost 23 of its 88 tanks and suffered 30 dead.[70] Meanwhile, the Panzer-Regiment 1 from 1. Panzer-Division had advanced to Kiernozia, where it ran into intense resistance. As at Ruszki, the German tanks had been separated from their supporting infantry and then ravaged by artillery and anti-tank fire. Nor were the Germans the only ones who learned to use anti-aircraft guns against tanks; the Polish 14th Anti-Aircraft Battery found that its 40mm Bofors guns performed well in the direct-fire role against tanks. Altogether, the 1. Panzer-Division lost 42 tanks, including ten Pz IV medium tanks, before withdrawing. The German attack had been a spectacular failure, demonstrating that Panzer-Divisionen could be stopped by well-led infantry divisions. The

German attacks failed because of the lack of air and artillery support and also because the Panzer units were too willing to advance into enemy positions without proper infantry support.

The Germans resumed mop-up operations west of the Bzura on 17 September, but failed to pre-empt the final Polish breakout attacks. Reinhardt was ordered to deploy his tired 4. Panzer-Division in blocking positions along the Bzura – which was more properly a mission for an infantry division. On the night of 18/19 September, the Poles attacked *en masse*, crossing the Bzura at multiple points north of Sochaczew, hoping to escape into the nearby Kampinos Forest. The 4. Panzer-Division could not stop this horde and suffered significant casualties as Poles fought their way through the division's thin cordon.[71] Reinhardt's division command post was attacked several times.[72] In total, perhaps 50,000 Polish troops succeeded in reaching the Kampinos Forest, although many of these – including Bortnowski – were scooped up by the Germans in the next few days. Amazingly, Kutrzeba and Knoll-Kownacki broke through to Warsaw with elements of the 4, 15 and 25 DPs and some of the cavalry. The 25 DP managed to reach Warsaw with four infantry battalions and several artillery batteries. While the units that reached Warsaw were in poor condition, they did contribute to the defence. However, the Poles had to abandon virtually all of their equipment in the pocket, including over 300 artillery pieces. Most of the captured Germans were recovered – the Poles could have shot them, but they did not. Many of the Poles who escaped across the Bzura would survive to fight again, in Poland with the resistance or in the West. Kapitan Jastrzębski succeeded in reaching England and served with RAF 302 Squadron until killed in the Battle of Britain.

After the final breakout effort, resistance within the pocket ended on 19 September. During the battle of the Bzura, the Germans estimated that they captured about 120,000 Polish troops and eliminated eight divisions, which was not entirely accurate. Since many of the escaping Polish troops donned civilian clothes, the Germans simply detained all military-age males they encountered, so some must have been civilians. Furthermore, the Germans were rather careless in guarding prisoners and many of them escaped within a few days. For example, Stefan Szymkowiak, an ON soldier attached to Army Poznań, was captured during the battle of the Bzura but soon escaped and returned home.[73] Yet there is no doubt that the Poles had suffered a major defeat, with at least 15,000 dead. At the end of the battle, Poland's last field armies had been crushed. In perspective, the ten-day battle of the Bzura was the largest and most successful Allied counter-offensive against the Germans in the first two years of the Second

World War. In contrast, the battle of Arras in May 1940 only lasted four hours and affected only one German division.

The German performance in the battle of the Bzura was lacklustre compared to the Kesselschlacht of 1941–42 or even their performance elsewhere in Poland. Even Manstein noted that the battle 'did not measure up' in actual results.[74] Blaskowitz's 8. Armee was caught by surprise and suffered over 9,000 casualties, including about 2,000 dead and 4,300 missing/captured.[75] Afterwards, the battered 30. Infanterie-Division was judged 'not combat capable' and pulled into reserve to refit. Rundstedt – who should have been co-ordinating this battle – provided little in the way of effective leadership. It took 12 German divisions, with significant help from the Luftwaffe, ten days to crush eight isolated Polish divisions and then they allowed one-quarter of the enemy personnel to escape. Furthermore, the terrain and weather were both favourable to the Germans. Given this result, heads should have rolled, beginning with Blaskowitz himself, but he continued to be given high-level assignments right up to the end of the war. One of the few officers who faced any repercussions for his performance was General Ulex, who was replaced as commander of the X Armeekorps one month after the battle.

List Overruns Southern Poland, 6–16 September

After the loss of Kraków on 6 September, Generał Szylling's Army Kraków continued its retreat to the Dunajec River, trying to put an obstacle between themselves and Generaloberst List's 14. Armee. The Śląsk Operational Group (23rd and 55 DPs) was redesignated as Operational Group Jagmin and the Bielsko Operational Group (6 DP, 21 DPG) was renamed the Boruta Operational Group. From Warsaw, Rydz-Śmigły announced that Army Kraków and Army Karpaty would be redesignated as Army Malopolska, which he hoped could make a stand on the Dunajec or the San River. These nomenclature changes had negligible effect on the situation. The 24th Infantry Division (24 DP), part of the strategic reserve, was assigned to Generał Dywizji Kazimierz Fabrycy's Army Karpaty and ordered to hold Tarnow and the southern portion of the Dunajec. However, the odds were against Army Kraków making a stand on the Dunajec since its five infantry divisions and two cavalry brigades were running out of supplies due to the collapse of their logistic system and the troops were exhausted because they had been retreating for days. Command and control was also breaking down, which led to confusion and disorder.

A 'simple thing', like arranging for bread to be sent to Dębica to feed the retreating troops, proved too difficult due to insufficient transport and disrupted telephone networks. Many troops simply scavenged potatoes from local fields and drank water from streams – which was no way to support an 80,000-man army. Various units, such as Pułkownik Walerian Młyniec's 156 PP (45 DP), were isolated by the German advance and were trying to catch up to Army Kraków before they were detected and destroyed. Stragglers and isolated detachments roamed the woods and villages, marching eastwards.

List's pursuit was led by Kleist's XXII Armeekorps (mot.), consisting of Veiel's 2. Panzer-Division and Hubicki's 4. leichte-Division. Oberst Wilhelm Ritter von Thoma, Legion Condor veteran, was in the vanguard, scattering the Polish 21 DPG with his Panzer-Regiment 3. Veiel's 2. Panzer-Division was temporarily slowed by the difficulty of resupply fuel after the capture of Kraków; Polish stragglers ambushed one fuel column and the Germans were still repairing destroyed bridges along their lines of communication. On the morning of 8 September, Major Janusz Rowiński's 3rd Battalion of the 5th Regiment of Podhale Rifles moved into the Niepołomicka Forest, 25km east of Kraków. The Polish troops were spotted by a local *Volksdeutsche*, Jakub Mattern, who reported their presence to troops from the 2. Panzer-Division. Elements of the 2. Panzer-Division immediately attacked the Polish battalion, killing at least 49, capturing others and scattering the rest. The fate of this battalion was typical for Polish units that found themselves left behind. However, there were survivors and they were aware of the role played by Jakub Mattern. In May 1943, a Polish underground court found Mattern guilty of assisting the enemy and he was executed by the Home Army.[76]

On List's left flank Vietinghoff's 5. Panzer Division and SS-Regiment 'Germania' acted as a semi-independent pursuit group and flank guard. Rundstedt ordered that 5. Panzer-Division should be prepared to co-operate with 10. Armee in reducing the Polish Kielce Operational Group, so it was focused to the north/north-east, rather than on pursuing Army Kraków. List was also more cautious than Blaskowitz and did not want his flanks bothered by Polish counter-attacks. On List's right flank, the XVIII Armeekorps moved to clear the rest of the Carpathian passes. Fabrycy's Army Karpaty retreated too quickly, failing to destroy bridges over the Dunajec at Nowy Sącz. On 8 September, 2. Gebirgs-Division captured Gorlice while Generalmajor Ludwig Kübler's 1. Gebirgs-Division secured the Dukla Pass. The Polish 2nd Mountain Rifle Brigade was caught by surprise at Krosno and destroyed.

Army Kraków was unable to make a stand on the Dunajec River. The 6 DP and 21 DPG tried to cross the river north-west of Tarnow on the night of 7/8 September but were attacked by Kleist's troops while in the process of crossing. Due to 'tank panic', the bridge was prematurely blown up, stranding many troops on the west bank. The 21 DPG was decimated and fewer than 5,000 of its troops made it across the Dunajec.[77] Likewise, much of the 6 DP was lost – only one infantry regiment and about ten artillery pieces made it across the river. The survivors headed towards Jarosław on the San River. Fabrycy ordered the 24 DP to abandon its positions on the Dunajec and retreat to the San River – against express orders from Rydz-Śmigły to support the 6 DP and 21 DPG. Kleist's motorized troops quickly bridged the Dunajec on the night of 8/9 September and Hubicki's 4. leichte-Division caught up with the retreating 24 DP near Tuchow and overran three of its battalions. Hubicki then bypassed the retreating Polish units to seize Dębica, then pressed on to Rzeszow. The German rapid advance had split the tenuous boundary between Army Kraków and Army Karpaty; Army Malopolska would never be a unitary entity. Polish forces were in full retreat, heading for the imagined safety of the San River, but Hubicki's 4. leichte-Division was already closer to that river. The Jagmin Operational Group from Army Kraków tried to make a stand at Sandomierz on the Vistula, but Viettinghoff's 5. Panzer Division captured the city on 9 September and the VIII Armeekorps was closing in from the south-west, with the 8. and 28. Infanterie-Divisionen.

The one Polish unit in Army Malopolska that managed to conduct an efficient retreat was Maczek's 10 BK. Thanks to his brigade's mobility, Maczek was able to stay just ahead of Kleist's Panzers and reach Jarosław on the San River by the morning of 10 September. The local commander had gathered four reserve infantry battalions and a few artillery batteries to defend this key point, which was insufficient to hold off Kleist.[78] Veiel's 2. Panzer-Division soon arrived and captured Jarosław by 2100 hours on 10 September. Maczek ordered the bridge over the San blown up and retreated towards Lwów. However, Hubicki's 4. leichte-Division crossed the San further south at Radymno. Many Polish prisoners and equipment were captured by the rapid enemy advance and it was clear that Army Malopolska, now headquartered in Lwów, would not be able to form a line behind the San. It was also plain that exhaustion was taking its toll on both sides. By this point, most of List's 'leg' divisions from the VIII and XVII Armeekorps were 80–100km behind the German spearhead and were struggling to keep up. Likewise, Szylling's retreating divisions were disintegrating. The Jagmin Operational Group (6th, 23rd and 55 DPs)

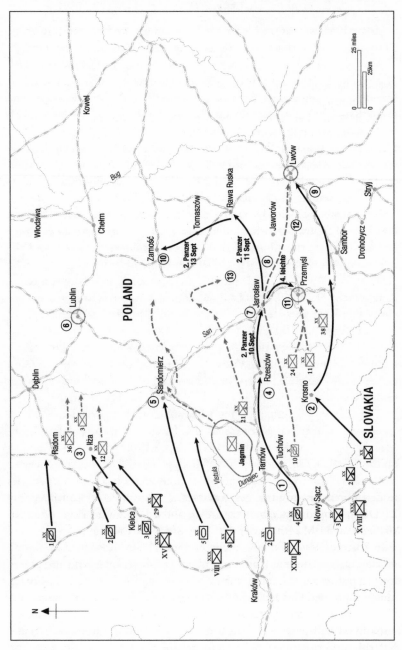

MAP KEY

1) 8 September. Army Kraków's attempt to make a stand on the Dunajec River fails.
2) 8 September. The 1. Gebirgs-Division destroys the Polish 2nd Mountain Rifle Brigade at Krosno.
3) 8–9 September. The XV Armeekorps (mot.) crushes part of Operational Group Kielce in the Battle of Iłza.
4) 9 September. The 4. leichte-Division bypasses retreating Polish units and reaches Rzeszow.
5) 9 September. The 5. Panzer-Division captures Sandomierz.
6) 9–10 September. Army Lublin forms to try to link up with Army Kraków.
7) 10 September. The 2. Panzer-Division captures Jarosław.
8) 11 September. Once across the San River, the XXII Armeekorps (mot.) divides to take Przemyśl and Rawa Ruska.
9) 12 September. The 1. Gebirgs-Division launches a surprise attack on the outskirts of Lwów.
10) 13 September. The 2. Panzer-Division advances through Tomaszów Lubelski to seize Zamość.
11) 13 September. Retreating Polish divisions reach Przemyśl. Two days later, after heavy fighting, the city is abandoned.
12) Night 15/16 September. The 11 DP overruns a battalion of the SS-Regiment 'Germania'.
13) 16 September. The Polish 21 DPG is surrounded and destroyed.

headed north-east towards Sandomierz, the Boruta Operational Group (21 DPG) moved eastwards on its own and the three divisions of Army Malopolska (11th, 24th and 38 DPs) headed towards Przemysl.

In Brześć, Rydz-Śmigły recognized that List's army was almost effortlessly overrunning southern Poland and that something had to be done to restore some kind of order. On the night of 10 September, Rydz-Śmigły appointed Generał Broni Kazimierz Sosnkowski to take command of Army Malopolska; by which he meant all forces in southern Poland.[79] Sosnkowski had been sidelined for years due to political disagreements with the Sanacja regime, but he was the most talented senior officer in the Polish Army. He immediately flew to Lwów to organize the defence of the city and to try and salvage something from the retreating wrecking of the frontier armies. When Sosnkowski arrived in Lwów he was amazed to find that this city of 316,000 residents was defended by only five battalions (two of which were ON) and a couple batteries of 75mm guns – roughly 3,500 troops. Generał Brygady Franciszek Sikorski*, who had been recalled from retirement, was in tactical command of the city's garrison. Rydz-Śmigły promised reinforcements for Lwów, including the reserve 35th Infantry Division (35 DP) from Grodno and the new 21st Light Tank Battalion (21 BCL), equipped with French R35s.

Once Kleist had a bridgehead across the San, he redirected Hubicki's 4. leichte-Division southwards to eliminate the Polish garrison at Przemyśl, which was the headquarters of the DOK X. The Poles had a garrison of about 8,000 troops in the town, along with several batteries of 105mm howitzers, so they were able to repulse Hubicki's initial attack on 11 September. It was critical for the Poles to hold Przemyśl as long as possible, since both the 11 and 24 DP were retreating towards it in order to escape towards Lwów. Once it was clear that the Poles would make a stand at Przemyśl, List directed the 7. Infanterie-Division and 2. Gebirgs-Division to converge on the town, although these formations were still two days march away. In order to prevent the other pieces of Army Kraków from reaching Lwów, Kleist sent the 2. Panzer-Division towards the north-east, to establish blocking positions near Rawa Ruska.

Sikorski had very little time to organize Lwów's defence since the lead elements of 2. Panzer-Division and 4. leichte-Division were across the San River and moving east by the evening of 12 September – which spelled disaster for Army Malopolska. Only the shortage of bridging material slowed Kleist's advance. In addition, Kübler's 1. Gebirgs-Division had steadily advanced through the Carpathians from Slovakia and had reached the outskirts of Lwów from the south. Fabrycy's Army Karpaty had completely failed in its mission to delay the advance of the XVIII Armeekorps. On the afternoon of 12 September, Kübler's advance guard – led by Oberst Ferdinand Schörner's Gebirgsjäger-Regiment 98 – launched a surprise attack on the south-west corner of the city which nearly succeeded. The Gebirgsjäger were elite troops but were handicapped by their limited artillery support, which reduced their ability to fight their way into a major city. Fortunately, the first train-load of Rydz-Śmigły's promised reinforcements arrived in Lwów on the night of 12/13 September with 6,500 troops from the reserve 35 DP and a

*Executed by the Soviet NKVD at Katyń Forest in 1940.

large shipment of ammunition. On the morning of 13 September, Kübler's 1. Gebirgs-Division attacked the north-west corner of the city and seized a key hill. Unable to storm the city, Kübler hoped to slowly encircle the city. Polish reinforcements continued to arrive in Lwów, including Maczek's 10 BK, and civilian volunteers created anti-tank barricades around the city.

Further adding to Polish problems, Ukrainian nationalists from the Organization of Ukrainian Nationalists (OUN) (which prior to the war had been funded by the German Abwehr) came out of hiding and instigated a vicious guerrilla campaign in Galicia. On the night of 12/13 September, a large group of armed OUN members seized control of the town of Stryj, 60km south of Lwów. Polish civilians in Stryj and nearby areas were murdered by Ukrainian nationalists. Local Polish commanders were obliged to scrape up an *ad hoc* force, built around a march battalion from the 49th Infantry Regiment (49 PP), to crush the rebellion. After two days of fighting, the rebellion in Stryj was crushed, but OUN rebels continued to plague the Poles in Galicia until the Soviet intervention.

Most of the LW's remaining operational aircraft had withdrawn to south-east Poland by this point: the Pursuit Brigade with about 50 fighters and the Bomber Brigade with 52 bombers. Daily sortie rates were low due to shortages of fuel and ground support crew at remote strips. One group of bombers operated from Hutniki airfield near Brody and was able to conduct 35 sorties on 12–14 September against German forces advancing in southern Poland. However, the Luftwaffe discovered Hutniki airfield and bombed it on the afternoon of 14 September and again the next morning, destroying 17 P.23b Karaś; this was the only time during the campaign that the Germans succeeded in destroying a large group of Polish aircraft on the ground. Due to fuel shortages, the bombers could not be evacuated in time. After this, the remaining Polish bombers were relocated to even more remote airfields such as Horodenka on the Romanian border.

While Lwów was improving its defences, Sosnkowski tried to rescue the Polish divisions that were trying to reach Przemyśl and cross the San. If these divisions could be saved, they could be used to reinforce the defence of Lwów. Sosnkowski flew to Przemyśl in a light aircraft to lead these isolated units in a breakout effort to reach Lwów. By the evening of 13 September, the 11th Infantry Division (11 DP) had reached Przemyśl but the Germans had nearly surrounded the city. The next day, Sosnkowski left a small rearguard in Przemyśl, then led the breakout of the three Polish divisions. In order to avoid the Luftwaffe, the units marched mostly at night and through forested areas. Fifteen kilometres south-east of Przemyśl, the 24 DP bumped into the 2. Gebirgs-Division and fought a nasty meeting engagement around the heavily forested village of Boratycze. After significant casualties on both sides, the Polish column managed to fight their way past the Gebirgsjäger by evening.[80] When Kleist learned that Polish units were escaping from Przemyśl, he accelerated the assault on the city and decided to send a motorized unit to block the Przemyśl-Lwów corridor; the SS-Regiment 'Germania' and the III./Artillerie-Regiment 109 (eight 15cm s.FH18 howitzers) were dispatched. An advance guard, consisting of SS-Hauptsturmführer Johannes-Rudolf Mühlenkamp's Kradschützen-Kompanie, established a blocking position in the village of Sadowa Wisznia, 40km east of Przemyśl. However, during the night of 13/14 September, two Polish infantry battalions from 38 DP overran this position. Mühlenkamp (who would later command the SS-Panzer-Division 'Wiking' in 1944) and ten of his men were captured and 19 killed.[81]

On the morning of 14 September, the German 7. Infanterie-Division attacked Przemyśl with strong air and artillery support. Nevertheless, the Polish rearguard battalions put up a very tough fight – suffering over 1,000 casualties – which prevented the Germans from achieving quick success. Having accomplished their mission, the garrison left the city during the night of 14/15 September. The Germans occupied the burning wreckage of Przemyśl on the morning of 15 September. Meanwhile, Sosnkowski's group continued to infiltrate eastwards. During the night of 15/16 September, elements of the 11 DP overran the III./'Germania' in the village of Mużyłowice, killing its commander, SS-Obersturmbannführer Heinrich Köppen, and 22 of his men. Around the same time, a regiment from the 38 DP overran the attached artillery unit in the nearby village of Czarnokonce, destroying most of the artillery, a battery of 8.8cm Flak guns and multiple vehicles.[82] The night combat was at close quarters and intense – two Polish company commanders were killed – but SS 'Germania' retreated in disorder.[83] Sosnkowski's group continued marching eastwards and by dawn were within 35km of Lwów. The 24 DP was in the best shape with 10,000 troops and 22 artillery pieces while the 11 DP still had about 8,000 troops and 30 artillery pieces. Alarmed by the failure of the Waffen-SS to stop Sosnkowski's group, Kübler was forced to detach blocking units from his own division to try and prevent these Polish reinforcements from reaching Lwów. The weakening of the German operation against Lwów led Maczek to spearhead a counter-attack with his brigade on 16 September that recovered some ground.

Lacking anti-tank guns and running low on supplies, the Gebirgsjäger could not stand up to Maczek's TKS tankettes and the Polish had better artillery support.

Aside from Lwów, the rest of Army Malopolska was unable to make a stand anywhere. Szylling continued to lead his Jagmin group (6th, 23rd and 55 DPs) north-east towards Zamość in order to link up with Piskor's Army Lublin. However, Veiel's 2. Panzer-Division quickly advanced through Tomaszów Lubelski and seized Zamość by 1700 hours on 13 September. The VII and VIII Armeekorps were also hard on Szylling's heels with five infantry divisions, advancing 20–25km per day. Nevertheless, the Jagmin Group managed to affect a link-up with Army Lublin south-west of Zamość on 16 September; Piskor assumed control of the combined force. By this point, the 2. Panzer-Division had left Zamość and Hubicki's 4. leichte-Division was left to screen a 30km-wide sector between Zamość and Tomaszów Lubelski. Piskor hoped to mount an attack in force on Tomaszów Lubelski, spearheaded by his best unit – Pułkownik Rowecki's Warsaw Armoured-Motorized Brigade – in order to break through the German cordon and escape southwards towards Lwów. Due to the general disorganization of the battered Polish units and shortage of supplies, a breakout effort would not be possible prior to 17 September. In order to gather another fuel for the attack, the Poles had to siphon petrol from non-essential vehicles and give it to Rowecki's brigade; 300 immobilized vehicles were then destroyed. Meanwhile, Generał Brygady Józef Kustron's 21 DPG broke off from Szylling's group in an effort to take a more direct route to Lwów but instead it was surrounded by the 45. Infanterie-Division near Oleszyce, 45km north-east of Przemyśl on 16 September. After a tough fight in which Kustron died leading a breakout attempt, the remnants of the division surrendered. Another group, led by Pułkownik Władysław Anders (consisting of the Kresowa, Nowogródzka and Volhynian Cavalry Brigades) was near Lublin and trying to make its way towards a link-up with Piskor's army as well. Although a large number of Polish units were still moving about in south-central Poland, the combat effectiveness of these formations was rapidly declining due to lack of supplies. On the night of 17/18 September, the city of Lublin with its population of 1.2 million was abandoned to the approaching German IV Armeekorps without a fight.

In light of the deteriorating situation everywhere, Rydz-Śmigły had already tasked Army Malopolska to maintain a corridor of retreat to neutral Romania (the so-called Przedmurza Rumańskiego or Romanian bridgehead), in the hope that remnants of the Polish Army could regroup there – or flee across the border, if necessary. When his headquarters in Brześć became threatened, Rydz-Śmigły moved to Młynów (near Dubno) on 13 September and then, two days later, moved to Kołomyja, only 70km from the Romanian border. The constant shifting of the Polish General Headquarters did more damage to Polish operational-level C^2 than German bombing and ensured that Rydz-Śmigły would play only a minor role in the Second Republic's final days. The 21 BCL, equipped with French R35 tanks, never reached Lwów but was instead sent to Stanisławów to protect the Romanian bridgehead – and Rydz-Śmigły's headquarters.

CHAPTER 7

Apotheosis

---

*'Warsaw will not be taken by assault, none of my soldiers will fall.
The Luftwaffe and artillery will destroy all subsistence and services.
In three or four days Warsaw will capitulate.'*
Adolf Hitler, 18 September 1939

Warsaw Under Attack, 9–16 September

Despite the failure of Reinhardt's initial assault on Warsaw's south-western suburb of Ochota on the afternoon of 8 September, Hoepner was determined to give it another go the next morning. Although the bulk of Richthofen's Stukas were diverted on this day to the Iłza sector, Major Spielvogel from II./LG 2 intended to provide air support for Reinhardt's next attack. Soon after dawn, Spielvogel decided to conduct a leader's reconnaissance in a Fieseler Storch but this did not go well – Spielvogel's aircraft was shot down by Polish anti-aircraft fire and he was killed.[1] Consequently, Reinhardt decided to rely upon his own divisional artillery, even though his forward observers were not in a position to observe targets concealed in the distant urban landscape. After a short, ineffective artillery preparation, the 4. Panzer-Division renewed its attack into the Ochota district at 0700 hours, with Oberst Hermann Breith's

Panzer-Regiment 36 on the left and Eberbach's Panzer-Regiment 35 on the right (each Panzer regiment had one battalion in the lead and one following in support). Infantry support was provided by Schützen-Regiment 12.[2] The Germans attacked on a broad front, nearly 5km in width – essentially a sweep and clear operation. Initially, the attack went well and the first two Polish street obstacles were breached, but sniper fire from rooftops and machine-gun fire from ground level soon pinned down much of the German infantry. Both Panzer-Regiments continued to advance along Warsaw's boulevards, but with less and less infantry still in support. On Wołoska Street, a single well-camouflaged 37mm anti-tank gun from the 40 PP's anti-tank battery fired at a range of just 100m and knocked out seven tanks from Panzer-Regiment 35. Oberleutnant Heinz-Günther Guderian, eldest son of General Guderian, was among those who had their tank disabled and had to flee on foot. Breith's advance was halted by a single 75mm gun from the 29th Light Artillery Regiment, which knocked out six tanks and two armoured cars. The Polish infantry from the 40 PP also engaged the German tanks at close range – infantry has the advantage in urban combat – throwing grenades and satchel charges at them. The Poles also tried to set Wołoska Street on fire with barrels of turpentine. Some German tanks ran onto mines, laid to discourage flanking movements. One platoon of three PZ II tanks from Panzer-Regiment 36 managed to penetrate as far as Narutowicza Square, but was stopped by a barricade. A Polish 7TP tank appeared and destroyed one of the Pz IIs, convincing the others to retire. After four hours of being battered and unable to make further progress, Reinhardt called off the attack. The German tanks retreated under cover of smoke grenades.

Reinhardt's 4. Panzer-Division lost at least 42–45 tanks on 9 September (30 from Panzer-Regiment 35 and 15 from Panzer-Regiment 36), plus a number of other vehicles. Eberbach's regiment was left with only one of its Pz IV medium tanks still operational, out of the original six. Prior to this action, no one had ever committed a large tank formation into a city and neither Reinhardt nor Hoepner could be sure how their Panzers would perform on the narrow streets of Warsaw – it was an experiment. However, the results were pretty clear – even armour supported by artillery and infantry was at a disadvantage in a city. Thereafter, German Panzer-Division commanders would try to avoid attacking into defended cities – at least until Stalingrad in 1942. Following this attack, 4. Panzer-Division shifted to a defensive posture, to repair its damaged tanks. Due to the strength of the Polish resistance, the Germans greatly exaggerated the size of the Polish garrison in the capital – which made it easier to explain away a tactical defeat. Reichenau told Hoepner to wait for 10. Armee's infantry to arrive, since they were better suited for city combat. However, the beginning of the Polish counter-offensive on the Bzura forced Hoepner to shift most of his XVI Armeekorps (mot.) to assist 8. Armee. The 31. Infanterie-Division was brought up to replace 4. Panzer-Division on the south-western outskirts of Warsaw. The Germans established themselves around Okęcie airfield, which was littered with wrecked and partly completed Polish aircraft.

While the German ground threat to Warsaw had temporarily ebbed, the Luftwaffe was still very much a threat. Pułkownik Stefan Pawlikowski's Pursuit Brigade had been reduced to just 16 operational fighters after six days of combat, but on 7 September it began to be reinforced with fighters withdrawn from army-level aviation units. Consequently, the Pursuit Brigade then possessed over 50 operational fighters – still a significant force if used at the right time and place. However, before the amalgamation process was complete, Pawlikowski was ordered to leave Warsaw and relocate his brigade to airfields around Lublin on 7 September. The hasty relocation left the Pursuit Brigade without fuel, ground support personnel or communications for several days. Just as the Pursuit Brigade was regaining some operational capability on 9 September, it was ordered to withdraw to the south-east corner of Poland, close to the Romanian border. Essentially, the Pursuit Brigade was out of action for the second week of the campaign, depriving both the capital and Polish field armies of even occasional air cover. On 16 September, the Pursuit Brigade scored its last victory, shooting down a German Hs 126 reconnaissance aircraft east of Sandomierz. As a result of the Pursuit Brigade's removal to south-east Poland – rather than German air superiority – the Polish capital was deprived of fighter cover. Instead, Warsaw would have to rely for air defence (*obrona przeciwlotnicza* or OPL) upon its limited complement of anti-aircraft artillery, numbering 24 40mm guns and 72 75mm guns (including eight of the new 75mm wz. 37 guns), but these point defence weapons were inadequate to cover the whole city.

Meanwhile, Generał Rómmel – now in command of Army Warsaw (Czuma remained as commander of the Warsaw garrison) – used the brief respite after Reinhardt's repulse to organize his forces, aided by his able chief of staff, Generał Brygady Tadeusz Tomaszewski. The Warsaw Defence Command divided the city into two sectors – the main one on the west side of the Vistula (which had 80 per cent of the city's population) and the secondary one on the east side. Initially, the bedrock of the defence rested upon five regular infantry battalions (the III/26 PP and I, II, III/40 PP from 5 DP and the II/41PP from 29 DP), along with their small contingent of support units. Since there were plenty of reservists, ON troops and civilian volunteers in Warsaw, Podpułkownik Jakub Chmura from the KOP was put in charge of forming them into a four-battalion regiment designated as the 360th Infantry Regiment (360 PP). One of the volunteer machine gunners in the II/360 was the 32-year-old runner Janusz Kusociński*, who had won a gold medal in the 1932 Los Angeles Olympic games. Two march battalions (IV/21 PP and IV/30 PP) provided additional infantry replacements. A labour brigade was also formed from volunteers, to dig trenches and help create street barricades. Although Rómmel was soon able to field over 10,000 troops, the main shortcoming of Army Warsaw was lack of fire support assets. Altogether, the garrison had about 40 75mm field guns, 12 120mm guns and 12 155mm howitzers, but these were spread over a fairly large area and most of the field guns were used in the direct-fire role. Anti-tank guns were in particularly short supply. On the positive side, ammunition stockpiles for most weapons was adequate for at least a week or two of fighting and there were several armament factories within the environs of Warsaw that could produce more, including the Zakłady Amunicyjne 'Pocisk' (ZAP) in the eastern suburb of Praga. The Norblin, Bracia Buch i T. Werner SA factory in central Warsaw was capable of producing up to two million rifle cartridges per month, as well as artillery ammunition. The state-run Armoury No. 2 in Praga was also capable of repairing damaged weapons and manufacturing machine guns.

Three days before the Germans arrived in Ochota, the Armoured Weapons Training Centre in Modlin had begun to form several small armoured units from its school personnel and training/testing vehicles.[3] All three companies were sent to Czuma's command to help defend the capital; these units consisted of:

- The 1st Light Tank Company, led by Kapitan Feliks Michałkowski. The company consisted of 11 7TP tanks (seven were the twin-turret version armed with two machine guns, the other four were armed with a 37mm gun).

*Executed by the Gestapo in 1940.

- The 2nd Light Tank Company, led by Kapitan Stanisław Grąbczewski. The company was provided with 11 factory-fresh 7TP tanks, some of which were improved models (the so-called '9TP' light tank).
- An armoured reconnaissance company, led by Kapitan Antoni Brażuk. The company was equipped with 11 TKS and TK3 tankettes.

Although his forces were limited, Rómmel did not intend to just passively wait in Warsaw for the end. Once the Germans were distracted by the battle of the Bzura, Rómmel took the opportunity to mount an active defence. On 10 September, he ordered Grąbczewski's 2nd Light Tank Company to mount an armoured raid in the north-west suburbs of Warsaw to the edge of the Kampinos Forest, hoping to open a pathway for units marching east from the Bzura. Grąbczewski's light tanks spent the entire day manoeuvring in this area and found that the 4. Panzer-Division was thinly spread and not expecting Polish tanks to sortie from the city. In the course of two meeting engagements, Grąbczewski's company destroyed two tanks from Panzer-Regiment 36, destroyed several trucks and captured some prisoners, then returned to the city at midnight. Buoyed by that success, Rómmel hoped to catch the Germans off-guard and recapture Okęcie airfield on the southern outskirts of Warsaw. This time, Rómmel planned to use both light tank companies to support an attack by the II./Infantry Regiment 360 The attack began from Mokotów at 0500 hours on 12 September, by which point the Poles probably knew that 4. Panzer-Division had been replaced by the 31. Infanterie-Division. Initially, the Polish attack went well, pushing back a German battalion (II./Infanterie-Regiment 82) towards the airport. German infantry did not like being attacked by more than 20 enemy tanks and retreated. However, as the Polish tanks and infantry continued to advance, they unexpectedly bumped into Infanterie-Regiment 33 (mot.) from the 13. Infanterie-Division (mot.) – an enemy unit that the Poles were unaware was near the capital. German defensive fire from their attached *Panzerjäger* (tank destroyers) was intense, knocking out seven Polish tanks. The surviving Polish tanks managed to cover the retreat of the Polish infantry, but Podpułkownik Chmura was killed.[4] Following the repulse of the Polish sortie on 12 September, ground combat activity around Warsaw diminished for a time, since the Germans were distracted by the battle of the Bzura and the Poles were trying to build up the Army of Warsaw. During this period, the city was not under siege since the Germans had not yet encircled the city and lines of communication

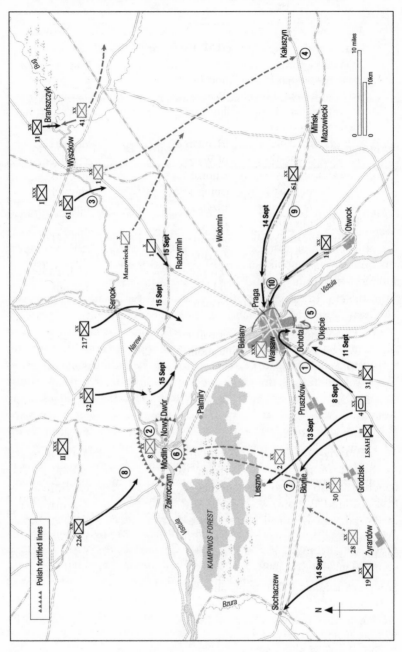

MAP KEY

1) 8–9 September. Two attempts by the 4. Panzer-Division to storm the south-west suburbs of Warsaw fail with heavy losses.
2) 9 September. The Modlin garrison establishes an all-around defensive perimeter.
3) 9 September. The German 61. Infanterie-Division conducts an assault crossing of the Bug west of Wyszków. The 11. Infanterie-Division crosses at Branszczyk. Operational Group Wyszków withdraws.
4) 11–12 September. The pursuing 11. Infanterie-Division catches up with the 1 DPL near Kałuszyn and there is a hard fought action, but the Polish units escape.
5) 12 September. Polish counter-attack against Okęcie airfield fails.
6) 13 September. Elements of Army Łódź reach Modlin.
7) 13 September. The LSSAH advances to Blonie and 4. Panzer-Division to Lesznoto try and block the retreat of Army Łódź.
8) 13–14 September. The German II Armeekorps begins investing Modlin.
9) 13–14 September. The German I Armeekorps pivots west to cut Warsaw's lines of communication.
10) 15 September. The I Armeekorps attack on Warsaw's eastern suburbs fails.

to eastern Poland were still open. Reichenau's 10. Armee only had the 31. Infanterie-Division and part of the 13. Infanterie-Division (mot.) south-west of the city. Aside from Warsaw and rescuing 8. Armee, Reichenau also had to divert forces to clear up stragglers from Army Prusy around Radom, west of the Vistula. Indeed, the German Army in Poland was so spread out at this point, pushing in every direction, that no single field army had a large force that could immediately move against Warsaw. Furthermore, Warsaw lay in the nebulous boundary zone between Heeresgruppe Nord and Heeresgruppe Süd, with neither army group yet assigned full responsibility for taking the city.

In order to capture a large city, it is imperative to isolate it, in order to prevent further reinforcements and supplies from getting in. Given that Warsaw had a pre-war population of over 1.2 million residents, the city simply could not stockpile enough food to withstand a long siege. The key position for Warsaw's fate was Wyszków, 50km north-east of the capital.

Even before Operational Group Wyszków abandoned its positions on the Narew, Generalleutnant Walter Petzel's I Armeekorps was preparing to cross the Bug River at Wyszków. Polish defences along the Bug were very thin – consisting primarily of the 1 DPL and Mazowiecka Cavalry Brigade near Wyszków, plus some remnants of the 31 and 41 DP. A smaller force, consisting of elements of the 33 DP and Podlaska Cavalry Brigade, was guarding the crossing sites at Brok. Although Operational Group Wyszków managed to blow up all the bridges over the Bug in this sector, the river did not prove a serious obstacle. At 0900 hours on 9 September, the German 61. Infanterie-Division conducted an assault crossing of the Bug west of Wyszków. Later in the day, the 11. Infanterie-Division crossed the Bug east of Wyszków at Brańszczyk. The 1 DPL conducted a successful counter-attack against the Brańszczyk bridgehead, but the 61. Infanterie-Division managed to build a pontoon bridge and was pouring across the Bug. Once it was clear that the Germans were across the Bug, Operational Group Wyszków began withdrawing towards the south-east.

The retreat of Operational Group Wyszków quickly turned into a disaster. The 11. Infanterie-Division caught up with the 1 DPL near Kałuszyn and tried to surround the Polish division. However, the 1 DPL made a bold night attack on 11/12 September to break through the attempted encirclement, which was highlighted by a mounted cavalry charge by the 4th squadron of the 11th Uhlans Regiment (Mazowiecka Cavalry Brigade). Infanterie-Regiment 44 suffered heavy casualties during the night action.[5] The Poles managed to escape southwards, but the 1 DPL was badly depleted. Further east, Panzer-Division Kempf and the 1. Infanterie-Division crossed the Bug east of Brok and quickly demolished the 33rd and 41 DPs by late on 10 September. Kempf then pushed south, far ahead of Korps Wodrig marching towards Garwolin to sever the Warsaw–Lublin highway. The only significant Polish force left east of Warsaw was Group Anders, formed from the Nowogródzka Cavalry Brigade and part of 10 DP. However, Anders was retreating to the south-east, away from Warsaw. Panzer-Division Kempf was unable to prevent Group Anders from slipping past and then found itself isolated and virtually immobilized for three days (12–14 September) since it was 30km beyond Korps Wodrig and Polish units were retreating across its lines of communication. After Korps Wodrig caught up, Panzer-Division Kempf was pulled back to regroup and refit. Yet with Warsaw now open to attack from the east, Bock directed Küchler on 13 September to complete the encirclement of Warsaw with Petzel's I Armeekorps (11. and 61. Infanterie-Division) as soon as possible. Although Bock ordered Küchler to capture the bridges over the Vistula, he cautioned him not to get drawn into costly city fighting.[6] General der Infanterie Adolf Strauß's II Armeekorps (32., 217. and 228. Infanterie-Divisionen) were ordered to deal with Polish resistance at the Modlin fortress.

However, Bock was unwilling to make a larger effort against Warsaw because he believed that the Polish Army was trying to regroup around Brześć.The knowledge that Rydz-Śmigły had relocated his headquarters to Brześć probably influenced Bock's decision-making process. Consequently, after crossing the Narew Guderian's XIX Armeekorps (mot.) (with 3. and 10. Panzer-Divisionen and 2. and 20. Infanterie-Divisionen (mot.)) was ordered to advance to Bielsk to disperse Polish forces in that area and then to push on to capture Brześć. By the evening of 13/14 September, Guderian's vanguard was within 30km of Brześć.[7] However, Rydz-Śmigły had left Brześć two days prior and no Polish army was forming in the city. Bock was also distracted with the idea of occupying north-east Poland to prevent Polish forces from regrouping around Białystok or Grodno. Falkenhorst was ordered to attack towards the north-east with his XXI Armeekorps, which led to the capture of Białystok on 15 September. Yet aside from the Podlaska and Suwalska Cavalry Brigades, there were no substantial Polish forces left in this sector. Bock had encouraged the dissipation of his army group's efforts by pursuing too many objectives, on divergent axes, at one time.As a result, a total of only three German infantry divisions (one from Heeresgruppe Süd and two from Heeresgruppe Nord) were committed against Warsaw by mid-September.Yet the level of command indecision displayed by the Germans in dealing with Warsaw is remarkably missing from most accounts of the 1939 campaign.

While the Germans dithered as to what to do about Warsaw, Polish units from the shattered frontier armies continued to trickle into the capital to reinforce Army Warsaw. On 13–14 September, survivors from Army Modlin reached Warsaw, including about five battalions from the 20 DP and Pułkownik Stanisław Sosabowski's 21 PP. Czuma immediately assigned Sosabowski to defend the Grochów district, on the east side of the Vistula, along with two battalions of volunteers. Sosabowski established his regimental command post near the vital 'Pocisk' ammunition factory. The 20 DP was assigned to defend the northern part of Praga.These tired formations had barely 24 hours to prepare defences before the first elements of Petzel's I Armeekorps reached the edge of the city on the morning of 15 September. Petzel decided to attack from the line of march – just as Hoepner had done – with the 11. Infanterie-Division making the main effort against Sosabowski's 21 PP in Grochów and the 61. Infanterie-Division on its right against the 20 DP in Praga.[8] After probing attacks in the morning, the German attacks escalated in the afternoon and attempted to push down Grochówska Avenue. Sosabowski's regiment put up fierce resistance and halted the German advance towards the Vistula bridges.[9] Nevertheless, Küchler's 3. Armee had succeeded in severing Warsaw's lines of communication to the east, although a small corridor remained open to Modlin.

Bock ordered Küchler to request that the Warsaw garrison surrender and on the morning of 16 September, Petzel sent a delegation under a white flag to discuss terms, but Rómmel had no interest in capitulation.[10] The Luftwaffe also sent He 111s from I./KG 4 over Warsaw to drop leaflets warning that the Germans would soon launch a major attack on the city unless the garrison surrendered.[11] At noon, Petzel resumed his attacks in the eastern suburbs, but made very little progress. The Poles launched several local counter-attacks which spoiled the German effort to push into Praga. By the end of 16 September, Warsaw was under loose siege, although neither 3. Armee on the east side of the Vistula nor 10. Armee on the west side had the strength to break into the city. Hitler and the OKH were not sanguine about an all-out assault into Warsaw due to the prospect of heavy casualties. Halder argued that food shortages and bombardment would quickly bring Warsaw to its knees.[12] For once, Hitler and his generals were in agreement and late on 16 September Hitler ordered major ground attacks in Warsaw suspended, although local actions could continue.

Meanwhile, Fortress Modlin continued to hold out and provided a haven for the survivors of the battle of the Bzura. Strauß's II Armeekorps made a few small attacks on the Polish defensive perimeter north of the Vistula but otherwise focused on gradually cutting off the narrow corridor that led to Warsaw. On 13 September, about 4,000 survivors from Army Łódź's Operational Group Piotrków (28th and 30 DPs) reached Modlin through the Kampinos Forest, along with Generał Brygady Wiktor Thommée. Rómmel ordered Thommée to take command of the Modlin fortress. By 16 September, Thommée had about 15,000 troops under his command, along with 96 artillery pieces and seven TK3 tankettes.[13] Although Modlin only had modest air defence capabilities, one battery of 40mm anti-aircraft guns in the fortress claimed to have shot down 24 German aircraft during the siege. Since Heeresgruppe Süd failed to adequately block the escape routes through the Kampinos Forest, more survivors from the Bzura continued to reach Modlin. Eventually, Thommée would amass nearly 40,000 troops under his command.

In eastern Poland, Guderian began his attack on Brześć on 14 September, even though the Germans knew that Brześć lay within the Soviet sphere of influence assigned by the Molotov–Ribbentrop Pact and that Soviet intervention in Poland was imminent. Brześć was the headquarters of DOK IX and was primarily a mobilization and supply base in event of war with the Soviet Union, but by mid-September most of its troops had been sent westwards. Before leaving Brześć on 11 September, Rydz-Śmigły appointed Generał Brygady Konstanty Plisowski*, a sickly cavalry officer who had retired years before, to organize the defence of the city. Plisowski had fewer than 4,000 troops at hand – just three 'march' battalions of reservists, the 56th Sapper Battalion, 18 light field guns and two light tank companies with a total of 36 obsolete FT17 tanks. When alerted to the German approach by aerial reconnaissance, Plisowski deployed blocking detachments north of the Brześć citadel to buy more time to organize the fortress for defence, but was unable to man the smaller satellite forts. Twelve FT-17s from the 113th Light Tank Company, a company of infantry and the Armoured Train No. 53 were assigned to delay the enemy advance.

Schaal's 10. Panzer-Division approached Brześć from the north, late on the morning of 14 September, led by I./Aufklärungs-Regiment 8 and II./Panzer-Regiment 8. Oberst Botho Elster, commander of Panzer-Regiment 8, decided to conduct a leader's reconnaissance and discovered that the Poles had not manned the city's outer defensive positions. Elster opted to mount an immediate attack, sending one tank company to occupy Fort No. 2 at 1430 hours. There was no resistance. Elster pushed on and his tanks reached the main train station in Brześć at 1539 hours. However at this point, the German vanguard came under fire from Armoured Train No. 53, which was armed with two 100mm howitzers and two 75mm guns. The Polish 113th Light Tank Company appeared and engaged the tanks of Oberstleutnant Ramsauer's II./Panzer-Regiment 8. Unfortunately, the slow-moving FT17s were no match for the German tanks and ten were quickly knocked out. As the German armour continued to advance into the city, they came under artillery and sniper fire. Eventually, the Polish troops retreated into the citadel, blocking the entrances with the remaining FT-17 tanks. With night approaching, Elster pulled his forces back to regroup.[14] The vanguard of 3. Panzer-Division also moved into the north-east environs of Brześć before sunset. During the night, the lead elements of the 20. Infanterie-Division (mot.) approached the north-west corner of Brześć. Guderian planned to attack Brześć the next day with all three divisions.

*Executed by the Soviet NKVD at Katyń Forest in 1940.

On 15 September, Guderian began the day by using his divisional artillery and Luftwaffe air support to pound the Brześć citadel. Following this 'softening up', he mounted several attacks upon the citadel during the afternoon, but each was repulsed in turn. Generał Plisowski was wounded during the day, but remained in command. Guderian launched another attack on 16 September, with the 10. Panzer-Division and 20. Infanterie-Division (mot.) – it failed. Amazingly, a 19th-century fortification, held by an outnumbered group of reservists, managed to fend off Germany's best divisions for over two days. At Brześć, German tanks were easily thwarted and the battle dragged on due to Guderian's mistake of cramming too many units into a small area. However, the Polish defenders had suffered heavy losses in the process and Plisowski decided to abandon the citadel during the night of 16/17 September. Despite the fact that the Germans had the citadel surrounded, the bulk of the garrison escaped during the night and escaped southwards to link up with Generał Brygady Franciszek Kleeberg's Independent Operational Group Polesie. Early on 17 September, Infanterie-Regiment (mot.) 76 entered the abandoned citadel.

The Soviet Invasion, 17–22 September

'The destruction of this state [Poland] in the present conditions
would mean one less bourgeois fascist state! What would be bad if,
as a result of the defeat of Poland, we extended the socialist
system to new territories and population?'

Stalin, 7 September 1939[15]

Despite signing a peace treaty with Poland in 1921, the Soviet Union almost immediately began a campaign of subversion in the eastern Kresy region to undermine Polish control over these provinces. First the OGPU in the 1920s, then the NKVD in the 1930s were directed to recruit from the Belarusian and Ukrainian populations in eastern Poland. With the support of the Moscow-based Comintern, the Communist Party of Western Belarus (KPBZ) was established in 1923 and demanded return of the eastern border provinces to the USSR – resulting in the suppression of the party by the Polish government. Consequently, the KPBZ went underground, conducting subversive activities and covertly receiving arms provided by the OGPU–NKVD; during the inter-war period members of the KPBZ conducted terrorist-style actions against Polish local officials and police in Kresy. One of the KOP's primary missions, aside from border protection, was to counter the illegal activities of the KPBZ. Meanwhile, the Communist Party of Poland (KPP) tried to act like a legitimate political party; it was allowed to participate in Polish elections but was regarded with great suspicion. Not surprisingly, the KPP was financed by Moscow and was regarded as a means to gain influence over Polish workers' organizations. However, Stalin changed his mind about the utility of these organizations in 1937–38; the leaders of the KPP were summoned to Moscow and executed as part of the great purge. Stalin ordered the KPBZ suppressed, but about 4,000 members were still active in eastern Poland at the start of the war.

Once *Fall Weiss* began, Stalin carefully monitored events in Poland, but he was in no hurry to enter an ongoing war. After the Anglo-French declared war on Germany, Stalin's preference was to maintain friendly relations with Germany under the terms of the Molotov–Ribbentrop Pact, but not to appear as a military ally. Fighting on the same side as the Third Reich would be even more of an ideological contradiction than the Soviet–German diplomatic rapprochement and endanger Moscow's control over the worldwide communist movement. As it was, many communists in the West were confused by the Molotov–Ribbentrop Pact. Instead, Stalin preferred to harvest the corpse of the Polish state, once the Wehrmacht had done the fighting, thereby remaining out of the international spotlight. Unlike Hitler, Stalin was not a risk-taker. In Warsaw, Rydz-Śmigły hoped that the Soviet Union would remain neutral but ordered the KOP to round up known members of the KPBZ in Kresy; hundreds were arrested.

The Soviet reluctance to initiate military operations against Poland was soon noted by the Germans. On the same day that the Anglo-French declared war on Germany, Ribbentrop sent a diplomatic note to Moscow asking when Soviet troops would cross into Poland. Two days later, Molotov replied that 'We agree with you that at the right time it will be absolutely necessary for us to begin concrete actions. We believe, however, that this time has not yet come.' On the same day, 5 September, the Politburo enacted measures which amounted to a partial military mobilization; reservists were called up for units in the military districts bordering Poland and military supplies were ordered. However, Soviet decision-making was opaque to the Germans and all that the OKH could see was that the Red Army were sitting on the sidelines, waiting for the Wehrmacht to deliver them their slice of Poland for free. Further German diplomatic queries were met by the response from Molotov on 10 September that the Soviets would not be ready for military intervention for another two to three weeks. In Moscow, Stalin preferred not to make a move until Warsaw had fallen, in which cause the Soviet Union could claim that it had not violated its non-aggression treaty with Poland.

The Soviet Invasion, 17–22 September 1939

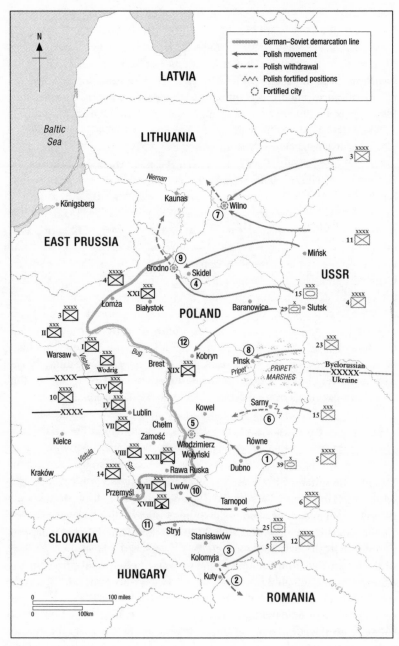

Map key

1) 17 September. The Soviet 39th Light Tank Brigade from 5th Army advances rapidly, overrunning both Dubno and Łuck, capturing over 15,000 Polish troops.
2) Night 17/18 September. The Polish Government and thousands of military personnel cross into Romania.
3) 18 September. The Soviet 5th Cavalry Corps occupies Kolomyja.
4) 18 September. Pro-Soviet uprising by armed KPZB members in town of Skidel.
5) 18 September. Polish efforts to regroup at Włodzimierz Wołyński are frustrated by the rapid Soviet advance.
6) 19–20 September. KOP units briefly defend the Sarny Fortified Area against the Soviet 15th Rifle Corps.
7) 20 September. Wilno is occupied by Soviet 3rd Army after a brief fight.
8) 20 September. Pinsk is occupied by the Soviet 23rd Rifle Corps.
9) 20–22 September, The Soviet 15th Tank Corps occupies Grodno after heavy fighting.
10) 22 September. Lwów surrenders to the Soviet 6th Army.
11) 22 September. The Germans turn the Drohobycz oilfield over to the Soviet 12th Army.
12) 22 September. The Soviet 29th Light Tank Brigade reaches Brest and Guderian hands the city over to the Red Army after a joint military parade.

Despite the spheres of influence delineated by the secret protocol of the Molotov–Ribbentrop Pact, the Germans and Soviets had not discussed in any detail what they would do with Poland. Hitler was committed to the destruction of Polish military capabilities but he was willing to countenance the existence of a rump Polish state, at least for a time. In order to get that rump state, the Polish government would have to sign a peace treaty, which Hitler regarded as a potential means to get the Anglo-French to drop their belligerent status. While the Poles were highly unlikely to sign any treaty with Hitler at this point – since he would surely crush the rump state once it had served its purpose – Halder's diary indicates that this idea was actively under discussion within the German High Command. Halder also noted that Hitler was mooting the idea of an independent West Ukraine; in other words, if the Red Army was not going to fight to gain the territory allotted under the secret protocol, then Hitler would decide what happened in this region.[16] While Hitler's political intentions are open to debate, it is clear that he never ordered the OKH to impose operational restrictions upon the Wehrmacht in regard to the agreed Soviet sphere of influence in eastern Poland. Indeed, right up to the moment of Soviet intervention, German forces from both army groups were still attacking full-force into areas that had been allotted to the Soviet Union.

It was the German push into eastern Poland which accelerated the Soviet timetable. On the afternoon of 14 September, Molotov informed the German ambassador in Moscow that 'the Red Army reached a state of readiness sooner than expected', and that Soviet military intervention was imminent. The German Foreign Ministry signalled its approval of the Soviet decision and noted that 'conditions may arise [in Poland] for the formation of new states' – a clear nod to the possibility of forming a rump Polish state. Earlier in the day, Marshal Kliment Voroshilov, minister of defence, issued a directive to the commanders of the Byelorussian and Kiev military districts, which contained guidance for the invasion of eastern Poland. In classic Stalinist style, the military district commanders were given only two days to prepare for an operation involving over 600,000 troops and 4,700 tanks. Logistic factors were simply ignored. Planning was rushed and amateurish. Few units even had maps of Poland. Furthermore, the rules of engagement provided to Soviet troops were extremely muddled; the troops were entering Poland as 'liberators' and should refrain from bombarding Polish towns and firing upon Polish troops – unless they resisted. On the other hand, Soviet propaganda had labelled the Poles as capitalist oppressors, so they were class enemies who deserved no restraint. Likewise, Soviet troops were told to avoid provoking German troops but could fire upon them, if necessary.[17]

The Red Army had to do its best to prepare an invasion force in the two days allotted, but not all units were ready in time. Polkovnik Ivan N. Russianov's 52nd Rifle Division, in the 4th Army, was a so-called 'Urai' division, assigned to construct and defend a fortified area – the unit had not been training for mobile warfare.[18] Even those units that had trained for mobile operations were hindered by low operational mechanical readiness of tanks and motor vehicles. In the Byelorussian military district, Komandarm II Mikhail P. Kovalyov would command four armies (3, 4, 10 and 11) and the Dzerzhinsky Cavalry-Mechanized Group; a total of

13 rifle divisions, six cavalry divisions and eight tank brigades. The 3rd Army was assigned to capture Wilno, the 11th Army to capture Grodno. In the Kiev military district, Komandarm I Semen K. Timoshenko formed three armies (5, 6 and 12) with a total of nine rifle divisions, seven cavalry divisions and eight tank brigades. The Soviet Air Force (VVS) could provide up to 2,000 aircraft (roughly 1,200 fighters, 600 bombers and 200 reconnaissance) to support the operation.

On the opposite side of the border, the Poles had sent most of their troops west to fight the Germans, leaving barely 12,000 KOP troops to guard the 1,400km long border with the Soviet Union. Generał Brygady Wilhelm Orlik-Rückemann, a Polish tank officer, was in charge of the KOP forces. He was in the process of reconstituting his KOP battalions with volunteers and older reservists when the Soviet invasion began. Although about 600,000 Polish troops were still under arms, they were either cooped up in places like Warsaw and Modlin, or retreating from the Germans – no reserves were left. More than half the remaining troops were heading south towards the Romanian bridgehead.

At 0315 hours on 17 September 1939, Wacław Grzybowski, the Polish ambassador in Moscow, was called to the Soviet Foreign Ministry.[19] Once there, Molotov's deputy, Vladimir Potyomkin, proceeded to begin reading a note which stated that:

> The Polish–German war has revealed the internal failure of the Polish state. Within ten days of military operations, Poland lost all its industrial areas and cultural centres. Warsaw as the capital of Poland does not exist anymore. The Polish government fell apart and shows no signs of life. This means that the Polish state and its government have virtually ceased to exist. Thus, the agreements concluded between the USSR and Poland are terminated. Left to itself and without leadership, Poland has become a convenient field for all sorts of coincidences and surprises that could pose a threat to the USSR. Therefore, being neutral until now, the Soviet government cannot continue to be neutral with regard to these facts. The Soviet government also cannot be indifferent to the fact that Ukrainians and Belarusians living in Poland, abandoned to their fate, are left defenceless. In view of this situation, the Soviet government has ordered the High Command of the Red Army to order its troops to cross the border and take under their protection the lives and property of the population of Western Ukraine and Western Belarus. At the same time, the Soviet government intends to take all

measures to rescue the Polish people from the ill-fated war, where it was plunged by its unwise leaders, and give them the opportunity to lead a peaceful life.[20]

Ambassador Grzybowski immediately refuted the notion that the Polish state had disintegrated and refused to accept the note. Later, Potyomkin would be in charge of pushing the Soviet narrative that the Germans were responsible for the Katyń Forest massacre. Forty-five minutes later, the first Soviet troops began crossing the Polish border. Nor did the Soviets respect the concept of Polish diplomatic immunity. Ambassador Grzybowski only avoided arrest due to the intervention of other senior members of the foreign diplomatic corps in Moscow, including the German ambassador, Friedrich-Werner Graf von der Schulenburg (who wanted to ensure that German diplomats abroad were granted immunity from reprisals). However, the Polish consul in Kiev, Jerzy Matusiński, received no such protection – he was arrested by the NKVD and executed a month later.[21]

Timoshenko's Ukrainian Front advanced quickly against minimal resistance. At most border crossing sites there were only squad-size detachments of Polish border guards, who were killed or captured. Rydz-Śmigły, who was still located with his staff in Kolomyja, was shocked by news of the Soviet invasion but immediately realized that Poland could not simultaneously fight both Germany and the Soviet Union. Thus, he ordered Orlik-Rückemann not to resist the Soviet invasion but to withdraw with all his troops towards the Romanian bridgehead. The same order was given to those units in south-central Poland that could reach the Romanian or Hungarian borders. However, Orlik-Rückemann and other local commanders ignored this order – they could not simply abandon the field to the hated enemy. Orlik-Rückemann was located in the one place near the border where there was still a significant KOP presence – in the Sarny Fortified Area, about 55km west of the Polish–Soviet border. Although still incomplete, the Sarny Fortified Zone had 207 concrete bunkers and a residual garrison of about 4,000 KOP troops. Komdiv Vasily I. Repin's 15th Rifle Corps (5th Army) advanced slowly towards the Sarny Fortified Zone, on a narrow front. It took the lead unit, the 60th Rifle Division, two days to advance to Sarny, which gave Orlik-Rückemann time to prepare his small garrison for combat. During the night of 18/19 September, the 60th Rifle Division, including a few T-26 tanks, crossed the Sluch River and began attacking the Polish bunkers before dawn. One Polish officer stated that the Soviet soldiers 'behaved like a herd of sheep' and advanced mindlessly into fields of fire, which cost them heavy casualties. However, the Soviets had heavy weapons and the Poles did not. In some cases, Soviet tanks drove right up to casemates and fired their main gun directly into apertures, stunning or killing the crews inside. Nevertheless, the Poles resisted for 24 hours, until bunkers were surrounded and the crews ran out of ammunition. On 20 September, Orlik-Rückemann ordered a retreat to the Styr River, where he hoped to regroup with other KOP units. In the battle of Sarny, one Polish battalion was destroyed, with 229 dead and 301 captured or missing. Soviet losses were in the hundreds.

Further south, the rest of the Soviet 5th Army advanced towards Dubno and Brody, while the 6th Army captured Tarnopol on the first day. Many Polish troops near the border were caught by surprise before they could react. In Dubno, Generał Brygady Stefan Strzemiński began evacuating the city but the sudden arrival of Kombrig Mikhail Bogomolov's 39th Light Tank Brigade (5th Army) at 0630 hours on the morning of 18 September cut off the escape of two regiments of reservists, totalling about 6,300 troops; the troops allowed themselves to be disarmed. From Dubno, Bogomolov pivoted north and reached Łuck at 1900 hours, capturing another 9,000 Polish troops. The remaining Polish troops in this area retreated west, with the intent of regrouping at Włodzimierz Wołyński. However, Bogomolov's 36th Light Tank Brigade advanced 8km during the night and attacked the town at dawn. The senior Polish officer in Włodzimierz Wołyński, Generał Brygady Mieczysław Smorawiński* (commander of the DOK II), agreed to Soviet surrender terms which stipulated that his troops would be disarmed but allowed to proceed south to Hungary. After the surrender, Smorawiński and his officers were arrested by the NKVD. Although Stalin's purges had wreaked great havoc on the Red Army, Bogomolov's performance indicates that there were still some talented and aggressive officers available.

Komdiv Vasiliy Gonin's 5th Cavalry Corps (12th Army), supported by tanks, headed straight for Rydz-Śmigły's headquarters in Kolomyja. Local KOP commanders attempted to form a line on the Dniestr River, but Soviet tanks reached the bridges before a defence could be organized. When Rydz-Śmigły heard an alarmist report that Soviet tanks were nearby – although they were still over 50km distant – he relocated to the village of Kuty, on the Romanian border. Józef Beck crossed the border

---

*Executed by the Soviet NKVD at Katyń Forest in 1940.

to meet with the Romanian ambassador to arrange for the passage of the Polish government through to the port of Constanta, where they hoped to embark for France. With luck, Rydz-Śmigły and other senior Polish leaders would be in Paris in a few weeks, where they could establish a government-in-exile. That was the tentative plan, anyway. Carton de Wiart, head of the British military mission (as he had been in 1919 too), tried to convince Rydz-Śmigły to remain on Polish soil, but was ignored.[22]

That evening, Rydz-Śmigły gave his final radio address, ordering military and government personnel to evacuate to Romania and Hungary. He ordered Warsaw and Modlin to continue resistance, but otherwise made no mention of Poles continuing the war either at home or abroad. It was a shameful speech for a Polish commander to make, containing a tone of abandonment. President Ignacy Mościcki, nearby in the town of Kosów, also made a radio address to the nation, calling on Poles 'to preserve the firmness of spirit and courage in the fight against soulless barbarians.' Unlike Rydz-Śmigły, Mościcki stated that the Polish government would transfer 'to the territory of one of our allies.'[23] After some deliberations with his staff, Rydz-Śmigły decided to cross the bridge over the Czeremosz River before dawn on 18 September, into internment in Romania. The rest of the Polish government followed suit, including President Mościcki, Prime Minister Składkowski and Foreign Minister Józef Beck. Now Poland was without a functioning government. The Soviet invasion also threatened the LW's remaining airfields in eastern Poland. Initially, Polish fighters engaged some Soviet aircraft, shooting down two SB-2 bombers and two reconnaissance aircraft, for the loss of one P.11C fighter.[24] Yet by the afternoon of 17 September, the surviving aircraft and personnel of the Pursuit and Bomber Brigades were crossing the border to Romania – leaving Poland without an air force.[25] The 21 BCL was also ordered to cross into Romania with its 34 R35 tanks, having seen virtually no action against the enemy. The Red Army occupied Kolomyja on 18 September and Stanisławów on 19 September, effectively eliminating the Romanian bridgehead.

Thousands more Polish troops crossed the border into Romania before the Red Army arrived, including the Second Department's Cipher Bureau. The three most important Polish code-breakers – Marian Rejewski, Henryk Zagalski and Jerzy Różycki – were all evacuated to Romania, then France; they managed to take two replica Enigma machines with them.[26] Poland was also able to evacuate the bulk of its gold reserves, about 75 tonnes, first to Romania, then to Dakar in French West Africa.

However, the Germans managed to seize $5 million in Polish gold reserves from customs facilities in Danzig.[27] A number of important persons were also flown out by special flights by LOT (the Polish national airline), including Józef Piłsudski's widow and his two daughters, who were flown from Latvia, to Sweden, to Norway and then Scotland.

When news of the Soviet invasion was announced, the KPZB began to conduct armed attacks in the north-east part of Poland. On 18 September, about 200 armed members of the KPZB took control of the town of Skidel, east of Grodno. However, Polish troops arrived the next day and dispersed the KPZB rebels; 30 of them were shot. Numerous other incidents occurred around Wilno, Grodno and Postway, as armed communist rebels sniped at Polish troops and policemen. In many towns, large numbers of Jewish residents also welcomed the Soviet invaders, which reinforced existing Polish prejudices that Jews were not loyal to the Second Republic.[28] In eastern Galicia, Ukrainian OUN nationalists also took the opportunity to conduct random violence and loot towns as the Polish Army retreated; about 600 Polish civilians were murdered.[29] One Polish convoy was ambushed by OUN rebels on the night of 18/19 September, resulting in 32 Polish soldiers killed. In a number of towns in Kresy, the Ukrainians and Belarussian population displayed banners welcoming the Soviet invaders.[30] As Polish authority waned, communist revolutionary committees moved to fill the vacuum, seizing power in towns. Once the Red Army arrived, KPBZ members donned red armbands and served as auxiliary militia, helping the NKVD to identify those people who supported the Second Republic.[31]

Some of the heaviest fighting against the Red Army occurred in north-east Poland, against Kovalyov's Byelorussian Front. Medvedev's 11th Army sent the 36th Cavalry Division and the 6th Light Tank Brigade to seize Wilno, supported by the 24th Cavalry Division and two light tank brigades from Komkor Vasily Kuznetsov's 3rd Army; altogether, a combined force of about 25,000 troops and 800 light tanks. The Soviet strike force was noticeably tank-heavy, but it had very little artillery and infantry – it was not a combined arms force of the kind that the Wehrmacht preferred to use in its vanguard elements. In Wilno, the Poles had a day to organize their defence, which was not impressive. Since the 1 DPL had been sent west, the only forces remaining in the city were three KOP battalions, three march (replacement) battalions for the 1 DPL, three volunteer battalions and one small cavalry squadron – a grand total of about 6,000 mostly untrained troops. The Wilno garrison was particularly short of heavy weapons, possessing fewer than a dozen 75mm field guns and a few anti-tank guns. Furthermore, the local commander in the city was indecisive, uncertain whether to defend the city, or to abandon the city and escape to Lithuania. The first elements of the 11th Army's 36th Cavalry Division reached the south-east suburbs of Wilno around 1700 hours on 19 September and skirmished with the KOP Battalion 'Troki'. It quickly became apparent to the defenders that they could not stop large numbers of tanks without anti-tank weapons and during the night, the Poles gradually began evacuating the city. On the morning of 20 September, the 6th Light Tank Brigade pushed into the city against significant resistance. The Poles managed to knock out five BT-7 tanks and a BA-10 armoured car, but they could not prevent the Soviets from seizing the bridges over the Neris River. The three KOP battalions marched westwards to internment in Lithuania (from whence quite a few would reach France) while the other units either tried to reach Grodno or broke up. The Soviets admitted 37 casualties in the fighting in Wilno, which was probably below the actual number.

Timoshenko sent his most capable force – Komkor Ivan V. Boldin's Dzerzhinsky Cavalry-Mechanized Group – to seize Grodno. The vanguard of this strike group was led by Komdiv Mikhail Petrov's 15th Tank Corps and the 21st Light Tank Brigade. Grodno was nearly 200km from the Soviet border, which would be the longest advance that Soviet tanks had ever made in a single bound up to this point. Fuel was a major problem for the armoured units since logistic planning was minimal prior to the invasion and the T-26 tank could only go about 90km on one load of fuel. Furthermore, many of the tanks were in mechanically poor condition – about 12 per cent of the BT-7 and 18 per cent of the T-26 tanks broke down on the road march.[32] Along the way, the Soviet tanks occupied Baranovichi, then continued west. In Grodno, the situation was confused. Generał Brygady Józef Olszyna-Wilczyński*, commander of the DOK III, believed that defending the city was hopeless since there were barely 2,000 reservists in two march battalions. He left the city on 19 September without appointing anyone to command the remaining garrison. Roman Sawicki, a mathematics teacher and deputy mayor, inserted himself into the command vacuum and began organizing a defence in co-ordination with junior military officers who remained in the city. Sawicki was able to

---

*Executed by the Soviet NKVD at Katyń Forest in 1940.

rally large numbers of teachers, students, scouts from the Polish Scouting Association (Związek Harcerstwa Polskiego or ZHP), policemen, firemen and other volunteers to dig trenches, erect barricades and fill incendiary bottles with petrol. While preparing their defence, the Poles also had to contend with armed KPBZ members and other pro-communist elements, who sniped at them from rooftops.

The first Soviet troops, from Petrov's 15th Tank Corps, approached Grodno from the south-east on the morning of 20 September. A reconnaissance company of BT-7 tanks was able to rush past the thinly manned outer positions, but was swarmed once it entered the city. In close combat, the Poles destroyed at least three BT-7 tanks with petrol bombs and damaged others, forcing the unit to withdraw. In particular, teenage Polish scouts attacked the tanks with reckless abandon; 19-year-old Janusz Budzanowski destroyed one BT with a petrol bomb but was mortally wounded by machine-gun fire from another tank. Later in the day, the Poles were reinforced by about 1,000 troops from the Reserve Cavalry Brigade 'Wołkowysk', but their lack of artillery and anti-tank weapons was telling. During the night of 20/21 September, the rest of the 15th Tank Corps reached the outskirts of Grodno and Petrov planned a full-scale attack for the next day. On the morning of 21 September, Petrov attacked the southern suburbs of Grodno with over 80 tanks and some motorized infantry. The Poles resisted fiercely, fighting street to street. Tadeusz Jasiński, a 13-year old volunteer, died after a failed attack on a Soviet tank with a petrol bomb. Gradually, the Soviets used their superior firepower to push their way towards the city centre, but by late afternoon Petrov's tankers were running out of fuel and ammunition. The Soviet attack paused for the rest of the day, enabling a large part of the garrison to escape to Lithuania. Roman Sawicki remained with the final rearguard to buy time for the others to escape and Petrov did not capture the rest of Grodno until noon on 22 September. About 1,000 Poles may have been captured in Grodno, at least 130 of whom were summarily executed by the NKVD.[33] The Soviets admitted suffering over 200 casualties in Grodno and the loss of 19 tanks. Interestingly, a fair number of those Poles who fought in the defence of Grodno survived to fight either in the West or at home in the Home Army.

As soon as the Red Army occupied areas, the NKVD was quick to move in. The Soviets were particularly keen to eliminate the Polish military settlers (*Osadnicy*) – of whom there were over 40,000 – who had moved into the Kresy region after the Russo-Polish War. Indeed, Soviet authorities branded the Osadnicy as 'enemies of the people' and treated them as the Kulaks had been treated in the 1920s. Ethnic Belarussians and Ukrainians were particularly helpful in eliminating the Osadnicy, then looting their property.[34] However, as military veterans, the Osadnicy often fought back. When NKVD troops arrived to arrest one retired Polish artillery officer, Adam Sielicki, he shot the first two dead with his pistol. The other NKVD soldiers then shot Sielicki down and riddled his corpse with bullets.

Surprisingly, the Wehrmacht continued attacking Polish forces in eastern Poland even after they learned of the Soviet invasion. Halder issued a stop order to the field armies, which was apparently *pro forma*. Indeed, after the Soviet intervention began German commanders seem to have lost interest in mopping up the remaining Polish units in favour of securing key terrain. After the fall of Brześć, Guderian's XIX Armeekorps (mot.) continued 50km east to Kobryń, where the 2. Infanterie-Division (mot.) was stopped by fierce resistance on 17–18 September from an improvised Polish division-size force, Pułkownik Adam Epler's 60th Infantry Division (60 DP). However, as Red Army units approached from the east, Epler broke off the action and headed south with his troops into the Pripet Marshes. On 20 September, the reconnaissance elements of Kombrig Semyon Krivoshein's 29th Light Tank Brigade, the vanguard of Komkor Vasily I. Chuikov's 4th Army, met Guderian's troops 24km north of Brześć. Although the meeting was amicable, it is amazing that no effort was made to establish liaison officers prior to actual physical link-up.

The 13. Infanterie-Division (mot.) had crossed the Vistula and seized Dęblin on 16 September. One of Poland's largest ammunition depots was located in the northern suburb of Stawach, which was still under control of Generał Brygady Bruno Olybrycht's reserve 39 DP. The depot had a vast stockpile of arms and ammunition, including 197,000 rifles, 3,000 rkm wz. 28 automatic rifles, 1,500 machine guns and 275 artillery pieces. However, Generał Dywizji Stefan Dąb-Biernacki, whom Rydz-Śmigły had placed in charge of the Northern Front, ordered Olybrycht to abandon Dęblin and march to join him at Chelm. Consequently, Olybrycht ordered his sappers to set the depot on fire; although some material was salvaged or moved elsewhere, the loss of arms and ammunition was a disaster.[35]

At Lwów, Kübler's 1. Gebirgs-Division still did not have the city surrounded. Since Sosnkowski's group (11th, 24th and 38 DPs) was still clawing its way towards Lwów through the Janów Forest, Kübler was forced to divide his forces, sending some troops west to block Sosnkowski.

An intense battle occurred in the Janów Forest on 17–18 September, with the German 7. Infanterie-Division attacking Sosnkowski's group from the west and the 44. Infanterie-Division from the north, while the Gebirgsjäger acted as an anvil in the east. The Luftwaffe was called in to bomb Sosnkowski's group, further disrupting it. Despite horrendous losses, Sosnkowski's group reached the outskirts of Lwów late on 19 September, just as Soviet troops reached the eastern side of the city. Only about 500 Polish troops made it into the city past the German cordon. The sole organized unit to reach Lwów was a reserve infantry battalion, led by Major Henryk Dyduch*. Sosnkowski ordered the remainder to break up into small groups and try to reach Hungary. List still wanted to try and capture Lwów before the Soviet arrival, but Sosnkowski's adventure had been a major distraction. The next day, Hitler ordered Rundstedt to disengage from Lwów and leave the city to the Red Army. Inside Lwów, Generał Brygady Władysław Langner (overall commander of the city) recognized that the situation was hopeless once the Soviets arrived, but did his best to save what could be saved. Maczek's 10 BK was the only unit in Lwów with the mobility to escape and Langner ordered Maczek to take his brigade to Hungary.[36] Amazingly, Maczek slipped out before the ring was closed around Lwów and his brigade moved nearly 200km in about 36 hours. With flags flying, Maczek and about 1,500 of his men crossed the Hungarian border on the morning of 19 September.[37] On 22 September, Langner finally agreed to accept generous surrender terms from Komkor Filipp I. Golikov's 6th Army – which were quickly violated. The NKVD immediately began arresting all Polish officers in the garrison. One of those arrested was Kapitan Józef Baran-Bilewski†, a reserve artillery officer and former head of the Polish athletic team at the 1932 Los Angeles Olympics.

List had also ordered the 5. Panzer-Division to secure the Drohobycz oilfield on 17 September – even though this was allocated to the Soviet sphere of influence. The Germans occupied Drohobycz for five days before turning it over to the Soviet 12th Army on 22 September. The attempted breakout of Piskor's Army Lublin at Tomaszów Lubelski on 18 September provided List with an additional excuse to keep his 14. Armee east of the agreed demarcation line for more than a week after the Soviet invasion. At 0700 hours on 18 September, Pułkownik

*Executed by the Soviet NKVD at Katyń Forest in 1940.
†Executed by the Soviet NKVD at Katyń Forest in 1940.

Rowecki's Warsaw Armoured-Motorized Brigade launched a surprise attack against elements of Hubicki's 4. leichte-Division at Tomaszów Lubelski. This action was the largest use of Polish armour during the 1939 campaign, with 22 7TP tanks from the 1 BCL under Major Stefan Majewski, a company with 12 Vickers light tanks and about 30–40 TKS tankettes; altogether about 75 armoured fighting vehicles. Rowecki attacked with two parallel mixed infantry–tank assault groups. The northern group managed to push back the Kavallerie-Schützen-Regiment 11 and take 160 prisoners, but lost four Vickers tanks and eight TKS, robbing the attack of momentum. The southern group, personally led by Major Majewski, was more successful and managed to overrun German infantry positions and fight its way into Tomaszów Lubelski by 1300 hours, causing some panic among Hubicki's troops. However, Hubicki called in Luftwaffe air support and used his artillery to smash up Polish troop concentrations. By the afternoon, the Polish attack was running out of fuel and ammunition and casualties were approaching 50 per cent. Kleist dispatched an armoured Kampfgruppe from 2. Panzer-Division at Rawa Ruska to the rescue, which suddenly appeared on the Polish right flank. Majewski decided to break off the attack and withdraw. Altogether, Rowecki lost 12 7TP and four Vickers tanks and expended most of his fuel.[38] Hubicki's 4. leichte-Division suffered about 300 casualties, including 79 dead.

Despite the losses suffered in the first attack, Piskor was determined to break through, since the German VII Armeekorps and VIII Armeekorps were closing in from the west. The German 27. Infanterie-Division was already attacking his westernmost units. The Army of Lublin was now virtually surrounded and its supplies of food, ammunition and fuel were nearly exhausted. The handful of remaining artillery batteries had just 70 rounds left. On the night of 18/19 September, Piskor attacked Tomaszów Lubelski with the 11 PP (23 DP) and his remaining tanks. However, the Germans had reinforced the town with an infantry battalion from the 28. Infanterie-Division and had 32 tanks in direct support, along with plenty of artillery. The Polish infantry was repulsed with heavy losses, forcing their tanks to withdraw. Only seven Polish light tanks and 2 TKS were still operational. By the late afternoon of 19 September, Piskor and Szylling knew that the situation was hopeless – they had over 5,000 wounded troops in the pocket and almost no supplies left. Piskor ordered documents burned and the destruction of any equipment that could not be carried. One last desperate effort would be made to break out, in small groups if necessary. At 2000 hours, the Polish 11 DP moved forwards in three assault groups based upon its regiments, supported by the last seven tanks. Generals Piskor and Szylling marched on foot, like the rest. Although the Poles fought fiercely, the German defences were too strong and most of the tanks were knocked out by PaK guns or ran out of fuel. After hours of fighting, two battalions of the German Infanterie-Regiment 63 (27. Infanterie-Division) launched a counter-attack from the north, which broke the back of the Polish breakout effort.[39] At 1020 hours on 20 September, Piskor decided that his troops were incapable of further fighting and decided to surrender. Rowecki allowed troops from his brigade to try and evade in small groups through the woods; he himself was able to evade capture and reach Warsaw. Szylling also tried to evade but was caught. Later, List's 14. Armee announced the capture of 11,000 troops around Tomaszów Lubelski and another 3,000 further south. Subsequently, the Germans handed most of these prisoners over to the Red Army. Although Army Lublin was destroyed, other separate Polish units in the vicinity, such as the Dubno Group, continued to try and push towards the Hungarian border.

Polkovnik Ivan O. Yarkin's 25th Tank Corps (12th Army) advanced rapidly, capturing a bridge across the Dniestr River at Halicz on 19 September and then bumped into the German 57. Infanterie-Division near Stryj in the late afternoon of 20 September. After negotiations, the Germans turned over the city two days later. In order to block Polish troops from crossing into Hungary, the 12th Army moved the 13th Rifle Corps to occupy positions along the southern border.

On the morning of 22 September, Krivoshein's 29th Light Tank Brigade reached Brześć. Guderian was obliged to withdraw his forces west of the Bug River under the terms of the Molotov–Ribbentrop Pact, but on his own authority he suggested a joint German–Soviet military parade in Brześć prior to handing over the city. Krivoshein agreed. The Germans set up a large banner at the edge of the city, which said in Cyrillic: 'Greetings to the saviours from your oppression'. Guderian set up a nice reviewing stand for himself and Krivoshein (who was Jewish) to review the troops, while a German military band played the *Internationale*. At 1600 hours, the joint military parade began, including elements of the German 20. Infanterie-Division (mot.) and a battalion of Soviet T-26 tanks. Guderian even arranged for Luftwaffe fighters to fly low over the reviewing stand during the parade, apparently to impress Krivoshein. Afterwards, Guderian's troops withdrew across the Bug. By the evening of 22 September, all of Poland's major cities – save for Warsaw – were in either German or Soviet hands. The withdrawal of German forces from eastern Poland was slow – the Soviets later claimed that the Germans wanted time to loot occupied areas – and implemented in stages. Indeed, the German withdrawal would not be completed until the end of September. In the interim, the OKH mandated a 25km-wide buffer between German and Soviet forces to prevent incidents.[40] Officially, Stalin regarded the Soviet military intervention in Poland as completed.

In London, the reaction to the Soviet invasion was to ignore it. At a cabinet meeting on the morning of 18 September, Halifax was quick to point out that the Anglo–Polish military alliance only pertained to German aggression, not Soviet aggression. Chamberlain stated that he regarded the Soviet invasion with 'indignation and horror' but was opposed to issuing a formal protest – despite the appeals of Count Edward Raczyński, the Polish ambassador in London. As long-time allies of Poland, the French government initially pushed for a formal protest to the Soviet Union. Instead, the British Cabinet demurred but did spend considerable time discussing the need to import timber from the Soviet Union.[41] The implication was clear: for Chamberlain and Halifax, maintaining economic relations with the Soviet Union was important, keeping faith with their Polish ally was not. On 20 September, Chamberlain spoke vapidly about the Soviet invasion in the House of Commons, saying that 'it was still too early to pronounce any final verdict on the motives or consequences of the Russian action.'[42] A few days later, David Lloyd George wrote an opinion piece in the *Sunday Express*, which aped Soviet propaganda and praised the Soviet government for 'liberating their kinsmen from the Polish yolk.'[43] In Paris, initial enthusiasm melted away as French communist deputies openly praised the Soviet invasion for 'liberating' Ukrainians and Byelorussians.[44] Eventually Daladier's cabinet decided upon a low-level diplomatic message to Moscow, which fell far short of a formal protest. Chamberlain's cabinet stated that since the French had delivered a formal message on the subject, there was no need for Britain to duplicate this effort.[45] Neither the British nor French cabinets discussed the possibility of breaking diplomatic relations with the Soviet Union or severing economic relations. Within a short period of time, British diplomats began referring to the Soviet action in Poland as an 'intervention', while German actions were still described as an invasion. Unlike Hitler, Stalin got his half of Poland without censure or serious reaction from Poland's unreliable Anglo-French allies.

Warsaw and Modlin, 17–29 September

*'Nie damy się! Wolimy zagrzebać się w gruzach niż
poddać się Niemcom.'*
[We will not give in! We prefer to bury ourselves in
rubble than surrender to the Germans.]

Popular Slogan in Warsaw during the Siege

After the battle of the Bzura ended, the Wehrmacht in Poland shifted its focus to crushing Polish resistance in Warsaw as quickly and painlessly as possible. However, this did not prove as easy as it might have seemed. It was already clear that Rómmel was not interested in surrender talks and that the Army of Warsaw had grown into a considerable force. Generał Brygady Wiktor Thommée's garrison in Modlin had also grown into a real nuisance. The lines of communication for Küchler's 3. Armee from East Prussia ran across the Narew and Bug, but this territory would soon have to be handed over to the Red Army in compliance with the terms of the Molotov–Ribbentrop Pact. Since Modlin blocked the logical alternative supply route for 3. Armee, Küchler would be logistically constrained until this thorn was removed.

Sensing that the campaign was all but over, the Luftwaffe had begun transferring bomber units to the western front, leaving Luftflotte 1 and Luftflotte 4 with just 91 level-bombers (three Gruppen of Do 17s from KG 77) instead of the 19 bomber Gruppen with nearly 600 bombers available at the start of the campaign. German ground forces were also extremely dispersed across Poland by 17 September and rather disorganized. Bock's Heeresgruppe Nord had 4. Armee spread out between Bialystok and Brześć, leaving only Küchler's threadbare 3. Armee in the Modlin–Warsaw region. Rundstedt's Heeresgruppe Süd had 8. Armee re-organizing around Kutno, 10. Armee was pushing east towards Lublin and 14. Armee was fighting between Zamość and Lwów. A number of divisions were already being pulled out of the line by the OKH to refit and re-organize. Consequently, the Poles in Modlin and Warsaw were given time to re-organize and strengthen their defences; throughout the Polish campaign, the Wehrmacht demonstrated a recurring failure to quickly finish off defeated enemy forces.

When the Soviet invasion began, the German siege of Warsaw was a half-hearted effort, with only Küchler's 3. Armee involved in direct combat against the Polish capital. Furthermore, Küchler could not focus all his resources against Warsaw since he had to assign two divisions (32. and 228. Infanterie-Divisionen) from Adolf Strauß's II Armeekorps to encircle the Modlin garrison. Even this force proved insufficient, as Thommée's garrison was reinforced by survivors of the battle of the Bzura. Eventually, Thommée had elements of four divisions with about 35,000 troops in Modlin, which was too big for II Armeekorps to handle alone. Bock was obliged to scrape up individual companies and part of Brigade Eberhardt to reinforce the thinly manned siege lines around Modlin.[46] Küchler also had difficulty trying to create siege lines around Warsaw and the capital maintained a functioning rail link with the Modlin garrison. Unknown to the Germans, the Poles still had a large stockpile of artillery ammunition stored in Palmiry, on the eastern side of the Kampinos Forest. While Küchler had the 11. and 61. Infanterie-Divisionen from Generalleutnant Walter Petzel's I Armeekorps (3. Armee) on the east side of the Vistula, there were large gaps in the north. Küchler was forced to assign the 1. Kavallerie-Brigade to the siege lines on the north-east side of Warsaw, since he lacked other readily available units. Petzel lacked the strength to make anything other than probing attacks and these did not go well. On 17 September, Sosabowski's 21 PP repulsed a German battalion-size attack and took 120 prisoners. The situation on the west side of the Vistula was even worse for the Germans, since the only significant force was the 31. Infanterie-Division from Reichenau's 10. Armee.

Given the porous nature of the German siege lines, thousands of troops from the battle of the Bzura continued to reach Warsaw from the north-west, through the Kampinos Forest. Reichenau sent the 1. leichte-Division into the forest on 18 September in an effort to block this avenue, expecting only disorganized stragglers. Instead, the 1. leichte-Division encountered General Brygady Abraham Roman's Wielkopolska Cavalry Brigade, which still possessed some of its TKS tankettes, artillery and anti-tank guns. The Polish cavalry brigade fought a series of vicious close-quarter battles in the forest north-west of Warsaw, demonstrating considerable tactical flair and aggressiveness. On the morning of 18 September, Roman sent his TKS tankettes ahead to reconnoitre a clear rout to Warsaw. Cadet Roman Edmund Orlik's platoon of three TKS tankettes reached the village of Pociecha, where he occupied an ambush position; Orlik's tankette was one of the few equipped with the new 20mm cannon, which gave him an anti-tank capability that other tankettes lacked. Soon thereafter, a tank platoon from the 1. leichte-Division approached and Orlik engaged the enemy column at a range of less than 100m. In moments, he destroyed three German tanks with rapid 20mm fire – probably two Pz-35t and one Pz IV – then disengaged. The German platoon leader, Prince Viktor Albrecht von Ratibor IV, died after being pulled from his burning tank. On the night of 18/19 September, dismounted cavalrymen from Roman's Wielkopolska Cavalry Brigade seized the village of Sieraków, 15km north-west of Warsaw. Among the prizes, the Polish cavalrymen captured 34 German trucks, loaded with fuel and supplies. Around 1000 hours on 19 September, the 1. leichte-Division launched a counter-attack at Sieraków but was repulsed with heavy losses from Polish anti-tank and artillery fire. Orlik claimed to have destroyed seven more tanks with his 20mm armed tankette, and overall German tank losses at Sieraków may have been as high as 31 destroyed.[47] On the night of 19/20 September, Roman's Wielkopolska Cavalry Brigade, including Orlik's tankettes, entered Warsaw; these were the only Polish armoured vehicles from the Bzura to reach the capital. The arrival of other elements of Army Poznań in Warsaw allowed Rómmel to form a tactical reserve of three infantry battalions.

Rómmel's army was also boosted by numerous civilian volunteers. Stanisław Mikołajczyk, a 38-year-old member of the Sejm joined the army and served as a private soldier. As in other Polish cities, teachers, students and women volunteered to serve in the Civil Guard (intended to fight fires and maintain order) or in labour units to dig trenches. The population of Warsaw were not apathetic but, rather, fully engaged in helping to defend their city.

Despite the fact that Polish units were slipping past the loose cordon to reinforce the Warsaw garrison, Rundstedt was slow to re-orient and re-organize Heeresgruppe Süd in order to make a greater contribution to the siege effort. Finally, on 19 September he assigned Blaskowitz's 8. Armee to move to Warsaw and deploy on the western side of the city for an eventual assault. At this point, 8. Armee consisted of General der Artillerie Emil Leeb's XI Armeekorps (18 and 19. Infanterie-Divisionen) and General der Kavallerie Maximilian von Weichs' XIII Armeekorps (10., 31. and 46. Infanterie-Divisionen). Blaskowitz was promised additional artillery and pioneer units, although it would take several days to transfer them from other formations, such as 10. Armee. Under the circumstances, neither Blaskowitz nor Küchler believed that they could mount a serious attack on Warsaw until at least 23 September. In the interim, the Germans pecked at Warsaw with limited air and artillery strikes. Hitler personally ordered 3. Armee to shell the Royal Castle, which was set afire. The flag of the President of Poland – who was now in Romania – still fluttered outside the castle, as its copper-plated roof buckled from the flames.[48] On 20 September, Stukas bombed Warsaw's main waterworks, smashing in the roof. Thereafter, the lack of water pressure made fire-fighting difficult and German artillery fire continually created new fires. The garrison was short on water, as well as food. Surplus army horses were already being eaten, although rations were still adequate. The next day, the Germans temporarily suspended the bombardment of Warsaw so that 800 foreign diplomats and their families could leave the city. Rainy and cloudy weather on 22–23 September impaired flight operations.

Küchler's 3. Armee dug trenches and laid barbed wire along its perimeter on the east side of the Vistula, and a First World War-style 'No Man's Land' developed in the space between German and Polish lines. German forward observers could see all the bridges over the Vistula and directed artillery fire against any movement detected over them – which made it difficult for the Poles to maintain contact with their forces in Praga. During daylight hours, there was little observable activity but the Germans used their mortars and light artillery to harass the enemy. The Poles had plenty of small arms ammunition but were running short of artillery ammunition and would only use it to repel enemy assaults. At night, the Poles conducted patrols and raids – which considerably annoyed the Germans. On 22 September, the German 61. Infanterie-Division conducted some probing attacks into the eastern suburb of Zacisze to test the defences – which proved quite strong. German artillery bombarded Praga, although not in great concentrations. Generaloberst Werner von Fritsch, the former head of the Heer whom Hitler had forced to resign in February 1938, had returned to the front as honorary colonel of his old regiment – Artillerie-Regiment 12 – which was part of Korps Wodrig. In truth, Fritsch was merely a supernumerary at this point and had no real duties. On 22 September, Fritsch and two other staff officers apparently decided to drive to the forward areas to observe German artillery fire. Near the front line, Polish troops fired on the trio of German officers and Fritsch was struck in the thigh; he bled out and died within a moment. Later that day, Hitler, Brauchitsch and Keitel arrived at 3. Armee headquarters and drove forwards to observe the bombardment of Praga from the tower of a church 5km from the front line.[49]

The Germans had difficulty amassing a pool of heavy artillery – with enough ammunition – to support a general offensive against Warsaw. Most of the Heeresartillerie (army and corps-level units) was stripped from 4. Armee and 10. Armee to reinforce 3. Armee and 8. Armee. In the rush to field new Panzer units, the Heer had focused on providing adequate numbers of field artillery for the new divisions (the 10.5cm l.FH18 and 15cm s.FH18 howitzers) but had neglected heavier artillery. German doctrine going back to Seeckt's Reichswehr had stressed mobility, not fighting in cities. Consequently, the largest weapon available in the Wehrmacht inventory in Poland was the Skoda 30.5cm howitzer, of which 17 had been seized in Czechoslovakia; it could hurl a 287kg high explosive (HE) projectile out to about 9–10km but had a very low rate of fire. Furthermore, the 20-ton Skoda weapon was difficult to move into place and required considerable support equipment. The best German-made weapon was the 21cm Mörser 18, which could fire a 113kg HE projectile out to 14–15km. Longer range came at the expense of greater barrel wear. However, Blaskowitz's 8. Armee was only provided with four 30.5cm howitzers and 12 21cm Mörser 18s, while Küchler's 3. Armee received just two 30.5cm and six 21cm howitzers; the Skoda howitzers fired a total of just 517 rounds during the campaign. The Heeresartillerie units also included over 160 10cm s.K18 cannon, which were good for counter-battery work but their flat trajectory was less useful in bombarding a large city. Altogether, 8. Armee fielded 612 artillery pieces (four 30.5cm, 12 21cm, 220 15cm, 136 10cm s.K18 and 240 10.5cm) and 3. Armee had 308 artillery pieces (100 15cm, 28 10cm and 180 10.5cm), for a grand total of 920 artillery pieces. Essentially, the German artillery park in September 1939 was useful for suppressing military targets and starting fires in cities, but lacked the punch to inflict much damage on fortified buildings or partly buried bunkers. Bock complained that the artillery barrages against Warsaw were too inadequate to be effective.[50] Indeed, the Wehrmacht would not be able to assemble a decent siege park until 1942 and only then with the help of more captured weapons.

While preparing for a grand assault on Warsaw, the XI Armeekorps was used to clear out the Kampinos Forest, along with the 29. Infanterie-Division (mot.). At the same time, Generał Brygady Mikołaj Bołtuć was leading a group of 5,000 troops from Modlin through Palmiry to Warsaw. On the morning of 21 September, the 29. Infanterie-Division (mot.) bumped into Bołtuć's group and discovered the Palmiry ammunition depot in the process. After a brief fight, Bołtuć's group slipped past but the Germans captured the depot. On the same day, Infanterie-Regiment 30 (18. Infanterie-Division) occupied Łomianki, severing the Warsaw–Modlin link and blocking Bołtuć's path to Warsaw. Before dawn on 22 September, Bołtuć attacked the German positions at Łomianki but failed to break though; he was killed leading a bayonet charge. Lacking heavy weapons, the Polish group was slaughtered, suffering an estimated 800 dead and most of the rest captured. Warsaw was finally isolated.

During this period, Kluge's 4. Armee returned to East Prussia, but some of its assets were transferred to Küchler's 3. Armee. Bock ordered that older East Prussian reservists could leave their units to assist with the harvest and the OKH authorized the release of Landwehr as well – clearly senior German officers felt that the shooting war was nearly over.

On 24 September, Blaskowitz issued final orders for the all-out assault on Warsaw while the Luftwaffe conducted air strikes to soften up the defences. At noon on 23 September, Mayor Stefan Starzyński continued to rally fighting spirit among the populace, giving a speech over Radio Warsaw referring to the 'magnificent, indestructible, great, fighting Warsaw'. Shortly thereafter, a German air raid knocked out the electrical power plant in Powisle, silencing Radio Warsaw. In another raid, the Germans scored a lucky hit which destroyed a large food warehouse in Praga. By 24 September, food in Warsaw was scarce and morale was impacted by the realization that no help of any kind was coming.

On the same day, Göring finally authorized the postponed Operation *Wasserkante* on Warsaw, hoping to crush morale in the city, but now Richthofen only had 400 aircraft available. The grand assault began with Richthofen orchestrating a series of mass air raids on the capital, beginning around 0700 hours on 25 September. Although eight Gruppen with 240 Ju 87 Stukas were used in the raids, each could only deliver a small bomb-load and their precision-ability was reduced by smoke and haze over the city from numerous fires. The Do 17s from KG 77 simply dumped their bombs indiscriminately in the city centre. Richthofen was forced to use 30 Ju 52 transports to drop incendiary bombs as well. Blaskowitz opened fire with his artillery soon after the air raids began. After two hours, Blaskowitz demanded that Richthofen halt the bombing, since the smoke it was producing prevented his own artillery from firing accurately. Hitler, who was present to watch the assault, simply told Richthofen to carry on, and the bombing and shelling continued throughout the day.[51] Altogether, Richthofen's 400 aircraft committed to the operation flew 1,176 sorties and dropped about 486 tonnes of high explosives and 72 tonnes of incendiaries. Most of the HE bombs dropped were 50kg and 250kg bombs. Polish anti-aircraft batteries, nearly out of ammunition, claimed only three enemy aircraft (two of which were Ju 52s).[52] The Poles referred to the bombardment as 'Black Monday' and it inflicted thousands of casualties, although the exact numbers are not known. It is known that about 25,000 Polish civilians died in Warsaw during the siege and recent estimates suggest that between 6,000 and 10,000 people were killed on 'Black Monday'.

While the bombers and artillery spent much of the day pounding Warsaw, several units in 8. Armee conducted preliminary operations to seize Polish defensive positions on the outer periphery of the city. Rundstedt and Blaskowitz focused far too much on the capture of the outer ring forts, all of which were 19th-century relics that had been demilitarized after the First World War. The real Polish defences were on the city streets, consisting of barricades and fortified buildings. In the south-west, the 10. Infanterie-Division attacked with two infantry regiments on line and advanced into the edge of the Mokotów district, while the 31. Infanterie-Division advanced on its left flank. In north-west Warsaw, the 18. Infanterie-Division launched a major attack on Fort IIa 'Babice', defended by Major Jacek Decowski's III/26 PP. Decowski's battalion had already been heavily pounded for some days, suffering heavy casualties, but managed to hold off the reinforced Infanterie-Regiment 51 for some time. By the time that the position was finally overrun, Decowski was badly wounded and his unit had suffered 60 per cent casualties. Along the Vistula, Podpułkownik Stanisław Małek made an equally determined stand with the 60th Infantry Regiment (60 PP) in the Bielany position. The German ground assault was underwhelming considering that so much planning had gone into it. Blaskowitz had only attacked with three of his five divisions, with both the 19. and 46. Infanterie-Divisionen not yet ready to join the assault. Nor did the 3. Armee forces on the east side of the Vistula attack Praga. Despite being heavily outnumbered and faced with superior firepower, Polish battalions had generally held their ground. The main problem for the Poles was that there were numerous fires in the city which could not be extinguished.

The main German ground assault on Warsaw commenced at 0600 hours on 26 September, with the hardest fighting occurring in the southern district of Mokotów and the western district of Wola. The 31. Infanterie-Division struck the II/40 PP hard in Wola, smashing its barricades with artillery and pushing the Polish battalion back 1,500m. In Mokotów, the 10. Infanterie-Division became embroiled in costly street fighting and was forced to deploy its field artillery in city streets to fire directly at enemy-held buildings. Polish defensive fire inflicted significant losses on the German infantrymen and artillerymen, who had not trained for city fighting. German pioneer units, such as Pionier-Bataillon 60, added their flamethrowers and demolition charges into the mix, but were not decisive. Instead, it was the constant pounding on the Polish units and the shortage of ammunition which gradually weakened the Polish defence. Virtually all of the civilian population had been living in basements and underground shelters for days, with little food or water, while the city burned around them.

Inside his underground headquarters beneath the Post Office and Savings Bank, Rómmel chaired a meeting of the city's defence council in order to weigh their options. Although the Army of Warsaw was still capable of resistance, probably for some days, the outcome would still be defeat. The question really came down to sparing the population from further unnecessary loss of life. Mayor Starzyński estimated that approximately 19,000 civilians were known dead and over 50,000 injured by the enemy bombardment. Several hospitals had been bombed and even those that had not could not cope with the flood of casualties. About 12 per cent of the buildings in the city were destroyed, including most of the critical services. The council decided to open talks with the Germans. Rómmel drafted a letter, requesting a 24-hour cease-fire in order to discuss surrender, and this letter was delivered under a white flag to Petzel's I Armeekorps during the afternoon of 26 September. In his diary, Bock claimed that he refused to grant any cease-fire and ordered his artillery units to intensify fire until the Poles agreed to unconditional surrender, but Sosabowski notes that a *de facto* cease-fire did occur after the parley.

Rómmel sent Kutrzeba to hammer out the surrender terms at Petzel's headquarters east of the city on 27 September. During the surrender negotiations, Bock engaged in an extremely petty exchange with the OKH, demanding that 3. Armee take the surrender of Warsaw, even though most of the recent ground fighting had been conducted by 8. Armee. This was the first foreign capital that the German Army had occupied in a long time and Bock wanted to get credit for it, no matter what Brauchitsch and Halder said. After hours of haggling over the telephone, Bock believed that he had got his way.[53] However, the OKH insisted that Blaskowitz would take the surrender and Kutrzeba arrived at the ruins of the Skoda plant in Rakowiec at 1300 hours on 28 September to sign the articles of capitulation. Under the terms of the agreement, the Germans agreed to release most of the Polish enlisted personnel within a few days, while the Poles agreed not to destroy still functional military equipment. However, once they learned of the surrender, many Polish commanders ordered the destruction of weapons and equipment to prevent its use by the Germans. Sosabowski ordered his regiment to dump machine-gun bolts and breach blocks from field guns into the Vistula.[54] Reactions on the Polish side varied: some were relieved that the fighting was over and they had survived, while others were grimly determined to continue the fight, either at home or abroad. At 1800 hours, the Army of Warsaw, over 120,000 strong, marched out of the still-smouldering city into captivity.

Modlin capitulated on the same day as Warsaw. Strauß's II Armeekorps had kept Thommée's garrison under daily bombardment but had not made any large-scale attack. Küchler reinforced Strauß with Panzer-Division Kempf, two more infantry divisions and some heavy artillery, including two 30.5cm howitzers and six 21cm Mörser 18s, with the intent of launching a major attack once Warsaw had fallen. However, Thommée's forces were desperately short of food, ammunition and medical supplies for his 4,000 wounded soldiers, which made it problematic how much longer the garrison could hold out. Late on 27 September, Thommée initiated negotiations with Strauß's II Armeekorps. At dawn the next morning, Thommée instructed all Polish troops in the Modlin garrison that negotiations were in progress and that they should cease firing and display white flags. During the negotiation phase, troops from the SS-Regiment 'Deutschland', part of Panzer-Division Kempf, decided to violate the cease-fire by attacking Polish troops near the village of Zakroczym on the western side of the Modlin pocket. Fort I near Zakroczym, although obsolete, was a critical position that anchored the western end of the Polish position. Kapitan Tadeusz Dorant, commander of the III/PPL (2 DPL), was in charge of the 200-man Polish garrison of the fort. Due to the cease-fire and the knowledge that a surrender was imminent, Dorant's troops were loitering unarmed outside the fort when the SS attacked around 0630 hours. Since they were not fired upon, the SS troops easily penetrated the Polish barbed wire obstacles and began gunning down the unarmed Polish troops. In an effort to intervene, Kapitan Dorant ran out of a bunker with his hands raised but was killed with a flamethrower. The SS troops killed over 50 Polish troops in this attack but the remaining Poles grabbed their weapons and fought back, killing 15 SS men and wounding 33. The fighting around the fort lasted nearly four hours and delayed Thommée's surrender.[55] After the garrison of 35,000 surrendered on 29 September, the SS troops killed some of the prisoners from 2 DPL (probably to eliminate witnesses), then treated the residents of the town of Zakroczym to a mediaeval-style sack; the SS-men looted the houses, then set them on fire, while casually murdering civilians who objected.

It is important to recognize that German armies had no recent experience handling such large numbers of prisoners – roughly 160,000 from just Warsaw and Modlin – nor had they made logistical preparations to accommodate such numbers. Prisoners typically spent the first week under open skies in fields, surrounded by some barbed wire. Although some German troops were brutal towards the Polish prisoners of war, they also could be very lackadaisical and many Poles slipped away. Sosabowski was one of those who did so, as was Tadeusz Komorowski – both men immediately joined the incipient Polish resistance. Stanisław Mikołajczyk escaped, made it to Hungary and then England, where he would play a key role in the Polish government-in-exile. For their part, the Germans reneged on the Warsaw surrender terms and refused to release enlisted prisoners; instead, most were eventually sent to Germany as forced labour.

The Last Battles, 23 September – 6 October 1939

'Tell the people that yesterday there was a battle. The war is not ended. Poles are fighting and will keep fighting.'
Generał Brygady Franciszek Kleeberg, 7 October 1939

By the third week of September, Generał Dywizji Stefan Dąb-Biernacki – the officer who had squandered Army Prusy in the first week of the campaign – found himself leading the Northern Front, the largest remaining fragment of the Polish Army, south towards the Hungarian border. On paper, the Northern Front comprised five infantry divisions (including 1 DPL and 10th, 33rd, 39th and 41 DPs), two infantry brigades formed from various bits and pieces and five cavalry brigades, plus an artillery train with 263 pieces. However, most of these units were well under strength and it was telling that the 39 DP, a reserve formation, was the only division even near full strength. Nor were the units concentrated; rather, they were dispersed over a wide area. Without a line of communication any more, the only supplies the Northern Front had were what they carried. Pułkownik Władysław Anders' cavalry group (Nowogródzka and Wołyńska Cavalry Brigades) had joined Dąb-Biernacki's Northern Command near Chelm, but marched on a parallel course towards Zamość. Of course, the German

VII Armeekorps was already there and the Red Army was approaching from the east.

Anders decided to try to break through the German cordon with his two cavalry brigades west of Tomaszów Lubelski, along the Wieprz River. Dąb-Biernacki's larger group tried to break through north of Tomaszów Lubelski, on a broad front. The German VIII Armeekorps, which had the 8. and 28. Infanterie-Divisionen around Tomaszów Lubelski, was still rounding up prisoners from the defeat of Army Lublin. The one advantage the Poles had was that the German forces in this area were packing up to move west to the demarcation border and did not expect that any major Polish forces were left in the vicinity. On the morning of 21 September, the Poles began bumping into German units south of Zamość and conducted a number of localized attacks. From the German viewpoint, they could not properly assess what they were up against and efforts to re-orient and counter-attack with VIII Armeekorps on 22 September proved fruitless because no major enemy units were encountered. The normal German tactical aggressiveness was impaired because Hitler had said that no more German blood should be shed east of the Vistula since it was being handed over to the Soviets – nobody wanted to suffer unnecessary losses in a campaign that was ending. Anders enjoyed the most success, thanks to some luck. By chance, around 0800 hours on 23 September his Nowogródzka Cavalry Brigade stumbled upon the lightly guarded command post of Generalleutnant Rudolf Koch-Erpach's 8. Infanterie-Division near Krasnobród. After a firefight, Generalleutnant Koch-Erpach and 100 of his troops were captured – the first German general captured in the Second World War. Anders had also broken through the German cordon and he headed south with his cavalry, and their prisoners.

In contrast, Dąb-Biernacki's main group could not get past the VIII Armeekorps' blocking positions around Tomaszów Lubelski, but spent their last strength trying to fight their way through. The elite 1st Legions Infantry Division was destroyed in the fighting. On the night of 23 September, Dąb-Biernacki abandoned his troops and fled south in civilian clothes – eventually reaching France. Generał Dywizji Emil Krukowicz-Przedrzymirski was left in charge of the disintegrating Northern Command and spent a couple more days trying to get past the German cordon, but failed. On 26 September, about 6,000 survivors from the 39th and 41 DPs surrendered, while other units broke up and tried to evade in small groups.

Anders continued to move south with about 2,500 cavalry. He was aided by the fact that the Germans were pulling out of this area and no longer hunting Polish stragglers. On 25 September, Anders encountered elements of the German XVIII Armeekorps north-east of Przemysl, which was moving back to the San River. The local German commander agreed to look the other way and Anders released his prisoners, including Generalleutnant Koch-Erpach. By the morning of 27 September, Anders' group was near Sambor and less than 120km from the Hungarian border. Unfortunately, Komdiv Dmitri Riabyshev's 4th Cavalry Corps had occupied the nearby village of Władypol and detected the Polish group. Rebuffing Anders' efforts to negotiate, Riabyshev attacked at once with his two cavalry divisions, supported by 60 tanks and armoured cars. The Polish cavalry put up a fight but it was grossly outnumbered and Anders' few remaining 75mm field guns quickly ran out of ammunition. Anders was wounded and over 1,000 of his troops were captured by the Soviets. Anders managed to escape southwards with several hundred survivors, but was captured the next day.

Two other Polish groups remained at large in eastern Poland: General Wilhelm Orlik-Rückemann's KOP Group with about 8,000 troops and Generał Brygady Franciszek Kleeberg's Independent Operational Group Polesie with over 15,000 troops. These two formations – which were operating outside of any chain of command – tried to operate in the space between the withdrawing Wehrmacht and the advancing Red Army in the waning days of the campaign. Orlik-Rückemann and Kleeberg tried to co-ordinate their operations but communications – even though the groups were within about 50km of each other – were sporadic. Kleeberg wanted to reach the arms storage depot in Dęblin – unaware that it had been destroyed – but even if they could resupply, there was no real plan other than to remain under arms as long as possible. Both groups tried to link up near Kowel, but this city had already been taken by the Soviet 5th Army.

Kleeberg was a model officer – one of the best in the Polish Army – having both a distinguished record in combat in the Russo-Polish War and a fine military education at the École Supérieure de Guerre in France. He possessed high morale and a sense of duty that enabled him to retain command authority with his troops despite the overall deteriorating military situation. He was also fortunate that he had equally motivated subordinates, such as Pułkownik Adam Epler, commander of the 60 DP. For all its flaws, the WP had commanders who could keep troops fighting and moving long after other armies would have packed it in.

Heading towards the Bug River, Orlik-Rückemann's group discovered elements of Pulkovnik Ivan N. Russianov's 52nd Rifle Division in the village of Szack on the morning of 28 September. Russianov's division was extremely spread out and only instructed to be on the lookout for 'bands of Polish officers', not a reinforced brigade-size group. Kapitan Timofey G. Nisenyuk, commander of the 411th Separate Tank Battalion (15 T-26s, 15 T-38s), thought a show of force would convince the Poles to surrender but when his tanks advanced in column they were shot to pieces by Polish 37mm anti-tank guns. Kapitan Nisenyuk was killed, seven of his tanks were destroyed and nine abandoned T-26 tanks were captured. Orlik-Rückemann sent a battalion-size force into Szack, which routed a Soviet anti-tank and headquarters unit in the village. Pulkovnik Russianov, the division commander, was knocked off his horse by a shell fragment in his arm and was forced to flee.[56] Despite this nice tactical victory, Orlik-Rückemann knew that the Red Army would react massively to this incident and he tried to withdraw to the north through a heavily wooded area. Komdiv Vasily I. Repin, commander of the 15th Rifle Corps, sent two infantry regiments and a reconnaissance battalion to cut off the Poles' escape route but only succeeded in trapping about 500 KOP troops near Mielnik. On the morning of 29 September these troops surrendered to the Soviet 112th Rifle Regiment; 18 Polish officers were shot after surrendering.

Kleeberg's Independent Operational Group Polesie was moving nearly parallel to Orlik-Rückemann's group and crossed the Bug north of Włodawa. Kleeberg fought and won two meeting engagements against the Soviet 143rd Rifle Division near Parczew on 28–29 September. The Soviet tactical performance in these actions was poor, resulting in over 500 casualties, including 60–100 captured. On 30 September, Orlik-Rückemann crossed the Bug south of Włodawa, about 50km south-east of Kleeberg's position. However, Repin's 15th Rifle Corps had not given up the pursuit and Orlik-Rückemann's group was spotted west of the Bug on the evening of 30 September. The next morning, a Soviet reconnaissance unit identified the Polish group along the eastern shore of Lake Wytyczno, 50km north-east of Lublin. After knocking out two Soviet T-37 reconnaissance tanks, Orlik-Rückemann ordered his troops to dig in along the edge of the lake. The KOP troops only had four 75mm guns left and were desperately short of ammunition. Around 0700 hours, Repin moved in to attack with the 253rd Rifle Regiment and a tank battalion, without artillery support. Polish defensive fire was initially heavy, inflicting over 100 casualties upon one Soviet battalion, but once the 75mm guns ran out of ammunition they could not keep the Soviet tanks at bay. One KOP battalion was mauled and about 300 of its troops surrendered. After five hours of fighting, Orlik-Rückemann gave the order to break up into small groups and try to evade to the north-west. He succeeded in reaching Lithuania and eventually England, but most of his troops were not so fortunate. The battle of Wytyczno was the last major clash between Soviet and Polish troops in the 1939 campaign.

Meanwhile, Luftwaffe aerial reconnaissance had detected Kleeberg's Independent Operational Group Polesie moving west towards Dęblin and Wietersheim's XIV Armeekorps (mot.) was notified. The Germans were uncertain about the size of the Polish force, but given that the campaign was all but over, they did not expect that it was a serious threat. A single battalion from Generalleutnant Paul Otto's 13. Infanterie-Division (mot.) was sent forwards to investigate. On the morning of 2 October, the Germans encountered strong Polish cavalry, supported by artillery, near the village of Kock. By this point, Independent Operational Group Polesie had grown to nearly 25,000 troops in three cavalry brigades and two reserve infantry divisions (50th and 60 DPs). Still overconfident, Otto sent only part of his division – three motorized infantry battalions and an artillery battalion under Oberst Gustav Fehn – forwards to crush the Poles. Since most of the Panzer units were already redeploying westwards, Otto had no armour support. Nor were any further Luftwaffe strikes authorized east of the Vistula. During the late afternoon of 2 October, the German motorized infantry pushed towards the village of Kock, which was held by two battalions of the 50th Infantry Division (50 DP). However, the Germans advanced with open flanks on either side, unaware that more Polish forces were in the vicinity. Kleeberg seized the opportunity to counter-attack with his cavalry brigades into the German flank, scattering the unwary III./Infanterie-Regiment 93 (mot.) and capturing 200 prisoners. Fehn fell back and requested Otto to send the rest of the division.

Before the rest of the 13. Infanterie-Division (mot.) arrived, Kleeberg tried to launch an attack on the morning of 3 October to crush Fehn's regimental-size group, but the 50 DP's infantry was repulsed by German artillery fire. Instead, the Polish cavalry jabbed at the German flanks most of the day, preventing Otto from regaining the initiative. Otto's division had also got itself into an odd position, in that the bulk of the Polish forces were now astride his line of communications back to the Vistula. Wietersheim finally realized that they were dealing with a large Polish force and released the 29. Infanterie-Division (mot.) to support Otto. On 4 October, Otto attacked westwards but barely budged the Polish lines and Polish cavalry kept getting around his flanks. Wietersheim was now under pressure to end this action, since the Germans were supposed to have already handed this area over to the Soviets. Otto attacked again on 5 October with more success, since the Polish troops were running out of ammunition. The 29. Infanterie-Division (mot.) also came up from the north-west, encircling most of Independent Operational Group Polesie. Finally, Kleeberg initiated surrender talks during the night of 5/6 October, although fighting did not stop until 1000 hours the next morning. Kleeberg gave his troops the option to try and evade on their own, but the bulk of his force – some 16,855 troops – surrendered at 1600 hours on 6 October.[57] The last major conventional resistance in Poland had been extinguished. However, the Germans were equally sloppy at herding the prisoners towards a POW camp near Radom and many escaped, including Pułkownik Adam Epler – who immediately joined the resistance.

Many other smaller armed groups, consisting of the remnants of shattered regiments and battalions continued to wander around Polish forests and remote areas, occasionally skirmishing with German or Soviet forces. The most significant was a cavalry detachment under Major Henryk Dobrzański ('Hubal'), who vowed that 'I will not take off my uniform until I die'. Leading a group of barely 50 soldiers south into the heavily wooded area north-west of Kielce, Major 'Hubal' fought a guerrilla war against the Germans until he was killed in April 1940. After this, the war in Poland would be carried on by covert resistance groups, who could blend in with the civilian population.

CHAPTER 8

Occupation

---

*'My colleagues and I felt it was an honour to be allowed
to help in conquering this area for our own nation and
for German culture.'*

Melita Maschmann, Hitler Youth Leader in Poland, November 1939

Campaign Analysis

In the space of five weeks, the Wehrmacht had defeated the fourth largest
army in Europe, smashed the Second Polish Republic and added 188,550
square kilometres of territory to the Third Reich. It was the first in a long
line of conquests for Hitler's war machine. Except for the initial stage
of the battle of the Bzura, the Germans held the initiative throughout
the campaign and Polish forces were quickly battered into pieces before
they could organize a more coherent defence. The test of combat had
validated both the Luftwaffe and the new motorized forces, although
definite room for improvement was noted. Although short, the Polish
campaign was intensely violent and hard-fought. While the Germans
had the initiative, the Poles proved capable of striking back whenever
favourable opportunities arose.

On 6 October 1939, Hitler presented the results of the campaign to the German people, in a speech delivered in the Reichstag. He stated that according to casualty lists up to 30 September, the total losses of the Wehrmacht were 10,572 killed, 3,404 missing and 30,322 wounded, for a total of 44,198 casualties. Later OKW records, updated to 5 October, state that the Wehrmacht suffered 8,842 killed in action, 5,079 missing and around 30,000 wounded. The exact German casualty figures for the Polish campaign have been slippery for a number of reasons. Some accounts include non-battle deaths, but most do not. The number of non-battle deaths, from accidents and other causes, was not insignificant. The missing figure shifted over time, as some personnel were reclassified as dead or presumed dead, while others remained missing. About 5,000 Wehrmacht military personnel fell into Polish hands during the brief campaign, but most were treated well and survived to be released by 5 October, despite Hitler's claim that the Poles had 'massacred' many German prisoners. Unlike the Wehrmacht, the WP honoured the Geneva Convention. Anyone missing by the time that the OKW lists were compiled on 5 October was likely dead or a deserter. Based upon the available evidence, the numbers stated by Hitler are reasonably accurate. Thus, in the final assessment, the Wehrmacht suffered approximately 13,900 dead in Poland. The Slovak Army, which saw only limited combat in southern Poland, suffered 18 dead, 11 missing and 46 wounded.

The bulk of German casualties – a total of 39,421 – were suffered by the Heer. The Luftwaffe came off relatively lightly, with a total of 953 casualties, including the permanent loss of about 300 flying personnel. About 18,000 personnel from the Waffen-SS and Allgemeine-SS participated in the campaign and they suffered a total of 732 killed in action, 163 non-battle deaths and 20 missing. Although it does not get much attention, the Germans did court-martial over 800 individuals as a result of misbehaviour during the Polish campaign; 503 were convicted of desertion and 27 were executed, 38 were convicted of treason and ten executed, 27 convicted of looting and 17 executed, 24 convicted of rape and seven executed, 20 convicted of murder but only one executed. The court-martial records indicate that the Wehrmacht was more concerned about offences against military discipline or disloyalty to the regime than offences committed against enemy civilians or prisoners. On 4 October, Hitler issued a general amnesty for any German soldiers convicted of crimes committed during the Polish campaign, so most of those court-martialled were eventually reinstated, including the 17 convicted rapists and 19 convicted murderers.

Table 4: German Personnel Casualties in the Polish Campaign

Service	Killed	Missing	Wounded	TOTAL
Heer	7,712	4,960	26,749	39,421
Luftwaffe	368	99	486	953
SS	732	20	N/A	N/A
Kriegsmarine	30	0	134	164
TOTAL	8,842	5,079	27,369+	41,290+

German material losses in Poland were significant, but not crippling. Of the approximately 2,800 German tanks committed to the Polish campaign, 236 were destroyed (listed as *Totalausfall* or total loss) and another 457 were damaged.[1] About 180 of the damaged tanks were eventually repaired but the rest were scrapped, so total German tanks losses in Poland were closer to the 500 mark. The loss of Pz I and Pz II tanks was virtually irrelevant since both were to be phased out as soon as possible, but the losses of the workhorse Pz III and Pz IV medium tanks were significant since monthly production barely exceeded losses in a short campaign. While these losses represented only about 18 per cent of the committed armour, the campaign had revealed the fragility of Germany's ability to maintain its motorized forces during even a short campaign. No lost tanks were replaced during *Fall Weiss* and shortages of spare parts severely impacted the ability of units to repair damaged vehicles. Guderian's dash to Brześć was impressive, but it quickly wore out his tank tracks and few replacements were available. By that point, the supply lines for his XIX Armeekorps (mot.) were over 300km long and the quartermaster depots in East Prussia could not push spares forwards quickly over the patchwork of dirt roads and pontoon bridges Guderian left in his wake. Indeed, it is incredible that the Wehrmacht went to war without a stockpile of rubber tyres for its trucks; during the Polish campaign, repair units could only replace 15 per cent of damaged tyres. On 4 October, the 1.leichte-Division reported that 'more than four weeks are needed to repair the Panzers if the repair parts arrive. All of the Panzerkampfwagen and 50 per cent of the artillery Zugmaschinen [prime movers] need new tracks. Due to these worn out tracks, Panzer-Regiment 11 will be immobilized after being transported by rail to its home garrison.'[2] German ground forces also lost 319 armoured cars (out of about 1,000 committed), 6,046 trucks and 5,538 motorcycles in Poland.[3] Hitler mandated that all motorized units would be refitted in Germany and ready for action within six weeks – i.e.

Table 5: German Tank Losses in the Polish Campaign

Type	Totalausfall	Monthly Production
Pz I	89	0
Pz II	83	5
Pz III	26	40
Pz IV	19	20
Pz 35 (t)	7	0
Pz 38 (t)	7	30
Pz Bef	5	10
TOTAL	236	105

by 16 November. This goal was not achieved.[4] Thus it can be concluded that while the German Panzer and motorized infantry units suffered only modest material losses in Poland, the mechanical wear and tear of just four weeks of manoeuvre warfare was sufficient to greatly reduce their combat effectiveness for the next two months.

The Luftwaffe flew about 33,000 sorties over Poland, of which 75 per cent were bombing missions. Altogether, the Luftwaffe dropped 20,205 tonnes of bombs during the Polish campaign.[5] Although the Bf 109E was a vastly superior fighter to the Polish P.11C, it did not perform particularly well in Poland, due to its short range and limited duration of flight. A total of 67 Bf 109s were lost or written off during the Polish campaign and another 59 damaged, but they scored no more than 52 victories. The sole Luftwaffe ace of the Polish campaign, Hauptmann Hannes Gentzen, Gruppenkommandeur of I./ZG 2 (equipped with the older Bf 109Ds) claimed six Polish aircraft – five P.23 Karaś and 1 P.37 Łoś – but no enemy fighters. Instead, the Bf 110C proved more useful over Poland, thanks to its longer endurance. Overall, the Luftwaffe lost 285 aircraft destroyed during the campaign, plus an additional 263 aircraft damaged. About 47 per cent of German aircraft losses were due to Polish fighter interceptions and 53 per cent to ground defences or other causes. Since around 60 per cent of the damaged aircraft were eventually scrapped, the Luftwaffe lost a total of about 415 aircraft in the Polish campaign – equivalent to one month of production. It should be noted, however, that even without a proper air defence network and obsolescent fighters the LW still managed to inflict very heavy losses on German reconnaissance aircraft – implying that lone aircraft had poor survivability over enemy airspace even in favourable conditions.

Table 6: Luftwaffe Losses Based on 5 October 1939, OKL
4. Abteilung Quartiermeister

Type	Lost	Damaged*	Total	% of Deployed	Monthly Production
Bf 109E	67	59	126	43%	110
Bf 110C	12	27	39	47%	40
He 111H/P	50	48	98	35%	110
Do 17Z	28	20	48	15%	50
Ju 87B, Hs 123	31	22	53	15%	33
Long-range Recon (Do 17P)	25	9	34	44%	5
Short-Range Recon (Hs 126)	32	43	75	40%	34
Seaplanes	8	3	11	N/A	25
Ju 52	12	32	44	N/A	36
Miscellaneous	9	2	11	N/A	20
TOTAL	285	263	548		463

*Damage assessed between 10% and 59%.

While the Luftwaffe leadership did not take any immediate steps to improve the range of the Bf 109E fighter, it did learn several other useful lessons as a result of *Fall Weiss*. The range of the Ju 87B Stuka was recognized as inadequate, so the improved Ju 87R went into production in late 1939 and was available in quantity for the French campaign; it had double the range of its predecessor. The Luftwaffe also learned that its battle damage assessment capabilities were inadequate. Post-campaign investigation of two aircraft factories at Mielec and Lublin – which the pilots bombing them had reported as destroyed – were found to be untouched. Similar results were found in regard to airfields and train stations – pilots proved to be poor at assessing the results of their own missions. Fortunately for the Allies, this was one area where the Germans decided that no improvement was necessary, which had considerable bearing on the Luftwaffe's ability to estimate the damage it was inflicting upon the RAF in the Battle of Britain.

Several sources have attempted to claim that the Wehrmacht greatly diminished its stockpiles of fuel and ammunition during the Polish campaign. It is true that Hitler embarked upon the Polish campaign despite the fact that the Wehrmacht had limited reserves of fuel and ammunition. In September 1939, Germany had a reserve of 480,000 tonnes of aviation fuel and 350,000 tonnes of motor fuel (petrol); monthly production was about 50,000 tonnes of aviation fuel and 93,000 tonnes of motor fuel.[6] During the five-week campaign, German ground forces consumed 60,000m³ (about 45,000 tonnes) of motor fuel, which was less than 13 per cent of the pre-war reserve. Likewise, Luftwaffe fuel use was relatively moderate. However, no significant fuel stocks were captured in Poland and once training and other operational requirements are factored in, the Polish campaign did represent a minor net loss. The ammunition utilization rate in the Polish campaign was serious, particularly for the Luftwaffe, but claims that the Luftwaffe used up 60 per cent of its stock of bombs in three weeks are wildly inaccurate.[7] Rather, OKL data shows that the Luftwaffe expended just 30 per cent of its bombs in five weeks, equivalent to roughly two months' production. The expenditure of artillery ammunition in Poland was moderate, averaging only 8–12 per cent of reserves of the most useful rounds. In most cases, monthly production exceeded use in Poland, so the net effect was minimal. As a result of the Polish campaign, Germany ramped up its ammunition production during the winter of 1939/40 in preparation for the Western campaign. Thus, the Wehrmacht's expenditure of artillery ammunition and bombs during the Polish campaign had minimal impact upon Germany's ability to conduct follow-on operations in the West. While ill-prepared to support an extended campaign, the Third Reich's industrial base was fully capable of mounting short campaigns, as long as there were recovery periods in between.

The fact that the Wehrmacht defeated Poland in five weeks should not conceal the reality that German operations often fell short of the perfection depicted by Dr Goebbels' propaganda machine. In operational

Table 7: Luftwaffe Expenditure of Bombs in Polish Campaign

Ordnance	Stockpile 1 Sep 39	Used in Polish Campaign	% of Pre–war Stockpile	Estimated Monthly Production
10kg	1,500,000	91,800	6%	0
50kg	700,000	289,000	41%	60,000
250kg	47,000	16,050	34%	20,000
500kg	9,000	1,650	18%	750
TONNAGE	66,250	20,205	30%	8,375

Table 8: Heer/Waffen-SS Expenditure of Artillery Ammunition in
Polish Campaign

Ordnance	Stockpile 1 Sep 39	Used in Polish Campaign	% of Pre-war Stockpile	Estimated Monthly Production
21cm Mörser 18	16,000	3,794	23%	12,000
15cm s.FH	3,100,000	296,560	9%	215,000
10cm s.K18	1,100,000	86,046	8%	66,000
10.5cm l.FH18	16,100,000	1,408,193	9%	690,000
8cm mortar	1,900,000	486,585	25%	775,000
7.5cm l.IG18	3,300,000	409,517	12%	220,000

terms, the Wehrmacht made two very noticeable mistakes which enabled the Poles to mount a serious counter-offensive on the Bzura. First, *Fall Weiss* failed to designate any significant force to engage Army Poznań and fix it in place or at least follow its retreat. Consequently, Army Poznań remained not only mobile and combat-effective, but became virtually invisible to Heeresgruppe Süd. Second, under the original *Fall Weiss* plan, Guderian's XIX Armeekorps (mot.) was supposed to keep attacking along the Vistula, crush Army Pomorze then link up with Hoepner's XVI Armeekorps (mot.) west of Warsaw – but this did not occur. Instead, thanks to a half-baked plan developed by Halder and Bock, Guderian's corps was pulled out of the line before Army Pomorze was fully destroyed and then carted across East Prussia to attack Brześć – an objective with no special significance. Guderian's Panzers were sidelined for nearly a week and then moved away from the decisive theatre around Warsaw to push into territory that the OKH already knew was assigned to the Soviets. While Hoth's XV Armeekorps (mot.) was relentlessly hounding Szylling's Army Kraków to extinction, Guderian was off chasing prestige targets – a mistake he would repeat in the Soviet Union in 1941. In most sources – even the definitive West Point military atlas – the German campaign is depicted as a double pincer attack, with 3. Armee and 10. Armee meeting at Warsaw; these depictions are erroneous because 3. Armee did not move through Modlin but instead headed east. The classic German double pincer attack on Warsaw took over two weeks to play out and there was no great link-up between Heeresgruppe Nord and Heeresgruppe Süd at Warsaw.

Although the German campaign in Poland may have seemed impressive in terms of operational manoeuvre, it was far from impressive in terms of operational logistics or intelligence. Guderian's and Hoepner's motorized corps quickly outran their supply lines and were frequently running out of fuel. Furthermore, German mobile tactics were still chained to a fixed logistic and support infrastructure back in Germany, with very little mobile support capability to sustain them as they pushed deeper into enemy territory. Maintenance units provided to motorized divisions did not have sufficient towing vehicles for efficient battlefield recovery or sufficient personnel to repair recovered vehicles in a timely manner. In addition to losing track of Kutrzeba's Army Poznań, Luftwaffe intelligence did a poor job finding the LW's dispersal airfields. Blaskowitz's 8. Armee was blissfully unaware of large Polish forces moving across his open left flank, while Küchler's 3. Armee seemed completely ignorant of the Polish fortifications that had been built during the summer of 1939. Against this opponent, these German deficiencies could be glossed over, but the same kind of arrogant disregard for operational logistics and intelligence would invite painful consequences during Operation *Barbarossa* in 1941.

At the tactical level, the Heer performed quite well, thanks to effective pre-war training and good leadership. Meeting engagements tended to be costly due to inadequate reconnaissance, and tactical bridge-building was often slow and impaired advances. On the other hand, German light anti-aircraft defences were mobile, excellent and lethal. The Waffen-SS units performed poorly in Poland, often unable to accomplish their missions and suffering inordinate casualties. On the whole, senior Heer commanders regarded the SS troops as ill-disciplined and more pre-occupied with brutalizing the civilian population and prisoners than focusing on their purely military tasks. However, the regime wanted to extoll the virtues of the SS, so their painful mistakes in Poland – such as the ambush of the SS-Regiment 'Germania'– were swept under the carpet. It was clear that German Panzers needed better armour to enable them to survive on a battlefield where the enemy had 37mm anti-tank guns. The Pz Is and Pz IIs were deathtraps on such a battlefield – unable to even cope with the 37mm armed Polish 7TP light tank – but they would have to be retained until more medium tanks became available. Even the Pz III and Pz IV medium tanks proved too thinly armoured and the next version of the Pz IV, the Ausf D model, added 20mm thick plates to the side armour and hardened the frontal armour. Nevertheless, most of the Panzers available in late 1939 were still poorly armed and poorly protected compared to the best French tanks.

On 7 October, Panzer-Division Kempf was disbanded and Panzer-Regiment 7 was assigned to the 10. Panzer-Division, while the Waffen-SS units were sent to form the SS-Verfügungs-Division. The experimental hybrid Heer-SS division concept was not judged favourably by either side and Himmler pressed for his own divisions. For his part, Hitler was so impressed by the performance of the Panzertruppen in Poland that he decided to increase the number of Panzer-Divisionen from six to ten. It had already been decided before *Fall Weiss* that the four leichte-Divisionen would eventually be converted into Panzer-Divisionen once sufficient tanks were available. In mid-October 1939, less than two weeks after the end of *Fall Weiss,* the 1., 2. and 3. leichte-Divisionen began converting into the 6., 7. and 8. Panzer-Divisionen. The 4. leichte-Division did not convert to the 9. Panzer-Division until January 1940. The handful of independent Panzer-Abteilungen were absorbed into the new divisions to flesh out their tank parks. The re-organization of the Panzer-Divisionen was an important step in ramping up the Heer's ability to fight a first class enemy such as the French, but it required months of effort to implement. By May 1940, the Heer had ten fully effective Panzer-Divisionen, which tipped the scales in the Wehrmacht's favour.

Politically, *Fall Weiss* produced mixed results for Hitler. The naysayers among the Wehrmacht who had warned that it would be impossible to limit the operation to Poland had been proved correct. Hitler's effort to offer peace to the Anglo-French on 6 October proved too vague and weighed down by previous dissimulations; having been branded as a flagrant aggressor and liar, he could not now negotiate his way out of a general European war. Chamberlain's cabinet took six days to concoct a rather mealy-mouthed response, which sought to avoid 'slamming the door' to the idea of a negotiated settlement, but also to avoid the appearance of making any concessions. While drafting the response, discussions in Chamberlain's cabinet indicate that there was limited support for making restoration of Poland a pre-condition for negotiation. Instead, the cabinet members considered the 'restoration of the rule of law' in Europe to be their primary objective. Eventually, Chamberlain delivered the response in the House of Commons on 12 October, which concluded that 'Either the German Government must give convincing proof of all sincerity of their desire for peace by definite acts and by the provision of effective guarantees of their intention to fulfil their undertakings, or we must persevere in our duty to the end. It is for Germany to make her choice.'[8] Had Hitler offered to restore some limited form of Polish autonomy in a rump state and demobilize parts of the Luftwaffe and Heer, he might have been able to woo the Chamberlain government into negotiations, but this did not coincide with his real plans. After *Fall Weiss*, Hitler's preference was to crush the Anglo-French, not make concessions to them.

According to Soviet data, the Red Army lost a total of 996 dead or missing and 2,002 wounded during the period of 17–25 September; however, this omits the battles of Władypol, Szack and Wytyczno which were fought on 27 September – 1 October. These later actions add at least another 820 casualties to the Soviet total, bringing them up to at least 1,227 dead and 2,588 wounded. Interestingly, Soviet data also reveals that 147 commanders (officers) were killed or disappeared during the brief campaign – an unusually high leadership loss.[9] Soviet material losses in Poland were minimal but that was due to the lack of significant Polish resistance. In truth, the Soviet invasion was a sucker punch delivered to an opponent that was already staggering from repeated blows from the Germans and lacking in resources to defend its eastern provinces. Soviet operational performance was good in theory – units were assigned objectives and they reached them – but logistic support was almost non-existent. Tactical performance was a bit better and a few units, such as Kombrig Mikhail Bogomolov's 39th Light Tank Brigade, performed very well. Other Soviet units allowed themselves to be bested by inferior Polish forces due to clumsy tactics and inept leadership. German officers noted the poor condition of most Soviet equipment and the sloppy appearance of troops, which influenced German strategic decision-making in 1940–41. Overall, the Red Army's performance in Poland hinted at organizational failure, but this was confirmed for the whole world to see two months later, when the Soviet Union attacked Finland. The same slap-dash approach to operational planning exhibited in Poland was applied to the Finnish scenario but failed disastrously in the face of a determined opponent. Nevertheless, Stalin was happy with the results in Poland – he had quickly gained territory and eliminated a traditional foe, while avoiding war with the Anglo-French. He judged that the Red Army's operational deficiencies could be corrected with more arrests, more beatings, more executions.

The results of *Fall Weiss* looked very different from the Polish perspective. In five weeks, the WP suffered 200,000 casualties, including 66,300 dead, from a total mobilized force of about 1.1 million.[10] In addition, 694,000 Polish military personnel were captured by the Germans, 250,000 by the Soviets and 1,350 by the Slovaks (who handed most of them over to the Soviets). There are no solid estimates of Polish civilian losses during the 1939 campaign, but they are generally believed to have been around 150,000 dead. During September 1939, at least 23,638 Polish military personnel escaped to Romania, 900 to Hungary and about 1,000 to Lithuania. Général Louis Faury, head of the French military mission to Poland, played a critical role in facilitating the transfer of Polish troops from Romania to France. Eventually, thousands more military-age males would flee through the Balkans during the winter of 1939/40, enabling the recreation of air and ground units in France.

About 75 per cent of the LW's personnel escaped to Romania, including 10,100 airmen. Pułkownik Stefan Pawlikowski, commander of the Pursuit Brigade, reached England and flew in support of the Dieppe Landing in 1942. He was killed in action during a fighter sweep over the English Channel in May 1943. Pułkownik Władysław Heller, commander of the Bomber Brigade, also reached England and died in a training flight in October 1943. The two highest-scoring Polish fighter pilots in 1939, Skalski Stanisław (142 Eskadra) and Dudwał Hieronim (113 Eskadra), each with four confirmed kills, both escaped to the West. Stanisław reached England and flew during the Battle of Britain, in North Africa and Sicily. He became the highest-scoring Polish pilot of the war, with 18 confirmed kills. When he returned to Poland in 1947 he was sentenced to death for 'espionage', which was commuted to life in prison, He was tortured by the communists and served eight years in prison. Eventually, he was rehabilitated. Dudwał Hieronim reached France and was killed in a dogfight with Bf 109s on 7 June 1940. Over 144 LW aircraft were flown to Romania, including 58 fighters, 27 P.37 Łos bombers, 19 P.23 Karaś and 40 reconnaissance aircraft; the Royal Romanian Air Force added a number of these aircraft to its own inventory. Given that the LW still had over 100 operational combat aircraft and 10,000 personnel left to evacuate to Romania, it is clear that the Luftwaffe failed in its mission to destroy this force

Altogether, the LW flew 2,540 sorties and lost 333 of 432 aircraft during the campaign, including about 35 LW aircraft mistakenly shot down by Polish anti-aircraft gunners. Of 1,181 pilots, the LW lost 171 dead or missing and 63 wounded, or 20 per cent casualties. Polish fighters flew 1,373 sorties and scored 107 victories (103 German and four Soviet aircraft), but lost 120 of 158 fighters and 50 pilots.[11] Polish bombers flew about 380 sorties, lost 142 aircraft and dropped 200 tonnes of bombs. Polish reconnaissance units flew 520 sorties and lost 80 aircraft. The P.23 Karaś suffered particularly, losing 55 of 114 available aircraft to enemy Flak and another 17 to enemy fighters. Given the circumstances, the LW performed reasonably well – its pilots inflicted some damage and most survived to fight the Luftwaffe another day, under better conditions.

The operational performance of the Polish Army was poor from the outset due to a faulty deployment plan, which led to an incoherent and unco-ordinated defensive effort. In no sector did the Polish border armies have anything like a continuous front, which allowed the Germans to bypass resistance centres and drive wedges between Polish divisions. Polish efforts to form defensive lines along favourable terrain features, such as the Warta River, were compromised before they even began. Reliance upon *ad hoc* operational group structures instead of proper corps headquarters proved disastrous and it was rare that a single commander could co-ordinate the efforts of two or more Polish divisions. Indeed, it is fair to say that the Germans won the campaign not so much due to technology or numbers, but because they could readily co-ordinate multiple divisions and the Poles could not. Due to Rydz-Śmigły's ill-judged decisions to leave Army Pomorze close to Danzig – then disband the Intervention Corps at the last moment – this critical army was set up for immediate defeat by Guderian's motorized units. Likewise, Army Poznań was deployed in a forward, exposed position with no real mission. However, the worst Polish operational mistake was the fumbling manner in which the operational reserve – Army Prusy – was quickly squandered and disorganized in an effort to reinforce the crumbling Army Łódź. While the last-minute mobilization did not help the WP's performance, the decision to abandon city after city without a major fight severely impacted the Polish Army's ability to deploy its reserve divisions and allowed the enemy to keep all the field armies on the run. Had the Germans been forced to deal with defended cities such as Poznań and Częstochowa, it would have reduced their ability to maintain their high operational tempo. The Germans would have been forced to detach divisions to reduce these cities, weakening their main effort. Sometimes commanders have to sacrifice some of their units in delaying actions for the greater good, but Rydz-Śmigły did not have this mindset.

At the tactical level, the performance of the Polish Army was generally good, with a few exceptions. Polish anti-tank weapons and artillery performed particularly well and when Polish units were able to fight with the advantage of fixed defences, they could inflict real damage. Polish cavalry units and the small number of tank units also performed quite well and it is interesting that the Wehrmacht failed to completely destroy any of the pre-war cavalry brigades until the final days of the campaign. Polish tactical aggressiveness – particularly the willingness to conduct night attacks – caught the Germans by surprise on several occasions. Overall, Polish troops were motivated and willing to suffer heavy losses to achieve an objective; in many cases, Polish troops fought to the death to defend positions. Unlike other armies that the Wehrmacht fought in 1940–41, Polish units did not disintegrate just because they were surrounded.

Politically, the September campaign was the death-knell for Pilsudski's flawed Second Republic. Pilsudski's desire to encompass the largest amount of territory in 1919–21 had saddled the Second Republic with unresolved territorial disputes with most of its neighbours and a sullen group of minorities (German, Byelorussian and Ukrainian) who proved to be a serious internal security risk. Endemic in-fighting between pro-Pilsudski and anti-Pilsudski factions also proved to be a serious handicap and meant that military command was based upon loyalty to the regime rather than ability. The Second Polish Republic was over-stretched and internally fragile, which made it a tempting target for aggressors.

Were the Poles doomed to defeat in September 1939? The question is not entirely fair since under the unfavourable circumstances that developed, Poland was essentially caught unprepared for a high-intensity war. Polish leaders had gambled – and lost – that they had enough time to create a strong domestic military-industrial base before either Germany or the Soviet Union attacked. Had this policy been granted more time, Poland would have been in a stronger position of military deterrence and less dependent on French military aid. What is often forgotten is just how rapidly the German military threat emerged. Until mid-1938, the Wehrmacht lacked sufficient Bf 109 fighters or modern tanks to achieve battlefield dominance over the Polish military. Had Hitler attacked Poland prior to 1939, the Polish military would have performed much better.

Poland's leadership did have the means to alter the course – if not the outcome – of a campaign against Germany by making different operational and strategic decisions. Had Rydz-Śmigły ordered each of the border armies to assign one regular and one reserve division to defend key cities – Modlin, Bydgoszcz, Poznań, Łódź, Częstochowa, Katowice and Kraków – the Germans would have been forced to divert a good portion of their infantry and artillery to besiege them, leaving far fewer forces to push into the Polish heartland. German operational methods were poorly suited to urban warfare and their firepower less effective, which is a weakness that the Poles could have anticipated and exploited. The remainder of the Polish armies, about 20 divisions, could have concentrated around Warsaw, Lublin and Lwów, using the Vistula as a shield – an approach recommended by the French. By concentrating their armies, the Poles could probably have gained local superiorities as they did on the Bzura, in order to gain some tactical victories. If the Poles had massed all their available tanks, motorized cavalry brigades and airpower under Army Warsaw from the beginning, they probably could have prevented the Germans from encircling or bombing the city for longer than they did in the actual campaign. With the two existing motorized cavalry brigades and two light tank battalions, the WP had the components to form a single mechanized division, which could have been used to spearhead counter-attacks. Enhanced Polish resistance would also probably have delayed Soviet entry, since Stalin was not interested in fighting a protracted campaign in Poland. Better leadership, such as Sosnkowski instead of Dąb-Biernacki, and earlier mobilization would likely have improved Polish performance in the campaign as well. Under these conditions, Polish military forces might have survived several more weeks and delayed Soviet intervention, thereby allowing more troops to escape to the West via Romania. Finally, the Polish General Staff should have anticipated the need to form guerrilla units in enemy occupied territory and could have created dispersed weapons stockpiles in remote areas and assigned reserve officers to lead resistance forces.

It is also possible that other countries could have delayed – if not prevented – the war that occurred in September 1939. Had the British government been more circumspect in the early 1930s about allowing the export of military technology such as the Vickers 6-tonne tank to the Soviet Union and aircraft engines to Germany, the pace of rearmament in both countries would have been delayed. Had the United States blocked companies from selling advanced industrial machinery to the Soviet Union, Stalin's First Five Year Plan would have been delayed, which would have inhibited the growth of the Red Army. Had Britain and France imposed economic sanctions upon Germany for violating the disarmament clauses of the Treaty of Versailles, Hitler's rearmament programme would have been starved of both resources and capital. Had Britain provided Poland with military loans prior to 1939, Poland could have accelerated its own rearmament plans. Instead, the leaders of the Western democracies not only failed to act effectively to prevent aggression in Europe, but they wittingly enabled it on multiple occasions by turning a blind eye as events unfolded before them.

Polish Resistance and Soviet–German Crimes, 1939–41

'The worst damage, however, which will accrue to the German national body from the present conditions, is the excessive brutality and moral depravity, which will spread in the shortest time like a plague. When high officials of the SS and police demand violent acts and commend them in public, then in a very short time only the violent will reign. Surprisingly fast, like-minded people and those with a bad temper are coming together to let off steam, as is the case in Poland, with their animal and pathological instincts. There is hardly any way to restrain them, for they must rightfully be authorized by official channels and feel justified in every cruelty.'

General Blaskowitz, February 1940

The authority of the government of the Polish Second Republic collapsed the moment that Rydz-Śmigły and his entourage crossed into Romania. Although promised quick transit to the West, Rydz-Śmigły, Mościcki and the rest of the Polish government were soon interned by the Romanian authorities and not allowed to leave the country. Just before leaving Poland, Mościcki had issued instructions to begin forming a government-in-exile in France, but it did not work out as he expected. The Polish ambassadors in Paris and London ignored Mościcki's candidate and engineered the selection of Władysław Raczkiewicz, who was technically third in line of succession as Marshal of the Senate, as the new president of the republic. The Polish government-in-exile was established in Angers, south-west of Paris. Since few members of the Sanacja regime had yet reached France, the new government was packed with many opponents of the regime. On 30 September, Raczkiewicz appointed General Władysław Sikorski to be prime minister and commander-in-chief of the Polish armed forces in exile. Two months later, Stanisław Mikołajczyk arrived via Hungary to join the Polish government-in-exile.

Meanwhile, in Poland, Hitler came to Warsaw on 5 October to witness a triumphal victory parade. All Polish citizens were ordered to remain indoors and the Germans took over 400 hostages, including Mayor Starzyński, to ensure that there were no incidents. Initially, the Wehrmacht administered occupied Poland, with Rundstedt as the titular head of the military government. Danzig, Upper Silesia and the Polish provinces of Poznań, Pomorze and Łódź were annexed to the Reich;

338

Poznań and Łódź were reformed into the Reichsgau Wartheland and SS-Obergruppenführer Arthur Greiser was put in charge of administering this region for the Reich. Greiser's first task was to remove the indigenous Polish population by any means necessary. Greiser was assisted by the Reichssicherheitshauptamt (Reich Main Security Office or RSHA) under Reinhard Heydrich, which was tasked with the removal of 8.9 million Poles from all annexed areas, so that the regions could be fully Germanized. Forster was put in charge of Reichsgau Danzig-Westpreußen, which encompassed Pomerania. Thousands of others were forcibly deported east, by armed members of the *Volksdeutscher Selbstschutz*. In the first five months of the German occupation, 87,000 Poles were deported from Danzig and 70,000 from Poznań.[12] Polish cities such as Bydgoszcz, Gdynia, Łódź and Poznań were renamed Bromberg, Gotenhafen, Litzmannstadt and Posen. In mid-October 1939, the Germans had already begun conscription of forced labour and eventually 1.7 million Polish civilians, including girls as young as 14, were sent to work in Germany.

Rundstedt and the rest of the Wehrmacht had little say in what transpired in the rest of occupied Poland, which was actually a power vacuum in which various SS and Gestapo security officials and their acolytes in the Volksdeutscher Selbstschutz units exercised real authority. On 25 October, the Wehrmacht transferred authority over occupied Poland to Hans Frank's General Government, located in Kraków.[13] Blaskowitz replaced Rundstedt as military commander in the east, but had little authority over the various SS, police and paramilitary units operating in Poland. Poles forcibly deported from the annexed provinces were dumped in the General Government, which usually left them destitute. Frank's mission was to reduce the Poles to abject servitude through a deliberate policy of brutality and denial of resources. Six days after assuming his position, Frank issued new guidelines that made many crimes punishable by death and a strict food rationing system that was guaranteed to lead to slow starvation. As soon as the fighting was over, a whole new breed of SS officials appeared out of the woodwork to begin a vicious campaign of winnowing out anyone in Polish society who might resist the New Order. Just a week after Bydgoszcz fell into German hands, SS-Brigadeführer Lothar Beutel, commander of Einsatzgruppe 4, executed approximately 150 Polish civilians near the city. SS-Oberführer Ludolf von Alvensleben, a career sociopath, led the way in taking actions to eliminate the Polish intelligentsia, clergy and other prominent citizens, beginning with mass arrests and executions in Pomerania. The RSHA absorbed the Einsatzgruppen, which spent the autumn of 1939 working through the lists (*Sonderfahndungsbuch Polen*) of Polish citizens, murdering thousands. SS-Brigadeführer Emil Rasch established the Soldau concentration camp near Mława in late September 1939, where SS troops under his command began executing members of the local Polish intelligentsia. Greiser also moved to crush the Catholic clergy, while in Kraków SS-Obersturmbannführer Bruno Müller arrested the entire staff of the Jagiellonian University. Although relatively few civilians were murdered in the first months of the German occupation, the groundwork was laid for more lethal measures. In May 1940, the SS began *AB-Aktion* (*Ausserordenliche Befriedungsaktion*; Extraordinary Pacification Operation) in Poland, arresting over 30,000 persons, of whom roughly 7,000 were executed, including Jews and Poles.

Both the Wehrmacht and the SS committed widespread looting in Poland. One of the beneficiaries of this looting was Heinz Guderian, who in 1942 was given a 2,000-acre estate in the Reichsgau Wartheland near the village of Głębokie.[14] The original owner was a Polish officer, Tadeusz Twardowski, who had been murdered by the NKVD in Katyń Forest. Hans Frank was a notorious looter, enriching himself with the spoils of war. The SS also initiated a programme under Himmler's direction to kidnap Polish children who appeared suitably Aryan. Thousands were abducted and sent to *Kinderlager* (child camps) and – if they passed medical exams – to be raised by German parents. Those children deemed not suitable were murdered.[15] Blaskowitz began complaining in writing to the OKH in November 1939 about the criminal actions being committed by the SS and police in Poland but was relieved of command in February 1940. Hitler referred to Blaskowitz's objections as 'childish.'[16]

It should be noted that the Wehrmacht did take measures to preserve the senior Polish military leadership that fell into its hands. The Germans captured seven of the nine senior Polish field commanders, except for Fabrycy and Dąb-Biernacki, who fled to England. All seven of these Polish generals survived German captivity. However, the 664,000 captured Polish enlisted soldiers were detained in rough prisoner-of-war (POW) camps in Poland for six months and were denied succour from the International Red Cross, since the German Foreign Ministry claimed that they were not POWs because Poland no longer existed. The 50,000 Jewish-Polish POWs were segregated and treated more harshly, with half dying during the first winter. Eventually, most of the Polish POWs were shipped off to Germany in 1940 for use as forced labourers, including clearing snow in the streets of Berlin and assisting with the harvests. Thousands of these forced labourers would perish from abuse and malnutrition over the next five years. No estimate has yet been made on the number of Polish POW deaths, but they were substantial and should be added to the total.

Before Warsaw surrendered, Rómmel ordered his deputy, Generał Brygady Michał Karaszewicz-Tokarzewski, to form an underground resistance movement to continue the fight against the Germans. A surprising number of officers from Army Warsaw were able to escape German captivity and Karaszewicz-Tokarzewski was able to form the first Polish resistance movement, known as the Service for Victory in Poland (Sluzba Zwyciestwu Polski or SZP), in just a few weeks. Stefan Rowecki was among those who joined the leadership cadre of the resistance. Although the core of the SZP was led by professional army officers, Karaszewicz-Tokarzewski was able to reach out and recruit volunteers from the general populace. Poland, with its long history of covert resistance to foreign occupiers, was fertile ground for developing an active guerrilla force. In November 1939, the SZP was redesignated as the Union for Armed Struggle (Zwiazek Walki Zbrojnej or ZWZ) and it was placed under the authority of the government-in-exile. When Kazimierz Sosnkowski reached France, Sikorski appointed him to command the ZWZ. However, there were a myriad of other resistance groups that formed in Poland that were not loyal to the government-in-exile, including the right-wing affiliated NSZ and the peasant-based BCh groups. The inability of these groups to work together hindered the evolution of the Polish resistance into a more effective organization for two years. In February 1942, the ZWZ transformed into the Home Army and the resistance had grown to 100,000 full-time and part-time members. By 1944, the Home Army would quadruple in size and was able to field battalion-size units during the Warsaw Uprising. However, the Home Army would continue the fight for Polish independence long after the Second World War had officially ended in Europe.

Unlike occupied countries in Western Europe, there was virtually no collaboration with the enemy in Poland. While some individuals betrayed others under interrogation to save themselves, there was no effort to work with the enemy. Nor did the Germans attempt to form Waffen-SS units with Poles, as they did with Belgians, Bosnians, Danes, Dutch, French and Norwegians. On the other hand, the ethnic Germans did collaborate with the occupation and they should not be considered as Poles, just like those Byelorussian communists and Ukrainian nationalists who collaborated with the Soviets. Many of the *Volksdeutsche* signed the *Volksliste*, certifying them as Germans. One who signed the list was the actor Igo Sym, who made a pro-Nazi propaganda film in conjunction with the Germans; in March 1941 Sym was assassinated by ZWZ agents to discourage similar collaboration.

As a result of the Soviet invasion of eastern Poland, the Soviet Union gained control over 12 million people, including about 250,000 Polish military personnel. Arrests and deportations of 'anti-Soviet elements' began almost immediately. Virtually all the Polish officers, about 9,000, were transferred to two NKVD-run camps in the Soviet Union: Kozel'sk and Starobel'sk. Another group of 4,700 border guards and KOP personnel were sent to a separate camp at Ostashkov. Władysław Anders was fortunate in that he was transferred to the Lubyanka prison in Moscow for special interrogation. The Polish enlisted soldiers were sent to work in labour camps in the Soviet Union. On 11 October, the Soviets bullied Lithuania into signing a treaty of mutual assistance, which ceded the city of Wilno to Lithuania but allowed the Red Army to station 20,000 troops in the country. Six months later, the Soviets annexed Lithuania by force. On 1 November, the Polish eastern provinces were formally annexed to the Soviet Union and on 29 November everyone living in the Kresy region was assigned Soviet citizenship. The NKVD ruthlessly weeded out hostile elements: around 250,000 were arrested and sentenced to hard labour in the Soviet Gulag and 65,000 were simply executed.[17] In February 1940, the Soviets began mass deportations from eastern Poland and in the next 16 months roughly 400,000 civilians were forcibly removed to Kazakhstan and Siberia; thousands died en route. Children as young as 14 were made to build railroads and work in mines, fed at near-starvation levels. One of the teenagers deported to Siberia was Wojciech Jaruzelski, who would one day be groomed by the Soviets to lead the armed forces of the Polish People's Republic. Another of those arrested by the NKVD was Ryszard Kaczorowski, a 20-year-old scouting instructor in Białystok, who was sent to the infamous Kolyma Gulag camp in north-east Siberia, along with thousands of his countrymen. Kaczorowski was one of the lucky ones – not only would he survive, but he would become the last president of the Polish government-in-exile in 1989–90. Despite the persistent efforts of the Polish government-in-exile, the British and French governments made no effort to demand that the Soviet Union release these prisoners. Adding insult to injury, Franklin D. Roosevelt's moronic vice president, Henry A. Wallace, visited the Kolyma Gulag camp in August 1944 and was completely hoodwinked by NKVD efforts to conceal the true nature of the facility. Wallace not only returned with an admiring report about the

Gulag camps, in which he believed all the workers were paid volunteers, but assisted in the production of a film about Kolyma which helped to deceive the American public about the true nature of Stalin's regime.[18]

The ZWZ attempted to form cells in eastern Poland but this effort was defeated by the NKVD's arrest of virtually anyone sympathetic to the Second Republic. In March 1940, Karaszewicz-Tokarzewski attempted to enter the Soviet zone, but was arrested by the NKVD and sent to the Lubyanka prison. On March 5, 1940, the Soviet Politburo decided that the Polish officers were 'sworn enemies of the Soviet regime' and ordered the NKVD to eliminate them. In April, the NKVD began executing the Polish prisoners in groups of 300 in secret, gradually emptying the Kozel'sk, Ostashkov and Starobel'sk camps. According to Soviet records, 4,421 Polish officers were murdered by the NKVD in the Katyń Forest near Smolensk in April 1940 and another 17,436 Poles in Kiev, Kharkov and other locations in the Ukraine. Thus, the Soviet regime murdered a total of 21,857 Allied military personnel.[19] The Soviet government then disavowed all knowledge of Polish officer prisoners. Although these murders were suspected by the Polish government-in-exile because all contact with the prisoners ceased in spring 1940, they were not confirmed until the Germans found the mass graves in Katyń in 1943.

Both Germany and the Soviet Union continued to exploit the annexed regions of Poland in 1940–41 and the Gestapo and NKVD co-operated in efforts to hunt down Polish resistance groups. The Germans regarded the Poles as race enemies, while the Soviets regarded them as class enemies. During this period, the British government did very little to assist their Polish allies, even though Sikorski was able to build up considerable Polish military forces in the West; these forces played an important role in the battle of Narvik, the Battle of Britain, the Battle of the Atlantic and the North African campaign. Once Germany invaded the Soviet Union in June 1941, Winston Churchill was eager to work with the Soviets and pressured Sikorski to resume diplomatic relations with the Soviet Union; this was a major insult to the Poles but they grudgingly accepted it as part of the obligation of being allies with Great Britain. As a result of the Sikorski–Mayski Agreement signed on 30 July 1941, which restored Soviet–Polish diplomatic relations, Stalin agreed to issue an amnesty for the remaining Polish prisoners in the Soviet Union. However, Stalin wanted to reform the Poles into divisions under Soviet command and use them as cannon fodder on the Eastern Front. He only grudgingly agreed to allow Anders and Karaszewicz-Tokarzewski (who were some of the few senior Polish officers still alive in Soviet custody) to leave the Soviet Union with some of the less fit personnel; in March 1942 31,189 Polish soldiers and 12,408 civilians left the USSR via Iran. Yet upon reaching Palestine, Anders' troops were so emaciated and sickly that it took months before these personnel were fit for military duty. Meanwhile, the NKVD used the Polish renegade Zygmunt Berling to form the 'Polish People's Army', which would operate on the Eastern Front under Soviet command.

German war crimes in Poland were acknowledged by the Western Allies, but relatively few were ever held accountable. Hans Frank was arrested by the US Army in 1945, tried at Nuremberg and hanged in 1946. SS-Oberführer Erich Naumann, commander of Einsatzgruppe 6 in Poland, was convicted for his crimes against Soviet civilians in 1941 and hanged in 1951. Arthur Greiser and Albert Forster were tried in Polish courts after the war and hanged. Three other SS officers involved in war crimes in Poland – SS-Obersturmbannführer Emanuel Schäfer and SS-Obergruppenführer Udo von Woyrsch and Bruno Müller – were tried after the war in German courts and received light prison sentences, then were released. Two other Einsatzgruppe commanders, SS-Standartenführer Bruno Streckenbach and SS-Brigadeführer Lothar Beutel, were not convicted due to lack of evidence. Ludolf von Alvensleben was eventually indicted for the campaign of murders he orchestrated in Poland but fled to Argentina after the war, which then refused his extradition.

Of course, none of the Soviet NKVD officials or Red Army officers who committed war crimes or crimes against humanity in Poland were ever indicted or even acknowledged by the West as criminals. Vasily M. Blokhin, the NKVD official who led the execution teams at Katyń Forest, was given the Order of the Red Banner by Stalin but was sacked after Stalin's death. Even though the United States received credible reporting that the Katyn Forest massacre had been the work of the NKVD, the Roosevelt administration actively worked to conceal Soviet guilt.[20] In Britain, the 1991 War Crimes Act restricted itself to acts committed by Germans or on German-occupied territory, but ignored similar Soviet crimes. Indeed, the Soviet Union was never held accountable for the vast human misery and suffering it inflicted on Poland and the other countries of eastern Europe.

Epilogue

Once the Polish Second Republic was smashed and the Third Reich and the Soviet Union now had a common border, their spirit of collaboration did not last long. Hitler benefited from Soviet economic trade while he prepared to attack in the West, thereby weakening the effects of the Allied naval blockade. By May 1940, the Wehrmacht had recovered from Case White and was ready to launch its long-awaited Western offensive. Amazingly, in just six weeks the Wehrmacht smashed the French, Belgian and Dutch armies and evicted the British Expeditionary Force from the continent. During the Western Campaign, the Wehrmacht demonstrated much-improved operational and tactical efficiency over its performance in Poland, and by June 1940 Hitler believed that German forces were virtually invincible. While Hitler had been pre-occupied in the West, Stalin had annexed the three Baltic states and Bessarabia. Once the Anglo-French allies were defeated, Hitler intended to renounce the Molotov–Ribbentrop Pact and attack the Soviet Union while his military forces were at peak efficiency. In June 1941, Hitler launched Operation *Barbarossa*, hoping to overrun the Soviet Union in a matter of weeks, as he had done Poland and France.

However, Hitler had not fully comprehended that the Wehrmacht's style of warfare could not simply be scaled up to defeat a country that was fifty times larger than either Poland or France. Indeed, the Wehrmacht met its match in the Soviet Union, where its lack of adequate preparations for a long war and arrogant disregard for intelligence, logistic and terrain/weather factors led to catastrophic failures. Rebounding from its own initial defeats thanks to superior pre-war industrial preparations, the Red

Army relentlessly pushed westwards and by July 1944 had reached the Vistula River and driven the Wehrmacht from eastern Poland. However, the Soviets paused outside Warsaw when the Home Army rose in rebellion against the Germans, allowing the SS to leisurely crush the uprising. Anglo-American efforts to aid the Home Army in Warsaw were rebuffed by Stalin, who wanted the Home Army eliminated. Indeed, as soon as the Red Army moved into eastern Poland, all pretence of co-operation with Polish forces controlled by the London government-in-exile ceased and the NKVD began arresting and murdering Home Army officers. The Red Army finally captured the burnt-out wreck of Warsaw and most of western Poland in January 1945. However, the Germans hung tenaciously onto Danzig and this city, where the war began, did not fall until 30 March 1945. In the harbour of Gotenhofen (Gdynia), the wreck of the pre-dreadnought *Schleswig-Holstein,* which had fired the first shots of the Second World War, lay rusting after having been belatedly sunk by RAF bombers.

Meanwhile, Poland's Western allies gradually sold out its interests during the war in order to retain good relations with Stalin. Soviet collusion with the Third Reich in 1939–40, Soviet criminal behaviour in Poland and the Katyń Forest massacre were all nonchalantly swept under the carpet by the American and British leadership. Western media and socialist labour leaders in the West continually churned out admiring reports about the valiant Red Army and its liberation of eastern Europe, ignoring the fact that it had helped to conquer four of these nations in 1939–40. Western appeasement of Hitler's pre-war aggression did not end, it simply morphed into appeasement of Stalin's aggressive behaviour and for the same reason – to avoid making greater military sacrifices to restore the pre-war status quo. The epitome of this craven sell-out occurred at the Tehran Conference in November 1943, where any hope for Poland's post-war independence was sacrificed on the altar of Allied solidarity. No Polish leaders were invited to discuss their post-war borders with the Soviets and they were brow-beaten into acquiescence, just as the Czechs had been by Chamberlain in 1938. At no point did the Anglo-Americans even consider threatening to reduce Lend Lease shipments to the Soviet Union in order to gain better terms for Poland and Czechoslovakia. While Churchill's inability to press Stalin was understandable to the Poles since it was clear that the British Empire was fading, it was harder for them to understand why the United States, with its military and economic power out-matching Soviet resources, was willing to concede eastern Europe without protest. Unfortunately, President Franklin D. Roosevelt was a sickly man, possessed of a cartoonish image of 'Uncle Joe' Stalin and advised by gullible men such as Henry Wallace and Harry Hopkins. At Yalta, Hopkins told Stalin that 'the United States had no special interests in Poland and would accept any government in Poland which was desired by the Polish people', then accepted Stalin's vague assent to 'free elections'.[1] Just as European leaders had thought they could 'manage' Hitler in the 1930s, the Americans believed that they could 'manage' Stalin to accept their vision for post-war Europe. Polish hopes for any kind of post-war freedom were ruined by British weakness and American ignorance.

So Poland passed from complete occupation by the Germans to complete occupation by the Soviets. The Polish People's Republic was foisted upon the Poles in 1947, with its leadership imported directly from Moscow. Stanisław Mikołajczyk returned to Poland but was defeated in rigged elections and many of his supporters were arrested; he was lucky to escape with his life. Instead, Bolesław Bierut, an NKVD agent, became the new president of Poland. Since Stalin refused to return any of the territory seized from Poland in 1939, the new Poland was moved 100km westwards to the Oder–Neise line, into seized German territory. The new communist government then deported ethnic Germans from their lands in order to Polonize them. In just a few years, Poland became a police state, ruthlessly suppressing anything or anyone that threatened the communist party. However, the communists were never able to stabilize Poland, whose people remained defiant to foreign-imposed rule. Former members of the Home Army, known as 'cursed soldiers', kept up an active guerrilla campaign until the last member was killed in 1963. In June 1956, widespread labour unrest occurred in Poznań, which required tanks and troops to put down, resulting in nearly 100 deaths. More riots in Gdynia in December 1970 led to troops firing upon workers with machine guns, killing at least 40. The Catholic Church in Poland – which was repressed by the regime – led the way towards building more effective civil resistance to undermine communist rule. The Solidarity trade organization, founded in 1980, was the vehicle of national deliverance. Although the regime, led in its final days by Wojciech Jaruzelski, tried intimidation and martial law to suppress Solidarity, in the end it was the regime that broke. In August 1989, the communist edifice of power in Poland rapidly crumbled and the first democratic elections resulted in the creation of the Third Polish Republic. On 17 September 1993, President Lech Wałęsa bid farewell to the last Russian soldiers leaving Poland – exactly 54 years after the initial invasion. Once the Russian troops were gone, the new Polish Republic moved to eliminate any remaining vestiges of the 54 years of occupation. Although modern Poland is now a democratic state with membership of NATO and the EU, the lessons of Case White and Katyń Forest have impressed upon its citizens the need to remain vigilant and not take freedom for granted.

Officer Rank Table

Poland	Germany	Soviet Union	United Kingdom
Marszałek Polski	Generalfeldmarschall	Marshal	Field Marshal
	Generaloberst	General armii	General
Generał Broni	General der ...	General-Polkovnik	Lieutenant General
Generał Dywizji	Generalleutnant	General-Leytenant	Major–General
Generał Brygady	Generalmajor	General-Mayor	Brigadier
Pułkownik	Oberst	Polkovnik	Colonel
Podpułkownik	Oberstleutnant	Podpolkovnik	Lieutenant-Colonel
Major	Major	Mayor	Major
Kapitan	Hauptmann	Kapitan	Captain
Porucznik	Oberleutnant	Starshiy leytenant	Lieutenant
Podporucznik	Leutnant	Leytenant	Second Lieutenant
		Mladshiy leytenant	

Abbreviations

GERMAN

AA	Aufklärungs-Abteilung (reconnaissance battalion)
AR	Aufklärungs-Regiment (mot.) (reconnaissance regiment)
AufklGr	Aufklärungsgruppe (reconnaissance group)
IR	Infanterie-Regiment (mot.)
JG	Jagdgeschwader (fighter group)
KG	Kampfgeschwader (bomber group)
Krad	Kradschützen-Bataillon (motorcycle battalion)
KSR	Kavallerie-Schützen-Regiment (mounted rifle regiment)
KüFlGr	Küstenfliegergruppe (coastal air group)
LG	Lehrgeschwader (demonstration group)
Ln-Abt	Luftnachrichten-Abteilung (Luftwaffe signals battalion)
MSK	Marinestosstruppkompanie (naval assault company)
OKH	Oberkommando des Heeres (High Command of the Army)
OKL	Oberkommando der Luftwaffe (High Command of the Air Force)
OKW	Oberkommando der Wehrmacht (High Command of the Armed Forces)
Pz	Panzer, also Pzkfw or Panzerkampfwagen (armoured fighting vehicle)
RM	Reichsmark (Germany currency; in 1939, $1 US = RM 2.5 or £1 = RM 12)

SdKfz	Sonderkraftfahrzeug (specialized vehicle)
SPW	Schützenpanzerwagen (armoured infantry vehicle)
SR	Schützen-Regiment (rifle regiment)
StG	Sturzkampfgeschwader (dive-bomber group)
VS	Verbrauchssatz (a basic load of fuel)
Z	Zerstörer (destroyer units)
ZG	Zerstörer-Geschwader (destroyer group)

POLISH

BK	Brygada Kawalerii (Cavalry Brigade)
CKM	Cekaem (heavy machine-gun unit)
COP	Centralny Okręg Przemysłowy (Central Industrial Region)
DOK	Dowództwo Okręgu Korpusu (Corps District Command)
KMW	Kierownictwo Marynarki Wojennej (Naval Directorate)
KOP	Korpus Ochrony Pogranicza (Border Protection Corps)
KPP	Komunistyczna Partia Polski (Polish Communist Party)
KSUS	Komitetu ds. Uzbrojenia i Sprzętu (Armaments and Equipment Committee)
LW	Lotnictwo Wojskowe (Polish Military Aviation)
M.S. Wojsk	Ministerstwo Spraw Wojskowych (Ministry of Military Affairs)
Oddział II	Second Department, or Division II, of the Polish General Staff (intelligence)
ON	Obrona Narodowa (National Defence, i.e. territorial units)
OPL	Obrona Przeciwlotnicza (air defence)
OWS	Obszar Warowny Śląsk (Fortified Region of Silesia)
OW	Oddział Wydzielony (independent detachment)
POW	Polska Organizacja Wojskowa (Polish Military Organization)
PPS	Polska Partia Socjalistyczna (Polish Socialist Party)
SG WP	Sztab Generalny Wojska Polskiego (Polish General Staff)
WP	Wojsko Polskie (Polish Armed Forces)
wz.	wzór (Model/Year)
zł	*złoty* (Polish currency; in 1939, \$1 US ≈ 5.2 zł or £1 ≈ 25 zł)

SOVIET

OGPU	Obyedinyonnoye gosudarstvennoye politicheskoye upravleniye pri SNK SSSR (Joint State Political Directorate)
NKVD	Narodnyy Komissariat Vnutrennikh Del (People's Commissariat for Internal Affairs)
RVS	Revolyutsionny Voyenny Sovyet (Revolutionary Military Council)
VVS	Voyenno-Vozdushnye Sily (Military Air Force)

Appendices

APPENDIX A: CASE WHITE ORDER OF BATTLE, 1 SEPTEMBER 1939

Polish 2nd Republic

President Ignacy Mościcki
Prime Minister Felicjan Sławoj Składkowski

High Command

- Marszałek Edward Rydz-Śmigły, commander-in-chief
- Generał Brygady Wacław Stachiewicz, Chief of the General Staff of the Polish Army

Ministry of Military Affairs

- Generał Dywizji Tadeusz Kasprzycki

Polish Army

Reserve of Supreme Command

- 11th Infantry Division (11 DP)
- 24th Infantry Division (24 DP)
- 21st Tank Battalion (R35)
- Czechoslovak Legion (forming) (Lieutenant-Colonel Ludvík Svoboda)*
- Armoured Train No. 15

---

*This battalion-size unit of Czech expatriates was in the process of forming in Poland when the German invasion began, but was not yet armed. It began to form into a combat unit on 3 September but was still only lightly armed by the time that it was forced to surrender to the Red Army.

Army Prusy (Armia Prusy) (Generał Dywizji Stefan Dąb-Biernacki)
- Northern Group
  - 13th Infantry Division (13 DP)
  - 19th Infantry Division (19 DP)
  - 29th Infantry Division (29 DP)
  - Wileńska Cavalry Brigade (Wileńska Brygada Kawalerii)
  - 1st Light Tank Battalion (7TP) (1 BCL)
- Southern Group (Generał Brygady Stanisław Skwarczyński)
  - 3rd Legions Infantry Division
  - 12th Infantry Division (12 DP)
  - 36th Infantry Division (36 DP)
- 22nd Mountain Infantry Division
- Army Support Units
  - 1st Heavy Artillery Regiment, 3rd Heavy Artillery Regiment, 50th Heavy Artillery Detachment
  - 81st Motorized Engineer Battalion

Army Pomorze (Armia Pomorze) (Generał Dywizji Władysław Bortnowski)
- Operational Group East (Generał Brygady Mikołaj Boltuc)
  - 4th Infantry Division (4 DP)
  - 16th Infantry Division (16 DP)
  - Jablomowo Local Defence Regiment
- Operational Group Czersk (Generał Brygady Stanisław Grzmot-Skotnicki)
  - Pomorska Cavalry Brigade (Pomorska Brygada Kawalerii)
  - Kościerzyna Detachment (2 ON battalions)
  - Chojnice Detachment (1st Rifle Battalion, 2 ON, 1 artillery battalion)*
  - Tczew Detachment (2nd Rifle Battalion)
- 9th Infantry Division (9 DP)
- 15th Infantry Division (15 DP)
- 27th Infantry Division (27 DP)
- Pomorska ON Brigade (6 ON battalions)
- Chełmska ON Brigade (7 ON battalions)
- Army Support Units
  - 6th Heavy Machine-gun Battalion
  - 46th Motorized Engineer Battalion
  - Armoured Train No. 14
  - Vistula Local Defence Regiment
  - Torun Local Defence Regiment

Army Modlin (Armia Modlin) (Generał Brygady Emil Przedrzymirski-Krukowicz)
- 8th Infantry Division (8 DP)

*The Polish Army organized 3 independent rifle battalions during the 1930s.

- 20th Infantry Division (20 DP)
- Nowogródzka Cavalry Brigade (Nowogródzka Brygada Kawalerii)
- Mazowiecka Cavalry Brigade (Mazowiecka Brygada Kawalerii)
- Warsaw ON Brigade
- Army Support Units
  ◦ 1st Heavy Machine-gun Battalion
  ◦ 1st Heavy Artillery Regiment (3 battalions with a total of 8 × 105mm, 8 × 120mm, 12 × 155mm)
  ◦ 60th Motorized Engineer Battalion
  ◦ Armoured Trains No. 13 and No. 15

Operational Group Wyszków (Generał Brygady Wincenty Kowalski)
- 1st Legions Infantry Division (1 DPL)
- 41st Infantry Division (Reserve) (partially mobilized)
- 1st Battalion/2nd Heavy Artillery Regiment
- Armoured Train No. 55

Independent Operational Group Narew (SGO Narew) (Generał Brygady Czesław Młot-Fijałkowski)
- 18th Infantry Division (18 DP)
- 33rd Infantry Division (33 DP) (incomplete)
- Podlaska Cavalry Brigade (Podlaska Brygada Kawalerii)
- Suwalska Cavalry Brigade (Suwalska Brygada Kawalerii)Osowiec Fortress Garrison (a reinforced KOP battalion)
- Group Support Units
  ◦ 2nd Heavy Machine-gun Battalion
  ◦ 53rd Motorized Engineer Battalion
  ◦ 81st Light Artillery Battalion

Army Poznań (Armia Poznań) (Generał Dywizji Tadeusz Kutrzeba)
- 14th Infantry Division (14 DP)
- 17th Infantry Division (17 DP)
- 12th Infantry Division (25 DP)
- Wielkopolska Cavalry Brigade (Wielkopolska Brygada Kawalerii)
- Podolska Cavalry Brigade (Podolska Brygada Kawalerii)
- Army Support Units
  ◦ 5th Heavy Machine-gun Battalion
  ◦ 47th Motorized Engineer Battalion
  ◦ Armoured Trains No. 11 and No. 12

Army Łódź (Armia Łódź) (Generał Dywizji Juliusz Rómmel)
- 2nd Legions Infantry Division (2 DPL)
- 10th Infantry Division (10 DP)
  ◦ 1st Cavalry Regiment KOP
- 28th Infantry Division (28 DP)

- Kresowa Cavalry Brigade (Kresowa Brygada Kawalerii)
- Sieradz ON Brigade
- Operational Group Piotrków (Generał Brygady Wiktor Thommée)
  - Wołyńska Cavalry Brigade (Wołyńska Brygada Kawalerii)
  - 30th Infantry Division (30 DP)
  - 2nd Battalion/4th Heavy Artillery Regiment (9 × 155mm)
  - 7th Heavy Machine-gun Battalion
- Army Support Units
  - 2nd Light Tank Battalion (7TP) (2 BCL)
  - 6th Heavy Artillery Regiment
  - 50th Motorized Engineer Battalion
  - 3rd Heavy Machine-gun Battalion
  - Armoured Trains No. 52 and No. 53

Army Kraków (Armia Kraków) (Generał Brygady Antoni Szylling)
- Operational Group Ślask (Generał Brygady Jan Jagmin-Sadowski)
  - 23rd Infantry Division (23 DP)
  - 55th Infantry Division (55 DP) (incomplete)*
  - Katowice Fortress Brigade Group† (Pułkownik Wacław Klaczyński)
  - 95th Heavy Artillery Detachment
- Operational Group Bielsko (Generał Brygady M. Boruta-Spiechowicz)
  - 1st Brigade Mountain Rifles KOP
    - 1st Infantry Regiment KOP
    - 2nd Infantry Regiment KOP
  - 6th Infantry Division (6 DP)
  - 21st Mountain Infantry Division
- 7th Infantry Division (7 DP)
- Krakowska Cavalry Brigade (Krakowska Brygada Kawalerii)
- 10th Motorized Brigade (10. Brygada Kawalerii) (Pułkownik Stanisław Maczek)
- Army Support Units
  - 4th Heavy Machine-gun Battalion
  - 64th Light Artillery Detachment
  - 1st Motorized Anti-Aircraft Battalion
  - 65th Motorized Engineer Battalion
  - Armoured Train No. 51

*The 55 DP was formed from ON battalions in late August 1939.
†This group consisted of 3 regular infantry battalions from the 23rd Infantry Division, one ON battalion and one artillery battalion equipped with 75mm guns.

Army Karpaty (Armia Karpaty) (Generał Dywizji Kazimierz Fabrycy)
- Operational Group Jasło
  - 2nd Mountain Rifle Brigade
  - 3rd Mountain Rifle Brigade
- Detachment 'Hungary'
  - 216th Infantry Regiment
  - Karpaty ON Brigade
- 1st Regiment Border Protection Corps (KOP)
- Army Support Units
  - 1st Motorized Artillery Regiment

Mobilization

Date (1939)	Unit	Assigned
4 September	41 DP (incomplete)	SGO Narew
	44 DP (incomplete)	Lodz Army
5 September	Warsaw Armoured-Motorized Brigade	
6 September	46th Squadron of Heavy Artillery (120mm)	Modlin Army
7 September	35 DP	
	47th Squadron of Heavy Artillery (120mm)	Modlin Army
	11th, 12th, 13th Squadrons of Heavy Artillery (6 × 220mm mortars each)	Modlin Army
9 September	38 DP	Army Karpaty
10 September	39 DP	Army Prusy
19 September	60 DP (incomplete)	OG Polisie

Polish Air Force (Lotnictwo Wojskowe)
- Commander – Generał Brygady Józef L. Zając

Brygada Pościgowa (Pursuit Brigade) (Pułkownik Stefan Pawlikowski)
- III/I Group
  - 111 Eskadra Kościuszkowska (10x P.11c)
  - 112 Eskadra (10x P.11c)
- IV/ Group
  - 113 Eskadra (10x P.11c)
  - 114 Eskadra (10x P.11c)
  - 123 Eskadra (10x P.7a)

Brygada Bombowa (Bomber Brigade) (Pułkownik Władysław Heller)
- II/2 Group
  - 21 Eskadra (10x P.23b)
  - 22 Eskadra (10x P.23b)

- IV/6 Group
  - 64 Eskadra (10x P.23b)
  - 65 Eskadra (10x P.23b)
- X/1 Group
  - 211 Eskadra (9x P.37b)
  - 212 Eskadra (9x P.37b)
- XV/I Group
  - 216 Eskadra (9x P.37b)
  - 217 Eskadra (9x P.37b)
- 55 Eskadra (10x P.23b)
- 16 Eskadra (7x Lublin R. XIIId)

Army Aviation
- Kraków Army
  - III/2 Group
    - 121 Eskadra (10x P.11c)
    - 122 Eskadra (10x P.11c)
  - 24 Eskadra (10x P.23b)
  - 23 Eskadra (7x RWD.14)
  - 26 Eskadra (7x Lublin R.XIIId)
- Poznań Army
  - Group III/3
    - 131 Eskadra (10x P.11c)
    - 132 Eskadra (10x P.11c)
  - 34 Eskadra (10x P.23b)
  - 33 Eskadra (7x RWD.14)
  - 36 Eskadra (7x Lublin R.XIIId)
- Pomorze Army
  - III/4 Group
    - 141 Eskadra (10x P.11c)
    - 142 Eskadra (10x P.11c)
  - 42 Eskadra (10x P.23b)
  - 43 Eskadra (7x Lublin R.XIIId)
  - 46 Eskadra (7x Lublin R.XIIId)
- Modlin Army
  - 152 Eskadra (10x P.11c)
  - 41 Eskadra (8x P.23b)
  - 53 Eskadra (7x RWD.14)
- Łódź Army
  - Group III/6
    - 161 Eskadra (10x P.11c)
    - 162 Eskadra (10x P.7a)

- ○ 32 Eskadra (10x P.23b)
- ○ 63 Eskadra (7x RWD 14)
- • Karpaty Army
  - ○ 31 Eskadra (10x P.23b)
  - ○ 56 Eskadra (7x Lublin R.XIIId)
- • Independent Operational Group Narew (SGO Narew)
  - ○ 151 Eskadra (10x P.7a)
  - ○ 51 Eskadra (10x P.23b)
  - ○ 13 Eskadra (7x RWD 14)

Type	Model	TOTAL
Fighters	P.11c	128
(158)	P.7a	30
Bombers	P.23b	114
(150)	P.37b	36
Reconnaissance	R. XIIId	49
(84)	RWD 14	35
TOTAL		392

Polish Navy (Marynarka Wojenna)

- • Counter-Admiral Józef Unrug, commander of the fleet
- • Vice-Admiral Jerzy Świrski, chief of staff

Destroyer flotilla (Dywizjon Kontrtorpedowców) (Kapitan Marynarki Roman Stankiewicz)
- • Destroyers (4) *Burza, Wicher, Blyskawica, Grom*

Submarine flotilla (Kontradmiral Adam Mohuczy)
- • Submarines (5) *Rys, Wilk, Zbik, Orzel, Sep*

Minelayer (1) *Gryf*
Minesweepers (6): *Czajka, Jaskolka, Mewa, Rybitwa, Czapla, Zuraw*
Gunboats (2): *General Haller, Komendant Pilsudski*

Land Coastal Command (Lądowa Obrona Wybrzeża, LOW) (Pułkownik Stanisław Dąbek)
Naval Brigade of National Defence (Morska Brygada Obrony Narodowej) (Podpułkownik Stanisław Brodowski)
- ○ 1st Naval Rifles Regiment (Podpułkownik Kazimierz Pruszkowski)
- ○ 2nd Naval Rifles Regiment (Podpułkownik Ignacy Szpunar)
- ○ Kashubian ON Battalion
- ○ Kartuzy ON Battalion

Coastal Defence Group (Grupa Obrony Wybrzeża) (Kapitan Stanislaw Zwartynski)
- Hel Fortified Region (Rejon Umocniony Hel) (Kontradmiral Włodzimierz Steyer)
  - Battery No. 31 (4 × 152mm), Battery No. 32 and No. 33 (2 × 105mm each)
- Westerplatte garrison (Major Henryk Sucharski) 209 soldiers

Naval Air Squadron (Morski Dywizjon Lotniczy) (Lublin R–VIII and Lublin R–XIII seaplanes)

German Reich
Führer: Adolf Hitler

High Command
Oberkommando des Heeres (OKH) (Generaloberst Walter Brauchitsch)
Oberkommando des Luftwaffe (OKL) (Reichsmarschall Hermann Göring)
Oberkommando der Kriegsmarine (OKM) (Großadmiral Erich Raeder)

Heer
Heeresgruppe Nord (Generaloberst Fedor von Bock)
- 3. Armee (General der Artillerie Georg von Küchler)
  - I Armeekorps (Generalleutnant Walter Petzel)
    - Panzer-Division Kempf (Generalmajor Werner Kempf)*
      - SS-Regiment 'Deutschland'
      - Panzer-Regiment 10
    - 11. Infanterie-Division
    - 61 Infanterie-Division
    - II./Artillerie-Regiment 37, II./Artillerie-Regiment 47, schwere Artillerie-Abteilung.506†
    - II., III./Flak-Regiment 11‡

*Panzer-Division Kempf was an *ad hoc* unit formed from mixed Heer and Waffen-SS sub-units. It was comprised of Panzer-Regiment 7 (2 battalions with a total of 164 tanks), SS-Regiment 'Deutschland', the SS-Artillerie-Regiment 'Totenkopf' and an SS reconnaissance unit, II./Artillerie-Regiment 47 (schwere) and Panzerabwehr-Abteilung 511. However, the formation did not have a full complement of support units. After the Polish campaign, this division was disbanded on 7 October 1939 and the sub-components eventually re-assigned to other divisions.
†Each German army-level heavy artillery battalion, *schwere Artillerie-Abteilung*, was typically equipped with a total of 4 10cm cannons and 8 15cm howitzers. Other Heeresartillerie artillery battalions were equipped with 8 15cm howitzers and a third battery with 10.5cm howitzers.
‡Luftwaffe anti-aircraft battalions were equipped with 24 × 2cm, 12 × 8.8cm Flak guns.

- XXI Armeekorps (Generalleutnant Nikolaus von Falkenhorst)
  - 21 Infanterie-Division
  - 228. Infanterie-Division
  - I./Panzer-Regiment 10 (74 tanks)
  - Maschinengewehr-Bataillon 9 (mot.)*
  - schwere Artillerie-Abteilung 511 (8 × 15cm), II./Artillerie-Regiment 57
  - I./Flak-Regiment.11
- Gruppe Brand (Generalmajor Albrecht Brand)
  - Brigade Goldap†
  - Brigade Lötzen‡
- Korps Wodrig (Generalleutnant Albert Wodrig)§
  - 1. Infanterie-Division
  - 12. Infanterie-Division
  - 1. Kavallerie-Brigade¶
  - Grenzwacht-Regiment 31**
- Army Reserves
  - 206. Infanterie-Division
  - 217. Infanterie-Division
  - Gruppe Medem††
  - Grenzwacht-Regimenter 1, 21
  - Panzerjäger-Abteilung 511 (mot.)
  - schwere Artillerie-Abteilung 536 (8 × 15cm)
  - Pioniere Bataillonen 42, 50, 505 (mot.)
  - Panzerzug 6, Panzerzug 7

*A motorized machine-gun battalion had a total of 995 troops, equipped with 51 heavy machine-guns, 12 3.7cm PaK and 181 motor vehicles.
†Brigade Goldap consisted of 7 battalions of Landwehr, Artillerie-Abteilung 161 and Panzerjäger-Abteilung 521. Total strength 7,771 troops, equipped with 12 10.5cm howitzers, 12 3.7cm PaK and 166 motor vehicles.
‡Brigade Lötzen consisted of 6 battalions of Landwehr and 3 artillery battalions in Artillerie-Regiment 161. Total strength 8,326 troops, equipped with 36 10.5cm howitzers, 8 7.5cm IG, 48 3.7cm PaK and 301 motor vehicles.
§On 1 October 1939 Korps Wodrig was redesignated as the XXVI Armeekorps.
¶The strength of the 1. Kavallerie-Brigade was 6,684 men and 4,552 horses. The brigade consisted of 2 mounted regiments and was partly motorized, with over 400 motor vehicles and 8 armoured cars.
**A 1,752-man border guard regiment consisted of 3 battalions, equipped with 8 3.7cm PaK and 144 light machine guns. The regiment relied primarily upon horses for mobility.
††Gruppe Medem consisted of one battalion of border guards, a machine-gun company, an artillery battery, and Pionier Bataillon 41. Altogether, 2,577 troops, 4 15cm howitzers and 244 motor vehicles.

- Separate paramilitary formations in Danzig (SS-Brigadeführer Johannes Schäfer)
  - SS-Heimwehr Danzig (SS-Obersturmbannführer Hans-Friedemann Götze)*
  - SS Wachsturmbann Eimann (SS-Sturmbannführer Kurt Eimann)†
  - Brigade Eberhardt (Police)‡ (Generalmajor Georg Friedrich-Eberhardt)
    - Verstärkter Grenzaufsichtsdienst (SA)
  - Einsatzgruppe V (SS-Standartenfürer Ernst Damzog)
- 4. Armee (General der Artillerie Günther von Kluge)
  - XIX Armeekorps (mot.) (General der Panzertruppe Heinz Guderian)
    - 3. Panzer-Division
      - Panzer-Lehr-Abteilung
    - 2. Infanterie-Division (mot.)
    - 20. Infanterie-Division (mot.)
    - II./Artillerie-Regiment 48, II./Artillerie-Regiment 68; schwere Artillerie-Abteilung 601
    - Nebelwerfer-Abteilung 2 (mot) (24 × 10cm mortars)
    - II./Flak-Lehr-Regiment, I./Flak-Regiment 61
    - Panzerzug 3
  - II Armeekorps (General der Infanterie Adolf Strauß)
    - 3. Infanterie-Division
    - 32. Infanterie-Division
    - II./Artillerie-Regiment 38, schwere Artillerie-Abteilung 436 (mot.), schwere Artillerie-Abteilung 604 (mot.) (4 × 15cm, 6 × 21cm Mörser)
    - I./Flak-Lehr-Regiment.
  - III Armeekorps (General der Artillerie Curt Haase)
    - 50. Infanterie-Division
    - Brigade Netze§
    - II./Artillerie-Regiment 39, II./Artillerie-Regiment 59
    - Panzerjäger-Abteilung 605¶

---

*The strength of the SS-Heimwehr Danzig was 1,550 men in 8 companies.

†SS Wachsturmbann Eimann was formed in July 1939 and was considered an armed reserve for Danzig SS-Standarte 36. The unit consisted of about 450 personnel.

‡Brigade Eberhardt (also known as Gruppe Eberhardt) was organized from 6 Danzig Landes-Polizei battalions (Polizei-Regimenter 1 and 2) and an artillery battalion (with 8 7.5cm guns and 6 10.5cm howitzers). During opening hostilities, it also had separate border guard and pioneer detachments attached.

§Brigade Netze had a strength of 11,836 personnel and consisted of Grenzwacht-Regimenter 22 and 52, Maschinengewehr-Bataillon 8 and schwere Artillerie-Abteilung 436.

¶The Panzerjager-Abteilung (mot.) was equipped with 36 3.7cm PaK anti-tank guns.

- Aufklärungs-Lehr-Abteilung*
○ Army Reserves
  ▪ 23. Infanterie-Division
  ▪ 218. Infanterie-Division
  ▪ schwere Artillerie-Abteilung 602
  ▪ Panzerjäger-Abteilung 560
  ▪ I., II./Flak-Regiment 411
○ Grenzschutz-Abschnitt-Kommando 1 (Generalleutnant Leonhard Kaupisch)
  ▪ 207. Infanterie-Division
  ▪ Grenzwacht-Regimenter 32, 42
  ▪ schwere Artillerie-Abteilung 611
○ Grenzschutz-Abschnitt-Kommando 2
  ▪ Grenzwacht-Regimenter 2, 12
  ▪ Artillerie-Abteilung 628
○ Grenzschutz-Abschnitt-Kommando 12
  ▪ Grenzwacht-Regimenter 3, 13, 23
  ▪ Artillerie-Abteilung 103
○ Einsatzgruppe IV (SS-Brigadeführer Lothar Beutel)
○ Heeresgruppe Nord Reserves
○ 10. Panzer-Division
○ 73. Infanterie-Division
○ 208. Infanterie-Division

Heeresgruppe Süd (Generaloberst Gerd von Rundstedt)
- 8. Armee (General der Infanterie Johannes Blaskowitz)
  ○ X Armeekorps (General der Artillerie Wilhelm Ulex)
    ▪ 24. Infanterie-Division
    ▪ II./Artillerie-Regiment 58 (mot.), II./Artillerie-Regiment 66 (mot.)
  ○ XIII Armeekorps (General der Kavallerie Maximilian von Weichs)
    ▪ 10. Infanterie-Division
    ▪ 17. Infanterie-Division
      • Infanterie-Regiment Leibstandarte SS Adolf Hitler (mot.)
      • I./Panzer-Abteilung 23
    ▪ II./ Artillerie-Regiment 46 (mot.), II./ Artillerie-Regiment 53 (mot.)
    ▪ II./Flak-Regiment 22
  ○ Grenz-Abschnitt-Kommando 13
  ○ Grenz-Abschnitt-Kommando 14
  ○ Army Reserves
    ▪ 30. Infanterie-Division

*This army-level reconnaissance battalion was equipped with 6 SdKfz 232 (8Rad) and 8 SdKfz 222 armoured cars.

- Maschinengewehr-Bataillon 6 (mot.)
- Panzerjäger-Abteilung 561
- I./ Flak-Regiment 33, I./Flak-Regiment 52
  ○ Einsatzgruppe III (SS-Obersturmbannführer Ludwig Fischer)
- 10. Armee (General der Artillerie Walter von Reichenau)
  ○ XI Armeekorps (General der Artillerie Emil Leeb)
    ▪ 18. Infanterie-Division
    ▪ 19. Infanterie-Division
    ▪ II./Artillerie-Regiment 55 (mot.), II./ Artillerie-Regiment 67 (mot.)
    ▪ I./Flak-Regiment 36
  ○ XVI Armeekorps (mot.) (General der Kavallerie Erich Hoepner)
    ▪ 1. Panzer-Division
    ▪ 4. Panzer-Division
    ▪ 14. Infanterie-Division
    ▪ 31. Infanterie-Division
    ▪ II./Artillerie-Regiment 60 (mot.), II./Artillerie-Regiment (mot.)
    ▪ Nebelwerfer-Abteilung 1 (mot) (24 × 10cm mortars)
    ▪ II./Flak-Regiment 23
  ○ IV Armeekorps (General der Infanterie Viktor von Schwedler)
    ▪ 4. Infanterie-Division
    ▪ 46. Infanterie-Division
    ▪ II./Artillerie-Regiment 40 (mot.), II./Artillerie-Regiment 50 (mot.), II./ Artillerie-Regiment 84 (mot.) (6 × 24cm howitzers), Art.Abt.624 (4 × 10cm cannons, 4 × 30.5cm howitzers)
    ▪ I./Flak-Regiment 711
  ○ XV Armeekorps (mot.) (General der Infanterie Hermann Hoth)
    ▪ 2. leichte-Division
    ▪ 3. leichte-Division
    ▪ Maschinengewehr-Bataillon 7 (mot.)
    ▪ Flak-Abteilung 93
  ○ XIV Armeekorps (mot.) (General der Infanterie Gustav von Wietersheim)
    ▪ 13. Infanterie-Division (mot.)
    ▪ 29. Infanterie-Division (mot.)
    ▪ II./Artillerie-Regiment 49 (mot.), II./Artillerie-Regiment 54 (mot.), II./Artillerie-Regiment 56 (mot.)
    ▪ Maschinengewehr-Bataillon 15 (mot.)
    ▪ I./Flak-Regiment 13
  ○ Army Reserves
    ▪ 1. leichte-Division
    ▪ Panzerjäger-Abteilung 563
    ▪ II./Artillerie-Regiment 115
    ▪ I./Flak-Regiment.13, I./Flak-Regiment 22, I./Flak-Regiment 43
  ○ Einsatzgruppe II (SS-Obersturmbannführer Emanuel Schäfer)

- 14. Armee (Generaloberst Wilhelm List)
  - ○ VIII Armeekorps (General der Infanterie Ernst Busch)
    - 5. Panzer-Division
    - 8. Infanterie-Division
    - 28. Infanterie-Division
    - 239. Infanterie-Division
    - SS-Regiment 'Germania'
    - Schwere Artillerie-Abteilung 641 (4 × 10cm cannons, 4 × 30.5cm howitzers), schwere Artillerie-Abteilung 607 (4 × 15cm cannons, 6 × 21cm Mörser), schwere Artillerie-Abteilung 631 (4 × 10cm cannons, 6 × 21cm Mörser), II./Artillerie-Regiment 44 (mot.), II./Artillerie-Regiment 64 (mot.)
    - Pionier-Bataillon 47 (mot.)
    - II./Flak-Regiment 38
  - ○ XVII Armeekorps (General der Infanterie Werner Kienitz)
    - 7. Infanterie-Division
    - 44 Infanterie-Division
    - 45. Infanterie-Division
    - Pionier-Bataillon 70 (mot.)
    - I., II./Artillerie-Regiment 109 (mot.)
    - Pionier-Bataillon 70 (mot.)
    - I./Flak-Regiment 7
  - ○ XVIII Armeekorps (General der Infanterie Eugen Beyer)
    - 2. Panzer-Division
    - 4. leichte-Division
    - 3. Gebirgs-Division
    - Pionier-Bataillon 85 (mot.)
    - III./Artillerie-Regiment 109
  - ○ XXII Armeekorps (mot.) (General der Kavallerie Ewald von Kleist)
    - 1. Gebirgs-Division
    - 2. Gebirgs-Division
    - Artillerie-Abteilung 422, Artillerie-Abteilung 445
  - ○ Field Army Bernolák (Major-General Ferdinand Čatloš)[*]
    - 1st Infantry Division Janošík (Slovakia)
    - 2nd Infantry Division Škultéty (Slovakia)
      - Ukrainian Legion[†]
    - 3rd Infantry Division Razus (Slovakia)

[*]The Slovak Army did not begin mobilizing until after the German invasion began and only the 1st Infantry Division was operational at the start. On 1 September, Field Army Bernolák had 13,351 troops, which increased to 32,880 by 10 September.
[†]A 300-man detachment of armed Ukrainian Nationalists from the OUN.

- Fast Troops Group Kalinčiak (Slovakia)*
  ○ Under Army Command
    ▪ I./Flak-Regiment 18
    ▪ Panzerzug 4
    ▪ Einsatzgruppe I (SS-Standartenführer Bruno Streckenbach)
- Heeresgruppe Süd Reserves
  ○ VII Armeekorps
    ▪ 27. Infanterie-Division
    ▪ 68. Infanterie-Division
    ▪ II./Artillerie-Regiment 43, II./Artillerie-Regiment 63
  ○ 62. Infanterie-Division
  ○ 213. Infanterie-Division
  ○ 221. Infanterie-Division
  ○ 252. Infanterie-Division
  ○ Artillerie-Abteilung 605, 629, 634
  ○ Panzerjäger-Abteilung 545

Luftwaffe
OKL Reserve
7./Ln.Abt. 100 (12x Ju 52/3m)
8./Ln.Abt. 100 (8x He 111H)
7. Flieger-Division (Generalmajor Kurt Student)
- Fallschirmjäger Regiment 1
- II./ Fallschirmjäger Regiment 2

Luftflotte 1 (General der Flieger Albert Kesselring)
- Directly under Luftflotte 1 Command
  ○ 1.(F)/121(11x Do 17)
  ○ 3.(F)/121(11x Do 17)
- 1. Fliegerdivision (Generalleutnant Ulrich Grauert)†
  ○ 2.(F)/121 (11x Do 17)
  ○ I.(J)/LG 2 (33x Bf 109E)
  ○ II./ZG 1 (48x Bf 109E)
  ○ I./ZG 1 (24x Bf 110C)
  ○ Stab., I./KG 1 (33x He 111H)
  ○ Stab., II/KG 26 (35x He 111H)
  ○ Stab., I., II., III./KG 27 (69x He 111P)

---

*This regimental-size mobile group was formed on 5 September and had 13 Czech-made tanks and 6 armoured cars.
†Grauert was killed by a Polish pilot from No. 303 Squadron on 15 May 1941, when his Ju 52 transport was shot down over France.

- I./KG 53 (29x He 111H)
- I./KG 152 (32x He 111H)
- II., III./ StG 2 (73x Ju 87)
- IV.(St)/LG 1 (36x Ju 87)
- Stab./Träger Flieger Gruppe II./186
  - 4./ Trägersturzkampfstaffel 186 (12x Ju 87B)
  - 5.,6./Trägerjagdgruppe 186 (46x Bf 109B/E)
- Stab./Kustenfliegergruppe 506
  - 1./KüFlGr 506 (He 60)
  - 2./KüFlGr 506 (Do 18)
  - 3./KüFlGr 506 (He 59)
  - 3./KüFlGr 706 (He 59)
- Lehrdivision (Generalmajor Helmuth Förster)
  - I.(Z)/LG 1 (29x Bf 110C)
  - Stab., I., II./KG 2 (72x Do 17)
  - II.(S)/LG 2 (37x Hs 123)
- Luftwaffenkommando Ostpreußen (Generalleutnant Wilhelm Wimmer)
  - I./JG 1 (46x Bf 109E)
  - I./JG 21 (37x Bf 109D)
  - Stab., II., III./KG 3 (70x Do 17Z)
  - I./ StG 1 (31x Ju 87, 3x Do 17)
  - 1.(F)/120 (12x Do 17)
- Luftgaukommando III (Berlin)
  - Stab., I./JG 2 (43x Bf 109E)
  - 10. (N)/JG 2 (9x Bf 109D)
- Luftgaukommando IV (Dresden)
  - Stab., I./JG 3 (41x Bf 109E)
  - I./JG 20 (36x Bf 109E)

Luftflotte 4 (General der Flieger Alexander Löhr)
- Directly under Luftflotte 4 Command
  - 3.(F)/123 (11x Do 17)
- 2. Fliegerdivision (Generalmajor Bruno Loerzer)
  - I./ZG 76 (29x Bf 110)
  - Stab., I., II., III./KG 4 (81x He 111P)
  - Stab., I., III./KG 76 (77x Do 17Z)
  - Stab., I., II., III./KG 77 (91x Do 17E)
  - I./StG 2 (32x Ju 87)
  - 3.(F)/122 (11x Do 17)
- Fliegerführer z.b.V (Generalmajor Wolfram Freiherr von Richthofen)
  - I./ZG 2 (45x Bf 109D)
  - Stab (J), II (S)/LG 2 (2x Bf 109E, 37 Hs 123)
  - I./StG 76 (21x Ju 87)

- ○ Stab., I., II./StG 77 (69x Ju 87, 6x Do 17)
- ○ 1.(F)/124 (9x Do 17)
- Luftgaukommando VIII (Breslau)
  - ○ I./JG 76 (45x Bf 109E)
  - ○ I./JG 77 (43x Bf 109)

Luftwaffe Operational Aircraft Deployed Against Poland, 1 September 1939

Type	Model	Luftflotte 1	Luftflotte 4	TOTAL
Fighter (487)	Bf 109	339	135	474
	Bf 110	53	29	82
Bombers (492)	Do 17	145	168	313
	He 111	198	81	279
	Ju 88	12*	0	12
Ground Attack (274)	Ju 87	154	122	276
	Hs 123	37	37	74
Reconnaissance (348)	Hs 126	88	69	157
	He 45/46	9	22	31
	Do 17	45	31	76
		1,080	694	1,774

Kriegsmarine

Naval Group East (Marinegruppe Ost) (Generaladmiral Conrad Albrecht)
- Battleships (2): *Schleswig Holstein, Schlesien*
- 3. Marinestosstruppkompanie (MSK) a 230-man naval commando unit under Oberleutnant Wilhelm Henningsen. Embarked on *Schleswig-Holstein*.

Commander Reconnaissance Forces (Vizeadmiral Hermann Densch)
- Light Cruisers (3): *Nürnberg, Leipzig, Köln*

Führer der Torpedoboote (Konteradmiral Günther Lütjens)
- Destroyers (9) *Leberecht Maass, Georg Thiele, Richard Beitzen, Friedrich Ihn, Erich Steinbinck, Friedrich Eckoldt, Bruno Heinemann, Wolfgang Zenker, Bernd von Arnim*
- 1st Minesweeper Flotilla: M1, M3, M4, M5, M7, M8, M111, M132
- S-Boot-Flotille: S11, S12, S18, S19, S20, S21, S22, S23
- Tender (1) *Tsingtau*

*The 12 Ju 88s in I./KG 25 were an experimental test unit that was made operational on the first day of the war.

APPENDIX B: RED ARMY ORDER OF BATTLE, 17 SEPTEMBER 1939

Byelorussian Front (Komandarm II Mikhail P. Kovalyov)

3rd Army (Komkor Vasily I. Kuznetsov)/Polotsk Group
- 4th Rifle Corps
  - 27th Rifle Division
  - 50th Rifle Division
- Lepelska Army Group
  - 5th Rifle Division
  - 24th Cavalry Division
  - 22nd Light Tank Brigade (T-26)
  - 25th Light Tank Brigade (T-26)

4th Army (Komkor Vasily I. Chuikov)/Slutsk Group
- 8th Rifle Division
- 29th Light Tank Brigade (T-26)
- 32nd Light Tank Brigade (T-26)
- 23rd Rifle Corps
  - 52nd Rifle Division
  - 143rd Rifle Division

10th Army (Komkor Ivan G. Zakharkin)
- 11th Rifle Corps
  - 6th Rifle Division
  - 33rd Rifle Division
  - 121st Rifle Division

11th Army (Komdiv Nikifor V. Medvedev)/Minsk Group
- 16th Rifle Corps
  - 2nd Rifle Division
  - 100th Rifle Division
- 3rd Cavalry Corps
  - 7th Cavalry Division
  - 36th Cavalry Division
- 6th Light Tank Brigade (BT-7)

Dzerzhinsky Cavalry-Mechanized Group (Komkor Ivan V. Boldin)
- 5th Rifle Corps
  - 4th Rifle Division
  - 13th Rifle Division
- 6th Cavalry Corps
  - 4th Cavalry Division
  - 6th Cavalry Division
  - 11th Cavalry Division

- 15th Tank Corps (Komdiv Mikhail Petrov)
  - 2nd Light Tank Brigade (234x BT-7)
  - 27th Light Tank Brigade (223x BT-7)
  - 20th Motorized Rifle Brigade
- 21st Heavy Tank Brigade (98x T-28, 30x BT-7)

Ukrainian Front (Komandarm I Semen K. Timoshenko)
5th Army (Komdiv Ivan G. Sovetnikov)/Shepetovskaya
- 8th Rifle Corps
  - 44th Rifle Division
  - 45th Rifle Division
  - 81st Rifle Division
- 15th Rifle Corps (Komdiv Vasily I. Repin)
  - 60th Rifle Division
  - 87th Rifle Division
- 36th Light Tank Brigade (BT)

6th Army (Komkor Filipp I. Golikov)/Volochysk Group
- 17th Rifle Corps
  - 96th Rifle Division
  - 97th Rifle Division
- 2nd Cavalry Corps
  - 3rd Cavalry Division
  - 5th Cavalry Division
  - 14th Cavalry Division
- 10th Heavy Tank Brigade (58x T-28, 20x BT-7)
- 38th Light Tank Brigade (142x T-26)
- 24th Light Tank Brigade (237x BT)

12th Army (Komkor Ivan V. Tyulenev)/Kamenetz–Podolsk Group
- 4th Cavalry Corps
  - 32nd Cavalry Division
  - 34th Cavalry Division
- 5th Cavalry Corps
  - 9th Cavalry Division
  - 16th Cavalry Division
- 25th Tank Corps (Polkovnik Ivan O. Yarkin)
  - 4th Light Tank Brigade (BT, T-37/38)
  - 5th Light Tank Brigade (BT, T-37/38) (Polkovnik Mikhail Katukov)
  - 1st Motor Rifle Brigade
- 13th Rifle Corps
  - 72nd Rifle Division
  - 99th Rifle Division

- 26th Light Tank Brigade (T-26)
- 23rd Light Tank Brigade (BT)

Front	Rifle Divisions	Cavalry Divisions	Tank Brigades	Motor Rifle Brigades
Byelorussian	12	6	8	1
Ukrainian	9	7	8	1
TOTAL	21	13	16	2

Unit	Authorized Strength	Artillery Support	Armoured Fighting Vehicles	Horses
Rifle Division	18,841	12 × 152mm 28 × 122mm 38 × 76mm	16 × T-38 12 × BA-10/20	6,208
Cavalry Division	8,000	8 × 122mm 8 × 76mm	30–45 × BT 10–15 × BA10	7,000
Heavy Tank Brigade	2,745		136 × T-28 37 × BT 30 × BA-10/20	
Light Tank Brigade (Cavalry)	2,745		238 × BT-7 24 × BA-10/20	
Light Tank Brigade (Infantry Support)	2,745		238 × T-26 24 × BA-10/20	

APPENDIX C: CHRONOLOGY

1918

1 November	The West Ukrainian People's Republic is established, sparking conflict with Poland over the city of Lviv.
11 November	Józef Piłsudski is appointed commander-in-chief of Poland's military forces. Three days later Piłsudski is declared head of stata, as well.
16 November	Piłsudski announces the re-creation of an independent Polish state, to be known as the Second Republic.
8 December	At Versailles, British diplomats propose the 'Curzon Line' as the eastern border of Poland – which is ignored by Piłsudski.
27 December	Polish insurgents start a rebellion in Poznań to seize the region from German authorities.

1919

4 January	French military mission to Poland arrives.
4/5 January	Attempted right-wing coup in Warsaw fails.
23 January	Czech forces seize the disputed Teschen region after a week-long border war with Polish forces.
12 February	British military mission to Poland arrives.
14 February	The Russo-Polish War begins.
20 April	First elements of Haller's Blue Army arrive in Poland from France. In addition, the French Military Mission to Poland arrives to assist the Polish military.
28 June	The Treaty of Versailles is signed. Pomerania is awarded to Poland, but the Allies coerce Poland into signing the Minority Treaty.
17 July	After Poland occupies Galicia and inflicts a military defeat on Ukraine, both sides agree sign a cease-fire.

1920

10 January	Poland is one of the founding members of the League of Nations.
7 May	Polish forces capture Kiev but are forced to abandon it one month later.
12–21 August	The battle of Warsaw results in a major Polish victory over the Red Army.
9 October	Polish forces seize Wilno from Lithuania.
15 November	The Free City of Danzig is established by the Treaty of Versailles.

1921

21 February	France and Poland sign a defensive alliance.
3 March	A five-year defensive alliance is signed with Romania.
17 March	The March Constitution is adopted by the Second Polish Republic.
18 March	The Treaty of Riga ends the Russo-Polish War.
20 March	League of Nations-run plebiscite in Upper Silesia.
20 October	The League of Nations divides Upper Silesia between Germany and Poland.

1922

16 April	The Treaty of Rapallo is signed, beginning German–Soviet economic and military co-operation.

1923

February	First covert Reichswehr military mission visits the USSR.
15 March	The League of Nation recognizes the Russo-Polish border established by the Treaty of Riga.

1925

16 October	The Locarno Treaties are signed, which open the door to German territorial revanchism n Eastern Europe.

1926

24 April	The Treaty of Berlin is signed by Germany and the USSR.
14 May	After a military coup, Piłsudski becomes *de facto* head of state.

1930

23 September	The Armoured Weapons Command is established in the M.S. Wojsk.

1931

31 December	At Poland's request, the French military mission is liquidated.

1932

14 June	The 'Wicher' Affair in Gdańsk leads to fleet expansion.
25 July	The Soviet–Polish Non-Aggression Pact is signed, effective for three years.

1933

30 January	Hitler becomes Chancellor of Germany.

28 May	The Nazi Party (NSDAP) receives a majority in the City of Danzig's parliamentary elections.
19 October	Germany quits the League of Nations.
31 October	The Nazis take control over the Danzig police force and begin using it as a tool of repression.

1934

26 January	The German–Polish Non-Aggression Pact is signed, effective for ten years.
5 May	The Soviet–Polish Non-Aggression Pact is extended to 1945.
2 August	After Hindenburg's death, Hitler becomes Führer.

1935

12 May	Piłsudski dies and is replaced by Marszałek Edward Rydz-Śmigły.

1936

6 September	Under the terms of the Rambouillet Accord, France provides a large loan to modernize the Polish military.

1937

12 March	Formation of National Defence (ON) battalions is authorized.

1938

30 September	As a result of the Munich Agreement, Germany acquires the Sudetenland from Czechoslovakia.
2 October	Polish forces seize Cieszyn (Teschen) back from Czechoslovakia.
24 October	Germany issues first demand to Poland, for return of Danzig (Gdańsk) and creation of a motorway across the corridor.
26 November	The USSR re-affirms the Non-Aggression Pact with Poland.
29 November	Hitler orders the OKW to plan a coup to seize Danzig at an opportune moment.

1939

5 January	Adolf Hitler presents the minister of foreign affairs, Józef Beck, with the proposal to connect Danzig to the Third Reich.
15 March	Germany occupies the rest of Czechoslovakia.
21 March	Ribbentrop tells Lipski that Germany will assert its rights to Danzig even through armed conflict.
22 March	Germany seizes the port of Memel from Lithuania.
	German newspapers begin reporting Polish 'atrocities' against German civilians in Poland.
23 March	Poland begins a partial mobilization.

31 March	Chamberlain's security guarantee to Poland.
3 April	The OKW issues a directive on preparations for war which has three optional plans: (1) border security, (2) *Fall Weiss* and (3) seizure of Danzig. Hitler orders that the Wehrmacht be ready to execute no later than 1 September.
6 April	Anglo-French mutual assistance pact with Poland.
11 April	Hitler confirms the OKW directive and states that the objective of *Fall Weiss* is to 'limit the war to Poland'.
28 April	Hitler denounces the German–Polish Non-Aggression Pact.
5 May	Beck's speech in the Sejm; he rejects German demands to join Gdańsk to Germany.
10 May	The OKW issues a follow-on directive, stating that the Luftwaffe and Kriegsmarine will prepare for economic warfare against Britain.[1]
12 May	Poland makes a formal request to Britain for financial aid to purchase defence equipment and supplies.
16 May	The OKH and OKM alert field commanders of intent to attack Poland.
19 May	Gamelin signs a military agreement with Poland, promising to begin a major offensive against Germany within 15 days of mobilization.
22 May	Germany and Italy sign the 'Pact of Steel'.
15 June	The OKH finalizes *Fall Weiss,* which calls for a pincer attack with two army groups from north and south to capture Warsaw.
17 June	Josef Goebbels delivers a strident, threatening speech in Danzig.
1 July	Britain offers limited military aid to Poland.
14 July	Poland rejects the British aid offer as unsatisfactory.
15 July	OKH issues a detailed operations order for *Fall Weiss.*
20 July	A German SA soldier kills a Polish border guard in Danzig.
10 August	The German ambassador in Warsaw is recalled to Berlin.
15 August	Germany closes its border crossing sites into Poland.
19 August	France grants Poland F 430 million in credits.
22 August	Hitler assembles his senior commanders at the Obersalzberg to state his intentions.
23 August	The Molotov–Ribbentrop Pact is signed in Moscow. Hitler orders that *Fall Weiss* will begin at 0430 hours on 26 August (Y-Tag). Poland orders emergency mobilization without public announcement.
24 August	The Nazi-dominated senate in Danzig declares *de facto* independence and begins arresting Polish officials in the city.

25 August	The battleship *Schleswig-Holstein* arrives in Danzig.
	The Anglo–Polish military alliance is signed.
	1930 hours, Hitler postpones *Fall Weiss*.
29 August	Britain and France convince Poland to delay general mobilization.
	Germany delivers an ultimatum to Poland.
30 August	Poland announces general mobilization.
31 August	0630 hours, Hitler orders Wehrmacht to deploy to attack positions. 1240 hours, Hitler issues Directive No. 1 to attack Poland the next morning.
1 September	*Fall Weiss* begins at 0445 hours.
3 September	1100 hours, Britain declares war on Germany.
	1700 hours, France declares war on Germany.
6 September	Kraków falls to the 14. Armee.
7 September	The Polish government leaves Warsaw; Marszałek Rydz-Śmigły moves the Polish GHQ to Brest.
	Britain finally agrees to provide a £5 million loan to Poland.
9 September	Lodz is occupied by the 8. Armee.
11 September	The Soviet ambassador to Poland is withdrawn.
13 September	Marszałek Rydz-Śmigły moves the Polish GHQ to Mlynow.
15 September	Marszałek Rydz-Śmigły moves the Polish GHQ to Kolomyja near the Romanian border.
17 September	The Soviet Union invades eastern Poland.
18 September	Marszałek Rydz-Śmigły and the Polish Government flee to Romania.
	Lublin falls to the German IV Armeekorps.
20 September	Hitler orders 14. Armee to cease attack on Lwów and allow Soviets to take it.
22 September	Lwów surrenders to the Soviet 12th Army. German forces begin pulling west of demarcation line.
27 September	The Warsaw garrison begins surrender talks with 3. Armee.
28 September	Battle of Szack: Polish border troops defeat the Soviet 52nd Rifle Division.
	Germany and the Soviet Union sign an agreement formally establishing the division of Poland into two zones.
29 September	The Army of Warsaw files out of the city to formally surrender.
4 October	Hitler issues a general amnesty for any German soldiers convicted of crimes committed during the Polish campaign.
6 October	After the battle of Kock, the last Polish forces surrender.

APPENDIX D: GERMAN MECHANIZED/ MOTORIZED UNIT ORGANIZATION & STRENGTH, 1939

Formation	Panzer-Abteilungen	Infantry	Motorcycle	Recon
1. Panzer-Division	I.,II./Pz.Regt. 1 I.,II./Pz.Regt. 2	I.,II./SR1	Krad 1	AA4
2. Panzer-Division	I.,II./Pz.Regt. 3 I.,II./Pz.Regt. 4	I.,II./SR2	Krad 2	AA5
3. Panzer-Division	I.,II./Pz.Regt. 5 I.,II./Pz.Regt. 6 Pz. Lehr-Abt.	I.,II./SR3	Krad 3	AA3
4. Panzer-Division	I.,II./Pz.Regt. 35 I.,II./Pz.Regt. 36	I.,II./SR12		AA7
5. Panzer-Division	I.,II./Pz.Regt. 15 I.,II./Pz.Regt. 31	I.,II./SR14		AA8
Panzer-Division Kempf	I.,II./Pz.Regt. 7	I.,II.,III./SS-'Deutschland'		SS-AA
10. Panzer-Division	I.,II./Pz.Regt. 8	I.,II.,III./IR 86		I./AR8
1. leichte-Division	I.,II./Pz.Regt. 11 Pz.Abt. 65	I.,II.,III./SR 4	Krad 6	AA 6
2. leichte-Division	Pz.Abt. 66	I.,II./KSR 6 I.,II./KSR 7		I.,II./AR 7
3. leichte-Division	Pz.Abt. 67	I.,II.,III./KSR 9		II./AR 8
4. leichte-Division	Pz.Abt. 33	I.,II./KSR 10 I.,II./KSR 11		I.,II./AR 9
2. Infanterie-Division (mot.)		I.,II.,III./IR 5 I.,II.,III./IR 25 I.,II.,III./IR 92		AA 2
13. Infanterie-Division (mot.)		I.,II.,III./IR 33 I.,II.,III./IR 66 I.,II.,III./IR 93		AA13
20. Infanterie-Division (mot.)		I.,II.,III./IR 69 I.,II.,III./IR 76 I.,II.,III./IR 90		AA 20

Formation	Panzer-Abteilungen	Infantry	Motorcycle	Recon
29. Infanterie-Division (mot.)		I.,II.,III./IR 15 I.,II.,III./IR 71		AA 29
Heerestruppen	I./Pz.Regt. 10 I./Pz.Regt. 23			Auf. Lehr
SS-'Germania' Regiment		I.,II.,III./ Germania		1 company
SS-LSSAH Regiment		I.,II.,III./ LSSAH		1 company

Sub-unit totals: 33 Panzer battalions, 69 motorized infantry battalions/ squadrons, 4 motorcycle battalions and 18 motorized reconnaissance battalions.

Panzer Strength in Selected Units

Formation	Pz I	Pz II	Pz III	Pz IV	Pz 35(t)	Pz 38(t)	Total Tanks*
1. Panzer-Division	93	122	26	56	0	0	297
2. Panzer-Division	124	155	6	17	0	0	302
3. Panzer-Division	122	176	43	32	0	0	373
4. Panzer-Division	183	130	0	12	0	0	325
5. Panzer-Division	152	144	3	14	0	0	313
Panzer-Division Kempf	61	81	3	9	0	0	154
10. Panzer-Division	57	74	3	9	0	0	143
1. leichte-Division	0	65	0	41	112	0	218
2. leichte-Division	41	42	0	0	0	0	83
3. leichte-Division	0	23	0	0	0	55	78
4. leichte-Division	34	23	0	0	0	0	57

*Excluding command tanks and other auxiliary vehicles.

Notes

INTRODUCTION

1. Esther B. Fein, 'Soviets Confirm Nazi Pacts Dividing Europe', *The New York Times*, August 19, 1989.
2. Martin Gilbert, *The Second World War: A Complete History* (New York: Henry Holt and Company, 1989), p. 2.
3. Donald Cameron Watt, *How War Came: The Immediate Origins of the Second World War, 1938–1939* (New York: Pantheon Books, 1989), p. 569.
4. John Keegan, *The Second World War* (New York: Viking Penguin, 1990), p. 44.
5. Gerhard Weinberg, *A World At Arms: A Global History of World War II* (New York: Cambridge University Press, 1994), p. 51.
6. Antony Beevor, *The Second World War* (New York, Little Brown and Company, 2012), p. 29.
7. Hanson W. Baldwin, *The Crucial Years, 1939–1941* (New York: Harper & Row Publishers, 1976), p. 67.
8. Richard J. Evans, *The Third Reich at War* (New York: Penguin Press, 2009), p. 4.
9. Weinberg, *World at Arms*, p. 49.
10. Beevor, p. 31.
11. Marek Piotr Deszczyński, *Polski eksport sprzętu wojskowego w okresie międzywojennym* [*Polish Export of Military Equipment in the Inter-war Period*] (Warsaw: Neriton, 1994), pp. 94–95.
12. Evans, p. 4.

CHAPTER 1: POLAND IS NOT LOST

1. Winston S. Churchill, *The Second World War*, Vol. 1 (Boston: Houghton Mifflin Co., 1948), p. 289.
2. Oscar Halecki, *A History of Poland* (New York: Barnes & Nobles Books, 1992), pp. 204–205.

3. Wacław Jędrzejewicz, *Piłsudski: A Life for Poland* (New York: Hippocrene Books, 1982), pp. 42–43.
4. Ibid., pp. 54–55.
5. Jesse Kauffman, *Elusive Alliance: The German Occupation of Poland in World War I* (Cambridge, MA: Harvard University Press, 2015), pp. 94–97.
6. Adam Zamoyski, *Warsaw 1920: Lenin's Failed Conquest of Europe* (London: Harper Collins Publishers, 2008), p. 17.
7. Halik Kochanski, *The Eagle Unbowed: Poland and the Poles in the Second World War* (Cambridge, MA: Harvard University Press, 2012), p. 22.
8. Zamoyski, p. 27.
9. Nigel Thomas, *Armies of the Russo-Polish War 1919–21* (Oxford: Osprey Publishing, 2014), p. 5.
10. Zbigniew Gwóźdź, *Polskie konstrukcje broni strzeleckiej* [*Polish Constructions of Small Arms*] (Warsaw: SIGMA-NOT, 1993), pp. 140–150.
11. Carole Fink, *Defending the Rights of Others: The Great Powers, the Jews, and International Minority Protection, 1878–1938* (New York: Cambridge University Press, 2004), pp. 122–123.
12. Titus Komarnicki, *Rebirth of the Polish Republic* (London: W. Heinemann, 1957), pp. 162, 236.
13. Anna M. Cienciala, 'British Policy Toward the Rebirth of Poland, 1914–1918', *Zeszyty Historyczne* [Historical Journal], Vol. 16 (1969), pp. 67–94.
14. Norman Davies, 'Lloyd George and Poland, 1919–20', *Journal of Contemporary History*, Vol. 6, No. 3 (July 1, 1971), pp. 142–143.
15. Italy delivered a total of 164 pieces (eight 210mm mortars, 12 149mm guns, 12 105mm howitzers and 132 75mm field guns). Andrzej Konstankiewicz, *Broń strzelecka i sprzęt artyleryjski formacji polskich i Wojska Polskiego 1914–39* [*Guns and Artillery Equipment of the Polish Armed Forces 1914–39*] (Warsaw: Uniwersytetu Marii Curie-Skłodowskiej, 2003), p. 51.
16. Norman Davies, *White Eagle/Red Star: The Polish–Soviet War 1919–1920 and the Miracle on the Vistula* (London: Pimlico, 2003), p. 41.
17. Janusz Cisek, *Kosciuszko, We Are Here! American Pilots of the Kosciuszko Squadron in Defense of Poland, 1919–1921* (Jefferson, NC: McFarland & Co., 2002).
18. Ronald Suny, *The Soviet Experiment: Russia, the USSR, and the Successor States* (New York: Oxford University Press, 2010), p. 120.
19. Kochanski, p. 21.
20. Ibid., pp. 200–205.
21. Davies, 'Lloyd George and Poland', p .152.
22. Jerzy B. Cynk, *The Polish Air Force at War: The Official History, Vol. 1, 1939–1943* (Atglen, PA: Schiffer Military History, 1998), pp. 36–37.
23. Davies, p. 153.
24. M. Epstein (ed.), *The Annual Register 1921* (London: Longmans, Green and Co., 1922), pp. 178–180.
25. Jędrzejewicz, p. 194.

26. John Grenville and Bernard Wasserstein, *The Major International Treaties of the Twentieth Century: A History and Guide with Texts* (New York: Routledge, 2013), p. 157.

CHAPTER 2: POLAND PREPARES FOR THE NEXT ROUND

1. Christoph M. Kimmich, 'The Weimar Republic and the German-Polish Borders', *The Polish Review*, Vol. 14, No. 4 (Autumn, 1969), p. 41.
2. Gwóźdź, p. 140.
3. Grzegorz Nowik, *Zanim złamano 'Enigmę' Polski radiowywiad podczas wojny z bolszewicką Rosją 1918–1920* [*Before Enigma Was Decoded: Polish SIGINT in the War with Bolshevik Russia 1918–1920*] (Warsaw: Wyd. Rytm, 2004), pp. 917–926.
4. First National Census of 30 September 1921 (Warsaw: Central Statistical Office of the Polish Republic, 1927).
5. Julian M. Skelnik, *Centrum Wyższych Studiów Wojskowych 1923–1933* [*Centre for Higher Military Studies 1923–1933*] (Gdynia: Armageddon, 2006).
6. Tomasz Kozieł, *Przemysł zbrojeniowy w Polsce w latach 1918–1939* [*The Arms Industry in Poland in the Years 1918–1939*] (14 March 2007) in Konflikty.pl. Found at http://www.konflikty.pl/historia/1918-1939/przemysl-zbrojeniowy-w-polsce-w-latach-19181939/.
7. Deszczyński, pp. 105–106.
8. Cynk, pp. 38–41.
9. Jędrzejewicz, p. 281.
10. Piotr Stefan Wandycz, *The Twilight of French Eastern Alliances, 1926–1936: French-Czechoslovak-Polish Relations from Locarno to the Remilitarization of the Rhineland* (Princeton, NJ: Princeton University Press, 1988), pp. 217–218.
11. Paul N. Hehn, *A Low, Dishonest Decade: The Great Powers, Eastern Europe and the Economic Origins of World War II* (New York: Continuum, 2005), pp. 68–69.
12. Gordon H. Mueller, 'Rapallo Reexamined: A New Look at Germany's Secret Military Collaboration with Russia in 1922', *Military Affairs*, Vol. 40, No. 3 (October 1976), pp. 109–110.
13. Gaines Post, *The Civil-Military Fabric of Weimar Foreign Policy* (Princeton, NJ: Princeton University Press, 1973), p. 102.
14. Ryszard Rybka, *Najlepsza broń. Plan mobilizacyjny 'W' i jego ewolucja* [The Best Weapon: Mobilization Plan 'W' and its Evolution] (Warsaw: Adiutor, 2010)
15. Tomasz Kośmider (ed.), *Planowanie wojenne i przygotowania obronne II Rzeczypospolitej* [*War Planning and Defence Preparations of the Second Polish Republic*] (Warsaw: National Defence Academy, 2012), pp. 73–74.
16. Kośmider, p. 76.
17. Cynk, p. 41.
18. Aleksander Wysocki, 'Zarys produkcji bojowych środków chemicznych w Polsce w latach 1918-1939' [Outline for the Production of Combat Chemicals

in Poland in the Years 1918–1939], *Biuletyn Wojskowej Służby Archiwalnej* [Bulletin Military Archival Service], No. 24 (2001).

19. Kimmich, pp. 37–45.

20. Josef Korbel, *Poland Between East and West: Soviet and German Diplomacy toward Poland, 1919–1933* (Princeton, NJ: Princeton University Press, 1965), p. 262.

21. Tomasz Wesołowski, *Limes Polonicus – gen. bryg. inż. Józef Burhardt (1863–1938) i jego koncepcja ufortyfikowania granic Rzeczypospolitej* [*Limes Polonicus – Gen. Brig. Eng. Józef Burhardt (1863–1938) and his Concept of Fortification of the Borders of the Polish–Lithuanian Commonwealth*] (Białystok: Military History Research Centre, 2012).

22. J. E. Kaufmann and R. M. Jurga, *Fortress Europe: European Fortifications of World War II* (Conshohocken, PA: Combined Publishing, 1999), pp. 265–27.

23. Adrian Carton de Wiart, *Happy Odyssey* (Barnsley, UK: Pen & Sword Books Ltd., 2007), p. 119.

24. Korbel, p. 133

25. Cynk, p. 60.

26. Jędrzejewicz, p. 329.

27. Adolf Hitler, *Mein Kampf* (Farmington, MN: Free Thought Books, 2016), p. 164.

28. Eugeniusz J. Kozłowski et al., *Wojna obronna Polski 1939 wybór źródeł* [*Defensive War of Poland 1939, Selected Sources*] (Warsaw: Ministry of National Defence, 1968), pp. 33–34.

29. Angus Maddison, *The World Economy: Historical Statistics* (Paris: OECD Publishing, 2003).

30. FM 100-5 *Operations* (Washington, DC: Department of the Army, June 1993), pp. 2–12.

31. Stanisław Sosabowski, *Freely I Served* (Nashville, TN: The Battery Press, 1982), p. 21.

32. Gwódźdź, pp. 140–150.

33. Wandycz, p. 185.

34. Konstankiewicz, pp. 51-53.

35. Jędrzej Korbal, 'Pancernym w szczeliny' [Armour in the Gaps], *Wojsko i Technika Historia* [*Military and Technical History*] (March 2018).

36. P. Rozwadowski, *Polskie armaty przeciwlotnicze 75 mm wz.36/37 oraz 40 mm Bofors* [*Polish Anti-aircraft Guns 75mm wz.36 / 37 and 40mm Bofors*], Typy Broni I Uzbrojenia nr. 183 (Warsaw, 1998).

37. Zdzisław Józef Cutter, *Polskie wojska saperskie w 1939 r.: organizacja, wyposażenie, mobilizacja i działania wojenne* [*Polish Sapper Troops in 1939: Organization, Equipment, Mobilization and Warfare*] (Częstochowa: Wydawnictwo Wyższa Szkoła Pedagogiczna, 2003).

38. Robert A. Doughty, 'French Anti-Tank Doctrine, 1940: The Antidote that Failed', *Military Review*, Vol. LVI, No. 5 (May 1976), pp. 36–48.

39. Marian Zacharski, *Operacja Reichswehra: kulisy wywiadu II RP* [*Operation Reichswehr: Behind the Intelligence of the Second Polish Republic*] (Poznań: Zysk I S-ka, 2013).

40. H. Ćwięk, *Rotmistrz Sosnowski. As wywiadu II Rzeczypospolitej* [*Captain Sosnowski, Intelligence Ace of the Second Polish Republic*] (Wydawnictwo Literackie: Kraków 2010).

41. Hugh Sebag Montefiore, *Enigma: The Battle for the Code* (Hoboken, NJ: John Wiley & Sons, Inc., 2000), pp. 44–45.

42. Steven Zaloga and Victor Madej, *The Polish Campaign 1939* (New York: Hippocrene Books, Inc., 1991), pp. 55–59.

43. Kazimierz Krzyzanowski, *Wydatki wojskowe Polski w latach 1918–1939* [*Military Expenditure of Poland in 1918–1939*] (Warsaw: Panstwowe Wydawnictwo Naukowe, 1976).

44. Zara Steiner, *The Triumph of the Dark: European International History 1933–1939* (Oxford: Oxford University Press, 2013), p. 284.

45. Zaloga and Madej, *The Polish Campaign*, pp. 12–13.

46. Zbigniew Landau, 'Poland and America: The Economic Connection 1918–1939', *Polish American Studies*, Vol. 32, No. 2 (Autumn, 1975), pp. 38–50.

47. Mark Harrison, *The Economics of World War II: Six Great Powers in International Comparison* (Cambridge, UK: Cambridge University Press, 1998), pp. 7–8.

48. Deszczyński, pp. 103–110.

49. Deszczyński, p. 91.

50. Michael Alfred Peszke, 'The Forgotten Campaign: Poland's Military Aviation in September, 1939', *The Polish Review*, Vol. 39, No. 1 (1994), p. 60.

51. Władysław Szarski, *Ośrodek Oporu Jastarnia i inne fortyfikacje stałe Helu* [*Resistance Centre Jastarnia and Other Permanent Fortifications Hel*] (Stowarzyszenie Przyjaciele Helu, 2010).

CHAPTER 3: THE THREAT EMERGES

1. Richard J. Overy, *The Dictators: Hitler's Germany and Stalin's Russia* (New York: W.W. Norton & Co., 2004), pp. 441.

2. James S. Corum, *The Roots of Blitzkrieg: Hans von Seeckt and German Military Reform* (Lawrence, KS: University Press of Kansas, 1992), p. 97.

3. James S. Corum, *The Luftwaffe: Creating the Operational Air War, 1918–1940* (Lawrence, KS: University Press of Kansas, 1997), pp. 86–87.

4. Corum, *The Roots of Blitzkrieg*, p. 98.

5. Richard Meredith, *Phoenix: The Phoenix is Reborn, 1918–1934*, Vol. 1 (Solihull: Helion & Company Ltd., 2016), pp. 211–214.

6. Corum, *The Roots of Blitzkrieg*, pp. 160–161.

7. Corum, *The Luftwaffe*, p. 117.

8. Albert and Joan Seaton, *The Soviet Army, 1918 to the Present* (Harrisonburg, VA: Meridian Books, 1986), p. 83.

9. Mary R. Habeck, *Storm of Steel: The Development of Armour Doctrine in Germany and the Soviet Union, 1919–1939* (Ithaca, NY: Cornell University Press, 2003), pp. 96–99.

10. William Manchester, *The Arms of Krupp 1587–1968* (New York: Little Brown and Company, 1968), pp. 352, 355.

11. Robin Higham (ed.), *Russian Aviation and Air Power in the Twentieth Century* (New York: Routledge, 1998), p. 167.

12. Corum, *The Roots of Blitzkrieg,* p. 108.

13. 'Cargoes of Munitions from Russia to Germany! Secret Plan between Reichswehr Officers and Soviets', *Manchester Guardian*, 3 December, 1926.

14. Ferenc A. Vajda and Peter Dancey, *German Aircraft Industry and Production, 1933–1945* (Warrendale, PA: SAE International, 1998), p. 10.

15. Thomas L. Jentz, *Panzertruppen*, Vol. 1 (Atglen, PA: Schiffer Publishing Ltd., 1996), p. 9.

16. Robert M. Citino, *The Path to Blitzkrieg: Doctrine and Training in the German Army, 1920–39* (Mechanicsburg, PA: Stackpole Books, 2008), pp. 223–227.

17. US Strategic Bombing Survey (USSBS), Motor Vehicle Industry Report, Table 3 (Washington, DC: Government Printing Office, 1947).

18. Adam Tooze, *The Wages of Destruction: The Making and Breaking of the Nazi Economy* (New York: Penguin Books, 2006), p. 26.

19. John W. Hiden, *The Weimar Republic* (New York: Routledge, 2014), p. 79.

20. Hitler's speech to the Industry Club in Düsseldorf, 21 January 1932. archive.org/details/HitlerAdolfAddressToTheIndustryClubInDuesseldorf On27thJanuary1932EN24S.Text.

21. Vajda and Dancey, p. 11.

22. Tooze, pp. 53–57.

23. J. Richard Smith and Eddie J. Creek, *Kampfflieger: Bombers of the Luftwaffe, 1933–1940* (Hersham, UK: Ian Allan Publishing Ltd., 2004), p. 5.

24. Peter C. Smith, *Dive Bomber!: Aircraft, Technology, and Tactics in World War II* (Mechanicsburg, PA: Stackpole Books, 2008), p. 117. Also, Helmut Erfurth, *Junkers Ju 87* (Bonn, Germany: Bernard & Graefe Verlag, 2004), p. 27.

25. *The Times*, 10 December, 1932.

26. Hanfried Schliephake, *Birth of the Luftwaffe* (Chicago: Henry Regnery Co., 1972), p. 32.

27. Jentz, p. 14.

28. Richard J. Overy, *The Dictators: Hitler's Germany and Stalin's Russia* (New York: W. W. Norton & Co., 2004), p. 441.

29. Walter J. Spielberger, *Panzer III and its Variants* (Atglen, PA: Schiffer Publishing Ltd., 1993), p. 8.

30. Corum, *The Luftwaffe*, pp. 247–248.

31. Mike Spick, *Luftwaffe Bomber Aces: Men, Machines, Methods* (London: Greenhill Books, 2001), p. 32.

32. Chris McNab, *MG 34 and MG 42 Machine Guns* (Oxford: Osprey Publishing, 2012), p. 13.

33. Tooze, p. 246.

34. Wesley K. Wark, *The Ultimate Enemy: British Intelligence and Nazi Germany, 1933–1939* (Ithaca, NY: Cornell University Press, 1985), p. 182.

35. Tooze, pp. 302–303.

36. Barton Whaley, *Covert German Rearmament 1919–39, Deception and Misperception* (Frederick, MD: University Press of America, 1984), p. 69.

37. Jentz, p. 48.

38. Richard J. Overy, 'German Air Strength 1933 to 1939: A Note', *The Historical Journal,* Vol. 27, Issue 2 (June 1984), pp. 465–471.

39. David M. Glantz, *The Military Strategy of the Soviet Union: A History* (London: Frank Cass, 1992), p. 92.

40. Figures for Soviet tanks and combat aircraft are estimates which have been calculated by the author from a variety of sources.

41. Oskar Munzel, *Die Deutschen gepanzerten Truppen bis 1945* [*The German Armoured Troops until 1945*] (Hamburg: Maximilian-Verlag, 1965), pp. 209.

42. Corum, *The Luftwaffe*, pp. 195–196.

43. Lucas Molina Franco and Jose Manrique Garcia, *Soldiers of von Thoma: Legion Condor Ground Forces in the Spanish Civil War 1936–1939* (Atglen, PA: Schiffer Publishing Ltd., 2008), pp. 18–19.

44. Jentz, p. 56.

45. Leo W. G. Niehorster, *German World War II Organizational Series, Vol. 1/II-1, 1st and 2nd Welle Army Infantry Divisions (1 September 1939)* (Milton Keynes: The Military Press, 2006), p. 3.

46. US Strategic Bombing Survey (USSBS), Motor Vehicle Industry Report, Table 3 (Washington, DC: Government Printing Office, 1947).

47. Jentz, p. 63.

48. 'Freyn Makes Russian Deal', *The New York Times,* August 4, 1928, p. 25.

49. Anthony C. Sutton, *Western Technology and Soviet Economic Development 1930–1945,* Vol. II (Stanford: Hoover Institution Press, 1973), pp. 10–11.

50. Sutton, pp. 137–138.

51. John Scott, *Behind the Urals: An American Worker in Russia's City of Steel (Bloomington, IN: Indiana University Press, 1989), p. 102.*

52. Sutton, p. 11.

53. Roger Munting, *The Economic Development of the USSR* (London: Palgrave Macmillan, 1982), p. 93.

54. David R. Jones, 'From Disaster to Recovery: Russia's Air Forces in the Two World Wars' in *Why Air Forces Fail: The Anatomy of Defeat* ed. Robin Higham (Lexington, KY: The University Press of Kentucky, 2006), pp. 268–270.

55. Tim Bean and Will Fowler, *Russian Tanks of World War II: Stalin's Armored Might* (St. Paul, MN: MBI Publishing Company, 2002), pp. 10-13.

56. Steven J. Zaloga, *T-26 Light Tank: Backbone of the Red Army* (Oxford: Osprey Publishing, 2015), pp. 6–7.

57. Steven J. Zaloga, *BT Fast Tank: The Red Army Cavalry Tank, 1931–45* (Oxford: Osprey Publishing, 2015), pp. 6–10.

58. Habeck, pp. 108–109.
59. Richard W. Harrison, *Architect of Soviet Victory in World War II: The Life and Theories of G. S. Isserson* (Jefferson, NC: McFarland & Company Inc., 2010), pp. 122–135.
60. Simon Sebag Montefiore, *Stalin: The Court of the Red Tsar* (New York: Vintage Books, 2003), pp. 221–227.

CHAPTER 4: COUNTDOWN TO WAR

1. Imperial War Museum Collection, LBY K. 91 / 2382, Hitler's speech extracted from the *News Chronicle*, March 16, 1939.
2. Hitler's speech to the Industry Club in Düsseldorf, 21 January 1932. https:// archive.org/details/HitlerAdolfAddressToTheIndustryClubInDuesseldorf On27thJanuary1932EN24S.Text
3. Steiner, pp. 22–23.
4. Ian Kershaw, *Hitler: 1889–1936 Hubris* (New York: W.W. Norton & Company, 1998), pp. 522–524.
5. Tooze, p. 69.
6. Hans-Erich Volkmann (ed.), *Wirtschaft und Rüstung am Vorabend des Zweiten Weltkrieges [Economy and Armaments on the Eve of World War II]*, 2nd edition (Düsseldorf: Droste, 1981), p. 85.
7. Albrecht O. Ritschl, 'Nazi Economic Imperialism and the Exploitation of the Small: Evidence from Germany's Secret Foreign Exchange Balances, 1938–1940', *The Economic History Review*, Vol. 54, No. 2 (May, 2001), pp. 329–330.
8. Neil Forbes, *Doing Business with the Nazis: Britain's Economic and Financial Relations with Germany, 1931–1939* (London: Frank Cass Publishers, 2000), pp. 97–128.
9. Frank McDonough, *Neville Chamberlain, Appeasement, and the British Road to War* (Manchester: Manchester University Press, 1998), pp. 141.
10. Hehn, p. 19.
11. A. J. Barker, *The Rape of Ethiopia 1936* (New York: Ballantine Books, Inc., 1971), pp. 56–57.
12. Steiner, pp. 112–127.
13. '50,000 Men March in Alsace-Lorraine', *The New York Times,* March 9, 1936.
14. J. T. Emmerson, *The Rhineland Crisis 7 March 1936, A Study in Multilateral Diplomacy* (Ames, Iowa: Iowa State University Press, 1977), pp.184–190.
15. Kochanski, p. 40.
16. Neil Short, *Germany's West Wall: The Siegfried Line* (Oxford: Osprey Publishing, 2004), pp. 9–10.
17. Scott A. Silverstone, 'The Legacy of Coercive Peace-Building: The Locarno Treaty, Anglo-French Grand Strategy, and the 1936 Rhineland Crisis' in *The Challenge of Grand Strategy: The Great Powers and the Broken Balance between the World Wars* ed. Jeffrey W. Taliaferro (Cambridge: Cambridge University Press, 2012), p. 8.
18. Steiner, pp. 256–257.
19. Ibid., pp. 331–332.

20. Norman H. Baynes (ed.), *The Speeches of Adolf Hitler: April 1922 – August 1939*, Vol. 2 (Oxford: Oxford University Press, 1942), p. 1368.

21. Ian Kershaw, *Hitler: 1936–1945 Nemesis* (New York: W. W. Norton & Company, 2000), pp. 76–78.

22. Heinz Guderian, *Panzer Leader* (New York: Ballantine Books, Inc., 1968), pp. 30–35.

23. Tooze, p. 246.

24. Kershaw, *Nemesis*, pp. 96–97.

25. Walter Gorlitz (ed.), *In the Service of the Reich: The Memoirs of Field Marshal Keitel* (New York: Cooper Square Press, 2000), pp. 66–68.

26. Klaus-Jürgen Müller (ed.), *General Ludwig Beck, Studien und Dokumente zur politische-militärischen Vorstellungswelt und Tätigkeit des Generalstabschefs des deutschen Heeres 1933–1938* [General Ludwig Beck, Studies and Documents on the Political-military Imagination and Activity of the Chief of Staff of the German Army 1933-1938] (Boppard am Rhein: H. Boldt, 1980), pp. 502–512.

27. P. E. Caquet, *The Bell of Treason: The 1938 Munich Agreement in Czechoslovakia* (London: Profile Books Ltd., 2018), p. 39.

28. Richard Overy, 'Germany and the Munich Crisis: A Mutilated Victory?' in *The Munich Crisis Prelude to World War II* ed. Igor Lukes and Erik Goldstein (London: Frank Cass, 1999), p. 201.

29. Allan Bullock, *Hitler and Stalin: Parallel Lives* (New York: Alfred A. Knopf, 1992), pp. 570–574.

30. Roger Manvell, *The Conspirators, 20th July 1944* (New York: Ballantine Books, Inc., 1971), pp. 35–37.

31. Caquet, p. 68.

32. Greg Baughen, *The Rise of the Bomber: RAF–Army Planning, 1919 to Munich 1938* (Croyden: Fonthill Media Ltd., 2016), pp. 223–224.

33. Henryk Batowski, *Kryzys Dyplomatyczny w Europie: Jesieri 1938–Wiosna 1939* [*The Diplomatic Crisis in Europe: Autumn 1938–Spring 1939*] (Warsaw: Ministry of National Defence, 1962), p. 155.

34. Guderian, pp. 39–41.

35. Anna M. Cienciala, *Poland and the Western Powers 1938–1939: A Study in the Interdependence of Eastern and Western Europe* (Toronto: University of Toronto Press, 1968), pp. 34, 141–143.

36. Cienciala, *Poland and the Western Powers*, p. 39.

37. Ibid., pp. 177–182.

38. H. G. Wells, *The Shape of Things To Come* (London: Penguin Books Ltd., 2005), pp. 105, 208–209.

39. Dieter Schenk, *Hitlers Mann in Danzig. Gauleiter Forster und die NS-Verbrechen in Danzig-Westpreußen* [*Hitler's Man in Gdansk. Gauleiter Forster and the Crimes in Gdansk West Prussia*] (Bonn: J. H. W. Dietz, 2000).

40. Bullock, pp. 534–535.

41. Herbert S. Levine, 'The Mediator: Carl J. Burckhardt's Efforts to Avert a Second World War', *The Journal of Modern History*, Vol. 45, No. 3 (September, 1973), p. 447.

42. Cienciala, *Poland and the Western Powers*, pp. 189–190.

43. Gerhard L. Weinberg, *Hitler's Foreign Policy 1933–1939: The Road to World War II* (New York: Enigma Books, 2005), p. 685.

44. Steiner, pp. 727–729.

45. Adam Lebor, 'Never mind the Czech gold the Nazis stole ...', *The Telegraph*, 31 July 2013.

46. Speech by Adolf Hitler in Memel, 23 March 1939, http://der-fuehrer.org/reden/english/39-03-23.htm, accessed 18 April 2019.

47. Watt, p. 333.

48. *Mobilizacja Marcowa 1939* [*Mobilization March 1939*], Centralne Archiwum Wojskowe (CAW), *Military Teki Archiwalne*, Vol. 2 (Warsaw, 2012).

49. Gorlitz (ed.), p. 84.

50. Anita J. Prazmowska, *Britain, Poland and the Eastern Front, 1939* (Cambridge: Cambridge University Press, 1987), pp. 46–47.

51. Wark, pp. 116–117.

52. Prazmowska, pp. 50–54.

53. House of Commons Debates, Debate 345, 31 March 1939, Cols. 2421-2.

54. Joachim Fest, *Hitler* (New York: Harcourt Brace Jovanovich, 1974), p. 578

55. Gorlitz (ed.), pp. 84–85.

56. 'OKW Directive for the Uniform Preparation of War by the Wehrmacht 1939/40, 11 April 1939' in *Fuehrer Conferences on Naval Affairs, 1939–45* ed. Jak P. Mallmann Showell (London: Greenhill Books, 2006), pp. 29–30.

57. Prazmowska, pp. 59–63.

58. Ibid., pp. 115, 120

59. Steiner, p. 200.

60. 'Poland repeats Danzig Warning to Hitler', *The Telegraph*, 22 July, 1939.

61. Prazmowska, pp. 120–129.

62. Martin S. Alexander, *The Republic in Danger: General Maurice Gamelin and the Politics of French Defence, 1933–1940* (Cambridge: Cambridge University Press, 1992), pp. 306–308.

63. Brian Bond, *British Military Policy Between the Two World Wars* (Oxford: Oxford University Press, 1980), pp. 314–318

64. Baughen, p. 227.

65. Prazmowska, pp. 95.

66. Tooze, pp. 308–309, 382.

67. 'OKW Directive for the Uniform Preparation of War by the Wehrmacht 1939/40, Part VI, 10 May 1939' in Showell, pp. 30–31.

68. Weinberg, *Hitler's Foreign Policy*, pp. 717–718.

69. Christopher Hibbert, *Mussolini: The Rise and Fall of Il Duce* (New York: Palgrave Macmillan, 2008), p. 107.

70. Kershaw, *Nemesis*, pp. 190–193.

71. Ibid., pp. 192–193.
72. Roger Manvell and Heinrich Fraenkel, *Goering: The Rise and Fall of the Notorious Nazi Leader* (New York: Skyhorse Publishing Inc., 2011), p. 210.
73. Milan Hauner, *Hitler: A Chronology of his Life and Time* (New York: Palgrave Macmillan, 2005), pp. 144–145.
74. Albert Speer, *Inside the Third Reich* (New York: Simon & Schuster, 1970), pp. 161–162.
75. John Keegan, *Rundstedt* (New York: Ballantine Books Inc., 1974), p. 65.
76. Christian Jansen and Arno Weckbecker, *Der 'Volksdeutsche Selbstschutz' in Polen 1939/40* [*The German Self-Defence Units in Poland, 1939/40*] (Munich: R. Oldenbourg, 1992).
77. *Poland in The British Parliament 1939–1945*, Vol. 850, compiled by the Jozef Pilsudski Institute of America (Trenton, NJ: White Eagle Printing Co., 1946), pp. 1001–1002.
78. Ryszard Dalecki, *Armia Karpaty w Wojnie Obronnej 1939* [*Army Carpathia in the Defensive War 1939*] (Rzeszów: Libra Publishing House, 2009).
79. Sosabowski, pp. 20–21.
80. Prazmowska, p. 97.
81. Watt, pp. 355–359.
82. Montefiore, *Enigma*, pp. 44–45.
83. Galeazzo Ciano, *Diary 1937–1943* (New York: Enigma Books, 2002), p. 558.
84. Stephen Kotkin, *Stalin: Waiting for Hitler, 1929–1941* (New York: Penguin Press, 2017), pp. 656–658.
85. Roger Moorhouse, *The Devil's Alliance: Hitler's Pact with Stalin, 1939–1941* (New York: Basic Books, 2014), p. 23.
86. Ibid., pp. 24–27.
87. Moorhouse, p. 27.
88. russia-insider.com/en/history/truth-about-soviet-german-non-aggression-pact-23rd-august-1939-and-its-secret-protocol
89. Tadeusz Piotrowski, *Poland's Holocaust: Ethnic Strife, Collaboration with Occupying Forces and Genocide in the Second Republic, 1918–1947* (London: McFarland & Co., Inc., 1998), p. 205.
90. Robert M. Kennedy, *The German Campaign in Poland 1939*, DA Pamphlet 20-255 (Washington, DC: Department of the Army, 1956), p. 63.
91. Niehorster, p. 56.
92. Klaus Gerbet (ed.), *Generalfeldmarschall Fedor von Bock: The War Diary, 1939–1945* (Atglen, PA: Schiffer Publishing Ltd., 1996), p. 41.
93. Klaus A. Maier et al., *Germany and the Second World War*, Vol. II (Oxford, Oxford University Press, 2015), p. 90.
94. Ibid., pp. 65–66.
95. Besondere Anordnungen für die Versorgung [Special Arrangements for Supply], No. 4, Ia, KTB, Band A, Akte II, AOK 10, 21 August – 4 September 1939, NAM (National Archives Microfilm), Series T-312, Roll 75, frame 7595213–7595214.

96. Franz Halder, *The Halder War Diary, 1939–1942* (Novato, CA: Presidio Press, 1988), pp. 28–31.
97. Kershaw, *Nemesis*, p. 209.
98. Gerbet (ed.), Bock diary, p. 34.
99. Cajus Bekker, *The Luftwaffe War Diaries: The German Air Force in World War II* (Boston: Da Capo Press, 1994), p. 25.
100. Clay Blair, *Hitler's U-Boat War: The Hunters, 1939–1942* (New York: Random House, 1996), p. 55.
101. M. J. Whitley, *Destroyer! German Destroyers in World War II* (Annapolis, MD: Naval Institute Press, 1983), pp. 97–98.
102. Operationsbefehl Nr. 1 für Linienschiff 'Schleswig-Holstein', Marine-Gruppenkommando Ost, 21 August 1939, KTB Linienschiff *Schleswig-Holstein*, 25 August – 30 November 1939 [War Diary of Battleship Schleswig-Holstein], NAM (National Archives Microfilm), Series T-1022, Roll 3863, PG 48503/b.
103. Watt, p. 484.
104. William L. Shirer, *Berlin Diary: The Journal of a Foreign Correspondent, 1934–1941* (Baltimore: Johns Hopkins University Press, 2002), pp. 183–186.
105. Marlis G. Steinert, *Hitler's War and the Germans: Public Mood and Attitude during the Second World War* (Athens, OH: Ohio University Press, 1977), pp. 41–42.
106. Halder, p. 33.
107. Aleksandr Narbut-Łuczyński, *U kresu wędrówki. Wspomnienia* [At the End of the Journey. Memories] (London: Gryf, 1966), pp. 333, 338–340.
108. Antoni Nawrocki, *Zabezpieczenie logistyczne wojsk lądowych sił zbrojnych II RP w latach 1936–39* [Logistics Security for Land Forces of the Second Polish Armed Forces in 1936–39] (Warsaw: Ulmak, 2002), p. 286.
109. Wendy von Well and Roman Gastager, *The Easter Bunnies: Long-distance Reconnaissance by the German Luftwaffe over Poland, France, England and the Atlantic 1938–1945* (Oxford: Trafford Publishing, 2006).
110. Ciano, p. 265.
111. Herbert Schindler, *Mosty und Dirschau 1939: Zwei Handstreiche der Wehrmacht vor Beginn des Polenfeldzuges* [Mosty and Dirschau 1939: Two Coups by the Wehrmacht Before the Start of the Polish Campaign] (Freiburg: Rombach & Co., 1971).
112. Gerbet (ed.), Bock diary, p. 37.
113. Józef Lipski, *Diplomat in Berlin, 1933–1939* (New York: Columbia University Press, 1968), pp. 592–593.
114. Anlagen 1 zum KTB, XVI Armeekorps, 19 August – 10 September 1939, NAM (National Archives Microfilm), Series T-314, Roll 567, frames 155–158.
115. David Kahn, *Hitler's Spies: German Military Intelligence in World War II* (Boston: Da Capo Press, 1978), p. 249.
116. Cynk, p. 67.
117. Michael Alfred Peszke, *Poland's Navy, 1918–1945* (New York: Hippocrene Books Inc., 1999), p. 36.
118. Hugh Trevor-Roper, *Hitler's War Directives, 1939–1945* (Edinburgh: Birlinn Ltd., 2004), p. 38.

119. Halder, p. 43.
120. Marek Fijałkowski, 'Wrzesień 1939 roku w zbiorach Muzeum Okręgowego w Pile' [September 1939 in the Collection of the District Museum in Piła] Niepodległość i Pamięć',Vol. 6/2, No. 15 (1999), p. 340.

CHAPTER 5: OPENING MOVES

1. Sonke Neitzel and Harald Welzer, *Soldiers: German POWs on Fighting, Killing, and Dying* (New York: Random House, 2012).
2. Heinz Nowarra, *Heinkel He 111: A Documentary History* (London, Jane's Publishing Ltd., 1980), p. 105.
3. Grzegorz Okoński, 'We wrześniu 1939 r. Poznań był bombardowany. Zginęło niemal 300 osób' [In September 1939, Poznań was Bombed. Almost 300 People Died], *Historia*, 25 August, 2016.
4. Bekker, p. 33.
5. Peter C. Smith, *Stuka Squadron: Stukagruppe 77 – the Luftwaffe's Fire Brigade* (Wellingborough, UK: Patrick Stephens Ltd, 1990), p. 36.
6. John Weal, *Messerschmitt Bf 110 Zerstörer Aces of World War 2* (Oxford: Osprey Publishing, 2012) p. 15.
7. Bartlomiej Belcarz and Tomasz J. Kopanski, *Polish Wings 3, PWS-10, Avia BH-33, PZL P.7a* (Sandomierz: Stratus, 2009), p. 38.
8. Richard P. Hallion, *Strike From the Sky: The History of Battlefield Air Attack, 1910–1945* (Tuscaloosa: University of Alabama Press, 1989), p. 134.
9. Ulf Balke, *Kampfgeschwader 100 'Wiking' – Eine Geschichte aus Kriegstagebüchern, Dokumenten und Berichten 1934–1945* (Stuttgart: Motorbuchverlag, 1995).
10. Cynk, p. 78.
11. Ibid., pp. 79–80.
12. Leszek Moczulski, *Wojna polska 1939* [*The Polish War of 1939*] (Warsaw: Bellona, 2017), p. 456.
13. Piotr Laskowski, 'Kompania szturmowa Kriegsmarine w walkkach na Westerplatte w 1939' [The Kriegsmarine Assault Company in the Fight at Westerplatte, 1939], *Przeglad Morski* [*Maritime Review*] (2008), pp. 58–59.
14. KTB Linienschiff *Schleswig-Holstein*, 25 August – 30 November 1939, NAM (National Archives Microfilm), Series T-1022, Roll 3863, PG 48503/b.
15. Watt, p. 535.
16. Polish Institute and Sikorski Museum London, Archives Ref. No Mar. A. II. 7/3 and, SR 17 903, f. 1–8.
17. Whitley, *Destroyer!*, p. 99.
18. Gerbet (ed.), Bock diary, p. 44.
19. Mariusz Borowiak, *Westerplatte, w obronie prawdy* [*Westerplatte, in Defence of the Truth*] (Warsaw: Alma Press, 2008).
20. Jarosław Tuliszka, *Westerplatte 1926–1939* (Gdansk: Adam Marszałek Publishing House, 2011), p. 245.

21. Polish Institute and Sikorski Museum London, Archives Ref. No Mar. A. II. 7/3 and, SR 17 903, f. 1–8.

22. Stanisław Strumph Wojtkiewicz, *Alarm Dla Gdyni* [*Alarm for Gdynia*] (Warsaw: Ministry of National Defence, 1977).

23. Bericht über die Beschießung der Südspitze 'Hela' am 25.9.1939, KTB Linienschiff *Schliesen*, 25 August – 30 September 1939, NAM (National Archives Microfilm), Series T-1022, Roll 2950, PG 48484.

24. Louis Paul Lochner, *What About Germany?* (New York: Dodd, Mead & Company, 1942), pp. 11–12.

25. Guderian, p. 50.

26. Veterans of the 3rd Panzer Division, *Armoured Bears: The German 3rd Panzer Division in World War II*, Vol. II (Mechanicsburg, PA: Stackpole Books, 2013), pp. 25–27.

27. Jakub Gackowski, 'Wielka Klonia – Świekatowo, 1–2 września 1939 roku', Biuletyn Historyczny (BURCHAT: świekatowo, 2009).

28. Guderian, p. 51.

29. Anna Charczuk, 'Walki 9 Dywizji Piechoty w składzie Armii "Pomorze" w korytarzu pomorskim we wrześniu 1939 r' [Combat of the 9th Infantry Division in the 'Pomerania' Army in the Pomeranian Corridor in September 1939], *Szkice Podlaskie* [Sketches of Poland], 16 (2008), pp. 67–78.

30. Jan Maliszewski, '35 pp w obronie Pomorza we wrześniu 1939 r' [35 pp in Defence of Pomerania in September 1939], *Wojskowy Przegląd Historyczny* [*Military Historical Review*], No. 2 (128) (1989), pp. 241–252.

31. Andrzej J. Lorbiecki and Marcin Wałdoch, *Chojnice 1939* (Warsaw: Bellona Publishing House, 2014).

32. Konrad Ciechanowski, *Armia Pomorze 1939* (Warsaw: Ministry of National Defence, 1982), p. 78.

33. Bekker, pp. 25–26.

34. Ciechanowski, pp. 97–98.

35. Ibid., pp. 80–84.

36. Robert Grochowski, 'w obronie Pomorza 1–6 wrzesnia 1939' [The Defence of Pomerania, 1-6 September 1939], Biuletyn Historyczny (BUKO, 2010).

37. Veterans of the 3rd Panzer Division, *Armoured Bears*, p. 32.

38. Olaf Popkiewicz, 'Dzień, w którym przestała istnieć 9. Dywizja Piechoty' [The Day when the 9th Infantry Division Ceased to Exist], *Odkrywca* [*Explorer*], 16 September, 2017.

39. Ia, Kriegstagebuch des Generalkommandos XIX. A.K. uber den Feldzug in Polen, June–September 1939, NAM (National Archives Microfilm), Series T-314, Roll 611, frame 596.

40. Christoph von Allmayer-Beck, *Die Geschichte der 21. (ostpr./westpr.) Infanterie-Division* [*The History of the 21st East Prussian Infantry Division*] (Munich: Schild Verlag GmbH, 1990), pp. 56.

41. Tomasz Chinciński, *Forpoczta Hitlera. Niemiecka dywersja w Polsce w 1939 roku* [*Hitler's Outpost: German Diversions in Poland in 1939*] (Gdańsk: Naukowe Schola, 2010).
42. Guderian, p. 54.
43. Ryszard Juszkiewicz, *Bitwa pod Mławą 1939* [*Battle of Mława, 1939*] (Warsaw: Książka i Wiedza, 1987).
44. Ic, Kriegstagebuch (KTB), I Armeekorps, September–October 1939, NAM (National Archives Microfilm), Series T-314, Roll 33, frame 944.
45. Ryszard Juszkiewicz, '1 Wrzesnia 1939 roku w swietle relacji uczestnikow bitwy granicznej Armii "Modlin"' [September 1, 1939, Reports From Participants of the Border Battle of the 'Modlin' Army] *Rocznik Mazowiecki* [Mazowiecki Yearbook] 21 (Muzeum Historii Polski, 2009), pp. 140–152.
46. Account by Kapitan Kazimierz Nowiński, 1 baterii, 20 PAL in Juszkiewicz, pp. 140–152.
47. IIa/IIb, Anlagen zum KTB, Heft 7, I Armeekorps, September–October 1939, NAM (National Archives Microfilm), Series T-314, Roll 33, frame 1122.
48. Ia, Kriegstagebuch (KTB), I Armeekorps, September–October 1939, NAM (National Archives Microfilm), Series T-314, Roll 33, frame 32.
49. Krzysztof Komorowski (ed.), *Boje Polskie 1939–1945. Przewodnik Encyklopedyczny* [*Polish Battles, 1939–1945, Encyclopedic Guide*] (Warsaw: Bellona, 2009), pp. 249–250.
50. Wim Brandt, 'Eine motorisierte Aufklärungsabteilung im der Polenfeldzug' [A Motorized Reconnaissance Detachment in the Polish Campaign], *Militär-Wochenblatt* 124, no. 25 (December 15, 1939).
51. Sosabowski, pp. 22–23.
52. Ibid., p. 24.
53. Gerbet (ed.), Bock diary, p. 45.
54. Tadeusz Jurga and Władysław Karbowski, *Armia Modlin 1939 r* (Warsaw: Ministry of National Defence, 1987), pp. 152–161.
55. Ryszard Juszkiewicz, *Walki o przedmościa Różan, Pułtusk, Płock 1939* [*Struggles for the Różan, Pułtusk and Płock Bridgeheads*] (Warsaw: MAKO, 1992), pp. 34–38.
56. Komorowski, p. 250.
57. Wehrmacht 10-Day Casualty Reports, 1939 [BA/MA RW 19/1379–1380].
58. Armeebefehl für den Angriff am X-Tag (29 August 1939) in Ia, Anlagen zum Kriegstagebuch (KTB), Akte II, AOK 10, 21 August – 4 September 1939, NAM (National Archives Microfilm), Series T-312, Roll 75, frame 595242.
59. Albert Krull, *Das Hannoversche Regiment 73* (Hannover, 1967), pp. 33–36.
60. Jochen Böhler, *Zbrodnie Wehrmachtu w Polsce* [*Wehrmacht Crimes in Poland*] (Krakow: Znak Publishing House, 2009).
61. Rudolf Lehmann, *Die Leibstandarte*, Vol. 1 (Winnipeg: J. J. Fedorowicz Publishing, 1987), pp. 148–150.

62. Lucjan Woźniak, 'Wrzesień 1939 w oczach ułana' [September 1939: In the Eyes of an Uhlan], Za i Przeciw, 1986, No. 36.

63. Hans Schäufler, Knight's Cross Panzers: The German 35th Panzer Regiment in WWII (Mechanicsburg: Stackpole Books, 2010), pp. 8–9.

64. Jentz, p. 103.

65. Andrzej Wilczkowski, Anatomia Boju: Wołyńska Brygada Kawalerii pod Mokrą, 1 września 1939 [Anatomy of a Battle: the Volhynian Cavalry Brigade at Mokra, 1 September 1939] (Łódź: Łódzkie, 1992).

66. Korpsbefehl für den Angriff, IV Armeekorps, 28 August 1939, KTB Nr. 1, 21 August – 30 September 1939, NAM (National Archives Microfilm), Series T-314, Roll 215, frame 295.

67. Ia, Kriegstagebuch, 4. Infanterie-Division, 24 August–12 October 1939, NAM (National Archives Microfilm), Series T-315, Roll 187, frame 550.

68. Ia, Kriegstagebuch, Feldzug in Polen, XV Armeekorps, 19 August – 13 October 1939, NAM (National Archives Microfilm), Series T-314, Roll 550, frame 234–235.

69. Schäufler, p. 9.

70. Adam Kurus, 'Częstochowa 1939: Zapomniana bitwa' [Częstochowa 1939: Forgotten Battle], Archeologia Wojenna, Vol. 3 (2012).

71. Hans von Tettau and Kurt Versock, Die Geschichte der 24. Infanterie-Division (Eggolsheim: Dörfler, 1956), p. 14.

72. Roman Abraham, Wspomnienia wojenne znad Warty i Bzury [War Memories from the Warta and Bzura] (Warsaw: Ministry of National Defence, 1990), pp. 19–20.

73. Romuald Szeremietiew, 'Garnizon Leszczyński WP w wojnie obronnej 1939 r' [The WP Garrison of Leszno in the Defensive War of 1939], Historia Wojskowa (September, 2010).

74. Ia, Kriegstagebuch, Feldzug in Polen, XV Armeekorps, 19 August – 13 October 1939 1939, NAM (National Archives Microfilm), Series T-314, Roll 550, frame 236–238.

75. David R. Higgins, Panzer II vs. 7TP: Poland 1939 (Oxford: Osprey Publishing, 2015), pp. 59–65.

76. Władysław Steblik, Armia Kraków 1939 (Warsaw: Ministry of National Defence, 1975), pp. 68–70, 114–120.

77. Steblik, pp. 154–155.

78. Janusz Ryt, Bitwa Pszczyńska 1939 [Battle of Pszczyńska 1939] (Pszczyna: Infopres, 2007), pp. 73–93.

79. Wilhelm Hertlein, Chronik der 7. Infanterie-Division München (Munich: Verlag F. Bruckmann, 1984).

80. Mark W. Axworthy, Axis Slovakia: Hitler's Slavic Wedge, 1938–1945 (New York: Axis Europa Books, 2002), p. 72.

81. Jerzy Majka, Invincible Black Brigade: Polish 10th Cavalry Brigade 1939 (Sandomierz: MMP Books, 2011), p. 76.

82. F. S. Kurcz, The Black Brigade (Harrow: Atlantis Publishing Co. Ltd., 1943), pp. 19–20.

83. Stanislaw Maczek, *Avec Mes Blindés* (Paris: Presses de la Cité, 1967), pp. 32–38.
84. Kurcz, p. 24.
85. Franciszek Skibiński, *Pierwsza pancerna* [*First Panzer*] (Warsaw: Czytelnik, 1979), pp. 23–30.
86. Franz Josef Strauss, *Die Geschichte der 2. (Wiener) Panzer-Division* (Eggolsheim: Dörfler, 2005), pp. 35–36.
87. Maczek, pp. 54–57.

CHAPTER 6: TOTAL WAR

1. Neitzel and Welzer.
2. Watt, p. 539.
3. Steiner, pp. 1010–1013 and Watt, pp. 544–545.
4. CAB 47 (39), 1 September, 1939, pp. 1–10.
5. CAB 24/288, Cabinet Defence Preparedness Committee, D.M. (39) 4th Meeting, September 1, 1939, pp. 1–3.
6. P. R. Stafford, 'The French Government and the Danzig Crisis: The Italian Dimension', *The International History Review*, Vol. 6, No. 1 (February, 1984), pp. 48–87.
7. CAB 48 (39), 2 September, 1939, pp. 9–10.
8. Watt, pp. 578–580.
9. CAB 49 (39), 2 September, 1939, p. 10.
10. Baughen, p. 222.
11. Max Hastings, *Bomber Command* (London: Pan Books, 2010), p. 53.
12. Howard Hughes, *The Holy Fox: The Life of Lord Halifax* (London: Head of Zeus Ltd., 2014), p. 239.
13. Foreign Relations of the United States Diplomatic Papers, 1939, General, Vol. I, 740.00116 European War 1939/12.
14. War Cabinet Meeting, W. M. (39) 1st Conclusions, 4 September, 1939, p. 3.
15. M. J. Whitley, *German Cruisers of World War Two* (Annapolis, MD: Naval Institute Press, 1985), p. 76.
16. Henrik Skov Kristensen, Claus Kofoed and Frank Weber, *Vestallierede luftangreb i Danmark under 2. Verdenskrig* [*Western Allied Air Attacks in Denmark during World War II*] (Aarhus: Aarhus University Publishing, 1988).
17. Martin Middlebrook, *The Bomber Command War Diaries* (Leicester: Midland Publishing, 2000), p. 24.
18. Blair, pp. 66–69.
19. War Cabinet Meeting, W. M. (39) 1st Conclusions, 3 September, 1939, pp. 3, 7.
20. War Cabinet Meeting, W. M. (39) 2nd Conclusions, 4 September, 1939, p. 12.
21. Keith Feiling, *The Life of Neville Chamberlain* (London: Macmillan & Co. Ltd., 1947), p. 417.
22. Robert Self, *Neville Chamberlain: A Biography* (London: Routledge, 2016), p. 383.

23. Peter Hoffman, *Stauffenberg: A Family History, 1905–1944* (Montreal: McGill-Queen's Press, 2003).

24. Jochen Böhler, Klaus-Michael Mallmann and Jürgen Matthäus, *Einsatzgruppen w Polsce [Einsatzgruppen in Poland]* (Warsaw: Bellona, 2009).

25. OKH, *Außerordentliche Regeln für Sicherheitsrichtlinien [Extraordinary Rules for Directives Concerning Security]*, 9 August, 1939, BA-MA, RH19-I/91, passage 5a, c. 21–22.

26. Böhler, *Zbrodnie Wehrmachtu,* pp. 113–114.

27. Ibid., p. 185.

28. Dziennik wojenny sztabu 32 Dywizji Piechoty z kampanii w Polsce [Military Journal of the Staff of the 32nd Infantry Division from the Campaign in Poland] (CAW, Central Military Archive, No. 4/33, 2012).

29. Jan Maliszewski et al., 'Wspomnienia dowódcy 35. pułku piechoty' [Memories of the Commander of the 35th Infantry Regiment] in *Żołnierze Września [Soldiers of September]* (Warsaw: PAX, 1971), pp. 61–67.

30. Gerbet (ed.), Bock diary, p. 45.

31. Guderian, pp. 54–55.

32. Jaroslaw Skora, *WWII 1939 Polish Fighter PZL P.11* (self-published, 2017), p. 64.

33. Nikolaus von Vormann, *Der Feldzug 1939 in Polen – Die Operationen des Heeres* (Weissenburg: Prinz-Eugen-Verlag, 1958), p. 78.

34. Jurga and Karbowski, pp. 152–154.

35. Ryszard Juszkiewicz, *Obrona Pułtuska i 13 pułk piechoty w wojnie 1939 roku [Pułtusk Defence and the 13th Infantry Regiment in the War of 1939]* (Mława: Stacja Naukowa, 2000).

36. Jochen Böhler, *Najazd 1939. Niemcy przeciw Polsce [Invasion 1939, Germany Against Poland]* (Krakow: Znak Publishing House, 2011), pp. 272–273.

37. Halder, pp. 52–53.

38. Ia, Anlage I z. KTB 1 mit Ib Anlagen., 10. Panzer-Division, 25 August – 14 September 1939, Series T-315, Roll 558.

39. Dominik Kasprzak, 'Wzmocniony polski polowy schron żelbetowy w Łomży' [Strengthened Polish Field Reinforced Concrete Shelter in Łomża], *Wojsko i Technika Historia* , May 2018.

40. Ia, Anlage z. KTB 1, 21. Infanterie-Division, 21 August – 30 September 1939, NAM (National Archives Microfilm), Series T-315, Roll 749, frame 519.

41. Ia, Kriegstagebuch 1 und Kriegsrangliste, XXI Armeekorps, August – October 1939, Series T-314, Roll 660.

42. Eugen Hadamovsky, *Blitzmarsch nach Warschau [Lightning March to Warsaw]* (Munich: Zentralverlag der NSDAP, 1940), pp. 175–179.

43. Allmayer-Beck, p.67.

44. Cynk, p. 84.

45. Guderian, pp. 56–59.

46. Higgins, pp. 64–66.

47. Stanisław Wyrzycki, *2 Pułk Piechoty Legionów* [*2nd Infantry Regiment of the Legions*] (*Warsaw: Ajaks, 2000*).

48. Walter Charles de Beaulieu, *Generaloberst Erich Hoepner* (Neckargemünd: Kurt Vowinkel-Verlag, 1969), pp. 30–31.

49. Halder, p. 51.

50. Schäufler, pp. 9–10.

51. Bekker, pp. 49–50.

52. Jan Przemsza-Zieliński, *Księga Wrześniowej Chwały Pułków śląskic* [*Book of the September Glory of the Silesian Regiments*], Vol. 2 (Katowice-Sosnowiec: Sowa-Press, 1993).

53. Lehmann, pp. 162–164.

54. Tettau and Versock, p. 19.

55. Ia, Tagesbuchaufzeichnungen aus dem Polenfeldzug, X Armeekorps, 26 August – 6 October 1939, NAM (National Archives Microfilm), T-314, Roll 441, F 960.

56. Erich von Manstein, *Lost Victories* (Novato: Presidio Press, 1982), p. 55.

57. Piotr Bauer and Bogusław Polak, *Armia Poznań w wojnie obronnej 1939* [*The Poznań Army in the Defensive War of 1939*] (Poznań: Poznań Publishing, 1982), p. 169.

58. Hubert Kazimierz Kujawa, *Księga lotników polskich poległych, zmarłych i zaginionych 1939–1946* [*Book of Polish Airmen Killed, Dead and Missing 1939–1946*] (Warsaw: Ministry of National Defence, 1989), p. 118.

59. Rolf Elble, *Die Schlacht an der Bzura im September 1939 aus deutscher und polnischer Sicht* [*The Battle of the Bzura in September 1939 from the German and Polish Point of View*] (Freiburg: Rombach, 1975), pp. 119, 125.

60. Krzysztofem Handke, *Pułkownik Władysław Wiecierzyński: dowódca 55. Poznańskiego Pułku Piechoty w Lesznie 1935–1939* [*Colonel Władysław Wiecierzyński: commander of the 55th Poznań Infantry Regiment in Leszno, 1935–1939*] (Leszno: Association of Reserve Officers 69 Leszno Anti-aircraft Regiment, 2010).

61. Elble, pp. 128–129.

62. Ibid., p. 139.

63. Tettau and Versock, pp. 22–23.

64. Bekker, p. 54.

65. Bauer and Polak, p. 310.

66. Robert M. Citino, *The German Way of War: From The Thirty Years War to the Third Reich* (Lawrence: University Press of Kansas, 2005), p. 264.

67. Elble, p. 251.

68. Tadeusz Jurga, *Bzura 1939* (Warsaw: Bellona, 2013), pp. 152–153.

69. Witold Engel, *Czołgi płonęły nad Bzurą* [*Tanks were Burning at the Bzura*] (Poznań: Drukarnia Naukowa 1992), pp. 73–75.

70. Schäufler, pp. 13–14.

71. Hans Reinhardt, 'Die 4. Panzerdivision vor Warschau und an der Bzura vom 9. 20.9.1939', *Wehrkund* 5 (1958), pp. 237–247.

72. Schäufler, p. 15.

73. BBC People's War website, www.bbc.co.uk/history/ww2peopleswar/stories/ 32/a2314432.shtml.
74. Manstein, *Lost Victories, p. 58*.
75. Alex Buchner, *Der Polenfeldzug 1939* (Leoni: Druffel Verlag, 1989).
76. Leopold Wójcik, '156 pułk piechoty we wrześniu 1939 roku' [156 Infantry Regiment in September 1939], *Zeszyty Historyczne ZBoWiD* No. 3 (Krakow, 1988).
77. Steblik, pp. 220–226.
78. Ibid., pp. 320–321.
79. Zaloga and Madej, *The Polish Campaign 1939,* p. 149.
80. Komorowski, pp. 49–50.
81. Wojciech Włodarkiewicz, *Lwów 1939* (Warsaw: Bellona, 2007), p. 117.
82. Ryszard Dalecki, 'Czy 38 DP Rez została rozbita 16.9.1939 r. pod Rodatyczami?' [Was the 38th Reserve Infantry Division Shattered on 16.9.1939 near Rodatycze?), *WPH*, No. 1 (February–March, 1971), p. 422.
83. Ia, 75 K/l Armeebefehle, 14 Armee, 30 August – 7 October 1939, NAM (National Archives Microfilm), Series T-312, Roll 477, frame 8067021.

CHAPTER 7: APOTHEOSIS

1. Bekker, p. 51.
2. Ludwik Głowacki, *Obrona Warszawy i Modlina 1939* [*Defence of Warsaw and Modlin 1939*] (Warsaw: Ministry of National Defence, 1985), p. 78.
3. Adam Jońca, et al., *Wrzesień 1939 – Pojazdy Wojska Polskiego* [*September 1939 – Vehicles of the Polish Army*] (Warsaw: WKŁ, 1990).
4. Janusz Odziemkowski, *Warszawa w wojnie obronnej 1939 roku* [*Warsaw in the defensive war of 1939*] (Warsaw: PWN, 1989), p. 103.
5. Werner Bux, *Weg und Schicksal der 11 Infanterie-Division* (Bad Manheim: Podzu Verlag, 1968), p. 13.
6. Gerbet (ed.), Bock diary, p. 53.
7. Guderian, pp. 58–61.
8. Ia, Kriegstagebuch., I Armeekorps, September – October 1939, NAM (National Archives Microfilm), Series T-314, Roll 33 and IIa/IIb, Anlagen zum KTB, Heft 7, I Armeekorps, September 1939, NAM (National Archives Microfilm), Series T-314, Roll 33, frame 1077.
9. Sosabowski, p. 35.
10. Ibid., pp. 37–38.
11. Bekker, p. 57.
12. Halder, p. 56.
13. Głowacki, pp. 150, 204.
14. Welf Botho Elster, *Die Grenzen des Gehorsams: das Leben des Generalmajors Botho Henning Elster in Briefen und Zeitzeugnissen* (Hildesheim: Olms, 2005), pp. 71–73.
15. Steiner, pp. 913.
16. Halder, pp. 51, 55.

17. Mikhail I. Meltyukhov, *Sovetsko-pol'skiye voyny: Voyenno-politicheskoye protivostoyaniye 1918–1939* [*Soviet–Polish Wars: The Military-Political Confrontation of 1918–1939*] (Moscow: Veche, 2001), pp. 279–285.

18. Ivan N. Russiyanov, *V boyakh rozhdennaya ...* [*In the Battles Born ...*] (Moscow: Military Publishing House, 1982).

19. Kotkin, p. 683.

20. Sikorski Institute, Documents on Polish–Soviet Relations, Vol. I, p. 46.

21. Wojciech Skóra, *Porwanie kierownika polskiej placówki konsularnej w Kijowie Jerzego Matusińskiego przez władze radzieckie w 1939 r.* [*Abduction of the Head of the Polish Consular Post in Kiev Jerzy Matusiński by the Soviet Authorities in 1939*], in *Polish Diplomacy in the East in the 20th and Beginning of the 21st Century* (Kharkov, 2010), pp. 414–437.

22. Carton de Wiart, p. 158.

23. Edward Rydz-Śmigły, Wacław Stachiewicz, et. al., *Wrzesień 1939 w relacjach i wspomnieniach* [*September 1939 in Relations and Memories*] (Warsaw: Ministry of National Defence, 1989), pp. 142–144.

24. Mirek Wawrzyński, 'Lotnictwo sowieckie w wojnie nad Polską wrzesień 1939 roku' [Soviet Aviation During the War against Poland September 1939], Part II, *Militaria i Fakty*, May–June 2003.

25. Cynk, p. 86.

26. Montefiore, *Enigma*, pp. 50–52.

27. Jean-François Bergier, 'Switzerland and Gold Transactions in the Second World War, Interim Report (of the independent commission of experts)' (Berne, 1998).

28. Piotrowski, pp. 49–50.

29. Jan T. Gross, *Revolution from Abroad: The Soviet Conquest of Poland's Western Ukraine and Western Belorussia* (Princeton: Princeton University Press, 2002), pp. 35–40, 50–53.

30. Wojciech Rodak, 'Śmierć Lachom! Piąta kolumna na Kresach we wrześniu 1939 r.' [Death to You! The Fifth Column in the Borderlands in September 1939] *Nasza Historia* (25 August, 2016).

31. Marek Wierzbicki, *Polacy i żydzi w zaborze sowieckim: Stosunki polski-żydowskie na ziemiach północno-wschodnich II RP pod okupacja sowiecka 1939-1941* [*Poles and Jews in the Soviet Partition. Polish–Jewish Relations in the North-eastern Territories of the Second Polish Republic under the Soviet Occupation of 1939–1941*] (Warsaw: Fronda, 2007), pp. 77–79.

32. Zaloga, *T-26*, p. 32.

33. Piotrowski, p. 145.

34. Janina Stobniak-Smogorzewska, *Osadnicy wojskowi a ludność żydowska na Kresach Wschodnich 1920–1940* [*Military Settlers and the Jewish Population in the Eastern Borderlands of 1920–1940*] (Warsaw: Rytm, 2003), p. 567.

35. Klemens Kurzyp, *Dęblin, Szkice z dziejów miejscowości i okolicy* [*Dęblin, Sketches from the History of the Town and the Area*] (Dęblin, 1994), pp. 152–153.

36. Wojciech Włodarkiewicz, *Obrona Lwowa 1939* [*The Defence of Lwów*] (Warsaw: Bellona, 1996), p. 106.
37. Maczek, pp. 99.
38. Wojciech Dziedzic, 'Polscy pancerniacy pod Tomaszowem Lubelskim' [Polish Tanks near Tomaszów Lubelski], *Rewizje Historyczne,* No. 12 (1994).
39. Heinz Greiner and Eberhard Ebeling, *Kriegeslehren in taktischen Beispielen aus dem Weltkrieg 1914/1918 und aus dem Polen-Feldzug 1939* [*War Lessons in Tactical Examples from the World War 1914/1918 and from the Polish Campaign 1939*] (Berlin: E. S. Mittler, 1941).
40. Halder, pp. 58, 60.
41. CAB 65-1, War Cabinet Meeting, W. M. (39) 19th Conclusions, 18 September, 1939, pp. 150–151, 154.
42. Keith Sword, *British Reactions to the Soviet Occupation of Eastern Poland in September 1939, The Slavonic and East European Review*, Vol. 69, No. 1 (January, 1991), p. 85.
43. 'What is Stalin up to?', *Sunday Express*, 24 September, 1939.
44. William M. Shirer, *The Collapse of the Third Republic: An Inquiry into the Fall of France in 1940* (New York: Da Capo Press, 1994), p. 531.
45. CAB 65-1, War Cabinet Meeting, W. M. (39) 21st Conclusions, 20 September, 1939, p. 165.
46. Gerbet (ed.), Bock diary, p. 55.
47. Abraham, pp. 218, 265.
48. Alexander Polonius, *Widziałem oblężenie Warszawy* [*I Saw The Siege of Warsaw*] (Poznań: Rebis, 2018).
49. Gorlitz (ed.), pp. 95–96.
50. Gerbet (ed.), Bock diary, p. 62.
51. Bekker, p. 58.
52. Smith and Creek, p. 64.
53. Gerbet (ed.), Bock diary, pp. 62–66.
54. Sosabowski, p. 44.
55. Ludwik Czyżewski, *Wspomnienia dowódcy obrony Zakroczymia w 1939 r.* [*Memories of the Commander of the Defence of Zakroczym*] (Warsaw: Książka i Wiedza, 1973), pp. 61–62, 87–95.
56. Russiyanov.
57. Tadeusz Grzeszkiewicz, 'Działania Samodzielnej Grupy Operacyjnej Polesie. Z relacji uczestnika walk' [Operations of the Polesie Independent Operational Group. From the Participant's Relationship], in *Wrzesień 1939 w relacjach i wspomnieniach* (Warsaw: Ministry of National Defence, 1989), p. 805.

CHAPTER 8: OCCUPATION

1. Jentz, p. 104.
2. Lukas Friedli, *Repairing the Panzers: German Tank Maintenance in World War 2*, Vol. 2 (Monroe, NY: Panzerwrecks, 2011), p. 127.

3. Zaloga and Madej, *The Polish Campaign*, p. 156.
4. Friedli, pp. 26–27.
5. Cynk, p. 89.
6. US Strategic Bombing Survey, Oil Division, Final Report, 1947, pp. 17–18.
7. Vajda and Dancey, p. 51.
8. War Cabinet Meeting, W. M. (39) 45th Conclusions, 12 October, 1939, pp. 370–372.
9. G. F. Krivoshein, *Soviet Casualties and Losses in the Twentieth Century* (London: Greenhill Books, 1997), p. 58.
10. Moczulski, p. 926.
11. Cynk, p. 90.
12. Sophie Hodorowicz Knab, *Wearing the Letter P: Polish Women as Forced Laborers in Nazi Germany, 1939–1945* (New York: Hippocrene Books, 2016).
13. Maier et. al, pp. 130–131.
14. Emmanuel Kreike (ed.), *Corrupt Histories* (Rochester: University of Rochester Press, 2004), p. 115.
15. Evans, pp. 31–32.
16. Sarah Ann Gordon, *Hitler, Germans, and the 'Jewish Question'* (Princeton: Princeton University Press, 1984), pp. 280–281.
17. Kochanski, pp. 128, 137.
18. Tim Tzouliadis, *The Forsaken: An American Tragedy in Stalin's Russia* (New York: The Penguin Press, 2008), pp. 220–226.
19. Note by the Chairman of the KGB at USSR Council of Ministers A.N. Shelepin on March 3, 1959, No 632-III with a proposal to liquidate all the cases of the operation carried out by the NKVD in accordance with the decision of the Central Committee of the CPSU (b) of March 5, 1940.
20. Krystyna Piorkowska, 'Anglojęzyczni świadkowie Katynia. Najnowsze Badania' [English-Speaking Witnesses to Katyn: Recent Research], *The Polish Review*, Vol. 58, No. 1 (2013), pp. 98–101.

EPILOGUE

1. Christopher D. O'Sullivan, *Harry Hopkins: FDR's Envoy to Churchill and Stalin* (Lanham: Rowman & Littlefield Publishing Group, 2015), p. 133.

APPENDICES

1. *Führer Conferences on Naval Affairs 1939–1945* (London: Chatham Publishing, 2005), p. 30.

Bibliography

PRIMARY SOURCES

CAB 23/100, Cabinet Meetings (39), Conclusions from 21 June to 3 September 1939.

CAB 65/1, War Cabinet Meeting, W. M. (39) Conclusions, from 3 September to 1 October, 1939.

Various records from the RG 242 series at the NAM (National Archives Microfilm) in College Park, Maryland, including: German army-level, corps-level and division-level records.

MEMOIRS AND DIARIES

Roman Abraham, *Wspomnienia wojenne znad Warty i Bzury* [*War Memories from the Warta and Bzura*] (Warsaw: Ministry of National Defence, 1990).

Galeazzo Ciano, *Diary 1937–1943* (New York: Enigma Books, 2002).

Ludwik Czyżewski, *Wspomnienia dowódcy obrony Zakroczymia w 1939 r.* [Memories of the Commander of the Defence of Zakroczym] (Warsaw: Książka i Wiedza, 1973).

Klaus Gerbet (ed), *Generalfeldmarschall Fedor von Bock: The War Diary, 1939–1945* (Atglen, PA: Schiffer Publishing Ltd., 1996).

Heinz Guderian, *Panzer Leader* (New York: Ballantine Books, Inc., 1968).

Franz Halder, *The Halder War Diary, 1939–1942* (Novato, CA: Presidio Press, 1988).

Stanislaw Maczek, *Avec Mes Blindés* (Paris: Presses de la Cité, 1967).

Aleksandr Narbut-Łuczyński, *U kresu wędrówki. Wspomnienia* [*At the End of the Journey. Memories*] (London: Gryf, 1966).

Zdzisław Pacak-Kuźmirski, *Reduta 56* (Warsaw: Ministry of National Defence, 1959).

Edward Rydz-Śmigły, Wacław Stachiewicz, et. al., *Wrzesień 1939 w relacjach i wspomnieniach* [*September 1939 in Relations and Memories*] (Warsaw: Ministry of National Defence, 1989).

Stanisław Sosabowski, *Freely I Served* (Nashville, TN: The Battery Press, Inc., 1982).

Skalski Stanisław, *Czarne krzyże nad Polską* [*Black Crosses over Poland*] (Warsaw: Ministry of National Defence, 1957).

Antoni Szylling, *Moje dowodzenie w roku 1939* [*My Command in 1939*] (Kraków: PAU, 2007).

Tadeusz Tomaszewski, *Byłem szefem Sztabu Obrony Warszawy w 1939 roku* [*I was the Head of the Warsaw Defence Staff in 1939*] *(London: Orbis, 1961)*.

Adrian Carton de Wiart, *Happy Odyssey* (Barnsley, UK: Pen & Sword Books Ltd., 2007).

SECONDARY SOURCES

Piotr Bauer and Bogusław Polak, *Armia Poznań w wojnie obronnej 1939* [*The Poznań Army in the Defensive War of 1939*] (Poznań: Poznań Publishing, 1982).

Jochen Böhler, *Zbrodnie Wehrmachtu w Polsce* [*Wehrmacht Crimes in Poland*] (Krakow: Znak Publishing House, 2009).

Konrad Ciechanowski, *Armia Pomorze 1939* (Warsaw: Ministry of National Defence, 1982).

Anna M. Cienciala, *Poland and the Western Powers 1938–39: A Study in the Interdependence of Eastern and Western Europe* (Toronto: University of Toronto Press, 1968).

Robert M. Citino, *The Path to Blitzkrieg: Doctrine and Training in the German Army, 1920–39* (Mechanicsburg, PA: Stackpole Books, 2008).

James S. Corum, *The Luftwaffe: Creating the Operational Air War, 1918–1940* (Lawrence, KS: University Press of Kansas, 1997).

Jerzy B. Cynk, *The Polish Air Force at War: The Official History, Vol. 1, 1939–1943* (Atglen, PA: Schiffer Military History, 1998).

Marek Piotr Deszczyński, *Polski eksport sprzętu wojskowego w okresie międzywojennym* [*Polish Export of Military Equipment in the Inter-war Period*] (Warsaw: Neriton, 1994).

Rolf Elble, *Die Schlacht an der Bzura im September 1939 aus deutscher und polnischer Sicht* [*The Battle of the Bzura in September 1939 from the German and Polish Point of View*] (Freiburg: Rombach, 1975).

Marius Emmerling, *Luftwaffe nad Polska 1939* [*Luftwaffe Over Poland, 1939*], 3 volumes (Armageddon, 2002–09).

Ludwik Głowacki, *Obrona Warszawy i Modlina 1939* [*Defence of Warsaw and Modlin 1939*] (Warsaw: Ministry of National Defence, 1985).

Jan T. Gross, *Revolution from Abroad: The Soviet Conquest of Poland's Western Ukraine and Western Belorussia* (Princeton: Princeton University Press, 2002).

Czesław Grzelak, *Warszawa we wrześniu 1939 roku. Obrona i życie codzienne* [*Warsaw in September of 1939, Defence and Daily Life*] (Warsaw: RYTM Publishing House, 2004).

Mary R. Habeck, *Storm of Steel: The Development of Armour Doctrine in Germany and the Soviet Union, 1919–1939* (Ithaca, NY: Cornell University Press, 2003).

Richard Hargreaves, *Blitzkrieg Unleashed: The German Invasion of Poland, 1939* (Mechanicsburg, PA: Stackpole Books, 2010).

Paul N. Hehn, *A Low, Dishonest Decade: The Great Powers, Eastern Europe and the Economic Origins of World War II* (New York: Continuum, 2005).

David R. Higgins, *Panzer II vs. 7TP: Poland 1939* (Oxford: Osprey Publishing, 2015).

Wacław Jędrzejewicz, *Piłsudski: A Life for Poland* (New York: Hippocrene Books, 1982).

Tadeusz Jurga and Władysław Karbowski, *Armia Modlin 1939 r* (Warsaw: Ministry of National Defence, 1987).

Ryszard Juszkiewicz, *Bitwa pod Mławą 1939* [*Battle of Mława, 1939*] (Warsaw: Książka i Wiedza, 1987).

Ryszard Juszkiewicz, *Walki o przedmościa Różan, Pułtusk, Płock 1939* [*Struggles for the Różan, Pułtusk and Płock Bridgeheads*] (Warsaw: MAKO, 1992).

Halik Kochanski, *The Eagle Unbowed: Poland and the Poles in the Second World War* (Cambridge, MA: Harvard University Press, 2012).

Krzysztof Komorowski (ed.), *Boje Polskie 1939–1945. Przewodnik Encyklopedyczny* [*Polish Battles 1939–1945, Encyclopaedic Guide*] (Warsaw: Bellona, 2009), pp. 249–250.

Andrzej Konstankiewicz, *Broń strzelecka i sprzęt artyleryjski formacji polskich i Wojska Polskiego 1914 – 39* [*Guns and Artillery Equipment of Polish and Polish Army Formations 1914 – 39*] (Warsaw: Wydawnictwo Uniwersytetu Marii Curie-Skłodowskiej, 2003).

Eugeniusz J. Kozłowski et al., *Wojna Obronna Polski, 1939* [*The Polish Defensive War, 1939*] (Warsaw: Ministry of National Defence, 1979).

Klaus A. Maier et. al., *Germany and the Second World War*, Vol. II (Oxford, Oxford University Press, 2015).

Mikhail I. Meltyukhov, *Sovetsko-pol'skiye voyny: Voyenno-politicheskoye protivostoyaniye 1918–1939* [*Soviet–Polish Wars: The Military-Political Confrontation of 1918–1939*] (Moscow: Veche, 2001).

Leszek Moczulski, *Wojna polska 1939* [*The Polish War of 1939*] (Warsaw: Bellona, 2017).

Roger Moorhouse, *The Devil's Alliance: Hitler's Pact with Stalin, 1939–1941* (New York: Basic Books, 2014).

Antoni Nawrocki, *Zabezpieczenie logistyczne wojsk lądowych sił zbrojnych II RP w latach 1936–39* [*Logistics Security for Land Forces of the Second Polish Armed Forces in 1936–39*] (Warsaw: Ulmak, 2002).

Leo W. G. Niehorster, *German World War II Organizational Series, Vol. 1/II-1, 1st and 2nd Welle Army Infantry Divisions (1 September 1939)* (Milton Keynes: The Military Press, 2006).

Michael Alfred Peszke, *Poland's Navy, 1918–1945* (New York: Hippocrene Books Inc., 1999).

Tadeusz Piotrowski, *Poland's Holocaust: Ethnic Strife, Collaboration with Occupying Forces and Genocide in the Second Republic, 1918–1947* (London: McFarland & Co., Inc., 1998).

Marian Porwit, *Obrona Warszawy. Wrzesień 1939 [Defence of Warsaw. September 1939]* (Warsaw: Czytelnik, 1979).

Anita J. Prazmowska, *Britain, Poland and the Eastern Front, 1939* (Cambridge: Cambridge University Press, 1987).

Anthony Read and David Fisher, *The Deadly Embrace: Hitler, Stalin and the Nazi-Soviet Pact 1939–1941* (New York: W. W. Norton & Company, 1988).

Vincent W. Rospond, *The Polish Army in 1939* (Point Pleasant, NJ: Winged Hussar Publishing, 2016).

William Russ, *Case White: The German Army in the Polish Campaign, September 1939* (Point Pleasant, NJ: Winged Hussar Publishing, 2017).

Władysław Steblik, *Armia Kraków, 1939* (Warsaw: Ministry of National Defence, 1975).

Zara Steiner, *The Triumph of the Dark: European International History 1933–1939* (Oxford: Oxford University Press, 2013).

Nikolaus von Vormann, *Der Feldzug 1939 in Polen – Die Operationen des Heeres* (Weissenburg: Prinz-Eugen-Verlag, 1958).

Wesley K. Wark, *The Ultimate Enemy: British Intelligence and Nazi Germany, 1933–1939* (Ithaca, NY: Cornell University Press, 1985).

Donald Cameron Watt, *How War Came: The Immediate Origins of the Second World War, 1938–1939* (New York: Pantheon Books, 1989).

Gerhard L. Weinberg, *Hitler's Foreign Policy 1933–1939: The Road to World War II* (New York: Enigma Books, 2005).

David G. Williamson, *Poland Betrayed: The Nazi–Soviet Invasions of 1939* (Mechanicsburg, PA: Stackpole Books, 2009).

Steven Zaloga and Victor Madej, *The Polish Campaign 1939* (New York: Hippocrene Books, Inc., 1985).

Apoloniusz Zawilski, *Bitwy polskiego września [Battles of Polish September]* (Kraków: Znak, 2009).

Index

References to maps are in **bold**.